The Sociology of Law

The Sociology of Law

Classical and Contemporary Perspectives

A. Javier Treviño

Routledge
Taylor & Francis Group

LONDON AND NEW YORK

First published 2008 by Transaction Publishers

Published 2017 by Routledge
2 Park Square, Milton Park, Abingdon, Oxon OX14 4RN
711 Third Avenue, New York, NY 10017, USA

Routledge is an imprint of the Taylor & Francis Group, an informa business

New material this edition copyright © 2008 by Taylor & Francis.
Copyright © 1996 by St. Martin's Press, Inc.

Library of Congress Catalog Number: 2007049544

Library of Congress Cataloging-in-Publication Data

Treviño, A. Javier, 1958-
   The sociology of law : classical and contemporary perspectives / A. Javier Trevino ; with a new introduction by the author.
      p. cm.
   Includes bibliographical references and index.
   ISBN 978-1-4128-0788-3
      1. Sociological jurisprudence. I. Title.

K370.T74 2008
340'.115--dc22

2007049544

ISBN 13: 978-1-4128-0788-3 (pbk)

For my parents,
Alberto T. Treviño *and* Carmen Inocencio Treviño

Contents

Preface

The purpose of this textbook is to introduce the student to the sociology of law by providing a coherent organization to the general body of literature in that field. As such, the text gives a comprehensive overview of theoretical sociology of law. It deals with the broad expanse of the field and covers a vast amount of intellectual terrain. This volume is intended to fill a gap in the literature since most textbooks in the sociology of law are insufficiently theoretical or else do not provide a paradigmatic analysis of sociolegal theories.

The content of this text consists of discussions of the works of scholars who have contributed the most to the cumulative development of the sociology of law. It surveys the major traditions of legal sociology but is not wedded to any one particular theoretical approach. Both the "classical," or nineteenth-century, and "contemporary," or twentieth-century, perspectives are covered. The student will see that nineteenth-century thought has directly influenced the emergence of twentieth-century theory.

One unique feature of this book is that key sociological and legal concepts, presented in bold print and italics, are defined, described, and illustrated throughout. Although the nature of the subject matter is highly theoretical and, at times, quite complex, I have made every effort to present the material in the most straightforward and intelligible form possible without compromising the integrity of the theories themselves. This textbook is intended for use in upper-division undergraduate and graduate courses. It is meant for such classes as the Sociology of Law, Law and Society, Law and Social Sciences, Sociolegal Studies, and Jurisprudence.

While much of the material is theoretical, empirical studies are also considered. My personal inclination, however, is always toward a qualitative (or nonquantitative) exposition of even the most statistically oriented of the studies. In order to better illustrate the concepts and theories discussed, historical as well as more recent examples are liberally employed throughout the book. I have taken these examples from a wide variety of sources, including literature, popular culture, and sociological works.

The ten chapters in this book are sequenced to follow a paradigmatic chronology and to build on the complexity of the material covered. For example, since Max Weber's sociology of law was largely influenced by the ideas of Karl Marx, the chapter on Weber follows the chapter on Marx. The sociolegal ideas of past and present theorists whose works have provided a foundation for further progress in legal sociology are discussed in depth. Some of the early contributors to the sociology of law who are prominently featured here have not always received the attention they deserve. They include, among others, Cesare Beccaria, Sir Henry Maine, Herbert Spencer, William Graham Sumner, Oliver Wendell Holmes, Roscoe Pound, and Karl N. Llewellyn. Biographical sketches of these and other theorists are provided in order to place their influential ideas in a broader perspective.

Also discussed are the theories of contemporary scholars like E. P. Thompson, Evgeny B. Pashukanis, Karl Renner, Richard D. Schwartz, Kai T. Erikson, Vilhelm Aubert, Ralf Dahrendorf, Joseph Gusfield, Talcott Parsons, Niklas Luhmann, Adam Podgorecki, Michel Foucault, Duncan Kennedy, Clare Dalton, and Richard Delgado.

This textbook contains lengthy chapters devoted to the insightful concepts of the three sociological theorists who rank above all others: Karl Marx, Max Weber, and Emile Durkheim. Their central ideas and arguments are considered in detail in Chapters 4, 5, and 6. I have made a special effort to critique the theories and methodologies of these classical thinkers for two interrelated reasons. First, critique permits us to delve deeper into their theoretical perspectives and consider issues and problems that Marx, Weber, and Durkheim could not, or chose not, to address. Second, critique allows us to extend and elaborate upon their theoretical proposals and make those proposals more relevant to contemporary society.

The two major sociological paradigms of structural-functionalism and conflict theory are covered in Chapters 7 and 8 respectively. In addition, an analysis of the more recent intellectual development in jurisprudence, critical legal studies, is provided in Chapter 9. This book largely takes a "macro" theoretical orientation to the study of legal sociology. I have made no sustained effort to include the "micro" theories and paradigms that have also informed the field.

Another distinctive feature of this volume is that it contains twenty-one essays written by some of the theorists presented in the text. The readings consist of "primary," or classical works, and "secondary," or more contemporary works written about, or that stem from, the classical works. All of the essays have been carefully edited for readability. I have taken special care to delete superfluous material and yet retain those passages crucial to a basic understanding of the authors' fundamental ideas.

Although all twenty-one of the essays are discussed thoroughly in the body of the text, the student is strongly advised to read the essays. While I have tried to remain faithful to the basic arguments and ideas in these important works, it is worth noting that the further removed the reader is from the original author, the more likely it is that the arguments and ideas will be misrepresented.

I have attempted to make theoretical connections within and between each chapter in order to give overall coherence to the volume. Because this work is intended to be comparative as well as expository, convergences and discrepancies between the theories will be pointed out periodically.

This volume represents an attempt to consolidate the vast amount of literature that has been produced in the sociology of law over the last century or so. Although the text seeks to provide a representative sample of the classical and contemporary works that have made important contributions to the field, it is, of course, not possible to mention every major treatise. In light of space limitations and other restrictions, some principle theorists and theories had to be omitted.

In short, this textbook endeavors to help the student of legal sociology accomplish three objectives:

1. Become informed about the progressive advancement of sociolegal theory.
2. Learn to analyze the law as a social phenomenon.
3. Develop a critical mode of thinking about issues relevant to the relationship between law and society.

I am grateful to the following reviewers for the many helpful comments and suggestions that they made on various drafts of the manuscript: Ronald L. Akers, University of Florida; Mark Cooney, University of Nevada-Las Vegas; Jurgen Gerber, Sam Houston State University; David F. Greenburg, New York University; William Kelly, University of Texas at Austin; Marvin Krohn, SUNY-Albany; Mindie Lazaarus-Black, University of Chicago; Matthew Ross Lippman, University of Illinois at Chicago; Edward Shaughnessy, John Jay College of Criminal Justice; and Victoria Swigert, College of the Holy Cross. None of these reviewers is responsible for the views expressed in the text. All errors remaining are my own.

I am also grateful to the following authors for granting me their kind permission to edit and reprint their works in this volume: Ronald L. Akers, University of Florida; Isaac D. Balbus, The University of Illinois at Chicago; William J. Chambliss, The George Washington University; Clare Dalton, Northeastern University School of Law; Duncan Kennedy, Harvard Law School; Lonn Lanza-Kaduce, University of Florida; Steven Spitzer, Suffolk University; Alan Stone, University of Houston; and Austin T. Turk, University of California, Riverside.

I want to thank Susan L. Kindel for first believing in the project. I wish to acknowledge the continuous moral support and intellectual influence provided me by my friend and mentor, Richard Quinney. Another friend, David O. Moberg provided words of encouragement throughout the writing of this book.

I also want to thank my former students Tania Sadek, Valerie L. Gunhus, and Ibis Smith Kinnart for organizing, typing, and proofreading the edited readings. I am indebted to the staff of the Marquette Law Library for helping me locate books, journals, articles, and various types of information necessary in researching this text. Robin Cork, Brian Dorband, Duane Strojny, Mary Mahoney, and Stephen Nelson were especially helpful in this regard.

The manuscript benefited immeasurably from Barbara Muller's review of the book's first five chapters and fifteen of the edited essays. Rich Wright's copyediting was exceptional. I am deeply grateful to several people at St. Martin's Press who were influential in making the text a reality. In particular, I would like to thank Louise Waller, Huntley McNair Funsten, Kerry Abrams, Bob Nirkind, Elizabeth Bast, Doug Bell, and especially Sabra Scribner. Sabra's intelligence, sensitivity, and professionalism saw me through the peaks and valleys of textbook writing. I could not have asked for a better editor.

The most important debt of all is to my wife, Nancy J. Treviño, who read every chapter, sometimes twice, and made numerous detailed suggestions for improvement. Without her support, patience, and understanding, this book would not have been possible.

A. Javier Treviño

Introduction to the Transaction Edition

Although the term "sociology of law" was first coined by the Italian legal philosopher Dionisio Anzilotti in 1892, and Eugen Ehrlich's *Grundlegung einer Soziologie des Rechts* appeared as early as 1913, it wasn't until the 1950s that American sociologists—inspired particularly by the works of Eastern European thinkers Ehrlich, Nicholas S. Timasheff, and Georges Gurvitch—became attentive to socio-legal concerns. Today, interest in law among sociologists and other social scientists reaches worldwide proportions.

In the United States, the popularity of law and society scholarship currently runs high as represented by organizational and literary endeavors such as the Law and Society Association (established in 1964) and its major literary organ, the *Law & Society Review*; the Sociology of Law section of the American Sociological Association; and the Law and Society division of the Society for the Study of Social Problems. Additionally, the American Bar Foundation publishes *Law & Social Inquiry*, a journal of empirical and theoretical studies that are both international and interdisciplinary and that make original contributions to an understanding of socio-legal processes. *Social & Legal Studies: An International Journal* (published in the United States) is yet another leading international forum for scholarship on law from a variety of perspectives within social theory.

In Europe, the sociology of law involves work and organization in various countries including Poland, the United Kingdom, the Scandinavian countries, and Spain, for example. The Polish Sociological Association established a Section of the Sociology of Law in 1961 and the Socio-Legal Studies Association was formed in 1990 in the U.K. Some of the leading European periodicals for socio-legal studies with an international readership include the *International Journal of the Sociology of Law, The Journal of Law and Society* (both published in Britain) and *Scandinavian Studies in Law* (published in Sweden).

Another indication of a global interest in socio-legal scholarship was the founding, in 1988, of the International Institute for the Sociology of Law by the International Sociological Association (Research Committee on Sociology of Law) and the Basque government. The Institute is located in the Old University of Oñati (Spain) and offers a Master's degree as well as an internationally recognized Doctorate in the field of Sociology of Law.

The sociology of law also commands the attention of scholars in Asia. For example, the Japanese Association of the Sociology of Law was formed as early as 1948. And in Korea, sociologists have shown earnest interest in socio-legal matters, at least since the 1970s. The Korean Law and Society Association, established in 1987, now publishes a biannual journal, the *Korean Journal of Law & Society*. In China, also in 1987, the first national symposium for sociology of law was held under the auspices of the Law Department of Peking University.

The Textbook's Purpose, Content, and Intent

The purpose of this textbook is to introduce students to the sociology of law, or legal sociology, by providing a coherent organization to the general body of literature in that field. Through its coverage of a vast intellectual terrain, this text engages the broad expanse of the field. This volume is intended to fill a gap in the literature since most textbooks in the sociology of law are insufficiently theoretical or else do not provide a paradigmatic analysis of socio-legal theories.

The content of this text consists of discussions of the works of those scholars who have contributed the most to the cumulative development of the sociology of law. It surveys the major traditions of legal sociology but is not wedded to any one particular theoretical approach. Both the "classical," or nineteenth-century, and "contemporary," or twentieth- and twenty-first-century, perspectives are covered. The student will see that nineteenth-century thought has directly influenced the emergence of current theoretical work.

One unique feature of this book is that key sociological and legal concepts—presented in bold print and italics—are defined, described, and illustrated throughout. Although the subject matter can be highly abstract and, at times, quite complex, every effort has been made to present the material in the most straightforward and intelligible form possible without compromising the integrity of the theories themselves. This textbook is intended for use in upper-division undergraduate and graduate courses. It is meant for such classes as the Sociology of Law, Law and Society, Law and Social Sciences, Socio-legal Studies, and Jurisprudence.

While the main focus is on theoretical analysis, empirical studies are also considered. Moreover, preference is given to a qualitative (or non-quantitative) exposition of even the most statistically oriented of the studies. In order to better illustrate the concepts and theories discussed, historical as well as more recent examples—taken from a wide variety of sources, including literature, popular culture, and social scientific works—are liberally employed throughout the book.

The ten chapters that comprise the text are sequenced to follow a paradigmatic chronology and to build on the complexity of the material covered. For example, since Max Weber's sociology of law was largely influenced by the ideas of Karl Marx, the chapter on Weber follows the chapter on Marx. The socio-legal ideas of past and present thinkers, whose works have provided a foundation for further development in legal sociology, are discussed in depth. Some of the early contributors to the sociology of law who are prominently featured here have not always received the attention they deserve. They include, among others, Cesare Beccaria, Sir Henry Maine, Herbert Spencer, William Graham Sumner, Oliver Wendell Holmes Jr., Roscoe Pound, and Karl N. Llewellyn. Biographical sketches of these and other thinkers are provided in order to place their influential ideas in a broader sociohistorical context. Also discussed are the theories of more recent scholars like E.P. Thompson, Evgeny B. Pashukanis, Karl Renner, Richard D. Schwartz, Kai T. Erikson, Vilhelm Aubert, Ralf Dahrendorf, Joseph Gusfield, Talcott Parsons, Niklas Luhmann, Adam Podgorecki, Michel Foucault, Duncan Kennedy, Clare Dalton, and Richard Delgado.

This textbook contains lengthy chapters devoted to the insightful ideas of the three sociological theorists who rank above all others: Karl Marx, Max Weber, and Emile Durkheim; their central concepts and arguments are considered in detail in Chapters 4, 5, and 6. Special effort has been made to critique the theories and methodologies of these classical thinkers for two interrelated reasons. First, critique permits us to delve deeper into their theoretical perspectives and consider issues and problems that Marx, Weber, and Durkheim could not, or chose not to, address. Second, critique allows us to extend and elaborate upon their conceptual proposals and to make those proposals more relevant to contemporary society.

The two major sociological paradigms of structural-functionalism and conflict theory are covered in Chapters 7 and 8 respectively. In addition, an analysis of the influential late twentieth-century intellectual development in jurisprudence, critical legal studies, is provided in Chapter 9.

This didactic commentary on the sociology of law largely takes a "macro," or structuralist, theoretical approach. No sustained effort is made to include the "micro," or interactionist, theories and paradigms that have also informed the field.

Theoretical connections are made within and between each chapter in order to give overall coherence to the volume. Because this work is intended to be comparative as well as expository, convergences and discrepancies between the various theories discussed are alluded to periodically.

This textbook is an attempt to survey the more salient conceptual statements that have been produced in legal sociology over the last 100 years or so. Although the text seeks to provide a representative sample of the classical and contemporary works that have made important contributions to the field, it is, of course, not possible to mention every major treatise. In light of space limitations and other restrictions, some principal theorists and theories had to be omitted. In particular, there are three main theoretical strands that are not discussed in this text, but that since its initial publication in 1996 have become influential in various quarters of the sociological study of law. These are Donald Black's pure sociology of law, feminist jurisprudence, and critical race theory, and they deserve brief mention.

Three Theoretical Strands for the Twenty-First Century

Donald Black, who has perhaps done more than anyone else to conceptually advance scholarship in law and society, has, for over a quarter-century, proffered a metatheoretical paradigm for the sociology of law (indeed for all of sociology). This paradigm—which Black calls "pure" sociology of law—conceptualizes law as a social, rather than a "people," phenomenon. It eschews psychology, one-dimensionality, microcosms/macrocosms, anthropocentrism, and teleological theory. It is in his world-classic text, *The Behavior of Law*, that Black first introduced his epistemological strategy of pure sociology. In that volume he also advanced the notion that the law "behaves"—that is, varies in quantity and style—in a predictable manner. Since then, several scholars have attempted to test Black's theory, with mixed results, in their examination of such practical matters as the handling of legal cases and the settlement of disputes.

The other important conceptual framework, feminist legal theory—or feminist jurisprudence—(briefly alluded to in Chapter 9) refers to a movement in socio-legal scholarship that analyzes and critiques law as a patriarchal institution. While the topics of interest to feminist jurisprudence are wide ranging, they tend to concentrate on legal issues that specifically pertain to the notion of evolving gender roles: equal protection law; discrimination in education, hiring, and promotion; comparable worth; the regulation of sexuality (prostitution and pornography) and reproduction (surrogacy, adoption, abortion); and the patriarchal bias in legislation and adjudication. Feminist jurisprudence borrows from several theoretical traditions including liberal, cultural, radical, Marxist, and socialist feminist approaches; critical legal studies; postmodernism; deconstruction; and psychoanalysis. Despite differences in perspective, feminist jurisprudence is, first and foremost, a critique of those legal principles, doctrines, and institutions that perpetuate *patriarchy*, the hierarchical social structure that subordinates women to men, and *sexism*, the prejudice against women. In the final analysis, feminist jurisprudence examines the relationship between law, gender, and equality in an effort to eliminate patriarchy.

The third socio-legal trend—critical race theory (CRT)—emerged as a pointed analysis of what the early twentieth-century African American sociologist, W.E.B. Du Bois, famously referred to as the "problem of the color line." Informed by transformative politics, first in the area of legal studies during the 1990s, CRT quickly permeated and invigorated other disciplines including sociology, justice studies, and education. A short distance past the threshold of the twenty-first century, critical race theory is now no longer new. And though it remains faithful to its original mandate of treating the social construction of race as central to the way that people of color are ordered and constrained in the United States, CRT has begun to move beyond the black-white paradigm and beyond vulgar racial essentialism to consider the racialized lives, the daily microaggressions inflicted upon various oppressed minorities such as Latinos, Asians, gays, Indians, and women of color. Thus, in recent years, CRT has quickly ramified into several area programs such as Latino/a critical studies (LatCrit), critical queer studies (QueerCrit), critical race feminism, and critical white studies, to name just some of the more salient ones. As such, CRT now grapples with such provocative and weighty socio-legal issues as immigration, language rights, sexism, internal colonialism, sexual oppression, transnationality, and citizenship status.

The Problem of the Rule of Law

Another important issue not considered in the 1996 edition of this textbook is the problem of the *rule of law*. Explicit treatment of this unquestioned notion—which has been a tacit, but most crucial, part of the received wisdom in socio-legal thinking—can only serve to further increase legal sociology's analytic power, its critical edge.

To begin with, legal sociologists have yet to self-reflexively examine their own deep cultural commitment to the rule of law. Thus far they have largely failed to recognize, or, more inexcusably, they have failed to admit, that any analysis of law and society is inextricably tied to the ontology of law's rule. While socio-legal scholars have been especially clever at formulating myriad concepts and theories that allow for various analyses of law in society, they have invariably done so from *within* the legal system. All issues pertaining to the social phenomenon of law—e.g., legal reform, legal evolution, legal reasoning, legal critique, etc.—are invariably discussed in terms of the form and substance of law, never over *whether* law, in general, should rule at all. The fact of the matter is that it has been the nature of legal sociology to operate internally to law's rule and, as such, for legal sociologists to proffer their theories within an order that they themselves legitimate.

Notwithstanding the critical legal scholars' talk of indeterminacy, the critical race theorists' arguments against colorblind legislation, and the Marxists' skepticism about worker's rights, all sociologists of law approach law—or as they like to say (and, in fact, as is articulated throughout this textbook) in an obvious gesture of legal reification, *the* law—from the perspective of its validity. Because they have no Archimedean point outside of law on which to stand, socio-legal scholars are not only incapable of launching a preemptive critique of law, more importantly, they cannot conceive of any modern society independent of a culture wholly permeated by law's rule. If legal sociology is to successfully forge a full-scale critique—in its analyses, explanations, and interpretations—of socio-legal phenomena, it must also explicitly question the core beliefs that justify the rule of law.

The Transaction Edition

This reissued edition, by Transaction Publishers, of *The Sociology of Law: Classical and Contemporary Perspectives* remains faithful to the three objectives of the original book; objectives that are as important today as they were in 1996. It endeavors to help the rising generation of students of legal sociology:

1. Become informed about the progressive advancement of socio-legal theory;
2. Learn to analyze law as a social phenomenon;
3. Develop a critical mode of thinking about issues relevant to the relationship between law and society.

In sum, it is hoped that this text will serve as a useful tool in students' intellectual education in the sociology of law, particularly as they undertake a survey of the field's trends and developments.

• 1 •

The Sociology of Law

This opening chapter introduces the reader to some of the general topics that will inform the next nine chapters. By way of addressing these topics we begin by posing three fundamental and pivotal questions: What is sociology? What is law? and What is the sociology of law? Although it is virtually impossible to give definitive answers to these questions, it is nevertheless necessary that we seriously consider them and, at minimum, attempt a tentative description of their concerns. The main purpose of this chapter is to provide an organizing theme to the study of the sociology of law.

Generally speaking, the sociology of law is concerned with explaining the relationship between law and society. This relationship compels the student of legal sociology to obtain a working knowledge of how the beliefs, practices, and organization of the law and of human society operate. The sections that follow will introduce us to this working knowledge. We begin by considering the question: What is sociology?

What Is Sociology?

We may define **sociology** as the study of: (1) human society, (2) the organization of social groups, (3) the social interactions of people, and (4) the meaning that people give to their social reality. Put another way, sociology is an "intellectual craft"; a way of looking at all things social (Mills, 1959). Because of the broad inclusiveness of its subject matter, sociology must often consult other knowledge-fields such as philosophy, history, political science, anthropology, economics, and law.

A wide array of topics are of interest to the sociologist. These topics include deviant behavior; the influence of health and illness on society; education; the urban environment; the family; religion; race and ethnic relations; the influence of politics on society; work and occupations; military life; and law. Consequently, sociology consists of many specialties or subfields such as the sociology of deviance, medical sociology, the sociology of education, urban sociology, the sociology of the family, the sociology of religion, the sociology of race and ethnic relations, political

1

sociology, the sociology of work and occupations, military sociology, and the sociology of law, or legal sociology.

Sociologists are typically interested in studying **social institutions,** or those forms of organization that are supported by, and meet the basic needs of a society. The major institutions found in most societies are the family, the economy, the polity (i.e., government or the state), education, religion, and law. In addition, all societies possess a type of skeletal framework or **social structure**—an organizational pattern of social relations. Making up the social structure are the basic components of society, which include the aforementioned institutions as well as *roles, statuses, norms, values,* and *ideology.*

The institutions themselves have a social structure. For example, the legal institution contains various **roles,** or patterns of behavioral expectations, in the form of legislators, judges, lawyers, and police officers. These individuals are assigned a distinct task or a set of tasks to perform in accordance with their obligations and within the context of the legal institution. Additionally, there are various **statuses,** or social positions, that correspond to the different roles. For instance, in the courtroom as well as in society at large, judges have traditionally held a higher social position than police officers. Consequently, relative to police officers, judges enjoy greater esteem, prestige, and honor. Moreover, there are certain **norms,** or social rules, that exist in the legal institution. Some of these norms include the following: state legislators must not make a law that contradicts the Constitution of the United States; all those present in the courtroom must rise as the judge enters and takes the bench; lawyers must, to the best of their ability, represent their clients; and police officers must not use excessive force when apprehending a suspect. Some of the major **values,** or standards of desirability and goodness, that are prevalent in the legal institution of the U.S. are the following: judges must not take bribes; members of Congress should represent the interests of their constituents; and the president is expected to be honest with the American people. Finally, a dominant **ideology,** or belief system, exists throughout society and informs most of the social institutions including the legal one. For instance, the general notion that all U.S. citizens have the right to life, liberty, and the pursuit of happiness, forms part of our cultural as well as legal ideology.

The Tools of the Craft

Much like practitioners in other knowledge-fields, sociologists utilize certain instruments or tools that aid them in learning more about society, its institutions, and social structure. Because most (though not all) of what sociologists study is, by its nature, intangible and abstract (namely, social institutions and social structures) so too must their tools, of necessity, be intangible and abstract. There are three main types of tools used by the sociologist: *concepts, theories,* and *paradigms.*

Concepts are ideas that represent some important features of the social world. Concepts take the form of words and, sometimes, phrases. Throughout this book we will examine a variety of sociological and legal concepts, some of which are simple, others more complex.

A **theory** is a set of interrelated statements, or propositions, that attempts to explain certain aspects of society and regular patterns of social behavior. It is through theories that sociologists endeavor to answer the larger social questions: Why do some people obey the law while others violate it? How do changes in society bring about corresponding changes in the law? Do some groups of people benefit more from legislation relative to other groups? Most of what is called "theory" in sociology is not stated formally. Indeed, much of sociological theory is amorphous and not always articulated in propositions. Thus, in this text, we will generally call theory any scholarly effort—formal or informal, structured or unstructured—that attempts to make sense of, and explain, sociolegal phenomena. Let us now look at the third type of tool used by the sociologist, the paradigm.

A **paradigm**—that is, a theoretical perspective, school of thought, or intellectual tradition—serves as an orientation that reflects a particular set of ideas and assumptions regarding the nature of people and society. Sociology has been called a "multiple paradigm science" because of the many competing theoretical perspectives that currently exist in the discipline (Ritzer, 1975). In other words, there are various ways of examining the social world and doing sociology. Each paradigm gives the sociologist a different view of social reality. Because no paradigm is wholly comprehensive, no one paradigm can provide all of the answers to all of the issues of social life. In this book we will be concerned principally with *structural-functionalism* and *conflict theory* since these are the two paradigms that have most influenced the sociology of law.

Generally, structural-functionalism is based on the assumption that society is a complex system made up of interdependent parts that work together to produce stability and consensus. Functionalists see law as a neutral entity that serves to resolve disputes and contribute to the integration of society. We will examine this paradigm in more detail in Chapter 7. By contrast, the conflict paradigm is based on the assumption that the antagonisms, hostilities, and struggles over power and scarce resources in society lead to social inequality. Conflict theorists view law as a weapon that is used by powerful social groups for the purpose of establishing, defending, and propagating their interests, values, and ideological beliefs. The conflict perspective will be featured in Chapter 8.

The Theorists and Premodern, Modern, and Postmodern Society

In this textbook we will also examine the work of those theorists who proposed, elaborated, and popularized the various concepts, theories, and paradigms relevant to the sociology of law. Among these theorists are jurists, legal scholars, philosophers, historians, and anthropologists. Most of the theorists, however, are either sociologists by training or else their work exhibits a strong sociological orientation. The sociolegal perspectives of three major theorists—Karl Marx, Max Weber, and Emile Durkheim—will be analyzed in Chapters 4, 5, and 6, respectively. The sociology of law—indeed, all of general sociology—has its theoretical basis in the ideas of these three thinkers of the nineteenth century. They rightly demand our serious consideration.

It is noteworthy that the theorists discussed in this book articulated their sociological statements in reference to societies situated in specific historical time periods and informed by different cultural values, goals, and ideologies. These temporal and cultural differences allow us to speak of three "pure" types of society: the *premodern*, the *modern*, and the *postmodern*.

The **premodern** characterizes Western societies before the eighteenth century as well as some contemporary cultures in the nonindustrialized parts of Asia, Africa, and Latin America. Premodern societies are guided by two interrelated ideologies. On the one hand, there is the "religious ideology" that views social phenomena as being endowed with, and controlled by, magical, mystical, and supernatural forces. On the other hand, there is the "ideology of the heroic" that ranks people on the basis of their degree of personal charisma, wisdom, and inspiration. These two ideologies combine to form a society organized around inherited social status and sacred authority. Thus, in premodern societies, the most influential individuals are those with the highest social status and the greatest sacred authority: warriors, priests, prophets, kings, tribal chiefs, patriarchs, slaveholders, landowners, and divinely inspired judges.

The **modern** characterizes Western society from the eighteenth century to the mid-twentieth century. Modern, Western society lays great stress on rationality, calculability, production, and predictability. Whereas premodern society is dominated by religion and magic, modern society is dominated by science and technology. Social phenomena, therefore, are explained through reason, logic, and observation. Modern thinking extols the notion that there exists an objective social reality composed of fixed and knowable entities.

In modernity the metaphor for life is the machine. Society is seen as a complex mechanical device with logical coherence; like a clock, for instance, made up of differentiated parts operating efficiently to maintain the whole. The large-scale organizations and institutions of modern society are structured bureaucratically. Modern society is also industrialized and largely engaged in the mass production of manufactured goods. Modern persons are viewed as time-conscious, task-oriented, rational agents who examine the facts and make decisions accordingly. People engage in contractual relationships with each other and orient their social actions toward the pursuit of gain.

Modern society's economy is capitalist, its politics liberal, its law formal. As such, modernity is premised on the notion of the private. Much importance is placed on the entitlement of rights for the private citizen, the private law of contract, and the ownership of private property. In modern societies the most influential people are scientists, technicians, industrialists, bureaucratic functionaries, specialists, and technically trained members of the bar. As we shall see, the majority of the social theorists featured in this book focus exclusively on modern society.

The **postmodern**, which has characterized Western society since the mid-twentieth century, is more difficult to depict because it is still in the making. Generally speaking, however, postmodern society involves the intensification and exaggeration—a travesty, so to speak—of modernity. Thus, relative to modernity, postmodern culture is much more differentiated and rational. Greater social differentiation brings about more narrow expertise and in postmodern society we find specializations and sub-specializations. Each specialization is a community of discourse with its own distinct language and therefore unable to communicate with other communities. There is, however, a state of *reflexivity*, or a circularity of communication and observation, within each specialized community. Differentiation also produces various viewpoints—different and competing ideologies—that give emphasis to relativity. Individuals in postmodern society are confronted with a *multiplicity of meanings* based on a rhetoric that is full of *paradoxes and contradictions*. Consequently, all truth claims are challenged, all narratives are discredited, and no ideology is granted a privileged position. Thus, three main traits of postmodern society are reflexivity, the multiplicity of meanings, and paradoxes and contradictions.

Postmodernism is a disconcerting mixture—a fragmentation and integration—of seemingly incompatible viewpoints and lifestyles. In postmodern culture traditional boundaries are blurred and re-formed. Elements that were previously seen as dichotomous now blend into each other: private/public, objective/subjective, form/substance, self/other. This blurring of traditional boundaries makes social reality more incoherent, indeterminate, and uncertain. In postmodern society relationships are highly mechanical, instrumental, and autonomous. Much greater emphasis is placed on rationality to the point that it becomes irrational. Social theorist George Ritzer calls this phenomenon the "irrationality of rationality" (1994:152ff). The result is that bureaucratic functioning becomes highly technical and less efficient. In short, present-day postmodern society is a confounded caricature of the past. Throughout this text we will see how the beliefs, practices, and organization of premodern, modern, and postmodern society impact on the law.

Having briefly, and thus superficially, considered the question, What is sociology?, we now turn our attention to the next logical question, What is law?

What Is Law?

In 1781 the German philosopher Immanuel Kant noted that jurists were still searching for a definition of law (1933:588, n.a). Over two hundred years later, no conclusive definition of the concept exists. This is not for want of trying, for numerous scholars have attempted to define the concept of law. For example, U.S. Supreme Court Justice Oliver Wendell Holmes (see Chapter 3) described it, very pragmatically, as "the prophecies of what the courts will do in fact" (1897:461). Similarly, another Justice, Benjamin N. Cardozo, defined law as "a principle or rule of conduct so established as to justify a prediction with reasonable certainty that it will be enforced by the courts if its authority is challenged" (1924:52). Legal philosopher Hermann Kantorowicz characterized law, very broadly (and ambiguously), as "a body of social rules prescribing external conduct and considered justiciable" (1980:79).

Anthropologists such as Bronislaw Malinowski, whose ideas we will discuss in Chapter 7, have also tried their hand at defining the law concept. According to Malinowski, "law is the specific result of the configuration of obligations, which makes it impossible for the native to shirk his responsibility without suffering for it in the future" (1982:49). Another anthropologist, E. Adamson Hoebel, states that "a social norm is legal if its neglect or infraction is regularly met, in threat or in fact, by the application of physical force by an individual or group possessing the socially recognized privilege of so acting" (1978:28).

Sociologists, too, have contributed their own share of definitions. For instance, Richard Quinney, whose theory of the social reality of crime is discussed in Chapter 8, regards law as "a body of specialized rules created and interpreted in a politically organized society" (1970:36). Legal sociologist Donald Black views law, very concisely, as "governmental social control" (1976:2). More recently, Steven Vago has stated that, "law consists of the behaviors, situations, and conditions for making, interpreting, and applying legal rules that are backed by the state's legitimate coercive apparatus for enforcement" (1994:8). But perhaps the most famous of all sociological definitions is that of Max Weber: "An order will be called *law* if it is externally guaranteed by the probability that physical or psychological coercion will be applied by a *staff* of people in order to bring about compliance or avenge violation" (1978:34). We will have opportunity to examine Weber's definition more closely in Chapter 5.

As we have already seen, law is regarded as one of the major institutions of society. As such, we may speak of the **legal institution**. Sociologist Alan V. Johnson (1977), for example, conceptualizes law as an institution composed of a body of statements and a set of organized activities that express or implement the body of statements. Other writers, such as Max Weber and Roscoe Pound, view the law as a **legal order**—"the regime of adjusting relations and ordering conduct by the systematic application of the force of a politically organized society" (Pound, 1971:300). Still others have referred to law as a "system" and thus make reference to the **legal system**. Legal scholar Lawrence M. Friedman (1975), for instance, argues that the law is a system, or an operating unit with definite boundaries, that has as its components a social structure, substance, and culture. Depending on which description best suits the discussion at hand, we will refer to law as an institution (Chapter 4), an order (Chapter 5), or a system (Chapter 7).

Law is also conceptualized differently depending on whether it is placed in the context of premodern, modern, or postmodern society. In premodern society the law consists of the sacred or extraordinary commands of the sovereign. In modern society the law is treated either as a formal and internally consistent, gapless system of rules or as a set of reciprocal rights and duties. In postmodern society the law is seen either as a reflexive system driven by paradoxes or as a set of discourses, or "stories," rife with contradictions.

Second only to law, *jurisprudence* is perhaps the most difficult concept to define. Because it means different things to different people, there is no consensus as to a nominal definition of the term. In this book we will use the term **jurisprudence** to refer to the philosophy of law, the science of law, and the study of legal doctrine.

What Is the Sociology of Law?

Now that we have attempted a description of the discipline of sociology and tried to conceptualize what is law, it is time to take a closer look at what is meant by the sociology of law. We begin with a definition. The **sociology of law**, or *legal sociology*, is an academic speciality within the general discipline of sociology that attempts to theoretically make sense of, and explain, the relationship between law and society, the social organization of the legal institution (order or system), the social interactions of all who come in contact with the legal institution and its representatives (police officers, lawyers, judges, legislators, etc.), and the meaning that people give to their legal reality. The sociology of law is not a self-contained knowledge-field. It shares much intellectual common ground with jurisprudence, criminology, the anthropology of law, the sociology of deviance, political sociology, and other kindred areas. For a better understanding of the sociology of law, let us briefly examine some of the major trends and developments that have characterized the subfield since the 1950s.

The intellectual trends and developments impacting on American legal sociology have been distinct and sundry. However, because these influences have been experienced relatively recently, it may be said that legal sociology is now only entering its middle stages of intellectual maturation. In the brief history that follows we chronicle legal sociology's evolution through two main periods, the 1950s–1970s and the 1980s–1990s.

The 1950s–1970s

Inspired by the works of European legal sociologists Eugen Ehrlich (1936), Nicholas S. Timasheff (1939), and Georges Gurvitch (1942), American sociologists begin to cultivate an interest in sociolegal theory during the 1950s. At this time some of Max Weber's theoretical writings on the sociology of law were translated into English. This collection, published as *Max Weber on Law in Economy and Society* (Rheinstein, 1954), introduced several generations of American sociologists to the legal thought of one of the greatest social thinkers of all time. The following year saw the publication of an abridged volume, *Law and Morality* (1955), that presented the psychosocial legal theory of Russian-Polish jurist Leon Petrazycki. Although the book was largely ignored, Petrazycki's unique theoretical approach nevertheless found a friendly reception among a handful of jurists and sociologists who made passing reference to it.

Despite the inroads that sociolegal theory was making into sociology, the general discipline of sociology, in the main, avoided analyzing law as a social phenomenon. Toward the end of the 1950s, F. James Davis (1957) did a content analysis of various sociology books in an attempt to determine how much emphasis law had had on general sociology. Davis found that, on average, writers of books on sociological theory devoted more space to law than did writers of introductory texts. However, some theoreticians completely omitted any mention of law, while almost all textbook writers attempted some general discussion of the law's place in society. On the basis of these data, Davis concluded that, generally speaking, the law did not have a well-recognized place in sociological thought and that, at present, sociology could not provide adequate knowledge of law for the sociology student.

By the end of the 1950s the sociology of law had evolved to the point where Philip Selznick (1959) felt comfortable assessing its past, present, and future. Accordingly, Selznick outlined three basic stages of legal sociology's intellectual development.

The first stage, which he calls the "primitive," or "missionary" stage, involves formulating a theoretical perspective. According to Selznick, a "not-very-sophisticated" sociological perspective was introduced to legal study by American legal scholars who were influenced by European thought, and by some of the more articulate appellate judges (Selznick, 1959:116). Although he does not say who these legal scholars and judges may be, we can safely assume that Selznick has in mind such people as Eugen Ehrlich, Nicholas Timasheff, Georges Gurvitch, and Leon Petrazycki, as well as Oliver Wendell Holmes, Roscoe Pound, and Karl Llewellyn (see Chapter 3).

Selznick states that the second stage of development, and the one that the sociology of law was about to enter (in 1959), belongs to the sociological craftsman. At this stage the sociologist utilizes survey and experimental research methods in conjunction with sociological concepts and theories in solving the law's practical problems. Many of the empirical studies mentioned throughout this book are illustrative of legal sociology's second stage of intellectual development.

Finally, during legal sociology's third and most advanced stage, the sociologist is to "explore the meaning of legality itself, to assess its moral authority, and to clarify the role of social science in creating a society based on justice" (Selznick, 1959:124). This third stage is perhaps now beginning to emerge with the recent popularity of critical legal studies (see Chapter 9).

During the early 1960s legal sociologist William M. Evan edited *Law and Sociology: Exploratory Essays* (1962). The book consists of essays written by eight legal scholars and sociologists who present their various views on law and society. This effort proved that an intellectual discourse between lawyers and sociologists was not only possible but exceedingly fruitful. At around the same time F. James Davis et al. published *Society and the Law: New Meanings for an Old Profession* (1962), a book that was essentially another symposium in which sociologists collaborated with lawyers.

The Law and Society Association was established in 1964 and its major literary organ, the *Law and Society Review*, was founded. This journal resulted from the "growing need on the part of social scientists and lawyers for a forum in which to carry on an interdisciplinary dialogue" (Schwartz, 1966:6).

The following year, Jerome Skolnick (1965) reviewed most of the major empirical work in sociolegal studies that had been done during the previous decade. Skolnick's review was a lengthy thirty-nine printed pages, indicating the perceived richness of the field at that time.

In 1968 several publications helped to further enhance legal sociology's visibility. For example, the appearance of the *International Encyclopedia of the Social Sciences* included the entry "The Sociology of Law" by Philip Selznick. *Norms and Actions: National Reports on Sociology of Law*, edited by Renato Treves and J. F. Glastra Van Loon, investigated the current state of sociolegal research and studies in several different countries including Scandinavia, Poland, and the United States. That same year one of the more popular textbooks in legal sociology, *Law and Society: A Sociological View* (1968), was published by New York University sociologist Edwin M. Schur. Many more texts were to follow.

In the early 1970s University of Virginia legal sociologist Donald Black began a discussion that was to have repercussions for legal sociology for years. Black (1972) argued forcefully that a "pure" sociology of law must be involved in scientifically analyzing legal life for the purpose of creating a general theory of law that can predict and explain every instance of legal behavior. Thus, for Black the sociology of law was to be a wholly conceptual, objective, and scientific endeavor free from the intrusion of values, morality, and politics. Black severely criticized those legal sociologists who are preoccupied with the "policy implications" of their research and who are engaged in evaluating the effectiveness of the law. In Black's view these sociologists confuse scientific questions with policy questions and thus severely retard the development of the sociology of law. At best, they offer an applied sociology of law that seeks to reform the legal order—at worst, sheer ideology.

Black's theoretical position is referred to as **positivism,** or the scientific doctrine asserting that: (1) the only valid knowledge is knowledge obtained from social phenomena endowed with objective reality; and (2) knowledge of objective reality can only be obtained from a position of value neutrality. Positivism underscores three basic principles of the scientific method:

> First, science can only know phenomena and never essences. The quest for the one correct concept of law or for anything else "distinctly legal" is therefore inherently unscientific. The essence of law is a problem for jurisprudence, not science. Second, every scientific idea requires a concrete empirical referent of some kind. A science can only order experience, and has no way of gaining access to non-empirical domains of knowledge. Accordingly, so far as such ideals as justice, the rule of law, and due process are without a grounding in experience, they have no place in the sociology of law. Third, value judgments cannot be discovered in the empirical world and for that reason are without cognitive meaning in science. . . . It is for this last reason that science knows nothing and can know nothing about the effectiveness of law. Science is incapable of an evaluation of the reality it confronts (Black, 1972:1092).

Berkeley sociologist Philippe Nonet (1976) vehemently rejected Black's positivism and called for a **normative,** or morally informed, approach in the sociology of law. According to Nonet, the normative approach will structure legal sociology in four ways:

1. The sociology of law needs to seriously consider those normative issues that are relevant to jurisprudence: legal, political, and historical issues; values; the adequacy, effectiveness, achievements, limitations, growth, and decline of various social arrangements. In other words, legal sociology needs to be more than just the scientific study of quantitative and measurable behavior.

2. The sociology of law must have redeeming value for policy. Thus, every project undertaken by the legal sociologist must have some practical utility and should not stand on its theoretical merits alone.

3. The sociology of law must take legal ideas seriously. That is to say that the sociologist cannot expect to capture all that really matters about the legal order without knowing something about the complicated and obscure arguments that are important to the lawyers. Put another way, sociologists who want to study law should become legally literate.

4. The sociology of law must integrate jurisprudence with policy analysis. In other words, legal sociology has to relate the moral dilemmas that concern jurisprudence to the evaluative research that concerns policy. In sum, Nonet calls for a "jurisprudential sociology," or a social science of law that speaks to the problems, and is informed by the ideas, of jurisprudence.

As we shall see throughout this book, much of the work currently being done in the sociology of law exhibits a certain degree of either the positivist or the normative theoretical approaches.

The 1980s–1990s

Similar to the sociological movement in law dominant during the first four decades of this century (see Chapter 3), critical legal studies (CLS) emerged during the 1980s and soon acquired a measured degree of prominence. And like the sociological movement in law, CLS arose not in departments of sociology but in the law schools. Be that as it may, much of CLS is highly sociological in orientation.

The chief goal of CLS is to critique the liberal legal doctrine found in most of the Western European and North Atlantic countries. The Critics maintain that liberal legal doctrine is rife with contradictions and inconsistencies. Harvard law professor Roberto Unger's article "The Critical Legal Studies Movement" (1983) is perhaps the most influential statement in CLS. In this article Unger posits that CLS "has undermined the central ideas of [liberal] legal thought and put another conception of law in their place. This conception implies a view of society and informs a practice of politics" (1983:563). The influence of CLS on jurisprudence as well as on sociology has continued to the present. Chapter 9 will deal exclusively with the critical legal studies movement.

In their article "The Sociology of Law: Where We Have Been and Where We Might be Going" (1989), Rita J. Simon and James P. Lynch look back on the state of the sociology of law during the 1980s and make two observations. The first concerns the matter of "grand theory," or a wide-encompassing macro description or explanation of sociolegal phenomena. Simon and Lynch contend that no grand theory had been proposed in legal sociology since Donald Black's *The Behavior of Law* (1976). Their second observation is directed at legal sociology's failure to compare law across cultures. While there have indeed been some studies on comparative legal systems and institutions, Simon and Lynch note that the majority of recent work in the sociology of law is not even implicitly comparative. Finally, they posit that, in order to draw the lessons for the future, it is fruitful to compare those areas where the sociology of law has fared well and less well.

In her 1989 presidential address to the Law and Society Association, Felice Levine surveyed the emergence of numerous sociolegal studies over the past twenty-five years. She concludes her survey by stating: "I end . . . with a sense of optimism flowing from our critiques, from our current agenda of work, and from what future law and societyists can and will accomplish as they depart from and link to our past" (1990:29).

The future of legal sociology is indeed an optimistic one. As we approach the twenty-first century we can begin to discern a few wispy images of trends yet to come that will aid in strengthening legal sociology, both theoretically and empirically. These trends include the formulation of a grand theory; an increased focus on the micro level of social analysis; a greater convergence of positivist and normative theoretical approaches; more empirical research in comparative socio-legal studies where non-Western legal systems are considered; the advancement of a legal sociology of peacemaking; more dialogue with practicing attorneys; more collaboration with legal sociologists in other countries; and the cultivation of closer relationships with other theoretical approaches such as autopoiesis (Chapter 7), deconstructionism (Chapter 9), feminist theory, and neo-Marxism. To be sure, these theoretical and empirical advances, some of which are already in the making, will promote a legal sociology more suitable to our postmodern world.

SUMMARY

This first chapter addressed the questions: What is sociology? What is law? What is the sociology of law? In the process of answering these questions, several issues of importance to legal sociology were highlighted. First, we looked at sociology's reliance on concepts, theories, and paradigms. Two of the major sociological paradigms that are featured in this book are structural-functionalism and conflict theory. Next, we mentioned the difficulties involved in rendering a conclusive definition of the law concept. Third, we defined sociology of law as an academic specialty that attempts to theoretically make sense of, and explain, the relationship between law and society, the social organization of the legal institution (order or system), the social interactions of all who come in contact with the legal institution and its representatives, and the meaning that people give to their legal reality. We concluded with a brief outline of some of the major trends and developments that have characterized legal sociology since the 1950s.

In the next chapter we commence our discussion of the substantive theories of legal sociology as we turn our attention to the foundational works on law and society. We begin by examining the classical theories of Cesare Beccaria, Sir Henry Maine, Herbert Spencer, and William Graham Sumner.

• 2 •

Foundational Works
on Law and Society

This chapter looks at four classical theorists who have had an indelible influence on contemporary views of law and society: Cesare Beccaria, Sir Henry Maine, Herbert Spencer, and William Graham Sumner. Although only Spencer and Sumner were sociologists per se, the concepts advanced by all four of these early writers provide a foundational knowledge-base on which to build and advance a modern sociology of law. As a consequence, we will see these theorists' notions concerning law and society reappear periodically throughout this book. Indeed, it is precisely because their works are pivotal to understanding the sociology of law that they are featured at the beginning of this text.

The purpose of this chapter is to show how Beccaria, Maine, Spencer, and Sumner were concerned with *social and legal change*. As such, they held two major ideas in common. First, they all believed that as the conditions of history change so will society's ideology, institutions, and values inevitably and concomitantly be altered (usually for the better). Near-contemporaries, Maine, Spencer, and Sumner expressed this idea of changing social conditions through the popular Victorian concept of evolution. Second, and related, all four classical thinkers believed that legal conceptions develop in a progressive fashion and, in so doing, they induce positive social reforms. These reforms produce, among other things, a fairer justice system, greater privatization of property, increased legal equality, and more effective regulation of immoral behavior. We begin by closely examining the writings of eighteenth-century Italian legal reformer, Cesare Beccaria.

Cesare Beccaria: Legal Reformer

Almost two and a half centuries after proposing his ideas for improving the legal and penal systems of Europe, Beccaria's philosophy remains an important topic of discussion in criminology and legal sociology. To be sure, he has long been considered a founder of the classical school of criminology and, as we shall presently see, his proposals have shaped the legal systems of several countries, including that of the United States.

Life and Influences

Cesare Bonesana, Marchese di Beccaria (1738–1794) studied law at the University of Pavia (Italy) and received his doctoral degree in 1758. Ten years later he was given the position of Professor of Political Economy in the Palatine School of Milan. Beccaria was not just an ivory tower intellectual, however; he also acquired practical experience in jurisprudence with his appointment, in 1771, to be "a councillor of state and a magistrate" (Phillipson, 1923:22).

Despite his various accomplishments, Beccaria is today best remembered for one singular achievement: in 1764, at the age of twenty-six, he produced the highly renowned essay, *On Crimes and Punishments*. This slim volume, first published anonymously, was a scathing indictment against the brutal abuses of the legal and penal systems of eighteenth-century continental Europe. In short, the treatise was a clarion call to radically transform the penal system and criminal procedure of the time.

Beccaria's ideas on penology were profoundly influenced by the social and philosophical thinking predominant during the eighteenth century's Age of Enlightenment. The main currents of the Age of Enlightenment as a philosophical movement were: (1) the celebration of reason; (2) the importance of humanitarian ideals; (3) the search for knowledge, freedom, and happiness; (4) the emphasis on truth; and (5) the critiquing of the existing social order. More specifically, Beccaria's notions about crimes and punishments were largely shaped by the Enlightenment philosophers—Thomas Hobbes (1588–1679), John Locke (1632–1704), Charles de Secondat Montesquieu (1689–1755), Francois-Marie Arouet de Voltaire (1694–1778), and Jean-Jacques Rousseau (1712–1778)—and their views of society as a social contract, and of human nature.

These philosophers regarded the basic feature of society as *contractual*. Society becomes contractual, they contended, when people surrender their innate pleasure-seeking proclivities to the political state and its laws. In other words, the individual citizen makes a bargain with the state in which he or she is concomitantly: (a) obligated to refrain from engaging in certain actions that are detrimental to society, and (b) entitled to receive certain protections that are beneficial to everyone. Thus, individuals surrender to the state some self-interests such as the freedom to do as they please, but in return they acquire from the state some needs such as peace and security. This consensual agreement preserves the social order by preventing what Thomas Hobbes called "a war of all against all."

The social contract is based on the doctrine of **utilitarianism,** or the ethical philosophy that argues that all social, political, and legal action should be directed toward achieving the greatest good for the greatest number of people. The terms of the social contract are specified in the laws. Inevitably, however, there are those individuals who will breach those terms (that is, break the laws) and punishments must be introduced to instill fear in these persons and prevent them, and others with similar intentions, from violating the contract in the future. Thus, the state, operating from a utilitarian perspective, relies on punishment as a way of protecting the law-abiding citizens (the majority) from the criminals (the minority).

The Enlightenment philosophers' view of human nature was predicated on three characteristics: *hedonism, free will,* and *rationality*. First, the philosophers believed that people are basically hedonistic. **Hedonism** refers to a way of life based on the belief that pleasure is the chief goal and pain the main factor to avoid in human existence. From this perspective, individuals are seen as motivated by self-seeking desires. Second, the philosophers believed that people have **free will** to choose their own course of action. Thus, in their view, there are no external influences, spiritual or otherwise, determining an individual's behavior. Finally, the Enlightenment thinkers believed that since people are **rational** they logically and systematically contemplate the consequences of their behavior; that people weigh the pros and cons of their actions. Taking these three characteristics of human nature into account—hedonism, free will, and rationality—Beccaria concludes that individuals violate the social contract because of a volitional, rational choice they make to achieve maximum pleasure at the cost of minimum pain. But, even though lawbreaking may be personally gratifying to individuals, it is, nevertheless, a threat to the happiness and welfare of society. With these ideas in mind, Beccaria was intent on establishing a fair and rational legal system based on the doctrine of utilitarianism. He was fully convinced that the judicial and penal practices of his day had to be altered because they were grossly unfair and highly irrational. We now consider some of Beccaria's recommendations for legal reform.

Legal Reform

Generally, the legal and penal systems of eighteenth-century Europe were extremely abusive and brutal. Owing to the fact that much of it was unwritten, the law was frequently applied in an uncertain, haphazard, and biased manner. Put another way, legal obscurity gave court magistrates enormous latitude in interpreting and administering the law. Moreover, the fact that judicial cases were arbitrarily decided by the magistrates created a high degree of legal unpredictability.

Beccaria was writing at a time when it was common for people to be accused of crimes without their knowledge. The corruption of prosecutors and judges was also a widespread problem during the eighteenth century. Judges were easily bribed and offenders of wealth and high status usually influenced the court's decision in their favor. In addition, because there was little or no due process of law, the accused lacked legal protections such as the right to a speedy and public trial by an impartial jury. Finally, many punishments involved a variety of agonizing torments and the majority of offenses carried the death penalty.

Much of the repressive and desultory nature of the laws and penalties of continental Europe stemmed from its **inquisitorial system of justice**. Inquisitorial procedure began with the presumption that defendants were guilty of having committed the offenses with which they were charged. Under this system magistrates were given the power not only to judge, but also to charge and prosecute the accused. Furthermore, extracting confessions through the use of torture was done so frequently and effectively that confession was called the "queen of the proofs."

The inquisitorial system's harshness derived chiefly from the fact that it was influenced by canon (church) law and Roman law. Concerning the influence of canon law on the inquisitorial system, criminologist Paul W. Tappan (1961) explains that during the fifteenth and sixteenth centuries the Catholic Church established a tribunal of Inquisitions called the Holy Office. The Holy Office, which dealt specifically with offenses against the faith, not only deprived alleged heretics of the benefits of legal procedure, it regularly used torture in eliciting confessions. The punishments that the Holy Office commonly employed for the violation of canon law were extremely severe and consisted of burning alive, confiscation of property, excommunication, the pillory, and mutilation (Tappan, 1961:42).

The advent of Protestantism in the sixteenth century did little to improve inquisitorial brutality. For example, under Protestant theology the penalty for adultery in Electoral Saxony was death by the sword. And for the crime of sacrilege, the offender was broken on the wheel (Tappan, 1961:42).

The influence of Roman law also contributed to the cruelties and inequities of the administration of justice in continental Europe:

> In France, where the law of the eighteenth century differed but little from that of the thirteenth, the Roman law was dominant, with its investment of broad discretion in the judges to determine both the definition of crime and the penalties to be imposed. The Criminal Ordinance of 1670 made quite detailed provisions for penalties, but they were similar to those of prior centuries: the death penalty in varied forms was applicable to numerous crimes; banishment was to Corsica, foreshadowing the later system of transportation; confiscation and civil death commonly accompanied these penalties; maiming, branding, flogging, the pillory, and the iron collar were employed as corporal penalties; consignment to the galleys and imprisonment for a term of years along with exile and servile public labor were designed as 'non-corporal afflictive punishment'; finally, a class of 'infamous punishments' was used, including public reproof, the deprivation of office or privileges, or other degrading penalties, these often combined with one of the other forms of penalty (Tappan, 1961:48–49).

In sharp contrast to the inquisitorial system of the Continent, England's **adversarial system of justice** provided several procedural safeguards. In English common law: (1) accusations were public; (2) the defendant was considered innocent until proven guilty; (3) the burden of proof was on the court; (4) the accused were allowed to confront their accusers; and (5) torture was not regularly practiced. To be sure, the English and the continental legal systems during the eighteenth century represented the two ends of a continuum (Currie, 1968:8).

In light of the abusive conditions on the Continent, Beccaria advances seven general recommendations for legal reform:

1. Beccaria declares that the legislature alone, and not the judiciary, should have the power to enact and interpret the law. Judges are not lawmakers and their responsibility must be limited to determining the guilt or innocence of the accused.

This clear demarcation between the legislature and judiciary we now refer to as "the separation of powers."

   2. Beccaria argues that because society's contractual nature does not discriminate between individuals on the basis of their social status, so too should the laws be applied equally regardless of a person's station in life. In other words, *all* citizens, whether they be aristocrats or commoners, are to be guaranteed the equal protection of the laws. In order to ensure against legal bias and inequity, Beccaria calls for the accused to be judged publicly by an impartial jury.

   3. Beccaria urges that the laws be written clearly and simply so that everyone is sure to understand them. In fact, he sees an inverse correlation between the comprehensibility of the laws and the crime rate: "When the number of those who can understand the sacred code of laws and hold it in their hand increases, the frequency of crimes will be found to decrease" (1988:17). Since not all laws were written down in the eighteenth century, individuals were often punished for actions they did not even know were crimes.

   4. Following the Enlightenment philosophers, Beccaria reasons that since people are rational it is only logical that the laws also be rational. A rational legal code requires that the laws be stated generally and systematically so that they can be applied uniformly to similar types of conduct. In order to avoid ambiguity it is necessary that the law communicate clearly which types of actions are generally permitted or generally prohibited.

   5. Beccaria recommends that the burden of proof be shifted from the accused to the court: "It pertains to the law, therefore, to indicate what evidences of crime justify detention of the accused, his subjection to investigation and punishment" (1988:19).

   6. During Beccaria's time there was no difference in treatment between the accused and the convicted. Attempting to rectify this injustice he writes that "a man accused of a crime, who has been imprisoned and acquitted, ought not to be branded with infamy" (1988:19). Thus, in Beccaria's view, a defendant found innocent of a criminal charge must not be stigmatized with a negative label.

   7. Beccaria vehemently denounces the secret accusations so prevalent in his day. Secret accusations not only encourage informers to lie, he says, they also create an atmosphere of suspicion where everyone is regarded as a potential enemy.

Beccaria's objective in proposing the aforementioned reforms was to devise a system of laws that reflected and responded to society's contractual character as well to people's natural predisposition to seek gratification, decide freely their own course of action, and engage in rational thought. Accordingly, Beccaria envisioned a legal system that administered justice in a fair, equitable, and logical manner. Let us now consider Beccaria's recommendations for reforming Europe's system of punishments.

Punishments

In eighteenth-century Europe, severe and cruel punishments were inflicted on offenders as a matter of course. The repressive punishments in vogue during that time included death by the gibbet, the mallet, the axe, by lashing, burning, breaking on the wheel, infamy, consignment to the galleys, branding, amputation of limbs, the pillory, and fastening to the horse's tail (Phillipson, 1923:32). Hundreds of offenses were punishable by death, usually in an aggravated fashion. French social historian Michel Foucault, for example, gives us a glimpse of the public torture and execution of Robert-Francois Damiens, the man accused of attempting to assassinate King Louis XV with a penknife. Damiens was executed in Paris in 1757, seven years prior to the publication of *On Crimes and Punishments*. The following account is taken from an eyewitness report:

> . . . Then the executioner, his sleeves rolled up, took the steel pincers, which had been especially made for the occasion, and which were about a foot and a half long, and pulled first at the calf of the right leg, then at the thigh, and from there at two fleshy parts of the right arm; then at the breasts . . .
>
> After these tearings with the pincers, Damiens, who cried out profusely, though without swearing, raised his head and looked at himself; the same executioner dipped an iron spoon in the pot containing the boiling potion, which he poured liberally over each wound. Then the ropes that were to be harnessed to the horses were attached with cords to the patient's body; the horses were then harnessed and placed alongside the arms and legs, one at each limb . . .
>
> . . . at each torment, he cried out, as the damned in hell are supposed to cry out, 'Pardon, my God! Pardon, Lord.' Despite all this pain, he raised his head from time to time and looked at himself boldly. The cords had been tied so tightly by the men who pulled the ends that they caused him indescribable pain. . . .
>
> The horses tugged hard, each pulling straight on a limb, each horse held by an executioner. After a quarter of an hour, the same ceremony was repeated. . . .
>
> When the four limbs had been pulled away, the confessors came to speak to him; but his executioner told them that he was dead, though the truth was that I saw the man move, his lower jaw moving from side to side as if he were talking. One of the executioners even said shortly afterwards that when they had lifted the trunk to throw it on the stake, he was still alive . . . (Foucault, 1979:3–5).

Approaching penology from a perspective of Enlightenment humanitarianism compelled Beccaria to inveigh against the barbaric use of torture. Highly developed in his own country of Italy, the application of torture was measured by degrees: *levis* (light), *gravis* (harsh), and *gravissima* (very harsh) (Phillipson, 1923:35). As a result of Beccaria's treatise and similar literature produced around that time, torture in particular, but also Europe's general modes of legal punishment, were severely criticized for their savagery. Beccaria and other penal reformers argued for the fair and utilitarian administration of punishment. Indeed, Beccaria's objective was to use punishment not as a form of retaliation but as a deterrent.

Beccaria sees aggravated and violent punishments as possessing an element of overkill. Accordingly, he argues that punishment must be proportional to the crime and must not exceed its reasonable limits. In his view, punishment should not be simply a means of exacting vengeance and tormenting the offender; instead its primary purpose should be to *deter*, or prevent future acts of criminality. Beccaria further maintains that for punishment to be an effective deterrent it must meet three criteria: *severity, swiftness,* and *certainty.*

Considering people's hedonistic nature, the **severity of punishment** should just slightly outweigh the pleasure derived from the crime. Anything over that calculation, Beccaria contends, is superfluous and tyrannical. Moreover, Beccaria states that subjecting the offender to intense forms of castigation is counterproductive to the goal of deterrence. To his way of thinking the severity of punishment serves to incite individuals to commit the very crimes it is intended to prevent.

Based on the principles of what would later be known as behavioral psychology, Beccaria argues that **swiftness of punishment** is necessary so that the connection between the pleasure of the crime and the pain of the penalty is resolutely impressed in people's minds. "To this end, Beccaria suggests that the accused should be tried as speedily as possible in order to reduce to a minimum the time that elapses between the commission of the crime and its punishment" (Monachesi, 1972:44).

According to Beccaria, the third condition, the **certainty of punishment,** is the most important for successful deterrence. If people believe that there exists a high probability of getting caught and punished for their criminal actions, they, as rational individuals, will refrain from engaging in that behavior. In sum, Beccaria's three criteria of severity, swiftness, and certainty *decrease* the likelihood that punishments will be motivated by the irrational desire for revenge and applied arbitrarily. Conversely, the three criteria *increase* the likelihood that punishments will be motivated by the utilitarian goal of deterrence and applied systematically.

Finally, a few words must be said about Beccaria's opposition to the death penalty. In Beccaria's view, capital punishment is neither useful, just, or necessary and he inveighs against it for two main reasons. First, he believes that the intensity and momentary action of the death penalty is far less potent as a deterrent to crime than is the prolonged and painful duration of life in prison. Second, Beccaria sees capital punishment as a form of legal homicide, no different from the homicide committed by the criminal. According to him, the death penalty is useless because it is an example of the very barbarity that it seeks to prevent.

In the conclusion to his treatise Beccaria tersely sums up his ideas about reforming the penal system: "In order for punishment not to be, in every instance, an act of violence of one or of many against a private citizen, it must be essentially public, prompt, necessary, the least possible in the given circumstances, proportionate to the crimes, dictated by the laws" (1988:99). Beccaria's ideas were truly radical at the time that he proposed them. Nevertheless, it is noteworthy that his recommendations for overhauling the grossly unjust legal and penal systems of eighteenth-century Europe did not fall on deaf ears.

Beccaria's Influence in Europe and America

As a result of Beccaria's *On Crimes and Punishments*, legal and penal reforms took place in various European countries including Prussia, Russia, Sweden, Austria, and France. While England's legal system was undoubtedly more progressive than that of the Continent's, the former was by no means free of injustice. Indeed, Beccaria's ideas spurred the English utilitarian philosopher and penologist Jeremy Bentham (1748–1832) to speak out against the legal abuses in his own country.

The popularity and impact of *On Crimes and Punishments* also extended across the Atlantic to North America. To be sure, its "spirit" can be found in documents central to the political development of the United States such as the Declarations of Causes and Independence, the Constitution, and the Bill of Rights (Caso, 1975: 13). For example, Beccaria's concern with the excesses of punishments is found in the doctrine of *proportionality* as stipulated in the Eighth Amendment to the U.S. Constitution: "Excessive bail shall not be required, nor excessive fines imposed, nor cruel and unusual punishments inflicted." Founding Fathers Thomas Jefferson and John Adams were influenced by, and quoted from, Beccaria's book. Benjamin Rush, a noted physician and signer of the Declaration of Independence, also made reference to Beccaria in an essay that Rush wrote on the injustices of capital punishment (Maestro, 1973:137–143).

Clearly, Beccaria's recommendations for legal and penal reform have had a great influence in both Europe and America. Be that as it may, today's legal and penal systems in the United States are still endowed with a measured degree of quirkiness and bias. For example, opponents of capital punishment have argued compellingly that the death penalty is unfairly and discriminatorily applied against members of disadvantaged groups, namely, African Americans and the poor.

We now turn our attention away from Beccaria's efforts at legal reform in eighteenth-century continental Europe and toward legal influences during the Victorian period in England and America. In so doing we focus on the statements made by three near-contemporaries concerning the law and social change, the legal historian Sir Henry Maine and sociologists Herbert Spencer and William Graham Sumner. We begin with Maine since it is in his work that we may locate the first seeds of contemporary sociology of law.

Sir Henry Maine: Social Historian of Law

Sir Henry Maine's classic work on ancient legal history, and his notions about how certain types of law are connected to particular types of society, continue to enthrall students of the anthropology of law and the sociology of law. In this section we examine Maine's explanation of how legal conceptions are a product of historical development.

Life and Influences

Henry James Sumner Maine (1822–1888) spent his early childhood at Henley-on-Thames, England, until 1829 when he enrolled at Christ's Hospital (a charitable school) in London. In 1840, he was awarded a scholarship to attend Pembroke College, Cambridge. Shortly after graduating from Pembroke, Maine began his research on ancient Roman law, an enterprise that would later prove highly advantageous to writing his famous book on that subject. In 1847, at the age of twenty-five, he became Professor of Civil Law at Cambridge University and three years later he was admitted to the bar. Maine served as Professor of Jurisprudence at Oxford until he became Professor of International Law at Cambridge in 1887.

Henry Maine published numerous lectures and articles on or around the theme of law and society. However, his major contributions to legal sociology stem chiefly from his first and most widely recognized book, *Ancient Law* (1861).

Maine's sociological analysis in *Ancient Law* involves tracing the historical development of archaic legal ideas (particularly those of Roman jurisprudence), and explaining their influence on modern social institutions. Nevertheless, despite his use of the historical-comparative method and his undeniable contributions to legal sociology, Maine did not actually produce a systematic theory explaining the ultimate origins of law. R. C. J. Cocks, who wrote a biography on Maine, explains that nowhere in *Ancient Law* does Maine attempt to apply an explanatory theory to all of his observations, and as a result there is no "Maineian" legal theory (1988:78). There are, however, strong grounds for regarding Maine, through the publication of his *Ancient Law*, as an important forerunner of modern sociology (Feaver, 1969: 58). For example, Maine clearly delineated a natural history of law (Pollock, 1970: xiv). Indeed, the initial popularity of this work, which appeared just shortly after Charles Darwin's *On the Origin of Species* (1859), is attributed to the fact that Maine explained the law's sociohistorical development in the sort of evolutionary terms that were popular during the Victorian era (Cocks, 1988:52).

In what follows we briefly examine the law's evolutionary development—from status to contract—as explained in *Ancient Law*.

From Status to Contract

Undoubtedly, Maine's most enduring contribution to the sociology of law is his proposal that societies undergo a transition from status to contract. In his view, this social evolution involves a move from giving legal emphasis to the individual's rights and duties based on *status*, or the social position derived from *family* relations, to giving legal emphasis to the individual's rights and duties based on *contract*, or those personal bargains resulting from *individual* will. Let us first consider the individual's legal status within the context of the early Roman family.

The family. According to Maine, the earliest of the progressive societies were organized into patriarchal family units. Indeed, "society" in premodern times was seen not as a collection of individuals, but as an aggregation of *families*.

In ancient Rome, the oldest male parent and head of the family, the *paterfamilias*, held *patria potestas*, or absolute "power of the father." As such, the paterfamilias could do as he pleased with his family members: from dictating the conditions of marriage and divorce to disposing of his wife, children, and slaves through adoption, sale, or death. In short, in the earliest of societies, the family, through the power of the despotic father, determined the individual's social status.

Maine regards the family of antiquity as the "original stock" from which proceeds, through "aggregation," and "as a system of concentric circles," the House, the tribe, and eventually the state. As this territoriality expands so too does the law's jurisdiction expand. The expansion causes the civil law to gain more influence over the family while the paterfamilias loses his influence and the children are liberated from their father. The gradual process of freeing the individual children from the familial bonds and absolute authority of the paterfamilias is illustrated in the evolution of Roman property law.

Originally, Roman children could not own property apart from their father because whatever they acquired was appropriated by him. The reason for this was that during the earliest Roman society the family was the dominant institution and all the members put their earnings into the common stock. Because individuals could own nothing independent of the family unit, private ownership was inconceivable.

However, Maine states that by the first years of the Roman Empire (ca. 31 B.C.E.) a series of changes began to take place in property law. The first major modification was that the civil law gradually curtailed much of the father's power and transferred it to the individual children. This transition was first evidenced when Emperor Augustus introduced the *castrense peculium*, or that law prohibiting the paterfamilias from seizing property that his sons acquired upon entering military service. By 300 C.E. the *quasi-castrense peculium* protected, from parental confiscation, everything that the sons earned as civil servants. A few years later the Emperor Constantine restricted the father's ownership of the estate his children inherited from their mother by introducing the idea of *usufruct*, or part ownership. Usufructus gave the paterfamilias only the privilege of taking produce from his children's property without damaging the property itself. Finally, in the fifth century, Justinian, emperor of the Eastern Roman Empire, stipulated in his legal code that the right of the paterfamilias to extract produce from his children's property was forfeited when the paterfamilias died.

In sum, the gradual weakening of the patria potestas eventually brought about the Law of Persons that focuses, not on the family but on the individual. We now look at how the individual's right to own private property continued to evolve in ancient Rome.

The individual. As noted previously, in the earliest Roman society the focus was on the family, not on the individual. However, as the sphere of civil law expanded, two fundamental changes took place with respect to the family and the individual. First, Roman civil law began to claim jurisdiction over family matters that were formerly under the exclusive control of the paterfamilias. Second, and related, the authority of the paterfamilias gradually diminished and the individual was subsequently emancipated from the family. In the most famous passage in *Ancient Law*, Maine explains the progress society makes in basing an individual's legal rights and duties on private contract rather than on familial status:

> Nor is it difficult to see what is the tie between man and man which replaces by degrees those forms of reciprocity in rights and duties which have their origin in the Family. It is Contract.

> The word Status may be usefully employed to construct a formula expressing the law of progress thus indicated, . . . All the forms of Status taken notice of in the Law of Persons were derived from . . . the powers and privileges anciently residing in the Family. If then we employ Status . . . to signify these personal conditions . . . we may say that the movement of the progressive societies has hitherto been a movement *from Status to Contract* (Maine, 1970:163–165).

In this section we have seen how Maine explains the relationship between legal change and the status-to-contract social evolutionary movement. This connection between law and society lies at the heart of legal sociology and is particularly salient in the work of Maine's fellow Briton and evolutionist, Herbert Spencer.

Herbert Spencer: Social Evolutionist

In the first chapter to his 1937 book, *The Structure of Social Action*, sociologist Talcott Parsons poses the rhetorical question, "Who now reads Spencer?" He then proceeds to pronounce as "dead" Spencer's social theory. Over half a century later, Parsons's question has now become an anachronism due to Herbert Spencer's refusal to remain "dead." In fact, contemporary social theorists cannot afford to refrain from reading Spencer's works. As we shall see, Spencer's ideas on social evolution furnish legal sociologists with an insightful account of the law's progressive development.

Life and Influences

Herbert Spencer (1820–1903) never received a formal education. Thus, unlike most of the theorists featured in this book, Spencer did not obtain a university degree. Indeed, the better part of Spencer's early instruction occurred at the home of his uncle, Thomas.

The lack of a university degree prevented Herbert from pursuing an academic career and as a result he found work as an engineer with the London and Birmingham Railway. However, when Thomas died he left Herbert a rather large inheritance. From then on, not requiring steady employment, Herbert was free to pursue his intellectual interests and writing. By the time of his death, Herbert Spencer (largely as a result of his writings, for he despised lecturing) had achieved prominence as one of the foremost intellectuals of Victorian England.

Spencer was highly selective of what he read. Accordingly, he seems to have had only scant acquaintance with some of the main contemporaneous trends in psychology, history, and philosophy. Ironically, Spencer was also one of the most erudite thinkers of the nineteenth century. This paradox has led sociologist Lewis Coser to remark caustically that "critics now seem to be of the opinion that deep down Spencer was a rather shallow philosopher" (1979:89).

Although he usually refused to acknowledge them, Spencer's intellectual influences were many. His political philosophy of **laissez-faire,** or *government nonintervention,* was in all likelihood derived from the writings of Scottish economist

Adam Smith (1723–1790). Spencer's doctrine of "survival of the fittest" was derived in part from the demographer Thomas Malthus's (1766–1834) idea that population pressures contributed to social progress. And it was because of French naturalist Jean-Baptiste Lamarck's (1744–1829) theory of biological evolution that Spencer was able to formulate his own theory of social evolution. Moreover, embryologist Karl Ernst von Baer's (1792–1876) theory that progress proceeds from homogeneity to heterogeneity shaped Spencer's explanation of social evolution. Finally, and perhaps most significantly, Charles Darwin's (1809–1882) concepts of "adaptation," "competition," and "natural selection" provided Spencer's work with an overarching theoretical framework. To be sure, Spencer's social and political philosophy has long been called **social Darwinism** because it argues for a laissez-faire approach to human social affairs and advances the notion that the strongest, most capable people will and should gain more in the struggle for survival than the weaker and less capable.

Principal Concepts in Spencer's Sociology

Our concern in this book is not with the entirety or even the bulk of Spencer's work. Our interest is limited to his statements concerning the origins and evolution of the law. As such, we need to briefly discuss those key sociological concepts utilized by Spencer in articulating his ideas on legal development and progression. Two principal concepts in Spencer's sociology are his notion of social evolution and the distinction that he makes between militant and industrial societies.

Social evolution. One of the concepts that Spencer articulates early in his writings and subsequently employs throughout his career is the notion of *evolution*. Spencer defines **evolution** as "an integration of matter and concomitant dissipation of motion; during which the matter passes from an indefinite incoherent homogeneity to a definite coherent heterogeneity; and during which the retained motion undergoes a parallel transformation" (1880:343). In his view, every aspect of the universe, including the societal, is subject to evolutionary change.

Applying his notion of social evolution Spencer suggests the idea that as society increases in population size and density, progressive changes in its structure and organization will result. The outcome of these changes is increased *differentiation*. That is to say that as society evolves, its institutions will experience greater *heterogeneity*, or differences, within and between each other. In Spencer's own words, "the transformation of the homogeneous into the heterogeneous is that in which progress essentially consists" (1899:10). Thus, the more advanced and heterogeneous is a society, the more elaborate and differentiated will be its political organization.

According to Spencer, social differentiation first arises in the political institution when one individual proclaims himself or herself chief and begins to exercise authority over the other individuals. As society continues to evolve it becomes more politically differentiated and produces a chief of chiefs. Later, with continued social evolution there develops an even more differentiated political system with its hierarchy of kings, local rulers, petty chiefs, and so on (Spencer, 1898, Vol. I:471–473). Depending on whether their political organization is relatively undifferentiated or relatively differentiated, Spencer classifies societies as either militant or industrial.

Militant and industrial societies. Spencer characterizes **militant societies**, like the ancient Egyptian and Inca empires, as being nearly always at war with other societies. In order to deal with external enemies threatening their existence, militant societies develop a centralized, and thus relatively undifferentiated, form of governmental authority. In other words, because militant societies require a regulative structure for mobilizing an army, the political organization that arises will be one of despotism. In this case a divinely inspired ruler possesses absolute power and exerts control over the religious, military, and political areas of life. Thus, he is at once the high priest, the commander-in-chief, and the political head. The ruler maintains political regulation through *compulsory cooperation*, or the fact that all citizens, combatants and noncombatants, are forced to take collective action in the war effort. The authoritarian government in militant societies suspends all civil rights and the citizen is allowed to pursue private ends only when the state has no need of him or her. In short, in militant societies the individual is owned by the state.

Relative to militant societies, **industrial societies**, like modern England and America, are more advanced in regard to social evolution, have little involvement in war, and are almost exclusively occupied with the production and distribution of goods. Indeed, societies of the industrial type are characterized not by external conflicts but by commercial or economic competition. Lacking external hostilities, these societies do not need to exercise authoritarian forms of social control. Instead, they possess a decentralized, or highly differentiated, form of governmental authority consisting of several rulers who must conform their decisions to the consensus of the citizens. And while the state may legislatively interfere in matters concerning wrongful violations of commercial transactions, in all other matters regarding the "natural competition" endemic to the industrial struggle for existence, Spencer staunchly advocates strict government nonintervention. Thus, in industrial societies political regulation is based on *voluntary cooperation*, or the fact that individuals are allowed to freely pursue their own private interests.

In sum, Spencer examines societies in reference to their stage of evolutionary development and their type of governmental authority. Spencer's idea of social evolution and his militant and industrial typologies are therefore fundamental to understanding his legal sociology. Let us now see how these concepts coincide with Spencer's thoughts regarding the origins and evolution of law.

The Origins and Evolution of Law

In his discussion of legal evolution in *The Principles of Sociology* (1898), Spencer suggests that law originates from five main sources corresponding to five evolutionary stages of sociolegal development: (1) the consensus of individual interests; (2) inherited custom; (3) the special injunctions of deceased leaders; (4) the will of the living ruler; and (5) the consensus of individual interests in reconstituted form. We now consider each of these stages of legal evolution in turn.

The consensus of individual interests. In the first stage of legal evolution, the laws emerge from the prevailing sentiments and ideas of a community. Because

these premodern societies usually have an underdeveloped governmental authority—
that is, they are devoid of a state apparatus—crimes are informally settled by
exacting private revenge on the guilty party. The revenge is private because it is not
executed by the state, but rather by the victim, the victim's relatives, or by the community at large. At this stage of legal development there is no real distinction made
between a **crime,** or an action regarded as public harm and a matter of concern for the political body, and a **tort,** or an action regarded as a personal injury and
a matter between private parties.

Societies practicing this kind of "lawless law" based on the consensus of individual interests include such North American Indian nations as the Chippewas,
Shoshones, Haidahs, and Cheyenne. For example, jurist Karl Llewellyn and anthropologist E. Adamson Hoebel found that, among the Cheyenne, where chastity
in women is highly prized, sexual assault is addressed by taking personal vengeance
on the offender:

> To disturb the [chastity belt], or to assault a girl, was a private delict of first
> magnitude. Unless the offender fled into temporary exile, he stood in dan-
> ger of death at the hands of women relatives of the outraged girl.
>
> As Dog stated it, the women relatives, when informed by a girl of her
> misfortune, charged the lodge of the boy, and laying about right and left,
> destroyed whatever of his goods came to hand and killed his horses. If the
> father of the boy was at home, he came out of the lodge and stood to one
> side to let them at it. Even the parents could lose thereby. Dog avers he has
> seen this done. He probably refers to Lone Elk, who forty years ago untied
> a girl's [chastity belt], according to the testimony of Black Wolf. In this
> case the mother destroyed all the property of the boy's parents (Llewellyn
> and Hoebel, 1978:177).

In communities like those of the Cheyenne, **lex talionis,** or the law of retribution, is supported, not by governmental authority (since it is not yet fully developed), but by popular opinion. Based on an ethic of reciprocity, lex talionis
attempts to equalize injuries or losses suffered as a result of the offense. Thus, at
this first stage of legal development there exists a special concern with the "equality
of claims among the individuals concerned" (Spencer, 1898, Vol. II:528) and a
wrong against any individual must be avenged.

Inherited custom. During the second stage of legal evolution, the ideas, sentiments, and cultural knowledge of premodern societies devoid of political organization stem from a rigid set of social rules called *customs.* **Customs** are injunctions
that constitute the code of conduct for the members of a community. The members
inherit the customs from their dead ancestors.

According to Spencer, the procedure for obtaining this type of inherited law
involves several steps. First, seeking help and guidance, the members of the community invoke the ghosts of their ancestors. Certain supplicatory processes and
shibboleths are employed by the community members when they desire a reply
from the previously deceased. Next, the message is conveyed through some medium such as a dream. Finally, upon receiving the reply, it becomes a precedent and

once the precedent is established, it constitutes the custom regulating people's behavior.

The point to be made here is that in the early stages of civilization, the customs bequeathed by past generations control public conduct to a far greater degree than the laws made by the living. Or, as the great American jurist Roscoe Pound has written, "law is often in very truth a government of the living by the dead" (1906/1937:180).

The special injunctions of deceased leaders. In the third stage of legal evolution, the dictates of the *distinguished* dead supplement the set of customs discussed above. The distinguished dead are persons, such as chiefs and kings, regarded as divine beings during life. Their commands and admonitions are especially revered and constitute a sacred code of conduct. The supernatural guidance of these distinguished leaders is communicated through dreams, ceremonial invocations, priests, oracles, and the like.

Violations of these divine laws are regarded as the most reprehensible crimes and are punished severely. Transgression carries harsh penalties because it is disobedience to authority. Indeed, Spencer refers to obedience as the law's principal mandate and insubordination as its principal offense. "The breaking of a law," writes Spencer, "is punished not because of the intrinsic criminality of the act committed, but because of the implied insubordination" (1898, Vol. II:536). This notion that a violation of the king's law is an offense against the king's authority is predominant in militant societies where the sovereign has absolute power and the relation of people to the monarch is servile.

During this third stage in the development of laws, because the ruler is viewed as a divine being, all social behavior, from the most mundane to the most momentous, is under the influence of religious authority. Consequently, "sacrificial observances, public duties, moral injunctions, social ceremonies, habits of life, industrial regulations, and even modes of dressing, stand on the same footing" (Spencer, 1898, Vol. II:535). And because all transgressions require religious penance, no distinction is made between sacred law and secular law.

The will of the living ruler. In the fourth stage of legal evolution, societies increase in size and complexity and begin to establish a more definitive political authority. At this point, new behaviors are not considered in the sacred code and the sovereign of such a society must enact certain rules to address these novel forms of comportment. For example, the Law of Moses written in the Pentateuch around 1490 B.C.E., lists hundreds of religious ordinances from the sumptuary laws detailing the types of garments and jewelry to be worn by the Hebrew priests to the proper way to make religious offerings. The sacred Law of Moses, however, does not instruct today's Israeli citizens on the safety procedures of automobile driving. This instruction is found in the secular statutes of the state of Israel.

The new rules enacted by the political body, however, lack the religious character of the previous sacred codes of conduct. A distinction can now be made between sacred and secular law. Thus, at this stage salient differences emerge between crimes against God and crimes against people.

The consensus of individual interests in reconstituted form. In the most recent stage of legal evolution, the secular law is divided into two parts. First, there is the law that originates from the despotic ruler's power. As we have already seen, this type of law, found predominantly in militant societies, has as its goal the maintenance of the ruler's absolute authority. Because obedience to the ruler is compulsory, inequality among the members of society is implied.

Second, there is the law, found in industrial societies, originating from the consensus of individual interests. In this case, the law contributes to the general welfare of society and obedience to it stems from voluntary cooperation. Equality is the essential characteristic of law rooted in the public will. All, regardless of status, are treated equally by the law.

In sum, in militant societies where compulsory cooperation is predominant, law is concerned with (a) regulating the *status* of individuals; (b) maintaining status inequality; and (c) enforcing authority. By contrast, industrial societies possessing a decentralized form of government are characterized by voluntary consensus and here law functions to (a) fulfill *contracts*, or business agreements; and (b) bring about social equality. As societies evolve toward the industrial type, law based on the consensus of individual interests comes to dominate and replace law based on the will of the ruler. Thus, we can see that, in much the same way as Henry Maine, Spencer also considers the evolution of law as progressing from status to contract.

Spencer's social Darwinist ideas about evolution, government nonintervention, and survival of the fittest found their ultimate expression in America in the writings of Yale sociologist William Graham Sumner. In the next section we examine Sumner's thoughts on social Darwinism and sociolegal change.

William Graham Sumner: Champion of the Middle Classes

William Graham Sumner presents law as the product of "folkways" and "mores." With these concepts he enhances our insight into the relationship between rights, customary law, and positive law. Moreover, as we shall see, Sumner's comments concerning the origins, definition, and development of law revolve around the notion of social Darwinism.

Life and Influences

William Graham Sumner (1840–1910) entered Yale University as a student in 1859. Upon graduating he set out for Europe and further study at the universities of Geneva, Göttingen, and Oxford. In 1866, Sumner returned to Yale as a tutor and six years later he was given the chair of Political and Social Science. He would remain at the University until his retirement in 1909. Sumner's thirty-seven years at Yale were truly colorful and eventful. During that time he taught the first sociology course in the U.S.; was involved in an academic-freedom controversy concerning his use of Spencer's *Study of Sociology* as a text; wrote his most famous book, *Folkways;* and was named the second president of the American Sociological Society.

Not long after Sumner's death, sociologist Harry Elmer Barnes captured the essence of Sumner's sociological ideas when he wrote: "The late Professor Sumner stands out as the great American exponent of the laissez-faire doctrine so inseparably associated with the name of Herbert Spencer" (1919:3). In addition to being a defender of Spencerian government nonintervention, Sumner was also a dogmatic advocate of the social Darwinist, and uniquely capitalist, tenets found in liberal political theory: self-reliance, rugged individualism, private property, freedom of contract, social evolution, the struggle for existence, and *the competition of life*, or "the rivalry, antagonism, and mutual displacement in which the individual is involved with other organisms by his efforts to carry on the struggle for existence for himself" (Sumner, 1940:16). Let us examine Sumner's ideological position concerning social Darwinism and the competition of life.

Social Darwinism and the Competition of Life

A champion of the middle classes and an apologist for the wealthy, Sumner extols the idea of the social and economic competition of life. According to him, this principle demands the elimination of those segments of the population considered socially unfit: the poor, the widowed, the orphaned, and the aged. Sumner, for instance, concurs with the idea of eliminating the elderly who have lost their capability, or struggle for existence, in tribal societies. In his view, the premodern custom of children killing their aged parents is nothing short of an act of mercy. This practice, says Sumner, "testifies to the fact that the first liberty of all, the liberty to exist, becomes an unendurable burden to the savage man when he becomes old" (1934:293).

In a similar social Darwinist vein, Sumner greatly disdains the impoverished masses because they are not able participants in the competition of life. Sumner, however, glorifies the "forgotten man" of the middle classes and describes him glowingly as honest, productive, self-supporting, industrious, clean, quiet, virtuous, patient, persevering, and independent. Sumner asserts that the average worker is neglected and ignored because he "makes no clamor," "asks no favors," and does not complain or beg. By contrast, the poor, whom Sumner refers to as "the petted classes," and "who constantly arouse the pity of humanitarians and philanthropists, are the shiftless, the imprudent, the negligent, the impractical, and the inefficient, or they are the idle, the intemperate, the extravagant, and the vicious" (1934:476). Sumner regards the poor as a social and financial burden on the "forgotten man" of the middle classes and states:

> If you care for the Forgotten Man, you will be sure to be charged with *not* caring for the poor. Whatever you do for any of the petted classes wastes capital. If you do anything for the Forgotten Man, you must secure him his earnings and savings, that is, you legislate for the security of capital and for its free employment; you must oppose paper money, wildcat banking and usury laws and you must maintain the inviolability of contracts. Hence you

must be prepared to be told that you favor the capitalist class, the enemy of the poor man (1934:495).

Sumner's contempt for the poor impels him to sermonize at length on the notion of the competition of life. Indeed, Sumner carries this concept through to his last major work *Folkways* (1906), in which he examines the role of law in society. It is to this book that we now turn.

Folkways and Mores

Folkways are habitual patterns of human behavior that operate on two levels. When engaged in by the individual, they are habits; when engaged in by the group, they are customs. Guided by biological instincts and the capacity to distinguish between pleasure and pain, humans, through trial and error, partake in certain habitual patterns of behavior that prove expedient in their struggle for social existence. Although largely unconscious, these folkways help individuals satisfy their needs of hunger, love, vanity, and fear. Children learn and internalize the folkways of their society through the processes involved in socialization: tradition, imitation, and authority.

Because the folkways emerge spontaneously, people are initially unaware of them or the process by which they arise. In time, however, the folkways gain wider currency and when universally adopted by the group, these localized habits become customs.

Sumner uses language as an example of a folkway. Language satisfies the basic human need to communicate and it is an essential mechanism for engaging in cooperative efforts such as war and industry. Initially, language consists of habit as individuals haphazardly develop it. Later, it becomes part of custom when learned and accepted by the group. Lastly, language is buttressed by the authority of tradition as it is passed on from one generation to the next.

When folkways become necessary for the welfare of society and are made conscious in the minds of individuals, they are transformed into *mores*. Sumner defines **mores** as "the ways of doing things which are current in a society to satisfy human needs and desires, together with the faiths, notions, codes, and standards of well living which inhere in those ways, having a genetic connection with them" (1940:59). An example of a more is patriotism. Patriotism gives a country an identity and an ideology of unity. It also provides for a society's continued existence as a nation-state.

Mores designate the *morality* of a society and dictate what is good, proper, appropriate, and worthy. They give order and form to social life by setting limits on human behavior. When they are stated in negative terms, mores are called **taboos**. In prohibiting such actions as cannibalism and incest, taboos make moral judgments as to what is necessary to society's well-being. Finally, out of mores arise rights and laws.

Rights and Laws

Sumner maintains that **rights,** or those ethical entitlements that are considered just, are assumed in mores. It follows, therefore, that rights cannot be enunciated prior to the development of mores. Indeed, rights—such as the right to life, liberty, and the pursuit of happiness—are never fully articulated, says Sumner, until through some later philosophical development, they find their expression in proverbs, maxims, and myths, or (imperfectly) in the laws. He argues that the modern philosophers invented the idea of *natural* rights so that they could introduce rights as jural notions in advance of the law (Sumner, 1934:360). But, says Sumner, since rights reside in mores they cannot be treated as matters of the law but only as matters of political philosophy. Thus, in his view, rights cannot properly be articulated in legal declarations such as the 1789 French Rights of Man or in constitutions such as the 1791 American Bill of Rights.

Because mores are a social phenomenon determined by culture, rights, as products of mores, are characterized by cultural relativity. In other words, what is considered a right in one society may not be so considered in another. Consequently, rights, according to Sumner, are not natural, inalienable, or God-given. Rights do not have their origin in some absolute and transcendent force, rather, they arise from the "we-group," or *in-group*.

The in-group exists in relation to the "others-group," or *out-group*. The members of an in-group share sentiments of peace and security. These feelings of fellowship are possible only because, in the struggle for existence, the in-group's relationship with the out-group is one of hostility and war. The in-group's peace and security can only be maintained through government and law.

So long as the members of an in-group enjoy peace and security they will refrain from disputing about rights. However, during difficult times, when the struggle for existence has been hard and people experience the pain of injustice, they will either demand their rights or protest that their rights have been violated (Sumner, 1934:361). Sumner contends that the complainants are the weaker, less capable parties involved in some conflict of interest. Thus, when these weaker parties who have been unsuccessful in their struggle for survival demand their rights, they are essentially saying that they want the rules in the competition of life changed. Rights, Sumner maintains, give the advantage to the weaker parties.

Despite his antipathy for individual rights, Sumner nevertheless recognizes that they provide benefits for the social structure. This is evident in his description of rights as "the rules of mutual give and take in the competition of life which are imposed on comrades in the in-group, in order that the peace may prevail there which is essential to the group strength" (1940:29). Whereas rights are nothing more than philosophical expressions, mores, says Sumner, are essential for the survival of society and must be reflected in the laws. We now consider how mores are related to two main types of law, *customary law* and *positive law*.

Sumner contends that premodern societies depend mainly on customs and taboos for their principal means of social control. These societies do not rely on legal rules enacted through legislation but on legal rules that are premised on custom, **customary law.** Customary law is rooted in the customs of the people and the reverence for the ancestors from whom they inherited their folkways. For instance, anthropologist E. E. Evans-Pritchard states that the Nuer, a cattle-herding people of the Sudan in Africa, have no written law and base their entire way of life, including issues of harm and **redress** (payment for harm done), on customary conventions. He gives the following account:

> In a strict sense Nuer have no law. There are conventional compensations for damage, adultery, loss of limb, and so forth, but there is no authority with power to adjudicate on such matters or to enforce a verdict. In Nuerland legislative, judicial, and executive functions are not invested in any persons or councils. Between members of different tribes there is no question of redress; and even within a tribe, in my experience, wrongs are not brought forward in what we call a legal form, though compensation for damage (*ruok*) is sometimes paid. A man who considers that he has suffered loss at the hands of another cannot sue the man who has caused it, because there is no court in which to cite him, even were he willing to attend it. I lived in intimacy for a year with Nuer and never heard a case brought before an individual or a tribunal of any kind, and furthermore, I reached the conclusion it is very rare for a man to obtain redress except by force or threat of force (1969:162).

Sumner concedes that customary law does sometimes take a written form. He offers the *Corpus Iuris Civilis*—the Eastern Roman Emperor Justinian's body of civil law that was compiled in 528–534 C.E.—as an example of written law that is grounded in custom. Justinian's *Corpus* makes two points that are consistent with Sumner's ideas on how mores are related to customary law. First, the *Corpus* states that Roman "law exists either in writing or unwritten form" (*Institutes* 1.2.3.). Second, the *Corpus* states that mores may be accepted as law because "everyday customs, which are approved by the users, imitate statute" (*Institutes* 1.2.9.). Indeed, Justinian equates mores with the law.

A second type of law is **positive law,** or those legal rules enacted by the legislature and written in the statutes. Positive law becomes possible only after reverence for the dead ancestors and their customs has diminished. But, in order for positive law to be truly effective in regulating human behavior, it is essential that it reflect the moral convictions of the people, or mores.

Sumner sees the regulation of different "immoral" behaviors as passing through three stages: mores, police regulations, and positive law. That a behavior comes under any one of these three influences depends on four general considerations: (1) whether there is adequate knowledge to formulate legal enactments with beneficial results; (2) whether a legal enactment has enough elasticity to permit the application of a variety of appropriate sanctions; (3) whether there is sufficient popular support for the enactment or for its legitimator, the government; and (4) whether the police have enough power to make people comply with the enactment (Ball et al., 1962:537–538).

Drug use, gambling, prostitution, and other such "immoral" behaviors increasingly come under the control of positive law and carry specific sanctions. These behaviors are no longer simply a matter of mores, but of law enacted by the legislature. According to Sumner, legal "enactments come into use when conscious purposes are formed, and it is believed that specific devices can be framed by which to realize such purposes in the society" (1940:56). Restated, this means that when people decide that they want to disallow certain behaviors that they consider to be immoral, they write laws that specifically prohibit these behaviors.

On the whole, mores exert an enormous influence over many aspects of social life. But as we have seen, through time, mores gradually begin to give way to the law. Nevertheless, Sumner states succinctly and emphatically that "stateways cannot change folkways" (Greenberg, 1959:2). In other words, no legislation enacted by the state can transform the mores of the people. Let us now, with Sumner, examine the relationship between law and social change.

Law and Social Change

Basing their arguments on Sumner's maxim that stateways cannot change folkways, legal sociologists have typically deduced that (1) law can never move ahead of mores and (2) any positive law that is not firmly rooted in mores cannot bring about social change. However, contrary to popular belief, Sumner is not opposed to all attempts at social change (Starr, 1925:625). Indeed, Sumner sees law not as a passive instrument, but as an active force to be employed in inducing fundamental social reform (Ball et al., 1961–1962:1962).

On the one hand, Sumner does contend that once mores are put to familiar and continued use, it is inevitable that they will resist social change. Additionally, he believes that individuals with political power as well as the general population are both likely to resist social reform. The power-holders will oppose any kind of alterations because they have a vested interest in preserving the status quo. Similarly, Sumner sees the masses as instinctively conservative because they "accept life as they find it, and live on by tradition and habit" (1940:45). For them social change is "irksome." On the other hand, Sumner holds that "no less remarkable than the persistency of the mores is their changeableness and variation" (1940:84). Mores change in response to the changing conditions of life and it is necessary to prosperity that mores are elastic and flexible enough to adapt to these transformations.

According to Sumner, crises occur when social innovations are introduced but old mores continue to persist. These crises can be solved through either revolution or reform. In *revolution*, old mores are dismantled but they are not replaced by new ones. *Reform*, by contrast, proposes only "an arbitrary action on the mores" and no sudden or large changes are intended (Sumner, 1940:113). Because positive law reflects the moral convictions of the community, for Sumner, positive law is preferred to unplanned and chaotic revolution as a way of inducing rational, imperative social change. However, in what is one of his most frequently quoted statements, Sumner cautions that "legislation, to be strong, must be consistent with the mores" (1940:55). The end result is that sociolegal changes that are congruent with mores are easily realized, but sociolegal changes that are opposed to mores require long and patient effort, if they are possible at all. To the extent that positive law *can* contribute to social reform, Sumner maintains that it is most expediently accomplished by consciously altering people's behavior through the establishment of ritualistic practices. Changing people's specific behavior through ritual induces corresponding changes in their thoughts and moral convictions. The new moral convictions constitute new mores.

SUMMARY

In this chapter we examined the foundational works of Cesare Beccaria, Sir Henry Maine, Herbert Spencer, and William Graham Sumner. We noted that all four of these early theorists endeavored to explain how the law induces social change, and how society's historical progression renders new legal conceptions. As such, these thinkers repeatedly underscored the intimate relationship extant between law and society.

We first discussed Cesare Beccaria's ideas for radically transforming eighteenth-century continental Europe's unfair and abusive inquisitorial system of justice. Inspired by the Enlightenment philosophers' views on society and human nature, Beccaria advanced several recommendations for legal and penal reform. In regard to legal reform Beccaria proposed that: (1) judges' powers be limited to determining guilt or innocence; (2) *all* accused citizens be judged publicly and by an impartial jury; (3) the laws be made comprehensible to everyone; (4) the laws be stated and applied generally and systematically; (5) the burden of proof be on the court; (6) defendants found innocent be restored their civil rights; and (7) all accusations be made public. In regard to penal reform, Beccaria proposed that punishment be used only for the purpose of deterrence. He further argued that for punishment to be an effective deterrent it must be severe, swift, and certain. Beccaria's main objective in recommending legal and penal changes was to make the judicial system more fair, equitable, and humanitarian.

We next discussed Sir Henry Maine's ideas concerning how law evolves as it is influenced by sociohistorical developments. According to him, law initially accords rights and duties on the basis of familial status and only later, as society progresses, does it accord rights and duties on the basis of private contract. Focusing on ancient jurisprudence to illustrate the status-to-contract development, Maine explains that Roman property law underwent a transformation from joint ownership by the family to private ownership by the person. In essence, two interrelated factors helped to institute the Law of Persons and the legal notion that individuals could own property solely on the basis of private contract: Roman civil law's jurisdictional limits gradually reached into the realm of the family; and legal notions like the castrense peculium, quasi-castrense peculium, and usufruct began to lessen the Roman father's legal power over his children. Both factors aided in releasing the individual from the family's domination and gave him or her the legal right to freely and willfully make personal bargains. In sum, the law's evolutionary development proceeds from status to contract.

Turning next to Herbert Spencer, we noted that his notion of social evolution and militant-industrial typologies help to put into sociohistorical context the law's development and progression. Accordingly, we began with a discussion of his idea that social evolution involves a transformation in society's structural organization that advances from homogeneity to heterogeneity. For Spencer, the degree of heterogeneity, or differentiation, that typifies a society's political organization determines if that society is of the militant or industrial variety. Militant societies have a relatively undifferentiated (centralized) form of government, are run by a despotic ruler believed to have religious authority, and strictly regulate citizens' behavior. Industrial societies have a relatively differentiated (decentralized) form of government, are run by several democratically elected officials who represent the consensual will of the majority, and only minimally regulate citizens' behavior (laissez-faire).

We further noted that Spencer saw law as evolving through five main chronological stages. First, in premodern societies with a rudimentary form of government, laws have their origin in the consensus of individual interests. Second, law is derived from the customs inherited from a community's dead ancestors. Third, the commands of dead rulers who were regarded as divinely inspired during life make up the sacred law. Fourth, societies with a more developed form of government have a sovereign or legislative body that enacts secular law to address new behaviors. Fifth, in militant societies with a centralized form of government, secular law originates from the absolute power of the ruler, and in industrial societies, with a less centralized form of government, secular law originates from the consensus of individual interests.

To conclude this chapter, we examined William Graham Sumner's statements concerning the relationship between, and evolutionary progression of, folkways, mores, rights, customary law, and positive law. Folkways, such as language and the use of money, consist of habitual patterns of behavior that help to satisfy basic human needs and fulfill the interests of life. Mores, such as patriotism and democracy, are moral standards that designate right-living and are necessary for the welfare of society. Rights, such as the freedom of self-expression, are ethical entitlements that are considered just and are assumed in the mores. Customary law consists of crystallization's of custom inherited from ancestors. Positive law, on the other hand, consists of those written legal rules that are enacted by the political body. The crux of Sumner's legal sociology was that positive law is efficacious in, regulating human behavior, and bringing about rational, imperative social change, only if it is compatible with the mores.

By focusing their analysis on social and legal change, Cesare Beccaria, Sir Henry Maine, Herbert Spencer, and William Graham Sumner provided a conceptual foundation on which the edifice of legal sociology could be constructed. In Chapter 3 we turn our attention to the work of the next generation of scholars who began to build the sociolegal edifice as they scrutinized and critiqued the reciprocal relationship between law, politics, and economics.

Ancient Law

Sir Henry Maine

Ancient Codes

The earliest notions connected with the conception, now so fully developed, of a law or rule of life, are those contained in the Homeric words "Themis" and "Themistes." "Themis," it is well known, appears in the later Greek pantheon as the Goddess of Justice, but this is a modern and much developed idea, and it is in a very different sense that Themis is described in the Iliad as the assessor of Zeus. It is now clearly seen by all trustworthy observers of the primitive condition of mankind that, in the infancy of the race, men could only account for sustained or periodically recurring action by supposing a personal agent. Thus, the wind blowing was a person and of course a divine person; the sun rising, culminating, and setting was a person and a divine person; the earth yielding her increase was a person and divine. As, then, in the physical world, so in the moral. When a king decided a dispute by a sentence, the judgment was assumed to be the result of direct inspiration. The divine agent, suggesting judicial awards to kings or to gods, the greatest of kings, was *Themis*. The peculiarity of the conception is brought out by the use of the plural. *Themistes*, Themises, the plural of Themis, are the awards themselves, divinely dictated to the judge. Kings are spoken of as if they had a store of "Themistes" ready to hand for use; but it must be distinctly understood that they are not laws, but judgments, or, to take the exact Teutonic equivalent, "dooms." "Zeus, or the human king on earth," says Mr.

Grote, in his History of Greece, "is not a law-maker, but a judge." He is provided with Themistes, but, consistently with the belief in their emanation from above, they cannot be supposed to be connected by any thread of principle; they are separate, isolated judgments. . . .

The literature of the heroic age discloses to us law in the germ under the "Themistes" and a little more developed in the conception of "Dike." The next stage which we reach in the history of jurisprudence is strongly marked and surrounded by the utmost interest. Mr. Grote, in the second part and ninth chapter of his History, has fully described the mode in which society gradually clothed itself with a different character from that delineated by Homer. Heroic kingship depended partly on divinely given prerogative, and partly on the possession of supereminent strength, courage, and wisdom. Gradually, as the impression of the monarch's sacredness became weakened, and feeble members occurred in the series of hereditary kings, the royal power decayed, and at last gave way to the dominion of aristocracies. If language so precise can be used of the revolution, we might say that the office of the king was usurped by that council of chiefs which Homer repeatedly alludes to and depicts. At all events from an epoch of kingly rule we come everywhere in Europe to an era of oligarchies; and even where the name of the monarchical functions does not absolutely disappear, the authority of the king is reduced to a mere shadow. He becomes a mere hereditary general, as in Lacedaemon, a mere functionary, as the

36

King Archon at Athens, or a mere formal hierophant, like the *Rex Sacrificulus* at Rome. In Greece, Italy, and Asia Minor, the dominant orders seem to have universally consisted of a number of families united by an assumed relationship in blood, and, though they all appear at first to have laid claim to a quasi-sacred character, their strength does not seem to have resided in their pretended sanctity. . . . [I]n the East aristocracies became religious, in the West civil or political, the proposition that a historical era of aristocracies succeeded a historical era of heroic kings may be considered as true, if not of all mankind, at all events of all branches of the Indo-European family of nations.

The important point for the jurist is that these aristocracies were universally the depositories and administrators of law. They seem to have succeeded to the prerogatives of the king, with the important difference, however, that they do not appear to have pretended to direct inspiration for each sentence. The connection of ideas which caused the judgments of the patriarchal chieftain to be attributed to superhuman dictation still shows itself here and there in the claim of a divine origin for the entire body of rules, or for certain parts of it, but the progress of thought no longer permits the solution of particular disputes to be explained by supposing an extrahuman interposition. What the juristical oligarchy now claims is to monopolize the *knowledge* of the laws, to have the exclusive possession of the principles by which quarrels are decided. We have in fact arrived at the epoch of Customary Law. Customs or Observances now exist as a substantive aggregate, and are assumed to be precisely known to the aristocratic order or caste. Our authorities leave us no doubt that the trust lodged with the oligarchy was sometimes abused, but it certainly ought not to be regarded as a mere usurpation or engine of tyranny. Before the invention of writing, and during the infancy of the art, an aristocracy invested with judicial privileges formed the only expedient by which accurate preservation of the customs of the race or tribe could be at all approximated to. Their genuineness was, so far as possible, insured by confiding them to the recollection of a limited portion of the community. . . .

From the period of Customary Law we come to another sharply defined epoch in the history of jurisprudence. We arrive at the era of Codes, those ancient codes of which the Twelve Tables of Rome were the most famous specimen. In Greece, in Italy, on the Hellenized sea-board of Western Asia, these codes all made their appearance at periods much the same everywhere, not, I mean, at periods identical in point of time, but similar in point of the relative progress of each community. Everywhere, in the countries I have named, laws engraven on tablets and published to the people take the place of usages deposited with the recollection of a privileged oligarchy. It must not for a moment be supposed that the refined considerations now urged in favor of what is called codification had any part or place in the change I have described. The ancient codes were doubtless originally suggested by the discovery and diffusion of the art of writing. . . .

But, whatever to a modern eye are the singularities of these Codes, their importance to ancient societies was unspeakable. The question— and it was one which affected the whole future of each community—was not so much whether there should be a code at all, for the majority of ancient societies seem to have obtained them sooner or later, and, but for the great interruption in the history of jurisprudence created by feudalism, it is likely that all modern law would be distinctly traceable to one or more of those fountain-heads. But the point on which turned the history of the race was, at what period, at what stage of their social progress, they should have their laws put into writing. In the western world the plebeian or popular element in each State successfully assailed the oligarchical monopoly, and a code was nearly universally obtained *early* in the history of the Commonwealth. But, in the East, as I have before mentioned, the ruling aristocracies tended to become religious rather than military or political, and gained, therefore, rather than lost in power; while in some instances the physical conformation of

Asiatic countries had the effect of making individual communities larger and more numerous than in the West; and it is a known social law that the larger the space over which a particular set of institutions is diffused, the greater is its tenacity and vitality. From whatever cause, the codes obtained by Eastern societies were obtained, relatively, much later than by Western, and wore a very different character. . . .

Legal Fictions

When primitive law has once been embodied in a Code, there is an end to what may be called its spontaneous development. Henceforward the changes effected in it, if effected at all, are effected deliberately and from without. . . .

I confine myself in what follows to the progressive societies. With respect to them it may be laid down that social necessities and social opinion are always more or less in advance of Law. We may come indefinitely near to the closing of the gap between them, but it has a perpetual tendency to reopen. Law is stable; the societies we are speaking of are progressive. The greater or less happiness of a people depends on the degree of promptitude with which the gulf is narrowed.

A general proposition of some value may be advanced with respect to the agencies by which Law is brought into harmony with society. These instrumentalities seem to me to be three in number, Legal Fictions, Equity, and Legislation. Their historical order is that in which I have placed them. . . .

. . . But now I employ the expression "Legal Fiction" to signify any assumption which conceals, or affects to conceal, the fact that a rule of law has undergone alteration, its letter remaining unchanged, its operation being modified. . . . The *fact* is in both cases that the law has been wholly changed; the *fiction* is that it remains what it always was. It is not difficult to understand why fictions in all their forms are particularly congenial to the infancy of society. They satisfy the desire for improvement, which is not quite wanting, at the same time they do not offend the supersti-

tious disrelish for change which is always present. At a particular stage of social progress they are invaluable expedients for overcoming the rigidity of law and, indeed, without one of them, the Fiction of Adoption which permits the family tie to be artificially created, it is difficult to understand how society would ever have escaped from its swaddling clothes, and taken its first steps towards civilization. . . .

The next instrumentality by which the adaptation of law to social wants is carried on I call Equity, meaning by that word any body of rules existing by the side of the original civil law, founded on distinct principles and claiming incidentally to supersede the civil law in virtue of a superior sanctity inherent in those principles. The Equity whether of the Roman Praetors of the English Chancellors, differs from the Fictions which in each case preceded it, in that the interference with law is open and avowed. On the other hand, it differs from Legislation, the agent of legal improvement which comes after it, in that its claim to authority is grounded, not on the prerogative of any external person or body, not even on that of the magistrate who enunciates it, but on the special nature of its principles, to which it is alleged that all law ought to conform. The very conception of a set of principles, invested with a higher sacredness than those of the original law and demanding application independently of the consent of any external body, belongs to a much more advanced stage of thought than that to which legal fictions originally suggested themselves.

Legislation, the enactments of a legislature which, whether it take the form of an autocratic prince or of a parliamentary assembly, is the assumed organ of the entire society, is the last of the ameliorating instrumentalities. It differs from Legal Fictions just as Equity differs from them, and it is also distinguished from Equity, as deriving its authority from an external body or person. . . .

Law of Nature and Equity

The Romans described their legal system as consisting of two ingredients. "All nations," says the

Institutional Treatise published under the authority of the Emperor Justinian, "who are ruled by laws and customs, are governed partly by their own particular laws, and partly by those laws which are common to all mankind. The law which a people enacts is called the Civil Law of that people, but that which natural reason appoints for all mankind is called the Law of Nations, because all nations use it." The part of the law "which natural reason appoints for all mankind" was the element which the Edict of the Praetor was supposed to have worked into Roman jurisprudence. Elsewhere it is styled more simply Jus Naturale, or the Law of Nature; and its ordinances are said to be dictated by Natural Equity (*naturalis aequitas*) as well as by natural reason. . . .

Primitive Society and Ancient Law

The effect of the evidence derived from comparative [historical] jurisprudence is to establish that view of the primeval condition of the human race which is known as the Patriarchal Theory. . . . The points which lie on the surface of the history are these:—The eldest male parent—the eldest ascendant—is absolutely supreme in his household. His dominion extends to life and death, and is as unqualified over his children and their houses as over his slaves; indeed the relations of sonship and serfdom appear to differ in little beyond the higher capacity which the child in blood possesses of becoming one day the head of a family himself. The flocks and herds of the children are the flocks and herds of the father, and the possessions of the parent, which he holds in a representative rather than in a proprietary character, are equally divided at his death among his descendants in the first degree, the eldest son sometimes receiving a double share under the name of birthright, but more generally endowed with no hereditary advantage beyond an honorary precedence. A less obvious inference from the Scriptural accounts is that they seem to plant us on the traces of the breach which is first effected in the empire of the parent. The families of Jacob and Esau separate and form two nations; but the families of Jacob's children hold

together and become a people. This looks like the immature germ of a state or commonwealth, and of an order of rights superior to the claims of family relation. . . .

. . . Law is the parent's word, but it is not yet in the condition of those *themistes* which were analyzed in the first chapter of this work. When we go forward to the state of society in which these early legal conceptions show themselves as formed, we find that they still partake of the mystery and spontaneity which must have seemed to characterize a despotic father's commands, but that at the same time, inasmuch as they proceed from a sovereign, they presuppose a union of family groups in some wider organization. The next question is, what is the nature of this union and the degree of intimacy which it involves? It is just here that archaic law renders us one of the greatest of its services and fills up a gap which otherwise could only have been bridged by conjecture. It is full, in all its provinces, of the clearest indications that society in primitive times was not what it is assumed to be at present, a collection of *individuals*. In fact, and in the view of the men who composed it, it was *an aggregation of families*. The contrast may be most forcibly expressed by saying that the *unit* of an ancient society was the Family, of a modern society the Individual. . . .

. . . In most of the Greek states and in Rome there long remained the vestiges of an ascending series of groups out of which the State was at first constituted. The Family, House, and Tribe of the Romans may be taken as the type of them, and they are so described to us that we can scarcely help conceiving them as a system of concentric circles which have gradually expanded from the same point. The elementary group is the Family, connected by common subjection to the highest male ascendant. The aggregation of Families forms the Gens or House. The aggregation of Houses makes the Tribe. The aggregation of Tribes constitutes the Commonwealth. . . .

On a few systems of law the family organization of the earliest society has left a plain and broad mark in the life-long authority of the Father or other ancestor over the person and property of his descendants, an authority which we may conveniently call by its later Roman name of Patria Potestas. . . . We may infer, I think, that a strong sentiment in favor of the relaxation of the Patria Potestas had become fixed by the time that the pacification of the world commenced on the establishment of the Empire. . . .

. . . No innovation of any kind was attempted till the first years of the Empire, when the acquisitions of soldiers on service were withdrawn from the operation of the Patria Potestas, doubtless as part of the reward of the armies which had overthrown the free commonwealth. Three centuries afterwards the same immunity was extended to the earnings of persons who were in the civil employment of the state. Both changes were obviously limited in their application, and they were so contrived in technical form as to interfere as little as possible with the principle of Patria Potestas. A certain qualified and dependent ownership had always been recognized by the Roman law in the perquisites and savings which slaves and sons under power were not compelled to include in the household accounts, and the special name of this permissive property, Peculium, was applied to the acquisitions newly relieved from Patria Potestas, which were called in the case of soldiers Castrense Peculium, and Quasi-castrense Peculium in the case of civil servants. Other modifications of the parental privileges followed, which showed a less studious outward respect for the ancient principle. Shortly after the introduction of the Quasi-castrense Peculium, Constantine the Great took away the father's absolute control over property which his children had inherited from their mothers, and reduced it to a *usufruct*, or life-interest. A few more changes of slight importance followed in the Western Empire, but the furthest point reached was in the East, under Justinian, who enacted that unless the acquisitions of the child were derived from the parent's own property, the parent's rights over them should not extend beyond enjoying their produce for the period of his life. . . . The tenacity of the Romans in maintaining this relic of their most ancient condition is in itself remarkable, but it is less remarkable than the diffusion of the Potestas over the whole of a civilization from which it had once disappeared. While the Castrense Peculium constituted as yet the sole exception to the father's power over property, and while his power over his children's persons was still extensive, the Roman citizenship, and with it the Patria Potestas, were spreading into every corner of the Empire. . . .

We have now examined all parts of the ancient Law of Persons which fall within the scope of this treatise, and the result of the inquiry is, I trust, to give additional definiteness and precision to our view of the infancy of jurisprudence. The Civil laws of States first make their appearance as the Themistes of a patriarchal sovereign, and we can now see that these Themistes are probably only a developed form of the irresponsible commands which, in a still earlier condition of the race, the head of each isolated household may have addressed to his wives, his children, and his slaves. But, even after the State has been organized, the laws have still an extremely limited application. Whether they retain their primitive character as Themistes, or whether they advance to the condition of Customs or Codified Texts, they are binding not on individuals, but on Families. Ancient jurisprudence, if a perhaps deceptive comparison may be employed, may be likened to International Law, filling nothing, as it were, except the interstices between the great groups which are the atoms of society. In a community so situated, the legislation of assemblies and the jurisdiction of Courts reach only to the heads of families, and to every other individual the rule of conduct is the law of his home, of which his Parent is the legislator. But the sphere of civil law, small at first, tends steadily to enlarge itself. The agents of legal change, Fictions, Equity, and Legislation, are brought in turn to bear on the primeval institutions, and at every point of the progress, a greater number of personal rights and a larger amount of property are removed from the domestic forum to the cognizance of the public tribunals. The ordinances of the government obtain gradually the same efficacy in private concerns as in matters of state, and are no longer liable to be overridden by the behests of a despot enthroned by each hearthstone. We have in the annals of Roman law a nearly complete history of the crumbling away of an archaic system, and of the formation of new institutions from the recombined materials, institutions some of which descended unimpaired to the modern world, while others, destroyed or corrupted by contact with barbarism in the dark ages, had again to be recovered by mankind. When we leave this jurisprudence at the epoch of its final reconstruction by Justinian, few traces of archaism can be discovered in any part of it except in the single article of the extensive powers still reserved to the living Parent. Everywhere else principles of convenience, or of symmetry, or of simplification—new principles at any rate—have usurped the authority of the jejune considerations which satisfied the conscience of ancient times. Everywhere a new morality has displaced the canons of conduct and the reasons of acquiescence which were in unison with the ancient usages, because in fact they were born of them.

The movement of the progressive societies has been uniform in one respect. Through all its course it has been distinguished by the gradual dissolution of family dependency and the growth of individual obligation in its place. The individual is steadily substituted for the Family, as the unit of which civil laws take account. The advance has been accomplished at varying rates of celerity, and there are societies not absolutely stationary in which the collapse of the ancient organization can only be perceived by careful study of the phenomena they present. But, whatever its pace, the change has not been subject to reaction or recoil, and apparent retardations will be found to have been occasioned through the absorption of archaic ideas and customs from some entirely foreign source. Nor is it difficult to see what is the tie between man and man which replaces by degrees those forms of reciprocity in rights and duties which have their origin in the Family. It is Contract. Starting, as from one terminus of history, from a condition of society in which all the relations of Persons are summed up in the relations of Family, we seem to have steadily moved towards a phase of social order in which all these relations arise from the free agreement of individuals. In Western Europe the progress achieved in this direction has been considerable. Thus the status of the Slave has disappeared—it has been superseded by the contractual relation of the servant to his master. The status of the Female under Tutelage, if the tutelage be understood of persons other than her husband, has also ceased to exist; from her coming of age to her marriage all the relations she may form are relations of contract. So too the status of the Son under Power has no true place in the law of modern European societies. If any civil obligation binds together the Parent and the child of full age, it is one to which only contract gives its legal validity. The apparent exceptions are exceptions of that stamp which illustrate the rule. The child before years of discretion, the orphan under guardianship, the adjudged lunatic, have all their capacities and incapacities regulated by the Law of Persons. But why? The reason is differently expressed in the conventional language of different systems, but in substance it is stated to the same effect by all. The great majority of Jurists are constant to the principle that the classes of persons just mentioned are subject to extrinsic control on the single ground that they do not possess the faculty of forming a judgment on their own interests; in other words, that they are wanting in the first essential of an engagement by Contract.

The word Status may be usefully employed to construct a formula expressing the law of progress thus indicated, which, whatever be its value, seems to me to be sufficiently ascertained. All the forms of Status taken notice of the in the Law of Persons were derived from, and to some extent are still colored by, the powers and privileges anciently residing in the Family. If then we employ Status, agreeably with the usage of the best writers, to signify these personal conditions only, and avoid applying the term to such conditions as are the immediate or remote result of agreement, we may say that the movement of the progressive societies has hitherto been a movement from *Status to Contract.* . . .

The Early History of Property

It will be necessary for us to attend to one only among these "natural modes of acquisition," Occupatio or Occupancy. Occupancy is the advisedly taking possession of that which at the moment is the property of no man, with the view (adds the technical definition) of acquiring property in it for yourself. The objects which the Roman lawyers called *res nullius*—things which have not or have never had an owner—can only be ascertained by enumerating them. Among things which *never had* an owner are wild animals, fishes, wild fowl, jewels disinterred for the first time, and land newly discovered or never before cultivated. Among things which *have not* an owner are moveables which have been abandoned, lands which have been deserted, and (an anomalous but most formidable item) the property of an enemy. In all these objects the full rights of dominion were acquired by the *Occupant*, who first took possession of them with the intention of keeping them as his own—an intention which, in certain cases, had to be manifested by specific acts. . . .

. . . The Roman lawyers had laid down that Occupancy was one of the Natural modes of acquiring property, and they undoubtedly believed that, were mankind living under the institutions of Nature, Occupancy would be one of their practices. . . .

. . . It is only when the rights of property have gained a sanction from long practical inviolability, and when the vast majority of the objects of enjoyment have been subjected to private ownership, that mere possession is allowed to invest the first possessor with dominion over commodities in which no prior proprietorship has been asserted. The sentiment in which this doctrine originated is absolutely irreconcilable with that infrequency and uncertainty of proprietary rights which distinguish the beginnings of civilization. Its true basis seems to be, not an instinctive bias towards the institution of Property, but a presumption, arising out of the long continuance of that institution, that *everything ought to have an owner*. When possession is taken of a "res nullius,"

that is, of an object which *is* not, or has *never* been, reduced to dominion, the possessor is permitted to become proprietor from a feeling that all valuable things are naturally the subjects of an exclusive enjoyment, and that in the given case there is no one to invest with the right of property except the Occupant. The Occupant, in short, becomes the owner, because all things are presumed to be somebody's property and because no one can be pointed out as having a better right than he to the proprietorship of this particular thing. . . .

. . . We have the strongest reason for thinking that property once belonged not to individuals nor even to isolated families, but to larger societies composed on the patriarchal model; . . .

. . . The history of Roman Property Law is the history of the assimilation of Res Mancipi to Res Nec Mancipi. . . .

The only *natural* classification of the objects of enjoyment, the only classification which corresponds with an essential difference in the subject matter, is that which divides them into Moveables and Immoveables. Familiar as is this classification to jurisprudence, it was very slowly developed by Roman law, from which we inherit it, and was only finally adopted by it in its latest stage. The classifications of Ancient Law have sometimes a superficial resemblance to this. They occasionally divide property into categories, and place immoveables in one of them; but then it is found that they either class along with immoveables a number of objects which have no sort of relation with them, or else divorce them from various rights to which they have a close affinity. . . . More over, the classifications of Ancient Law are classifications implying superiority and inferiority; while the distinction between moveables and immoveables, so long at least as it was confined to Roman jurisprudence, carried with it no suggestion whatever of a difference in dignity. The Res Mancipi, however, did certainly at first enjoy a precedence over the Res Nec Mancipi, . . . [T]he objects of enjoyment honored above the rest were forms of property known first and earliest to each particular community, and dignified therefore emphatically with the designation of *Property*. On the other hand, the articles not enumerated among the favored objects seem to have been placed on a lower standing, because the knowledge of their value was posterior to the epoch at which the catalogue of superior property was settled. They were at first unknown, rare, limited in their uses, or else regarded as mere appendages to the privileged objects. Thus, though the Roman Res Mancipi included a number of moveable articles of great value, still the most costly jewels were never allowed to take rank as Res Mancipi, because they were unknown to the early Romans. . . .

I proceed to notice one or two more contrivances by which the ancient trammels of proprietary right were more or less successfully relaxed, premising that the scheme of this treatise only permits me to mention those which are of great antiquity. On one of them in particular it is necessary to dwell for a moment or two, because persons unacquainted with the early history of law will not be easily persuaded that a principle, of which modern jurisprudence has very slowly and with the greatest difficulty obtained the recognition, was really familiar to the very infancy of legal science. There is no principle in all law which the moderns, in spite of its beneficial character, have been so loath to adopt and to carry to its legitimate consequences as that which was known to the Romans as Usucapion, and which has descended to modern jurisprudence under the name of Prescription. It was a positive rule of the oldest Roman law, a rule older than the Twelve Tables, that commodities which had been uninterruptedly possessed for a certain period became the property of the possessor. . . . Usucapion did not lose its advantages till the reforms of Justinian. But as soon as law and equity had been completely fused, and when Mancipation ceased to be the Roman conveyance, there was no further necessity for the ancient contrivance, and Usucapion, with its periods of time considerably lengthened, became the Prescription which has at length been adopted by nearly all systems of modern law.

I pass by with brief mention another expedient having the same object with the last, . . . I speak of the Cessio in Jure, a collusive recovery, in a Court of Law, of property sought to be conveyed. . . .

Laws

Herbert Spencer

§ 529. If, going back once more to the primitive horde, we ask what happens when increase of numbers necessitates migration—if we ask what it is which causes the migrating part to fall into social arrangements like those of the parent part, and to behave in the same way; the obvious reply is that the inherited natures of its members, regulated by the ideas transmitted from the past, cause these results. That guidance by custom which we everywhere find among rude peoples, is the sole conceivable guidance at the outset.

To recall vividly the truth set forth in § 467, that the rudest men conform their lives to ancestral usages, I may name such further illustrations as that the Sandwich Islanders had "a kind of traditionary code . . . followed by general consent;" and that by the Bechuanas, government is carried on according to "long-acknowledged customs." A more specific statement is that made by Mason concerning the Karens, among whom "the elders are the depositaries of the laws, both moral and political, both civil and criminal, and they give them as they receive them, and as they have been brought down from past generations" orally. Here, however, we have chiefly to note that this government by custom, persists through long stages of progress, and even still largely influences judicial administration. Instance the fact that as late as the fourteenth century in France, an ordinance declared that "the whole kingdom is regulated by 'custom,' and it is as 'custom' that some of our subjects make use of the written law." Instance the fact that our own Common Law is mainly an embodiment of the "customs of the realm," which have gradually become established: its older part, nowhere existing in the shape of enactment, is to be learnt only from textbooks; and even parts, such as mercantile law, elaborated in modern times, are known only through reported judgments, given in conformity with usages proved to have been previously followed. Instance again the fact, no less significant, that at the present time custom perpetually reappears as a living supplementary factor; for it is only after judges' decisions have established precedents which pleaders afterwards quote, and subsequent judges follow, that the application of an act of parliament becomes settled. So that while in the course of civilization written law tends to replace traditional usage, the replacement never becomes complete.

And here we are again reminded that law, whether written or unwritten, formulates the rule of the dead over the living. In addition to that power which past generations exercise over present generations by transmitting their natures, bodily and mental; and in addition to the power they exercise over them by bequeathed private habits and modes of life; there is this power they exercise through these regulations for public conduct handed down orally or in writing. Among savages and in barbarous societies, the authority of laws thus derived is unqualified; and even in advanced stages of civilization, characterized by much modifying of old laws and making of new ones, conduct is controlled in a far greater degree by the body of inherited laws than by those laws which the living make.

I emphasize these obvious truths for the purpose of pointing out that they imply a tacit ancestor-worship. I wish to make it clear that when asking in any case—What is the Law? we are asking—What was the dictate of our forefathers? And my object in doing this is to prepare the way for showing that unconscious conformity to the dictates of the dead, thus shown, is, in early stages, joined with conscious conformity to their dictates.

§ 530. For along with development of the ghost-theory, there arise the practice of appealing to ghosts, and to the gods evolved from ghosts, for directions in special cases, in addition to the general directions embodied in customs. There come methods by which the will of the ancestor, or the dead chief, or the derived deity, is sought; and the reply given, usually referring to a particular occasion, originated in some cases a precedent, from which there results a law added to the body of laws the dead have transmitted.

The seeking of information and advice from ghosts, takes here a supplicatory and there a coercive form. The Veddahs, who ask the spirits of their ancestors for aid, believe that in dreams they tell them where to hunt; and then we read of the Scandinavian diviners, that they "dragged the ghosts of the departed from their tombs and forced the dead to tell them what would happen:" cases which remind us that among the Hebrews, too, there were supernatural directions given in dreams as well as information derived from invoked spirits. This tendency to accept special guidance form the dead, in addition to the general guidance of an inherited code, is traceable in a transfigured shape even among ourselves; for besides conforming to the orally declared wish of a deceased parent, children are often greatly influenced in their conduct by considering what the deceased parent would have desired or advised: his imagined injunction practically becomes a supplementary law.

Here, however, we are chiefly concerned with that more developed form of such guidance which results where the spirits of distinguished men,

regarded with special fear and trust, become deities. . . .

. . . Not forgetting the tradition that by an ancient Cretan king, a body of laws was brought down from the mountain where Jupiter was said to be buried, we may pass to the genesis of laws from special divine commands, as implied in the Homeric poems. Speaking of these Grote says:

> The appropriate Greek word for human laws never occurs: amidst a very wavering phraseology, we can detect a gradual transition from the primitive idea of a personal goddess, Themis, attached to Zeus, first to his sentences or orders called Themistes, and next by a still farther remove to various established customs which those sentences were believed to satisfy—the authority of religion and that of custom coalescing into one indivisible obligation.

Congruous in nature was the belief that "Lycurgus obtained not only his own consecration to the office of legislator, but his laws themselves from the mouth of the Delphic God." To which add that we have throughout later Greek times, the obtainment of special information and direction through oracles. Evidence that among the Romans there had occurred a kindred process, is supplied by the story that the ancient laws were received by Numa from the goddess Egeria; and that Numa appointed augurs by whose interpretation of signs the will of the gods was to be ascertained. Even in the ninth century, under the Carolingians, there were brought before the nobles "articles of law named *capitula*, which the king himself had drawn up by the inspiration of God." . . .

. . . [T]he above evidence makes it amply manifest that, in addition to those injunctions definitely expressed, or embodied in usages tacitly accepted from seniors and through them from remote ancestors, there are further injunctions more consciously attributed to supernatural beings—either the ghosts of parents and chiefs who were personally known, or the ghosts of more ancient traditionally known chiefs which have been magnified into gods. Whence it follows that originally, under both of its forms, law embodies the dictates of the dead to the living.

§ 531. And here we are at once shown how it happens that throughout early stages of social evolution, no distinction is made between sacred law and secular law. Obedience to established injunctions of whatever kind, originating in reverence for supposed supernatural beings of one or other order, it results that at first all these injunctions have the same species of authority. . . .

. . . That among the Hebrews there existed a like connexion, is conspicuously shown us in the Pentateuch; where, besides the commandments specially so-called, and besides religious ordinances regulating feasts and sacrifices, the doings of the priests, the purification by scapegoat, &c., there are numerous directions for daily conduct—directions concerning kinds of food and modes of cooking; directions for proper farming in respect of periodic fallows, not sowing mingled grain, &c.; directions for the management of those in bondage, male and female, and the payment of hired laborers; directions about trade-transactions and the sales of lands and houses; along with sumptuary laws extending to the quality and fringes of garments and the shaping of beards: instances sufficiently showing that the rules of living, down even to small details, had a divine origin equally with the supreme laws of conduct. . . .

Originating in this manner, law acquires stability. Possessing a supposed supernatural sanction, its rules have a rigidity enabling them to restrain men's actions in greater degrees than could any rules having an origin recognized as natural. They tend thus to produce settled social arrangements; both directly, by their high authority, and indirectly by limiting the actions of the living ruler. As was pointed out in § 468, early governing agents, not daring to transgress inherited usages and regulations, are practically limited to interpreting and enforcing them: their legislative power being exercised only in respect of matters not already prescribed for. . . .

While the unchangeableness of law, due to its supposed sacred origin, greatly conduces to social order during those early stages in which strong restraints are most needed, there of course results an unadaptiveness which impedes progress when there arise new conditions to be met. Hence come into use those "legal fictions," by the aid of which nominal obedience is reconciled with actual disobedience. Alike in Roman law and in English law, as pointed out by Sir Henry Maine, legal fictions have been the means of modifying statutes which were transmitted as immutable; and so fitting them to new requirements: thus uniting stability with that plasticity which allows of gradual transformation.

§ 532. Such being the origin and nature of laws, it becomes manifest that the cardinal injunction must be obedience. Conformity to each particular direction presupposes allegiance to the authority giving it; and therefore the imperativeness of subordination to this authority is primary.

That direct acts of insubordination, shown in treason and rebellion, stand first in degree of criminality, evidently follows. . . . When Abraham, treating Jahveh as a terrestrial superior . . . , entered into a covenant under which, for territory given, he, Abraham, became a vassal, circumcision was the prescribed badge of subordination; and the sole capital offense named was neglect of circumcision, implying insubordination: Jahveh elsewhere announcing himself as "a jealous god," and threatening punishment "upon the children unto the third and fourth generation of them that hate me." And the truth thus variously illustrated, that during stages in which maintenance of authority is most imperative, direct disloyalty is considered the blackest of crimes, we trace down through later stages in such facts as that, in feudal days, so long as the fealty of a vassal was duly manifested, crimes, often grave and numerous, were overlooked.

Less extreme in its flagitiousness than the direct disobedience implied by treason and rebellion, is, of course, the indirect disobedience implied by breach of commands. This, however, where strong rule has been established, is regarded as a serious offense, quite apart from, and much exceeding, that which the forbidden act intrinsically involves.

Its greater gravity was distinctly enunciated by the Peruvians, among whom, says Garcilasso, "the most common punishment was death, for they said that a culprit was not punished for the delinquencies he had committed, but for having broken the commandment of the Ynca, who was respected as God." . . . And then, beyond the criminality which disobeying the ruler involves, there is the criminality involved by damaging the ruler's property, where his subjects and their services belong wholly or partly to him. In the same way that maltreating a slave, and thereby making him less valuable, comes to be considered as an aggression on his owner—in the same way that even now among ourselves a father's ground for proceeding against a seducer is loss of his daughter's services; so, where the relation of people to monarch is servile, there arises the view that injury done by one person to another, is injury done to the monarch's property. . . . Our own history similarly shows us that, as authority extends and strengthens, the guilt of disregarding it takes precedence of intrinsic guilt. " 'The king's peace' was a privilege which attached to the sovereign's court and castle, but which he could confer on other places and persons, and which at once raised greatly the penalty of misdeeds committed in regard to them." Along with the growing check on the right of private revenge for wrongs—along with the increasing subordination of minor and local jurisdictions—along with that strengthening of a central authority which these changes imply, "offenses against the law become offenses against the king, and the crime of disobedience a crime of contempt to be expiated by a special sort of fine." And we may easily see how, where a ruler gains absolute power, and especially where he has the *prestige* of divine origin, the guilt of contempt comes to exceed the intrinsic guilt of the forbidden act. . . .

While, then, in that enforced conformity to inherited customs which plays the part of law in the earliest stages, we see insisted upon the duty of obedience to ancestors at large, irrespective of the injunctions to be obeyed, which are often trivial or absurd—while in the enforced confor-

mity to special directions given in oracular utterance by priests, or in "themistes," &c., which form a supplementary source of law, we see insisted upon the duty of obedience, in small things as in great, to certain recognized spirits of the dead, or deities derived from them; we also see that obedience to the edicts of the terrestrial ruler, whatever they may be, becomes, as his power grows, a primary duty.

§ 533. What has been said in the foregoing sections brings out with clearness the truth that rules for the regulation of conduct have four sources. Even in early stages we see that beyond the inherited usages which have a quasi-religious sanction; and beyond the special injunctions of deceased leaders, which have a more distinct religious sanction; there is some, though a slight, amount of regulation derived from the will of the predominant man; and there is also the effect, vague but influential, of the aggregate opinion. Not dwelling on the first of these, which is slowly modified by accretions derived from the others, it is observable that in the second we have the germ of the law afterwards distinguished as divine; that in the third we have the germ of the law which gets its sanction from allegiance to the living governor; and that in the fourth we have the germ of the law which eventually becomes recognized as expressing the public will.

Already I have sufficiently illustrated those kinds of laws which originate personally, as commands of a feared invisible ruler and a feared visible ruler. But before going further, it will be well to indicate more distinctly the kind of law which originates impersonally, from the prevailing sentiments and ideas, and which we find clearly shown in rude stages before the other two have become dominant. . . . By which facts we are reminded that where central authority and administrative machinery are feeble, the laws thus informally established by aggregate feeling are enforced by making revenge for wrongs a socially imposed duty; while failure to revenge is made a disgrace, and a consequent danger. In ancient Scandinavia, "a man's relations and friends who had not revenged his death, would instantly have lost that reputation which constituted their principal security." So that, obscured as this source of law becomes when the popular element in the triune political structure is entirely subordinated, yet it was originally conspicuous, and never ceases to exist. And now having noted the presence of this, along with the other mingled sources of law, let us observe how the several sources, along with their derived laws, gradually become distinguished.

Recalling the proofs above given that where there has been established a definite political authority, inherited from apotheosized chiefs and made strong by divine sanction, laws of all kinds have a religious character; we have first to note that a differentiation takes place between those regarded as sacred and those recognized as secular. . . . But in historical Athens, "the great impersonal authority called 'The Laws' stood out separately, both as guide and sanction, distinct from religious duty or private sympathies." And at the same time there arose the distinction between breach of the sacred law and breach of the secular law: "the murderer came to be considered, first as having sinned against the gods, next as having deeply injured the society, and thus at once as requiring absolution and deserving punishment." . . . In the words of Sir Henry Maine, there were "laws punishing *sins*. There were also laws punishing *torts*. The conception of offense against God produced the first class of ordinances; the conception of offense against one's neighbor produced the second; but the idea of offense against the State or aggregate community did not at first produce a true criminal jurisprudence." . . . The Mishna contains many detailed civil laws; and these manifestly resulted from the growing complication of affairs. The instance is one showing us that primitive sacred commands, originating as they do in a comparatively undeveloped state of society, fail to cover the cases which arise as institutions become involved. In respect of these there consequently grow up rules having a known human authority only. By accumulation of such rules, is produced a body of human laws distinct form the divine laws; and the offense of disobey-

ing the one becomes unlike the offense of disobeying the other. . . .

And this brings us to the differentiation of equal, if not greater, significance, between those laws which derive their obligation from the will of the governing agency, and those laws which derive their obligation from the *consensus* of individual interests—between those laws which, having as their direct end the maintenance of authority, only indirectly thereby conduce to social welfare, and those which, directly and irrespective of authority, conduce to social welfare: of which last, law, in its modern form, is substantially an elaboration. Already I have pointed out that the kind of law initiated by the *consensus* of individual interests, precedes the kind of law initiated by political authority. Already I have said that though, as political authority develops, laws acquire the shape of commands, even to the extent that those original principles of social order tacitly recognized at the outset, come to be regarded as obligatory only because personally enacted, yet that the obligation derived from the *consensus* of individual interests survives, if obscured. And here it remains to show that as the power of the political head declines—as industrialism fosters an increasingly free population—as the third element in the triune political structure, long subordinated, grows again predominant; there again grows predominant this primitive source of law—the *consensus* of individual interests. We have further to note that in its redeveloped form, as in its original form, the kind of law hence arising has a character radically distinguishing it from the kinds of law thus far considered. Both the divine laws and the human laws which originate from personal authority, have inequality as their common essential principle; while the laws which originate impersonally, in the *consensus* of individual interests, have equality as their essential principle. Evidence is furnished at the very outset. For what is this *lex talionis* which, in the rudest hordes of men, is not only recognized but enforced by general opinion? Obviously, as enjoining an equalization of injuries or losses, it tacitly assumes equality of claims among the individuals concerned. The principle of requiring "an eye for an eye and a tooth for a tooth," embodies the primitive idea of justice everywhere: the endeavor to effect an exact balance being sometimes quite curious. . . . A kindred effort to equalize in this literal way, the offense and the expiation, occurs in Abyssinia; where, when the murderer is given over to his victim's family, "the nearest of kin puts him to death with the same kind of weapon as that with which he had slain their relative." As the last case shows, this primitive procedure, when it does not assume the form of inflicting injury for injury between individuals, assumes the form of inflicting injury for injury between families or tribes, by taking life for life. . . .

But now the truth to be noted is that, with the relative weakening of kingly or aristocratic authority and relative strengthening of popular authority, there revives the partially suppressed kind of law derived from the *consensus* of individual interests; and the kind of law thus originating tends continually to replace all other law. . . . Of course in our transition state the change is incomplete. But the sympathy with individual claims, and the *consensus* of individual interests accompanying it, lead to an increasing predominance of that kind of law which provides directly for social order; as distinguished from that kind of law which indirectly provides for social order by insisting on obedience to authority, divine or human. With decline of the *régime* of status and growth of the *régime* of contract, personally derived law more and more gives place to impersonally derived law; and this of necessity, since a formulated inequality is implied by the compulsory cooperation of the one, while, by the voluntary cooperation of the other, there is implied a formulated equality.

So that, having first differentiated from the laws of supposed divine origin, the laws of recognized human origin subsequently redifferentiate into those which ostensibly have the will of the ruling agency as their predominant sanction, and those which ostensibly have the aggregate of private interests as their predominant sanction; of which two the last tends, in the course of social evolution, more and more to absorb the first. Necessarily, however, while militancy continues, the absorption remains incomplete; since obedience to a ruling will continues to be in some cases necessary.

Folkways and Mores

William Graham Sumner

Definition and Mode of Origin of the Folkways

If we put together all that we have learned from anthropology and ethnography about primitive men and primitive society, we perceive that the first task of life is to live. Men begin with acts, not with thoughts. Every moment brings necessities which must be satisfied at once. Need was the first experience, and it was followed at once by a blundering effort to satisfy it. It is generally taken for granted that men inherited some guiding instincts from their beast ancestry, and it may be true, although it has never been proved. If there were such inheritances, they controlled and aided the first efforts to satisfy needs. Analogy makes it easy to assume that the ways of beasts had produced channels of habit and predisposition along which dexterities and other psychophysical activities would run easily. Experiments with newborn animals show that in the absence of any experience of the relation of means to ends, efforts to satisfy needs are clumsy and blundering. The method is that of trial and failure, which produces repeated pain, loss, and disappointments. Nevertheless, it is a method of rude experiment and selection. The earliest efforts of men were of this kind. Need was the impelling force. Pleasure and pain, on the one side and the other, were the rude constraints which defined the line on which efforts must proceed. The ability to distinguish between pleasure and pain is the only psychical power which is to be assumed. Thus ways of doing things were selected, which were expedient. They answered the purpose better than other ways, or with less toil and pain. Along the course on which efforts were compelled to go, habit, routine, and skill were developed. The struggle to maintain existence was carried on, not individually, but in groups. Each profited by the other's experience; hence there was concurrence towards that which proved to be most expedient. All at last adopted the same way for the same purpose; hence the ways turned into customs and became mass phenomena. Instincts were developed in connection with them. In this way folkways arise. The young learn them by tradition, imitation, and authority. The folkways, at a time, provide for all the needs of life then and there. They are uniform, universal in the group, imperative, and invariable. As time goes on, the folkways become more and more arbitrary, positive, and imperative. If asked why they act in a certain way in certain cases, primitive people always answer that it is because they and their ancestors always have done so. A sanction also arises from ghost fear. The ghosts of ancestors would be angry if the living should change the ancient folkways. . . .

The Folkways Are a Societal Force

The operation by which folkways are produced consists in the frequent repetition of petty acts, often by great numbers acting in concert or, at least, acting in the same way when face to face

50

with the same need. The immediate motive is interest. It produces habit in the individual and custom in the group. It is, therefore, in the highest degree original and primitive. By habit and custom it exerts a strain on every individual within its range; therefore it rises to a societal force to which great classes of societal phenomena are due. Its earliest stages, its course, and laws may be studied; also its influence on individuals and their reaction on it. It is our present purpose so to study it. We have to recognize it as one of the chief forces by which a society is made to be what it is. Out of the unconscious experiment which every repetition of the ways includes, there issues pleasure or pain, and then, so far as the men are capable of reflection, convictions that the ways are conducive to societal welfare. These two experiences are not the same. The most uncivilized men, both in the food quest and in war, do things which are painful, but which have been found to be expedient. Perhaps these cases teach the sense of social welfare better than those which are pleasurable and favorable to welfare. The former cases call for some intelligent reflection on experience. When this conviction as to the relation to welfare is added to the folkways they are converted into mores, and, by virtue of the philosophical and ethical element added to them, they win utility and importance and become the source of the science and the art of living.

Folkways Are Made Unconsciously

It is of the first importance to notice that, from the first acts by which men try to satisfy needs, each act stands by itself, and looks no further than the immediate satisfaction. From recurrent needs arise habits for the individual and customs for the group, but these results are consequences which were never conscious, and never foreseen or intended. They are not noticed until they have long existed, and it is still longer before they are appreciated. Another long time must pass, and a higher stage of mental development must be reached, before they can be used as a basis from which to

deduce rules for meeting, in the future, problems whose pressure can be foreseen. The folkways, therefore, are not creations of human purpose and wit. They are like products of natural forces which men unconsciously set in operation, or they are like the instinctive ways of animals, which are developed out of experience, which reach a final form of maximum adaptation to an interest, which are handed down by tradition and admit of no exception or variation, yet change to meet new conditions, still within the same limited methods, and without rational reflection or purpose. From this it results that all the life of human beings, in all ages and stages of culture, is primarily controlled by a vast mass of folkways handed down from the earliest existence of the race, having the nature of the ways of other animals, only the topmost layers of which are subject to change and control, and have been somewhat modified by human philosophy, ethics, and religion, or by other acts of intelligent reflection. We are told of savages that "It is difficult to exhaust the customs and small ceremonial usages of a savage people. Custom regulates the whole of a man's actions,—his bathing, washing, cutting his hair, eating, drinking, and fasting. From his cradle to his grave he is the slave of ancient usage. In his life there is nothing free, nothing original, nothing spontaneous, no progress towards a higher and better life, and no attempt to improve his condition, mentally, morally, or spiritually."[1] All men act in this way with only a little wider margin of voluntary variation. . . .

Process of Making Folkways

Although we may see the process of making folkways going on all the time, the analysis of the process is very difficult. It appears as if there was a "mind" in the crowd which was different from the minds of the individuals which compose it. Indeed some have adopted such a doctrine. By autosuggestion the stronger minds produce ideas which when set afloat pass by suggestion from mind to mind. Acts which are consonant with the ideas are imitated. There is a give and take between man and man. This process is one of development. New suggestions come in at point after point. They are carried out. They combine with what existed already. Every new step increases the number of points upon which other minds may seize. It seems to be by this process that great inventions are produced. Knowledge has been won and extended by it. It seems as if the crowd had a mystic power in it greater than the sum of the powers of its members. It is sufficient, however, to explain this, to notice that there is a cooperation and constant suggestion which is highly productive when it operates in a crowd, because it draws out latent power, concentrates what would otherwise be scattered, verifies and corrects what has been taken up, eliminates error, and constructs by combination. Hence the gain from the collective operation is fully accounted for, and the theories of *Völkerpsychologie* are to be rejected as superfluous. Out of the process which has been described have come the folkways during the whole history of civilization. . . .

Definition of the Mores

When the elements of truth and right are developed into doctrines of welfare, the folkways are raised to another plane. They then become capable of procluding inferences, developing into new forms, and extending their constructive influence over men and society. Then we call them the mores. The mores are the folkways, including the philosophical and ethical generalizations as to societal welfare which are suggested by them, and inherent in them, as they grow. . . .

Why Use the Word Mores?

"Ethica," in the Greek sense, or "ethology," . . . would be good names for our present work. We aim to study the ethos of groups, in order to see how it arises, its power and influence, the modes of its operation on members of the group, and the various attributes of it (ethica). "Ethology" is a very unfamiliar word. It has been used for the mode of setting forth manners, customs, and mores in satirical comedy. The Latin word "mores" seems to be, on the whole, more practically convenient and available than any other for our purpose, as a name for the folkways with the connotations of right and truth in respect to welfare, embodied in them. The analysis and definition above given show that in the mores we must recognize a dominating force in history, constituting a condition as to what can be done, and as to the methods which can be employed.

Mores Are a Directive Force

Of course the view which has been stated is antagonistic to the view that philosophy and ethics furnish creative and determining forces in society and history. That view comes down to us from the Greek philosophy and it has now prevailed so long that all current discussion conforms to it. Philosophy and ethics are pursued as independent disciplines, and the results are brought to the science of society and to statesmanship and legislation as authoritative dicta. We also have *Völkerpsychologie*, *Sozialpolitik*, and other intermediate forms which show the struggle of metaphysics to retain control of the science of society. The "historic sense," the *Zeitgeist*, and other terms of similar import are partial recognitions of the mores and their importance in the science of society. It can be seen also that philosophy and ethics are products of the folkways. They are taken out of the mores, but are never original and creative; they are secondary and derived. They often interfere in the second stage of the sequence,—act, thought, act. Then they produce harm, but some ground is furnished for the claim that they are creative or at least regulative. In fact, the real process in great bodies of men is not one of deduction from any great principle of philosophy or ethics. It is one of minute efforts to live well under existing conditions, which efforts are repeated indefinitely by great numbers, getting strength from habit and from the fellowship of united action. The resultant folkways become coercive. All are forced to conform, and the folkways dominate the societal life. Then they seem true and right, and arise into mores as the norm of welfare. Thence are produced faiths, ideas, doctrines, religions, and philosophies, according to the stage of civilization and the fashions of reflection and generalization.

Consistency in the Mores

The tendency of the mores of a period to consistency . . . is greatly strengthened when people are able to generalize "principles" from acts. This explains the modern belief that principles are causative. The passion for equality, the universal use of contract, and the sentiments of humanitarianism are informing elements in modern society. Whence did they come? Undoubtedly they came out of the mores into which they return again as a principle of consistency. Respect for human life, horror at cruelty and bloodshed, sympathy with pain, suffering, and poverty (humanitarianism), have acted as "causes" in connection with the abolition of slavery, the reform of the criminal law and of prisons, and sympathy with the oppressed, but humanitarianism was a generalization from remoter mores which were due to changes in life conditions. The ultimate explanation of the rise of humanitarianism is the increased power of man over nature by the acquisition of new land, and by advance in the arts. When men ceased to crowd on each other, they were all willing to adopt ideas and institutions which made the competition of life easy and kindly.

The Mores of Subgroups

Each class or group in a society has its own mores. This is true of ranks, professions, industrial classes, religious and philosophical sects, and all other subdivisions of society. Individuals are in two or more of these groups at the same time, so that there is compromise and neutralization. Other mores are common to the whole society.

Mores are also transmitted from one class to another. . . .

Laws

Acts of legislation come out of the mores. In low civilization all societal regulations are customs and taboos, the origin of which is unknown. Positive laws are impossible until the stage of verification, reflection, and criticism is reached. Until that point is reached there is only customary law, or common law. The customary law may be codified and systematized with respect to some philosophical principles, and yet remain customary. The codes of Manu and Justinian are examples. Enactment is not possible until reverence for ancestors has been so much weakened that it is not longer thought wrong to interfere with traditional customs by positive enactment. Even then there is reluctance to make enactments, and there is a stage of transition during which traditional customs are extended by interpretation to cover new cases and to prevent evils. Legislation, however, has to seek standing ground on the existing mores, and it soon becomes apparent that legislation, to be strong, must be consistent with the mores.[2] Things which have been in the mores are put under police regulation and later under positive law. It is sometimes said that "public opinion" must ratify and approve police regulations, but this statement rests on an imperfect analysis. The regulations must conform to the mores, so that the public will not think them too lax or too strict. The mores of our urban and rural populations are not the same; consequently legislation about intoxicants which is made by one of these sections of the population does not succeed when applied to the other. The regulation of drinking places, gambling places, and disorderly houses has passed through the above-mentioned stages. It is always a question of expediency whether to leave a subject under the mores, or to make a police regulation for it, or to put it into the criminal law. Betting, horse racing, dangerous sports, electric cars, and vehicles are cases now of things which seem to be passing under positive enactment and out of the unformulated control of the mores. When an enactment is made there is a sacrifice of the elasticity and automatic self-adaptation of custom, but an enactment is specific and is provided with sanctions. Enactments come into use when conscious purposes are formed, and it is believed that specific devices can be framed by which to realize such purposes in the society. Then also prohibitions take the place of taboos, and punishments are planned to be deterrent rather than revengeful. The mores of different societies, or of different ages, are characterized by greater or less readiness and confidence in regard to the use of positive enactments for the realization of societal purposes.

How Laws and Institutions Differ from Mores

When folkways have become institutions or laws they have changed their character and are to be distinguished from the mores. The element of sentiment and faith inheres in the mores. Laws and institutions have a rational and practical character, and are more mechanical and utilitarian. The great difference is that institutions and laws have a positive character, while mores are unformulated and undefined. There is a philosophy implicit in the folkways; when it is made explicit it becomes technical philosophy. Objectively regarded, the mores are the customs which actually conduce to welfare under existing life conditions. Acts under the laws and institutions are conscious and voluntary; under the folkways they are always unconscious and involuntary, so that they have the character of natural necessity. Educated reflection and skepticism can disturb this spontaneous relation. The laws, being positive prescriptions, supersede the mores so far as they are adopted. It follows that the mores come into operation where laws and tribunals fail. The mores cover the great field of common life where there are no laws or police regulations. They cover an immense and undefined domain, and they break the way in new domains, not yet controlled at all. The mores, therefore, build up new laws and police regulations in time.

NOTES

1. *Journal of the Anthropological Institute of Great Britain*, XX, 140.
2. In the reigns of Theodosius and Honorius, imperial edicts and rescripts were paralyzed by the impalpable, quietly irresistible force of a universal social need or sentiment.—Dill, *Rome from Nero to M. Aurel.*, 255.

• 3 •

The Sociological Movement in Law

In the previous chapter we saw how the foundational works of Beccaria, Maine, Spencer, and Sumner reveal the intricate relationship between law and society. In this chapter we devote our attention to those twentieth century legal thinkers who instigated the sociological movement in law that has deepened our understanding of political and economic influences on the legal order. The **sociological movement in law** is an organized critique of *legal formalism*, or the doctrine in law that was dominant from the latter part of the nineteenth century to the 1940s, the time when the United States was emerging as an industrialized nation. The sociological movement in law sought to replace legal formalism with alternative forms of jurisprudence that are more predictive, pragmatic, and positivistic.

This chapter discusses the work of three American legal thinkers who affected those alternative forms of jurisprudence, Oliver Wendell Holmes, Roscoe Pound, and Karl Llewellyn. These three thinkers' philosophies of law, known as *sociological jurisprudence* and *American legal realism*, are practical, action-oriented, and informed by empirical sociology. Their goal is to fulfill and safeguard the immediate needs and interests of an ever-changing society. However, before we discuss the works of Holmes, Pound, and Llewellyn, let us first examine the historical events that led to the development of the sociological movement in law.

The Sociological Movement in Law: Prediction, Pragmatism, and Positivism

On the whole, scholars (Horwitz, 1975, 1977, 1992; Gilmore, 1977; Kennedy, 1980; Mensch, 1982; Friedman, 1985) agree that one fundamental change occurred in American legal thought at around the time of the Civil War and another at around the time of World War I. Karl Llewellyn refers to the jurisprudence that flourished during the period between the American Revolution and the Civil War, as the *Grand Style*. After the Civil War the Grand Style gave way to the Formal Style or, *legal formalism*. In the brief historical account that follows, we shall see

55

how the practical and flexible jurisprudence called the Grand Style was gradually replaced by the abstract and rigid jurisprudence called legal formalism.

The Grand Style

According to William Twining (1973), Professor of Jurisprudence at University College, London, during the 1840s and 1850s, the Grand Style of jurisprudence was epitomized in the American courts and in the thought of such influential judges as John Marshall, James Kent, Benjamin Cardozo, and Learned Hand. The **grand style** of judging is based on what Llewellyn calls "situation sense." By this he means that in all court decisions three circumstantial factors must be considered by the judge: (1) the context in which the legal facts are embedded, (2) the consequences of the law, and (3) the knowledge, experience, and values of the judge and the court (Llewellyn, 1960:60). In other words, when it comes to adjudication, the Grand Style emphasizes experience, "horse sense," and intuition. Although legal precedent is carefully regarded, what is truly important in the Grand Style is the creative fashioning of court opinions to the practical needs of a living society. Thus, a judge rendering a decision according to the Grand Style is less likely to consider abstract legal principles that are applied systematically to the *generalities* of the case, and more likely to consider extralegal factors like political and economic influences having a specific bearing on the *particulars* of the case. Let us see how the Grand Style emerged at the end of the eighteenth century and how liberal political theory contributed to its eventual demise.

Liberal Political Theory

Immediately following Independence from Great Britain in 1776, the new American Republic found itself without a homegrown body of legal precepts. The only law that most American lawyers and judges of the post-Revolutionary era were familiar with was the common law of England. Thus, the legal system of the United States, in large measure, had to be based on, and developed from, English common law. What is more, the only legal sources available to the Americans were the treatises of English jurists Sir Edward Coke (1552–1634), whose reports were compiled in the late sixteenth and early seventeenth centuries, and Sir William Blackstone (1723–1780), whose *Commentaries on the Laws of England* were published between 1765 and 1769. Generally regarded as the most authoritative guide on English common law, Backstone's *Commentaries* were widely read by American jurists. The *Commentaries* were particularly important as American law borrowed heavily, albeit selectively, from them.

During the half century following the Revolutionary War, many American lawyers and judges had set as their task the "Americanization" of the common law. Indeed, because there were precious few cases previously decided in accordance with the burgeoning legal system of the United States, these jurists had to tailor their court opinions to fit the social needs and developments of the new country. In other words, the lawyers and judges of the early nineteenth century, in Grand Style, applied the law to the specific conditions of the time.

Despite the supreme concern with concrete social issues, equally as important to the U.S. legal system were those universal principles derived from the moral precepts comprising **natural law,** or that set of conduct rules said to be intrinsic to human behavior. Natural law's moral precepts consist of such basic human needs as self-preservation, control of aggression, and allocation of limited resources. The universal principle that seemed to require the most zealous protection during the early nineteenth century was the right to private property (Mensch, 1982:20). Indeed, Blackstone himself had stated that, "The right of property . . . is founded in the law of nature, and is antecedent to all civil regulations" (as cited in Miller, 1965:224–225). And, as we shall see, the right to private property would come to play a pivotal role in the economic development of the United States.

Owing to the interplay between natural law and the common law, there developed an uneasy relationship between the *morality* of natural law, which valued doing what is right for the public good, and the *commercial utility* of common law, which underscored engaging in ventures that were economically profitable for private persons. This incompatibility between morality and commercial utility directly challenged the *liberal political theory* expressed in the U.S. Constitution guaranteeing equality of opportunity to every American. Generally speaking, the Constitution gives everyone the right to life, liberty, and private property. Liberal political theory, or **liberalism,** maintains that citizens have the freedom to do as they please, within the context of their *private* world, without having to worry about governmental (i.e., legal) intervention. Thus, at the center of liberalism is the ideology of laissez-faire, or the policy that there be no government or legal interference in private economic matters. In addition, liberalism demands that the state protect private rights of individuals such as the **freedom of contract,** or the constitutionally protected entitlement to make and enforce economic bargains.

These liberal ideals notwithstanding, the amorphous blend of morality and commercial utility that made up early nineteenth century law, was highly ambiguous. As such, it was too inadequate for safeguarding the private rights of the individual from the public power of the state (Mensch, 1982:22–23). Thus, in order to protect the economic interests of people and corporations, a sphere of pure private law was sharply delineated and clearly distinguished from the sphere of public (i.e., state and federal) law. The judiciary was given the job of policing the boundaries of the two spheres. The outcome of all these efforts converted the Grand Style of adjudication into a highly integrated conceptual scheme that gave coherence not just to the law, but to liberal political theory in general (Mensch, 1982:23). That integrated conceptual scheme was legal formalism. Let us now turn our attention to the decades following the Civil War and examine legal formalism's influence on American jurisprudence.

Legal Formalism

Karl Llewellyn cogently describes the procedure of legal formalism as judicial opinions running "in deductive form with an air or expression of single-line inevitability" (1960:38). Whereas the Grand Style looked to the specifics and practicality of social needs in its judicial decision-making, legal formalism creates a system of law that is highly logical, general, and conceptualist. By *conceptualism* is meant "the theory that there are a number of [legal] principles which can be stated in schematic form" (Radin, 1931:826). Conceptualism assumes, therefore, that there exists a rationally connected scheme of preexisting legal precepts that can be discovered by judges. Thus, **legal formalism** refers to the process whereby judges derive legal rules from abstract principles and then mechanically apply those rules, through logical and deductive reasoning, in deciding the outcome of a case. Legal formalism was especially popular in the period from 1870 to 1940.

But what were the social circumstances that led to the advent of legal formalism? Harvard law professor Morton J. Horwitz states that as merchant and entrepreneurial groups gained increased political and economic power, they began to forge an alliance with the legal profession to advance their own interests through a transformation of the legal system (1975:251). Clearly, by the end of the Civil War in 1865, the golden age of American business entrepreneurship had begun. As legal historian Lawrence Friedman explains, "this was the factory age, the age of money, the age of the robber barons, of capital and labor at war" (1985:339). Moreover, the period between 1850 and 1900 is considered the climax of laissez-faire.

Most of all, American entrepreneurship required a legal system with a high degree of generality and logic: Generality ensured entrepreneurs that the courts would not interfere too specifically in their business transactions; logic gave greater predictability to the legal outcome of these business transactions. Thus, as the U.S. was transformed from an essentially agrarian subsistence economy to an increasingly market-oriented society, the law, which, through the Grand Style, had previously been regarded as the expression of the public morality, was by the middle of the nineteenth century seen as reflecting and maintaining the interests of the rich and powerful. Roscoe Pound (1938:83–84) states that the role of economics in our legal history has been to raise new needs and wants. Accordingly, the pressures of new economic interests required that the Grand Style of adjudication be reshaped to serve these new needs and wants.

If, during the post-Revolutionary era, the Grand Style was needed to produce a unique American legal system, its practicality and flexibility were no longer necessary once the major beneficiaries of that transformation had amassed their vast fortunes. One way in which the wealthy and powerful could benefit further was if the basic premise of the new jurisprudence emphasizing self-interest was somehow disguised. The best manner of hiding the fact that the law promoted and legitimated economic self-interest, cutthroat competition, and similar essential practices of a liberal, market-oriented society, was by creating a system of law that gave the appearance of being self-contained, apolitical, and that made legal reasoning seem like mathematics (Horwitz, 1975:252). This type of jurisprudence provided an advantage for the newly powerful economic groups in that, because the legal system was said to be neutral in every way, the government was prevented from using the law to redistribute the wealth equally to all segments of society. This, then, was the birth of legal formalism.

In sum, legal formalism represents the successful efforts by mercantile and entrepreneurial groups to transform the law to serve their interests, leaving them to conceive of law as a fixed and inexorable system of logically deducible rules

(Horwitz, 1975:256). The following sections will show how the twentieth century sociological movement in law took part in a large-scale revolt against legal formalism by continuously emphasizing the inextricable connection between law, politics, and economics. Oliver Wendell Holmes, whose work we discuss next, was the first to instigate the sociological movement in law as he underscored the practical necessities of life and critiqued the formalism and conceptualism of late-nineteenth-century American jurisprudence.

Oliver Wendell Holmes, Jr.

The great-grandson of a judge of the Suffolk County probate court and the grandson of a justice of the Massachusetts Supreme Judicial Court, Oliver Wendell Holmes, Jr. (1841–1935) was born to a Brahmin family in Boston. As tradition demanded, Holmes attended Harvard College and later Harvard Law School. Shortly after publishing *The Common Law* in 1881 he accepted an appointment to the Massachusetts Supreme Judicial Court. In 1902, President Theodore Roosevelt appointed him an Associate Justice of the U.S. Supreme Court. After thirty active years on the bench, Holmes resigned his position on the Court because of failing health. Oliver Wendell Holmes died two days shy of his ninety-fourth birthday.

Holmes, to be sure, never formulated a truly systematic theory of jurisprudence. His philosophy of life and law—whether expressed in his books, speeches, letters, or judicial opinions—was ambivalent, unclear, and even contradictory. Holmes's inconsistencies notwithstanding, an orientation that is decidedly sociological does run through most of his work. But it is in *The Common Law* (1881) that his sociolegal approach finds its best expression.

Holmes's Sociolegal Approach

Generally accepted as commonplace today, Holmes's explanation of how the law emerges and unfolds was revolutionary, even heretical, when he first proposed it in the late nineteenth century. According to him, it is not the judicial system per se, but society that determines which legal rules are to survive and how they will be used. Holmes points out the close association between law and society when he writes: "The law embodies the story of a nation's development" (1963:5).

In contradiction to the formalist legal doctrine of the time, holding that the law consisted of eternal truths that, through logical and deductive reasoning, yield certain rules, Holmes emphatically asserts that the law relies on fluid rules that are contingent upon the needs and demands of the social environment. In what is arguably the most famous passage in *The Common Law*, he states:

> The life of the law has not been logic: it has been experience. The felt necessities of the time, the prevalent moral and political theories, intuitions of public policy, avowed or unconscious, even the prejudices which judges share with their fellow-men, have had a good deal more to do than the syllogism in determining the rules by which men should be governed. The law embodies the story of a nation's development through many

centuries, and it cannot be dealt with as if it contained only the axioms and corollaries of a book of mathematics. In order to know what it is, we must know what it has been, and what it tends to become. We must alternately consult history and existing theories of legislation. But the most difficult labor will be to understand the combination of the two into new products at every stage (1963:5).

The keynote of Holmes's argument is that the law emerges and develops according to the considerations of what is expedient to the community. Holmes's approach is highly pragmatic in that he considers law to be inextricably connected to the practical experiences of everyday life. Common law doctrine would not have survived, Holmes contends, were it not "supported by an appearance of *good sense*" (1963:26, emphasis added).

From the foregoing passage of his famous treatise, we may conclude that Holmes sees the law as emanating from one primary source: the actual feelings and demands of the community. He does not believe, however, that the law results from a general agreement of communal wishes. Indeed, for him it is not consensus, but social *conflict* that determines which public policies will be enacted into law and which ones will fall by the wayside. Consequently, Holmes regards the true source of law as "the will of the de facto supreme power of the community" (1873:583). That is to say that in the Darwinian struggle for social existence, the public policy that becomes law is the one that satisfies the needs, interests, and preferences of the group with the political and economic power to impose its will, by force if necessary, on all the other groups in society. Holmes describes this process as "the struggle for life among competing [legal] ideas, and of the ultimate victory and survival of the strongest" (1899:449). Thus, for Holmes, the "law embodies beliefs that have triumphed in the battle of ideas and then have translated themselves into action" (1953:294–295).

In sum, Holmes's sociolegal approach views the law's development as being contingent on what a discordant society, at any given point in time, determines to be its most pressing political and economic needs and interests. Holmes's empirical view of the nature of law stands in sharp contrast to the more doctrinaire view provided by legal formalism. We now analyze, in some detail, Holmes's critique of legal formalism.

Holmes's Critique of Legal Formalism

Of all of Holmes's speeches, "The Path of the Law" (1897) is arguably the most controversial because he exposes as "fallacies" two fundamental and interrelated assumptions of legal formalism: the law is inseparably linked with, and relies upon, a system of moral standards; and the law is made up of a complete and inclusive set of fixed axioms from which judicial opinions can be logically and deductively derived and cases settled once and for all. Going beyond a mere critique of legal formalism, Holmes also proposes an alternative jurisprudence that is predictive, positivistic, and pragmatic. Let us, along with Holmes, examine formalism's assumptions and their misconceptions.

Law and morality. Holmes begins by dispelling the myth and mystique that the law is an esoteric body of abstract dogma. According to him, the law is little more than "a well-known profession" (1897:457). Holmes sees the law, very pragmatically, as a business. Moreover, the goal of the lawyer as a practitioner of that business is to *predict* if his or her client will go to jail, be fined, or acquitted. Accordingly, Holmes gives a highly practical definition of law: "The prophecies of what the courts will do in fact, and nothing more pretentious, are what I mean by the law" (1897:461).

Holmes maintains that in order for a lawyer to predict what course of action the court will take regarding a case, he or she must look at the law from the point of view of the "bad man." The bad man, says Holmes, does not care for moral standards or ethical rules but only for the material consequences that practical knowledge of the law enables him to predict. Holmes's "bad man" principle, and thus his view of the law, is not just pragmatic, it is also based on scientific empiricism, or *positivism:* an approach that looks only at the offender's concrete social action. What the law considers and punishes, Holmes posits, is not the offender's motives, intentions, or morals, but the observable outward facts of his conduct. Let us employ an account provided by Holmes in *The Common Law* to illustrate this point.

A man who intentionally sets fire to his own house, his private property, is not **liable** (legally responsible) for the crime of **arson** (the malicious and unlawful burning of a building). However, he *is* guilty of arson if his neighbor's house, being in close proximity to his own, is burned as a result. The law punishes the man for the harm he did to his neighbor regardless of the man's intentions. Thus, a crime is said to have been committed based only on the consequences of the man's actions. According to Holmes, law only works within the sphere of the senses and is wholly indifferent to the morality of conscience. That is to say that the standards of the law are external standards.

By downplaying subjective thought and focusing instead on empirical behavior, Holmes distinguishes between the legal (which is concerned with what *is*) and the moral (which is concerned with what *ought* to be). In so doing he paves the way for a positivistic understanding of the law. Thus, contrary to what the proponents of legal formalism had maintained, Holmes argues that the practical operations of the law are not supported by moral standards.

Law and logic. As we have already seen, Holmes poignantly states in *The Common Law* that, the life of the law has *not* been logic, but practical experience. Thus, the second assumption of legal formalism that Holmes sets out to falsify is the notion that the law is derived through logic and that legal rules can be worked out like mathematics from some general axioms of conduct.

Holmes maintains that lawyers and judges are trained to reason according to the method of syllogistic logic. He notes that this is the mode of thinking with which they are most comfortable. In addition, judges believe that by applying logical reasoning to a case, they can arrive at a judicial decision that is certain and absolute. However, in Holmes's view, judicial decision-making is not a logico-deductive exercise with judges finding and applying predetermined legal postulates.

According to him, the opinion that a judge renders in a case is not determined by logical inference but by the shifting wishes and feelings of the social group with the most power. To illustrate the close association that Holmes sees between social power and judicial decision-making, let us take as an example the gas-stokers strike that took place in London in 1872.

For reasons that are not readily apparent, a gas-stoker, who was also a member of the gas-stokers' labor union, was discharged from his job. The union's demand that the company reinstate the stoker was to no avail. Five union leaders refused to work until the company complied with their demand.

In a criminal trial that lasted only one day, the five union leaders were convicted of **conspiracy** (an agreement by two or more persons to do something unlawful) to break a contract of employment that they had made with their company. The company charged that the men, by refusing to work, had interfered with the company's ability to carry on its private business. The defendants were found guilty and each was sentenced to one year in jail.

The outcome of the case was critiqued on the grounds that the courts favored the dominant power group—the company—and that the law was biased. Holmes, however, agreed with the court's decision. For him "the nub of the problem was not whether the court had imposed a burden upon one class of society but whether the court had assessed accurately the dominant power in the community and resolved the conflict to reflect that balance of power" (Aichele, 1989:127).

In addition, Holmes contends that because judges must consider the various ends and desires of the competing social groups, court decisions are not certain and absolute, but constantly changing and relative (1899:460–461). Holmes believes that science evaluates which of society's ends and desires are the strongest. In deciding a case, science will simplify the judge's selection by revealing which of the competing public policies is more useful to a particular society and more responsive to the actual feelings and demands of a particular time.

Holmes stated that while at that time the lawyer dominated the rational study of law, in the future it would be the statistician and the "master of economics" who would be influential in developing a positivist legal science capable of weighing social ends and desires (1897:469). Holmes could just as easily have included the "master of sociology" to his list, but it was up to his intellectual heir, Roscoe Pound, to consider more fully sociology's role in American legal thought. Let us see how Pound, through his program of sociological jurisprudence, also inveighs against the basic tenets of legal formalism.

Sociological Jurisprudence

As legal sociologist Alan Hunt (1978) points out, the origins of **sociological jurisprudence** cannot be fully understood without first situating it in its proper sociohistorical context. In this section we begin by looking at some of the social, political, and economic factors that were influential in promoting a jurisprudence that was sociological in orientation. We end with a discussion of the theory that is the cornerstone of sociological jurisprudence, Roscoe Pound's theory of social interests.

The rise of sociological jurisprudence is crucially interwoven with the vast institutional and ideological transformations taking place in the United States during the first quarter of the twentieth century. At this time the U.S. was shedding its frontier image and entering a period of modernity, an era characterized by increased urbanization (largely as a result of massive immigration) and industrialization. Rapid social change, triggered in part by enormous economic growth, helped the country achieve its status as a major world power. In the process, however, this rapid change also conceived immense social problems characterized by new and sharper levels of tension and conflict: poor working conditions in factories, political corruption, crowded city slums, the growth of the impoverished masses, the cartelization of the American economy, and the like.

Typically sluggish in keeping up with the changing times, the American legal system entered the twentieth century in its traditional nineteenth-century guise, as formalist jurisprudence. Formalist jurisprudence, being congruent with the liberal political theory of the post-Civil War period, had previously kept legal intervention and regulation in social and economic matters to a bare minimum. This laissez-faire policy, however, did not mean the end of legal regulation. It merely meant shifting the responsibility of control from "artificial" entities such as the state to "natural" ones such as the marketplace. The self-regulating market was said to be guided by such universal principles as occupational specialization, the growth of wealth, and self-interest.

The notion of universal principles—that is, unchanging rules, fixed axioms, and general absolutes—also affected the academic disciplines of biology, economics, and sociology. Indeed, during the nineteenth century there existed an intense preoccupation with the idea that general absolutes governed the social and natural worlds. For instance, we have already seen that Herbert Spencer regarded evolution as a universal principle. Thus, it was only a matter of time before legal formalism was likewise attracted to the universal principle. However, not long into the new century, biology, economics, and sociology took a sharp methodological turn and abandoned the attempt to deduce knowledge from fixed axioms. By contrast, legal formalism persisted in tenaciously holding on to the traditional notion of universal principles and this made the law rigid and unyielding. Noting the law's inability to keep up with social progress, Roscoe Pound complained that "law has always been dominated by ideas of the past long after they have ceased to be vital in other departments of learning" (1910:25). Accordingly, legal formalism ran into the problem of not being able to adapt to the changing conditions of the time. Or, as Pound saw it, there existed a discrepancy between the *law in books* and the *law in fact*. Legal formalism revealed its inadequacy in meeting the social ends about which Holmes had previously been concerned. Put another way, the law was unable to satisfy current human interests.

With this sociohistorical context as background we may now examine sociological jurisprudence and the ideas of its chief proponent, Roscoe Pound.

Roscoe Pound

Roscoe Pound (1879–1964) was the first son of a Lincoln, Nebraska district court judge. At the age of thirteen, Pound entered the University of Nebraska where he majored in botany. He graduated in 1888 and the following year received his M.A. degree. Pound attended Harvard Law School for one year in 1889–1890, and thereafter never undertook any other formal study of the law or completed the prescribed requirements for a law degree. The scantiness of a legal education notwithstanding, Pound become Professor of Law at Northwestern University in 1907. Later, he spent one year at the University of Chicago Law School before he was appointed Professor of Law at Harvard in 1910. In 1913 Pound was made Professor of General Jurisprudence and shortly thereafter became dean of the Harvard Law School. Whatever one may say of Roscoe Pound, one thing is certain: more than any other jurist of his time, "he wanted to work more directly and immediately with the law in its service to people living together in society" (Sayre, 1948:6).

Pound introduced sociological jurisprudence in an address that he delivered before the American Bar Association in 1906. In this speech Pound calls for the reform and modernization of what he saw as an antiquated system of legal justice. "Law," he remarks in characteristically bold fashion, "is often in very truth a government of the living by the dead" (1906/1937:180). This speech is pivotal in American legal history because it marked the beginning of a new movement in law that shook, challenged, and disturbed the orthodoxy of legal formalism. As John H. Wigmore (1937), one-time dean of the Northwestern School of Law, so eloquently put it, Pound's speech was "the spark that kindled the white flame of [legal] progress."

Pound sees legal formalism as scientific and, according to him, one main benefit of science is that it transforms law into a reasoned body of principles for the administration of justice. As such, science endows the law with a certain degree of logic, precision, and predictability. Put another way, a scientific jurisprudence reduces the judges' biases, ignorance, and the possibility of corruption because it prevents his or her departure from clearly articulated, predetermined rules. Pound, however, devotes much of his time to pointing out the shortcomings of a jurisprudence that is too scientific:

> Law is not scientific for the sake of science. Being scientific as a means toward an end, it must be judged by the results it achieves, not by the niceties of its internal structure; it must be valued by the extent to which it meets its ends, not by the beauty of its logical processes or the strictness with which its rules proceed from the dogmas it takes for its foundation (1908:605).

In Pound's view, legal formalism's overly scientific bent had transformed lawmaking and judicial decision-making into an abstract and artificial enterprise. Moreover, he notes that lawyers, in regarding science as something to be pursued for its own sake, tend to forget the true purpose of law, which is to fulfill and safeguard society's needs, wants, and interests. In addition, legal formalism's rigid exposition of hard-and-fast rules prevents the law from adjusting itself to society's changing conditions. As a result, the law had become a static entity and lost its practical function in dealing with the realities of everyday life.

Formalist jurisprudence, with its a priori concepts and logico-deductive reasoning, had become a *mechanical jurisprudence,* or as legal philosopher Herbert Morris refers to it, a "slot-machine jurisprudence" where "each case falls within a rule. The facts are simply put into the appropriate slot; the judge pulls the lever and the 'logically compelled' decision comes out" (1960:202). Pound urges jurists to reject these technical operations of legal formalism and accept a more realistic and action-oriented "jurisprudence of ends." The central question to be considered, according to Pound, should be: How will a rule or decision operate in practice? His objective in asking this question is to attain a pragmatic legal science that makes rules fit cases instead of making cases fit rules.

Pound maintains that the conceptual, artificial, and technical nature of legal formalism had created a discrepancy between the written law and the more down-to-earth sentiments of the American people. That is to say, that the law's rigidity prevents it from considering the practical needs, wants, and interests of the individuals the law is meant to be serve. Accordingly, Pound posits that formalist "legal theory and doctrine reached a degree of fixity before the conditions with which law must deal today had come into existence" (1907:608). However, he notes optimistically, that with the rise and growth of political science, economics, and sociology, the time is ripe for a new tendency in legal scholarship that will consider the relations of law to society, a tendency that Pound labels sociological jurisprudence.

"In the past fifty years the development of jurisprudence has been affected profoundly by sociology," wrote Roscoe Pound in 1927. In truth, it was Pound himself who, more than any other American legal thinker before him, brought sociology fully into the realm of law. The consequence of this effort is that his sociological jurisprudence significantly promoted the recognition of law as a social phenomenon (Hunt, 1978:19).

According to sociologist Gilbert Geis (1964), the sociological components of Pound's jurisprudence are derived largely from the writings of sociologists Albion Small, Lester Ward, and most especially, E. A. Ross, who was a colleague of Pound's at the University of Nebraska. Greatly influenced by Ross's ideas on social control, Pound focuses on the law's social character and examines its influence on society. Accordingly, Pound defines law as a "highly specialized form of social control, carried on in accordance with a body of authoritative precepts, applied in a judicial and administrative process" (1942/1968:41). The notion of social control provides Pound's jurisprudence with a sociological starting point.

To be sure, Pound conceived a unique movement in law by bringing together his own judicial ideas with strands of American sociology. The influence of sociology on his legal thinking is apparent throughout his work, but it is perhaps most evident in an early attempt by him to describe sociological jurisprudence:

> The characteristic marks of the sociological jurists of the present are that they study law as a phase of social control and seek to understand its place in the whole scheme of the social order; that they regard the working of law rather than its abstract content; that they think of law as a social institution which may be improved by intelligent human effort and hold it the duty of jurists to discover the means of furthering and directing that effort; and that they lay stress upon the social purposes which law subserves rather than upon theories of sanction (Pound, 1927:326).

In sum, Pound's jurisprudence is undoubtedly sociological because it treats law not as a conceptual and logical system of formal rules, but as an institution operating within a larger societal context that functions to regulate social processes with the objective of securing and protecting society's interests. With this notion of law in mind, we are now ready to discuss Pound's explanation of how the law accomplishes its objective, his theory of social interests.

Pound's Theory of Social Interests

There is no exaggeration in saying that Pound's **theory of social interests** lies at the very heart of sociological jurisprudence. In fact, it is in all likelihood the only truly sociological theory that he ever formulated. Although Pound, in his various writings, continued to revise and elaborate on the theory, he, nevertheless, consistently advances three types of interests: the individual, the public, and the social. We will not be concerned with individual interests because they are largely tangential to our sociological analysis of Pound's jurisprudence. Further, because most commentators agree that public interests are simply a subtype of social interests, we will only look at what Pound has to say about the latter.

Because Pound's notion of social interests evolved through the years, we may put together a composite description and define **social interests** as the prevalent claims, demands, desires, or expectations that human beings collectively seek to satisfy and that society must recognize and protect through the law (Pound, 1942/ 1968:66; 1943:2; 1959, vol. III:16). Because the law protects social interests they are given the status of legal rights. Put slightly differently, a right is a legally protected social interest.

Pound regards social interests as empirical entities because they are to be found solely in the law and legal processes of society. In other words, social interests are not abstract presuppositions derived, through logical deduction, from such determinist sources as theology or philosophy. According to Pound, the social interests can be inferred only through the empirical investigation of such objective data as court decisions, legislative declarations, and what is written in various works referring to the law. "The first step in such an investigation," writes Pound, "is a mere survey of the legal order and an inventory of the social interests which have pressed upon lawmakers and judges and jurists for recognition" (1943:17). Through a painstaking and thorough analysis of hundreds of legal documents, Pound inventories the social interests that have been asserted in "civilized society" (i.e., European countries in general, and England and the United States in particular) and which must be legally recognized and achieved in order to maintain that society. He then proposes six broad categories of social interests and their subcategories.

I. *The social interest in the general security* refers to society's claim to be secure against those patterns of behavior that threaten its existence. This social interest takes five forms:

1. *The physical safety of the people.*
2. *The general health of the population.*
3. *The peace and public order.*
4. *The security of acquisitions,* or the demands that **titles** (documents that show formal ownership of property) are not vulnerable to indefinite attack.

5. *The security of transactions* refers to society's demands that previous commercial exchanges are not subject to indefinite inquiry, so as to unsettle credit and disturb business and trade.

II. *The social interest in the security of social institutions* refers to society's claim that its fundamental institutions be secure from patterns of behavior that threaten their existence or impair their efficient functioning. This social interest takes four forms:

1. *The security of domestic institutions.*
2. *The security of religious institutions.*
3. *The security of political institutions.*
4. *The security of economic institutions.*

III. *The social interest in the general morals* refers to society's claim to be secure against patterns of behavior deemed offensive to the moral sentiments of the general population.

IV. *The social interest in conservation of social resources* refers to society's claim that the goods of existence are not needlessly and completely wasted. This social interest takes two forms:

1. *The use and conservation of natural resources.*
2. *The protection and training of dependents and defectives.* ("Dependents" include minors and "defectives" include the mentally handicapped).

V. *The social interest in general progress* refers to society's claim that the development of human powers and of human control over nature for the satisfaction of human wants go forward. This social interest takes two forms:

1. *Economic progress.*
2. *Political progress.*

VI. *The social interest in the individual life* refers to society's claim that each individual be able to live a human life in accordance with the standards of the society. This social interest takes three forms:

1. *Individual self-assertion.* (This claim is expressed in those cases where self-help is allowed).
2. *Individual opportunity* refers to society's claim that all individuals have fair, reasonable, and equal opportunities.
3. *Individual conditions of life* refers to the claim that each individual be assured at least the minimum living conditions which society can provide at that point in time.

Pound's theory of social interests is true to the first and fundamental question he would have us ask: How will a rule or decision operate in practice? That is to say, what practical utility does the law have in addressing social interests? Further, Pound is quite convinced that the jurist must rely on sociology, and its use of positivistic investigation, to ascertain the de facto claims articulated by people over a span of time. Put another way, Pound believes that sociology can identify those social interests that must be secured in order to maintain a "civilized" society.

Through his program of sociological jurisprudence, Pound succeeded in directing the attention of the legal establishment of his time to the practical concerns of the study of law and to the law's relationship with society. Pound constantly underscores the social character of law and for this he deserves, along with Oliver Wendell Holmes, to be recognized as a leading figure of the sociological movement in law. All this notwithstanding, however, it was only a matter of time before Pound's legal philosophy was replaced by another. That other philosophy of law came to be known as American legal realism.

American Legal Realism

American legal realism is a pragmatic jurisprudence that, fueled by skepticism, is highly critical of the contention that legal formalism possesses a high degree of certainty, predictability, and uniformity. As was the case with sociological jurisprudence, legal realism emerged, in the late 1920s, during a period of profound social change in American society. The second decade of the twentieth century was ripe for the rise of such a movement in the law. It was a time when the values and ideals of the Progressive era, its optimism and cheerfulness, had been swept away by the global upheaval created by World War I. The result was "the decay of confidence in progress and the growth of a climate of suspicion from which the world has never quite recovered" (Savarese, 1965:181). "Earnestness, a favorite state of the prewar years," writes University of Virginia law professor G. Edward White, "was replaced by cynicism; social responsibility gave way to alienation, virtuousness appeared as hypocrisy" (1972:1014).

Along with the First World War, two other events, the stock market crash of 1929 and the resulting Great Depression, marked a repudiation of some basic assumptions about American culture that had been fostered by Progressivism. Consequently, a more skeptical, even cynical, set of ideas replaced the optimism of the Progressive era: prosperity was not permanent; capitalism, whether regulated or not, was not omnipotent; people were not capable of mastering their economic environment; and the future is not necessarily an improvement upon the past. And thus, "one by one the truths of early twentieth century America were exposed as myths. The gap between illusion and reality seemed ever-widening" (White, 1972:1017).

Despite the skepticism brought on by the aforementioned social events, an optimistic belief, a kind of unwavering faith, in science endured. Throughout most of the nineteenth century, academic interest had focused principally on the impressive achievements of the natural and the physical sciences and on their methods of research. But by the end of World War I the term "science" increasingly included the behavioral and social sciences, most notably psychology, cultural anthropology, and sociology. Infused by this faith in science, it was only natural that the realists would set out to discover how it was that the empirical method of *induction*—a technique that places emphasis on the collection, observation, and recording of facts—applies to the social sciences in general and the law in particular. Ultimately, the realists' objective was the development of an empirical science of law.

Of all the behavioral sciences, psychology, and in particular some of its then novel variants, behaviorism and Freudian psychoanalysis, most influenced legal realism. And of the social sciences it was sociology that proved an inspiration to the realists in their investigations of the *law in action*. Perhaps the one major impact that psychology had on the realists was in presenting them with the notion that human behavior was idiosyncratic and irrational and that it could be studied empirically. Accordingly, the realists believed that once the human mind had been explained by science, its effect on society and the legal institution could be better understood.

Without a doubt, however, the greatest contribution to legal realism was the fact that in the intellectual community of the 1920s (especially in the humanities and social sciences) there had been a reaction against abstractions and universal principles and a movement toward the idea of a changing and developing society. In short, there existed, at the time, an intellectual trend rejecting conceptualism but accepting of pragmatism (Kalman, 1986:15).

The Influence of Pragmatism

In 1957 political scientist Julius Paul stated that "if we were to study the history of western thought since 1850, perhaps the most important writers of the past century in terms of their impact on modern American jurisprudence would be Marx, Darwin, Comte, Freud, James and Dewey" (1957:37). To be sure, the last two thinkers on Paul's list—the pragmatist philosophers William James and John Dewey—had a most notable influence on the development of legal realism.

A prominent American thinker, William James (1842–1910) may be considered the father of pragmatist philosophy. **Pragmatism,** (derived from the Greek word meaning "action"), was generally regarded as the dominant philosophy in the U.S. during the 1920s and 1930s. James describes pragmatism as an "attitude of orientation" that consists of "looking away from first things, principles, 'categories,' supposed necessities; and of looking towards last things, fruits, consequences, facts" (1938:204). Thus, in order to achieve knowledge of the truth, James maintains that we should begin by considering the practical facts, actions, and results of an event; only secondarily should we be concerned with the fixed and pre-established concepts relating to those facts, actions, and results. It was this empirical orientation that developed in the realists a skepticism towards the conceptualist reasoning of legal formalism. Accordingly, it became obvious to the realists that legal rules did not logically and systematically determine judicial decisions that allegedly were to serve as truth for all time. Applying his pragmatism to the law, James (1975) critiques formalism as he points out that legal principles are fluid, not absolute; they change every time a new factor is introduced in a case.

Equally significant to legal realism were the teachings of John Dewey (1859–1952), the most influential American philosopher. Through his pragmatism, or more accurately his *instrumentalism*, Dewey attacks the long-held notions about the role of formal logic and syllogistic reasoning in the law. Indeed, Dewey's views about using instrumentalism probably had a greater impact upon legal realism than the ideas of any other professional philosopher (Rumble, 1968:72).

Dewey contends that the deductive method of formalist jurisprudence, which begins the reasoning process with a coherent system of pre-established premises, is of little value when it comes to such practical matters as a lawyer advising a client on what he or she should do in a case of litigation. What is truly important, Dewey argues, is how a legal idea actually works and how it is experienced in practice. Dewey advances a "logic relative to consequences rather than to antecedents, a logic of prediction of probabilities rather than one of deduction of certainties" (1924:26).

Accordingly, Dewey proposes instrumental thinking as a substitute for the rigid deductive procedure of legal formalism. His instrumentalism calls for the use of an inductive logic of the law that is based on empiricism. Thus, his logic begins not with the abstract premise of a legal rule but with the concrete conclusion of a case. This is a more experimental and flexible logic than that previously advanced by formalist jurisprudence because it inquires into the probable outcome of a legal decision.

For Dewey, the consequences of a case produce practical experience that yields the best methods to be used in logical reasoning. These methods are then studied and the causes of what makes them work are discovered. Dewey's instrumentalism makes logic an empirical science and adds credence to Holmes's statement that the actual life of the law has not been deductive logic, it has been practical experience.

Realism, Sociology, and Society

As we have seen, the realists' skepticism led them to reject the logico-deductive syllogisms of judicial decision-making as well as the emphasis on conceptualism advanced by formalist jurisprudence. Indeed, the realists' pragmatic bent directed them to focus on the *realities* of the law. As such, the realist movement enlarged the field of the legally relevant by considering extralegal, or social and psychological, factors influencing the judges' decision in a particular case. This empirical focus on the realities of law is what Pound was referring to when he distinguished between "law in books" and "law in fact."

How the judge decides the case was of the utmost interest to the realists, but so was another very practical matter: *What* the decision of a case would be. Both considerations deal with legal certainty. To be sure, the work of some realists is characterized by an abiding concern with enabling the practicing lawyer to make more accurate predictions regarding the outcome of cases. Clearly, many of the realists, albeit with some notable exceptions, "accept the prediction theory of law as their basic theme for devising a science of law" (Moskowitz, 1966:482).

The realist movement consisted of a large and divergent group of jurists, law professors, and practicing lawyers representing a wide variety of theoretical viewpoints. Despite their conceptual differences, however, the realists shared the empiricism of science in critiquing legal formalism.

Lon L. Fuller (1934), one of legal realism's most outspoken critics, considers Karl Llewellyn the person most representative of the movement as a whole for three reasons: (1) Llewellyn's view of realism was distinctly middle-of-the road; (2) Llewellyn had written extensively and his writings constitute a fairly comprehensive exposition of realist jurisprudence; and (3) more than any other realist, Llewellyn revealed the philosophical approach that was implied in his work. In what follows we shall examine how Llewellyn combines legal realism with sociology.

Karl N. Llewellen: a realist's realist. Karl Nickerson Llewellyn (1893–1962) spent most of his childhood and adolescence in Brooklyn, New York. In 1911 he enrolled at Yale and fell "under the spell" of William Graham Sumner. Although he had died in 1910, Sumner's ideas continued to flourish at Yale. As a consequence of having been influenced by Sumner's sociology, "before he reached law school, Llewellyn came to the study of law with a predisposition to see law as a social institution embedded in its surrounding culture" (Twining, 1973:94). Llewellyn graduated from Yale Law School in 1918 and spent most of his career teaching at Columbia University Law School. In 1951 he accepted an appointment at the University of Chicago Law School where he remained until his death.

G. Edward White regards Llewellyn's article, "A Realistic Jurisprudence—The Next Step" (1930a), as the first self-conscious statement of legal realism. Here Llewellyn makes a distinction between "paper rules" and "real rules." *Paper rules* are "the accepted doctrine of the time and place—what the books there say 'the law' is" (Llewellyn, 1930a:448). *Real rules,* by contrast, are convenient shorthand symbols for the concrete actions, or tangible practices, of the courts, administrative agencies, and public officials. Accordingly, Llewellyn's definition of the law is a very pragmatic one: "what officials [of the law] do about disputes is, to my mind, the law itself" (1930b:12).

Determining whether the courts abide by paper rules or real rules requires undertaking a pragmatic approach to studying how judicial cases are ultimately decided. Relying on a behaviorist, or what he calls a "behavior-content," approach in analyzing real rules, Llewellyn proposes that the legal reference point be shifted away from the conceptual principles of legal formalism and toward an empirical study of the observable behavior of the courts and those affected by the courts. By 1949, however, Llewellyn had moved beyond examining the law as mere social behavior and began highlighting the sociological concept of "institution" in his analysis:

> I should wish to gather in also not only active conduct but the relevant attitudes and relevant lines of *in*action, and the *inter*actions of any portion of the institution with any other institution; and the machinery for recruiting and for breaking in the institution's specialized personnel; and a dozen or so obvious elements in any living major complex of the "institution" sort. Indeed the first direct contribution of the "law" discipline to sociology lies just here (1949:453).

Basic tenets of legal realism. For Llewellyn, legal realism is not so much a formal "school" as it is a "movement in thought and work about law." Furthermore, in his view, it was not likely that there would ever be a formal school of realists because there is no fundamental set of beliefs on which they all agreed. The realists were free agents doing their separate and distinct work. Nevertheless, despite the divergent interests of the individual realists, in his second major article,

"Some Realism About Realism" (1931), Llewellyn lists several basic tenets that all realists share. We shall discuss six of these tenets.

The first tenet consists of an idea that may be divided into two parts: (1) the law is not a static, a priori structure but rather a fluid and ever-changing process; and (2) the judiciary (not just the legislature) creates law.

Second, is the idea that the law is not just an end in itself but a means to attaining desired social ends. Thus, it follows that the law needs to be evaluated in terms of what ends it achieves. In other words, the purpose of the law is to serve society and the law is good if it contributes something positive to society. Conversely, the law is bad if it contributes something negative to society. Following this line of thinking, many of the realists engaged in a judicial activism that required instigating social change through measured reforms in legislation and public policy. Indeed, several of the more reform-minded realists actively participated in the New Deal agencies set up by President Franklin D. Roosevelt during the Great Depression of the 1930s. For instance, Thurman Arnold (1891–1969), Jerome Frank (1889–1957), and William O. Douglas (1898–1980) served with the Securities and Exchange Commission; Felix Cohen (1907–1953) with the Department of the Interior; and Herman Oliphant (1884–1939) with the Department of Treasury.

Third, the realists advance the idea that society changes at a faster rate than does the law. Thus, they maintain that the law requires continuous re-examination to determine its relevance to the society it purports to serve.

Fourth, the realists argue that "is" and "ought" must be temporarily separated in order to achieve an objective science of the law. Put another way, Llewellyn is saying that for the purposes of empirical study all value judgments as to what ought to be done in the future with respect to any part of the law should be suspended for a time. Realism's first task is to inquire into what is objectively known in the present. Such an investigation is accomplished through direct observation, description, and causal analysis.

Fifth, the realists distrust the concepts of legal formalism insofar as these concepts: (1) purport to describe what courts or people are actually doing, and (2) claim to predict judicial outcome.

Finally, the realists reject the legal formalist idea that doctrinal rules and concepts are the principal factors determining court decisions. The realists contend that this formalist notion involves rationalizing judicial outcome so that it is congruent with the doctrinal legal rules and concepts. Instead, Llewellyn argues that situation sense should determine the judicial opinion and the judge should "take at least one fresh look" at the facts of the case (1960:293).

Llewellyn's descriptive tenets of the realist movement may be summarized as follows: "the program implicit in legal realism was detailed, objective study of law as an instrument to achieve desired ends and in the context of a changing society" (Yntema, 1960:320).

Clearly, the influence of legal realism on American jurisprudence has been significant. Its effects have been particularly felt by legal education (the law school curriculum no longer clings as tightly to the formalism of the nineteenth century as it once did), research (a considerable number of sociolegal studies now focus on the empirical investigation of the law in action), the judiciary (judges understand that social factors play a role in their decision making), and the practicing bar (lawyers now consider the practical consequences of the law in action as well as the law in the books). The popular maxim, "Realism is dead; we are all Realists now," has become a reality.

As Alan Hunt reminds us, today's legal sociology "has its roots, not only in the American sociological tradition, but more immediately in the legacy of American legal realism" (1978:37). Keeping this in mind will help us to better understand contemporary sociology of law.

SUMMARY

In this chapter we discussed the efforts of American jurists Oliver Wendell Holmes, Roscoe Pound, and Karl Llewellyn. Through their academic works and judicial activism these three theorists instigated the organized revolt against legal formalism, or the sociological movement in law, which underscored the interplay between law, politics, and economics.

That doctrine in law that enjoyed hegemony from the 1870s to the 1940s—legal formalism—refers to the process of adjudication whereby judges logically deduce legal rules from a complete and inclusive set of fixed axioms and subsequently apply those rules in rendering a judicial opinion. Legal formalism became a self-contained system of law that was highly logical, general, conceptualist, and (allegedly) apolitical. In buttressing such basic principles of liberalism as the freedom of contract, the right to private property, laissez-faire ideology, economic competition, and individual self-interest, legal formalism concomitantly benefited the economic and political interests of the late-nineteenth-century merchant and entrepreneurial groups.

We saw that Holmes, Pound, and Llewellyn not only critiqued legal formalism, they also endeavored to replace it with alternative legal philosophies—sociological jurisprudence and legal realism—that were predictive, pragmatic, and positivistic. Informed by empirical sociology, sociological jurisprudence and legal realism had as their main objective to fulfill the practical needs of a transmutable society.

Looking first at Oliver Wendell Holmes, we noted that his sociolegal approach emphasized the law's reliance on the actual feelings and demands of everyday life. According to him, it is not a logical, general, conceptualist, and "apolitical" legal doctrine that determines which laws will survive and how they will be implemented; rather, the law emerges and develops in accordance with the changing needs and interests of those social groups with the most political and economic power.

Holmes therefore took a pragmatic approach to the law and saw it as an enterprise in which the practicing lawyer is concerned with predicting the outcome of a court decision involving his or her client. Thus, by "law" Holmes meant nothing more than "the prophecies of what the courts will do in fact." In his view, a positivist legal science would disclose which of the competing needs and interests best fulfills the actual feelings and demands of a society. As such, Holmes believed that the empirical sciences of statistics and economics would predict which proposed policies would be enacted into law.

Next, we turned to the ideas of Roscoe Pound, the chief architect of sociological jurisprudence. Pound's main criticism against legal formalism was that its artificial and technical processes had made the law impractical and thus irrelevant in meeting society's needs. Pound, therefore, proposed a jurisprudence that was more realistic and pragmatic because it was concerned not with the law's conceptualist procedures but with society's practical ends. This jurisprudence was also more sociologically oriented than legal formalism because it regarded the law as an institution of social control whose ultimate goal is to preserve the interests of a "civilized" society. We defined social interests as those predominant claims that people want satisfied and that society must legally protect. Pound listed six generic types of social interests dealing with:

1. General security
2. The security of social institutions
3. General morals
4. The conservation of social resources
5. General progress
6. Individual life

We concluded this chapter by discussing another alternative to formalist legal doctrine, American legal realism, or that inductive jurisprudence that repudiated conceptualist reasoning and focused on the practical facts, actions, and outcomes of a judicial case. We then examined the ideas of the person who best represented legal realism, Karl N. Llewellyn, and noted that he distinguished the doctrine of the law (paper rules) from what he considered to be more noteworthy: the tangible practices of legal officials (real rules). Llewellyn saw the law, very pragmatically, as what the officials of the law *do* about legal disputes. Accordingly, Llewellyn suggested that in order to truly understand the law's actual workings, jurisprudence must empirically study the social behavior of judges, lawyers, defendants, and plaintiffs. Later, Llewellyn gave wider focus to his jurisprudence by treating the law as a social institution and considering its cultural values, social practices, and recruitment and socialization techniques. Finally, we discussed six tenets of legal realism proposed by Llewellyn:

1. Judicial decision-making is and must be consciously involved in lawmaking.
2. Jurists must be actively involved in implementing laws that help society achieve its desired ends.
3. Jurists must ensure that the law keeps pace with societal changes.
4. Jurists must temporarily put aside the philosophical question of what "ought to be" so that they can develop an objective legal science dealing with the empirical question of what "is."
5. The paper rules of legal formalism do not reflect the court's real rules nor can they predict the court's outcome.
6. The paper rules of legal formalism do not determine the court's outcome.

The sociological movement in law, as articulated chiefly by Oliver Wendell Holmes's sociolegal approach, Roscoe Pound's sociological jurisprudence, and Karl Llewellyn's legal realism, demystified the law by plucking it from the metaphysical sphere of universal principles and placing it squarely in the social sphere of political and economic influences.

In the next three chapters we discuss the classical perspectives of three social thinkers who preceded the sociological movement in law and who also focused on political and economic influences: Karl Marx, Max Weber, and Emile Durkheim. We will see how the Marxian, Weberian, and Durkheimian perspectives employ the sociological orientation as these three theorists consider law within the wider context of modern, liberal, capitalist society.

The Path of the Law

Oliver Wendell Holmes

When we study law we are not studying a mystery but a well-known profession. We are studying what we shall want in order to appear before judges, or to advise people in such a way as to keep them out of court. The reason why it is a profession, why people will pay lawyers to argue for them or to advise them, is that in societies like ours the command of the public force is entrusted to the judges in certain cases, and the whole power of the state will be put forth, if necessary, to carry out their judgments and decrees. People want to know under what circumstances and how far they will run the risk of coming against what is so much stronger than themselves, and hence it becomes a business to find out when this danger is to be feared. The object of our study, then, is prediction, the prediction of the incidence of the public force through the instrumentality of the courts. . . .

I wish, if I can, to lay down some first principles for the study of this body of dogma or systematized prediction which we call the law, for men who want to use it as the instrument of their business to enable them to prophesy in their turn, and, as bearing upon the study, I wish to point out an ideal which as yet our law has not attained.

The first thing for a business-like understanding of the matter is to understand its limits, and therefore I think it desirable at once to point out and dispel a confusion between morality and law, which sometimes rises to the height of conscious theory, and more often and indeed constantly is making trouble in detail without reaching the point of consciousness. You can see very plainly that a bad man has as much reason as a good one for wishing to avoid an encounter with the public force, and therefore you can see the practical importance of the distinction between morality and law. A man who cares nothing for an ethical rule which is believed and practiced by his neighbors is likely nevertheless to care a good deal to avoid being made to pay money, and will want to keep out of jail if he can.

I take it for granted that no hearer of mine will misinterpret what I have to say as the language of cynicism. The law is the witness and external deposit of our moral life. Its history is the history of the moral development of the race. The practice of it, in spite of popular jests, tends to make good citizens and good men. When I emphasize the difference between law and morals I do so with reference to a single end, that of learning and understanding the law. For that purpose you must definitely master its specific marks, and it is for that that I ask you for the moment to imagine yourselves indifferent to other and greater things.

I do not say that there is not a wider point of view from which the distinction between law and morals becomes of secondary or no importance, as all mathematical distinctions vanish in presence of the infinite. But I do say that that distinction is of the first importance for the object which we are here to consider,—a right study and mastery of the law as a business with well understood limits, a body of dogma enclosed within definite lines. I have just shown the practical reason for saying so. If you want to know the law and nothing else, you must look at it as a bad man, who cares only for the material consequences which such knowledge enables him to predict, not as a good one, who finds his reasons for conduct, whether inside the law or outside of it, in the vaguer sanctions of conscience....

Take the fundamental question, What constitutes the law? You will find some text writers telling you that it is something different from what is decided by the courts of Massachusetts or England, that it is a system of reason, that it is a deduction from principles of ethics or admitted axioms or what not, which may or may not coincide with the decisions. But if we take the view of our friend the bad man we shall find that he does not care two straws for the axioms or deductions, but that he does want to know what the Massachusetts or English courts are likely to do in fact. I am much of his mind. The prophecies of what the courts will do in fact, and nothing more pretentious, are what I mean by the law.

Take ... a notion which as popularly understood is the widest conception which the law contains;—the notion of legal duty. ... We fill the word with all the content which we draw from morals. But what does it mean to a bad man? Mainly, and in the first place, a prophecy that if he does certain things he will be subjected to disagreeable consequences by way of imprisonment or compulsory payment of money. But from this point of view, what is the difference between being fined and being taxed a certain sum for doing a certain thing? That his point of view is the test of legal principles is shown by the many discussions which have arisen in the courts on the very question whether a given statutory liability is a penalty or a tax. On the answer to this question depends the decision whether conduct is legally wrong or right, and also whether a man is under compulsion or free. Leaving the criminal law on one side, what is the difference between the liability under the mill acts or statutes authorizing a taking by eminent domain and the liability for what we call a wrongful conversion of property where restoration is out of the question? In both cases the party taking another man's property has

to pay its fair value as assessed by a jury, and no more. What significance is there in calling one taking right and another wrong from the point of view of the law? It does not matter, so far as the given consequence, the compulsory payment, is concerned, whether the act to which it is attached is described in terms of praise or in terms of blame, or whether the law purports to prohibit it or to allow it. If it matters at all, still speaking from the bad man's point of view, it must be because in one case and not in the other some further disadvantages, or at least some further consequences, are attached to the act by the law. The only other disadvantages thus attached to it which I ever have been able to think of are to be found in two somewhat insignificant legal doctrines, both of which might be abolished without much disturbance. One is, that a contract to do a prohibited act is unlawful, and the other, that, if one or two or more joint wrongdoers has to pay all the damages, he cannot recover contribution from his fellows. And that I believe is all. You see how the vague circumference of the notion of duty shrinks and at the same time grows more precise when we wash it with cynical acid and expel everything except the object of our study, the operations of the law. ...

This is not the time to work out a theory in detail, or to answer many obvious doubts and questions which are suggested by these general views. I know of none which are not easy to answer, but what I am trying to do now is only by a series of hints to throw some light on the narrow path of legal doctrine, and upon two pitfalls which, as it seems to me, lie perilously near to it. Of the first of these I have said enough. I hope that my illustrations have shown the danger, both to speculation and to practice, of confounding morality with law, and the trap which legal language lays for us on that side of our way. For my own part, I often doubt whether it would not be a gain if every word of moral significance could be banished from the law altogether, and other words adopted which should convey legal ideas uncolored by anything outside the law. We should lose the fossil records of a good deal of history and the majesty got from ethical associations, but by ridding ourselves of an unnecessary confusion we should gain very much in the clearness of our thought.

So much for the limits of the law. The next thing which I wish to consider is what are the forces which determine its content and its growth. You may assume, with Hobbes and Bentham and Austin, that all law emanates from the sovereign, even when the first human beings to enunciate it are the judges, or you may think that law is the voice of the Zeitgeist, or what you like. It is all one to my present purpose. Even if every decision required the sanction of an emperor with despotic power and a whimsical turn of mind, we should be interested none the less, still with a view to prediction, in discovering some order, some rational explanation, and some principle of growth for the rules which he laid down. In every system there are such explanations and principles to be found. It is with regard to them that a second fallacy comes in, which I think it important to expose.

The fallacy to which I refer is the notion that the only force at work in the development of the law is logic. In the broadest sense, indeed, that notion would be true. The postulate on which we think about the universe is that there is a fixed quantitative relation between every phenomenon and its antecedents and consequents. If there is such a thing as a phenomenon without these fixed quantitative relations, it is a miracle. It is outside the law of cause and effect, and as such transcends our power of thought, or at least is something to or from which we cannot reason. The condition of our thinking about the universe is that it is capable of being thought about rationally, or, in other words, that every part of it is effect and cause in the same sense in which those parts are with which we are most familiar. So in the broadest sense it is true that the law is a logical development, like everything else. The danger of which I speak is not the admission that the principles governing other phenomena also govern the law, but the notion that a given system, ours, for instance, can be worked out like mathematics from some general axioms of conduct. This is the natural error of the schools, but it is not confined to

them. I once heard a very eminent judge say that he never let a decision go until he was absolutely sure that it was right. So judicial dissent often is blamed, as if it meant simply that one side or the other were not doing their sums right, and, if they would take more trouble, agreement inevitably would come.

This mode of thinking is entirely natural. The training of lawyers is a training in logic. The processes of analogy, discrimination, and deduction are those in which they are most at home. The language of judicial decision is mainly the language of logic. And the logical method and form flatter that longing for certainty and for repose which is in every human mind. But certainty generally is illusion, and repose is not the destiny of man. Behind the logical form lies a judgment as to the relative worth and importance of competing legislative grounds, often an inarticulate and unconscious judgment, it is true, and yet the very root and nerve of the whole proceeding. You can give any conclusion a logical form. You always can imply a condition in a contract. But why do you imply it? It is because of some belief as to the practice of the community or of a class, or because of some opinion as to policy, or, in short, because of some attitude of yours upon a matter not capable of exact quantitative measurement, and therefore not capable of founding exact logical conclusions. Such matters really are battle grounds where the means do not exist for determinations that shall be good for all time, and where the decision can do no more than embody the preference of a given body in a given time and place. We do not realize how large a part of our law is open to reconsideration upon a slight change in the habit of the public mind. No concrete proposition is self-evident, no matter how ready we may be to accept it, not even Mr. Herbert Spencer's Every man has a right to do what he wills, provided he interferes not with a like right on the part of his neighbors. . . .

So much for the fallacy of logical form. Now let us consider the present condition of the law as a subject for study, and the ideal toward which it tends. We still are far from the point of view which I desire to see reached. No one has reached it or can reach it as yet. We are only at the beginning of a philosophical reaction, and of a reconsideration of the worth of doctrines which for the most part still are taken for granted without any deliberate, conscious, and systematic questioning of their grounds. The development of our law has gone on for nearly a thousand years, like the development of a plant, each generation taking the inevitable next step, mind, like matter, simply obeying a law of spontaneous growth. It is perfectly natural and right that it should have been so. Imitation is a necessity of human nature, as has been illustrated by a remarkable French writer, M. Tarde, in an admirable book, "Les Lois de l'Imitation." Most of the things we do, we do for no better reason than that our fathers have done them or that our neighbors do them, and the same is true of a larger part than we suspect of what we think. The reason is a good one, because our short life gives us no time for a better, but it is not the best. It does not follow, because we are all compelled to take on faith at second hand most of the rules on which we base our action and our thought, that each of us may not try to set some corner of his world in the order of reason, or that all of us collectively should not aspire to carry reason as far as it will go throughout the whole domain. In regard to the law, it is true, no doubt, that an evolutionist will hesitate to affirm universal validity for his social ideals, or for the principles which he thinks should be embodied in legislation. He is content if he can prove them best for here and now. He may be ready to admit that he knows nothing about an absolute best in the cosmos, and even that he knows next to nothing about a permanent best for men. Still it is true that a body of law is more rational and more civilized when every rule it contains is referred articulately and definitely to an end which it subserves, and when the grounds for desiring that end are stated or are ready to be stated in words.

At present, in very many cases, if we want to know why a rule of law has taken its particular shape, and more or less if we want to know why it exists at all, we go to tradition. We follow it into the Year Books, and perhaps beyond them to the customs of the Salian Franks, and somewhere in the past, in the German forests, in the needs of Norman kings, in the assumptions of a dominant class, in the absence of generalized ideas, we find out the practical motive for what now best is justified by the mere fact of its acceptance and that men are accustomed to it. The rational study of law is still to a large extent the study of history. History must be a part of the study, because without it we cannot know the precise scope of rules which it is our business to know. It is a part of the rational study, because it is the first step toward an enlightened skepticism, that is, toward a deliberate reconsideration of the worth of those rules. When you get the dragon out of his cave on to the plain and in the daylight, you can count his teeth and claws, and see just what is his strength. But to get him out is only the first step. The next is either to kill him, or to tame him and make him a useful animal. For the rational study of the law the black-letter man may be the man of the present, but the man of the future is the man of statistics and the master of economics. It is revolting to have no better reason for a rule of law than that so it was laid down in the time of Henry IV. It is still more revolting if the grounds upon which it was laid down have vanished long since, and the rule simply persists from blind imitation of the past. . . .

I trust that no one will understand me to be speaking with disrespect of the law, because I criticize it so freely. I venerate the law, and especially our system of law, as one of the vastest products of the human mind. No one knows better than I do the countless number of great intellects that have spent themselves in making some addition or improvement, the greatest of which is trifling when compared with the mighty whole. It has the final title to respect that it exists, that it is not a Hegelian dream, but a part of the lives of men. But one may criticize even what one reveres. Law is the business to which my life is devoted, and I should show less than devotion if I did not do what in me lies to improve it, and, when I perceive what seems to me the ideal of its future, if I hesitated to point it out and to press toward it with all my heart. . . .

A Survey of Social Interests

Roscoe Pound

There has been a notable shift throughout the world from thinking of the task of the legal order as one of adjusting the exercise of free wills to one of satisfying wants, of which free exercise of the will is but one. Accordingly, we must start today from a theory of interests, that is, of the claims or demands or desires which human beings, either individually or in groups or associations or relations, seek to satisfy, of which, therefore, the adjustment of relations and ordering of conduct through the force of politically organized society must take account. I have discussed the general theory of interests, the classification of interests, and the details of individual interests in other places. It is enough to say here that the classification into individual interests, public interests, and social interests was suggested by Jhering. As I should put it, individual interests are claims or demands or desires involved immediately in the individual life and asserted in title of that life. Public interests are claims or demands or desires involved in life in a politically organized society and asserted in title of that organization. They are commonly treated as the claims of a politically organized society thought of as a legal entity. Social interests are claims or demands or desires involved in social life in civilized society and asserted in title of that life. It is not uncommon to treat them as the claims of the whole social group as such.

But this does not mean that every claim or demand or desire which human beings assert must be put once for all for every purpose into one of these three categories. For some purposes and in some connections it is convenient to look at a given claim or demand or desire from one standpoint. For other purposes or in other connections it is convenient to look at the same claim or demand or the same type of claims or demands from one of the other standpoints. When it comes to weighing or valuing claims or demands with respect to other claims or demands, we must be careful to compare them on the same plane. If we put one as an individual interest and the other as a social interest we may decide the question in advance in our very way of putting it. For example, in the "truck act" cases one may think of the claim of the employer to make contracts freely as an individual interest of substance. In that event, we must weigh it with the claim of the employee not to be coerced by economic pressure into making contracts to take his pay in orders on a company store, thought of as an individual interest of personality. If we think of either in terms of a policy we must think of the other in the same terms. If we think of the employee's claim in terms of a policy of assuring a minimum or a standard human life, we must think of the employer's claim in terms of a policy of upholding and enforcing contracts. If the one is thought of as a right and the other as a policy, or if the one is thought of as an individual interest and the other as a social interest, our way of stating the question may leave nothing to decide.

In general, but not always, it is expedient to put claims or demands in their most generalized form, *i.e.*, as social interests, in order to compare them. . . .

A generation ago, as a matter of course, we should have relied upon logical deduction. We should have deduced the several social interests as presuppositions of generalized social existence. But schemes of necessary presuppositions of law or of legal institutions seem to me to be at bottom schemes of observed elements in actual legal systems, systematically arranged, reduced to their lowest terms, and deduced, as one might say, to order. I doubt the ability of the jurist to work out deductively the necessary jural presuppositions of society in the abstract.

At one time it seemed that a more attractive starting point might be found in social psychology. One need only turn to the list of so-called instincts in any of the older social psychologies in order to see an obvious relation between interests, as the jurist now uses that term, or what we had been wont to call natural rights or public policies, on the one hand, and these "instincts" or whatever they are now called, on the other hand. Thus in McDougall's *Social Psychology* we used to find an instinct of repugnance and "predisposition to aesthetic discrimination." In jurisprudence we must consider a social interest in aesthetic surroundings which the law is beginning grudgingly to recognize. In McDougall we used to find an instinct of self-abasement, and in jurisprudence we must consider the so-called right of privacy. Again, to take so-called instincts with which the law has always had much to do, there is evident relation between the "instinct of pugnacity" and the law as to self-defense; between the "instinct of self-assertion" and the anxiety of the law that the will of the individual shall not be trodden upon; between the "instinct of acquisition" and individual interests of substance and the social interest in the security of acquisitions; between the "instinct of gregariousness" and loyalty and veracity as tendencies or habits connected therewith, and the social interest in the security of transactions. But in the last two decades, after a bitter controversy among sociologists and social psychologists, and redefinitions and substitute categories, most of what was accepted a generation ago in this connection has been pretty much given up. Certainly we can no longer build

on McDougall's scheme and such definitions and classifications as are suggested today are remote from what we need in jurisprudence.

If we may not rely upon logical deduction nor upon a theory and classification of what were formerly called instincts, there remains a less pretentious method which may none the less be upon surer ground. If legal phenomena are social phenomena, observation and study of them as such may well bear fruit for social science in general as well as for jurisprudence. Why should not the lawyer make a survey of legal systems in order to ascertain just what claims or demands or desires have pressed or are now pressing for recognition and satisfaction and how far they have been or are now recognized and secured? This is precisely what has been done in the case of individual interests, in the schemes of natural rights, although the process has usually been covered up by a pretentious fabric of logical deduction. The same method may well be applied to social interests, and this should be done consciously and avowedly, as befits the science of today. It is true that objection has been made to this because the same social interest appears behind many legal institutions and doctrines and precepts, and legal institutions and doctrines and precepts almost always have behind them, not one social interest or a simple adjustment or compromise of two, but a complex harmonizing of many. Yet it is of the first importance to perceive this, to note what those interests are, to see how they are adjusted or harmonized or compromised, and to inquire why it is done in this way rather than in another. The first step in such an investigation is a mere survey of the legal order and an inventory of the social interests which have pressed upon lawmakers and judges and jurists for recognition.

In such a survey and inventory, first place must be given to the social interest in the general security—the claim or want or demand, asserted in title of social life in civilized society and through the social group, to be secure against those forms of action and courses of conduct which threaten its existence. Even if we accept Durkheim's view that it is what shocks the general conscience, not what threatens the general security, that is repressed, I suspect that the general conscience reflects experience or superstition as to the general safety. A common-law judge observed that there would be no safety for human life if it were to be considered as law that drunkenness could be shown to negative the intent element of crime where a drunk man kills while intoxicated though he would never do such a thing when sober. It should be noted how the exigencies of the general security outweighed the traditional theory of the criminal law.

This paramount social interest takes many forms. In its simplest form it is an interest in the general safety, long recognized in the legal order in the maxim that the safety of the people is the highest law. It was recognized in American constitutional law in the nineteenth century by putting the general safety along with the general health and general morals in the "police power" as a ground of reasonable restraint to which natural rights must give way. In another form, quite as obvious today but not so apparent in the past, before the nature and causes of disease were understood, it is an interest in the general health. In another form, recognized from the very beginnings of law, it is an interest in peace and public order. In an economically developed society it takes on two other closely related forms, namely, a social interest in the security of acquisitions and a social interest in the security of transactions. The two last came to be well understood in the nineteenth century, in which they were more or less identified with individual interests of substance and individual interests in freedom of contract. Yet a characteristic difference between the law of the eighteenth century and the law of the nineteenth century brings out their true nature. Eighteenth-century courts, taking a purely individualist view, regarded the statute of limitations as something to be held down as much as possible and to be evaded in every way. Lord Mansfield in particular, under the influence of natural-law ideas and thinking of the statute only as an individual plea which enabled the individual interest of a plaintiff to be deprived of legal security, sought out numerous astute contrivances to get around its most obvious

provisions. If one said, "I am ready to account, but nothing is due you," if he made provision in his will for the payment of his "just debts," if his executors advertised, notifying those who had "just debts" owing them to present their claims, in these and like cases it was held there was an acknowledgment sufficing to take a barred debt out of the statute. Modern courts came to see that there was something more here than the individual interests of plaintiff and defendant. They came to see that the basis of the statute was a social interest in the security of acquisitions, which demands that titles shall not be insecure by being open to attack indefinitely, and a social interest in the security of transactions which demands that the transactions of the past shall not be subject to inquiry indefinitely, so as to unsettle credit and disturb business trade. If we compare the French rule, *en tout cas de meuble possession vaut titre*, with the Roman doctrine that no one can transfer a greater title than he has, if we note the growth of the idea of negotiability in the law everywhere, and in our law both by legislation and by judicial decision, we may see something of how far recognition of the social interest in the security of transactions went in the maturity of law.

Other examples of recognition of the security of transactions may be seen in the presumption as to transactions of a corporation through its acting officers, the stress which the courts put upon *stare decisis* in cases involving commercial law, and the doctrine allowing only the sovereign to challenge *ultra vires* conveyances of corporations. As to recognition of the social interest in the security of acquisitions, note the insistence of the courts upon *stare decisis* where rules of property are involved. In such cases it is an established proposition that it is better that the law be settled than that it be settled right.

Second, we may put the social interest in the security of social institutions—the claim or want or demand involved in life in civilized society that its fundamental institutions be secure from those forms of action and courses of conduct which threaten their existence or impair their efficient functioning. Looking at them in chronological order, this interest appears in three forms.

The first is an interest in the security of domestic institutions, long recognized in the form of a policy against acts affecting the security of domestic relations or in restraint of marriage. Legislation intended to promote the family as a social institution has been common. There is a policy against actions by members of the family against each other. Today, although the law is becoming much relaxed, this social interest is still weighed heavily against the individual claims of married persons in most divorce legislation. It still weighs heavily against individual claims in the law as to illegitimate children. At times this has been carried so far that great and numerous disabilities have attached to such children lest recognition of their individual interests should weaken a fundamental social institution. The movement to give independence to married women has had collateral effects of impairing the security of this interest, and the balance is not easy to make nor to maintain. The tendency to relax the rules which formerly obtained is brought out in *Russell v. Russell*, in which two of the five law lords dissented as to application of the policy of "preservation of the sanctity of married life," and *Fender v. St. John Mildmay*, in which again two of five law lords dissented as to the rule concerning the validity of a promise of marriage before a divorce proceeding has been finally determined. There are, however, recent cases which tend to uphold the policy formerly well established.

> It is no doubt too soon to be sure of even the path which juristic thought of the immediate future will follow. But increased weight given to the social interest in the individual life in the concrete, instead of upon abstract liberty, seems to be indicated. There is an emphasis upon the concrete claims of concrete human beings. . . . Family law, in which there must be a balance between the security of social institutions and the individual life, is necessarily much affected by such a change.

In another part of the law, the social interest in the security of domestic institutions still weighs heavily, in comparison, however, with the general security. A wife is not to be held as accessory after the fact for harboring a felon husband or for helping him escape. The common law does not require a wife to choose between fidelity to the relation of husband and wife and duty to the state. Also legislation as to mothers' pensions proceeds at least in large part upon this interest.

A second form is an interest in the security of religious institutions. In the beginning this is closely connected with the general security. A chief point of origin of the criminal law, of that part of the law by which social interests as such are directly and immediately secured, is in religion. Sacrifice of the impious offender who has affronted the gods, and exclusion from society of the impious offender whose presence threatens to bring upon his fellows the wrath of the gods, are, in part at least, the originals of capital punishment and of outlawry. Religious organization was long a stronger and more active agency of social control than political organization. In the Anglo-Saxon laws the appeals or exhortations addressed to the people as Christians are at least as important as the threats addressed to them as subjects. One of the great English statutes of the thirteenth century recites that Parliament had met to make laws "for the common Profit of holy Church, and of the Realm." It is only in relatively recent times that we have come to think of blasphemy as involving no more than a social interest in the general morals, of Sunday laws only in terms of a social interest in the general health, of heresy as less dangerous socially than radical views upon economics or politics, or of preaching or teaching of atheism as involved in a guaranteed liberty. Today what was formerly referred to this interest is usually referred to the social interest in the general morals. Questions as to the interest in the security of religious institutions have been debated in all lands.

In a third form the interest is one in the security of political institutions. This interest has weighed heavily in much twentieth century legislation too familiar to require more than mention. When the public called for such legislation for the security of political institutions, absolute constitutional guarantees of free speech and natural rights of individual self-assertion, which in other times had moved courts to refuse to enjoin repeated and undoubted libels, lest liberty be infringed, were not suffered to stand in the way. If the individual interests involved had been conceived less absolutely and had been looked at in another light, as identified with a social interest in the general progress, they might have fared better.

Perhaps a fourth form of the interest in the security of social institutions should be added, namely, an interest in the security of economic institutions. Formerly, these were chiefly commercial. Today industrial institutions also must be taken into account. Judicial recognitions of a social interest in the security of commercial institutions are numerous. In a leading case in which it was determined that a bank note payable to bearer passed current the same as coin, Lord Mansfield grounded the judgment "upon the general course of business, and . . . the consequences to trade and commerce: which would be much incommoded by a contrary determination." More than one decision in the last generation on labor law seems to go upon an interest in maintaining the industrial regime in the face of persistent pressure from the claims of organized workingmen. Some of the policies to be considered presently under the social interest in general progress might be referred to this head.

Third, we may put the social interest in the general morals, the claim or want or demand involved in social life in civilized society to be secured against acts or courses of conduct offensive to the moral sentiments of the general body of individuals therein for the time being. This interest is recognized in Roman law in the protection of *boni mores*. It is recognized in our law by policies against dishonesty, corruption, gambling, and things of immoral tendency; by treating continuity menaces to the general morals as nuisances; and by common-law doctrine that acts contrary to good morals and subversive of general morals are misdemeanors. It is recognized in equity in the maxim that he who comes into equity must come with clean hands. Similar provisions are to be found in the private law and in the criminal law in other lands. Obstinately held ideas of morality may in time come in conflict with ideas arising from changed social and economic conditions or newer religious and philosophical views. In such cases we must reach a balance between the social interest in the general morals, and the social interest in general progress, taking form in a policy of free discussion. What was said above as to free speech and writing and the social interest in security of social institutions applies here also.

Fourth, there is the social interest in conservation of social resources, that is, the claim or want or demand involved in social life in civilized society that the goods of existence shall not be wasted; that where all human claims or wants or desires may not be satisfied, in view of infinite individual desires and limited natural means of satisfying them, the latter be made to go as far as possible; and, to that end, that acts or courses of conduct which tend needlessly to destroy or impair these goods shall be restrained. In its simplest form this is an interest in the use and conservation of natural resources, and is recognized in the doctrines as to *res communes*, which may be used but not owned, by the common law as to riparian rights and constitutional and statutory provisions where irrigation is practiced, by modern game laws, by the recent doctrines as to percolating water and surface water, and by laws as to waste of natural gas and oil. There has been a progressive tendency to restrict the *ius abutendi* which the maturity of law attributed to owners. A crowded and hungry world may yet weigh this interest against individual claims to free action still further by preventing destruction of commodities in order to keep up prices, or even cutting off the common-law liberty of the owner of land to sow it to salt if he so desires. At times overproduction of agricultural products has led to proposals for restriction of the owner's *ius utendi* by regulation of what crops he may raise. At other times there are projects for administrative appointment of receivers of agricultural land cultivated or managed by the owner "in such a manner as to prejudice materially the production of food thereon. . . ." Restrictions with respect to housing proceed on another aspect of this same social interest.

A closely related social interest is one in protection and training of dependents and defectives. It might from one point of view be called an interest in conservation of the human assets of society. In one form it was recognized long ago in the common-law system by the jurisdiction of the chancellor, representing the king as *parens patriae*, over infants, lunatics, and idiots. This jurisdiction has had a significant development in recent times in the juvenile court, and an extension to youthful offenders beyond the period of infancy is being urged. Again, there has been an extension of the idea of protection and training of dependents, on one hand to the reformation of mature delinquents, and on another hand to protection of the mature who are yet economically more or less dependent. This has gone a long way in recent times in social security or social insurance legislation and in small loan legislation. The latter has had a historical background in the interference of equity to prevent oppression of debtors and necessitous persons. Also after the first world war there was legislative recognition of a social interest in rehabilitation of the maimed. Much of the legislation referred to runs counter to the insistence upon abstract individual liberty in the juristic theory of the last century. It was formerly often pronounced arbitrary and so unconstitutional by courts whose dogmatic scheme could admit no social interest other than the general security. There has been a significant widening of the field of legally recognized and secured social interests. But for the most part the claims or demands here considered are better treated in connection with the social interest in the individual life.

Fifth, there is the social interest in general progress, that is, the claim or want or demand involved in social life in civilized society, that the development of human powers and of human control over nature for the satisfaction of human wants go forward; the demand that social engineering be increasingly and continuously improved; as it were, the self-assertion of the social group toward higher and more complete development of human powers. This interest appears in three main forms, an interest in economic progress, an interest in political progress, and an interest in cultural progress. The social interest in economic progress has long been recognized in law and has been secured in many ways. In the common law it is expressed in four policies: the policy as to freedom of property from restrictions upon sale or use, the policy as to free trade and consequent policy against monopoly, the policy as to free industry, which has had to give much ground in recent legislation and judicial decision, and the policy as to encouragement of invention, which is behind patent legislation and there comes in conflict with the policy as to free trade. All of these policies have important consequences in everyday law. It may be thought that some of them should be classified rather as forms of a social interest in the security of economic institutions. As I read the cases, however, these demands have pressed upon courts and jurists from the standpoint of their relation to economic progress. If that relation fails, they are not likely to maintain themselves. Likewise the law has long recognized a social interest in political progress. In American bills of rights, and in written constitutions generally, a policy of free criticism of public men, public acts, and public officers, and a policy of free formation, free holding, and free expression of political opinion are guaranteed as identified with individual rights. Moreover, at common law, the privilege of fair comment upon public men and public affairs recognizes and secures the same interest. But the third form, the social interest in cultural progress, has not been recognized in the law so clearly. It may be said to involve four policies: a policy of free science, a policy of free letters, a policy of encouragement of arts and letters, and a policy of promotion of education and learning. The last two have been recognized to some extent in copyright laws and in American constitutional provisions for the promotion of higher learning. The first two have made their way more slowly because of conflict or supposed conflict with the security of religious and political institutions.

Closely connected with the interest in cultural progress is a social interest in aesthetic surroundings, which recently has been pressing for legal recognition. Fifty years ago, Sir Frederick Pollock could say with assurance that our law ignored aesthetic relations, and, comparing the English with the French in this respect, could quote Hood's lines:

> Nature which gave them the goût
> Only gave us the gout.

In the United States, courts and legislatures were long engaged in a sharp struggle over billboard laws and laws against hideous forms of outdoor advertising. For a time also the interest pressed in another way in connection with town planning legislation. It is significant that the courts are now ready to admit a policy in favor of the aesthetic as reasonable and constitutionally permissible.

Last, and in some ways most important of all, as we now are coming to think, there is the social interest in the individual life. One might call it the social interest in the individual moral and social life, or in the individual human life. It is the claim or want or demand involved in social life in civilized society that each individual be able to live a human life therein according to the standards of the society. It is the claim or want or demand that, if all individual wants may not be satisfied, they be satisfied at least so far as is reasonably possible and to the extent of a human minimum. Three forms of this social interest have been recognized in common law or in legislation: individual self-assertion, individual opportunity, and individual conditions of life. The first, the interest in free self-assertion, includes physical, mental, and economic activity. In Spencer's scheme of natural rights, they appear as a "right of free motion and locomotion," a "right of free exchange and free contract," deduced as a sort of free economic motion and locomotion, a "right of free industry," deduced expressly as a modern outgrowth of free motion and locomotion, as a right of free economic activity, a "right of free religious belief and opinion" and a right of free political belief and opinion, the two last being deduced also as modern developments of the same natural right of free motion and locomotion. These are deduced from a "law of equal freedom" which is taken to have

been discovered by observation of social phenomena and verified by further observation. Without the aid of his "law of equal freedom" he might have found them by observation of the policies set forth in the law books. The old common-law policy in favor of freedom, the doctrine that one may justify by his natural liberty of action, except where his action takes the form of aggression and so threatens the general security, and in part the policy of free industry, are examples of recognition of a social interest in individual physical self-assertion. The policy in favor of free speech and free belief and opinion, although related also to the social interest in political progress, must be referred in part to a social interest in individual mental self-assertion. Policies favoring free trade and free industry are in part referable to a social interest in free economic self-assertion.

But the most important phase of the social interest in individual self-assertion, from the standpoint of modern law, is what might be called the social interest in freedom of the individual will—the claim or interest, or policy recognizing it, that the individual will shall not be subjected arbitrarily to the will of others. This interest is recognized in an old common-law policy which is declared in the Fifth and Fourteenth Amendments. If one will is to be subjected to the will of another through the force of politically organized society, it is not to be done arbitrarily, but is to be done upon some rational basis, which the person coerced, if reasonable, could appreciate. It is to be done upon a reasoned weighing of the interests involved and a reasoned attempt to reconcile them or adjust them. This policy obviously expresses political and juristic experience of what modern psychology has discovered as to the ill effects of repression. For example, it is more and more recognized today in our penal legislation and in our treatment of offenders. It has come to be recognized particularly of late as a result of pressure upon courts and lawmakers for security in the relation of employer and employee. It is coming to be recognized also in juristic thought in another connection as sociological theories of property replace metaphysical theories. There are many signs of a growing feeling that complete exclusion of all but him whom the law pronounces owner from objects which are the natural media of human existence or means of human activity, must be measured and justified by a reasoned weighing of the interest on both sides and a reasoned attempt to harmonize them or to save as much as we may with the sacrifice of as little on the part of the excluded, no less than on the part of the owner, as we may.

I have called a second form the social interest in individual opportunity. It is the claim or want or demand involved in social life in civilized society that all individuals shall have fair or reasonable (perhaps, as we are coming to think, we must say equal) opportunities—political, physical, cultural, social, and economic. In American thinking we have insisted chiefly on equal political opportunities, since in the pioneer conditions in which our institutions were formative other opportunities, so far as men demanded them, were at hand everywhere. But a claim to fair physical opportunities is recognized in public provision of parks and playgrounds and in public provisions for recreation; the claim to fair cultural opportunities is recognized by laws as to compulsory education of children (although the social interests in general progress and in dependents are also recognized here) as well as by state provisions for universities and for adult education; the claim to fair social opportunities is recognized by civil rights laws; and the claim to fair economic opportunities is recognized, for example, in the legal right to "freedom of the market," and in the so-called "right to pursue a lawful calling," which is weighed with other social interests in regulating training for and admission to professions.

In a third form, an interest in individual conditions of life, the social interest in the individual life appears as a claim that each individual shall have assured to him the conditions of at least a minimum human life under the circumstances of life in the time and place. I have said minimum, which certainly was all that was recognized until relatively recent times. But perhaps we should now say reasonable or even equal. A claim for equal conditions of life is pressing and we can't put the

matter as to what is recognized with assurance as we could have done a generation ago. Moreover, the scope of generally asserted demands with respect to the individual life is obviously growing. The Roman law recognized a policy of this sort, and it has long been recognized in American legislation. In weighing individual interests in view of the social interest in security of acquisitions and security of transactions, we must also take account of the social interest in the human life of each individual, and so must restrict the legal enforcement of demands to what is consistent with a human existence on the part of the person subjected thereto. The Roman law imposed such a limitation in a number of cases in what is called the *beneficium competentiae*. At common law there were restrictions on what could be taken in distress for rent, and the thirteenth century statute providing for execution by writ of *elegit* exempts the debtor's oxen and beasts of the plow and half of his land. In the United States and recently in continental Europe, this policy is given effect in homestead laws and in exemptions from execution. In the latter, the social interest in the family as a social institution is also a factor. But nineteenth-century opposition to homestead and exemption laws, and in Europe to the *beneficium competentiae*, is significant. The nineteenth century sought to treat such cases as if they involved nothing more than the individual interests of the parties to the debtor-creditor relation, or, if a social interest was considered, sought to think only of the general security, which here takes the form of security of transactions. Other recognitions of this interest may be seen in restrictions on the power of debtors or contractors to saddle themselves with oppressive burdens, as in the doctrines of equity heretofore referred to, as in usury laws, and more recently in "loan shark" legislation. A notable instance in recent judicial decision may be seen in the English doctrine as to covenants not to exercise the calling for which one has trained himself. Statutes forbidding contracts by laborers to take their pay in orders on company stores, and as to conditions and hours of labor, minimum wage laws, child labor laws, and housing laws, are recognitions of the same interest.

Again, when the law confers or exercises a power of control, we feel that the legal order should safeguard the human existence of the person controlled. Thus the old-time sea law, with its absolute power of the master over the sailor, the old-time ignominious punishments, that treated the human offender like a brute, that did not save his human dignity—all such things are disappearing as the circle of recognized interests widens and we come to take account of the social interest in the individual life and to weigh that interest with the social interest in the general security, on which the last century insisted so exclusively.

Such in outline are the social interests which are recognized or are coming to be recognized in modern law. Looked at functionally, the law is an attempt to satisfy, to reconcile, to harmonize, to adjust these overlapping and often conflicting claims and demands, either through securing them directly and immediately, or through securing certain individual interests, or through delimitations or compromises of individual interests, so as to give effect to the greatest total of interests or to the interests that weigh most in our civilization, with the least sacrifice of the scheme of interests as a whole.

Some Realism about Realism—Responding to Dean Pound

Karl N. Llewellyn

Ferment is abroad in the law. The sphere of interest widens; men become interested again in the life that swirls around things legal. Before rules, were facts; in the beginning was not a Word, but a Doing. Behind decisions stand judges; judges are men; as men they have human backgrounds. Beyond rules, again, lie effects: beyond decisions stand people whom rules and decisions directly or indirectly touch. The field of Law reaches both forward and back from the Substantive Law of school and doctrine. The sphere of interest is widening; so, too, is the scope of doubt. *Beyond rules lie effects*—but do they? Are some rules mere paper? And if effects, what effects? Hearsay, unbuttressed guess, assumption or assertion unchecked by test—can such be trusted on this matter of what law is *doing?*

The ferment is proper to the time. The law of schools threatened at the close of the century to turn into words—placid, clear-seeming, lifeless, like some old canal. Practice rolled on, muddy, turbulent, vigorous. It is now spilling, flooding, into the canal of stagnant words. It brings ferment and trouble. So other fields of thought have spilled their waters in: the stress on behavior in the social sciences; their drive toward integration; the physicists' reexamination of final-seeming premises; the challenge of war and revolution. These stir. They stir the law. Interests of practice claim attention. Methods of work unfamiliar to lawyers make their way in, beside traditional techniques. Traditional techniques themselves are reexamined, checked against fact, stripped somewhat of confusion. And always there is this restless questing: what *difference* does statute, or rule, or court-decision, make?

Whether this ferment is one thing or twenty is a question; if one thing, it is twenty things in one. But it is with us. It spreads. It is no mere talk. It shows results, results enough through the past decade to demonstrate its value.

And those involved are folk of modest ideals. They want law to deal, they themselves want to deal, with things, with people, with tangibles, with *definite* tangibles, and *observable* relations between definite tangibles—not with words alone; when law deals with words, they want the words to represent tangibles which can be got at beneath the words, and observable relations between those tangibles. They want to check ideas, and rules, and formulas by facts, to keep them close to facts. They view rules, they view law, as means to ends; as only means to ends; as having meaning insofar as they are means to ends. They suspect, with law moving slowly and the life around them moving fast, that some law may have gotten out of joint with life. This is a question in first instance of fact: what does law *do*, to people, or for people? In the second instance, it is a question of ends: what *ought* law to do to people, or for them? But there is no reaching a judgment as to whether any specific part of present law does what it ought, until you can first answer what it is doing now. To see this, and to be ignorant of the answer, is to start fermenting, is to start trying to find out.

All this is, we say, a simple-hearted point of view, and often philosophically naive—though it has in it elements enough of intellectual sophistication. It denies very little, except the completeness of the teachings handed down. It knows too little to care about denying much. It affirms ignorance, pitched within and without. It affirms the need to know. Its call is for intelligent effort to dispel the ignorance. Intelligent effort to cut beneath old rules, old words, to get sight of current things. It is not a new point of view; it is as old as man. But its rediscovery in any age, by any man, in any discipline, is joyous.

Speak, if you will, of a "realistic jurisprudence." And since the individual workers who are the cells of ferment cry their wares, find their results good, see the need for more workers, more results, speak, if you will (as Dean Pound has) of a *Call for a Realist Jurisprudence*. If advance is insistent on advancing further, such a call there is. But it is a call which rests on work done as well as on work to do, on experience as well as on hope, on some portion of past experiment proved useful as well as on perceived need for further experiment.

Dean Pound has discussed the call and the ferment. One portion of his discussion calls in turn for our attention. He welcomed the ferment. He described it. The general terms in which he described the fermenters we seemed to recognize: "the oncoming generation of American law teachers"; "our younger teachers of law" who are insistent on realistic jurisprudence; "the new juristic realists"; "the new school . . . current juristic realism." These general designations we say, we seemed to recognize (except the "school"). There were more specific attributes which also struck responsive chords: "By realism they mean fidelity to nature, accurate recording of things as they are, as contrasted with things as they are imagined to be, or wished to be." "Insistent . . . on beginning with an objectively scientific gathering of facts." "Psychological exposure of the role of reason in human behavior, of the extent to which so-called reasons come after action as explanations instead of before action as determining factors, has made a profound impression upon the rising generation of jurists." "Looking at precepts and doctrines and institutions with reference to how they work or fail to work,

and why." "There is a distinct advance in their frank recognition of the alogical or non-rational element in judicial action which the legal science [philosophy?] of the nineteenth century sought to ignore." If these were attributes of the "new realists," we knew who they were. We rejoiced that a scholar of Dean Pound's standing and perspective found much in their fermenting to appreciate. We agreed with him that it was important for the older thinking and the newer to make contact. . . .

II. Real Realists

What, then, *are* the characteristics of these new fermenters? One thing is clear. There is no school of realists. There is no likelihood that there will be such a school. There is no group with an official or accepted, or even with an emerging creed. There is no abnegation of independent striking out. We hope that there may never be. New recruits acquire tools and stimulus, not masters, nor over-mastering ideas. Old recruits diverge in interests from each other. They are related, says [Jerome—ed.] Frank, only in their negations, and in their skepticisms, and in their curiosity.

There is, however, a *movement* in thought and work about law. The movement, the method of attack, is wider than the number of its adherents. It includes some or much work of many men who would scorn ascription to its banner. Individual men, then. Men more or less interstimulated—but no more than all of them have been stimulated by the orthodox tradition, or by that ferment at the opening of the century in which Dean Pound took a leading part. Individual men, working and thinking over law and its place in society. Their differences in point of view, in interest, in emphasis, in field of work, are huge. They differ among themselves well-nigh as much as any of them differs from, say, Langdell. Their number grows. Their work finds acceptance.

What one does find as he observes them is twofold. First (and to be expected) certain points of departure are common to them all. Second (and this, when one can find neither school nor striking likenesses among individuals, is startling) a cross-relevance, a complementing, an interlocking of their varied results "as if they were guided by an invisible hand." A third thing may be mentioned in passing: a fighting faith in their methods of attack on legal problems; but in these last years the battle with the facts has proved so much more exciting than any battle with traditionalism that the fighting faith had come (until the spring offensive of 1931 against the realists) to manifest itself chiefly in enthusiastic labor to get on.

But as with a description of an economic order, tone and color of description must vary with the point of view of the reporter. No other one of the men would set the picture up as I shall. Such a report must thus be individual. Each man, of necessity, orients the whole to his own main interest of the moment—as I shall orient the whole to mine: the workings of case-law in appellate courts. Maps of the United States prepared respectively by a political geographer and a student of climate would show some resemblance; each would show a coherent picture; but neither's map would give much satisfaction to the other. So here. I speak for myself of that movement which in its sum is realism; I do not speak of "the realists"; still less do I speak *for* the participants or any of them. And I shall endeavor to keep in mind as I go that the justification for grouping these men together lies not in that they are *alike* in belief or work, but in that from certain common points of departure they have branched into lines of work which seem to be building themselves into a whole, a whole planned by none, foreseen by none, and (it may well be) not yet adequately grasped by any.

The common points of departure are several.

1. The conception of law in flux, of moving law, and of judicial creation of law.

2. The conception of law as a means to social ends and not as an end in itself; so that any part needs constantly to be examined for its purpose, and for its effect, and to be judged in the light of both and of their relation to each other.

3. The conception of society in flux, and in flux typically faster than the law, so that the prob-

ability is always given that any portion of law needs reexamination to determine how far it fits the society it purports to serve.

4. The *temporary* divorce of Is and Ought for purposes of study. By this I mean that whereas value judgments must always be appealed to in order to set objectives for inquiry, yet during the inquiry itself into what Is, the observation, the description, and the establishment of relations between the things described are to remain as *largely as possible* uncontaminated by the desires of the observer or by what he wishes might be or thinks ought (ethically) to be. More particularly, this involves during the study of what courts are doing the effort to disregard the question what they ought to do. Such divorce of Is and Ought is, of course, not conceived as permanent. To men who begin with a suspicion that change is needed, a permanent divorce would be impossible. The argument is simply that no judgment of what Ought to be done in the future with respect to any part of law can be intelligently made without knowing objectively, as far as possible, what that part of law is now doing. And realists believe that experience shows the intrusion of Ought-spectacles *during the investigation of the facts* to make it very difficult to see what is being done. On the Ought side this means an insistence on informed evaluations instead of armchair speculations. Its full implications on the side of Is-investigation can be appreciated only when one follows the contributions to objective description in business law and practice made by realists whose social philosophy rejects many of the accepted foundations of the existing economic order. (*E.g.*, Handler *re* trade-marks and advertising; Klaus *re* marketing and banking; Llewellyn *re* sales; Moore *re* banking; Patterson *re* risk-bearing.)

5. Distrust of traditional legal rules and concepts insofar as they purport to *describe* what either courts or people are actually doing. Hence the constant emphasis on rules as "generalized predictions of what courts will do." This is much more widespread as yet than its counterpart: the careful severance of rules *for* doing (precepts) from rules *of* doing (practices).

6. Hand in hand with this distrust of traditional rules (on the descriptive side) goes a distrust of the theory that traditional prescriptive rule-formulations are *the* heavily operative factor in producing court decisions. This involves the tentative adoption of the theory of rationalization for the study of opinions. It will be noted that "distrust" in this and the preceding point is not at all equivalent to "negation in any given instance."

7. The belief in the worthwhileness of grouping cases and legal situations into narrower categories than has been the practice in the past. This is connected with the distrust of verbally simple rules—which so often cover dissimilar and non-simple fact situations (dissimilarity being tested partly by the way cases come out, and partly by the observer's judgment as to how they ought to come out; but a realist tries to indicate explicitly which criterion he is applying).

8. An insistence on evaluation of any part of law in terms of its effects, and an insistence on the worthwhileness of trying to find these effects.

9. Insistence on *sustained and programmatic attack* on the problems of law along any of these lines. None of the ideas set forth in this list is new. Each can be matched from somewhere; each can be matched from recent orthodox work in law. New twists and combinations do appear here and there. What is as novel as it is vital is for a goodly number of men to pick up ideas which have been expressed and dropped, used for an hour and dropped, played with from time to time and dropped—to pick up such ideas and set about *consistently, persistently, insistently to carry them through*. Grant that the idea or point of view is familiar—the results of steady, sustained, systematic work with it are not familiar. Not hit-or-miss stuff, not the insight which flashes and is forgotten, but sustained effort to force an old insight into its full bearing, to exploit it to the point where it laps over upon an apparently inconsistent insight, to explore their bearing on each other by the test of fact. . . .

· 4 ·

The Marxian Perspective

In the preceding chapter we saw that the sociological movement in law challenged some of the most basic judicial assumptions held by formalist legal doctrine. In addition, we noted that the major figures involved in this movement were all jurists (judges, lawyers, and legal scholars), their contributions to the sociology of law thus made from *within* the legal profession. Our survey of the development of modern legal sociology now takes a different direction by focusing on the three most influential social theorists of the nineteenth century: Karl Marx, Max Weber, and Emile Durkheim.

Although Marx and Weber had acquired university training in law, neither made legal practice their lifelong career. By profession, Weber and Durkheim were professors of economics, political science, education, and sociology, while Marx's early jobs were in journalism. The contributions of Marx, Weber, and Durkheim to the sociology of law were made from *outside* of the legal profession. Consequently, their theoretical perspectives differ from those of sociological jurisprudence and legal realism. As we have seen, the chief goal of sociological jurisprudence and legal realism was to analyze the law in order to critique its formalist doctrine. In this chapter and the next two chapters we shall see that the chief goal of Marx's, Weber's, and Durkheim's legal sociology is to analyze the law in order to better understand society.

The concepts and theories that these three men formulated have greatly enriched our knowledge of legal sociology, and for this reason we devote one chapter to each of their theoretical perspectives. We begin with Karl Marx and the Marxian perspective.

Karl Marx: The Sociologist as Social Critic

During the past 150 years, Marx's theories have often been the subject of heated debate and endless interpretation. But whatever else these theories may explain, we may say that the Marxian perspective is first and foremost involved in a *critique* of the economic system known as *capitalism*. As we will see, it is through critique that Marx reveals the *conflicts* and *contradictions* inherent in capitalism and its epiph-

93

emomena, including law. Marx's writings, therefore, tend to be polemical, ideological, and almost always focused on matters dealing with the economy. Thus, it
is as a critic of capitalist society that we may best understand Karl Marx and his
theoretical perspective. We now briefly examine his life and those intellectual
influences that prepared him to become one of the leading social critics of the nineteenth century.

Life and Influences

The eldest son of a lawyer, Karl Marx (1818–1883) was born in Trier, in the
German Rhineland of Prussia. At the age of seventeen, he became a law student at
the University of Bonn. The following year Marx transferred to the University of
Berlin where he attended Fredrich Karl von Savigny's (1719–1861) lectures on
jurisprudence. Shortly after arriving in Berlin, however, Marx came in contact with
the thoughts of idealist philosopher Georg Hegel (1770–1831). This turn of events
led him to abandon his legal studies and concentrate solely on philosophy. Four
years later, Marx received his doctorate in philosophy from the University of Jena.

Marx was blacklisted by the Prussian Minister of Education for his radical tendencies, thus preventing him from pursuing an academic career. He consequently
turned to journalism and in 1842 became chief editor of the liberal-radical newspaper *Rheinische Zeitung*. Because Marx wrote many inflammatory articles against
the government in Berlin, the government censored the paper after only fifteen
months in operation. However, it was through his association with the *Rheinische
Zeitung* that Marx met his lifelong friend and collaborator Friedrich Engels (1820–
1895). Although Engels wrote much on his own, his major work was produced in
collaboration with Marx. Owing to this joint authorship, it is sometimes difficult to
distinguish between the ideas of the two men.

Marx's intellectual influences were many and varied. However, it is Georg Hegel
who had the most lasting influence on him. Hegel's philosophy was premised
on the notion of the **dialectics.** Dialectical thinking involves the threefold process
of *thesis, antithesis,* and *synthesis.* Hegel maintained that for every idea, or **thesis,**
that can be conceived, the opposite idea, or **antithesis,** is also possible. In other
words, if idea "A" exists, then "-A" also exists. The assertion is that any particular
thesis can be realized and comprehended only in relation to its antithesis: "good"
and "evil," "black" and "white," "on" and "off." Moreover, every thesis contains its
own inherent contradictions in its antithesis. These contradictions will inevitably
result in the demise of the thesis, and a new product, called the **synthesis,** emerges
from the unity of two opposites. At this point another dialectical process begins as
the synthesis becomes the thesis and then encounters its antagonistic antithesis
thus forming yet another synthesis, and so forth. The upshot of the dialectics is
that there exists a logical, but conflictual, pattern in the development of human
consciousness.

As we shall see later in this chapter, the Hegelian *dialectical form of argumentation,* which the young Marx was adroit at using, is intended to reveal the internal
contradictions of a legal idea or issue. Before considering Marx's unique way of
legal reasoning, however, we must first discuss some of the principal concepts that

constitute his larger theoretical perspective. These concepts will help us to better understand the neo-Marxist legal theories to be examined later in this chapter.

Principal Concepts in Marx's Sociology

The concepts on which Marx relied to articulate his theoretical perspective are numerous, diverse, and complex. He adopted these concepts from various philosophic, economic, and historical sources. Terms such as *historical materialism, mode of production*, and *base and superstructure*, have now become permanent features in the Marxian lexicon. As a matter of fact, it is impossible to discuss intelligently the Marxian perspective without using these terms. In what follows we first discuss some of the most fundamental Marxian concepts and then employ them to understand the legal sociology of Marx and the neo-Marxians.

Historical materialism. Marx appropriated Hegel's notion of the dialectics and used it to formulate his theory of **historical materialism.** That is to say that Marx took the dialectic from the level of metaphysical abstraction and utilized it to explain the dynamics of concrete socioeconomic life. Applied in this manner the dialectic constitutes a set of universal principles that govern the systematic progression of human history.

In the opening paragraphs of the *Manifesto of the Communist Party* (1848), Marx and Engels boldly declare that "the history of all hitherto existing society is the history of class struggles." According to Marx, all Western civilizations have been characterized by socioeconomic conflicts, tensions, and antagonisms that exist between the haves and the have nots, the powerful and the powerless. Marx believes that in the short run, socioeconomic conflict is detrimental to the lower classes of society because it leads to their oppression and exploitation. In the long run, however, socioeconomic conflict contributes to the dialectical progression of society because only through class conflict can the existing socioeconomic system be destroyed and replaced by another.

In *The German Ideology* (1845–1846), Marx identifies six successive socioeconomic stages of history: primitive communism, slave society, feudalism, capitalism, socialism, and communism. We will first look at the three precapitalist stages, and then focus on capitalism and examine its more salient features. Lastly, we will conclude with a brief discussion of socialism and communism.

The six socioeconomic stages of history. As Marx viewed history, during the first stage of *primitive communism* small-scale hunting and gathering societies were prevalent. People came together in communities that had a simple division of labor: the men tracked and killed wild game, while the women tended the fires, foraged for food, and cared for the young. The idea of private property did not exist. Instead, there was tribal ownership of all things necessary for survival: food, water, land, tools, and the like. In this preclass society, all basic resources were held in common.

The second socioeconomic stage of development began in antiquity with the emergence of private property. Not only did people own land, dwellings, and beasts of burden, they also owned human beings as chattel. A *slave economy* characterized ancient Greece and Rome, with slave labor a major element in the production of subsistence goods in those societies. The result was the emergence of two major groups of oppressors and oppressed, the citizens and the slaves.

The third socioeconomic stage of history was the system of land ownership, called *feudalism*, that developed in Europe during the Middle Ages. This type of society relied primarily on an agrarian economy in which the produce was cultivated on arable land owned by the feudal lord and an enserfed peasantry lived on the estate as tenants of the landowner. In return for the right to occupancy the serfs paid labor rent, worked the land, and were entitled to a small percentage of the yield that they produced. Although the majority of the serfs were legally free, they possessed no legal rights against the landowners and were thus frequently subject to heavy demands of rent, taxes, and other payments. Further, while the serfs had effective possession of their huts, plows, and tools, they were not proprietors.

Marx's analysis of primitive communism, slave economy, and feudalism is rather cursory when compared to the attention which he pays to **capitalism,** or that economic system which depends on industrialization and private ownership and allows individuals to freely pursue monetary profit through the exchange of goods. Since, in his view, capitalism is just as oppressive as the three previous socioeconomic systems of history, Marx devotes the bulk of his work to a critical study of its many features.

Although several "types" or "phases" of capitalism have been identified by both Marxist and non-Marxist scholars, we will here be concerned only with that specific type of capitalism to which Marx and Engels directed their major criticisms: **industrial capitalism.** Achieving prominence during the mid-1800s, particularly in England, industrial capitalism relied extensively on the use of power-driven machinery with the objective of manufacturing commodities on a large scale for the purpose of selling them on the open market. Thus, it may be said that industrial capitalism was basically a market economy of commodity production.

We can identify several distinguishing features that characterize industrial capitalism. First, private ownership of the means of production prevails. Second, commodities are produced and sold for the sole purpose of private gain or profit-making. Third, labor power is considered a commodity that may be bought and sold and money is regarded as the universal medium of exchange. In addition, competition is encouraged among the capitalists who own the means of production, as well as among the workers who sell their labor power. Finally, an ideology of laissez-faire, the strongly held belief that private initiative in the development and production of commodities must not be restrained by government, is paramount. Implied in each one of these features of capitalism is the idea of class conflict.

Although the concept of *class* is central to Marxian social thought, neither Marx nor Engels rendered a specific definition of the term. Thus, we may say with Oxford University social theorist Isaiah Berlin that a class is "a group of persons in a society whose lives are determined by their position in the productive arrangements which determine the structure of that society" (1973:127).

While Marx recognized that several groupings existed in capitalist society, he nevertheless insisted that there were two main antagonistic social classes: the capitalist class, or *bourgeoisie*, and the working class, or *proletariat*. The social relations between these two classes split society into opposed camps of ruler and oppressed.

The **bourgeoisie**, the economically dominant class, owns and controls the material forces of production: human labor, raw materials, land, tools, machinery, technologies, and factories. In their effort to obtain maximum profits for the commodities that they produce, the bourgeoisie exploit the proletariat by not paying them the full value of the labor power they expend. In other words, the capitalists pay their workers the bare minimum—just enough to keep them alive and working. The **proletariat**, then, is that propertyless and subordinate social class "which procures its means of livelihood entirely and solely from the sale of its labor" (Engels, 1975a:341). Because the workers' labor power is bought and sold by the bourgeoisie, the workers themselves are treated as salable commodities and not as human beings.

Another concept important in Marxist thought is **alienation**, a state of estrangement or separation that occurs when the consequences of people's actions are in contradiction to, or removed from, their creations, motives, needs, and goals. Under capitalism, alienation takes four general forms:

1. The worker is alienated from his or her labor because he or she has sold it for wages.
2. The worker is alienated from the product of his or her labor because he or she has no control over the product.
3. The worker is alienated from himself or herself as a human being.
4. The worker is alienated from others, with the relationship between capitalist and worker, for example, one of mutual indifference as human relations are reduced to commodity exchanges.

In a broader sense, Marx's concept of alienation is related to his theory of needs. In Marx's view, humans manipulate their material conditions for the purpose of meeting certain social necessities. People, for example, create a system of laws in order to satisfy their need for predictability of behavior as well as their need for protection of persons and property. Before long, however, the legal system acquires a life of its own. Thus, it is seen by people not as something that they created, but as an objective institution possessing eternal, impersonal authority in its own right. The result is that individuals become estranged from, and governed by, their own creations.

The social institutions, including the law, and the ideologies (e.g., moral, intellectual, and religious beliefs, values and habits of life, scientific ideas, and legal thought) are instruments required by the bourgeoisie to protect their industrial, commercial, and financial interests and to ensure their continuance as the dominant class. These institutions and ideologies are seen by capitalists and workers alike as being desirable and part of the "natural" order of things. Although they are mere epiphenomena that express or reflect the capitalist economic mode of production, the institutions and ideologies are nevertheless seen as mysterious forces and become objects of great reverence. In this context, Engels maintains that the legal system "appears as an independent element which derives the justification for its existence . . . from its own inner foundations, ... People forget that their [law]

derived from their economic conditions of life" (1955:623). Only when the proletariat is able to demystify these distorted images of bourgeoisie ideology can it
achieve true revolutionary consciousness and pave the way for socialism.

In *The German Ideology*, Marx contends that all human societies, if they are to
survive, must have a particular **mode of production,** or an economic system by
which goods and services are produced, exchanged, and distributed. We have already seen that there existed three precapitalist modes of production in the Western world: primitive communism, slavery, and feudalism. The mode of production
under capitalism, however, is more much complex, comprised of both the *material
forces of production* and the *social relations of production.*

The **material forces of production** allow people to act on and transform their
social world for the purpose of producing their means of existence. These forces
consist of labor power, the means of production, and the raw materials of production. **Labor power** refers to our mental and physical ability to perform work,
the **means of production** are the industrial technologies needed to produce goods
(e.g., tools, machines, and factories), and the **raw materials of production** consist
of natural resources like land, water, coal, and iron ore.

The material forces of production give rise to the **social relations of production,** or the relations that exist among individuals with respect to the ownership of
productive forces. In Marx's view, the social relations of production that emerge
under capitalism may be described generally as follows: the members of the ruling
class privately own and control the means of production while the members of the
oppressed class own only their labor power, which they are forced to sell in exchange for wages. The ruling class legally owns as property (i.e., as a good or "commodity") the labor power of the workers. Consequently, the social relations of
production are, in their legal form, transformed into property relations.

Marx refers to a society's mode of production as its **economic base.** The
economic base largely determines society's **superstructure,** which consists of the
various social institutions (political, legal, etc.) as well as the various ideologies.
Because the superstructure has its foundation in the economic base, a change in the
latter will bring about a corresponding change in the former.

As Marx explains, the economic base of capitalism has a determining influence
on the form and content of the legal superstructure. For example, when the law
prohibits, through rules and sanctions, the forcible taking of other people's possessions, it serves to support the fundamental capitalist notion of the private ownership of the means of production. Similarly, the law of contract helps to facilitate
the widespread exchange of commodities that is crucial to the maintenance of a
free-market economy. Thus, for Marx, "legislation, whether political or civil, never
does more than proclaim, express in words, the will of the economic relations"
(1900:83).

But it is not only the political and legal superstructures that are influenced by
the base, so too are our ways of thinking. One of Marx's best known aphorisms
states, "It is not the consciousness of men that determines their existence, but their
social existence that determines their consciousness" (Marx, 1972:21). Despite the
apparent finality of this statement, it must be pointed out that Marx did not believe
that the economic base had a unidirectional casual influence on people's conscious-

ness. He merely wished to imply that, "in the last instance," it is the economic base that forms and gives meaning to our modes of thought.

Marx believed that the social revolution that would usher in the socioeconomic stage of socialism can only occur when the material forces of production come in conflict with the social relations of production. This conflict is the catalyst behind the progression of society.

Marx was fully convinced of capitalism's inevitable collapse. According to him, capitalist society would be replaced by a fifth, intermediary stage of socioeconomic development called **socialism.** Socialism involves the abolition of private ownership of the means of production. The means of production are instead owned collectively and the idea is that production is to be used for the public good, not for private gain. Thus, under socialism, land, industry, and technology as well as the major superstructural institutions such as medicine and education are centralized in the hands of the state.

Before socialism could be realized, however, the proletariat had to achieve **class consciousness,** a subjective awareness of their position within the production process. In Marx's view, only after the workers have become aware of their oppression and exploitation at the hands of the bourgeoisie can they organize themselves and forcibly overthrow the existing conditions of production. The proletarian revolution is thus the antithesis of capitalism. Socialism, as the synthesis, emerges from the class struggle between the working class and the bourgeoisie.

Finally, Marx's sixth and ultimate socioeconomic stage of historical development is **communism,** which he regarded as humanity's inevitable destiny. This final stage is characterized by both a communitarian mode of production and the abolition of all social classes resulting in the disappearance of class oppression. It is at this point in history that Marx felt people would achieve self-determination and realize true emancipation, becoming free of all forms of alienation. Perhaps the best description of the social relations of production in the communist society is given by Marx in *Critique of the Gotha Program* when he states: "From each according to his ability, to each according to his needs!"

In the sections that follow we shall examine Marx and Engels' political thinking at the start of their careers and before the maturation of their theory of historical materialism. We focus on this early period, the 1840s, because most of their specific and detailed comments on the law were made at this time. At this point in their intellectual development, Marx and Engels see law as an instrument utilized by the ruling classes to protect and advance their economic and political interests. We begin by looking at what Marx had to say about law, customary rights, and private property.

Law, Customary Rights, and Private Property

Between October 25 and November 3, 1842, Marx wrote, for the *Rheinische Zeitung,* a series of five articles entitled "Debates on the Law on Thefts of Wood." In these articles he deals with the proceedings of the Rhine Provincial Assembly concerning the proposal of a law prohibiting the gathering of wood in the Rhenish

forests. Marx severely criticizes this vague new law created from revisions made in
the Forestal Theft Act of 1837. In addition to the Rhineland, several German states
had similarly revised their legal codes:

> That of Baden, for example, enacted in 1833, contained 220 sections
> establishing rules and punishments for nearly every detail of forest appro-
> priation. In Thuringia and Saxe-Meiningen similar codes were estab-
> lished. Written permits were required for berry and mushroom gathering.
> Dead leaves and forest litter could be gathered for fodder only "in extreme
> cases of need." The topping of trees for May poles, Christmas trees, rake
> handles, wagon tongues, etc., was punishable by fine and prison (Line-
> baugh, 1976:13).

The Social Context

The Rhenish peasants—that is, the agrarian proletariat—had traditionally
been given common use-rights of the forests. Thus, they were in the practice of
carting away dead timber from the woodlands for their own use. The customary
right of allowing the poor to help themselves to surplus subsistence goods is an
ancient one. Hebrew law in the Old Testament, for example, required that glean-
ings of the harvest be left in the fields for the needy and the stranger and others
who had no land to harvest (see Leviticus 19:9–10). Charitable acts such as these
formed a central component of subsistence rights, which constituted the "moral
economy" (Thompson, 1991) of the poor, that continued through the Middle Ages
and beyond.

During the nineteenth century, in western Prussia where the proportion of
forest to arable lands was three to four, a similar customary subsistence right had
served to safeguard the Rhenish peasantry against natural and economic disaster.
For example, during the spring women and children would scour the fields along
the Rhine and its tributaries, cutting thistles and nettles, digging up the roots of
couch grass, and collecting various kinds of weeds and leaves to use as winter
fodder. The abundance of the forests provided fuel, forage, materials for houses,
farm equipment, and food. However, scarcities caused by the agrarian crises of the
1820s and the growing needs of industry led to a restriction on the gathering of
wood. According to legal historian Peter Linebaugh, "the crisis hitting the Rhenish
farming population made these riches all the more necessary to survival. At the
same time, access to them was becoming progressively restricted with the inexorable expropriation of forest rights" (1976:11).

As manufacturing became increasingly dependent on the agrarian production
of wood, the poor's wood-gathering rights were being gradually eroded. During
the first four decades of the nineteenth century the commercial value of timber
increased precipitously with the expansion of those markets that relied on the use
of wood. Railroad construction, for example, required beech for the making of
railway ties. In addition, growing industrialization increased the demand for oak
since it was widely used in the construction of machinery; shipbuilding depended
on Rhenish hardwoods such as oak, elm, cherry, and ash for its supply of spars,

masts, yards, staves, and knees; and the expansion of the coalfields brought with it a demand for mining timbers (Linebaugh, 1976:12).

As a consequence of industry's increasing reliance on agrarian products, the peasants' customary right to gather wood in the forests came under attack. At bottom was the issue of a dialectical conflict that had developed between the emergence of capitalism and the last remnants of common ownership of the land. This conflict took the form of "a brutal struggle to expropriate the masses of the people" (Mehring, 1966:41). As Linebaugh points out, criminalizing the peasant's appropriation of forest products "represented an important moment in the development of German capitalism" (1976:6).

Furthermore, by 1841 more than one-half of the Rhenish forests had come under the ownership and control of the Prussian government. This meant that the forests fell under the jurisdiction of the police and deputies of the Forstmeister of the Ministry of the Interior in Berlin. As a consequence of the forest police's aggressive enforcement of the law, prosecutions for wood stealing increased dramatically. In 1836, approximately three-quarters of all criminal prosecutions brought forward in Prussia concerned wood pilfering and other forest offenses such as poaching and trespassing. That same year, in Baden, there was one conviction of wood stealing for every 6.1 inhabitants. In 1841 there was a conviction for every 4.6 inhabitants, and in 1842 one for every four (Mehring, 1966:41; Linebaugh, 1976:13).

The Contradictions in the Law

Marx inveighed against the proposed law on thefts of wood because he believed that only the poor would be vulnerable to prosecution. He based his arguments on the fact that the law was rife with contradictions (Cain and Hunt, 1979:6).

Many of the law's contradictions were quite obvious. For example, on the one hand the law was intended to protect the forests by allowing their natural regeneration, by preventing the violent and unplanned clearing of the woods, and by preventing the depletion of the fertility of the soil. On the other hand, as Marx points out, the law was used by the rich Rhenish forest owners to protect and advance their own private interests. The law, to be sure, advantaged the forest owners because it gave them the right to force violators to work for them. The law also stated that the fines imposed on the violator as well as all compensation for damaged property were to be remitted to the forest owner.

This contradiction illustrates that while the law was at one time intended to protect the public interest, it was subsequently used to benefit the private interests of the forest owners. Thus, states Marx, "Our whole account has shown how the Assembly degrades the executive power, the administrative authorities, the life of the accused, the idea of the state, crime itself, and punishment as well, to the *material means of private interest*" (1975a:259). Marxist legal scholar Paul Phillips concisely summarizes Marx's argument when he states that "the whole tenor of [Marx's] articles is that the effect of the law is to subordinate all to 'private interest'" (1980:14).

Legal sociologists Maureen Cain and Alan Hunt (1979:6) maintain that, because "the rights of the poor are formless,"—that is, since they emerge from practices based on tradition and not from legislatures—it is almost inevitable that those rights will contradict the written law. Another contradiction arises when the customary rights of the poor, who have no property, conflict with the law of private property. In other words, the notions of "nonownership" and "ownership" are diametrically opposed to each other.

In light of these inherent contradictions, Marx argued that the poor's customary rights should not be suppressed. In advocating for the preservation of these rights he located their historical origin in an ambiguous, medieval idea of property. According to Marx, "all customary rights of the poor were based on the fact that certain forms of property were indeterminate in character, for they were not definitely private, but neither were they definitely common property, being a mixture of private and public right, such as we find in all the institutions of the Middle Ages" (1975a:232–233). Through time, though, this indeterminate form of property was transformed into something that was clearly privately owned, resulting in the poor's practice of wood gathering being regarded as a crime: stealing and trespassing. The proposed law did not, however, distinguish between the gathering of wood that had fallen on its own (i.e., dry twigs and branches) and timber that had been hewed. Thus, the taking of fallen wood and felled wood were both considered theft and similarly punished. Accordingly, Marx proposes that "if the law applies the term theft to an action that is scarcely even a violation of forest regulations [i.e., the taking of fallen wood], then the law *lies*, and the poor are sacrificed to a legal lie" (1975a:227). He then points to the law's dialectical self-demise by asking a rhetorical question: "And does not this crude view, which lays down a common definition for different kinds of action and leaves the difference out of account, itself bring about its own destruction?" (1975a:228).

According to Marx, the state, in criminalizing the gathering of fallen wood, was acting on behalf of the particular interests of the private landowners. It was biased and immoral. The state therefore was not expressing its true essence, which is, according to Hegel's notion of the ideal state, that of universal altruism.

Additionally, the composition of the Provisional Assemblies—where membership consisted of one-half country gentry, one-third urban landowners, and one-sixth peasant landowners (Mehring, 1966:37)—guaranteed that they enacted legislation that served private interests. Mehring contends that through his examination of the proceedings of the Rhine Provisional Assembly, "Marx wished to show what might be expected of a class assembly of private interests when once it seriously set about the task of legislating" (1966:42).

Political economy and the law. Several scholars have commented on the stage of Marx's theoretical development at the time he wrote his articles on the law on thefts of wood. Marx's biographer Franz Mehring maintains that, at this juncture, Marx's "reasoning is still based on considerations of justice and not yet of economics" (1966:41–42). Paul Phillips, by contrast, states that these articles illustrate Marx's "first major instance of the use of economic interests to explain a legal act" (1980:13). Moreover, in Peter Linebaugh's view these articles "first forced Marx to realize his ignorance of political economy" (1976:6). Regardless of whether Marx had, in 1842, taken an economic approach in his analysis of law, one thing is certain: he had not yet developed his formal theory of class struggle. Be that as it may, it is fair to say, along with Linebaugh, that "Marx's articles on the theft of wood expressed an important moment in the dynamics of [capitalist] accumulation and class relations" (1976:9).

Let us now look at another historical analysis of legal and property relations focusing on several themes considered by Marx: class exploitation, the treatment of property as an opportunity for profit making, and the use of legislation by the propertied class to perpetuate its social and economic interests. For this we turn to the work of English social historian E. P. Thompson and his commentary on the Black Act.

The Black Act. An English forest law known as the Black Act was ordered by the House of Commons and enacted in May 1723. The act, which was to remain in operation for only three years, kept being renewed, extended, and enlarged until it was finally made perpetual in 1758. Because it was so loosely drafted, the law was extremely inclusive and its penalties very severe. The act created over fifty new capital offenses including numerous crimes against the public order, the person, and, most significantly, property. Thompson refers to it as "an astonishing example of legislative overkill" (1975:196).

The property offenses legislated against took place in forest areas—that is, private estates with deer parks or fisheries—owned by the nobility and the local gentry. Thompson provides a general description of these offenses:

> The main group of offenses was that of hunting, wounding or stealing red or fallow deer, and the poaching of hares, conies or fish. These were made capital if the persons offending were armed and disguised, and, in the case of deer, if the offenses were committed in any of the King's forests, whether the offenders were armed and disguised or not (1975:22).

The "Blacks" were forest villagers—farmers and hunters—who organized themselves as a group of deer-slayers and poachers. Mounted and armed, and blackening their faces with soot and grease to disguise themselves, the Blacks hustled the forest officers, killed the deer, and cut down timber in the forests. But there was more to blacking than the commission of simple acts of predatory crime. Thompson maintains that the Blacks' attacks on forests and parks were actually "retributive in character and concerned less with venison as such than with the deer as symbols (and as agents) of an authority which threatened [the Blacks'] economy, their crops, and their customary agrarian rights" (Thompson, 1975:64). The Blacks, in Thompson's view, were armed foresters forcibly defending their claims of land cultivation, wood-taking, hunting, and grazing. Indeed, it is in this manner that the forest had traditionally provided a livelihood for hundreds of poor families.

For example, whenever a fall of timber took place it was the custom of the forest villagers to gather bundles of twigs and small tree branches for their own use. By the 1720s, however, the villagers' customary use-rights were severely encroached upon by the expansion of the landed gentry's private ownership of the forests, fisheries, deer parks, and game preserves. In an effort to keep out poachers and other trespassers, the landowners enclosed these properties with high walls, hedges, and wrought-iron fences, in effect denying the villagers' claims to common right usage.

The natural resources in these estates—timber, quarries, gravel- and sand-pits, peat bogs, and so on—had their economic value greatly enhanced as commercial demand for them increased. Thus, while the tenant farmers and village cottagers used the forests as a means of subsistence, the landholders exploited the forests for capital accumulation. According to Thompson, "the forest conflict was, in origin, a conflict between users and exploiters" (1975:245). Thompson baldly describes the poor villagers' situation as follows:

> The very roof-beams which housed their practical economy were being eaten away, by money and by law, above their heads. During the eighteenth century one legal decision after another signaled that the lawyers had become converted to the notions of absolute property ownership, and that . . . the law abhorred the messy complexities of coincident use-right. . . . The rights and claims of the poor, . . . were simply redefined as crimes: poaching, wood-theft, trespass (1975:241).

In effect, custom was criminalized.

The Whigs—those members of Parliament with great power and wealth—created the Black Act and in the process attempted to define blacking not as simple deer stealing but as treason and sedition against the government. These drafters and executants of the act saw the agrarian disturbances created by the Blacks as an emergency necessitating an immediate response. In point of fact, this "emergency" was merely an opportunity for the Whigs to use the law to protect those interests that they felt were most threatened: their property and status. To be sure, it was at this time that the law was elevated to a more prominent role than at any other period in English history. "Moreover, eighteenth-century law was concerned less with relations between persons than with relations between property, or claims upon property" (Thompson, 1991:35)

The status of the great gentry demanded ostentatious display of their property and deer parks were part of this display. Thus, blacking was the emergency that acted upon the Whig's sensibilities as members of the propertied class. According to Thompson, "property and the privileged status of the propertied were assuming, every year, a greater weight in the scales of justice, until justice itself was seen as no more than the outworks and defenses of property and of its attendant status" (1975:197). With the passage of the Black Act there occurred an ideological shift in what was regarded as a category of "crime," which now "was not an offense between men . . . but an offense against property" (1975:207). Thompson makes it clear that the Whigs' enactment of the Black Act was not a premeditated or conspiratorial response to be used for terrorizing the forest villagers, but a consequence of the opportunities that the rich and powerful had available to them. The fact remains, however, that during the eighteenth century, "the law was employed as an instrument of agrarian capitalism, . . . [and] [i]f it is pretended that the law was impartial, . . . then we must reply that this pretense was class fraud" (Thompson, 1991:175–176). Thompson's historical account of the Black Act is consistent with Marx and Engels' notion of law as an instrument manipulated by the economically advantaged classes for their own private gain.

We now turn our attention to those laws that deal not with the socioeconomic issue of property relations, but with the sociopolitical issue of freedom of expression: the censorship laws.

The Censorship Laws

Several of Marx's early writings during the 1840s deal with the issue of law and censorship of the press. In this section we examine some of these works, looking particularly at the dialectical form of argumentation that Marx employs to demolish his opponents' reasoning by revealing the internal contradictions of their positions and advancing his own point of view. At this time in his career Marx shared Hegel's philosophical conception of law as a type of existence of freedom. Marx's description of censorship—"criticism as a monopoly of the government" (1975b:159)—regards censorship as the antithesis of freedom. A censorship law, therefore, is a contradiction in terms.

The New Censorship Instruction

The Prussian King Friedrich Wilhelm IV, recently ascended to the throne, saw himself as a supporter of the freedom of the press. Consequently, on December 24, 1841, he, through the Prussian government, issued a censorship instruction that, relative to the old censorship decree of 1819, relaxed its excessive regulations on the press. In actuality, however, this new instruction imposed greater restrictive measures.

In early 1842, Marx wrote an essay—"Comments on the Latest Prussian Censorship Instruction"—that he sent to the magazine, *Die Deutschen Jahrbücher*, decrying the king's directive. According to Franz Mehring, this article "represents the beginning of Marx's political career" (1966:33). The gist of Marx's argument was that legal safeguards concerning censorship should be stated precisely and leave as little as possible to governmental discretion (Adams, 1972:47). In an ironic turn of events, the essay was censored by the Prussian government before it could appear. It was, however, published the following year in Switzerland in the Young Hegelian journal *Anekdota Philosophika*.

Marx's goal in his essay is to argue, in true dialectical fashion, that the censorship instruction undermines itself because of its internal inconsistencies. "The *new censorship instruction*," writes Marx, "becomes entangled in [its] dialectic. It contains the contradiction of itself doing, and making it the censor's duty to do, everything that it condemns as anti-state in the case of the press" (1975c:121). In short, the instruction is irrational and thus antithetical to the very essence of the state, which, according to Hegel, is the ethical embodiment of reason.

Another contradiction is revealed as Marx points out that, on the one hand the new instruction tells censors to permit a frank discussion of the internal affairs of Prussia. On the other hand, however, the old censorship decree of 1819 (which was still in effect) prohibited any critique of Prussian affairs. Further, censorship relying on secrecy and arbitrariness, says Marx, is wholly incompatible with the law's basic essence of publicity and universality.

Marx's most condemning attacks are directed at the new censorship instruction for stating that press criticisms about the government and its laws are permitted as long as these criticisms are "decent and their tendency well-meaning." The new instruction, however, does not say what constitutes tendency. In Marx's view, the law against tendency appears to punish writers for what they *think* and not for what they *do*. As Marx argues, the law—and, by implication, the state—can exist only in the world of deeds and acts. Because the restriction against tendency condemns thoughts and motives, it goes beyond the proper sphere of law; it is, in fact, lawlessness.

The new censorship instruction further demanded that the state censors approve the appointment of all editors of the daily press. Moreover, the instruction specifically required that editorial writers have "scientific qualification," "position," and "character." The censors, on the other hand, need only possess, in the vaguest of terms, "a tested frame of mind" and "ability."

Assessing the relationship between writer and censor—that is, the relationship between the former's expressions of political tendency and the latter's arbitrary and subjective authority—Marx states:

> *All objective standards* are abandoned, everything is finally reduced to the *personal* relation, and the censor's *tact has* to be called a guarantee. What then can the censor violate? Tact. But tactlessness is no crime. What is threatened as far as the writer is concerned? His existence. What state has ever made the existence of whole classes depend on the tact of individual officials? (1975c:129).

We now turn our attention to a series of articles written by Marx that are the key to understanding his general theory of historical materialism (Adams, 1972: 56,54). In these articles Marx critiques the Rhine Assembly's debates on the freedom of the press.

Debates on the Freedom of the Press

The *Rheinische Zeitung* was founded in Cologne in January 1842 and Marx became its editor a short nine months later. The following year Marx resigned the editorship in protest of the censorship law that required the press to submit all of its material to a censor. The newspaper itself had been previously banned for its subversive tendencies.

Marx's first contribution to the publication was a series of six articles published in May 1842 and entitled "Debates on Freedom of the Press and Publication of the Proceedings of the Assembly of the Estates." Although Marx was not yet a socialist at the time, these articles show the earliest form of Marx's political thought.

In these articles Marx deals with the debates of the Sixth Rhine Province Assembly, which sat in session from May 23 to July 25, 1841, in Düsseldorf. The debates took place around the issues of press freedom and the publication of the assembly proceedings. Concerning the latter issue, King Friedrich Wilhelm IV had previously tried to encourage the provincial assemblies to publish a report of the proceedings without publicizing the names of the speakers. His suggestion, however, was vehemently opposed by the assembly speakers themselves.

In his articles, Marx selects for discussion the arguments of a representative of each of the four estates of the Rhine province: the princes, the knights, the towns, and the peasants. He then "refutes each argument with elaborate logic and sometimes with equally elaborate satire, but the interests of his reply lies in his contention that the press is everywhere expressive of a people's mind and spirit" (Adams, 1972:52–53). In the finest dialectical tradition, Marx turns the speakers' arguments against themselves. His most cutting remarks are leveled at the two speakers who were the most vocal and passionate opponents of a free press: the speaker representing the princely estate and the speaker representing the knightly estate.

The speaker from the princely estate. Harboring a deep prejudice against the press, the princely speaker contends that all of society's defects, from the national debt to social revolution, are the direct result of excesses on the part of the press. For him, censorship is a lesser evil than freedom of the press. Marx is quick to remind the speaker that from 1819 to 1830—those years known as the "literary period of strict censorship" in Prussia—philosophy (to mention just one literary field) was censored in the German language. "The philosophical field ceased to speak German," writes Marx, "for German had ceased to be the language of thought. The spirit spoke in incomprehensible, mysterious [i.e., foreign] words because comprehensible [i.e., German] words were no longer allowed to be comprehended" (1975b:140). This period of severe censorship was disastrous for the development of German literature and served also to quell the spirit of the German people. "Finally," Marx asks, "does the [princely] speaker think that the national defects of a free press are not just as much national defects of the censors? Are the censors excluded from the historical whole? Are they unaffected by the spirit of a time?" (1975b:145).

The speaker from the knightly estate. Concerning the publication of the assembly's debates in the daily newspapers, the speaker of the knights maintains that the manner in which the proceedings are published is an issue to be decided by the assembly members in accordance with their "inner convictions" and should not be a matter of concern to the public. Marx retorts that the publication of the debates is intended for the province and not for the estates, and then asks sarcastically whether the estates belong to the province or the province to the estates. Marx, moreover, does not consider the assembly members trustworthy regarding the publication of their own proceedings.

Freedom and Censorship

Relying on the dialectical form of argumentation, Marx maintains that censorship contradicts the essential nature, or inner character, of the press, which is to be free. In his view, the free press serves as the watchful eye of a people's soul. "It is the spiritual mirror in which a people can see itself" (Marx, 1975b:165). A censored press, by contrast, leads only to hypocrisy and passivity. Because censorship cannot be part of the essence of freedom, a censored press is therefore not a press at all. "The essence of the free press," states Marx, "is the characterful, rational, moral essence of freedom. The character of the censored press is the characterless monster of unfreedom. . . . In order to really justify censorship, the speaker [of the knights] would have to prove that censorship is part of the essence of freedom of the press" (1975b:158).

Moreover, since the essence of law is also freedom, a censorship law is a meaningless contradiction. A censorship law has only the *form* of a law, but it can never be a real law. It is, in fact, nothing more than a police measure. As Marx puts it, "laws are in no way repressive measures against freedom, any more than the law of gravity is a repressive measure against motion" (1975b:162).

Finally,

> *A censorship law is an impossibility* because it seeks to punish not offenses but opinions, because it cannot be anything but a *formula for the censor*, because no state has the courage to put in general legal terms what it can carry out in practice through the agency of the censor. For that reason, too, the operation of the censorship is entrusted not to the courts but to the police (Marx, 1975b:166).

The Prussian Press Bill

Five years after the dissolution of the *Rheinische Zeitung*, Marx again turned his attention to the Prussian Press Bill. This time he wrote about it in a brief article that appeared in the *Neue Rheinische Zeitung*.

After producing some of their most impressive works in which they elaborated the basic principles of scientific communism, Marx and Engels settled in Cologne and founded the *Neue Rheinische Zeitung* as a replacement for its predecessor. Cologne appeared to be the most logical place from which to publish the new revolutionary newspaper, as the city had retained the more liberal press laws of the Code Napoleon from the time when it had been occupied by the French. Beginning with the newspaper's first issue on June 1, 1848, until it was completely suppressed by the government on May 19, 1849, Marx and Engels wrote about 220 articles for the publication.

"The Prussian Press Bill," published in July 1848, was written by Marx in reaction to a new bill that had been introduced before the Rhine Provincial Assembly by the Prussian Minister of Finance, David Justus Hansemann. This new bill proposed to extend the existing press law to all of Prussia and increase the severity of its sanctions. Because this was to be a law which dealt with **libel,** or written defamation, it prohibited the press from publishing statements accusing a state official of engaging in a crime, or any action that puts him in public contempt. The punishment for violating this new law was to be three months to three years imprisonment. Moreover, "if the libel was committed against state officials in relation to their official business, the normal punishment can be *increased by a half*" (Marx, 1973:135).

Marx sees the bill as an attack on the freedom of the press. "From the day when this law comes into force," he writes, "the [Prussian] officials will be able, unpunished, to commit any arbitrary, tyrannical, or illegal action; they will be free to flog and to order floggings, to arrest and imprison without trial; the only effective control, the press, will have been made ineffective" (Marx, 1973:136). Marx maintains that the Prussian Press Bill serves only to protect incompetent government officials.

Like Marx, Engels also inveighed against the imposition of press censorship. In July 1842 he wrote a short essay for the *Rheinische Zeitung* entitled "On the Critique of the Prussian Press Laws." Engels' main criticism in this article concerns section 151 of the Prussian Penal Code, which states: "Whosoever causes dissatisfaction by *insolent, disrespectful* criticism and *mockery* of the laws of the land and government edicts shall incur the penalty of detention in prison or fortress from six months to two years" (emphasis added). Engels considers it a legislative mistake to place the terms "insolent" and "disrespectful" side by side because it only leads to confusion. He points out that disrespect refers to an unintentional act of **negligence,** or the failure to exercise a reasonable amount of care in a situation that causes harm to someone, whereas insolence presupposes malicious intent or ill will. It is possible, therefore, to be disrespectful without being insolent. Nevertheless, by putting these two concepts under the same heading, Prussian law assumes that all disrespectful criticism of governmental affairs seeks to intentionally provoke dissatisfaction and is therefore punishable.

Engels makes the same argument concerning "disrespect" and "mockery." Although these two concepts are quantitatively and qualitatively different from each other, they nevertheless carry the same penalty. The whole confusion is caused by the law's incorporation of the word "disrespectful," which is extremely ambiguous. Engels posits that "such a vague concept, such latitude for subjective interpretation, should not be present in the Criminal Code, least of all where difference of political views is *bound* to come into play and where the judges are not jurymen but servants of the state" (1975b:307). Engels' assessment of section 151 of the Prussian Penal Code is that it "contains a mixture and confusion of heterogeneous legislative and press-police definitions" (1975b:310).

Thus far in this chapter, we have introduced some of Marx's more fundamental concepts, including dialectics, historical materialism, industrial capitalism, the mode of production, the social relations of production, the economic base, the superstructure, and the idea that law is an instrument utilized by the bourgeoisie to protect and advance their economic and political interests. Having briefly discussed these and other foundational concepts, we then turned our attention to Marx and Engels' commentary on the laws dealing with the theft of wood and the censorship of the press. By using the dialectical form of argumentation, which reveals the law's internal contradictions, Marx and Engels demonstrate that these laws are used by the ruling classes to their advantage.

We first considered Marx's explanation why the law on thefts of wood made it a crime for the peasants to take dead timber from the Rhenish forests. Marx argues that this law advantaged the rich forest owners because the peasants who violated the law were forced to work for them. In addition, as German capitalism came to rely more and more on the industrial use of forest products, it became necessary for the Rhine Provincial Assembly to propose the law on the thefts of wood and deny the poor their customary right to gather fallen wood.

We then turned out attention to an examination of Marx's ideas concerning class exploitation, the treatment of property as an opportunity for profit making, and the propertied class's use of legislation to perpetuate its interests. In so doing we looked closely at the English forest law called the Black Act. The Black Act made it illegal for English forest villagers to exercise their customary use-rights to cultivate the land, gather wood, hunt, and fish. Social historian E. P. Thompson shows that the Black Act criminalized the villagers use-rights so that the propertied class could exploit the forest for profit making.

Finally, we looked at what Marx and Engels had to say about the censorship law. Relying again on the dialectical form of argumentation, Marx illustrates that Prussia's new censorship instruction contains its own inherent contradictions. First, Marx argues that the censorship instruction is completely antithetical to the state's ethical embodiment of reason. Second, he states that although the new instruction allowed criticism of Prussia's political affairs, the old instruction, which was still in effect, prohibited such criticism. Third, Marx maintains that the secrecy of censorship is antithetical to the publicity of law.

Marx and Engels' statements about the laws dealing with wood theft and censorship constitute a large portion of the Marxian perspective in legal sociology. We now continue by analyzing the writings of those scholars who have attempted to formulate their legal theories within the Marxian perspective.

Neo-Marxian Contributions to the Marxian Perspective

As we have seen thus far, Marx and Engels wrote a handful of newspaper articles critiquing specific pieces of legislation that they perceived to benefit the ruling class at the expense of the other segments of society. Marx and Engels, however, never identified law as a major theoretical problem. Indeed, there is no coherent Marxian theory of law because, despite their scattered comments on the subject, law never constituted a specific object of inquiry for either of these men. What we have instead is a Marxian *analysis* of law that makes "use of elements of theory and concepts drawn from the Marxist tradition" (Hunt, 1981:92–93).

We now peruse the substantive contributions that neo-Marxian scholars Evgeny Pashukanis, Isaac Balbus, Karl Renner, and Alan Stone have made in the construction of a Marxian theory of law. Much of this material relies on the ideas mentioned in the first part of this chapter. Additionally, there are three concepts that will help to clarify a good amount of what will be discussed in the sections that follow: (1) *instrumentalism and structuralism*, (2) *the labor theory of value*, and (3) *the fetishism of commodities.*

A Marxian analysis of law is premised on two distinct theoretical approaches: instrumentalism and structuralism. An early perspective in Marxian legal analysis, **instrumentalism** attributes the law's content to the direct manipulation of the bourgeoisie. Marx and Engels illustrate this idea in *The German Ideology* when they maintain that law is but a creation of the ruling class:

> The individuals who rule . . . besides having to constitute their power in the form of the State, have to give their will, . . . a universal expression, . . . as law—an expression whose content is always determined by the relations of this class, as the civil and criminal law demonstrates in the clearest way possible (1964:357).

Because it is developed and promoted by the bourgeoisie, law is inevitably going to reflect the interests of that class. Instrumentalist Marxists argue that the state and its institutions—the law, the courts, and the police—are tools that help the capitalist class to maximize profits and control the working class. For example, Marxist criminologist Richard Quinney has written: "The state is organized to serve the interests of the dominant economic class, the capitalist ruling class. Criminal law is an instrument of the state and ruling class to maintain and perpetuate the existing social and economic order" (1974:16).

Since the late 1970s, **structuralism** has become the central approach within the Marxian analysis of law. The structural Marxists maintain that the development of the law's form and content is attributable to three interrelated but partially independent spheres of influence unified by the capitalist mode of production: the *political*, the *ideological*, and the *economic*. Although these three spheres work together to maintain a socioeconomic order that is generally beneficial to the bourgeoisie, they also limit the bourgeoisie's control of the state and its institutions. Consequently, the state routinely pursues such legislative policies as welfare laws, rent restriction, and antitrust laws, which are contrary to the immediate interests of the capitalist class (Beirne, 1979a:379). Structural Marxists contend that the law is *relatively autonomous* from ruling-class interests. Marx explains the interests of the ruling class through his labor theory of value.

The basis of Marx's labor theory of value is his analysis of commodities. A **commodity** is "an object outside of us, a thing that by its properties satisfies human wants of some sort or another" (Marx, 1962:35). The intrinsic utility of a commodity gives it a *use-value*, an emphasis on the unique characteristics peculiar to each commodity. Hence, each commodity is qualitatively different from every other commodity. Under capitalism, commodities are produced for sale on the open market and thus acquire exchange-value. According to Marx, **exchange-value** appears as "a quantitative relation, as the proportion in which values in use of one sort are exchanged for those of another sort" (1962:36). Restated, under capitalism commodities are exchanged, not on the basis of their inherent utility, but on the basis of their value (price). Further, commodities are generally exchanged in proportion to their value. Their value is determined by the amount of human labor power (in the form of brains, nerves, and muscles) and labor time (measured in hours, days, weeks, etc.) required to produce them. Accordingly, commodities that were qualitatively unequal are now quantitatively equal if the same amount of labor power and labor time is expended in their production. Under capitalism, money becomes the universal measure of value as well as the universal medium for exchanging or circulating commodities on the market.

relative independence from the superstructure of society

Marx depicts the simplest form of commodity circulation as C-M-C: the capitalist sells commodities (C) for money (M) and then uses that money to buy more commodities (C). Another, more interesting, form of commodity circulation that Marx illuminates is M-C-M'. In this case the capitalist uses money (M) to purchase a commodity (C) and then sells it for more money (M') to make a profit. When the capitalist uses money, in the form of wages, to purchase the commodity of labor power from the worker, the profit that the capitalist makes in this transaction is called **surplus value.**

The value of labor power (i.e., the amount of wages that the capitalist pays to the worker), is "determined, as in the case of every other commodity, by the labor-time necessary for the production" of the products that the capitalists intends to sell (Marx, 1962:170). In order to keep labor power circulating on the market, the capitalist pays the worker a minimum level of subsistence so that he or she keeps having to return to work.

The capitalist uses the worker's labor power to the point at which its use has created value equal to that paid to him or her in wages. In order to make a profit, the capitalist then extracts an excess of labor power from the worker. Exploitation occurs when the capitalist appropriates the net product the worker produces and does not pay the worker in full for the energy and time expended in producing that product. The capitalist makes the worker engage in what Marx calls "surplus labor" because he or she has worked longer than is necessary to obtain subsistence. The capitalist now owns a product whose value is greater than the amount paid to produce it. When this product is sold the capitalist then acquires surplus value in the form of money and makes a profit. Surplus value refers to that value created by the worker and appropriated by the capitalist, but for which the worker remains unpaid.

Finally, the **fetishism of commodities** occurs when people forget it is their labor that gives a product its value and existence. Instead, they begin to lose control over what they produce when they start to believe that the value of a commodity is a natural property of the thing itself. Commodity fetishism is a type of alienation because people see commodities as having an independent existence that then becomes coercive of the individual. Commodity fetishism distorts people's perception of their social world. Instead of seeing commodities as products of their own creation, they see them as natural, permanent, and unchangeable.

Furthermore, since commodities are regularly exchanged in a capitalist economy, they attain a stability in their value relative to other commodities, meaning that all commodities are equal because they have a value that can be measured, and all can be exchanged through the universal commodity of money. Money conceals the inherent differences in commodities that existed prior to their exchange. To perceive the objective world in terms of money means that the particular qualities (use-values) of things are lost. Money transforms the uniqueness of things into an abstract, universal value.

Having discussed structuralism, Marx's labor theory of value, and the idea that commodities are fetishized, we are now in a position to analyze E. B. Pashukanis's notion of law as a representation of the commodity form.

Law as a Representation of the Commodity Form '

Evgeny B. Pashukanis (1891–1937) was the preeminent Marxist legal theorist in Soviet Russia during the 1920s and early 1930s. This recognition came from his formulation of the **commodity exchange theory of law** that Pashukanis presented in his major treatise *The General Theory of Law and Marxism*, first published in Moscow in 1924.

Prior to Pashukanis, the dominant Marxist-Leninist view regarding law was informed by the instrumentalist approach whereby law is seen as the expression of the will of the bourgeoisie. It was believed that the bourgeoisie used the law to oppress the working class, but during the transition to communism the law would be used to destroy the bourgeoisie. As we shall see, Pashukanis's commodity exchange theory of law is more complex and sophisticated than this.

The commodity exchange theory of law. Pashukanis patterned his commodity exchange theory of law after Marx's analysis of value in Volume 1 of *Capital*. Simply put, Marx maintains that, in capitalist society, commodities are bought and sold on the market, not on the basis of their use-value, but on the basis of their exchange-value.

Pashukanis claims that by applying Marx's ideas about commodity exchange to jurisprudence, he, Pashukanis, can identify the historical period at which the real essence or *form* of law arose. Further, he sees as his goal "to present a sociological interpretation of the legal form and of the specific categories which express it" (1989:107).

Pashukanis begins with the premise that the most fundamental and abstract juridical concepts, such as "legal norm," "legal relation," and "legal subject," are ultimately expressions of economic social relationships: in particular, they are expressions of the commercial transactions that take place in a capitalist economy. What is more, the central categories of a market exchange economy—commodities, use-value, exchange-value—correspond closely to the juridical concepts.

Pashukanis asserts that the regulation of social relationships requires rules or norms, although not all norms are legal norms and not all social relationships are legal relationships. Under certain social conditions, however, the regulation of social relationships does assume a legal form. The task for the Marxist jurist, then, is to determine which conditions give social relationships their legal form and at what point in history those conditions emerge.

Pashukanis argues that the origins of the legal regulation of social relationships lie at the point in which the private interests of economic competitors come into conflict. "It is dispute, conflict of interest," says Pashukanis, "which creates the legal form" (1989:93). Consequently, the reciprocal interaction and exchange relationship between commodity traders—buyers and sellers of property—is reflected in the legal social relationship. That is to say, the logic of the social relationships of commodity exchange is analogous to the logic of legal concepts, and it is precisely in commercial transactions that the origin of law is to be found. Pashukanis insists that as long as the trading (buying and selling) of property persists, the law will be needed to facilitate and regulate the exchange process of private enterprise. "The ideal of law," writes American jurist Lon L. Fuller, "is realized at the same time as the ideal of the market; both present man as the trader, as an autonomous agent setting his relations with his fellows" (1949:1161). Consequently, all law is inherently bourgeois because it mirrors the form of economic exchange.

Only with the emergence of bourgeois society do relationships between people appear as relationships between *economic objects* and *legal subjects*. People are treated as economic objects when they circulate themselves on the market. This phenomenon is most apparent when the workers sell their labor power, as a commodity, to the capitalists. Moreover, a market economy regards people as commodity owners who possess the legal right to buy and sell their private property. They are seen as legal subjects because operating in the process of commodity exchange are the abstract rights and duties of the commodity traders. Accordingly, it is under capitalism that the treatment of people as economic objects and legal subjects realizes its purest form.

Legal equality obscures social inequality. Pashukanis maintains that there exists a parallel between the logic of the commodity form and the logic of the legal form. Both forms, he says, are universal equivalents that attempt to equalize entities—commodities and people—that are inherently unequal. Qualitatively distinct commodities appear as equal in the commercial transactions of competitive market capitalism because it is here that they are all given a value and can be exchanged through the mediation of another commodity, money. Commodities thus become fetishized and are treated as though they have living human powers, taking on an existence of their own. Additionally, in the relationship of commodity exchange real concrete people are transformed into abstract political citizens—legal subjects—when they become the bearers of the right to buy and sell as they choose.

As such, people with qualitatively distinct needs and interests are treated as equal before the law. Thus, it is said that they *all* have the right to engage in the free (i.e., uncoerced) and equal (i.e., fair) circulation of commodities. This notion, however, disguises the social inequality (class differences) inherent in the power relationship between capitalists and workers. In the contract of employment, for example, the legal rights and duties given the workers means only that they are free to be exploited equally by the capitalists. In other words, the capitalist class oppresses the proletariat by promoting the illusion that the worker *freely and willingly* enters into a contract with the employer. The fact of the matter is that too often the worker, out of a desperate need for survival, is forced to sell his or her labor power in exchange for whatever wages the employer, with an eye toward extracting surplus value, is willing to pay. Hence, the employment contract is not so freely and willingly entered into, nor is it a relationship in which each party recognizes the other as equal vis-à-vis the transaction. Nevertheless, if not in substance, at least in the abstract, all traders must *appear* to possess contractual freedom and equality of legal rights, for these are the conditions needed by the money economy to ensure the smooth and constant circulation of commodities.

In the United States, legal equality is provided for in the "equal protection" clause of the Fourteenth Amendment of the Federal Constitution. The clause guarantees all citizens **due process of law**—fair and equal treatment and representation before the law—irrespective of their race, gender, ideological conviction, or social class.

On the other hand, under feudalism (with its admixture of private/public property and limited economic trade), the specific rights and duties that persons held had their basis, not in a general legal concept, but on their specific social positions. Precisely because medieval society was a hierarchical one of fixed roles—lords, serfs, and so forth—rights were thought of as naturally and inherently unequal (Simmonds, 1985:142). According to Pashukanis, feudalism "completely lacked any notion of a formal legal status common to all citizens" (1989:119). The customary privileges and special immunities peculiar to the various social ranks prevented the emergence of the "average" legal person, possessor of universal rights. Max Weber tells us that during feudalism the legal order was "a mere bundle of assorted privileges" (1978:843). The law was not applied uniformly and equally to all, and justice was based on a person's status.

With the onset of capitalism—the most developed historical type of commodity-producing society—rights could no longer be identified with the persons occupying unequal statuses. After all, in a market-exchange economy characterized by fierce competition, equivalence and contractual freedom are necessary elements for organizing and facilitating the circulation of commodities; that is, for encouraging autonomous individuals to engage in negotiating, bargaining, and contracting. Therefore, any inequality of rights must be seen as the result of market transactions. Prior to entering any such transactions, all property owners need to possess formal equal rights in regard to buying and selling. Thus, "only when bourgeois relations are fully developed does law become abstract in character" (Pashukanis, 1989:120).

Owing to the fact that under competitive capitalism the actual inequality of concrete rights must be explained by reference to transactions freely entered into by the legal subject, contract is the central concept in the process of commodity exchange. It is also the central legal premise on which all aspects of law are based. Accordingly, conflicts of interest—that is, disputes between contracting parties—are the essential preconditions for the emergence of the legal form.

Where no contractual disputes exist, technical norms may be employed out of expediency but such norms will not take a legal form. In other words, technical norms do not regulate private transactions involving reciprocal rights and duties. Pashukanis provides an apt example for distinguishing between legal and technical norms: "the legal norms governing the railways' liability are predicated on private claims, private, differentiated interests, while the technical norms of rail traffic presuppose the common aim of, say, maximum efficiency of the enterprise" (1989:81).

The state. For Pashukanis, even the state, which he characterizes as a "political" and "legal" phenomenon, is also sometimes only an expression of the commercial transactions of the market. The *political state* employs the technical norms of administration based on the principle of expediency. The *legal state*, by contrast, acts as an impartial third party, arbitrating contractual disputes between contending traders and enforcing legal norms that give clarity and stability to the commodity exchange relations.

In Marx's base-superstructure metaphor, commodity exchange relations have a very close affinity to the economic base. As Pashukanis has indicated, commodity exchange relations are also contractual (private) relations. Further, private relations are simply the legal expression of exchange relations. It follows, then, that the superstructural state is an epiphenomenon that is derived from commodity exchange—that is, private law—relations.

Based on the preceding argument, Pashukanis arrives at two major conclusions. The first is that all law is necessarily private law because it emanates from commodity exchange. Indeed, Pashukanis claims that public law "is only able to exist as a reflection of the private-law form in the sphere of [the state], otherwise it ceases to be law entirely" (1989:103–104). The other conclusion is that the state and public law are secondary elements while commodity exchange relations, including their legal form (private law), are primary. For Pashukanis, then, the superstructural legal state would become irrelevant with the total demise of the capitalist economic base.

Criminal law. Pashukanis also applies his commodity exchange theory of law to the areas of crime and punishment. For him, the notion of retribution in criminal law directly mirrors the processes involved in economic exchange where the two "contracting" parties are the offender and the state. The state metes out proportional punishment (the principle of equivalency) to the offender in retaliation for the harm done to the victim. Punishment is therefore calculated: the severity of punishment must equal the severity of the crime. Pashukanis regarded the criminal code as a kind of price list that set the price (in terms of punishment) appropriate for each criminal offense.

Pashukanis is perhaps most convincing when comparing the procedures of the market-exchange economy with the procedures involved in the administration of criminal justice:

> Bourgeois administration of the law sees to it that the transaction with the offender should be concluded according to all the rules of the game; in other words, anyone can check and satisfy themselves that the payment was equitably determined (public nature of court proceedings), the offender can bargain for his liberty without hindrance (adversary form of the trial) and can avail himself of the services of an experienced court broker to this end (admission of counsel for the defense), and so on. In a word, the state's relations with the offender remain throughout well within the framework of fair trading (1989:183).

The withering away of law. Pashukanis confidently predicted that law (that is, legal norms and the legal state) would die out or "wither away" with the complete elimination of bourgeois commodity exchange. He believed that the legal superstructure would become superfluous and disappear with the advent of communism and upon the abolition of private property relations. Under communism, the relations of production and exchange and all other social relations would be governed, not by legal norms, but by the technical (administrative) norms employed by the political state. Consequently, policy, economic planning, and administration would replace law, and the future communist society would be free of legal coercion. Put another way, the transition from capitalism to communism was to be a transition from social relations regulated in accordance with the principle of equivalency to social relations regulated in accordance with the principle of expediency. → *easy*

To be sure, Pashukanis's commodity exchange theory of law has had no shortage of critics (see Kelsen, 1955; Sumner, 1979, 1981; Hirst, 1979, 1980; Mullin, 1980; Binns, 1980; Warrington, 1981; Milovanovic, 1981; Simmonds, 1985). Still, others (Kinsey, 1978; Edleman, 1979; Picciotto, 1979; Beirne and Sharlet, 1980; Redhead, 1982; Arthur, 1989; Hunt, 1991) have favorably acknowledged his efforts at pioneering a Marxian theory of law. It is the political scientist Isaac Balbus, however, who has rendered the most sympathetic development of Pashukanis's theory. Thus, it is to Balbus's work that we now turn.

The relative autonomy of law. Like Pashukanis, Balbus also rejects the simplistic instumentalist approach to law. For Balbus, law is not merely an instrument, a tool, directly under the control of the bourgeoisie. Nor does he accept the *formalist* argument that the legal order is self-sufficient and thus immune to extralegal influences, including those of the capitalist system. Instead, as a structural Marxist, Balbus' position toward the law is one of "relative autonomy." → *relative independence*

Two distinct but related theoretical currents flow concomitantly from Balbus's position. The first is that, in democratic societies like the United States, the ruling class may not directly manipulate the law for the purpose of protecting its interests. In this sense, we may say that the law *is* autonomous from the wishes of the ruling class. The second theoretical current is that the commodity form of capitalist society, as Pashukanis has already shown, is reflected in the legal form. Thus, we may say that the legal system *is not* autonomous from the capitalist system. Let us see how Balbus explains these two theoretical currents.

The idea that in the U.S. the ruling class may not flagrantly violate legal procedure in order to protect its economic and political interests is illustrated by Balbus in his *The Dialectics of Legal Repression* (1973). Balbus looks at the ghetto revolts of the mid-1960s and how the criminal courts successfully punished—that is, legally repressed—the participants in these revolts. He identifies as the "dialectics of legal repression" the conflict resulting from the two competing interests that the courts had to consider in responding to the dissident rebels who sought to change the existing economic and political order. On the one hand, the courts had to quickly put an end to the collective violence and deflect revolutionary potential in the interest of restoring public *order*. On the other hand, the courts had to provide due process of law (legal equality) to all citizens regardless of their ideological convictions, maintaining their *legitimacy* by ensuring that the rebels did not receive unfair and unequal treatment under the law. The courts' balancing of order and legitimacy led to "repression by formal rationality" (Balbus, 1973:11). (For an in-depth analysis of the concepts of legitimacy and formal rationality, see Chapter 5).

Repression by formal rationality means that the courts employ due process of law for the purpose of quelling the uprisings so that they can simultaneously restore order and maintain legitimacy. By employing due process of law, the courts criminalize the rebels' behavior and thus depoliticize the uprisings and defuse revolutionary potential:

> The "criminalization" process entailed in repression by formal rationality also serves to delegitimate whatever demands emerge from the collective violence. Demands which arise from "criminals" are unlikely to receive a hearing and thus less likely to be voiced in the first place. Once the process of criminalization is under way, public debate is not likely to center over the substantive grievances of the participants but rather over the severity of punishment which they merit: criminals do not have just grievances; criminals deserve to be punished. Repression by formal rationality thus makes it unlikely that the claims and grievances of the participants in collective violence will be addressed to, or accepted by, significantly large numbers of people (Balbus, 1973:12).

Repression by formal rationality is one way in which the state maintains the economic and political status quo favoring the ruling class. However, the ruling class itself does not have a direct hand in manipulating the law for its own ends. Thus, the law is autonomous from the influences of the ruling class. We now look at how the law is inextricably connected to the capitalist system.

Balbus agrees with Pashukanis that there does indeed exist a parallel or "homology" between the legal form and the commodity form. Just as Marx had shown that commodities are fetishized, so also does Balbus contend that persons with different needs and interests are fetishized when they are transformed into legal subjects who possess formal rights and duties. Because of the law, then, people take on the abstracted form of individual *citizens*—objects of exchange—"who exist in order to represent, and be represented by, other individual citizens" (Balbus, 1977:575). Accordingly, the legal form defines distinctions of need and interest out of political existence and "replaces" them with the abstraction of equal rights, and the flesh-and-blood individual with the abstraction of the legal person. Although they are not politically recognized, the socioeconomic inequalities of capitalist society nevertheless continue to exist.

Balbus maintains that the law produces and reinforces illusory forms of equality. As such, it simultaneously prevents "the formation of the class consciousness necessary to the creation of a substantively more equal society" and contributes "significantly to the persistence of a capitalist system" (1977:577,580). Ironically, the legal order retains its legitimacy even as it perpetuates these illusions. To be sure, the legal order is not usually called into question. The reason for this, explains Balbus, is that the legal order is fetishized and hence does not ordinarily allow individuals to even *think* about challenging it. Legal fetishism occurs when people see the law as having a life of its own and then attribute society's existence to the law. They do not know or have forgotten that the law has its origins in society, rather than the other way around. "When Society is held to be a result of the Law, rather than the Law to be a result of one particular kind of society, then the Law by definition is unproblematical" (Balbus, 1977:583).

In sum, Balbus supports his notion of the law's relative autonomy by showing that the law is autonomous from the will of the capitalist class, but that it is not autonomous from the capitalist system: the legal form is fetishized in the same way as the commodity form. In the next section we examine the work of another neo-Marxist, Karl Renner, and his efforts to construct a theory of law suitable for both capitalist and socialist societies.

Private Law Institutions

Like Pashukanis, the Austrian jurist Karl Renner (1870–1950) used Marx's remarks in *Capital* as a "springboard for his own efforts to document the relations of law and economics" (Grace and Wilkinson, 1978:94). Unlike Pashukanis, how-ever, "Renner took seriously the problems of socialist legality and the role and function of law in the transition to socialism" (Kinsey, 1983:11). Renner was a member of a group of socialist thinkers meeting in Vienna, the Austro-Marxists, who "were mainly interested in the development of Marxism as sociology" (Bot-tomore, 1978:3). In his book *The Institutions of Private Law and their Social Functions*, first published in 1904, Renner relies on the Marxian perspective for constructing a sociological theory of law.

Form and function. Renner's sociological theory of law analytically separates the form of legal institutions from their *social functions*—"the factual results of their application" (Kahn-Freund, 1949:3). (For a fuller account of the social functions of law, see Chapter 7). Renner's main focus is on the impact that economic forces and patterns of social change have on the functioning of those legal institutions—namely, property and contract—that belong to the sphere of private law. More narrowly, these institutions, whose forms Renner considers to be stable and rela-tively immutable, include *ownership*, the *contract of employment*, and the legal asso-ciation in the form of the *joint-stock association*.

Renner belongs to the formalist school of jurisprudence (see Chapter 3) that views the law as a logically consistent and self-sufficient system of *norms*, that is, laws defining "certain repeated patterns of social interaction" (Blum, 1985:66). Legal norms and institutions are seen as being abstract and quite indifferent toward their social functions. We may say, then, that Renner fetishizes the law. Moreover, it follows from his formalist position that all private legal institutions are "neutral" in that they are neither feudal, capitalist, nor socialist.

Renner's particular orientation toward the law yields two unique conceptual-izations. First, because he adopts the Austro-Marxist notion of society as an asso-ciation of individuals (Hirst, 1979:123), the law is ultimately nothing more than a series of commands addressed by one individual to another. Despite this individu-alism, Renner conceives of society as a supra-individual entity that may at times be "conscious" of its social existence and economic needs. Second, contrary to the crude economic determinism dominant at the time, Renner sees the legal super-structure and the economic base as being involved in a dialectical interaction in which they are mutually conditioning and subservient to each other: "the law is as much bound up with economics as economics is bound up with the law" (Renner, 1949:251). To be sure, the law and the economy as autonomous systems do in-fluence one another, but only in a limited way. Renner makes it clear that, in general, "economic change does not immediately and automatically bring about changes in the law" (1949:252). Nevertheless, to the extent that alterations in the economic base do produce changes in the legal institutions (their norms and their functions), the changes usually occur only after a considerable time lag. During this time lag the legal norms may not accurately reflect the actual conditions of society. Renner assures us, however, that there are periods when the legal and economic systems are not contradictory but instead complement each other: "There is always a moment in the history of human institutions when the legal system is the adequate expression of economic relations, when superstructure and [base] are in conformity" (1949:83).

Renner contends that legal institutions perform social and economic functions. In order to achieve the ultimate end of every society—the preservation of the species—all economic systems must engage in the production of the means of existence. Legal institutions perform their social function when they are used to expedite the production and distribution of goods necessary for survival. When several legal institutions operate concomitantly to help a particular economic system achieve its goals of production, distribution, and consumption, they are fulfilling their *economic function*. Moreover, as socioeconomic conditions change, the legal institution's functions may undergo a process of dynamic transformation, but its specific legal norms usually remain stable. "Fundamentally," says Renner, "the norms which make up the law have remained absolutely constant, and yet an enormous revolution has occurred without any changes of norms" (1949:88–89).

In most cases, the transformation of the social functions is scarcely noticed and not really understood because society is not yet fully conscious of its own existence. Socialism, however, is a society that is "conscious of itself" and therefore subjectively aware of the legal norms that it needs. In Renner's view it is not necessary to abolish property and contract; the "elasticity" of these legal institutions allows them to adapt to the changed socioeconomic conditions as their legal norms are replaced with new ones (For an illustration of how this happens empirically, see McManus, 1978). Engels, for example, recognized that during the transition from feudalism to capitalism the legal *form* is preserved while the legal *content* is considerably modified: "It is possible, as happened in England, in harmony with the whole national development, to retain in the main the forms of the old feudal laws while giving them a bourgeois content; in fact, directly reading a bourgeois meaning into the feudal name" (1959:235). Similarly, property and contract would remain primary legal institutions in capitalism as well as in socialism, though with different economic functions. As we will see, property and contract eventually acquire a socializing function.

At this juncture, it is significant to point out that Renner did not see the transition to socialism as taking the form of class struggle and the proletarian revolution. In his mind, economic "development by leaps and bounds is unknown" and the economic base "knows evolution only, not revolution" (1949:253). Renner thus made himself a revolutionary only in regard to the legal norms that shape the state and the relations of its citizens (Blum, 1985:64). Or, as Marxist legal scholar Richard Kinsey has tersely put it, Renner's revolution "is a revolution of re-form" (1983:21).

The orders of labor, power, and goods. The effort to keep production, distribution, and consumption going requires that every economic system—whether feudal, capitalist, or socialist—use its legal institutions to regulate or "order" itself in three different ways. First, it must impose on its members the compulsion to labor. Second, it must have the power to command so that it retains its ability to coordinate and organize. And finally, it must determine the manner in which goods are possessed. Thus, every society must have an "order of labor," an "order of power," and an "order of goods."

Socialism, according to Renner, is a conscious and therefore rational effort at regulating labor, power, and goods in the interest of all. Capitalism, by contrast, "denies its own consciousness." Under this system, where free labor and a free market are paramount, it is denied that people are forced to work or that goods are allocated in a manner planned and organized by the state. Because of its fetishized legal concepts of "free employment" (all people are free to work how and for whom they wish) and "private property" (all people have the equal capacity to own property as well as the right of **disposal**—to do what they please with their property), capitalism creates the illusion that it can operate without the legal regulation of labor and goods. (Moreover, with its concept of "legal person," i.e., the citizen as possessor of universal rights, capitalism only minimally admits to an order of power).

De facto bourgeois society, however, does indeed have orders of labor and goods, but they are not made explicit in the legal institutions. Instead, capitalism claims that it is not society (i.e., the state), but rather the natural forces of the laissez-faire marketplace (Adam Smith's "invisible hand") that govern production, distribution, and consumption. The fact of the matter is that the legal institutions of capitalism half-consciously *organize* (though they do not consciously *regulate*) the forces of production. For example, the institution of private property orders goods by giving **possession**—control—of a business only to the owner of that business; it orders labor when it allows the business owner to give commands to his workers; and it orders power when, through the law of succession to property, it governs the replacement and appointment of managerial positions. Thus, by changing its function, but without necessarily changing its form, the institution of property shows that it can adapt to a great many social circumstances. Contract also "remains one and the same legal institution, though it may serve an infinite variety of purposes . . . marriage as well as prostitution" (Renner, 1949:51).

Before we examine the legal institution of contract, and in particular the contract of employment in industrial capitalism, we must first briefly look at how the concept of ownership operated during the age of simple commodity production.

During the age of simple commodity production, the comprehensive legal institution of property was principally concerned with ownership and the order of goods. At this time the law of property was all that was needed for coordinating production, distribution, and consumption in the self-sufficient "house" (household/ workshop/cultivated land). Here, all the means of existence and "nearly all of their material components are physically combined into a universal, self-contained and organic world of objects that derives its individuality from the person of the owner" (Renner, 1949:84). As an independent small producer, the owner-worker of the house was given absolute dominion over his or her household and had complete control over a variety of tangible goods (tools, furniture, and other "things") necessary for the family's livelihood. Thus, at this point in time the superstructural institution of property law corresponded well with the economic conditions of simple commodity production. In other words, the right of ownership served all the economic functions of production.

The contract of employment. With the evolutionary development of industrial capitalism and large-scale production, the law of property shifted its concern to capital and the orders of labor and power. Since, on its own, the law of property could not endow goods with surplus value, it relied on a complementary institution for assistance: the contract of employment. Supplemented by the employment contract, the law of property was now able to give the capitalist ownership of an intangible commodity—the labor power of the worker. Thus began the transformation of simple commodity to industrial capitalism.

The institution of property took on a new application. It became part of the order of labor. However, it also became part of the order of power because the capitalist, through the employment contract, exercised domination over the subordinate workers; a phenomenon that Renner describes as "the draconian control of alien labor-power" (1949:292). The bourgeois capitalist has the right to dictate the terms and conditions under which the workers are to labor. Furthermore, the concept of the legal person no longer performed its social function in regard to the workers. Because the capitalist employer owned the workers' labor power, the workers' universal rights were no longer relevant (at least not during their time on the job). And, as we have already seen, the employment contract was never an equal transaction to begin with. Renner does note, though, that in the half century following the death of Karl Marx the contract of employment had become increasingly "socialized," thus giving equality of bargaining to the employer-employee relationship. By this he means that in holding a status or "position" (i.e., membership) in a labor union or in a comparable trade association, the workers had gained many legal rights and protections that were previously unknown.

As we saw in Chapter 2, according to Henry Maine progressive societies have developed from status to contract. Renner, on the other hand, posits that individuals acquire more rights and protections as they go from status in feudalism, to contract under capitalism, and back to status or "position" in a public institution or legal association. Renner also seems to imply that state regulatory agencies, such as today's National Labor Relations Board (NLRB) and the Occupational Safety and Health Administration (OSHA), and public law, like the Federal Insurance Contributions Act (social security) and the Federal Labor Standards Act (minimum wage), will pave the way for the development of a rationally ordered or regulated society, that is, socialism. Regulatory agencies, public law, and legal associations will, therefore, displace the institutions of private law, including contract. We now turn our attention to one specific form of legal association that Renner regarded as a major vehicle in the transformation to socialism, the joint-stock association.

The joint-stock association. Up to this point most of our discussions have centered around that specific type of capitalism that most occupied Marx's attention, industrial capitalism. However, between 1883, when Marx died, and 1904, when Renner published his sociological theory of law, a new, distinct phase of capitalism had begun to emerge: finance capitalism.

In his highly influential book *Finance Capital* (1910), Rudolf Hilferding (also a member of the Austro-Marxist school) proposes that **finance capitalism**—the highest stage of capitalist development up to that time—arose from the intimate relationship between industrial capital, whose profits are obtained through the appropriation of surplus-value, and financial capital, whose profits are obtained on the basis of interest. In the former case, the bourgeois capitalist realizes the bulk of his or her revenue through the exploitation of the workers' labor power. In the latter case, the finance capitalist makes his or her revenue from speculative investments.

Renner analyzes the centralization and concentration of finance capital in the **joint-stock association,** a business enterprise where the finance capitalist owns *shares* (portions) of *stock* (goods sold for profit). This means that the shareholder is only passively involved in the enterprise and "ownership becomes a mere title to a portion of the surplus value" (Hirst, 1979:125). It also means, as Marx, Hilferding, and Renner point out, that the joint-stock association separates the shareholder from the actual control of the means of production. In other words, because formal ownership and real control have now been divorced, the capitalist no longer has possession of the productive forces. Managers, directors, and other personnel in salaried positions are the ones who actually direct the company's day-to-day operations. Thus, while industrial capitalism was previously run by the owners, finance capitalism is now run by managers. Moreover, in contrast to the bourgeois capitalist of industrial capitalism, the shareholder of finance capitalism is relatively powerless because he or she has handed over his or her "social power of command" to the salaried employees. And, since Renner sees law as a series of commands addressed by one individual to another, the influence of private law (contract) in the owner-employee relationship is no longer present. Marx refers to this entire process as "private production without the control of private property" (1962, Vol. 3:429). He sees an inherent contradiction at work here, a contradiction that he claims will lead to the "abolition of the capitalist mode of production within the capitalist mode of production itself" (1962, Vol. 3:429). In Marx's view, this dialectic acts as a driving force in the transition to socialism.

According to Marx, in the joint-stock association, private capital (the personal wealth of individual capitalists) is superseded by social capital (the combined shares of associated investors). Capital is said to have acquired a social character because the shareholder is only one of many who own a small percentage of a large number of corporations. They are therefore not engaged in a private entrepreneurial undertaking but in a cooperative venture. The concentration of social capital in the form of joint stock in turn converts private property into social property (the property of associated investors). Renner, and Marx before him, referred to this phenomenon as the *socialization of the forces of production.* Indeed, Renner saw this process as the transfer of industrial property from private to public ownership.

Under finance capitalism, the shareholder's legal ownership of private property (the business enterprise) no longer fulfills the economic function of production and traditional private property becomes superfluous as a way of organizing the "socialized" production forces. Within the province of the joint-stock association, the legal institution of private property not only becomes irrelevant, it also becomes an impediment to evolutionary progression. The joint-stock association, says Renner, "has thus deprived [private] property of all functions connected with social production and reproduction, making [private] property itself an inoperative and antisocial institution, to which only one function is left, that of obstructing the future development of society" (1949:220).

To be sure, the joint-stock association anticipates socialism because it represents the implementation of a progressively more rational system of regulated production (Kinsey, 1983:27). Socialism, as a society conscious of its economic needs, can, through legislation, change the form of the institution of private property so that it corresponds with the socialized conditions of production as manifested in joint stock. Therefore, contrary to Pashukanis, the law will not simply wither away with the abolition of private property. Instead, the socialist state will very much rely on the functional efficiency of the institutions of public law to rationally regulate social property in the interest of all. For Renner, a socialist legality is not only possible it is indispensable.

By generally combining and extending the ideas of Renner, Pashukanis, and Balbus, another neo-Marxist scholar, Alan Stone, has developed a theory explaining the connection between law and economy: the theory of essential legal relations. We conclude this chapter with a discussion of that theory.

The theory of essential legal relations. Alan Stone (1985) came across the concept of essential legal relations while carefully examining the works by Marx and Engels. In a capitalist society, the **essential legal relations,** that is, "the legal expressions or images of the central components of the capitalist economic [base]" (Stone, 1985:54), consist of property, contract, credit, and combination (as exemplified by the joint-stock association). Stone considers these legal expressions as being absolutely fundamental to capitalism since without them capitalism would not be able to operate or maintain itself. Consequently, because of their key position in the economic system, the degree to which the essential legal relations may vary in form is strictly limited.

Stone maintains that the essential legal relations are in one sense superstructure (and thus linked to legal doctrine and particular court decisions), and in another sense a reflection of the economic base. Between the base and the superstructure there is a hierarchical series of intermediate links. These descending links, which are structured in order of importance, are as follows.

First are the *essential legal relations* that are integrally connected with the economic base. Second, derived from the essential legal relations, are their subsidiary or lower order legal concepts, which Stone calls *derivative subrelations.* (The derivative subrelations of property include lease, easement, sale, and mortgage. Those of credit consist of security, bankruptcy, lien, etc.). Finally, premised upon the derivative subrelations and residing at the level of superstructure are the *specific legal rules.* So important is this hierarchy of linkages that Stone calls it "the glue that holds a capitalist society together" (1985:64).

By way of illustrating the hierarchy, let us take as an example the essential legal relation of **contract for sale of goods**—an agreement made between a seller and a buyer involving the transfer of goods for a price. Suppose Smith contracts to sell his car to Jones for $2,000, delivery to be in two days. Stemming from contract is the derivative subrelation of **assignment of rights,** the transfer of rights by one party to another party. Now suppose Smith assigns his right to the $2,000 to Brown. A derivative subrelation under assignment is **delegation of performance,** or entrusting another party with the duty to transfer the goods. Smith then delegates to Brown the duty to deliver the car to Jones. Two legal rules that, in turn, arise from these derivative subrelations are found in the *Uniform Commercial Code:* "[1] A party may perform his duty through a delegate unless otherwise agreed or unless the other party has a substantial interest in having his original promisor perform or control the acts required by the contract . . . [2] Unless otherwise agreed all rights of either seller or buyer can be assigned" (UCC 2–210 (1),(2)).

Stone explains how the superstructural judicial system operates within the framework of these hierarchical linkages: "Courts, confronted with particular matters, accept the essential legal relation, consider the functions and purposes of the derivative subrelation, and then seek to render a best decision consistent with the derivative subrelation's principle function" (1985:58). To be sure, different courts often render diverse, and at times conflicting, judicial opinions. Nevertheless, the legal system will generally tolerate these contradictory decisions provided that they do not seriously challenge the essential legal relations. In truth, they are almost never questioned. Judges, lawyers, and legislators generally accept "the underlying notions contained within essential legal relations in much the same way that table manners are accepted and employed, without rationally considering them or demanding moral justifications" (Stone, 1985:60). As long as the notions of private property, contract, credit, and combination—which express core economic relations—are not questioned, they serve to maintain and perpetuate the capitalist economic mode of production. Put another way, they serve to "protect and further an unequal allocation of resources in society" (Stone, 1985:65). Thus, it follows that the legal system is a system of the capitalist class. And, much like Renner's legal institutions, Stone's essential legal relations persist over a period of time.

SUMMARY

In this chapter we considered some of the concepts crucial to understanding the Marxian perspective. Among these concepts are three that are central: historical materialism, base and superstructure, and the dialectical form of argumentation.

First, Marx's theory of historical materialism gives us a dialectical view of the progression of society through six successive socioeconomic stages: primitive communism, slave economy, feudalism, capitalism, socialism, and communism. Marx directed his major criticisms at capitalism and the manner in which the proletariat is exploited under this economic system.

Second, in Marx's view, capitalism's economic base has a determining influence on the form and content of the legal superstructure. The law therefore protects the basic tenets of the capitalist mode of production (e.g., private property, exchange of commodities) and also advances the political and economic interests of the bourgeoisie.

Third, we saw how the dialectical form of argumentation, or that manner of reasoning that reveals the internal contradictions of an idea, was employed by Marx and Engels to inveigh against legislation believed to be exploitative of the proletariat. Such legislation included the law on thefts of wood and the censorship laws.

The law on thefts of wood prohibited the Rhenish peasants from gathering wood in the forests. As such, the law undermined the customary use-rights that had traditionally allowed the peasants to cart away dead timber for their very survival. As industrialized capitalism increased its reliance on forest products, the law on thefts of wood made it a crime for the peasants to appropriate these products.

The censorship laws imposed excessive regulations on the Prussian press, and Marx pointed out the internal contradictions of these laws. One of the main contradictions that Marx reveals through his dialectical form of argumentation is that because the essence of the law is freedom, a censorship law is not a real law. Rather, it is a repressive police measure that punishes not offenses but opinions.

Marx and Engels' critical analyses of the law on thefts of wood and the censorship laws underscore the notion residing at the heart of the Marxian perspective on the sociology of law: that *the law is used by the ruling classes to their advantage.*

We then turned our attention to the writings of neo-Marxists E. B. Pashukanis, Isaac Balbus, Karl Renner, and Alan Stone, and their attempts to formulate their legal theories within the Marxian perspective.

In his commodity exchange theory of law, E. B. Pashukanis argued that there exists a parallel between the logic of the commodity form and the logic of the legal form. That is to say that juridical concepts such as "legal norm," "legal relation," and "legal subject," are ultimately expressions of the commercial transactions taking place in a capitalist society. Thus, Pashukanis predicted that law would wither away with the complete elimination of bourgeoisie commodity exchange.

We then saw how Isaac Balbus developed further Pashukanis's thesis that the legal and commodity forms are homologous. Balbus maintained that just as the commodity form is fetishized, so too is the legal form fetishized. Legal fetishism occurs when people attribute society's existence to the law. As such, the legal system is accepted as part of the natural order of things and seldom, if ever, criticized. Balbus's keynote is that the law may be described as having *relative autonomy.* That is to say that while the law is not directly manipulated by the bourgeoisie, the law does, to be sure, mirror the basic tenets of the market economy.

Next, we turned our attention to the theoretical ideas of neo-Marxist Karl Renner. Renner's interest was on the influence that socioeconomic changes have on the form and function of the private law institutions of property ownership and the employment contract. Renner postulated that while the practical application of these institutions' legal norms would change as society evolved from feudalism to capitalism, their structures, or repeated patterns of social interaction, would nevertheless remain the same. Thus, in Renner's view, property and contract would be similar legal institutions under both feudalism and capitalism. The case of socialism, however, is somewhat different.

Unlike capitalism, Renner saw socialism as an economic system that is "conscious" of itself. That is to say that socialism has an awareness of the legal norms it needs to rationally regulate labor, power, and goods, so that it can properly coordinate production, distribution, and consumption. Accordingly, socialism, in order to realize itself, requires the socializing function of legal institutions such as labor unions and legal associations such as the joint-stock association. The labor union socializes, or gives a social character to the employment contract, as it provides the workers with certain legal rights and protections. Similarly, the joint-stock association socializes property by legally combining the shares of associated investors. As such, both the labor union and the joint-stock association help to pave the way for the development of socialism.

We concluded this chapter with a discussion of Alan Stone's theory of essential legal relations. Essential legal relations, as expressions of the core economic relations of capitalism, are part base and part superstructure and consist of contract, credit, combination, and property. Derived from the essential legal relations are the derivative subrelations, which in the case of property consist of lease, easement, sale, and mortgage. Specific legal rules are enacted from the derivative subrelations. Stone's point is that while the legitimacy of specific legal rules may be questioned from time to time, the legitimacy of the essential legal relations—contract, credit, combination, and property—are almost never questioned.

In sum, this chapter gave us a comprehensive overview of law from one of the most important theoretical orientations in sociology, the Marxian perspective. In the next chapter we discuss law from the Weberian perspective.

Debates on the Law on Thefts of Wood[1]

Karl Marx

. . . In our account of the Assembly debates on the law on thefts we are directly describing the *Assembly's debates on its legislative function*.

At the very beginning of the debate, one of the urban deputies objected to the *title* of the law, which extends the category of *"theft"* to include simple offenses against forest regulations.

A deputy of the knightly estate replied: "It is precisely because the pilfering of wood is not regarded as theft that it occurs so often."

By analogy with this, the legislator would have to draw the conclusion: It is because a box on the ear is not regarded as murder that it has become so frequent. It should be decreed therefore that a box on the ear is murder.

Another deputy of the knightly estate finds it "still more risky not to pronounce the word 'theft', because people who become acquainted with the discussion over this word could easily be led to believe that the Assembly does not regard the pilfering of wood also as theft."

The Assembly has to decide whether it considers pilfering of wood as theft; but if the Assembly does not declare it to be theft, people could believe that the Assembly really does not regard the pilfering of wood as theft. Hence it is best to leave this ticklish controversial question alone. It is a matter of a euphemism and euphemisms should be avoided. The forest owner prevents the legislator from speaking, for walls have ears.

The same deputy goes even further. He regards this whole examination of the expression "theft" as "a dangerous preoccupation with *correcting formulations* on the part of the plenary assembly."

After these illuminating demonstrations, the Assembly voted the title of the law.

From the point of view recommended above, which mistakes the conversion of a citizen into a thief for a mere negligence in formulation and rejects all opposition to it as grammatical purism, it is obvious that even the *pilfering of fallen wood* or the gathering of dry wood is included under the heading of theft and punished as severely as the stealing of live growing timber.

It is true that the above-mentioned urban deputy remarks:

> Since the punishment could run to a long term of imprisonment, such severity would lead people who otherwise followed an honest path on to the path of crime. That would happen also because in prison they would be in the company of inveterate thieves; therefore he considered that the gathering or pilfering of dry fallen wood should be punished by a simple police penalty.

Another urban deputy, however, refuted him with the profound argument "that in the forest areas of his region, at first only gashes were made in young trees, and later, when they were dead, they were treated as fallen wood."

It would be impossible to find a more elegant and at the same time more simple method of making the right of human beings give way to that of young trees. On the one hand, after the adoption

128

of the paragraph, it is inevitable that many people not of a criminal disposition are cut off from the green tree of morality and cast like fallen wood into the hell of crime, infamy and misery. On the other hand, after rejection of the paragraph, there is the possibility that some young trees may be damaged, and it needs hardly be said that the wooden idols triumph and human beings are sacrificed!

The supreme penal code[2] includes under theft of wood only the pilfering of hewn wood and the cutting of wood for the purpose of theft. Indeed—our Provincial Assembly will not believe it—it states:

> If, however, in daytime someone takes fruit for eating and by its removal does no great damage, then, taking into account his personal position and the circumstances, he is to be punished by civil (therefore, not criminal!) "proceedings."

The supreme penal code of the sixteenth century requests us to defend it against the charge of excessive humanity made by a Rhine Province Assembly of the nineteenth century, and we comply with this request.

The gathering of fallen wood and the most composite wood theft! They both have a common definition. The appropriation of wood from someone else. Therefore both are theft. That is the sum and substance of the far-sighted logic which has just issued laws.

First of all, therefore, we call attention to the *difference* between them, and if it must be admitted that the two actions are essentially different, it can hardly be maintained that they are identical from the legal standpoint.

In order to appropriate growing timber, it has to be forcibly separated from its organic association. Since this is an obvious outrage against the tree, it is therefore an obvious outrage against the owner of the tree.

Further, if felled wood is stolen from a third person, this felled wood is material that has been produced by the owner. Felled wood is wood that has been worked on. The natural connection with

property has been replaced by an artificial one. Therefore, anyone who takes away felled wood takes away property.

In the case of fallen wood, on the contrary, nothing has been separated from property. It is only what has already been separated from property that is being separated from it. The wood thief pronounces on his own authority a sentence on property. The gatherer of fallen wood only carries out a sentence already pronounced by the very nature of the property, for the owner possesses only the tree, but the tree no longer possesses the branches that have fallen from it.

The gathering of fallen wood and the theft of wood are therefore essentially different things. The objects concerned are different, the actions in regard to them are no less different; hence the frame of mind must also be different, for what objective standard can be applied to the frame of mind other than the content of the action and its form? But, in spite of this essential difference, you call both of them theft and punish both of them as theft. Indeed, you punish the gathering of fallen wood more severely than the theft of wood, for you punish it already by declaring it to be theft, a punishment which you obviously do not pronounce on the actual theft of wood. You should have called it murder of wood and punished it as murder. The law is not exempt from the general obligation to tell the truth. It is doubly obliged to do so, for it is the universal and authentic exponent of the legal nature of things. Hence the legal nature of things cannot be regulated according to the law; on the contrary, the law must be regulated according to the legal nature of things. But if the law applies the term theft to an action that is scarcely even a violation of forest regulations, then the law *lies*, and the poor are sacrificed to a legal lie. . . .

You will never succeed in making us believe that there is a crime where there is no crime, you will only succeed in converting crime itself into a legal act. You have wiped out the boundary between them, but you err if you believe that you have done so only to your advantage. The people sees the punishment, but it does not see the crime, and because it sees punishment where there is no crime, it will see no crime where there is punishment. By applying the category of theft where it ought not to be applied, you have also exonerated it where this category ought to be applied.

And does not this crude view, which lays down a common definition for different kinds of action and leaves the difference out of account, itself bring about its own destruction? If every violation of property without distinction, without a more exact definition, is termed theft, will not all private property be theft? By my private ownership do I not exclude every other person from this ownership? Do I not thereby violate his right of ownership? If you deny the difference between essentially different kinds of the same crime, you are denying that crime itself is *different from right*, you are abolishing right itself, for every crime has an aspect in common with right. Hence it is a fact, attested equally by history and reason, that undifferentiated severity makes punishment wholly unsuccessful, for it does away with punishment as a success for right.

But what are we arguing about? The Assembly, it is true, repudiates the difference between gathering fallen wood, infringement of forest regulations, and theft of wood. It repudiates the difference between these actions, refusing to regard it as determining the character of the action, when it is a question of the *interests of the infringers of forest regulations*, but it recognizes this difference when it is a question of the *interests of the forest owners*.

Thus the commission proposes the following addition: "to regard it as an aggravating circumstance if growing timber is hewn or cut off with edged tools and if a saw is used instead of an axe."

The Assembly approves this distinction. The same keen-sightedness which so conscientiously distinguishes between an axe and a saw when it is a matter of its own interests, is so lacking in conscience as to refuse to distinguish between fallen wood and growing wood when it is a question of other people's interests. The difference was found to be important as an aggravating circumstance but without any significance as a mitigating circumstance, although the former cannot exist if the latter is impossible.

The same logic occurred repeatedly during the debate.

In regard to § 65, an urban deputy desired "that the *value* of the stolen wood also should be used as a measure for fixing the punishment", "which was opposed by the commission's spokesman as *unpractical.*"

The same urban deputy remarked in connection with § 66: "in general there is missing from the whole law any statement of value, in accordance with which the punishment would be increased or diminished."

The importance of value in determining punishment for violations of property is self-evident.

If the concept of crime involves that of punishment, the actual crime calls for a measure of punishment. An actual crime has its limit. The punishment will therefore have to be limited in order to be actual, it must be limited in accordance with a principle of law in order to be just. The problem is to make the punishment the actual consequence of the crime. It must be seen by the criminal as the necessary result of his act, and therefore as *his own act*. Hence the limit of his punishment must be the limit of his act. The definite *content* of a violation of the law is the limit of a definite crime. The *measure* of this content is therefore the measure of the crime. In the case of property this measure is its *value*. Whereas personality, whatever its limits, is always a whole, property always exists only within a definite limit that is not only determinable but determined, not only measurable but measured. Value is the civil mode of existence of property, the logical expression through which it first becomes socially comprehensible and communicable. It is clear that this objective defining element provided by the nature of the object itself must likewise be the objective and essential defining element for the punishment. Even if legislation here, where it is a matter of figures, can only be guided by external features so as not to be lost in an infinitude of definitions, it must at least regulate. It is not a question of an exhaustive definition of differences, but of establishing differences. But the Assembly was not at all disposed to devote its distinguished attention to such trifles.

But do you consider then that you can conclude that the Assembly completely excluded value in determining punishment? That would be an ill-considered, unpractical conclusion! The forest owner . . . —does not merely demand to be compensated by the thief for the simple general value. He even gives this value an individual character and bases his demand for special compensation on this poetic individuality. We can now understand what the commission's spokesman understands by *practical*. The practical forest owner argues as follows: This legal definition is good insofar as it is useful to me, for what is useful to me is good. But this legal definition is superfluous, it is harmful, it is unpractical, insofar as it is intended to be applied to the accused on the basis of a purely theoretical legal whim. Since the accused is harmful to me, it stands to reason that everything is harmful to me that lessens the harm coming to him. This is practical wisdom.

We unpractical people, however, demand for the poor, politically and socially propertyless many what the learned and would-be learned servility of so-called historians has discovered to be the true philosopher's stone for turning every sordid claim into the pure gold of right. We demand for the poor a *customary right*, and indeed one which is not of a local character but is a customary right of the poor in all countries. We go still further and maintain that a customary right by its very nature can *only* be a right of this lowest, propertyless and elemental mass. . . .

The customary rights of the aristocracy conflict by their *content* with the form of universal law. They cannot be given the form of law because they are formations of lawlessness. The fact that their content is contrary to the form of law—universality and necessity—proves that they are *customary wrongs* and cannot be asserted in opposition to the law, but as such opposition they must be abolished and even punished if the occasion arises, for no one's action ceases to be wrongful

because it is his custom, just as the bandit son of a robber is not exonerated because banditry is a family idiosyncrasy. If someone intentionally acts contrary to law, he is punished for his intention; if he acts by custom, this custom of his is punished as being a bad custom. At a time when universal laws prevail, rational customary right is nothing but the *custom of legal right*, for right has not ceased to be custom because it has been embodied in law, although it has ceased to be *merely* custom. For one who acts in accordance with right, right becomes his own custom, but it is enforced against one who violates it, although it is not his custom. Right no longer depends on chance, on whether custom is rational or not, but custom becomes rational because right is legal, because custom has become the custom of the state.

Customary right as a *separate domain* alongside legal right is therefore rational only where it exists *alongside* and *in addition to law*, where custom is the *anticipation* of a legal right. Hence one cannot speak of the customary rights of the privileged estates. The law recognizes not only their rational right but often even their irrational pretensions. The privileged estates have no right of anticipation in regard to law, for law has anticipated all possible consequences of their right. Hence, too, the customary rights are demanded only as a domain for *menus plaisirs*, in order that the same content which is dealt with in the law inside its rational limits should find in custom scope for whims and pretensions outside these rational limits.

But whereas these customary rights of the aristocracy are customs which are contrary to the conception of rational right, the customary rights of the poor are rights which are contrary to the customs of positive law. Their content does not conflict with legal form, but rather with its own lack of form. The form of law is not in contradiction to this content, on the contrary, the latter has not yet reached this form. Little thought is needed to perceive how *one-sidedly* enlightened legislation has treated and been compelled to treat the *customary rights of the poor*, of which the various *Germanic* rights[3] can be considered the most prolific source.

In regard to *civil law*, the most liberal legislations have been confined to formulating and raising to a universal level those rights which they found already in existence. Where they did not find any such rights, neither did they create any. They abolished particular customs, but in so doing forgot that whereas the wrong of the estates took the form of arbitrary pretensions, the right of those without social estate appeared in the form of accidental concessions. This course of action was correct in regard to those who, besides right, enjoyed custom, but it was incorrect in regard to those who had only customs without rights. Just as these legislations converted arbitrary pretensions into legal claims, insofar as some rational content of right was to be found in those pretensions, they ought also to have converted accidental concessions into necessary ones. We can make this clear by taking the monasteries as an example. The monasteries were abolished, their property was secularized, and it was right to do so. But the accidental support which the poor found in the monasteries was not replaced by any other positive source of income. When the property of the monasteries received some compensation, the poor who lived by the monasteries were not compensated. On the contrary, a new restriction was imposed on them, while they were deprived of an ancient right. This occurred in all transformations of privileges into rights. A positive aspect of these abuses—which was also an abuse because it turned a right of one side into something accidental—was abolished not by the accidental being converted into a necessity, but by its being left out of consideration.

These legislations were necessarily one-sided, for all customary rights of the poor were based on the fact that certain forms of property were indeterminate in character, for they were not definitely private property, but neither were they definitely common property, being a mixture of private and public right, such as we find in all the institutions of the Middle Ages. For the purpose of legislation, such ambiguous forms could be grasped only by understanding, and understanding is not only one-sided, but has the essential function of making the world one-sided, a great and remarkable work, for only one-sidedness can extract the particular from the unorganized mass of the whole and give it shape. The character of a thing is a product of understanding. Each thing must isolate itself and become isolated in order to be something. By confining each of the contents of the world in a stable definiteness and as it were solidifying the fluid essence of this content, understanding brings out the manifold diversity of the world, for the world would not be many-sided without the many one-sidednesses.

Understanding therefore abolished the hybrid, indeterminate forms of property by applying to them the existing categories of abstract civil law, the model for which was available in Roman law. The legislative mind considered it was the more justified in abolishing the obligations of this indeterminate property towards the class of the very poor, because it also abolished the state privileges of property. It forgot, however, that even from the standpoint of civil law a twofold private right was present here: a private right of the owner and a private right of the non-owner; and this apart from the fact that no legislation abolishes the privileges of property under constitutional law, but merely divests them of their strange character and gives them a civil character. If, however, every medieval form of right, and therefore of property also, was in every respect hybrid, dualistic, split into two, and understanding rightly asserted its principle of unity in respect of this contradictory determination, it nevertheless overlooked the fact that there exist objects of property which, by their very nature, can never acquire the character of predetermined private property, objects which, by their elemental nature and their accidental mode of existence, belong to the sphere of occupation rights, and therefore of the occupation right of that class which, precisely because of these occupation rights, is excluded from all other property and which has the same position in civil society as these objects have in nature.

It will be found that the customs which are customs of the entire poor class are based with a sure instinct on the *indeterminate* aspect of property; it will be found not only that this class feels an urge to satisfy a natural need, but equally that it feels the need to satisfy a rightful urge. Fallen wood provides an example of this. Such wood has as little organic connection with the growing tree as the cast-off skin has with the snake. Nature itself presents as it were a model of the antithesis between poverty and wealth in the shape of the dry, snapped twigs and branches separated from organic life in contrast to the trees and stems which are firmly rooted and full of sap, organically assimilating air, light, water and soil to develop their own proper form and individual life. It is a physical representation of poverty and wealth. Human poverty senses this kinship and deduces its right to property from this feeling of kinship. If, therefore, it claims physical organic wealth for the predetermined property owners, it claims physical poverty for need and its fortuity. In this play of elemental forces, poverty senses a beneficent power more humane than human power. The fortuitous arbitrary action of privileged individuals is replaced by the fortuitous operation of elemental forces, which take away from private property what the latter no longer voluntarily foregoes. Just as it is not fitting for the rich to lay claim to alms distributed in the street, so also in regard to these *alms of nature*. But it is by its *activity*, too, that poverty acquires its right. But its act of *gathering*, the elemental class of human society appoints itself to introduce order among the products of the elemental power of nature. The position is similar in regard to those products which, because of their wild growth, are a wholly accidental appendage of property and, if only because of their unimportance, are not an object for the activity of the actual owner. The same thing holds good also in regard to gleaning after the harvest and similar customary rights.

In these customs of the poor class, therefore, there is an instinctive sense of right; their roots are positive and legitimate, and the form of *customary right* here conforms all the more to nature because up to now the *existence of the poor class itself* has been a *mere custom* of civil society, a custom which has not found an appropriate place in the conscious organization of the state.

The debate in question affords an example of the way in which these customary rights are treated, an example which exhaustively illustrates the method and spirit of the whole procedure.

An urban deputy opposed the provision by which the gathering of bilberries and cranberries is also treated as theft. He spoke primarily on behalf of the children of the poor, who pick these fruits to earn a trifling sum for their parents; an activity which has been permitted by the owners *since time immemorial* and has given rise to a *customary right* of the children. This fact was countered by another deputy, who remarked that

> in his area these berries have already become articles of commerce and are dispatched to Holland by the barrel.

In *one locality*, therefore, things have actually gone so far that a customary right of the poor has been turned into a *monopoly* of the rich. That is exhaustive proof that common property can be monopolized, from which it naturally follows that it must be monopolized. The nature of the object calls for monopoly because private property interests here have invented this monopoly. The modern idea conceived by some money-grabbing petty traders becomes irrefutable when it provides profit for the age-old Teutonic landed interest.

The wise legislator will prevent crime in order not to have to punish it, but he will do so not by obstructing the sphere of right, but by doing away with the negative aspect of every instinct of right, giving the latter a positive sphere of action. He will not confine himself to removing the *impossibility* for members of one class to belong to a higher sphere of right, but will raise their class itself to the *real possibility* of enjoying its rights. But if the state is not humane, rich and high-minded enough for this, it is at least the legislator's absolute duty not to convert into a *crime* what circumstances alone have caused to be an *offense*. He must exercise the utmost leniency in correcting as a social *irregularity* what it would be the height of injustice for him to punish as an anti-social crime. Otherwise he will be combating the social instinct while supposing that he is combating its anti-social form. In short, if popular customary rights are suppressed, the attempt to exercise them can only be treated as the simple *contravention of a police regulation*, but never punished as a crime. Punishment by police penalties is an expedient to be used against an act which circumstances characterize as a superficial irregularity not constituting any violation of the eternal rule of law. The punishment must not inspire more repugnance than the offense, the ignominy of crime must not be turned into the ignominy of law; the basis of the state is undermined if misfortune becomes a crime or crime becomes a misfortune. Far from upholding this point of view, the Provincial Assembly does not observe even the elementary rules of legislation.

The petty, wooden, mean and selfish soul of interest sees only one point, the point in which it is wounded, like a coarse person who regards a passer-by as the most infamous, vilest creature under the sun because this unfortunate creature has trodden on his corns. He makes his corns the basis for his views and judgment, he makes the one point where the passer-by comes into contact with him into the only point where the very nature of this man comes into contact with the world. But a man may very well happen to tread on my corns without on that account ceasing to be an honest, indeed an excellent, man. Just as you must not judge people by your corns, you must not see them through the eyes of your private interest. Private interest makes the one sphere in which a person comes into conflict with this interest into this person's whole sphere of life. It makes the law a *rat-catcher*, who wants only to destroy vermin, for he is not a naturalist and therefore regards rats only as vermin. But the state must regard the infringer of forest regulations as something more than a wood-pilfer, more than an *enemy to wood*. Is not the state linked with each of its citizens by a thousand vital nerves, and has it the right to sever all these nerves because this citizen has himself arbitrarily severed *one* of them? Therefore the state will regard even an infringer of forest regulations as a human being, a living member of the state, one in whom its heart's blood

flows, a soldier who has to defend his Fatherland, a witness whose voice must be heard by the court, a member of the community with public duties to perform, the father of a family, whose existence is sacred, and, above all, a citizen of the state. The state will not light-heartedly exclude one of its members from all these functions, for the state amputates itself whenever it turns a citizen into a criminal. Above all, the *moral* legislator will consider it a most serious, most painful, and most dangerous matter if an action which previously was not regarded as blameworthy is classed among criminal acts.

Interest, however, is practical, and nothing in the world is more practical than to strike down one's enemy. "Hates any man the thing he would not kill?" we are already told by Shylock. The true legislator should fear nothing but wrong, but the legislative interest knows only fear of the consequences of rights, fear of the evil-doers against whom the laws are made. Cruelty is a characteristic feature of laws dictated by cowardice, for cowardice can be energetic only by being cruel. Private interest, however, is always cowardly, for its heat, its soul, is an external object which can always be wrenched away and injured, and who has not trembled at the danger of losing heart and soul? How could the selfish legislator be human when something inhuman, an alien material essence, is his supreme essence? *"Quand il a peur, il est terrible,"* ["When he is afraid, he is terrible"] says the *National* about Guizot. These words could be inscribed as a motto over all *legislation inspired by self-interest*, and therefore by *cowardice....*

Previously, when innocent persons were turned into criminals, when in connection with the gathering of fallen wood a deputy remarked that in prison they were brought into contact with inveterate thieves, prisons were said to be *good*. Suddenly reformatories have been metamorphosed into institutions for corruption, for at this moment it is of advantage to the interests of the forest owner that prisons corrupt. By reform of the criminal is understood *improvement of the percentage of profit* which it is the criminal's noble function to provide for the forest owner.

Interest has no memory, for it thinks only of itself. And the *one* thing about which it is concerned, itself, it never forgets. But it is not concerned about contradictions, for it never comes into contradiction with itself. It is a constant improviser, for it has no system, only *expedients*.

Whereas humane and rightful motives have no part to play except

> Ce qu'ua bal nous autres sots humains, Nous appelons faire tapisserie, [What, at a ball, we simple folk call being wallflowers.]

expedients are the most active agents in the argumentative mechanism of private interest. Among these expedients, we note two that constantly recur in this debate and constitute the main categories, namely, *"good motives"* and *"harmful results."* We see sometimes the spokesman for the commission, sometimes another member of the Assembly, defending every ambiguous provision against hostile shafts of objections by means of the shield of shrewd, wise and good motives. We see every conclusion drawn from the standpoint of right rejected by referring to its harmful or dangerous results. Let us examine for a moment these extensive expedients, these expedients *par excellence*, these expedients covering everything and a little more.

Interest knows how to denigrate right by presenting a prospect of harmful results due to its effects in the external world; it knows how to whitewash what is wrong by ascribing good motives to it, that is, by retreating into the internal world of its thoughts. Law produces bad results in the external world among bad people, wrong springs from good motives in the breast of the honest man who decrees it; but both, the good motives and the harmful results, have in common the peculiar feature that they do not look at a thing in relation to itself, that they do not treat the law as an independent object, but direct attention away from the law either to the external world or to their own mind, that therefore they maneuver *behind the back of the law.* . . .

What then are harmful results? Harmful is that which is harmful to the interests of the forest owner. If, therefore, the law does not result in the furtherance of his interests, its results are harmful. And in this respect interest is keen-sighted. Whereas previously it did not see what was obvious to the naked eye, it now sees even what is only visible through a microscope. The whole world is a thorn in the side of private interest, a world full of dangers, precisely because it is the world not of a single interest but of many interests. Private interest considers itself the ultimate purpose of the world. Hence if the law does not realize this ultimate purpose, it becomes inexpedient law. *Law which is harmful to private interests* is therefore *law with harmful results.*

Are *good motives* considered to be better than harmful results?

Interest does not think, it calculates. Motives are its figures. Motive is an incentive for abolishing the basis of law, and who can doubt that private interest will have many incentives for doing so? The goodness of a motive lies in the casual flexibility with which it can set aside the objective facts of the case and lull itself and others into the illusion that it is not necessary to keep one's mind on what is good, but that it suffices to have good thoughts while doing a bad thing.

Resuming the thread of our argument, we mention first of all a side line to the noble deeds recommended to the Herr Burgomaster.

> The commission proposed an amended version of § 34 along the following lines: if the accused demands that the warden who drew up the charge be summoned, then he must also deposit with the forestry court *in advance* all the costs thereby incurred.

The state and the court must not do anything gratis in the interests of the accused. They must demand payment in advance which obviously in advance makes difficult any confrontation of the warden making the charge and the accused.

A noble deed! Just one single noble deed! A kingdom for a noble deed! But the only noble deed proposed is that which the Herr Burgomaster has to perform for the benefit of the Herr Forest Owner. The burgomaster is the representative of noble deeds, their humanized expression, and the series of noble deeds is exhausted and ended for ever with the burden which was imposed with melancholy sacrifice on the burgomaster.

If, for the good of the state and the moral benefit of the criminal, the Herr Burgomaster must do more than his duty, should not the forest owners, for the sake of the same good, demand *less* than their *private interest* requires?

One might think that the reply to this question had been given in the part of the debate already dealt with, but that is a mistake. We come to the *penal provisions*.

A deputy from the knightly estate considered that the forest owner would still be inadequately compensated even if he received (over and above the simple replacement of the value) the amount of the fine imposed, which would often not be obtainable.

An urban deputy remarked:

The provisions of this paragraph (§ 15) could have the most serious consequences. The forest owner would receive in this way *threefold* compensation, namely: the value, then the four-, six-, or eightfold fine, and in addition a special sum as compensation for loss, which will often be assessed quite arbitrarily and will be the result of a fiction rather than of reality. In any case, it seemed necessary to him to direct that the special compensation in question should be claimed at once at the forestry court and awarded in the court's sentence. It was obvious from the nature of the case that proof of loss sustained should be supplied separately and could not be based merely on the warden's report.

Opposing this, the spokesman and another member explained how the *additional value* mentioned here could arise in various cases indicated by them. The paragraph was adopted.

Crime becomes a lottery in which the forest owner, if he is lucky, can even win a prize. There can be additional value, but the forest owner, who already receives the simple value, can also make a

profitable business out of the four-, six-, or eightfold fine. But if, besides the simple value, he receives special compensation for loss, the four-, six-, or eightfold fine is also sheer profit. If a member of the knightly estate thinks the money accruing as a fine is an inadequate guarantee because it would often not be obtainable, it would certainly not become more obtainable by the value and the compensation for loss having to be recovered as well. We shall see presently how this difficulty of receiving money from the accused is overcome.

Could the forest owner have any better insurance for his wood than that instituted here, whereby crime has been turned into a source of income? Like a clever general he converts the attack against him into an infallible opportunity for a profitable victory, since even the additional value of the wood, an economic fantasy, is turned into a substance by theft. The forest owner has to be guaranteed not only his wood, but also his wood business, while the convenient homage he pays to his business manager, the state, consists in not paying for its services. It is a remarkable idea to turn the punishment of crime from a victory of the law over attacks on it into a victory of selfishness over attacks on selfishness.

In particular, however, we draw the attention of our readers to the provision of § 14, which compels us to abandon the customary idea that *leges barbarorum* are laws of barbaric peoples. *Punishment* as such, the restoration of the law, which must certainly be distinguished from restitution of the value and compensation for loss, the restoration of private property, is transformed from a *public punishment* into a *private compensation*, the fines going not to the state treasury, but to the private coffers of the forest owner.

True, an urban deputy stated: "This is contrary to the dignity of the state and the principles of correct criminal jurisprudence", but a deputy from the knightly estate appealed to the Assembly's sense of right and fairness to protect the rights of the forest owner, that is to say, he appealed to a *special* sense of right and fairness.

Barbaric peoples order the payment of a definite monetary compensation (atonement money) to the injured person for a definite crime. The notion of public punishment arose only in opposition to this view, which regards a crime merely as an injury to the individual, but the people and the theory have yet to be discovered which are so complacent as to allow an individual to claim for himself both the private punishment and that imposed by the state.

The Assembly of the Estates must have been led astray by a complete *qui pro quo*. The law-giving forest owner confused for a moment his two roles, that of legislator and that of forest owner. In one case as a forest owner he made the thief pay him for the wood, and in the other as a legislator he made the thief pay him for the thief's *criminal frame of mind*, and it quite accidentally happened that in both cases it was the forest owner who was paid. So we are no longer faced by the simple *droit du seigeur*. We have passed through the era of public law to the era of double patrimonial right, patrimonial right raised to the second power. The patrimonial property owners have taken advantage of the progress of time, which is the refutation of their demands, to usurp not only the private punishment typical of the barbaric world outlook, but also the public punishment typical of the modern world outlook.

Owing to the refunding of the value and in addition a special compensation for loss, the relation between the wood thief and the forest owner has ceased to exist, for the infringement of forest regulations has been completely abolished. Both thief and property owner have returned to their former state in its entirety. The forest owner has suffered by the theft of wood only insofar as the wood has suffered, but not insofar as the law has been violated. Only the sensuously perceptible aspect of the crime affects him, but the criminal nature of the act does not consist in the attack on the wood as a material object, but in the attack on the wood as part of the state system, an attack on the right to property as such, the realization of wrongful frame of mind. Has the forest owner any private claims to a law-abiding frame of mind on the part of the thief? And what is the multiplication of the punishment for a repetition of the

offense except a punishment for a criminal frame of mind? Can the forest owner present private demands where he has no private claims? Was the forest owner the state, prior to the theft of wood? He was not, but he becomes it after the theft. The wood possesses the remarkable property that as soon as it is stolen it bestows on its owner state qualities which previously he did not possess. But the forest owner can only get back what has been taken from him. If the state is given back to him—and it is actually given him when he is given not only a private right, but the state's right over the law-breaker—then he must have been robbed of the state, the state must have been his private property. Therefore the wood thief, like a second St. Christopher, bore the state itself on his back in the form of the stolen wood.

Public punishment is satisfaction for the crime to the reason of the state; it is therefore a right of the state, but it is a right which the state can no more transfer to private persons than one person can hand over his conscience to another. Every right of the state in relation to the criminal is at the same time a right of the criminal in relation to the state. No interposing of intermediate links can convert the relation of a criminal to the state into a relation between him and the private persons. Even if it were desired to allow the state to give up its rights, i.e., to commit suicide, such an abandonment of its obligations on the part of the state would be not merely negligence, but a crime.

It is therefore as impossible for the forest owner to obtain from the state a private right to public punishment as it is for him to have any conceivable right, in and for himself, to impose public punishment. If, in the absence of a rightful claim to do so, I make the criminal act of a third person an independent source of income for myself, do I not thus become his accomplice? Or am I any the less his accomplice because to him falls the punishment and to me the fruit of the crime? The guilt is not attenuated by a private person abusing his status as an legislator to arrogate to himself rights belonging to the state because of a crime committed by a third person. The embezzling of public, state funds is a crime against the state, and is not the money from fines public money belonging to the state?

The wood thief has robbed the forest owner of wood, but the forest owner has made use of the wood thief to purloin the *state itself*. How literally true this is can be seen from § 19, the provisions of which do not stop at imposing a fine but also lay claim to the *body and life* of the accused. According to § 19, the infringer of forest regulations is handed over completely to the forest owner, for whom he has to perform *forest labor*. . . .

. . . In the unbridled pursuit of private interest you came up against the law itself as an obstacle and you treat it as such. You haggle and bargain with it to secure the abrogation of a basic principle here and there, you try to silence it by the most suppliant references to the right of private interest, you slap it on the shoulder and whisper in its ear: these are exceptions and there are no rules without an exception. You try, by permitting the law as it were terrorism and meticulousness in relation to the enemy, to compensate it for the slippery ease of conscience with which you treat it as a guarantee of the accused and as an independent object. The interest of the law is allowed to speak insofar as it is the law of private interest, but it has to be silent as soon as it comes into conflict with this holy of holies.

The forest owner, who himself *punishes*, is so consistent that he himself also *judges*, for he obviously acts as a judge by declaring a sentence legally binding although it has no legal validity. How altogether foolish and impractical an illusion is an impartial judge when the legislator is not impartial! What is the use of a disinterested sentence when the law favors self-interest! The judge can only puritanically formulate the self-interest of the law, only implement it without reservation. Impartiality is then only in the form, not in the content of the sentence. The content has been anticipated by the law. If the trial is nothing but an empty form, then such a trifling formality has no independent value. According to this view, Chinese law would become French law if it was forced into the French procedure, but *material law* has its own *necessary, native form of trial*. Just as the rod

necessarily figures in Chinese law, and just as torture has a place in the medieval criminal code as a form of trial, so the public, free trial, in accordance with its own nature, necessarily has a public content dictated by freedom and not by private interest. Court trial and the law are no more indifferent to each other than, for instance, the forms of plants are indifferent to the plants themselves, and the forms of animals to their flesh and blood. There must be a *single* spirit animating the trial and the law, for the trial is only the *form of life of the law*, the manifestation of its inner life.

The pirates of Tidong[4] break the arms and legs of their prisoners to ensure control over them. To ensure control over wood thieves, the Provincial Assembly has not only broken the arms and legs but has even pierced the heart of the law. We consider its merit in regard to re-establishing some categories of our trial procedure as absolutely nil; on the contrary, we must acknowledge the frankness and consistence with which it gives an unfree form to the unfree content. If private interest, which cannot bear the light of publicity, is introduced materially into our law, let it be given its appropriate form, that of secret procedure so that at least no dangerous, complacent illusions will be evoked and entertained. We consider that at the present moment it is the duty of all Rhinelanders, and especially of Rhenish jurists, to devote their main attention to the *content of the law*, so that we should not be left in the end with only an empty mask. The form is of no value if it is not the form of the content.

The commission's proposal which we have just examined and the Assembly's vote approving it are the climax to the whole debate, for here the Assembly itself becomes conscious of the *conflict between the interest of forest protection and the principles of law*, principles endorsed by our own laws. The Assembly therefore put it to the vote whether the principles of law should be sacrificed to the interest of forest protection or whether this interest should be sacrificed to the principles of law, and *interest outvoted law*. It was even realized that the whole law was an *exception to the law*, and therefore the conclusion was drawn that *every* exceptional provision it contained was permissible. The Assembly confined itself to drawing consequences that the legislator had neglected. Wherever the legislator had forgotten that it was a question of an exception to the law, and not of a law, wherever he put forward the legal point of view, our Assembly by its activity intervened with confident tactfulness to correct and supplement him, and to make private interest lay down laws to the law where the law had laid down laws to private interest.

The Provincial Assembly, therefore, *completely fulfilled its mission*. In accordance with its *function*, it represented a definite *particular interest* and treated it as the final goal. That in doing so it trampled the law under foot is a *simple consequence of its task*, for interest by its very nature is blind, immoderate, one-sided; in short it is lawless natural instinct, and can lawlessness lay down laws? Private interest is no more made capable of legislating by being installed on the throne of the legislator than a mute is made capable of speech by being given an enormously long speaking-trumpet.

It is with reluctance that we have followed the course of this tedious and uninspired debate, but we considered it our duty to show by means of an example what is to be expected from an *Assembly of the Estates of particular interests* if it were ever seriously called upon to make laws. . . .

NOTES

1. *Proceedings of the Sixth Rhine Province Assembly. Third Article. Debates on the Law on Thefts of Wood* is one of the series of articles by Marx on the proceedings of the Rhine Province Assembly from May 23 to July 25, 1841. Marx touched on the theme of the material interests of the popular masses for the first time, coming out in their defense. Work on this and subsequent articles inspired Marx to study political economy. He wrote about this in the preface to his *A Contribution to the Critique of Political Economy* (1859): "In the year 1842–43, as editor of the *Rheinische Zeitung*, I first found myself in the embarrassing position of having to discuss what is known as material interests. Debates of the Rhine Province Assembly on the theft of wood and the division of landed property; the official polemic started by Herr von Schaper, the Oberpräsident of the Rhine Province, against the *Rheinische Zeitung* about the condition of the Mosel peasantry, and finally the debates on free trade and protective tariffs caused me in the first instance to turn my attention to economic questions."

   Exerpts from the speeches by the deputies to the Assembly are cited from *Sitzungs-Protokolle des sechsten Rheinischen Provinzial-Landtags*, Koblenz, 1841.

2. Marx refers to the Criminal Code of Karl V (*Die peinliche Halsgerichtsordnung Kaiser Karls V. Constitutio criminalis Carolina*), approved by the Reichstag in Regensburg in 1532; it was distinguished by its extremely cruel penalties.

3. The reference is to the so-called barbaric laws (*leges barbarorum*) compiled in the fifth–ninth centuries which were records of the common law of various Germanic tribes (Franks, Frisians, Burgundians, Langobards [Lombards], Anglo-Saxons and others).

4. *Tidong*—a region in Kalimantan (Borneo).

Commodity Form and Legal Form: An Essay on the "Relative Autonomy" of the Law

Isaac D. Balbus

I. Introduction

In this essay I attempt to outline the essentials of a Marxian theory of law. This theory, as we shall see, entails a simultaneous rejection of both an *instrumentalist* or reductionist approach, which denies that the legal order possesses any autonomy from the demands imposed on it by actors of the capitalist society in which it is embedded, and a *formalist* approach, which asserts an absolute, unqualified autonomy of the legal order from this society. The instrumentalist approach—whether pluralist or crude-Marxist—conceives of the law as a mere instrument or tool of the will of dominant social actors and thus fails even to pose the problem of the specific *form* of the law and the way in which this form articulates with the overall requirements of the capitalist system in which these social actors function.[1] The formalist approach, on the other hand, locates and describes the specificity of the legal form but, insofar as it treats this form as a closed, autonomous system whose development is to be understood exclusively in terms of its own "internal dynamics," is likewise unable even to conceptualize the relationship between the legal form and the specifically capitalist whole of which it is a part.[2] In short, neither approach is capable of explaining why a specifically legal form of the exchange of people is inextricably intertwined with a specifically capitalist form of the exchange of products. It is precisely that problem to which this essay is addressed.

The debate between the instrumentalists and the formalists—which has dominated legal theory for at least two hundred years and continues to flourish today—has always been extraordinarily misleading. It is characterized by a false dichotomy which arises from an inadequate starting point shared by *both* approaches, i.e., the assumption that the law must be judged "autonomous" to the extent that it functions and develops independently of the *will* of the extralegal social actors. Given this common conceptual terrain, their dispute is necessarily and merely a dispute over the "facts;" formalists "discover" that the law is independent of the will of social actors, and thus conclude that it is "autonomous," whereas instrumentalists "find," to the contrary, that the law is directly responsive to the will of these actors and thus conclude that the law is "not autonomous." Neither understands that the answer to the question whether the law is independent of the will of social actors *in no way* disposes of the question whether the law is autonomous from the capitalist *system* of which these actors are the agents. Even more: the formulation that *to the degree that the law does not respond directly to the demands of powerful social actors it is autonomous, in the sense that it functions and develops according to its own internal dynamics* omits the possibility that the law is not autonomous from, but rather articulates with and must be explained by, the systemic requirements of capitalism precisely because it does *not* respond directly to the demands of these actors. In other words, it is one thing to argue that the legal order is autonomous from the preferences of actors outside this order, but quite another to argue that it is autonomous from the capitalist system (un-

140

less one were to commit the "voluntarist" error of equating the preferences of actors with those activities that must be performed if the system in which they function is to survive). Indeed, I will try to demonstrate that it is precisely because the law *is* autonomous in the first sense that it is *not* autonomous in the second or, to put it another way, that the relative autonomy of the legal form from the will of social actors entails at the same time an essential *identity* or homology between the legal form and the very "cell" of capitalist society, the commodity form. Thus the Marxian theory of the "relative autonomy" of the law, which I am proposing, cannot be understood as a *compromise* between the instrumentalist and formalist positions; rather it purports to *transcend* the opposition between these positions by rejecting the common conceptual terrain on which they are based and elaborating a wholly different theoretical terrain. This requires a brief summary of Marx's analysis of the logic of the commodity form.

II. The Logic of the Commodity Form

This logic, Marx tells us in the first chapter of Volume I of *Capital*, is that of a "mysterious," twofold and, in fact, contradictory reality. A commodity, to begin with, is a use-value: it is a qualitatively distinct object which exists to fulfill a qualitatively distinct, concrete human need and has been brought into existence by a qualitatively distinct form of labor, which Marx calls "concrete labor." In their role as use-values different commodities are thus *not* equal to one another; their inequality corresponds to the unequal labors that produced them. At the same time, however, a commodity is also an object of exchange, or an exchange-value: it exists and is valued not only, and not immediately, because it is used but also and rather because it can be exchanged for another commodity. The existence of exchange-value, or what Marx simply calls value, thus presupposes that qualitatively distinct and otherwise incommensurable commodities enter into a formal relationship of equivalence

with one another, i.e., that qualitatively different objects become what they are not: *equal*. This relationship of equivalence, in turn, is facilitated by the existence of a particular commodity, money, which with the development of capitalism becomes the *universal economic equivalent* by means of which the value of every other commodity can be expressed. Money, in other words, permits all products to assume a formal identity so that they can become, in Marx's suggestive phrase, "citizens of that world [of commodities]" (1967:63), that is, they can all stand for or be *represented* by each other. The fully developed commodity form, or the money form, thus entails a common *form* which is an abstraction from, and masking of, the qualitatively different *contents* of the objects and the concrete human needs to which they correspond: "The memory of use-value, as distinct from exchange-value, has become entirely extinguished in this incarnation of pure exchange-value" (Marx, 1973:239–40).

This abstraction from, and masking of, the content or quality of the object is only made possible by a prior abstraction from, and masking of, the concrete labor that produced it. The common form that is exchange-value can only exist as the expression of the one form that is common to all the qualitatively different labors that bring objects into existence, i.e., of labor-power understood as an abstract, undifferentiated expenditure of energy over a given period of time, or what Marx calls abstract labor. Thus, in order for commodities to become equal to one another, i.e., in order for exchange-value to exist, concrete, qualitatively different labors must become what they are not: *equal*. The result is that the "memory" of concrete labor is "extinguished" along with that of use-value.

The logic of the commodity form is thus that of a *double movement from the concrete to the abstract, a double abstraction of form from content, a twofold transmutation of quality into quantity*. The transformation of commodities from unequal to equal objects parallels, and is made possible by, a transformation of the labor which produces them from unequal to equal. In order for commodities *to be what they are*, both the unequal objects and the unequal labor which has produced them must *become what they are not*, i.e., equal. Thus the commodity form has its origin in concrete human needs and creative labor, but it "possesses the peculiar capacity of concealing its own essence from the human beings who live with it and by it" (Lefebvre, 1969:47), i.e., by virtue of the double mystification inherent in the commodity form, human beings necessarily "forget" that commodities owe their existence to human needs and to the activity in which people have engaged both to produce and fulfill these needs. The commodity form, in other words, is an economic form that necessarily functions *independently* of, or *autonomously* from, the will of the subjects who set it in motion. Thus the *fetishism of commodities:* the masking of the link between commodities and their human origin gives rise to the appearance, the ideological inversion, that commodities have living, human powers. Products appear to take on a life of their own, dominating the very human subjects who in fact bring them into existence but who no longer "know" this. Commodity fetishism thus entails a profound reversal of the real causal relationship between humans and their products: humans, the subjects who create or cause the objects, become the object, i.e., are "caused" by the very objects which they have created and to which they now attribute subjectivity or causal power. Human life under a capitalist mode of production becomes dominated by the passion to possess the commodity's living power, especially the power of that one commodity, money, that makes possible the possession and accumulation of all other commodities. Thus money is transformed from a means of exchange into the very end or goal of human life itself.

III. The Logic of the Legal Form

. . . I shall argue that the logic of the legal form and the logic of the commodity form are one and the same.

If, in a capitalist mode of production, products take on the form of individual *commodities*, people take on the form of individual *citizens;* the exchange of commodities is paralleled by the exchange of citizens. A citizen, in turn, is every bit as "mysterious," twofold, and in fact contradictory a reality as a commodity. An individual citizen, to begin with, is a qualitatively distinct, concrete subject with qualitatively distinct human needs or interests. In this aspect of their existence, then, individual citizens are manifestly *not* equal to one another, an inequality which corresponds to the uniqueness of the human activities and the networks of social relationships from which their needs or interests derive. At the same time, however, individual citizens are not only, and not immediately, subjects with needs but also and rather objects of exchange who exist in order to represent, and be represented by, other individual citizens. The existence of political exchange or representation thus requires that qualitatively distinct individuals with otherwise incommensurable interests enter into a formal relationship of equivalence with one another, i.e., that the qualitatively different subjects become what they are not: *equal.* This relationship of equivalence, in turn, is made possible by the law which, with the development of capitalism, becomes the *universal political equivalent* by means of which each individual is rendered equal to every other individual, so that any one individual can represent any other. The fully developed legal form thus entails a common *form* which is an abstraction from, and masking of, the qualitatively different *contents* of the needs of subjects as well as the qualitatively different activities and structures of social relationships in which they participate. Thus the legal form, in Marx's words, "makes an abstraction of real men"[3] which is perfectly homologous to the abstraction that the commodity form makes of "real products." Let us look more closely at the legal form in order to clarify the way in which it is able to perform this abstraction, as well as the consequences of this operation.

A. The Law as Universal Political Equivalent

The formality, generality, and "autonomy" of the law—captured in Weber's concept of "formal legal rationality" and summarized by Professor Trubek . . . (1972)—preclude the qualitatively different interests and social origins of individuals from entering into the calculus of political exchange, just as the formality, generality, and "autonomy" of money preclude the qualitatively different use-values of commodities, and the unique labor that produces them, from being recognized in the calculus of economic exchange. The "blindness" of the legal form to substantive human interests and characteristics thus parallels the blindness of the commodity form to use-value and concrete labor, and if the commodity-form functions to "extinguish" the "memory" of use-value and concrete labor, so too the legal form functions to extinguish the memory of different interests and social origins. As Marx puts it:

> The [legal] state abolishes, after its fashion, the distinctions established by birth, social rank, education, occupation when it decrees that birth, social rank, education, occupation are *non-political* distinctions; when it proclaims, without regard to these distinctions, that every member is an *equal* partner in popular sovereignty. [1972a:31]

The legal form thus defines distinctions of interest and origin *out of political existence*, just as the commodity form defines distinctions of use and labor out of economic existence. And, just as the commodity form "replaces" use-value and concrete labor with the abstractions of exchange-value and undifferentiated labor-power, the legal form "replaces" the multiplicity of concrete needs and interests with the abstractions of *"will"* and *"rights,"* and the socially differentiated individual with the abstraction of the *juridical subject* or the legal person. Pashukanis was perhaps the first Marxist after Marx to specify what might be called the common *mode of substitution* underlying both the commodity form and the legal form:

> In the same way that the natural multiformity of the useful attributes of a product is in commodities merely a simple wrapper of the value, while the concrete species of human

labor are dissolved in abstract labor as the creator of value—so the concrete multiplicity of the relationships of a man to a thing comes out as the abstract will of the owner, while all the specific peculiarities distinguishing one representative of the species *homo sapiens* from another are dissolved in the abstraction of man in general as a juridic subject. [1951: 163][4]

The subject of "equal rights" substitutes for the concrete subject of needs, and the abstract legal person substitutes for the real, flesh-and-blood, socially differentiated individual. Thus we are in the presence of the same double movement from the concrete to the abstract, the same twofold abstraction of form from content, that characterizes the commodity form.

B. Equality, Individuality, and Community

The "equality" established and protected by the legal form is thus purely formal insofar as it is established in and through an abstraction from the real social inequalities of capitalist, class society, which nevertheless continue to exist, of course, even if denied "political" recognition. Thus "the political suppression of private property not only does not abolish private property, [but] actually presupposes its existence" (Marx, 1972a:31). The formality of legal equality, however, does not prevent it from having substantive consequences which are anything but equal and are in fact *repressive*. On the one hand, the systematic application of an equal scale to systemically unequal individuals necessarily tends to reinforce systemic inequalities; this, of course, was the force of Anatole France's famous, ironic praise of "the majestic equality of the French law, which forbids both rich and poor from sleeping under the bridges of the Seine." Thus Marx argues that the right of "equality" guaranteed by the legal form is "a right of inequality, in its content, like every other right" (1968:324). On the other hand, and probably even more importantly, legal equality functions to mask and occlude class differences

and social inequalities, contributing to a "declas-
sification" of politics which militates against the
formation of the class consciousness necessary to
the creation of a substantively more equal society.
Thus the "political suppression of private property"—legal equality—makes it that much harder
to eliminate private property and its attendant
class inequalities, since it works to prevent "property" and "class" from entering into the universe
of political discourse.

Similarly, the "individuality" established and
protected by the legal form is illusory insofar as it
is established in and through an abstraction from
the concrete, social bases of individuality and is
thus a "pure, blank individuality" (Marx, 1843:
481) bereft of any qualitative determinations and
differences. Just as the commodity form divorces
the concrete use-value existence of the commodity from its formal existence as exchange-value,
recognizing only the latter as constitutive of the
"individuality" of the commodity, so the legal
form splits off the concrete social existence of the
individual from his or her existence as a formal
object of political exchange and recognizes only
the latter as definitive of his or her individuality.
And a form that defines individuals as individuals
only insofar as they are severed from the social
ties and activities that constitute the real ground
of their individuality necessarily fails to contribute
to the recognition of genuine individuality.

The only form of individuality common to all
members of a capitalist society, moreover, is the
individualism and egotism of commodity exchang-
ers, which is in fact the real (and thus "false")
content of the formal individuality produced and
guaranteed by the legal form. The indifference to
qualitatively different needs "announced" in and
through the abstractions of "will" and "rights"
parallels, and is made possible through, a system
of commodity exchange whose individual agents
are necessarily indifferent to reach other's reciprocal needs and are rather obliged to treat each
other as a mere means to their own purely "private" ends (1973:242, 245). The juridical person,
in other words, is merely the political persona of
the individual whose social existence is instrumen-

tal, self-interested and alienated; the individual, in short, who fails to act as a *social* individual
aware of the inseparable relationship between his
or her development and the development of every
other individual.

> Political emancipation is the reduction of
> man, on the one side, to the egoistic member
> of civil society, to the egoistic, independent
> individual, on the other side to the citizen, to
> the moral person. [1972a:44][5]

Thus the commitment of the legal form to individuality is ultimately illusory, because the individuality it recognizes and presupposes is in fact
an alienated form of individuality—individualism.
The commitment becomes doubly illusory, moreover, once we recognize the contributions of the
legal form to the persistence of the very capitalist
mode of production which makes genuine individuality impossible.

Much the same can be said about the kind of
"community" produced by the legal form. Insofar
as the legal order establishes its universality, and
its citizens define their communality, through an
abstraction from the real social differences and interests that separate the members of capitalist society and set them against one another, Marx argues
that it entails an "illusory community" (1972b:159)
which "satisfies the whole man in an imaginary
manner" (1969:127).

> In the [legal] state . . . the individual . . . is
> the imaginary member of an imaginary sov-
> ereignty; he is robbed of his real individual
> life and filled with an unreal universality.
> [1972a:32]

> In order to be a real citizen and have political
> significance and efficacy, he must leave his
> social reality, abstract himself from it and re-
> turn from its whole organization into his
> individuality, for the only existence that he
> finds for his citizenship is his pure, blank in-
> dividuality. [1843:494]

The community of citizens is thus purely formal,
i.e., bereft of real content, because the real content of life in capitalist society is overwhelmingly

particularistic, rather than universalistic, in character. As such, the community produced in and through the legal order is as "imaginary" as that produced by religion; it is a "heavenly" sphere which "soars or seems to soar above ... the limitations of the profane world" (Lefebvre, 1969: 129–30). Indeed, Marx argues that the legal form is, in essence, a *religious form:*

> Up to now, the political constitution has been the religious sphere, the religion of the people's life, the heaven of their universality in contrast to the particular mundane existence of the actuality. [1843:436]

> The individual leads, not only in thought, in consciousness, but in reality, a heavenly and an earthly life, a life in the political community wherein he counts as a member of the community, and a life in civil society, where he is active as a private person, regarding other men as means, degrading himself as a means and becoming a plaything of alien powers. *The political state is related to civil society as spiritualistically as heaven is to earth.* [1972a:32, emphasis added][6]

Thus the "community" produced by the legal form is no more real than the "heaven" produced by a religious system.

Notwithstanding its purely formal, imaginary character, however, this "community" entails substantive consequences of the highest order. If citizenship is at bottom a religion, then it is an *opiate* in the twofold sense both of dulling and distorting perception of reality, and providing a substitute gratification which compensates for the misery of reality and makes it bearable. On the one hand, membership in the illusory political community blurs the perception of the real, mundane class-based and thus particularistic communities in which people live, providing the basis for appeals to an abstract "common interest" or "public interest" which militate against the recognition of class interests. On the other hand, the political community provides individuals with a compensation for the absence of communal relationships

within their everyday existence in the same manner that the perfection of "heaven" compensates for, and thus allows the believer to bear, the imperfections of earthly existence. For both reasons, the "community" produced by the legal form contributes decisively to the reproduction of the very capitalist mode of production which makes genuine community impossible.

Thus the legal form both produces and reinforces illusory, rather than genuine, forms of equality, individuality, and community. At the same time, as I have suggested, these illusory forms contribute significantly to the persistence of a capitalist system which necessarily precludes the realization of genuine equality, individuality, and community. . . .

C. "Legitimation"

The foregoing analysis has important implications for a theory of the "legitimation" and/or "delegitimation" of the legal form, and thus, of the capitalist state. Those who would argue that delegitimation can result from the failure of law to live up to its "promises" (i.e., from the gap between its promises and its performance) fail to understand that the legitimation of the legal order is not primarily a function of its ability to live up to its claims or "redeem its pledges" but rather of the fact that *its claims or pledges are valued in the first place.* As long as "formality," "generality," and "equality before the law" are seen as genuine human values, even gross and systematic departures from these norms in practice will not serve to delegitimate the legal order as a whole, but will at most tend to delegitimate specific laws and specific incumbents of political office who are responsible for these laws. Consider, for example, legal practices that systematically and obviously violate the principle of "equality before the law," such as those that result in rich individuals receiving more lenient treatment than poor individuals who have been convicted of comparable crimes. Such practices may in fact delegitimate particular judges and particular court systems, but they will not delegitimate the legal order itself, insofar as the delegitimation of the former does not call into question, but

rather is based on the affirmation of, a central criterion of the legal order, equal treatment irrespective of class position. In other words, those who
would object to the rich individual receiving more
lenient treatment than the poor, on the grounds
that the law should be indifferent to the distinction between rich and poor—that rich and poor
alike should receive the same penalty for the same
crime—would, in that very condemnation of the
judges and courts responsible for the differential
treatment, be affirming the legitimacy of the legal
order. Thus a "critical analysis of the relationship
between claim and reality," *pace* Trubek, is *not*, in
"itself a source of possible change towards a more
humane society," unless and until this "critical
analysis" also entails a critique of the legitimacy of
the value underlying the claim itself.[7] . . .

. . . An adequate theory of legitimation and/or
delegitimation would therefore have to explain
why the *logic* of the legal order as such, in contrast
to particular laws or legal practices, is ordinarily
accepted as unproblematical, and is not called into
question in the name of a radically different logic.

D. The Fetishism of the Law

The legal form is normally not called into question, I would argue, because the form itself ordinarily precludes the possibility of performing this
critical operation. The calling into question of
the legal order presupposes individuals who conceive themselves as subjects evaluating an object
which they have created and over which they have
control. It is just this presupposition, however,
which is nullified by the perverse logic of the legal
form; this form creates a fetishized relationship
between individuals and the Law in which individuals attribute subjectivity to the Law and conceive themselves as its objects or creations. Under
these conditions, the calling into question and
subsequent delegitimation of the legal order is literally "unthinkable."

The fetishism of the Law of which I am speaking appears in many guises. The most sublime is
probably the formalist theory of law itself, insofar
as this theory conceptualizes the law as an "independent," "autonomous" reality to be explained

according to its own "internal dynamics," i.e.,
conceives it as an independent subject, on whose
creativity the survival of the society depends. The
most ridiculous is undoubtedly the celebration of
"Law Day," during which we are asked to pay
homage to the God-Law. The most frequent, if it
is possible to judge from the numerous discussions
I have had with undergraduate students over the
past decade, is the common refrain: "If we didn't
have the Law everyone would kill each other." All
these instances, and many others, are simply variations on the common theme of legal fetishism, in
which individuals affirm that they owe their existence to the Law, rather than the reverse, inverting
the real causal relationship between themselves
and their product. And all these instances thus preclude the possibility of evaluating the legal form,
since it is impossible to evaluate an entity which is
conceived of as the independent source of one's
existence and values. When Society is held to be a
result of the Law, rather than the Law to be a result of one particular kind of society, then the Law
by definition is unproblematical. Or, to put it
another way, the answer to the legitimation question—why do citizens support the legal order?—
is, above all, the fact that *the citizens of this order
ordinarily do not and cannot ask this question.*

Thus under conditions of legal fetishism the
legal order appears not as an object of rational
choice undertaken by autonomous subjects, but
rather as an autonomous subject itself, whose
very existence requires that individuals "objectify"
themselves before it. According to Marx, the legal
State is a power

> which has won an existence independent of
> the individuals . . . a social power . . . [which]
> appears to the individuals . . . not as their own
> united power, but as an alien force existing
> outside of them, of the origin and goal of
> which they are ignorant, which they thus can-
> not control, and which on the contrary passes
> through a peculiar series of phases and stages
> independent of the will and the action of men,
> nay even being the prime governor of these.[8]

Here Marx is arguing that legal fetishism parallels
commodity fetishism, that the legal form, like the

commodity form, necessarily functions *independently* of, or *autonomously* from, the power or will of the subjects who originally set it in motion but do not know, or have forgotten, that they have done so. And, as in the case of the commodity form, the "deification" of the universal equivalent rests on the obfuscation of "origins" produced by the abstraction of the legal form. Just as the masking of the link between commodities and their human origins in use-value and concrete labor necessarily gives rise to the appearance or ideological inversion that commodities, and especially their universal equivalent, money, have living, human powers, so the abstraction from and masking of the different human needs and social origins carried out by the legal form necessarily produces the illusion that the Law—as the universal political equivalent—has a life of its own. The corollary to human relationships becoming abstract and reified (thing-like) is that things— be they material products or legal "products"— become personified, i.e., take on human characteristics. Commodity fetishism and legal fetishism are thus two inseparably related aspects of an inverted, "topsy-turvy" existence under a capitalist mode of production in which *humans are first reduced to abstractions, and then dominated by their own creations.* . . .

IV. Conclusion

It should now be clear why the "relative autonomy" of the law does not preclude, but rather necessarily entails, an essential identity or homology between the legal form and the commodity form. The homology between the legal form and the commodity form guarantees both that the legal form, like the commodity form, functions and develops autonomously from the preferences of social actors *and* that it does *not* function and develop autonomously from the system in which these social actors participate. Stated otherwise, the autonomy of the Law from the preferences of even the most powerful social actors (the members of the capitalist class) is not an obstacle to, but rather a prerequisite for, the capacity of the

Law to contribute to the reproduction of the overall conditions that make capitalism possible, and thus its capacity to serve the interests of capital as a *class*. . . .

NOTES

1. Despite their obvious opposition, there is no *theoretical* difference between a Pluralist and an Instrumentalist-Marxist approach to law. Both bypass entirely the problem of the form or structure of the legal order in order to conceive it as a direct reflection of consciously articulated and organized pressures. Thus the difference between them is merely empirical: Pluralists deny that there is a systematic bias to the interplay of pressures; Instrumentalist Marxists argue that this interplay is dominated by specifically capitalist interests. For a powerful critique of Legal Pluralism, see Tushnet (1977). For an influential critique of Instrumentalist Marxism, which contributed significantly to its rejection, by now almost universal, see Poulantzas (1973). The debate between Nicos Poulantzas and Ralph Miliband, which has been carried out over the past decade in the pages of *New Left Review*, is also instructive, as is the critique of Marxist Instrumentalism developed by Claus Offe (1972), as well as the analysis of David Gold, Clarence Lo, and Erik Wright (1975).
2. Tushnet (1977) occasionally lapses into this formalist position in his otherwise excellent critique of Lawrence Friedman's Pluralist Instrumentalism.
3. Quoted in Lefebvre (1969:127).
4. Only after "working out" the homology between the commodity form and the legal form did I discover that Pashukanis had developed essentially the same analysis roughly fifty years ago! Almost all subsequent Marxist work on the law is, unfortunately, a regression from the standard established by Pashukanis's pioneering effort. The concept "mode of substitution" derives from Goux (1972).
5. The legal state, like monotheistic religion, presupposes an individual who is incapable of acting as a social being in his or her everyday life. "Political democracy is Christian in the sense that man . . . every man, is there considered a sovereign being; but it is uneducated unsocial man . . . man as he has been corrupted, lost to himself, alienated, subjected to the rule of inhuman conditions . . . by the whole organization of our society—in short man who is not *yet* a real species-being" (1972a:37).

6. Thus, as Goux (1972) has noticed, Marx argues that the monotheistic religious form, as well as the legal form, is homologous with the commodity form. "Money is . . . the god among commodities" (1973: 221).

7. In arguing that the gap between "ideals" and performance in and of itself can be delegitimating, Trubek appears to misunderstand Habermas's account of the possibilities of a "legitimation crisis." The latter requires "a questioning . . . of the norms that . . . underlie . . . action," and not merely a demonstration that these norms are violated in practice (1975:69). Habermas, on the other hand, fails to develop a theory of fetishism, proposed in the following section of this essay, which would account for why this "questioning" ordinarily does not and cannot take place.

8. *The German Ideology*, quoted in Ollman (1971:219). Ollman's conception of the State as a "value relation" was an insightful contribution to my effort to work out the homology between legal form and commodity form.

REFERENCES

Baudrillard, Jean. 1972. *Pour une Critique de l'Economie Politique du Signe*. Paris: Gallimard.

Esping-Anderson, Gosta, Roger Friedland, and Erik O. Wright. 1976. "Modes of Class Struggle and the Capitalist State," 4–5 *Kapitalistate* 186 (Summer)

Galanter, Marc. 1976. "Theories of Legalization and Delegalization." Paper presented to the Annual Convention of the American Political Science Association, Chicago, September 2–5.

Gold, David A., Clarence Y. H. Lo, and Erik Olin Wright. 1975. "Recent Developments in Marxist Theories of the Capitalist State," 27(5) *Monthly Review* 29 (October); 27(6) *Monthly Review* 36 (November).

Goux, Jean-Joseph. 1972. *Freud, Marx: Economie et Symbolique*. Paris.

Habermas, Jurgen. 1975. *Legitimation Crisis*. Boston: Beacon Press.

Lefebvre, Henri. 1966. *Le Language et la Société* Paris: Gallimard.

———. 1969. *The Sociology of Marx*. New York: Vintage Books.

Marx, Karl. 1843. *The Critique of Hegel's Philosophy of the State*, MEGA I i (1) 481.

———. 1967. *Capital*, vol. I. New York: International Publishers.

———. 1968. "Critique of the Gotha Program," in *Karl Marx and Frederick Engels, Selected Works*, vol. I New York: New World Paperbacks.

———. 1972a. "On the Jewish Question," in Robert C. Tucker (ed.) *The Marx-Engels Reader*. New York: Norton.

———. 1972b. "The German Ideology," in Robert C. Tucker (ed.) *The Marx-Engels Reader*. New York: Norton.

———. 1973. *Grundrisse: Foundation of the Critique of Political Economy*. Translated by Martin Nicolaus. Harmondsworth, England: Penguin Books.

Offe, Claus. 1972. *Class Rule and the Political System: On the Selectiveness of Political Institutions*. Unpublished.

———. 1973. "The Abolition of Market Control and the Problem of Legitimacy," 1 *Kapitalistate* 109; 2 *Kapitalistate* 73.

Ollman, Bertell. 1971. *Alienation: Marx's Conception of Man in Capitalist Society*. Cambridge: Cambridge University Press.

Pashukanis, E. B. 1951. "The General Theory of Law and Marxism," in Hugh W. Babb (trans. and ed.) *Soviet Legal Philosophy*. Cambridge, Mass: Harvard University Press.

Poulantzas, Nicos. 1973. "The Problem of the Capitalist State," in Robin Blackburn (ed.) *Ideology in Social Science*. New York: Vintage Books.

Trubek, David M. 1972. "Max Weber on Law and the Rise of Capitalism," [1972] *Wisconsin Law Review* 720.

Tushnet, Mark. 1977. "Perspectives on the Development of American Law: A Critical Review of Friedman's 'History of American Law,'" [1977(1)] *Wisconsin Law Review* (forthcoming).

The Place of Law in the Marxian Structure-Superstructure Archetype

Alan Stone

IV. Structure and Superstructure

The starting point for any Marxist conception that seeks to relate law to the economic structure of society is Marx's famous 1859 Preface to *The Critique of Political Economy*, in which he stated:

> In the social production which men carry on they enter into definite relations that are indispensable and independent of their will. These relations of production correspond to a definite stage of development of their material powers of production. The sum total of these relations of production constitutes the economic structure of society—the real foundation, on which rise legal and political superstructures and to which correspond definite forms of social consciousness. The mode of production in material life determines the general character of the social, political and spiritual processes of life. It is not the consciousness of men that determines their existence, but, on the contrary, their social existence determines their consciousness (Marx, 1911: 11, 12).

Some preliminary observations are in order. First, as the above quotation indicates, the term "superstructure" includes a wide range of human activities—indeed, virtually every facet of life not specifically located in economic production; that is, every facet of life except "the totality of the operations aimed at procuring for a society its material means of existence" (Godelier, 1976:60). Thus, superstructure includes the beliefs of persons operating within a given society, cultural artifacts such as works of art, and the institutional rules such as laws that guide conduct within a society. It is fair to ask whether Marx's claim here is that the mode of production can be shown to determine religious preferences, styles of music, and the particular laws governing domestic relations in some direct, mechanical manner. If so, the wide variety of cultural, religious, intellectual, and other differences among contemporary capitalist societies would require us to reject Marx's hypothesis out of hand, "for such a position implies that the economic base is ultimately (if not immediately) self-sufficient and that its spontaneous development is the sole determinant of social evolution" (Jessop, 1982:11).

This simplistic view (known as economism) was common among many prominent Marxists in the period following the death of Engels in 1895 and for this reason has been attributed by some to Marx and Engels. But, as we will see, a very different construction of the language is possible.

Second, the quoted language in the above text appears to be inconsistent with other Marx-Engels texts insofar as it applies to law, and it is even inconsistent with other language in the 1859 Preface. Later in the same paragraph Marx asserts: "At a certain stage of their development, the material forces of production in society come in conflict with the existing relations of production or—*what is but a legal expression for the same thing*—with the property relations within which they had been at work before" (1911:12; emphasis added). Some scholars, comparing the two quoted portions of the 1859 Preface, have suggested a confusing and, perhaps, inconsistent dualism (Tushnet, 1983:281; Plamenatz, 1955:30, 31). Is property law part of the superstructure and consequently an effect of the economic structure, or is it simply a "legal expression" of the economic structure? While one must admit that the text is ambiguous, a closer examination of this and other Marx-Engels texts, together with the introduction of certain additional concepts, can clarify the apparent ambiguity and, more importantly, provide a framework that reveals connections between the law and economy that make for an underlying unity in the law of capitalist states.

How can one reconcile language that suggests a "legal expression" is synonymous with a part of the "economic structure" with language that suggests that all elements of the superstructure are separate from and somehow caused or shaped by the "economic structure"? Some Marxists have thrown away the dichotomy as it applies to law, claiming it is untenable (Thompson, 1975:261). To do so implies that Marx and Engels were intellectually confused not only in the Preface to the *Critique of Political Economy* but in many other places as well. Indeed, the structure-superstructure dichotomy is one of the cornerstones of both the Marxist view of society in stasis and the Marxist conception of historical change. As O'Hagan has observed, the dichotomy is critical to Marxism for several reasons. The superstructure helps to "maintain a stable system in which power over production and enjoyment of products is thus unequally allocated.... [Superstructures] ... impose a level of unity, cohesion and integration 'over and above' the disunited and indeed antagonistic interests of the classes composing the society" (O'Hagan, 1981:86). They both present particular interests as the general interests of society and provide sets of enforceable rules.

It is possible to reconcile the apparently inconsistent formulations on law when we turn from the rather compressed Preface to other texts

which suggest that the notion of legal superstructure contains two quite distinct, but related, concepts. In his 1888 essay, "Ludwig Feuerbach and the End of Classical German Philosophy," Engels distinguishes "essential legal relations" from the law (or judicial practice). The former phrase embraces those essential legal conceptions that are central to a capitalist economic order, such as property, contract, and credit. Essential legal relations must be distinguished from the particular laws that are based upon them (Engels, 1959:235, 236). Thus, the underlying notion of credit must be distinguished from the particular provisions of the Uniform Commercial Code, and the underlying concept of property must be distinguished from local landlord-tenant laws.

Although they employ different terminology, other Marx and Engels texts supply further support for this interpretation. *The German Ideology* of 1845–46 provides several such examples:

> Private property is a form of intercourse necessary for certain stages of development of the productive forces; a form of intercourse that ... cannot be dispensed with in the production of actual [capitalist] material life ... Because property ... as in all epochs is bound up with definite conditions, first of all economic, which depend on the degree of development of the productive forces and intercourse—conditions which inevitably acquire a legal and political expression (Marx and Engels, 1976:355, 356).

While not very artfully framed, the ideas are akin to those of Engels quoted above. The forms of intercourse (or essential legal relations) are integrally connected with the economic system; these in turn give rise to particular legal and political rules and institutions. Elsewhere in *The German Ideology* Marx and Engels refer to the "productive forces and ... the intercourse corresponding to these" as conditioning particular conceptions, laws, etc. (1976:36). Again, "All [production] relations can be expressed in language only in the form of concepts.... These general ideas and concepts are looked upon as mysterious forces ... [and] are further elaborated and given a special significance by politicians and lawyers" (1976:363).

In exploring the distinction between production relations and the concepts that refer to them, I will use the method employed by Marx in developing his structure of capitalism—the method of abstraction (Marx, 1973:100–108). Marx began by provisionally assuming away all social relations except those that he viewed as fundamental (capital and labor), developing abstract categories that were intended to elucidate the fundamentals of that relationship, and then gradually reintroducing other relationships and facts (Sweezy, 1942: 11–20). My approach is the same.

I begin with "essential legal relations," by which I mean the legal relations that mirror and legally define the fundamental economic relationships in a society. In a capitalist society these would include property and contract. Thus, one must employ these essential legal relations to comprehend the commercial, industrial, and employment relationships of a capitalist society—any capitalist society. As we will see, the concept of essential legal relations facilitates the understanding of linkages between the economy, on the one hand, and such lower order legal concepts as lease or easement as well as particular legal rules and decisions, on the other. And while one must be alert to the danger of reifying such essential legal relations as contract or property, one must be equally alert to the danger of disregarding the subjective content of action which is ordinarily expressed in conceptual terms. These concepts are parts of actors' meanings as they undertake action; they are not simply categories imposed by an observer (Weber, 1977:109–15).

The concept of essential legal relations also addresses one of the criticisms raised by Kamenka in his review of Marxist discussions of the law. He criticizes the incapacity of many Marxists to distinguish laws that are central to a legal system from laws that could be changed tomorrow without affecting the character of the legal system (or economic system, one may add) (Kamenka, 1981:476). In other words, not all laws and legal concepts—even in such areas as contract or property—are of equal importance. The question is which are most fundamental. We will see that, starting from the concept of essential legal relations, it is possible to structure legal concepts and rules in order of importance despite the mass of particulars. First, however, we must examine the concept of essential legal relations, beginning with a discussion of the economic base—in this case capitalism.

V. Capitalism and Essential Legal Relations: Property and Contract

The term "capitalism" is traceable to nineteenth-century socialist theoreticians, of whom Marx was the most important. Although Marx did not attempt to fully define the term, his writings form the basis for a broad consensus on the essential characteristics of capitalism. The most important of these characteristics, according to Marx, is that "the owner of the means of production . . . finds the free worker available, on the market, as the seller of his own labor" (Marx, 1977:274). These relations give rise to one class that owns the means of productions, including factories, mines, mills, raw materials, and machines, and another class that sells its labor power to the former in a free market. This relationship between classes is to be distinguished from one in which one class legally controls the persons of others for laboring purposes (slavery), or in which certain obligations (or mechanisms for remission) are owed from one to another as a result of tradition or status (feudalism), as well as from many other sorts of arrangements.

Capitalism, as Marx conceived it, is inescapably tied to certain ideas and arrangements that are realized in and guaranteed by law. The first of these is contract. The essence of a contract consists of a promise by one party to do something in return for a specific act or promise on the part of another party. It is a voluntary arrangement, "freely" entered into by both parties, and so stands in sharp contrast to obligations owed as a result of either one's status or enslaved condition. The relationships between the capitalist and the laborer, seller and buyer, and creditor and bor-rower are contractual at their core. A prerequisite for capitalism in the realm of the labor bargain as well as in other areas of commercial life is the recognition and enforceability of contracts by the state.

The second distinguishing feature of capital-ism that cannot thrive without law is the private *ownership* of the means of production. Prior to the sixteenth century in Britain and elsewhere, the notion of property was quite different from the one developed in conjunction with capitalism. The feudal concept of "property" embodied both common and private property, a sense of social obligation requiring the performance of duties, and a sense of stewardship in the use of person-ality and land. But with the coming of capitalism, the idea of a communal interest in property with-ered away, as did the senses of stewardship and social obligation (Larkin, 1969: Chs. 1 and 2). Under capitalism "property is equated with pri-vate property—the right of a natural or artificial person to exclude others from some use or benefit of something. . . . Whereas in pre-capitalist soci-ety a man's property had generally been seen as a right to a revenue, with capitalism property comes to be seen as a right in or to material things" (MacPherson, 1975:105). The conceptual change is reflected in the fact that property became more freely alienable and open to more uses, with the principal restrictions on the use of property being those assumed by contractual agreement and those imposed by the obligation not to interfere with other property owners in the enjoyment of their rights (Holdsworth, 1946:105).

The essential legal relations of contract and property came to cover more and more of the social relationships in evolving capitalist society. As Marx observed, "Whenever, through the de-velopment of industry and commerce, new forms of intercourse have been evolved (e.g., insurance companies, etc.) the law has always been com-pelled to admit them among the modes of acquir-ing property" (Marx and Engels, 1976:92). To which we might add that they are also subject to the contract relationship. Thus, stock certificates, commodities futures, options, and an array of other devices employed in commerce and industry have come to be embraced within the essential legal relations of contract and property. These are, in Habermas' terminology, "necessary to con-stitute the mode of production and maintain it" (Habermas, 1973:53). Their usefulness in order-ing the many kinds of activities and transactions that help establish the economic foundations of capitalism renders them essential to the system.

VI. Capitalism and Essential Legal Relations: Credit and Combination

But capitalism requires still more. Specifically, cap-italism requires credit and the capacity to enlarge capital by combining with other sources of wealth. Credit and combination, both contractual rela-tionships, are essential legal relations that enable capitalism to expand.

Most production in a capitalist society is not for the personal use of the producers but is instead for sale at a profit. The capitalist engages in the processes of manufacture, distribution, and sale to turn a profit. In Marx's direct language, the pro-duction of goods simply for their utility "must therefore never be treated as the immediate aim of the capitalist; nor must the profit on any single transaction. His aim is rather the unceasing move-ment of profit-making" (Marx, 1977:254). There are two important aspects to this description. First, the capitalist is interested in the continual repetition of the profit cycle and not simply in a single instance of profit-making. General Motors does not seek to sell its 1985 automobiles so that is can distribute the proceeds to its employees and shareholders and then exit from business. Rather, it arranges its activities so that it can produce and sell its products in continuous cycles of profitabil-ity, symbolized by Marx's "M-C-M'." The capi-talist uses money (M) to purchase commodities such as labor power, raw materials, machines, and the like (C), intending the cycle to result in more money than the amount originally expended (M'). And the cycle repeats.

Credit, as Veblen noted, may be divided into two subcategories: "(a) that of deferred payments in the purchase and sale of goods . . . and (b) loans or debts . . ." (Veblen, 1932:49). The need for credit follows from the M-C-M' cycle, with its goal of ever-increasing profits. Unless credit is employed in the M-C part of the cycle, barter and available cash constitute the only means of payments, sharply limiting profit-making opportunities. Credit also aids those with profit-making potential who do not have immediate access to the resources needed to realize this potential. Most directly, credit can increase the size of M, allowing more commodities (C) to be purchased in any particular cycle, with the concomitant potential of an M' of greater magnitude. Credit also aids the unceasing quest for profit-making since it can speed up each cycle by providing money for additional investments before earlier investments have been fully paid off.

In short, the *unceasing* pursuit of profit-making requires the establishment and development of a credit system for a variety of reasons. Credit, then, constitutes a third essential legal relation, and with the rise of capitalism became a regular institution of economic life rather than the exceptional phenomenon it had been (Mandel, 1968:217).

For many of the same reasons, combining with others is central to capitalism. The institution of contract allows one to reach an agreement not only with an adversary (e.g., buyer-seller or capitalist-employee) but also with those who share an interest in collaboration. Both types of combination are important, but the former is defined almost entirely by contractual agreement, while the latter, although rooted in contract, extends beyond it. Indeed, Coase (1937) has shown that the organizing authority and integrative activity of a business firm reduce the costs of negotiating and entering into many individual contracts, while Williamson (1975) suggests that the complete absorption of one business organization by another, the ultimate in combination, is a way to avoid the uncertainties of contractual relationships.

Because of the enhancement of capital, skill, and market power that combinations allow, it is natural in capitalism to seek allies in the pursuit of greater wealth. One special form of combination, the investment stock company, dramatically expands the ability of people to participate in the ownership of the means of production and provides the capitalist a means of greatly enhancing the available resources. Of course, combinations such as guilds, religious orders, monasteries, and towns existed in the pre-capitalist era (Davis, 1961: Chs. III and IV; Carr, 1909:161, 162). Indeed, these earlier forms of combination supplied many of the key ideas essential to combinations that arose under capitalism, including perpetual succession and management by elected representatives (Kramer, 1928). Nevertheless, these early forms of combination had characteristics antithetical to those that make the later forms part of the essential legal relations of combination under capitalism. Early corporate forms were rife with: (1) restrictions on which activities could be pursued, (2) membership qualifications, (3) training requirements, and (4) restrictions on the ability of members to deal with nonmembers (Scott, 1951:1–6).

Thus, the idea of essential legal relations, which, I argue, is the starting point in understanding Marx and Engels' theory of the relationship between economic structure and the superstructures, refers to the legal expressions or images of the central components of the capitalist economic structure. The essential legal relations pervade subsidiary concepts (i.e., sale or mortgage) as well as other aspects of the legal order. For example, many crimes (burglary, robbery, fraud, etc.) and torts (trespass, strict liability) are premised upon the essential legal relations in that concepts like contract and property are essential to an understanding of what is wrongful about these acts. Similarly, other legal rules may modify or erode essential legal relations (such as environmental regulations or minimum wage laws). Notwithstanding these tensions, which constitute much of the politics of modern capitalist societies (and which I discuss later), the fundamentals of essential legal relations remain. For otherwise capitalism as a system could not survive. This is true almost as a matter of definition. The economic and legal concepts are that close.

VII. The Structure of Hierarchy

In seeking to understand the Marxian conception of structure-superstructure and the law's place within it, it is important to note first that there are many segments of the superstructure (philosophy, religion, culture, law, politics). While it is appropriate for some purposes to distinguish between structure and superstructure as two separate and distinctive spheres, such a sharp bifurcation obscures linkages. Although essential legal relations are in one sense superstructure, in another sense they are the reflection of structure ("a legal expression" for "relations of production"). As such they can be linked not only to the structure but also to other elements of the superstructure, such as the arts and politics, and to less essential aspects of the legal culture, such as decisions in particular cases. In all cases the linkages are hierarchical, for superstructural elements and their included aspects may be conceived of as relatively further from the structure or nearer to it. We determine the "distance" from the structure by the number of intermediate links and the centrality of the particular superstructural segment or included aspect to the functioning of the base.

To take a simple example, high culture is far less critical to the functioning of the economic base than are essential legal relations. Capitalism can function effectively under a wide variety of cultural arrangements without significantly impeding its daily operations, but a breakdown of such essential legal relations as property or contract will destroy the basis for fundamental capitalist operations. Similarly, capitalism can accommodate its operations to a variety of specific laws on a particular subject, but the range of acceptable variations in essential legal relations is far more limited. Certainly, Marx in giving preeminence to the structure meant no more than that the productive state and social relations of society influence or color the activities in distant areas of superstructures, such as the artistic aspects of culture (Marx, 1973:110,111). A particular violinist, for example, may accept, reject, or be indifferent to the mode of production with virtually no effect on the health of the capitalist system. It is perhaps true that the mode of production may ultimately frame his or her discourse, experience, and understanding but if so, it allows for a wide range of thought and behavior that can be exhibited within the system's constraints. This room for human discretion applies to other superstructural segments (including law) as well.[1]

Let us return now to the Preface, which *apparently* stated that the legal supersturcture is determined by the structure but also told us that property relations are but the legal expression of the relations of production. The key to clearing up the apparent inconsistency is understanding that Marx was referring to different things. In the first instance he was speaking about the legal superstructure, while in the second instance the reference was to the essential legal relations to which the legal superstructure is linked. The apparent confusion, as G. A. Cohen acutely observes, stems from the fact that there was simply "no attractive alternative" to describing production relations except in legal terms (Cohen, 1978:224, 230). Cohen goes on to note that the economic system requires a specified, orderly set of essential legal relations in order to function and maintain itself on a continuing basis. The economic structure and essential legal relations are connected without intermediation. In that way essential legal relations are but an expression of the economic structure, even though they are at the same time part of one of the superstructural segments. A person undertaking an act, such as entering into a business contract, may simultaneously experience the process as an economic, legal, ideological, and perhaps even religious activity, but while structure and superstructure are thus simultaneously cojoined, they are also separate since the objective institutions, associative relationships, and legitimation structures of each segment are different (Godelier, 1976:62, 64; Weber, 1968: Pt. 1 Chs. I and II).[2]

VIII. Mediation and Derivative Subrelations

Our next task is to move from essential legal relations to the particulars of legal decision-making. This will be done in two steps. The first is to show how particular decisions and doctrines are derived from essential legal relations. The second is to show how public law and judicial rulings that conflict with the accumulation interests of the capitalist class fit in.

Engels has written:

> Still higher ideologies, that is, such as are still further removed from the material economic basis, take the form of philosophy and religion. Here the interconnection between conceptions and their material conditions of existence becomes more and more complicated, more and more obscured by intermediate links. But the interconnection exists (Engels, 1959:237).

Implicit in this statement is the idea that if we are to understand the "higher ideologies," we must attend to the intermediate links. An important set of links may, consistent with Marx's scheme, be called "derivative subrelations." In the legal sphere the derivative subrelations are legal conceptions that fall between essential legal relations and particular rules. Thus, property is an essential legal relation. Under it are such derivative subrelations as easement, lease, and the like. Derivative subrelations of credit include security, bankruptcy, lien, etc. From these derivative subrelations flow particular legal rules and further subrelations. In both cases distance from the economic structure is a function of the number and quality of mediating subrelations.[3] For example, assignment is a derivative subrelation under contract, but delegation of performance is a derivative subrelation under assignment in descending order from the structure. Particular legal rules (i.e., where personal performance is required under a contract, a substitute's performance does not discharge the contractor's duty), in turn, flow from the lower derivative subrelations.

One merit of this view is that it accords with the manner in which the Anglo-American judicial system works. Essential legal relations, the expression of economic structure, give rise to derivative subrelations. Courts, confronted with particular matters, accept the essential legal relation, consider the functions and purposes of the derivative subrelation, and then seek to render a best decision consistent with the derivative subrelation's principal function. Since there is room for differences in judgment in this process, different courts can adopt different particular rules. . . . Moreover, this dynamic accords with the differences that exist in human behavior. Judges are not omniscient. They can be stupid or wrong, just as they can be farsighted and brilliant. They are not constrained by a "dominant ideology" or by more direct influences of economic interests to reach those specific decisions that will *best* constitute and maintain the mode of production. And the system for its part can tolerate suboptimal and even occasionally antagonistic decisions at the case level.

This system of transmission from economic structure to the decisions of individual judges shows a structure of causation that is, at once, complex and flexible yet constraining. The fundamentals—essential legal relations—are set and nearly universally accepted, part of the "taken for granted" social order.[4] If they should become widely questioned, this would indicate that the economic structure itself is being widely questioned. From these essential legal relations, judicial and legislative officials seek to derive consistent subrelations to meet particular problems or resolve particular cases. So long as the essential legal relations are taken as the starting point, those actors who create the derivative subrelations and the particular legal rules under them will develop a jurisprudence compatible with the structurally defined system although they act neither conspiratorially nor consciously on behalf of a class or ruling group.

Not only can the system allow creative and flexible decision-making within the framework set by the essential legal relations, but it can also tolerate the mistakes, the inefficiencies, and the conscious or unconscious attempts at subversion that are inevitable when decisions are entrusted to a multitude of variously motivated human agents. For example, the developing law of business corporations in nineteenth-century America displayed many twists and turns before ultimately abandoning size limitations, restrictions on indebtedness and the consideration for which stock may be given, and other provisions that limited corporate growth and capital accumulation. Despite these restraints and inefficiencies, the system was nevertheless capitalist, and eventually the principles of liberal general incorporation were reached (Dodd, 1936:38). Similarly, as Engels observed, the different ways in which legal rules from older societies are adapted to capitalist ones can result in more or less efficient coordination between the structure and legal superstructure (Engels, 1959: 235, 236; Hall, 1977:57, 58).

To summarize thus far, paying attention to the Marxian idea of structure and superstructure allows us to understand how the economic structure and the activities of judicial decision-makers are linked to the making of specific decisions that constitute and maintain the mode of production. Linkages move along the following path:

structure

▼

essential legal relations

▼

derivative subrelations

▼

particular rules

This does not mean that particular rules may not alter or modify derivative subrelations, for they may. But most legal activity occurs in a routinized pattern in which the category hierarchically above is not questioned. A judge rendering a decision on a question of negotiable instruments does not ordinarily challenge the derivative subrelation of negotiability and will certainly not question the essential legal relation of contract. Thus, without resorting to crude instrumentalism, this construction shows how legal agents act to support capitalist social relations, and at the same time it accords with the manner in which legal

decisions are made. Moreover, it allows us to detect signals indicating that the mode of production is being seriously challenged. When an economy's essential legal relations are openly challenged, we know that this is the case.

Such a challenge occurs when the "justice" of the allocative biases inherent in essential legal relations is subject to question. The conception of contract, for example, includes the notions that people are "free" to enter into them and that, with only certain exceptions, the terms arranged by the parties must not be upset by courts. An alternative ethic which is inimical to the capitalist system would have the state determine the "correct" terms for every bargain in the context of some theory of distributive justice. Similarly, as G. A. Cohen argues, the implicit claim of the property system that it is just and proper may be challenged. "Now every actual piece of private property . . . either is or is made of something which was once the private property of no one. . . . We must ask, apart from how he in particular got it, how the thing came to be (anyone's) private property in the first place, and examine the justice of that transformation" (Cohen, 1981:15).

But, while philosophers may sometimes ponder such questions, this is generally not done in the real world. Ordinarily, legal actors accept the underlying notions contained within essential legal relations in much the same way that table manners are accepted and employed, without rationally considering them or demanding moral justifications. In this way, through biases built into the very concepts with which the law works, essential legal relations *help* to establish and maintain social conformity as well as what Antonio Gramsci termed "social hegemony"—ruling group homogeneity in the face of a diversity of particular societal interests (Gramsci, 1971:12, 13, 146, 195, 247, 261; Sumner, 1979:256, 257).

IX. Public Law and Social Conflict

Now that I have shown how particular decisions and doctrines are derived from essential legal relations, it is time to turn to public law and rules in apparent conflict with the accumulation interests of the capitalist class. The sequence of discussion is intended to follow Marx's method of abstraction, starting from the most fundamental aspects of capitalist law and incorporating other aspects of the capitalist legal system in steps. For this reason I started with activities in the realm of private law that help maintain the economic system. The next step is to incorporate public law into the analysis.

I begin with the observation that capitalist societies have proved remarkably flexible and adaptive. Innumerable rules and changes over time have occurred in every capitalist society. The law of America or England that prevails in the 1980s is obviously different from prevailing law in those nations 50 or 100 years before. Nevertheless, the essential legal relations and most derivative subrelations have persisted. The problem, then, is to show how the ideas developed thus far can embrace such change and the constant core. This task requires us to examine public law and politics in capitalist society. In doing so, we must confront the fact that many rules in the modern state conflict with the direct interests of the capitalist class. Nor can we take comfort in the thesis suggested by some that every rule in apparent conflict with capitalist interests is nothing more than a concession by the capitalist class designed to assure the quiescence of their enemies. Like the crude instrumentalism that preceded it, this perspective is contradicted by a fair look at the contents and operations of modern capitalist legal systems.

Let us start with a modified reiteration of Pashukanis' view that much of the law in a capitalist society is a reflection of generalized commodity exchange, which presupposes an atomized economy of individual units engaged in trading transactions with other units (Pashukanis, 1978: 85, 93–97). An economy of this sort is characterized by legal relations between individuals involving, for example, A entering into a contract with B and then perhaps suing B for a breach of that contract. A and B may be two businessmen, buyer and seller, employer and employee, or virtually any other pair of contracting parties. The abstractness of the essential legal relationship of

contract can embrace any relationship with adverse interests, as Pashukanis observes. But just as the law both facilitates and is shaped by the pursuit of individual gain, which is inherent in a capitalist society, so too it can facilitate and be shaped by collaborative efforts directed toward the same goal. A and B might, for example, enter into a partnership and together contract with C to purchase goods for less than either could have purchased them alone or, without contracting, they might agree not to compete in the same market. The two-person case, whether it involves a contract or not, can, of course, be extended to almost any number of similarly situated individuals who perceive that their well-being will be enhanced by extended collaborative efforts; for example, a trade association or a cooperative research venture.

Such collaboration produces interest groups, which are based upon the divisions in a capitalist society. Bukharin has outlined a number of dimensions along which divisions exist that commonly give rise to such groups. These include: (1) *size* (big business and small business), (2) *policy interest* (importers and exporters), (3) *vocation* (financiers and industrialists), (4) *industry* (insurance and commercial banking), (5) *firm* (AT&T and IBM.). *Intermediate classes* (such as managers, bureaucrats, and professionals), *transitional classes* (remnants of old orders), and *déclassé groups* outside the structure of production, distribution, and exchange may develop joint interests at variance with the interests of other groups (Bukharin, 1965: 276–92). Some of these divisions are more likely to be within classes than between them. Nor is the working class exempt from interest group fragmentation. For example, Marx expected the savings bank, designed to promote working-class saving and thrift, to "lead to a split between that portion of the working class which takes part in the savings banks and the portion which does not" (Marx, 1976:427). But ties to the economic system, through savings bank deposits or other links, are not the only bases on which working-class divisions may arise. The Marxian framework can extend to the range of intraclass divisions that occur in real life, whether based on race, sex, religion, neighborhood, or some other dividing dimension. Nor is it surprising, given a Marxian framework, to find that group life mirrors the self-seeking life of the individual, for whom essential legal relations generate the central rules for the allocation of resources.

Groups, like individuals, may use the devices of private law to attain their ends. The collective bargaining agreement is a contract, just as is an individually negotiated wage agreement, and groups have the same control over their property as individuals have over theirs. In addition, groups, unlike individuals, are often able to induce the state to reallocate resources to them through legislation and/or administrative action. Indeed, groups often form for just this purpose. Thus, both public and private law are potential ways of advancing wealth in a capitalist society.[5]

Public law, then, under capitalism is usually not a reflection of class divisions, although some public laws such as labor legislation or those governing the distribution of the tax burden may be. More typically, interest groups representing segments of classes employ available processes before courts, legislatures, and administrative decision-makers to gain advantages over other interest groups. For example, the history of federal and state banking legislation in this country is a history of conflict, victory, failure, and compromise among local, regional, and national commercial banks, credit unions, investment banks, etc. There can be many outcomes of such battles, and it is impossible in a few sentences to present a full-scale theory that explains the variety of outcomes in the numerous public policy areas in which such conflicts arise.

Several observations, however, are in order. First, in the name of the "public interest," laws can be enacted to fulfill any of the functions described by Habermas. For example, laws affecting monetary policy can be enacted to promote the economy. Such laws can originate from either interest group activity or the public-spiritedness of public officials. Second, groups from the economically dominant class in competition with other segments of the dominant class can ally themselves with groups from other classes, to whom concessions will have to be made. For example, domestic automobile companies and the automobile workers' union may align themselves against automobile importers. Finally, it is entirely possible in a democracy for groups representing segments of inferior classes to prevail frequently in their battles with segments of the dominant classes. Divisions within the dominant class, its relative lack of concern about a subject, the threat of cost-imposing lower-class actions (such as strikes) are among the factors that can lead to this result. Yet even such defeats are consistent with capitalist domination so long as the fundamental legal relations are not challenged.

Consider utility regulation as an example. Public utilities enter into large numbers of contracts with their subscribers, who are "free" to reject the service and provide alternatives (such as a solar home heating system). Sometimes a utility can offer various grades of service from which users can select. In these respects, the contract device remains intact and the essential legal relations remain unquestioned; contracts are honored and the utility's ownership of its property is not challenged. However, a utility is often an area's sole supplier of an essential service and so is in a position to extract monopoly profits. To forestall this, consumers, including other powerful capitalist interests, demand legal protection. The usual solution is a law establishing a public utility commission. Such commissions are usually given the power to affect the *terms* of the contract or the *uses* of the utility's property, but they cannot destroy or transform the essential legal relations themselves. In other words, the regulations limit the discretion of individuals or groups to make certain choices in employing essential legal relations, derivative sub-relations, and particular rules. These restrictions may be relatively tight, such as the requirement that a particular rate should be charged, or they may be relatively loose, such as the Federal Trade Commission's prohibition against false advertising, which precludes certain kinds of misleading messages without specifying what must be said. Whatever the restrictions, however, the essential legal relations are at their core respected, and those aspects of the legal superstructure that are isomorphic with elements of the economic base remain to foster the accumulation of wealth under capitalism even if the segment of the capitalist class that controls public utilities cannot take full advantage of the subrelations ordinarily derived from them.

Indeed, freedom to contract or deal with property has never been absolute. There have been illegal or unenforceable contracts and limitations on the use of property for as long as these legal concepts have existed. But the fact that there are rules, exceptions to the rules, limitations, and exceptions to the exceptions does not negate the conclusion that a capitalist society's fundamental operations are based upon a chain that leads from structure through essential legal relations to particular rules. This is the glue that holds a capitalist society together. Various interest groups are able to change aspects of their positions through the legal institutions the state provides. Sometimes these efforts focus on public law and at other times private law is used to establish particular rules or decisions. The outcomes of such efforts may make the mode of production more efficient, or they may make it less efficient. They may represent the effective actions of one group or another (Habermas, 1973:53, 54). Each effort requires separate investigation, but they all operate within a framework of essential legal relations.

We have already seen that these essential legal relations, although part of the legal superstructure, express core economic relations. It is also important to note that they are incorporated into the political superstructure as well. While an analysis of the capitalist state is beyond the scope of this article, it follows from our discussion of essential legal relations that if they are embedded in the political superstructure, the state in a capitalist society is a state of the capitalist class, even when the class loses important political and legal battles to others. The essential legal relations under capitalism, inconsistently but on balance, serve to protect and further an unequal allocation of resources in society. A challenge to the

essential legal relations means that the economic order is being fundamentally attacked.

NOTES

1. The capitalist structure, because of its individualistic competitive base, may allow substantially more room for discretion than other economic structures. For example, to hold people to a feudal economic system may require far greater constraints in other superstructural segments to maintain the legitimacy of the order than those required by capitalism.

2. Contrast the construction that Collins offers in his admirable book. Addressing the constitutive problem (law as a reflection of structure, yet superstructure), Collins argues that legal rules "subsume existing customs leaving them redundant as guides to correct behavior" (Collins, 1982: 88). The customs, in turn, originate in the practices necessary to the mode of production and the mechanisms needed to control deviance. The content of the law, Collins goes on, is thus superstructural because it is determined by the "dominant ideology as it is represented in customary standards of behavior," but it is also part of the structure "to the extent of being the sole institution giving [relations of production] concrete form and detailed articulations. Thus law is superstructural in origin but because of its metanormative quality it then may function in the material base" (1982:88, 89). Collins' argument, although solving the constitutive problem on a theoretical plane, leaves too much unresolved. The idea of a "dominant ideology" does not help us to specify doctrines and laws for examination, whereas the concept of essential legal relations does. Moreover, although Collins' view concedes a hierarchy and elaboration of law, the concept of "dominant ideology" provides no guidance about how to organize such a structure. The concept of essential legal relations, as I shall show shortly, does. Furthermore, merely giving the concept of dominant ideology a central role does not help elucidate the linkages between the economic structure and daily judicial and administrative decisions. Nor does it help us to understand how ideas in conflict with the dominant ideology, like environmentalism, arise, and how these ideas are translated into legal rules. As we will see in the discussion of public law below, the concept of essential legal relations helps us to place such laws in the context of a capitalist legal order.

3. I do not wish to be understood as saying that distance is *necessarily* inversely related to importance to the structure. It is entirely consistent with my formulation that a change in something distant from the economic structure can have a major impact on the structure. For this reason I use the word "quality" in the above sentence.

4. The processes by which the fundamentals are taken for granted are complex and would require a separate paper to explore fully. Here I shall simply mention some of the important considerations. First, the essential legal relations are encountered as part of our early socialization in much the same way that table manners, habits of dress, and so on are inculcated. An adult settling a dispute between two children battling over a toy will reward it to one of them, announcing that it "belongs to X." The word "property" is not used, but the concept and attributes are (Levi-Strauss, 1967:19). Such instruction continues onward from childhood through adulthood, and in most cases the essential legal relations become ingrained. Second, a capitalist society invests considerable effort in developing a coherent ideology regarding the importance and fairness of the essential legal relations. Courts, law schools, and the elites in these and other institutions exert pressures and guide others to work with (i.e., accept) the essential legal relations. Finally, we should not underestimate the high costs of replacing the essential legal relations with others. Most people are unwilling to incur the effort required to supplant existing essential legal relations.

5. To treat private law as if it were completely eclipsed by public law in the day-to-day workings of a capitalist society, as some scholars have done (Tushnet, 1978:99; Fraser, 1978:167), is to seriously distort the larger picture. Indeed, most of a capitalist society's daily transactions, such as sales, are covered by the mundane common law rules of the private law. To suggest, as Fraser (1978) does, that corporatism, consisting of a grand alliance of government agencies, trade unions, and corporate organizations, has destroyed private autonomy is seriously misleading.

REFERENCES

Adler, Max. 1978. "Ideology as Appearance," in T. Bottomore and P. Goode (eds.) *Austro-Marxism.* Oxford: Clarendon Press.

Beirne, Piers and Richard Quinney (eds.). 1982. *Marxism and Law.* New York: John Wiley.

Bottomore, Tom. 1978. "Introduction," in T. Bottomore and P. Goode (eds.), *Austro-Marxism.* Oxford: Clarendon Press.

Bukharin, Nikolai. 1965. *Historical Materialism.* New York: Russell & Russell.

Cain, Maureen and Alan Hunt (eds.). 1979. *Marx and Engels on Law.* New York: Academic Press.

Carr, Cecil Thomas. 1909. "Early Forms of Corporateness," in Association of American Law Schools (eds.), *Select Essays in Anglo-American Legal History,* Vol. 3. Boston: Little, Brown.

Coase, R. H. 1937. "The Nature of the Firm," 4 *Economica (New Series)* 386.

Cohen, G. A. 1978. *Karl Marx's Theory of History.* Princeton: Princeton University Press.

———. 1981. "Freedom, Justice and Capitalism," 126 *New Left Review* 3.

Collins, Hugh. 1982. *Marxism and Law.* New York: Oxford University Press.

Davis, John P. 1961. *Corporations.* New York: Capricorn Books.

Dodd, E. Merrick. 1936. "Statutory Developments in Business Corporation Law, 1886–1936," 50 *Harvard Law Review* 27.

Engels, Frederick. 1959. "Ludwig Feuerbach and the End of Classical German Philosophy," in L. S. Feuer (ed.), *Marx and Engels: Basic Writings on Politics and Philosophy.* Garden City, NY: Anchor Books.

Fraser, Andrew. 1976. "Legal Theory and Legal Practice," 44 Arena 123.

———. 1978. "The Legal Theory We Need Now," 40 *Socialist Review* 147.

Godelier, Maurice. 1976. "The Object and Method of Economic Anthropology," in D. Seddon (ed.), *Relations of Production.* London: Frank Cass.

Gordon, Robert W. 1980. "Review: Freyer's *Forums of Order,*" 54 *Business History Review* 223.

Gramsci, Antonio. 1971. *Selections from the Prison Notebooks.* New York: International Publishers.

Habermas, Jurgen. 1973. *Legitimation Crisis.* Boston: Beacon Press.

Hall, Stuart. 1977. "Rethinking the Base and Superstructure Metaphor," in J. Bloomfield (ed.), *Class, Hegemony and Party.* London: Lawrence & Wishart.

Holdsworth, William. 1946. *Essays in Law and History.* Oxford: Clarendon Press.

Jessop, Bob. 1982. *The Capitalist State.* New York: New York University Press.

Kamenka, Eugene. 1981. "Demythologizing the Law," *Times Literary Supplement* 475 (May 1).

Kramer, Stella. 1928. *The English Craft Gilds.* Oxford: Oxford University Press.

Larkin, Paschal. 1969. *Property in the Eighteenth Century.* New York: Howard Fertig.

Lempert, Richard O. 1983. "From the New Editor," 17 *Law & Society Review* 3.

Levi-Strauss, Claude. 1967. *Structural Anthropology.* Garden City, NY: Anchor Books.

MacPherson, C. B. 1975. "Capitalism and the Changing Concept of Property," in E. Kamenka and R. S. Neale (eds.), *Feudalism, Capitalism and Beyond.* London: Edward Arnold.

Mandel, Ernest. 1968. *Marxist Economic Theory,* Vol. 1. New York: Monthly Review Press.

Marx, Karl. 1911. *Critique of Political Economy.* Chicago: Charles H. Kerr.

———. 1973. *Grundrisse.* Harmondsworth: Penguin.

———. 1976. "Wages," in Karl Marx and Frederick Engels, *Collected Works,* Vol. 6. New York: International Publishers.

———. 1977. *Capital.* Vol. I. New York: Vintage Books.

Marx, Karl and Frederick Engels. 1976. "The German Ideology," in Karl Marx and Frederick Engels, *Collected Works,* Vol. 5. New York: International Publishers.

McLennan, Gregor. 1981. *Marxism and the Methodologies of History.* London: Verso Editions.

Moore, Stanley. 1980. *Marx On the Choice Between Socialism and Communism.* Cambridge, MA: Harvard University Press.

O'Hagan, Timothy. 1981. "On the Withering Away of Superstructures," in J. Mepham and D. H. Ruben (eds.), *Issues in Marxist Philosophy,* Vol. IV. Brighton, England: Harvester Press.

Pashukanis, Evgeny B. 1978. *Law and Marxism: A General Theory.* London: Ink Links.

Plamenatz, John. 1955. *German Marxism and Russian Communism.* New York: Harper & Row.

Popper, Karl R. 1959. *The Logic of Scientific Discovery.* New York: Basic Books.

Renner, Karl. 1949. *The Institutions of Private Law and Their Social Functions.* London: Routledge & Kegan Paul.

Scott, William Robert. 1951. *The Constitution and Finance of English, Scottish and Irish Joint Stock Companies to 1920,* Vol. I. New York: Peter Smith.

Sparks, Richard F. 1980. "A Critique of Marxist Criminology," 2 *Crime and Justice: An Annual Review of Research* 159.

Sumner, Colin. 1979. *Reading Ideologies.* New York: Academic Press.

Sweezy, Paul. 1942. *The Theory of Capitalist Development.* New York: Oxford University Press.

Thompson, E. P. 1975. *Whigs and Hunters.* New York: Pantheon.

Tushnet, Mark. 1978. "A Marxist Analysis of American Law," 1 *Marxist Perspectives* 96 (Spring).

———. 1983. "Review: Collins' *Marxism and Law,*" 68 *Cornell Law Review* 281.

Veblen, Thorstein. 1932. *The Theory of Business Enterprise.* New York: New American Library.

Weber, Max. 1968. *Economy and Society,* 3 Vols. New York: Bedminster Press.

———. 1977. *Critique of Stammler.* New York: Free Press.

Williamson, Oliver E. 1975. *Markets and Hierarchies: Analysis and Antitrust Implications.* New York: Free Press.

· 5 ·

The Weberian Perspective

The theoretical orientation that was laid out by German sociologist Max Weber is the second perspective that has had a significant influence on the sociology of law. The purpose of this chapter is to demonstrate how this perspective looks to political, religious, and economic factors ·in explaining the law's formulation and application. It is this eclectic approach that distinguishes the Weberian perspective from the Marxian and Durkheimian perspectives discussed in this text. Moreover, it is important to keep in mind that all three of these perspectives form the core of classical sociological theory.

This chapter begins with a discussion of some of Max Weber's key concepts and how he used them to explain (a) the three forms of political authority through which law is created and made effective, (b) the four types of lawmaking and lawfinding and their connection with religious influences, and (c) the effect that the capitalist economic system had on the emergence of continental Europe's unique legal system. The chapter concludes by looking at how certain scholars in recent years have analyzed, critiqued, and extended Weber's concept of legitimacy, his "England problem," and his dialogue with the ghost of Marx.

Max Weber: The Eclectic Scholar

Although Marx and Engels did not identify law as a major theoretical problem, Max Weber most certainly did. To be sure, Weber produced a fairly coherent sociology of law in his magnum opus, *Economy and Society*. This monumental work, which Weber began toward the end of his life and never completed, helped to establish him as one of the most erudite legal scholars of all time. Not only did he develop his legal sociology in this work, it is here that he also produced his theories of political sociology, sociology of religion, and sociology of economics. Weber's expansive sociological knowledge allowed him to thoroughly analyze various legal systems within the context of different cultures, at several periods in history, and at the subjective as well as the objective levels of social reality. Let us see how Weber's life and influences prepared him to be the author of *Economy and Society*.

163

Life and Influences

Max Weber (1864–1920) was born in Erfurt, Thuringia (Germany). His father, whom the young Weber initially attempted to emulate, was a lawyer and a politician. During the Bismarck period in Germany, the senior Weber sat in the Prussian House of Deputies and in the Reichstag (Imperial Parliament) as a member of the National Liberal party. By contrast, Max Weber's mother was a deeply religious Calvinist woman who rejected the affairs of the world. She tried to instill in the young Weber the strict standards of hard work, ascetic behavior, and personal morality. It is easy to see that Weber's sociological work in law, politics, and religion was largely inspired by his parents' personal interests.

After completing high school in 1882, Max Weber attended the University of Heidelberg, where he was enrolled as a law student. After two more years at the universities of Berlin and Göttingen, he took his first examination in law.

Weber studied Roman, German, and commercial law at the University of Berlin. In the fall of 1894, at the age of thirty, he accepted a full professorship in economics at Freiburg University and not long thereafter accepted the chair in political science at the University of Heidelberg. Weber's interests in law and politics merged in his role as consultant to a commission charged with the drafting of the new constitution for the Weimar Republic. Toward the end of his life, Weber joined the faculty at the University of Munich where he delivered his well-known lectures "Politics as a Vocation" and "Science as a Vocation."

Although several intellectual trends had a profound impact on Weber's work, chief among them was German **historicism.** This was an academic movement that (1) emphasized the uniqueness of different cultures; (2) highlighted the organic nature of cultures; (3) adopted the idea that the authenticity of organic cultures comes from their "subjective" nature (inner meanings, emotional states, spiritual experiences, etc.); (4) relied on the method of *Verstehen*, or understanding, to grasp the meaning of the subjective; and (5) focused on the political state as an expression of cultural ideas and uniqueness (see Westby, 1991:321–323). From these five features of German historicism, Weber was able to formulate some of the most powerful concepts in all of sociology.

Principal Concepts in Weber's Sociology

In the opening portions of *Economy and Society*, Weber sets forth two of several concepts that he considers to be fundamental to sociology: the *ideal type* and *rationality*. It is imperative that we become intimately acquainted with these and related concepts in order to truly appreciate Weber's statements about law and society.

Ideal types. Weber's sociology, and most of sociology in general, cannot be fully appreciated without reference to the concept of the ideal type. An **ideal type** is a methodological tool that aids the sociologist in subjectively understanding (*Verstehen*) complex cultural phenomena (e.g., law, political authority, and economic activity). It is an analytical model that does not exist in concrete reality. Consequently, no real-life example will correspond exactly to the ideal type as a pure form. In Weber's own words:

An ideal type is formed by the one-sided *accentuation* of one or more points of view and by the synthesis of a great many diffuse, discrete, more or less present and occasionally absent *concrete individual* phenomena, which are arranged according to those one-sidedly emphasized viewpoints into a unified *analytical* construct. . . . In its conceptual purity, this mental construct . . . cannot be found empirically anywhere in reality. It is a *utopia*. Historical research faces the task of determining in each individual case, the extent to which this ideal-construct approximates to or diverges from reality (1949:90).

In Weber's view, the ideal type is inductively derived from the real social world. As a mental construct, the ideal type underscores the important features of social structure (the organizational pattern of social relations) as well as of **social action** (the meaningful conduct of individuals).

The ideal type allows the sociologist to talk generally and abstractly about something specific and concrete. It also provides a yardstick with which to compare and contrast empirical social phenomena. Moreover, the ideal type helps to easily identify those cases that diverge or deviate from its stylized depiction. Let us look at two social phenomena—*bureaucracy* and *capitalism*—as examples of ideal types.

Weber described the ideal-typical bureaucracy as having the following salient characteristics:

1. There are fixed "offices" that are generally ordered by impersonal rules (i.e., laws or administrative regulations).
2. Regular organizational activities are structurally distributed as official duties.
3. Only qualified staff can perform these duties.
4. Offices are hierarchically structured according to levels of graded authority. This means that there exists a firmly ordered system of super- and subordination.
5. There is a democratic system of recruitment and a regular system of appointment and promotion based solely on certified qualifications of technical competence.
6. The office continues to exist regardless of who occupies it.
7. The management of the office is based upon written documents ("the files").
8. There is a separation of official from personal activities.
9. There is a thorough and expert training of staff performing the specialized duties of the office.
10. Administrative duties demand the full working capacity of the expert official.
11. There are regular and fixed salaries paid to staff officials.
12. The office administration follows general, abstract rules, which are more or less stable, more or less exhaustive, and can be learned (Gerth and Mills, 1978:196–198; Weber, 1969:343–345).

No real-life bureaucracy, whether it be a hospital, a business corporation, an army, or university, will conform, in every respect, to all of the above characteristics. Some organizations will undoubtedly be more bureaucratically structured than others. Nevertheless, this ideal-typical bureaucracy that Weber has sketched shows us which social structures and social actions are highly bureaucratic and which are not. Let us now look at those features that make up the ideal-typical economic activity that Weber referred to as *modern industrial capitalism.*

Weber describes modern industrial capitalism (to be referred to as "capitalism" from here on) as "the industrial provision for the needs of a human group." He further explains that "a rational capitalistic establishment is one with capital accounting, that is, an establishment which determines its income yielding power by calculation according to the methods of modern bookkeeping and the striking of a balance" (1950:275). Weber then goes on to list seven "presuppositions" that constitute the ideal type capitalism because they are indispensable to its development:

1. The appropriation of all the physical means of production—land, machinery, technology—as the disposable property of independent private industrial enterprises.
2. The freedom of the open market, that is, the absence of any arbitrary, unpredictable government interference with commercial transactions and property arrangements. In other words, there is a fully developed doctrine of laissez-faire.
3. The mechanization of technology for the production and distribution of commodities.
4. Calculability and predictability in the adjudication and administration of law.
5. Free labor, that is, workers must be legally and economically compelled to sell their labor on the market without restrictions.
6. The commercialization of economic life.
7. Financial speculation on the open market.
   (Weber, 1950:275–278).

These two examples of ideal types—the bureaucracy and capitalism—are said to involve some of the most rational forms of social structure and social action that exist in the modern Western world. Second only to the ideal type, the notion of rationality is the other concept that is central to the Weberian perspective.

Rationality. For Weber, the most important ideal types are based on **rationality.** Indeed, we may say that rationality, in regard to both social action and social structure, is the concept around which the whole of Weber's sociology revolves (including, as we shall see, his sociology of law). Although there is no general agreement among scholars as to what exactly Weber meant by rationality, we may nevertheless isolate six interrelated components that make up the concept. For a list of these six components we rely on sociologist Arnold Eisen (1978).

1. Underlying all rationality is *purpose;* that is, a person's conscious intent to achieve a particular end. Purposeful social action lowers the degree of arbitrariness involved because the person voluntarily chooses which means to take in attaining a desired result. Predictability is increased. If, for instance, your goal is to finish reading this chapter before dinner, then you will utilize those means—time and effort—needed to ensure completion of that goal.

2. *Calculability* makes for rational social action when means and ends are computed to determine certainty. For example, if I weigh the pros and cons of engaging in behavior "A" with the pros and cons of engaging in behavior "B," then I am estimating, with some degree of probability, the outcome of my actions. Put another way, there is a calculation of means and ends.

3. *Control* makes for rationality because it reduces the randomness of social action. If I can control my behavior or social environment, I can then predict, with a high degree of certainty, what will happen.

4. Rationality has a quality of the *logical*. This means that all interrelated social actions internally cohere in a systematic fashion and are performed in an efficient manner. Let us take as an example the following scenario: A group of five students is to write a term paper that consists of five sections. The most expedient way to do the assignment is for each student to write one section. Although they work separately on their own sections, the students must also work cooperatively to ensure that the sections come together in such as way that there are no gaps or contradictions in the paper as a whole.

5. *Universality* is a component of rationality. In other words, if there is a degree of abstractness to the logic involved concerning a social structure or social action, then its method will hold true no matter what the particular content may be. In law, for example, codified general rules are applied uniformly to a variety of specific behaviors. For instance, a penal code does not (typically) determine the crime of theft on the basis of what was stolen, or on the basis of whether the offender's family was in vital need of the food that he or she took. The formal legal rules simply determine if a theft was committed. (The law does, of course, distinguish between different kinds of theft: burglary, robbery, embezzlement, and so forth. And the jury may make even further distinctions and determinations based on the particulars—substantive issues—of a given case. To be sure, the behavior of jurors may constitute social action that is not, from the point of view of formal procedure, rational).

6. Rationality connotes a *systematic* method of organization that relates parts to whole in the most efficient manner for achieving the desired results.

Weber believed rationality to be the distinguishing hallmark of Western civilization. He noted that this leading trend toward increased rationalization had greatly impacted the development of numerous sectors of social life, including science, religion, music, architecture, the economy, politics, and law. When comparing Western civilization with the Orient (India, China, the Middle East). Weber found a lack of rationality in the latter societies. That is to say, that, relatively speaking, in Oriental culture there was less emphasis on calculability, efficiency, predictability, logic, and universality. For instance, law and justice in the West were administered according to formal and rational procedures and impersonal and universal rules. By contrast, justice in the East was dispensed in a highly irrational way; that is, in accordance with the intuitive decisions made by the judges or sultans based on their personal experiences and a variety of extralegal (i.e., ethical, political, and religious) factors. This made the administration of justice an extremely arbitrary, ambiguous, and unpredictable phenomenon.

Eisen describes a rational legal system as follows:

> Rational law, . . . possesses a logic which both systematically integrates all relevant materials, and itself defines what materials shall in fact be relevant . . . Law is consciously ordered and systematically set forth in abstract concepts and formal procedures, a structure which attempts universal scope and promises impersonal judgment, a system so calculable in its workings, says Weber at one point, that the judge or jury might be compared to a machine which takes in the facts at one slot, and delivers the verdict from another (1978:61).

(The reader will recall from Chapter 3 that this kind of mechanical, slot-machine, conceptual, or formalist jurisprudence is what Oliver Wendell Holmes, Roscoe Pound, and the legal realists were reacting against.)

Throughout the remainder of this chapter, we will employ Weber's two major concepts—rationality and the ideal type (in particular, the two ideal types of bureaucracy and capitalism)—in making sense of his sociology of law. Because Weber's legal sociology is closely associated with certain relations between law and political and administrative organizations, we begin by applying the concepts of rationality and the ideal type to these topics.

Three Forms of Political Authority

In this section we examine the relationship between Weber's political, religious, and legal sociologies. In so doing we arrive at an understanding of how the different forms of political domination rely on various degrees of sacredness for creating the law and making it more effective.

According to Weber, all political and administrative organizations, which are bureaucratically structured, possess the ability to dominate. He defines **domination** as the "probability that certain specific commands (or all commands) will be obeyed by a given group of persons" (1978:212). Domination, Weber tells us, can be either *legitimate* or *illegitimate*. In other words, there are essentially two ways of getting subordinates to obey commands. One way is to physically or psychologically coerce them into submission. This means that brute force is administered to ensure compliance to the orders issued. In such a case, people may obey only because they fear reprisal. Weber refers to this type of domination as illegitimate because it is not seen as valid or justified by the subordinates. Under these circumstances, the power of a political organization is highly unstable and exceedingly difficult to maintain over a long period of time.

A second and less costly way of ensuring compliance to commands is through legitimate domination, or what Weber calls **authority.** Under authority an order is considered valid and the subordinates voluntarily submit to it because they believe that the order itself and the commands of the leader are rightful or "deserved."

Consequently, because subordinates genuinely accept the order through a sense of duty there is little need for proactive coercion.

What most concerned Weber, and what played a central role in his sociology of law, were the three forms of political authority that he identified as the *charismatic*, the *traditional*, and "the crowning achievement of Western civilization" (Bendix, 1962:385), the *rational-legal*. These three forms are ideal types; thus, when they occur in historical reality they occur as combinations, mixtures, adaptations, or modifications. In what follows we examine the three ideal types of political authority through which the law is created and made effective.

Charismatic Authority

Charismatic authority rests on the emotional devotion of followers to the *extraordinary* character of a leader. Weber uses the term "charisma" to refer to

> a certain quality of an individual personality by virtue of which he is set apart from ordinary men and treated as endowed with supernatural, super-human, or at least specifically exceptional powers or qualities. These are such as are not accessible to the ordinary person, but are regarded as of divine origin or as exemplary, and on the basis of them the individual con-cerned is treated as a leader (1969:358–359).

In the case of charismatic authority, the followers submit to the leader's de-mands "because of their belief in the extraordinary quality of the specific *person*. . . . The legitimacy of charismatic rule thus rests upon the belief in magical powers, revelations, and hero worship" (Gerth and Mills, 1978:295–296).

Charismatic qualities based on magical or heroic powers and deeds, says Weber, can be found in a variety of persons including judges, saviors, the religious "berserk," and the shaman. However, Weber's main exemplars of the charismatic leader were the Hebrew prophets—e.g., Amos, Isaiah, Jeremiah, Ezekiel, Hosea, and the like.

By "prophet" Weber means "a purely individual bearer of charisma, who by virtue of his mission proclaims a religious doctrine of divine commandment" (1978: 439). In many cases the prophet was also a lawgiver, that is, "a personage who in a concrete case has been assigned the responsibility of codifying a law system-atically or of reconstituting it" (Weber, 1978:442). The law given by the prophet would, of course, be considered sacred and charismatic. The best example of a prophet-lawgiver is Moses, whose formulation of the Hebrew law (as found in the Torah) served to transform the Israelites into a newly unified people.

Weber maintains that the Hebrew prophets had a distinctive concern with social reform. To be sure, charismatic authority often acts as a revolutionary force. This explains why leaders with exceptional qualities are especially in demand dur-ing periods of emergency, crisis, or societal tension. The rise of a charismatic figure may well lead to social change and renewal. "In a revolutionary and sovereign man-ner," states Weber, "charismatic domination transforms all values and breaks all traditional and rational norms" (1978:1115).

Charismatic authority, however, is highly irrational because it is not premised on reason, but on emotional loyalty; that is, on the fact that the disciples enthusiastically accept their leader's power as divinely inspired. In other words, charismatic authority, in its decision-making process, does not rely on rational deductions from universal principles. As a consequence, "charismatic domination knows no abstract laws and regulations and no formal adjudication. Its 'objective' law flows from the highly personal experience of divine grace and god-like heroic strength" (Weber, 1978:1115). Charismatic adjudication may therefore be exercised, on a case-by-case basis, through any number of decision-making techniques rooted in subjective meaning: prophetic revelation, the oracle, sagacious discernment. Consider, as an example of the latter, King Solomon's reliance on intuitive judgment in settling the following dispute:

> Then two women . . . came to the king and stood before him. And one woman said . . . "it happened on the third day after I gave birth, that this woman also gave birth to a child, and we were together. . . . And this woman's son died in the night because she lay on it. So she arose in the middle of the night and took my son . . . and laid her son in my bosom. And when I rose in the morning to nurse my son, behold, he was dead; but when I looked at him carefully in the morning, behold he was not my son. . . ." The other woman said, "No! For the living one is my son, and the dead one is your son." . . . And the king said, "Get me a sword. . . . Divide the living child in two, and give half to one and half to the other." Then the woman whose child was the living one spoke to the king, . . . "Oh, my lord, give her the living child, and by no means kill him." But the other said, ". . . divide him!" Then the king answered and said, "Give the first woman the living child, and by no means kill him. She is his mother." When all Israel heard of the judgment which the king had handed down, they feared the king; for they saw the wisdom of God was in him to administer justice (1 Kings 3:16–28).

We may say that charisma is the strongest source of legitimacy because it directly transforms the mundane social relationship between leader and followers into an eternal relationship of superhuman quality. "The distinctiveness of Weber's charismatic authority, . . . lies in its *direct* legitimation of domination, in contrast to the other types of authority in which legitimation is mediated either by law or by tradition" (Miyahara, 1983:384). We now, with Weber, turn to that type of authority legitimated by tradition.

Traditional Authority

Traditional authority rests on "an established belief in the sanctity of immemorial traditions and the legitimacy of those exercising authority under them" (Weber, 1978:215). This type of authority is typically an inherited status in that it is handed down from the past and made valid by custom. Examples of traditional authority are found in the person of the paterfamilias, the pharaoh, the king, and the feudal landlord.

Traditional authority is premised on the claim by the leaders, and a belief on the part of the followers, that there is a sacred quality, not with the leader as a person as in the case of charismatic authority, but rather with time-honored rules and powers. In this case, the status of the leader is that of a personal master and the subjects obey out of a personal loyalty and devotion to him or her.

Weber distinguishes between four forms of traditional authority. The earliest form, **gerontocracy,** involves domination by those elders who are most familiar with the sacred traditions. The second form, **patriarchalism,** involves masters who rule their households. "Patriarchalism means the authority of the father, the husband, the senior of the house; . . . the rule of the master and patron . . . of the lord over the domestic servants and household officials . . . of the patrimonial lord and sovereign prince . . . over the 'subjects'" (Gerth and Mills, 1978:296). In other words, patriarchalism is a personal relationship of authoritative respect for the paternal head of the family by those in his household who are physically and mentally dependent on him. And, since there is no need for coercion, neither gerontocracy nor patriarchalism have an administrative staff to enforce the leader's demands.

A later form of traditional domination is **patrimonialism.** Under patrimonialism the ruler's personal "household" expands greatly to include an entire regime. Thus, a governmental administrative staff and military force become imperative in carrying out the ruler's will. The personal dependents of the master become the political subjects of the patrimonial ruler.

Despite the development of a governmental administration staffed with a variety of retainers, patrimonial authority nevertheless remains bound to tradition. The ruler is regarded as "the good king," the "father of his people" who sees to the welfare of his subjects. Moreover, devotion to the father of his people is inculcated in the subjects. Under a patrimonial system, the law, such as it is, is very arbitrary and thus irrational: "the prince gives commands from case to case according to his entirely free discretion; to the extent that there is no place for the concepts of either 'law' or 'right'" (Weber, 1978:843).

An even later form of traditional authority is **feudalism** as developed in medieval Europe and Japan. In this case, not subjects, but "socially prominent allies" (Bendix, 1962:295), that is, warriors (e.g., knights or samurai), give a contractual oath of loyalty to their leader. Although these warriors were vassals, they were nevertheless free because they could terminate the contractual oath at any time, the lord could not impose duties on the vassals arbitrarily, and, unlike the political subjects of the patrimonial system, the feudal vassals did not become personally dependent on the lord.

Weber tells us that during feudalism there was essentially no difference between lawmaking and adjudication. The legal order was irrational because the law was based on concrete matters at hand and not on a uniform and logical system of legal procedure. For example, if the king, as a matter of personal favoritism, granted some special privilege to a notable who came before the court, that privilege had to be respected in deciding his case. In other words, under a system of privilege, the law was not applied uniformly and equally to all; rather, justice was decided in accordance with a person's status. Indeed, Weber states that during feudalism all adjudication was nothing more than "negotiation, bargaining, and contracting about 'privileges,'" (1978:844). This process turns the legal order into "a mere bundle of assorted privileges" (Weber, 1978:843).

All four of the aforementioned forms—gerontocracy, patriarchalism, patrimonialism, and feudalism—may be seen as structural variations of traditional authority. According to Weber, all traditional authority is, at bottom, irrational because there exists "a realm of free arbitrariness and favor of the lord, who in principle judges only in terms of 'personal,' not 'functional' relations" (Gerth and Mills, 1978:296). Let us now look at that rational type of authority that is impersonal and has its basis in bureaucracy.

Rational-Legal Authority

Rational-legal authority rests "on a belief in the legality of enacted rules and the right of those elevated to authority under such rules to issue commands" (Weber, 1978:215). This type of domination is derived from an exhaustive and logically consistent system of abstract and impersonal rules that have been codified into written documents—namely, the statutory laws. In addition, it is legitimized on the basis of the enactment of the rules in accordance with formal procedure. In other words, under rational-legal authority the law validates and justifies itself.

Under rational-legal authority the superior is obeyed, not by virtue of personal faith or custom, as in the case of charismatic and traditional authority, but rather by virtue of the formal legality of his or her commands. Furthermore, the superior giving the orders must in turn comply with the impersonal system of legal rules. This is a very different situation from the absolute monarch who, under the patrimonial system of traditional authority, issued commands at his or her discretion but was not subject to those commands.

Although rational-legal authority appears in many historical circumstances, Weber deliberately points out that it achieved its prominence in modern Western society. Moreover, Weber is most interested in rational-legal authority as it appears in its bureaucratized form. Indeed, he considers the modern bureaucracy "the purest type of exercise of legal authority" (1978:220) because it emphasizes efficiency of administration. When applied to judicial decision-making, bureaucratic rational-legal authority with its emphasis on calculability, produces, as Weber exaggeratedly puts it, "the modern judge as a vending machine into which the pleadings are inserted together with the fee and which then disgorges the judgment together with its reasons mechanically derived from the Code" (Rheinstein, 1966:354). The main difference between rational-legal authority and the irrational authority based on charisma or tradition is that the latter two forms involve personal and arbitrary rule rather than impersonal and precise rule.

The ideal type rational-legal authority is based on several interdependent factors:

1. The legal rules are rationally made; that is, they are established on the grounds of expediency or on some ultimate value or both.

2. The legal rules form an internally consistent (gapless) system. They are abstract, intentionally made, and applied to individual cases in accordance with previously established formal procedures.
3. The superior is subject to the impersonal legal order.
4. Obedience is given by the subordinate only in his or her capacity as a member of the bureaucratic organization.
5. Obedience is given only to the impersonal legal order and not to the superior as an individual.
   (Weber, 1978:217–218)

The appearance of bureaucratized rational-legal authority in modern Western civilization resulted in the gradual emergence of the modern political state. The primary characteristics of this type of government consist of the following:

1. It possesses an administrative and legal order subject to change by legislation.
2. Its administrative staff engages in organized corporate duties that are regulated by legislation.
3. It claims binding authority over all action taking place in its jurisdiction.
4. It regards the use of force as legitimate only in so far as it either permits or prohibits coercion within its jurisdiction.
   (Weber, 1978:156)

Modern Western governments no longer take the form of patrimonial traditional authority—i.e., absolute monarchy. Under a system of legal dominance, authority is embodied in the *legal order*, and not in an individual. In other words, political authority in democratic societies is temporarily held by government officials elected to *office* (e.g., the President of the United States and members of Congress). These officials hold limited power and only for the time they remain in office. Additionally, and at least with the case of members of Congress, they are expected to enact laws in accordance with formal procedures (e.g., those procedures stipulated in the federal constitution). And finally, and perhaps most significantly, they are also expected to comply fully with these laws. Weberian sociologist Reinhard Bendix tersely explains the relationship between democracy, bureaucracy, and rational-legal authority:

> Bureaucracy developed with the support of democratic movements that demanded equality before the law and legal guarantees against arbitrariness in judicial and administrative decisions. As an opposition to the existing system of privilege and arbitrary powers, these demands clearly favored an impersonal exercise of authority governed by rules and a recruitment of officials from all social strata solely on the basis of technical qualification. In meeting these demands bureaucratic organizations had a leveling effect; the people subject to the law and the officials who exercised authority under the law became formally equal (1962:437).

In this section we saw that the three forms of authority through which law was created and made effective—the charismatic, the traditional, and the rational-legal—are closely connected with bureaucratically structured political and administrative organizations. In the section that follows we briefly focus on Weber's concept of law, lawmaking, and lawfinding.

Law, Lawmaking, and Lawfinding

In *Economy and Society*, Weber produces a working definition of the term *law:* "An order will be called *law* if it is externally guaranteed by the probability that physical or psychological coercion will be applied by a *staff* of people in order to bring about compliance or avenge violation" (Weber, 1978:34). Let us see how he arrived at this definition.

We begin with the concept of social action. Weber posits that **social action** occurs when "the acting individual attaches a subjective meaning to his behavior." Additionally, Weber states that "action is 'social' insofar as its subjective meaning takes account of the behavior of others and is thereby oriented in its course" (1978:4). In typical fashion, Weber then proceeds to list four ideal types of social action. Action may be rationally purposeful, value-rational, affectual, or traditional.

Rationally purposeful action occurs when "the end, the means, and the secondary results are all rationally taken into account and weighed" (Weber, 1978:26). In other words, a person is oriented toward a particular goal and, in an instrumental manner, calculates the means and ends of his or her behavior. **Value-rational action** is characterized by the consciously determined pursuit of some ethical, aesthetic, or religious value or cause. In this case, there may not be a great deal of regard for immediate practical consequences. **Affectual action** is motivated by the emotions (passions and feelings) of the individual. Such behavior is not based on reason and may be highly impulsive. **Traditional action** is behavior that is fixed by habit or custom. It is generally unreflective and "almost automatic." Regardless of their degree of rationality, all four types of social action refer to behavior that is meaningful to individuals within the context of social relationships.

In building his definition of law, Weber further identifies three types of social action that have been co-opted into the social structure: usage, custom, and convention. By **usage** Weber refers to social action that occurs on a regular basis; for example, eating three meals a day. If the regular social action is long-standing, it is called a **custom.** In the case of custom, conformity is not demanded and there are no external sanctions for its violation. Customary social action, however, can be oriented to the idea that there exists some **legitimate order**—"a [valid] set of ought ideas which are held in the minds of people" (Rheinstein, 1966:lxvii). An order is called a **convention** when behavior is regulated by "the expression of approval or disapproval on the part of those persons who constitute the environment of the actor" (Weber, 1978:319). A convention gives rise to a sense of duty or obligation because failure to comply with normative expectations will provoke the disapproval of others. Most conventions, however, are "characterized by the very absence of any coercive apparatus, i.e., of any, at least relatively clearly delimited, group of persons who would continuously hold themselves ready for the special task of legal coercion through physical or psychological means" (Weber, 1978:320).

Law, on the other hand, is a convention regulated by "specialized personnel for the implementation of coercive power (enforcement machinery: priests, judges, police, the military, etc.)" (Weber, 1978:326). Weber considers "law" to be a social order that is regarded as legitimate and that relies on a group of officials charged with implementing forceful actions or threats to enforce that order. In the next section we look at how the four types of legal thought help to bolster Weber's explanation of the judicial processes of lawmaking and lawfinding.

As Weber sees it, legal thought, or the judicial process, consists of lawmaking and lawfinding: these are the practices that involve creating the law (e.g., legislation) and applying the law once created (i.e., adjudication or judicial decisionmaking). Weber tells us that lawmaking and lawfinding can be rational (guided by clear and general rules) or irrational (not guided by clear and general rules). According to Weber *rationality* refers to generalization; that is, "the reduction of reasons relevant in the decision of concrete individual cases to one or more 'principles,' i.e., legal propositions" (1978:655). Conversely, *irrationality* means that the case is not governed by general principles, but rather is regarded on the basis of its own unique merits. Accordingly, every case is treated differently and similar cases will have varying outcomes. The results are unpredictable.

In addition, lawmaking and lawfinding can proceed rationally or irrationally according to means that are either *formal* (applying rules and procedures that are internal to the legal system) or *substantive* (applying rules and procedures that are external to the legal system). "Law . . . is formal," says Weber, "to the extent that, . . . only unambiguous general characteristics of the facts of the case are taken into account" (1978:656–657). Substantive law, by contrast, employs a wide range of extralegal criteria (e.g., ethical, political, and religious considerations) in deciding the case.

Four Types of Legal Thought

The above analysis yields, for Weber, four ideal-type categories of legal thought: (1) the formal irrational, (2) the substantive irrational, (3) the substantive rational, and (4) the formal rational. We will look at each of these systems of lawmaking and lawfinding in turn.

Formal Irrational Thought

Formal irrational thought is guided by individual rules that are derived from legal sources. In a legal order that is formally irrational, disputes are decided on the basis of such mysterious techniques as magic, an oracle, a prophetic revelation, or an ordeal. In regard to both lawmaking and lawfinding, these techniques are beyond the control of the intellect. This means that, because they possess a mysterious quality, no proof is offered as to what the "real truth" in a dispute may actually be. It also means that the verdict is rendered but no reasons are given to justify it. Nevertheless, the process for arriving at the judgment is said to be formal because there are certain fixed rules that specify the appropriate procedures to be employed when invoking an answer from the oracle. To be sure, these procedural rules must be

rigorously followed because "even the slightest deviation from the magically effective formula renders the whole [process] void" (Weber, 1978:761). On the other
hand, this mode of legal thought is highly irrational because it places its faith on
magical or divine powers, thus making it virtually impossible to reasonably anticipate in advance the verdict of the case. As legal philosopher Anthony T. Kronman
puts it, "In the case of an oracle, past decisions, unsupported by reasons, provide
only minimal guidance in predicting the outcome of future litigation" (1983a:82).

Let us take as an example of this type of oracular adjudication the method used
by Aaron, the high priest of the ancient Hebrews, in determining Yahweh's judgment in matters pertaining to Israel. Exodus 28 describes in detail the holy garments to be worn by the Hebrew priests. Included as part of the garments is the
"breastpiece of judgment." Exodus 28:30 states, "And you shall put in the breastpiece of judgment the Urim and the Thummim, and they shall be over Aaron's
heart when he goes in before the Lord; and Aaron shall carry the judgment of
the sons of Israel over his heart before the Lord continually." The Urim and
Thummim were sacred stones that were placed in a pouch behind the breastpiece.
When an inquiry from God was sought, the priest was to reach into the pouch and
randomly pick a stone. If the stone was Thummim, the answer was "yes"; if Urim,
it was "no."

The procedure of Urim and Thummim, as a form of charismatic legal revelation, was a *formal* one because the judgment was to be sought by the priest alone
and only in the manner prescribed. It was also *irrational*, however, because the
answer was completely random and unpredictable.

Substantive Irrational Thought

Substantive irrational thought is guided by individual rules derived from
nonlegal sources. In a substantive irrational legal order, lawmakers or lawfinders
make judicial decisions in an arbitrary manner because they are not guided solely
by general legal rules and procedures. This type of juristic thought is substantive
because the case is decided on the basis of an indiscriminate mixture of legal and
extralegal criteria; that is, on ethical, political, ideological, moral, and emotional considerations. Furthermore, it is irrational to the extent that even similarly situated
litigants will be treated differently. As a result of the extreme arbitrariness involved
in this kind of adjudication, the outcome of even like cases is impossible to predict.

Weber tells us that this ideal type of legal thought closely resembles the
khadi-justice of the Moslem judge who presides in the sharihah court. The khadi
judge, as a holder of charismatic and traditional authority, sits in the marketplace
of an Islamic town and arbitrates disputes that arise between buyers and sellers. He
decides cases, not in reference to explicit and universal rules or procedures, but
according to personal insight. The khadi bases his subjective judgment on the
particular features of each individual case and on emotive religious considerations.
And, much like the example of King Solomon above, the ad hoc decision appears
to be predicated solely on the judge's free discretion.

An extreme example of substantive irrational justice is found in the parable,
"The Lady, or the Tiger?" As the story has it, a semibarbaric king of great char-

ismatic authority constructed'an arena as his "great scheme of retribution and reward," for persons accused of various criminal offenses.

> When all the people had assembled in the galleries, and the king, surrounded by his court, sat high up on his throne of royal state on one side of the arena, he gave a signal, a door beneath him opened, and the accused subject stepped out into the amphitheatre. Directly opposite him, on the other side of the enclosed space, were two doors, exactly alike and side by side. It was the duty and the privilege of the person on trial, to walk directly to these doors and open one of them. He could open either door he pleased: he was subject to no guidance or influence but the aforementioned impartial and incorruptible chance. If he opened the one, there came out of it a hungry tiger, the fiercest and most cruel that could be procured, which immediately sprang upon him, and tore him to pieces, as a punishment for his guilt. . . . But, if the accused person opened the other door, there came forth from it a lady, the most suitable to his years and station that his majesty could select among his fair subjects; and to this lady he was immediately married, as a reward of his innocence (Stockton, 1902:2–3).

In this case the method of adjudication is *substantive* because the judgment is not rendered by the king in accordance with a body of legal rules and procedures; it is instead left up to chance, destiny, and fate. The technique is *irrational* because even though we can calculate the probability of the accused being found guilty or innocent as a fifty-fifty chance, the outcome is unpredictable. And while the process does, to be sure, possess on the face of it a certain degree of "fairness," there is also a great deal of uncertainty.

Substantive Rational Thought

Substantive rational thought is guided by general rules derived from nonlegal sources. In a substantively rational legal order, lawmakers and lawfinders make use of unambiguous general principles that are deduced either from religion or from "ethical imperatives, utilitarian and other expediential rules, and political maxims" (Weber, 1978:657). In other words, substantive rational law is guided by postulates of a system other than that of law itself. Nevertheless, relative to the other two modes of legal thought discussed, this type allows for greater predictability of case results.

An illustration of substantive rational law is found in the rock edicts of the Buddhist Emperor Asoka (ca. 264–226 B.C.E.). These edicts, which closely followed the religious and spiritual precepts of the Buddha, were implemented as laws designed to equalize the social status between the religious cultural elite and the lay population of India.

> One of these edits . . . declares that glory and renown do not bring much profit unless the people obey the law of piety. But to do so is difficult. It requires the utmost exertion and complete renunciation, and these are extraordinarily difficult for people of high rank—clearly a pointed reminder to the nobility of the time. Thus the "fruit of exertion . . . is not to be obtained by the great man only; because even the small man can by

exertion win for himself much heavenly bliss." And for this purpose an edit declared, "Let small and great exert themselves." Such deliberate leveling tendencies were already implicit in the religious ideas of the Buddha and were made explicit by the Emperor Asoka, indicating, according to Weber, that the secular rulers used religious appeals to satisfy the emotional needs and ensure the peacefulness of the population (Bendix, 1962:168–169).

This illustration shows that a substantively rational mode of juristic thought is, in effect, "lawmaking by a prince or other ruler aimed at the implementation of an ethically based 'welfare policy'" (Kronman, 1983a:77). In other words, the objective is to bring about social changes that are congruent with certain ethical considerations. This type of jurisprudence, which is grounded in traditional and charismatic authority, is *substantive* because no separation is made between the law and other religious and political ideals. On the other hand, this form of legal thought is *rational* to the extent that the unambiguous and uniform rules of an extra-legal doctrinal system (Buddhism, in the case of Asoka) are strictly adhered to.

Formal Rational Thought

Formal rational thought is guided by general rules derived from legal sources. In a formally rational legal order, universal rules are clearly stated in written documents and applied uniformly to all similar cases and litigants. In addition, only criteria that are internal to the legal system are considered and there exists a high degree of predictability of case results.

This type of legal doctrine can be broken down further into two subtypes: the *extrinsically formal rational* and the *logically formal rational*. These subtypes are two ways of determining which criteria are legally relevant to a case. In the extrinsic type, which Weber associated with the common law of England, the emphasis is on "sense-data." In other words, only those events and occurrences that have a tangible presence and can be perceived by the human senses have any legal significance. Examples of those concrete factual characteristics that are particularly pertinent to the externally formal rational law include the objective happening of an event, the **actus reus** (wrongful deed), and the "mechanistic remedy of vengeance" (Weber, 1978:884–885).

On the other hand, the logically formal type of legal thought, which Weber identified with the civilian codes of modern continental Europe, was especially rational because "the legally relevant characteristics of the facts are disclosed through the logical analysis of meaning" (Weber, 1978:657). In emphasizing *meaning*, Weber is alluding to the use of *Verstehen* as an "attitude-evaluation" or a "kind of interpretation [that] seeks to construct the relations of the parties to one another from the point of view of the 'inner' kernel of their behavior, from the point of view of their mental 'attitudes'" (1978:884). In other words, motive, **mens rea** (state of mind), and psychological attitude become pertinent to the case. The salient issue here is that Weber considered social action—the purposes and intentions of human conduct—and no other kind of behavior, as relevant to the law.

In emphasizing *logical analysis*, Weber is saying that this form of juristic thought is especially rational because it is a self-contained and internally coherent system "which tries to proceed upon the basis of general principles and to maintain consistency in the sense of avoiding contradictions within itself" (Rheinstein, 1966: liv). Logical formal rational jurisprudence lends itself to the highest degree of systemization.

For Weber, formally rational legal thought is *logical* insofar as "definitely fixed legal concepts in the form of highly abstract rules are formulated and applied" in a syllogistic manner (1978:657). As we saw in Chapter 3, logical thinking consists of deductive reasoning.

Finally, Weber pointed out that the logically formal rational method of legal thought was not to be found in the legal systems of the Orient. Indeed, it was uniquely a product of Western civilization with its impersonal and specialized professional roles of judges and lawyers. It constituted the method of the civilian codes as developed in continental Europe during the twelfth century and attained its highest expression in the teachings of the German Pandectists in the nineteenth century. This type of juristic thought is also the dominant legal form in our postmodern society based, of course, on bureaucratic, rational-legal authority.

Perhaps no other writer since Weber has depicted so descriptively the maze-like bureaucratic structure of the administration of law as did Franz Kafka (who was himself trained in the law) in his novel *The Trial*. The nightmarish world that Kafka creates in this book is filled with a variety of bureaucratic, low- and high-level legal functionaries occupying small, cramped offices: warders, inspectors, examining magistrates, clerks of inquiries, chief clerks of the court, judges, and lawyers. The protagonist Joseph K. states, "The ranks of officials in this judiciary system mounted endlessly, so that not even the initiated could survey the hierarchy as a whole" (Kafka, 1956:149). It is a bureaucracy characterized by an extreme dependence on documentation and a highly technical and obtuse language. Joseph K., who has been arrested on a charge that is never revealed, seeks the advice of a painter who has some acquaintance with the judiciary system. The painter tries to explain the labyrinth of the bureaucratic hierarchy to K.:

> I forgot to ask you what sort of acquittal you want. There are three possibilities, that is, definite acquittal, ostensible acquittal, and indefinite postponement. . . . [With ostensible acquittal you are] only ostensibly free, or more exactly, provisionally free. For the Judges of the lowest grade . . . haven't the power to grant a final acquittal, that power is reserved for the highest Court of all, . . . I can also tell you how in the regulations of the Law Court offices the distinction between definite and ostensible acquittal is made manifest. In definite acquittal the documents relating to the case are said to be completely annulled, . . . That's not the case with ostensible acquittal. The documents remain as they were, except that the affidavit is added to them and a record of the acquittal and the grounds for granting it. The whole dossier continues to circulate, as the regular official routine demands, passing to the higher Courts, being referred to the lower ones

again, and thus swinging backwards and forwards with greater or smaller oscillations, longer and shorter delays (Kafka, 1956:191; 197–198).

Kafka, to be sure, is here depicting a fictitious judiciary system. However, many real-life persons, who as litigants, lawyers, judges, and jurors have had personal involvement with the court processes, would probably not regard Kafka's depiction as being too farfetched in describing our American court system. The point of the matter is that a formal rational legal order requires a highly bureaucratic administrative organization.

Weber's four ideal types of lawmaking and lawfinding—the formal irrational, the substantive irrational, the substantive rational, and the formal rational—form the crux of his sociology of law. But it may be said that, at bottom, Weber's sociology of law is really an attempt to answer one main question: How did formal rational legal thought evolve in modern Western civilization and what prevented its development elsewhere? Accordingly, Weber further attempted to identify those ideas and institutions that promoted as well as hindered the development of formal rational law in Europe. This is the issue to which we next devote our attention.

The Emergence of Formal Rational Law in Europe

In this section we examine the effect that capitalism had on the emergence of a rational legal order. We should take note, however, that in his sociological explanations, Weber seldom, if ever, sees a direct, unilinear, monocausal relationship between social phenomena. This is not to say that Weber is not interested in cause-and-effect relationships; he most certainly is. However, because Weber is well aware of the complexities of social life, rather than speaking strictly in terms of cause and effect, he often chooses to emphasize the close harmony that exists between two or more social factors. In other words, a *convergence*, and not a direct determining influence, may usually be found among several more or less independent events and occurrences by virtue of the fact that they have an *elective affinity* for each other.

As concerns the connection between economic and legal activity, the notion of elective affinity is perhaps best illustrated by Weber in the following statement: "Economic situations do not automatically give birth to new legal forms; they merely provide the opportunity for the actual spread of a legal technique if it is invented" (1978:687). It is with this idea of elective affinity in mind that we begin our analysis of some of those general tendencies that served as catalysts in the historical development of a formally rational legal system in Europe.

Rationalizing Social Tendencies

According to Weber, three social tendencies helped to rationalize the legal system of Europe. These tendencies were the *secularization of the law*, the *involvement of laymen in the adjudication process*, and the *development of the bureaucratic form of government*.

Due in large measure to the fact that during the Republican period of Rome (509 B.C.E.–31 B.C.E.) the priests were not permitted to interfere in matters of everyday life, sacred law became separated from secular law at a relatively early date in the West. Contrast this situation with that of India, where the Brahman priests ruled with great charismatic authority until a much later time period. Because of this theocratic influence, religious and secular laws were not differentiated in India and other Asian societies. In Europe, on the other hand, the Christian church very clearly demarcated the jurisdiction under cannon and under secular law. This development paved the way for "the consequent growth of legal formalism in the development of the modern state" (Bendix, 1962:403). In other words, the law's substantive irrationality was eliminated once the charismatic, mysterious, and prophetic features stemming from religion were discarded. Put another way, the secularization of the law is a fundamental prerequisite of legal rationality (Bendix, 1962:401).

During the medieval period in Europe, the jurisdiction of the secular laws was expanded as the monarch's legal domination was gradually extended. Eventually, new secular laws were enacted through the magisterial power of the official charged with the administration of justice. "The common element in these legal innovations," writes Bendix, "was the adoption of more rational procedures in lieu of the older forms of legal revelation and folk justice" (1962:404). For instance, the royal writs issued by King Henry II of England (1154–1189) instituted one of these rational procedures. The writs granted the litigant the right to interrogate twelve citizens sworn to give truthful testimony concerning what they knew about the disputed **seisin** (possession of land for an indeterminate amount of time) in question. This procedure replaced the more arbitrary one of *trial by ordeal*, where the accused was subjected to life-threatening tests by way of determining guilt or innocence, the result being regarded as divine judgment. Moreover, the notion of the "jury" emerged with the acceptance of the verdict of twelve jurors rather than deriving the verdict from the previous unpredictable modes of oracular adjudication. "The jury thus promoted the 'rationalization' of the law by substituting the deliberation of laymen for the verdict of an oracle" (Bendix, 1962:404).

The third driving force that prompted the rationalization of the law in Europe was the development of the bureaucratic form of administration.

> The prince desired "order" as well as "unity" and cohesion in his realm. These aims emerged not only from technical requirements of administration but also from the personal interests of his officials: legal uniformity renders possible employment of every official throughout the entire area of the realm, in which case career chances are, of course, better than where every official is bound to the area of his origin by his ignorance of the laws of any other part of the realm. . . . [O]fficialdom is generally interested in "clarity" and "orderliness" of the law (Weber, 1978:848).

These and other rationalizing tendencies of the West notwithstanding, Weber was most interested in analyzing the connection between formal legal rationality and modern industrial capitalism. However, unlike Marx—with his notion of economic determinism—Weber, for reasons already discussed, saw a convergence, not a determining influence, between the two phenomena. Indeed, "for Weber, law relates to the economic in a variety of different and complex directions which cannot be reduced to a simple deterministic formula" (Turner, 1981:319). Let us now examine the elective affinity extant between law and capitalism.

Law and Capitalism

Just as only the West could have produced a formal rational system of law, so, too, only in the modern Western world could be found "rational capitalistic enterprises with fixed capital, free labor, the rational specialization and combination of functions, and the allocation of productive functions on the basis of capitalistic enterprises, bound together in a market economy" (Weber, 1978:165). As noted previously, Weber listed the calculability and predictability in the adjudication and administration of law as one of the seven presuppositions that constitute the pure form of modern industrial capitalism. Moreover, Weber stated that modern industrial capitalism is rational to the extent that it relies on *capital accounting*. A business enterprise practices capital accounting when it "determines its income-yielding power by calculation according to the methods of modern bookkeeping and the striking of a balance" (Weber, 1950:275). It stands to reason then, that a rational economic action like capital accounting would have a necessary convergence with a rational legal action like formal rational lawmaking and lawfinding. Both types of action promote each other's development.

Weber identifies three different ways in which formal legal rationality fostered rational capitalist activity, which, by Weber's account, consists chiefly of budgetary management and profit making (Kronman, 1983:125–127). First, this type of juristic order produced a relatively stable set of rules that provided certain legal rights or *guarantees* to parties engaging in contractual transactions. These guarantees also gave to the contractual relationship a modicum of certainty and predictability. "To the person who finds himself actually in possession of the power to control an object or a person the legal guaranty gives a specific certainty of the durability of such power. To the person to whom something has been promised the legal guaranty gives a higher degree of certainty that the promise will be kept" (Weber, 1978: 667). By guaranteeing that contracts will be enforced according to previously known rules, the legal order increases the probability that promises, once made, will be kept. In this way, the law encourages the making of contracts and other forms of entrepreneurial activity upon which a market exchange depends.

A second way in which formal rational law may advance rational economic action is by introducing certain *legal techniques* that are indispensable to the development of an economic system with a high degree of calculability and predictability. Weber cites the laws of agency and of negotiable instruments as examples of legal techniques that had a tremendous impact on the rationalization of modern finance. **Agency** refers to the relationship in which one person (the agent) acts for or represents another (the principle) with the latter's consent. "Every rational business organization," Weber contends, "needs the possibility of acquiring contractual rights and of assuming obligations through temporary or permanent agents." **Negotiable instruments** refer to signed legal documents containing an unconditional promise or order to pay a certain sum of money (e.g., bills of exchange, notes, checks). According to Weber, advanced trade requires "a method by which transfers can be made legally secure and which eliminates the need of constantly testing the title of the transferor" (Weber, 1978:681–682). Ancient Roman commerce had to get along without these technical devices because instruments in writing were not promoted until the seventh century. However, agency and free negotiability are legal techniques that are quite "indispensable for a modern capitalist society" (Weber, 1978:682).

Aside from the fact that budgetary management and profit making had to be encouraged in a growing market economy, two problems also needed to be addressed and settled. First, there had to be a way of clearly determining where it was that every member and every official of a business organization legally stood in relation to each other. Similarly, there had to be a way of clearly determining the legal position of the organization "and of the legitimation of its organs in both contractual transactions and in procedure" (Weber, 1978:706). In other words, the legal duties and expectations of people and corporations required specific articulation within the context of capitalist activity. The technical legal solution to these two problems was found in the concept of the juristic person (Weber, 1978:706). The **juristic person** or "juristic personality" (an impersonal concept which is applied to flesh and blood individuals as well as to corporations), is an abstract bearer of universal rights and duties. This concept made responsibility, liability, and expectation (and not magic, prophecy, or privilege) the central foci of purposive contracts. Moreover, the notion of an abstract juristic person serves two purposes: it treats all "persons" equally, and it gives predictability, uniformity, and calculability to legal and economy activity. In reference to business corporations, Weber calls the concept of the juristic person, "the most rational actualization of the idea of the legal personality of organizations" (1978:707). Furthermore, the idea of the juristic person "was compatible with a mode of production such as capitalism that needed autonomous entities competing in a formally free state" (Milovanovic, 1989:97).

Thus, it is with the aid of legal techniques and concepts like agency, negotiability, and the juristic person that the modern legal order has facilitated the operations of profit-making business enterprises. Without such legal techniques, commerce can be rationalized only to a limited degree (Kronman, 1983a:126).

Finally, a third way in which the formal rational legal order may promote rational economic activity is through *legislation* created specifically for the purpose of encouraging certain kinds of economic relations (Weber, 1978:667). For example, the *capital gains tax* allows the payment of taxes on profits made on the sale of capital assets at a lower rate than that applicable to ordinary income. This legislation, which is part of the Internal Revenue Code, is intended to stimulate market-exchange activity.

We may say, then, that a formally rational legal system contributed to the emergence and development of modern industrial capitalism by introducing guaranteed rights, legal techniques, and legislation. More generally, however, Weber has shown us that only within a sociohistorical context, where certain religious, political, and economic factors converge, could a formal rational legal system be realized. And since it is in modern Western Europe that these factors were present in their required form, it was only there and then that the law became formally rational.

In the preceding sections we have seen how Max Weber's sociology of law stands in close theoretical proximity to his sociology of religion, his political sociology, and his sociology of economics. That is to say that in Weber's view the law's development and application can best be understood when we consider such extralegal factors as the religious, the political, and the economic.

In an effort that brings together political and religious influences into his legal sociology, Weber identifies three ideal types of authority to illustrate the political process by which the law is created and given legitimacy. He tells us that charismatic and traditional authority have about them a quality of the sacred while rational-legal authority is devoid of all religious influences. Weber also states that there are four types of lawmaking and lawfinding that can be distinguished on the basis of whether or not they are (a) guided by clear and general rules; and (b) informed by ethical, political, and religious criteria. In a legal order that is formal rational, general rules are clearly stated in written documents and ethical, political, and religious criteria are not considered. Finally, we looked at what is perhaps the most central question in Weber's sociology of law: How did formal rational legal thought evolve in modern Western civilization? In answering this question, Weber examined the European legal system's elective affinity with the secularization of the law, the laicization of the adjudication process, the bureaucratization of political administration, and perhaps most significantly, the emergence of an economic activity that consists of budgetary management and profit making: modern industrial capitalism.

Despite Weber's penchant for continuously listing fairly complex terms and giving them similar sounding names, these concepts are crucial to understanding the major theses that form his legal sociology. By drawing, then, upon these and other concepts that will be introduced shortly, we will now be able to examine intelligently some of the theoretical statements that neo-Weberian scholars have advanced in recent years.

Neo-Weberian Contributions to the Weberian Perspective

Before we begin our analysis of the neo-Weberian contributions to the Weberian perspective, it is essential that we briefly glance at a couple of Weber's methodological ideas; namely, his insistence on the need of a value-free sociology and his use of *Verstehen*. These two ideas will help us to understand more fully the recent contributions and critiques that have been advanced in regard to Weber's concept of legitimacy.

Weber inveighed against the sociologist taking a value stand toward the social phenomena under study. Whatever his or her ethical opinion, the sociologist qua scientist is not to endorse any particular set of beliefs. To recognize beliefs is one thing, to support those beliefs is quite another. Indeed, Weber was very dogmatic about the fact that it is necessary that the social scientist remain completely neutral and refrain from making value judgments.

However, Weber argued that since social action is value directed, it is important that sociologists see values as objects of investigation. In other words, because people's beliefs compel them to act in certain ways, in order to truly comprehend social action the sociologist has to engage in an interpretive understanding of people's belief system or values. This analysis of values, however, must be conducted in the same way as an analysis of other empirically observable facts: in an objective manner. Any analysis that is not objective is biased and distorted and therefore not scientifically valid. Sociology must always strive to be a value-free science. As such, sociology is to be an analytical, and not an evaluative, discipline. As an analytical discipline, sociology's concern is with the interpretation of meaning and the explanation of causal relationships.

Weber's thinking in sociology was profoundly influenced by German historicism. As indicated previously, this academic movement looked at the inner meanings, emotional states, and spiritual experiences of organic cultures. This emphasis compelled Weber to consider the subjective meaning of all social phenomena. Accordingly, Weber describes sociology as "a science concerning itself with the interpretive understanding of social action and thereby with a causal explanation of its course and consequences" (1978:4). In explaining the cause-and-effect relationships between two or more kinds of social action (e.g., the charismatic leader's issuing of commands and the followers adherence to those commands) or social activity (e.g., the formulation of a legal order with a high degree of calculability and predictability and the increasing prominence of contractual business transactions), Weber advanced the concept of *Verstehen*. As a type of *interpretive understanding* of cultural phenomena (actions and activity), *Verstehen* was to aid the sociologist in interpreting those phenomena in terms of existing values. Sociology, then, engages in the interpretive understanding of values.

Weber distinguishes between two kinds of interpretive understanding. Direct *observational understanding*, he wrote, involves "deriving the meaning of an act or symbolic expression from immediate observation without reference to any broader context," while *explanatory understanding* involves placing "the particular act in a broader context of meaning involving facts which cannot be derived from immediate observation of a particular act or expression" (Weber, 1978:58, n.7).

In the remainder of this chapter we will continue to examine of some of the more salient themes in Max Weber's sociology of law, but this time we do so with the benefit of several theoretical developments that have taken place in the field since Weber's death. In particular, we will look at three main issues: Weber's concept of legitimacy, his "England problem," and his theoretical connection with the thought of Karl Marx. With the two methodological ideas of a value-free sociology and *Verstehen* we are now in a position to consider some of the theoretical statements and critiques made by contemporary scholars Martin Spencer, David Campbell, Alan Hyde, and Tom R. Tyler about Weber's concept of legitimacy and its relation to the social order.

Legitimacy

We have seen that a leader's authority is said to be legitimate when subordinates, through a sense of duty or obligation, voluntarily submit to his or her commands. Legal sociologist Gerald Turkel notes that, compared to power based on coercion, legitimate authority is based on *consensus* among superiors and subordinates (1980:23). This is to say that subordinates freely choose to obey their superiors on the basis of shared beliefs and values. Consensus, as a matter of cooperative social action, is the fundamental issue underlying legitimation.

What is said about the influence of personal authorities (e.g., industrial managers, judges, and elected representatives) also applies to *social orders* (political institutions such as Congress, political systems such as democracy, legal institutions such as the courts). People's beliefs in the legitimacy of a social order are premised on how they orient themselves to that order. Social action, says Weber, "may be guided by the belief in the existence of a legitimate order. The probability that action will be so governed will be called the 'validity' of the order in question" (1978:31). In other words, the greater the validity of a social order, the more obligated that people will feel toward it, and the more likely they are to accept its rules, principles, or commands. In addition, people, through their volitional acts of compliance, affirm it as a just order. Suppose that an attorney shows up in court at precisely the time that the judge has scheduled her case. She makes her punctual appearance not just out of habit, self-interest, or fear of being reprimanded, but because she believes she "ought" to do so. We may say that the attorney willingly adheres to the directives of the judge (as a representative of the judicial system) because she has a perceived obligation to obey his and the system's authority.

All social orders rely on legitimation to help maintain the stability and efficiency of their authority relations. Put another way, only through sufficient compliance can society function effectively. This legitimation, Weber has told us, generally has its basis in either affective or rational social action. In the next section, however, we look at that type of authority whose legitimacy is founded on higher moral principles.

Value-rational authority. Some neo-Weberians, like sociologist Martin Spencer, have expanded Weber's ideas about the legitimacy of authority. In so doing, Spencer has succeeded in developing a fourth ideal type of authority whose legitimacy is premised on an attitude not previously considered by Weber. This fourth type, **value-rational authority,** is informed by moral principles and can be used to explain the exercise of power in the higher levels of government.

According to Spencer (1970), Weber's comments on the three legitimate forms of authority—the *charismatic*, the *traditional*, and the *rational-legal*—are related to his comments on legitimate social orders. We had earlier defined legitimate order as "a [valid] set of ought ideas which are held in the minds of people" (Rheinstein, 1966:lxvii). Let us now employ Spencer's more detailed description and regard a legitimate social order as "a normative system which is upheld by the belief in the actors of its binding quality or rightness." (1970:123). Weber lists four ways by which people ascribe legitimacy to a social order:

(a) By tradition; a belief in the legitimacy of what has always existed; (b) by virtue of affectual attitudes, especially emotional, legitimizing the validity of what is newly revealed or a model to imitate; (c) by virtue of a rational belief in its absolute value, thus lending it the validity of an absolute and final commitment; (d) because it has been established in a manner which is recognized to be *legal* (1969:130).

We may label these four bases of legitimacy to a social order as *tradition, affectual attitudes, absolute-value,* and *rational-legal.*

Spencer states that Weber, in his discussions of orders and authority, is, in essence, dealing with the structure of social interactions. Weber identifies the components that make up this structure and give it stability as *authority* (or the rightful commands of a leader that are considered binding), and *norms* (or rules of conduct toward which people orient their actions). Spencer then finds three sets of relationships between Weber's three types of authority and three of the four types of legitimate norms cited above. These three relationships may be stated as follows:

1. The prophetic leader's *charismatic authority* generates *affectually legitimated norms* (sacred laws), which have their legitimate basis in the *affectual* (emotional) *attitudes* of his followers.
2. *Traditionally legitimated norms,* which have their legitimate basis in *usage* (custom), give the patriarchal master *traditional authority* over his subjects.
3. *Rational-legal norms,* which have their legitimate basis in "a manner which is recognized to be *legal,*" (that is, in formal *procedure*) give the high-level bureaucrat *rational-legal authority* over the lower level functionaries.

Spencer contends that all seven of the "fundamental postures" or categories of legitimacy—(1) charismatic authority, (2) traditional authority, (3) rational-legal authority, (4) traditionally legitimated norms, (5) affectually legitimated norms, (6) absolute-value norms, and (7) rational-legal norms—can be subsumed under two basic attitudes of legitimacy: *affectual* and *value-rational attitudes.* As previously indicated, affectual attitudes of social action are based on the emotions (passions and feelings) of the individual. Affectual attitudes, according to Spencer, are found in categories one, two, four, and five above. The value-rational attitudes of social action, on the other hand, are characterized by the consciously determined pursuit of some ethical, aesthetic, or religious value or cause. Such attitudes may be found in categories three, six, and seven above.

Spencer explains that the legitimacy of category six, that of absolute-value norms, is premised on the notion of "natural law," or law that relies on higher moral principles. An example of this type of legitimacy is found in civil rights legislation. It may be said that people comply with such legislation because they believe in the higher principles—the absolute values—of "equality" and "freedom." Furthermore, in Spencer's view, the type of legal thought that best typifies absolute-value norms is substantive rationality. The reader will recall that in a substantively rational-legal order, use is made of unambiguous general principles that may be derived from religion and a variety of extralegal sources.

In making all of the these conceptual connections Spencer has succeeded in constructing a new variety of authority beyond Weber's three-fold classification of the charismatic, the traditional, and the rational-legal. Spencer's calls this fourth type *value-rational authority.* Unlike rational-legal authority, which is precipitated by *formal law,* value-rational authority is derived from *substantive moral principles.* Spencer distinguishes between the two types of authority:

> Rational-legal authority is typically located in bureaucracies and exists in relation to specific laws that define its precincts. Value-rational authority

is typically found in the higher realms of political office—president, prime minister, chancellor or even constitutional monarch, and exists in relation to principles. Thus if legal rational authority is celebrated as an administration of laws, not of men, value-rational authority is a government of principles, not of men (1970:130).

Value-rational authority has greater explanatory power than Weber's rational-legal type in regard to analyzing the legitimacy of leaders who hold electoral offices in democratic political institutions; leaders such as the President of the United States, members of Congress, and the governors of the states. While rational-legal authority may, prima facie, account for the president's legitimate domination (based on the U.S. Constitution and other laws), it does not "explain certain curious waxings and wanings of presidential authority" (Spencer, 1970:129). For example, the authority of a president elected to office by a minority of the popular vote may be somewhat suspect because it is not based on the higher principle of "the will of the majority." In this case, the attainment of authority does not have the consent of the governed. In democratic societies, the consent of the governed is an extralegal ultimate value underlying the formal laws of the Constitution that legitimize the president's domination.

While Spencer extends Weber's three ideal types of authority by developing a fourth type, value-rational authority, the two theorists that we consider next, David Campbell and Alan Hyde, engage in a deliberate *critique* of the Weberian notion of legitimacy. Indeed, it is through the method of critique that neo-Weberian scholars have also refined and advanced Weber's ideas about legitimacy. We begin with a discussion of Campbell's critical comments concerning Weber's value-free approach to the empirical study of legitimacy.

Value freedom and legitimacy. According to David Campbell (1986), there is a contradiction in Weber's value-free explanation of legitimacy. As we have already seen, Weber's methodological approach is intended to help the sociologist-as-investigator achieve an empirical understanding of the subjective beliefs that persons hold about the legitimacy of a particular social order. Because sociologists are to be ethically neutral, they are forbidden to assess the "truth" of these beliefs. Campbell contends that Weber's value-free approach is impossible to carry out and that those scientific commentaries that purport to have carried it out merely conceal the value judgments they necessarily contain. In addition, Campbell proposes that the hidden expression of specific value judgments is, in fact, "intrinsically *required*" by Weber's sociological analysis of legitimacy. Let us see how Campbell backs up his assertions.

Campbell maintains that people's values are at the root of their beliefs in legitimacy. Therefore, the sociologist must understand those values so that legitimacy can be seen as a specific form of people's orientation to an order of authority. Weber, however, warns that for scientific purposes "it is only the probability of orientation to the subjective *belief* in the validity of an order which constitutes the valid order itself" (1978:33). In other words, the sociologist, as a scientist, must not be involved in making evaluations about the correctness of the beliefs in legitimacy under consideration. The sociologist need only be concerned with the degree of probability that a person will act a certain way in relation to a social order that that person sees as valid. Put another way, the sociologist should simply take note of the person's belief (as an empirical matter of fact) and ignore the substance of the value (as an ethical matter of conscience) that supports the belief. "When Weber holds that beliefs in legitimacy maintain the stability of an order of domination he by no means wishes to confer any actual legitimacy upon that order. He merely wants to point to the empirical significance of validity" (Campbell, 1986:210).

However, Weber's alleged objectivity is not sustained. Indeed, his "own sociological accounts can always be seen to take a value stance with regard to the legitimations discussed" (Campbell, 1986:212). How is it that Weber manages to surreptitiously inject his own values into his sociology? Campbell posits that Weber does so in two ways. First, Weber engages in a "continuous reservation" concerning people's value-based beliefs about a social order that they consider to be legitimate. In other words, Weber is skeptical of the meanings people give to legitimacy. And second, Weber effectively provides explanations that coincide, not with people's value-based self-understanding of the social order, but with Weber's own theoretical scheme of legitimate authority.

Through his methodological technique of *Verstehen*, Weber proposes to understand both legitimacy and social action. But Campbell claims that of the four ideal typic social actions that Weber presents—the rationally purposeful, the value-rational, the affectual, and the traditional—only rationally purposeful social action possesses meaning that can be fully comprehended sociologically. Because the other three types have a lower degree of rationality, they do not easily lend themselves to observational understanding. That is to say, because their meaning cannot be known empirically, a causal explanation is not possible. Weber therefore primarily focuses his causal explanations on rationally purposeful, and thus more predictable, social actions rather than on irrational, unpredictable social actions based on ethical, aesthetic, or religious values, emotions, or habit.

In regard to the study of legitimacy, *Verstehen* is used to understand the meaning of a person's beliefs concerning an order of domination that he or she considers to be legitimate. Weber's ultimate intention is to determine empirically if such an order has stability. Campbell claims that Weber's determination to do both—that is, on the one hand, to understand the meaning of a person's belief concerning a social order and, on the other, to determine if that order has stability—is contradictory. The contradiction becomes apparent when Weber sets out to *explain* (as opposed to merely *understand*) the basis of a belief in legitimacy. For example, Weber explains that the legitimacy of the patriarchal form of traditional authority (that is, that relation between master and servant) is based on "an established belief in the sanctity of immemorial traditions" (1978:215). But, says Campbell, this causal explanation may or may not jibe with the servant's self-understanding of the authority relation. Contrary to Weber, the servant may give legitimacy to patriarchal authority because of, "let us say, [the servant's] belief in the natural givenness of hierarchy" (Campbell, 1986:216). Thus, Weber's explanation is not based on the subordinate's conscious intended meaning of an order of domination, but on *Weber's* ideal typic understanding of an order of domination. Campbell's illustration shows very clearly that Weber sometimes forcibly fits his empirical explanations into his conceptual constructs. As political scientist Robert Grafstein points out, "Weber's strategy is to project meanings into the participants, who are then held to take these meanings as motives for their behavior" (1981:472).

In sum, according to Campbell, only legitimate authority that is based on rationally purposeful social action can be truly analyzed in a value-free manner. By contrast, the traditional and charismatic types of authority, which are based on irrational forms of social action, cannot, despite Weber's contentions, be explained in a value neutral way.

Another critique of Weber's notion of legitimacy is rendered by legal sociologist Alan Hyde. So critical is Hyde of Weber's thesis that legitimacy fosters obedience to the law, that Hyde recommends abandoning the concept of legitimacy altogether.

Abandoning the concept of legitimacy. In his article "The Concept of Legitimation in the Sociology of Law" (1983), Hyde questions Weber's theory of legitimacy on two points: (1) that people's belief in legitimacy influences their behavior, and (2) that the more people believe in the legitimacy of a social order, the more likely that they will obey its norms. Hyde also finds untenable the extended argument that the courts, through their formal procedures and legal decisions, influence people's beliefs in the legitimacy of the law. Hyde's article is important because it empirically demonstrates why a concept that Weber regarded as central to his political and legal sociology—formal legitimacy—is virtually irrelevant in explaining why everyday people obey the law.

Although Weber acknowledges that there are, in reality, a wide variety of motives for obedience, he nevertheless singles out three ideal type motives: *habit*, *self-interest*, and *legitimacy* (1978:31). Weber further admits that all legal and political orders are based ultimately on physical or psychological coercion; that is, on the *fear of sanctions*. Consequently, Hyde's question is: If we can explain a whole array of social actions as the result of habit, self-interest, and the fear of sanctions, do we really need the concept of legitimacy as an explanation of obedience to the law? Reformulated, the question becomes: Does the law legitimate anything? More specifically, we may ask with Hyde: If people comply with the legal decisions handed down by the courts, why do they do so? Let us see how Hyde addresses these questions as he reveals Weber's theoretical shortcomings.

In Weber's view, rational-legal authority (this is the type of authority that our courts possess in deciding legal cases) is legitimated by the correctness of formal legal procedure. "Today," says Weber, "the most common form of legitimacy is the belief in legality, the compliance with enactments which are *formally* correct" (1978:37). In other words, under Weber's model the law's legitimation does not depend on the specific legal *rules* but on the formal *procedures* that guide the formulation of legal rules and the outcome of judicial decisions. Hyde refers to this model as **formal legitimation.** He points out, however, that other theorists focus on **substantive legitimation,** or the supposition that legal rules are legitimated because they reflect the substantive moral values of the population.

Scholars have also differed on what it is that judicial decisions legitimate. Some have argued that they legitimate an entire social *order* (e.g., a political system such

as democracy). Others maintain that judicial deci⟨
norm (legal statute) they pronounce as well as the po⟨
gress or the president, that enact or act upon the norm in⟨
however, that none of these scholars have looked at what the⟨
to say about the legitimizing influence that judicial decision⟨
belief and behavior.

Hyde finds that empirical studies simply do not support the ⟨
of formal legitimation. These studies show that people know very lit⟨
the courts are doing, have a low opinion of the few judicial decisions a⟨
they do know, and, most importantly, care a great deal more about the su⟨
moral values, or content, behind a judicial decision than they do about the ⟨
procedure that was followed in rendering the decision.

It follows, however, that because people have little knowledge about the norm⟨
that the courts pronounce, then norm legitimation and order legitimation are irrelevant. Further, because people have a low opinion of the courts, any compliance
with the court's legal decisions has to be attributed to either motives of self-interest
or the fear of sanctions. Finally, because there is little popular awareness about the
courts' doings, people's obedience to the law cannot be based on legitimacy (that
is, a belief in its "rightness") rooted in either formal procedure or substantive moral
values. As Hyde states, "legitimacy cannot be shown to be as significant in explaining obedience as rational calculation, including evaluation of self-interest and
sanctions" (1983:426). In sum, because legitimacy does not explain why ordinary
people obey the law, Hyde suggests that we abandon the concept.

Legitimacy and procedural justice. Compared with Hyde's analysis, legal researcher Tom Tyler in his book, *Why People Obey the Law* (1990), has arrived at a
very different conclusion concerning voluntary legal compliance. Tyler undertakes
a longitudinal study that examines the issue of compliance from the instrumental
and normative perspectives. The **instrumental perspective on procedural justice** suggests that disputants assess the fairness of judicial procedure based on the
degree to which they are able to directly or indirectly attain a settlement that is
favorable to them. In other words, where people feel that they have control over
decisions, they believe that the procedure is fair; where they feel they lack control,
they believe it is unfair. By contrast, the **normative perspective on procedural
justice** views disputants as being more concerned with the normative issues involved in the judicial process—issues such as neutrality, lack of bias, honesty, efforts
to be fair, politeness, and respect for citizen's rights—and as being less concerned
with determining the outcome.

In his study, Tyler seeks to understand compliance to legal authorities (police
officers and judges) from the instrumental and normative perspectives. In the
instrumental perspective, the disputants, as a matter of self-interest, will attempt to
indirectly attain a decision favorable to their case by controlling the presentation of
evidence—that is, by having the opportunity to speak and state their opinions to
the legal authority. Under these conditions, the disputants want to control the
process of the case in order to control the *decision*. In the normative perspective, the
disputants also value the opportunity to present their side of the story to the

...ence the judicial decision, but
...at they can feel that they have

...ho had had recent personal
...dents generally felt that they
...state their case. At the same
...low *decision control,* or little
...r's findings clearly revealed
...respondents than was deci-
...s react to their experiences
...g an opportunity to state
...he case.

...judicial procedure, Tyler
...o obey the legal authority
...und that neither process
...the respondents' perceived obliga-
...other hand, both types of control had effects concern-
...for legal authorities. However, process control, not decision control,
was the issue that really mattered because people want to be treated politely and
have respect shown for their rights. "This reinforces the suggestion that people
value the opportunity to state their case and feel more fairly treated if they receive
it, even if it does not affect the decisions made" (Tyler, 1990:127). If people perceive that they have been treated fairly (i.e., ethically, neutrally, honestly, politely),
they will generally be supportive of legal authorities. This support enhances the authorities' legitimacy, and legitimacy, of course, plays an important role in promoting behavioral compliance with the law.

Tyler's empirical data are consistent with Weber's thesis that rational-legal authority is legitimated by formal procedure. According to Tyler, "procedural justice
is the key normative judgment influencing the impact of experience on legitimacy. . . . Views about authority are strongly connected to judgments of the fairness of the procedures through which authorities make decisions" (1990:162). In
short, legitimacy is based not only on instrumental issues of short-term self-interest
(positive outcome), but is primarily based on normative issues (fair procedure).

In this section we noted that Weber's concept of legitimacy and the issues that
surround it have been found wanting by David Campbell and Alan Hyde. On the
other hand, Martin Spencer and Tom Tyler consider Weber's idea of legitimacy
extremely helpful in explaining why it is that people obey the law. Additionally,
Tyler has found empirical support for the concept's continued application. Nevertheless, whether Weber's notion of legitimacy is critiqued positively or negatively,
there can be no doubt that the statements made by these scholars have greatly enhanced our knowledge of a concept that is central to Weber's sociology of law.

In the following section we look at other criticisms made against Weber. In
particular, we analyze those comments advanced by several neo-Weberians on what
is perhaps the most glaring problem in Weber's sociology of law, the England
problem.

191

The England Problem

As noted earlier in this chapter, in Weber's view, a correspondence exists between a logically formal rational system of law, which provides calculable and predictable judicial outcomes, and market exchange capitalism, which relies on such outcomes to ensure efficient contractual relations and guaranteed rights. But from what Weber tells us it is difficult to determine a causal (successive) relationship between the two phenomena. On the one hand, Weber states that "capitalism has not been a decisive factor in the promotion of that form of rationalization of the law which has been peculiar to the continental West" (1978:892). On the other hand, the reverse explanation, that rational law facilitated the emergence of capitalism, becomes untenable in light of the situation in England.

Capitalist development began in England some 150 years before it did on the Continent, without the benefit of a law that was formally rational. As we shall now discuss, English common law can scarcely be said to constitute itself as a gapless and internally consistent body of abstract rules. This deviant case has been referred to as Weber's "England problem" (Trubek, 1972:747). The English legal system presented Weber with a theoretical problem because of the irrational features of its common law. Let us briefly look at some of these features.

The irrational features of the common law of England. Weber very clearly regarded the practices of lawmaking and lawfinding in England to be substantively irrational. That is to say, English lawmakers and lawfinders were not guided by general rules and procedures nor did they decide a case solely on the basis of legal criteria. Weber states several reasons why English common law is substantively irrational.

Weber explains that the "empirical justice" (substantive irrationality) of English common law had its basis in **stare decisis** (from Latin meaning "to adhere to," or the policy that the courts must stand by prior judicial decisions—that is, legal precedent must be followed). He defines **empirical justice** as "formal judgments rendered, not by subsumption under rational concepts, but by drawing on 'analogies' and depending on and 'interpreting' concrete 'precedents'" (Weber, 1978:976). In Weber's view, then, the English legal system of precedent was irrational because it depended on induction as its method; that is, it relied on empirical propositions derived from particular facts. This method allows for the introduction of factors that are not only extralegal but that are also irrelevant to the judicial process. Thus, one reason why English law is substantive irrational is "because of the overriding emphasis that the system places upon the fact situation at the expense of the general principles of law" (Hunt, 1978:123–124).

Another factor that contributed to the law's substantive irrationality was the fact that England developed a small, elite group of judges and lawyers who had significant influence in shaping English legal thought, legal education, and the legal profession. This elite group had a charismatic nature about it, and the group's influence was largely whimsical. "Alongside all this," says Weber, "we find the patriarchal, summary and highly irrational jurisdiction of the justices of the peace. They deal with the petty causes of everyday life and, . . . represent a kind of khadi justice" (1978:891). Further, the jury, which had emerged as an institution in England after the royal edits of King Henry II, was an irrational form of "popular justice" because it gave no reasons to justify its verdict.

In examining the historical record, English legal historian David Sugarman (1987) shows empirically that certain "peculiarities of the English" contributed to the irrational nature of their legal system. These peculiarities are related to legal content, form, and training; judicial corruption and abuses; and the elitism of the legal profession.

Regarding the content of the law, Sugarman points out that although capitalism required clearly defined rights, in England such concepts as "absolute private property" and "freedom of contract" were open to a variety of meanings; all of which accentuated the law's irrational character. Additionally, laws important to business and industry, such as those governing partnerships and companies, were notoriously complex and ambiguous throughout most of England's Industrial Revolution. Moreover, despite the intricacy and uncertainty surrounding the law regulating unincorporated associations, it was not until the late-nineteenth century that incorporation replaced the partnership as the dominant form of business organization in England. Finally, many of the modern principles governing contract law and torts were developed much later than one would expect; that is, *after* the country's market-exchange economy had been allowed to mature.

Concerning the form of law, Sugarman contends that a striking feature of the English legal system was its deliberately unprincipled nature: the accumulative features of case and statute law. This unprincipled character was inevitable given the fact that local, customary, state, and informal norms and institutions existed alongside each other. Lawyers took advantage of the law's flexibility, discretion, and inherently open-ended character to carve out semiautonomous legal regimes for their clients. This made the legal system a patchwork of rules and jurisdictions. We may add that this patchwork was partially due to England's failure to codify its law and accept Roman law and its adherence to rational technique.

As concerns training in the law, England developed its legal instruction along empirical lines; that is, in the form of the apprenticeship. Professional and university legal education were almost nonexistent in that country during the time of the Industrial Revolution. Until the nineteenth century, English legal science did not consist of statues logico-deductively derived from abstract principles by university-trained doctors of the law; rather, it consisted of "lawyers law" produced by practicing attorneys.

As regards judges and the courts, corruption was rampant in England until at least the 1860s. During the eighteenth and nineteenth centuries, patronage, emoluments, sinecures, and perquisites were used by the state to bribe, remunerate, or honor the judiciary and the legal profession. Abuses by the courts were another form of judicial irrationality. For example, the Privy Council, which acted as the court of final appeal, would often reverse the decisions of the Dominion courts without preparing written judgments and usually with only three judges sitting. Also, the Law Lords of the House of Lords—the highest court in England—did not see themselves as professional judges. "During this period many high court appointments were political rather than based on their potential qualities as judges" (Sugarman, 1987:29).

As pertains the legal profession, in the nineteenth century the English bar was highly elitist and had become a near monopoly of the urban professional and business classes as well as the landed gentry. This made for a very conservative and reform-resistant bar. Indeed, the history of the English bar can be depicted as involving a series of minor crises that it absorbed without any major reforms. "In short, the bar has been pre-eminently successful in thwarting the efforts of those who have sought to 'modernize' it (in the Weberian sense)" (Sugarman, 1987:31).

The irrationalities of England's legal order have been pointedly satirized by no less an acute observer of nineteenth-century English life than Charles Dickens. In his works, Dickens repeatedly derides the irrational legal fictions so prevalent in English law at the time (Stone, 1985). *Bleak House,* for instance, is full of sardonic statements about the Court of Chancery—a court of remedy whose procedure is based on **equity** (i.e., unwritten principles of fairness as applied to each individual case) rather than on clearly formulated legal rules. Another such example is found in *Oliver Twist,* where Dickens mocks the injustice that results from the legal supposition that a wife acts under the direction of her husband. The law therefore holds the husband accountable for his wife's actions. Declares Mr. Bumble, "If the law supposes that . . . the law is a ass—a idiot" (Dickens, 1966:354).

In contrast to the substantive irrationality of English law, the legal systems of Italy, Spain, France, Germany, and the Netherlands were much more formally rational. At the time that Weber was writing, most of continental law had been codified, as exemplified by the French Civil Code of 1804. Continental law therefore constituted itself into an internally coherent and highly systematized legal doctrine. Systematization was especially characteristic of the Pandectist legal science of Germany under the influence of the jurist Friedrich Karl von Savigny, who, despite his antipathy toward codification, argued that the law must have a precision that resembles "a technical expression of geometry" (1986:38). To be sure, Weber considered the abstract Pandectist Civil Code, prepared in 1887 and finally implemented in 1900, to be the best expression of logically formal rational law. Continental law, with its autonomy, generality, and universality (those unique features that gave it a relatively high degree of rationality), was especially conducive to the needs of industrial capitalism. Let us now see how the neo-Weberian scholars explain the rise of a highly rational economic activity (capitalism) in a country (England) with a highly irrational system of law (the common law).

Law and economy in England. Due in large measure to Weber's intellectual honesty, he did not shy away from England's unique historical situation. He duly noted that in that country "the degree of legal rationality is essentially lower than, and of a type different from, that of continental Europe." Further, "English law-finding is not, like that of the Continent, an 'application' of 'legal propositions' logically derived from statutory texts." Finally, "it may indeed be said that England achieved capitalistic supremacy among the nations not because but rather in spite of its judicial system" (1978:890, 891, 814).

Some neo-Weberians (Albrow, 1975:22; Trubek, 1972; 1986) propose that Weber's treatment of the English situation reveals difficulties and in some cases outright contradictions in his entire discussion of the relations of law and economy.

Others account for the English situation in ways that do not completely refute Weber's thesis.

David Sugarman (1987) very effectively explains away the England problem. He argues that conceptualizations of modern society that are grounded in sharp dichotomies—e.g., the irrational/rational—are nothing more than caricatures and artificial devices that have no basis in empirical reality. He thus sets out to demonstrate that the evolutionary path to modernity and the emergence of a market-exchange economy in England "entailed a complex juxtaposition of the 'rational' and 'irrational' . . . rather than simple, stark discontinuities conjured up within a linear historical periodization" (Sugarman, 1987:3). Consequently, despite the irrational and antiformalistic characteristics listed above, the English legal system also possessed certain distinctive features that made it formally rational. Sugarman gives several examples: the English gentry, unlike the nobilities elsewhere, were not exempt from the law; English jurist Jeremy Bentham had made persuasive arguments in favor of legal codification; and "liberal reforms on a variety of fronts continued after 1870 undercutting further dimensions of 'pre-modern' England" (1987:41).

When we consider the various features that made English law formally rational, it is easy to see that for Weber there was no simple, cause-and-effect relationship between rational law and calculative economic activity. Instead, his approach was multicausal, and Sugarman contends that Weber "argued that a variety of forces had shaped the development of legal systems (professional, economic, social and political)" (1987:12). Sugarman maintains that because it was never Weber's intention to draw a positive and direct link between law and capitalism, Weber never had an England problem with which to contend.

Sociologist Herbert Treiber (1985:840) takes a slightly different track and suggests that Weber saw an elective affinity, and not a causal relation, between law and economics. In this view, various social and legal forces converge at a particular time and place and subsequently create the opportunity for capitalism to flourish. In the end it may be said that "the existence of logically formal rational law is a *necessary*, but not, it must be stressed, a *sufficient* condition for the emergence of capitalism" (Hunt, 1978:122; Beirne, 1979b:126). Other scholars give different explanations to the England problem.

Legal sociologist Maureen Cain (1980), for one, maintains that even though the English situation did not fit neatly into Weber's theoretical analysis of the causal relationship between logically formal rational law and an economic system based on means-ends calculation (namely, profit making and budgetary management), Weber was nevertheless able to explain the deviant case. Weber did so by arguing that despite the irrational features of the common law, the English were able to develop "a system of calculable and predictable adjudication finely attuned to the needs of the emergent capitalist class" (Cain, 1980:75). The English legal system, Cain suggests, did this in two ways:

> For the development of capitalism two features of Common Law have been relevant and both have helped to support the capitalist system. Legal training has been primarily been in the hands of the lawyers from among whom also the judges are recruited, i.e., in the hands of a group which is

active in the service of the propertied, and particularly capitalistic, private interests and which has to gain its livelihood from them. Furthermore and in close connection with this, the concentration of the administration of justice at the central courts in London and its extreme costliness have amounted almost to a denial of access to the courts for those with inadequate means (Weber, 1978:891–892).

Restated, the common law, with its relative flexibility, constructed a two-tiered legal system: one for capitalist interests and one for the petty causes of everyday life. In sum, Cain posits that, albeit limited, the rational features of the English legal system operated where it really mattered, in the area of commerce.

Sociologist of law Alan Hunt (1978) explains Weber's handling of the England problem somewhat differently than does Cain. He suggests that the emergence of capitalism took place in England because the legal system there was able to use its backward features to its advantage. Thus, Hunt proposes the idea that Weber formulated a theory of the "advantages of backwardness." For example, the late development of the rational concept of corporation (i.e., the juristic person) resulted in the advantage of producing many other practical forms of corporate organization that were advantageous to capitalistic development (see Weber, 1978:722ff). As a result, states Weber, "these very elements of 'backwardness' in the logical and governmental aspects of legal development enabled business to produce a far greater wealth of practically useful legal devices than had been available under the more logical and technically more highly rationalized Roman law" (1978:688). All these factors notwithstanding, Hunt maintains that Weber ultimately fails to advance a coherent solution to the England problem.

In contrast to the explanations given by Cain and Hunt, legal sociologist Sally Ewing's (1987) account of the England question is truly novel. She contends that when Weber explained the relationship between law and economics, he focused not on the logically formal rationality of legal *thought*, but on the formal rational administration of *justice*. Ewing underscores the point that this formal justice is a sociological and not a juristic phenomenon because "it refers to how rules are mechanically applied, not to how they ought to be developed" (1987:489, n.6). Moreover, formal justice is "abstract and bound by strict procedure, and guarantees the legal certainty essential for calculability in economic transactions" (Ewing, 1987:489).

Ewing contends that a formal rational administration of justice could exist, and did in fact exist, alongside the two systems of European legal thought: the logically formal rational (i.e., Continental code law) and the substantive irrational (i.e., English common law). And indeed, formal justice—precisely because it established guaranteed rights that gave predictability to market exchanges—transformed the common law into "a formal, rational legal system in the sociological sense" (Ewing, 1987:499). As a consequence of formal justice, both Continental code law and English common law were able to establish and enforce contractual relations. Furthermore, "to the extent that each system defended the freedom of contract and protected guaranteed rights, the capitalist economic order could thrive" (Ewing, 1987:499). Thus, Ewing concludes: "English common law, for all its substantive irrationality from the juridical point of view, was, from the sociological perspective, a system that operated according to the principles of formal justice and was therefore ideally suited to the needs of capitalism" (1987:500). Her point is that there never was any England problem.

One of the earliest statements on the England problem was put forth by University of Wisconsin legal scholar David Trubek in his article "Max Weber on Law and the Rise of Capitalism" (1972). According to Trubek, it is with the England problem that the ambiguities and contradictions inherent in Weber's sociology of law are most clearly revealed. Trubek asserts that Weber gave three highly inconsistent general explanations for the deviant case.

First, Trubek says, Weber maintains that while the English legal system offered a low degree of calculability, it nevertheless was able to assist the bourgeoisie by denying justice to the lower class. States Weber: "the high cost of litigation and legal services amounted for those who could not afford to purchase them to a denial of justice . . . This denial of justice was in close conformity with the interests of the propertied, especially the capitalist, classes" (1978:814).

Second, Weber considered the English situation to be a unique historical event. England could achieve rational economic development in spite of its irrational legal system. The conditions that made capitalism possible in England were not present elsewhere.

Third, the English legal system, while far from a model of logically formal rationality, was sufficiently calculable to support capitalism since judges were favorable to capitalists and also adhered to precedent. Thus, says Weber, modern capitalism could arise in a place like England where the "lawyers who, in the service of their capitalist clients, invented suitable forms for the transaction of business, and from whose midst the judges were recruited who were strictly bound to precedent, that means, to calculable schemes" (1978:1395). Trubek posits that Weber's three inconsistent explanations of the England problem demonstrate that "Weber had no clear image of English history."

To be sure, Weber's thesis—that a logically formal rational system of law facilitates the emergence of capitalism—appears, at least on the face of it, to be largely unfounded in the case of England. Be that as it may, Weber's most central effort at explaining the connection between capitalism's exploitative effects and the law's rationalization has a discernible Marxist quality that may serve to give it added credence. We now turn to that connection.

Weber's Dialogue with the Ghost of Marx

In 1945, social theorist Albert Salomon wrote: "Max Weber, the historian of law, the political scientist and economist, became a sociologist in a long and intense dialogue with the ghost of Karl Marx" (1971:596). Since that time, several scholars have not only acknowledged Weber's general "dialogue" with Marx but have also pointed out that the former's sociology of law was substantially influenced by the latter. Weber's relationship to Marxism, however, was decidedly ambivalent; that is, while they shared some common ground, there were strong disagreements between the two thinkers. In what follows we will explore some of the similarities and divergencies between Weber and Marx.

Bourgeois materialism. Weber emphatically rejected the Marxian notions of historical materialism and economic determinism. Repudiating any monocausal analysis, Weber believed that in addition to economic factors, other influences, such as the political, the religious, and ideological, also had a very real impact on the conditions of social life. To Weber, these influences were more than mere epiphenomena of the economic mode of production. He therefore took great pains to show that the formal rationality of European law could be explained by various noneconomic factors, such as the diversity of political power relationships and the relations between the theocratic and the secular powers. For Weber, causal social relations are more complex and indeterminate than Marx had supposed them to be.

Weber also disagreed with Marx's hopeful vision of the future, refuting what he considered to be the utopian notions of socialism: the historically inevitable proletarian revolution, the collapse of capitalism, and the emergence of a socialist economy. "A progressive elimination of private capitalism is theoretically conceivable," wrote Weber, "although it is surely not so easy as imagined in the dreams of some literati who do not know what it is all about" (1978:1401).

Weber differed from Marx in another important respect: he was proud to call himself "bourgeois." Indeed, Weber had, in the 1920s, been commonly referred to as "the bourgeois Marx." British sociologist Martin Albrow (1975) contends that Weber's sociology of law could best be labeled "bourgeois materialism" because Weber does not focus on the antagonism between the capitalists and the proletariat; instead he dissolves society into a number of conflicting but interdependent interests, none more basic than others.

Capitalist interests and formal justice. Despite the aforementioned differences between Weber and Marx, both theorists do share some intellectual commonalties. To be sure, Weber, in his sociology of law, did utilize important aspects of the Marxian analysis of capitalist society. Like Marx, Weber attributed (at least in part) the development of the modern legal system to the economic needs of the bourgeois class. For example, he explained that in order to protect their business exchanges the bourgeoisie had to promote a rational (i.e., highly predictable and calculable) legal system with guaranteed rights. Thus, states Weber, legal guaranty was sought by "bourgeois interests, which had to demand an unambiguous and clear legal system, that would be free of irrational administrative arbitrariness . . . , that would also offer firm guaranties of the legally binding character of contracts, and that . . . would function in a calculable way" (1978:847). Simply put, rational law and formal justice legitimize capitalism and thus serve the interests of the economically powerful class. Weber states that "in an increasing expanding market, those who have market interests constitute the most important group. Their influence predominates in determining which legal transactions the law should regulate by means of power-granting norms" (1978:669).

Weber also seems to share a Marxian orientation in regard to the topic of legal freedoms. For example, Weber tells us that formal justice is advantageous to capitalist interests when it alleges that everyone, regardless of status or privilege, has the legal equality and guaranteed right to establish a business corporation. The

practical fact of the matter, however, is that only the bourgeoisie, not the proletariat, will be establishing such corporations.

Because it is in the area of contract law that Weber's views most closely
approximate those of Marx, we will now consider what Weber had to say about the
exploitative effects of contractual freedom.

Freedom and contract law. In an attempt that is somewhat reminiscent of the
efforts of Sir Henry Maine, Weber traced the historical evolution of contract law.
Very simply, a **contract** is an agreement between two or more parties that creates
legally enforceable rights and duties for the parties involved. According to Weber,
in a precapitalist economy (e.g., during antiquity and feudalism) the law operates to
define a person's relations and privileges with regard to others in accordance with
the person's social status. Thus, at this point in history, the law was primarily concerned with the "contract of fraternization," or **status contract.** The status contract was a means by which "a person was to become somebody's child, father, wife,
brother, master, slave, kin, comrade-in-arms, protector, client, follower, vassal, subject, friend, or quite generally, comrade" (Weber, 1978:672). This type of contract
had a magical significance because, although nothing tangible changed or was exchanged, a social transformation occurred in the person's status.

Let us take the marriage contract as an example. When two individuals marry
each other, their status or social standing changes because society now views them
as a couple and endows them with those rights and duties that are endemic to the
matrimonial relationship. The status contract creates a fraternal bond, a sort of
brotherhood and comradeship, between the parties involved in the relationship.

With the emergence of capitalism, however, the status contract, which was
seen as an obstruction to the development of a market economy, dissipated. It soon
became obvious that a new kind of contractual association was needed. As the
bourgeoisie increasingly gained power it demanded certain legal rights. In particular it sought protection against government interference in business as well as
autonomy to coordinate its commercial transactions. Simply put, the bourgeoisie
wanted complete freedom of contract in the sphere of economic exchange. The
legal system thus established the market-oriented money contract, or the **purposive contract.**

Unlike the status contract, the purposive contract has nothing to do with
fraternal relationships or affectual attitudes. It is instead designed to deal only with
the rational transactions of business. Weber baldly describes the purposive contract
as "a specific, quantitatively delimited, qualityless, abstract, and . . . economically
conditioned agreement" (1978:674). With the purposive contract, agreements are
made, not with comrades and in the spirit of brotherliness, but with strangers and
for the expressed purpose of obtaining money or material goods or for satisfying
certain needs. This type of contract was peculiar to, and necessary for, those business activities endemic to an exchange-market economy. It gave a greater degree of
predictability and calculability to all commercial transactions. For instance, it made
it easier for the capitalists to reliably calculate their chances of profit and loss.

Let us now see how the idea of contractual freedom in a capitalist society has
benefited the bourgeoisie and created relationships bereft of affectual expressions.

Consent or coercion? Weber states that a formal rational-legal order is intended to decrease constraint and increase individual freedom by giving people the right to exchange goods, personal work, and services as they wish and without interference by a third party. In other words, individuals are now at liberty to enter into contractual agreements based on their voluntary consent rather than on their personal qualities or status. However, the bourgeoisie has used the contract to increase its freedoms at the expense of the other social classes.

Weber recognizes that, for classes other than the bourgeoisie, the freedom of contract is more limited under capitalism than it ever was under previous economic systems. To take but one of Weber's illustrations: freedom of **testation**—the disposition of personal property by will—has either been eliminated or severely restricted in modern times. One way in which testation had been limited is through the French Civil Code's abolition of **primogeniture** (the right of the eldest son to inherit his father's estate). According to legal philosopher Anthony Kronman, Weber hinted that primogeniture and the other legal devices used to restrict testation were imposed by the bourgeoisie against the aristocracy in the former's struggle to gain economic and political power (1983a:113–114).

Worker exploitation is another sphere in which the bourgeoisie has relied on the notion of contractual freedom to further its own economic interests. Under capitalism, where the differences of property distribution and economic power are guaranteed by contract law, contractual freedom actually operates to exploit the workers: "The formal right of a worker to enter into any contract whatsoever with any employer whatsoever does not in practice represent for the employment seeker even the slightest freedom in the determination of his own conditions of work" (Weber, 1978:729). For example, although a worker—an unemployed single mother, let us say—is legally free to pursue a part-time job with anyone she wishes, the employer holds an advantaged contractual position because he can force his terms on her by saying that only full-time work is available, "take it or leave it." In this case, her economic powerlessness imposes a significant restriction on her freedom of contract. Formal law thus benefits the capitalists by strengthening their ability to coerce the workers.

Weber also states that in a highly rational market economy the legal notion of free contract creates social relationships that are purely instrumental and devoid of expressive passions and feelings. That is to say, when engaging in business transactions people's social actions must be rationally purposeful. The competitive nature of the market forces the contracting parties to calculate precisely the means for achieving their desired end of profit making. Although it gives predictable results to the contractual association, this type of mechanical exchange weakens the fraternal bonds of comradeship and kinship. In language that approximates Marx's concept of alienation, Weber explains that the market community is the most impersonal relationship into which humans can enter with one another. "The reason for the impersonality of the market is its matter-of-factness, its orientation to the commodity and only to that. . . . there are no obligations of brotherliness or reverence, and none of those spontaneous human relations that are sustained by personal unions" (Weber, 1978:636). Weber is clearly referring to the alienation that arises from the highly rational market economy of capitalism. It is therefore informative to compare and contrast Weber's thoughts on alienation with those of Marx.

The iron cage. While not specifically using the term "alienation," Weber's treatment of that state of estrangement that occurs when the consequences of people's actions are removed from their creations, motives, needs, and goals is nevertheless pervasive throughout his discussion of the trend toward increased rationalization. According to Weber, *alienation*—the separation of the workers from the means of production—is determined by technical and economic factors. Simply put, technical factors have to do with the efficiency of production while economic factors deal with the maximization of profit. Efficient productivity in the bureaucratized workplace requires that management subject the workers to a stringent organizational discipline. Additionally, profit making requires calculability, and calculability suppresses human values and needs. In both cases, the emphasis is on increased rationality, a process that results in heightened feelings of estrangement between the workers and the means of production as well as the means of administration. The end result is that the workers are treated as mere objects or commodities. In language very similar to that of Marx, Weber states that:

> the characteristic feature of our present situation is that private enterprise, which is associated with private bureaucracy and therefore with the separation of the worker from the means of production, controls a domain which has never before in the history of the world possessed both these characteristics together to the same extent—namely the domain of industrial production. Furthermore, this process goes together with the mechanization of production within the factory, which results in local concentration of workers in one and the same space, bondage to the machine and a common work discipline within the machine shop or the mine. It is this discipline, above all, which gives its particular tone to the present-day form of "separation" between the worker and the means of production (Runciman, 1980:252).

But, Weber contends, it is not just the workers who are estranged; so, too, are the capitalist entrepreneurs. The entrepreneurs' unrelenting pursuit of the highest profits possible "presupposes the *battle of man with man*" (Weber, 1978:93). Restated, the strict competitiveness required of the autonomous participants in the marketplace upholds the "rational" striving for money and power but subordinates "irrational" human values and wants. As Weber vividly puts it, "the pursuit of wealth, stripped of its religious and ethical meaning tends to become associated with purely mundane passions" (1958:182). This means that the rational, profit-seeking participants in a capitalist economy—whom Weber describes as "specialists without spirit, sensualists without heart" (1958:182)—relate to each other in wholly impersonal terms, thus compounding the problem of alienation. It also means that the process of estrangement will inevitably continue with the irresistible advance of bureaucratization. The principle of rationalism in all social spheres—the economic, administrative, technical, and the legal (with its rational-legal authority, formal rational law, juristic personality, purposive contract, etc.)—has trapped people in a cultural "iron cage" from which there is no escape. The historical fate of the modern world—the iron cage of rationality—is characterized by systematization and disenchantment. The systematization of life imprisons us in a mess of bureaucratic rules and regulations that contribute to our loss of freedom. The disenchantment of the world means a denial of all religious and magical qualities, which leads to our loss of meaning. The prophet, the charismatic hero, and the khadi judge have now been replaced by the bureaucratic functionary, the "organization man," and the legal technician.

While Marx optimistically saw the end of alienation and the beginning of human emancipation in the decay of capitalism, Weber, in his pessimism, saw no way out of the modern world's "shell of bondage." Regardless of which economic mode of production may be in place, capitalism or socialism, a highly bureaucratic administrative machinery will always exist because both systems require rational planning. Indeed, Weber believed that matters are made worse under socialism because it is a totally planned economy, which means that it is *more* rational than capitalism. Weber asserted that in modern industrial society, the separation of the workers from the means of production has become a *technical* necessity (Marcuse, 1968:212). Both capitalism and socialism will inevitably produce a highly impersonal social order.

Legal rationalization only serves to contribute to industrialized society's "mechanized petrification." Kronman succinctly states Weber's view of rational law in modern society:

> The rationalization of law has limited individual autonomy by subjecting the layman to an increasing dependence on legal specialists—a consequence that parallels the similar loss of autonomy in the capitalist factory and modern bureaucratic organization. . . . The modern legal order, too, represents a "shell of bondage", an "iron cage" in which the individual's power of self-control is increasingly limited by the continuous and irreversible growth of "the technical elements in the law"—a process that resembles (indeed, is merely one aspect of) the "irresistible advance of bureaucratization" characteristic of modern political and economic life (1983a:174–175).

SUMMARY

The goal of this chapter has been to present some of the most significant themes that constitute the sociology of law from the Weberian perspective. As such, we discussed Max Weber's eclectic approach as he looked to political sociology, the sociology of religion, and the sociology of economics in explaining the law's formulation and application. In other words, in Weber's view, the law's development can best be understood when we consider such extralegal factors as the political, the religious, and the economic.

Weber's sociology of law revolves around the concept of rationality. According to Weber, rationality was the distinguishing hallmark of modern Western civilization. Within the context of the Western world's rationality, we discussed the three theses that form the core of Weber's legal sociology.

First, we analyzed the three ideal types of political authority through which the law is created and made effective: the charismatic, the traditional, and the rational-legal. Each of the three types relies on various degrees of sacredness and each is closely connected with bureaucratically structured political and administrative organizations.

Second, we looked at Weber's four types of lawmaking and lawfinding and their connection with religious influences: the formal irrational, the substantive irrational, the substantive rational, and the formal rational. Weber stated that the formal rational legal order requires a highly bureaucratic administrative organization and is uniquely a product of Western civilization.

Third, we discussed the effect that capitalism had on the emergence of continental Europe's unique legal system. The larger question that we addressed was: How did formal rational legal thought evolve in the modern Western world and what prevented its development elsewhere? A partial answer to this question revealed that there had to exist an elective affinity between formal legal rationality and modern industrial capitalism.

We then turned our attention to the contributions that neo-Weberians have made to the Weberian perspective with regard to the concept of legitimacy, Weber's England problem, and Weber's dialogue with the ghost of Karl Marx.

In regard to legitimacy, we begin with a discussion of how certain scholars have recently analyzed, critiqued, and expanded Weber's ideas about the legitimacy of authority. Martin Spencer developed a new variety of authority—value-rational authority—whose legitimacy is premised on absolute-value norms.

Next, we saw how David Campbell pointed out the contradiction in Weber's allegedly value-free explanation of legitimacy. Weber's contradiction becomes apparent when he attempts to explain, instead of to understand, the basis of a belief in legitimacy. Campbell contends that Weber's explanations are not based on the *actor's* belief in the legitimacy of an order of domination, but on *Weber's* ideal typic knowledge about an order of domination.

Finally, Alan Hyde empirically demonstrated why formal legitimacy is virtually irrelevant in explaining why everyday people obey the law. He stated that people care a great deal more about the substantive moral values behind a judicial decision than they do about the formal procedure that was followed in rendering that decision.

Continuing with our discussion of legitimacy, we looked at how Tom Tyler sought to understand, from the instrumental and normative perspectives, why people obey the law. Tyler found that disputants are primarily concerned with normative issues (fair procedure) involved in the judicial process. His findings were consistent with Weber's thesis that rational-legal authority is legitimated by formal procedure.

In focusing on Weber's England problem, we considered how this problem resulted from the fact that capitalism, as a highly rational economic activity, arose in England despite that country's highly irrational system of common law. In attempting to explain Weber's England problem, some neo-Weberian scholars have suggested that the English situation reveals difficulties and in some cases outright contradictions in Weber's discussion of the relations of law and economy. Others account for the English situation in ways that do not completely refute Weber's thesis that a logically formal rational system of law facilitates the emergence of capitalism.

We concluded this chapter with an examination of Weber's theoretical connection with the thought of Karl Marx. Although there existed some strong disagreements between the two thinkers, they also shared some intellectual commonalities. We noted that it is in the area of contract law, and more specifically on the topic of the exploitative effects of contractual freedom, that Weber's views most closely approximate those of Marx. Finally, in comparing and contrasting Weber's thoughts on alienation with those of Marx, we saw that legal rationalization contributes to alienation as people's freedom is limited by the law's increased technicality.

This chapter gave a view of legal sociology from the Weberian perspective. In the next chapter we will consider legal sociology from the Durkheimian perspective.

Categories of Legal Thought

Max Weber

...A body of law can be "rational" in several different senses, depending on which of several possible courses legal thinking takes toward rationalization. Let us begin with the seemingly most elementary thought process, viz., generalization, i.e., in our case, the reduction of the reasons relevant in the decision of concrete individual cases to one or more "principles," i.e., legal propositions. This process of reduction is normally conditional upon a prior or concurrent analysis of the facts of the case as to those ultimate components which are regarded as relevant in the juristic valuation. Conversely, the elaboration of ever more "legal propositions" reacts upon the specification and delimitation of the potentially relevant characteristics of the facts. The process both depends upon, and promotes, casuistry. However, not every well-developed method of casuistry has resulted in, or run parallel to, the development of legal propositions of high logical sublimation. Highly comprehensive schemes of legal casuistry have grown up upon the basis of a merely paratactic association, that is, of the analogy of extrinsic elements. In our legal system the analytical derivation of "legal propositions" from specific cases go hand in hand with the synthetic work of "construction" of "legal relations" and "legal institutions," i.e., the determination of which aspects of a typical kind of social or consensual action are to be regarded as *legally* relevant, and in which logically consistent way these relevant components are to be regarded as *legally* coordinated, i.e., as being in "legal relationships." Although this latter process is closely related to the one previously described, it is nonetheless possible for a very high degree of sublimation in analysis to be correlated with a very low degree of constructional conceptualization of the legally relevant social relations. Conversely, the synthesis of a "legal relationship" may be achieved in a relatively satisfactory way despite a low degree of analysis, or occasionally just because of its limited cultivation. This contradiction is a result of the fact that analysis gives rise to a further logical task which, while it is compatible with synthetic construction, often turns out to be incompatible with it in fact. We refer to "systematization," which has never appeared but in late stages of legal modes of thought. To a youthful law, it is unknown. According to present modes of thought it represents an integration of all analytically derived legal propositions in such a way that they constitute a logically clear, internally consistent, and, at least in theory, gapless system of rules, under which, it is implied, all conceivable fact situations must be capable of being logically subsumed lest their order lack an effective guaranty. Even today not every body of law (e.g., English law) claims that it possesses the features of a system as defined above and, of course, the claim was even less frequently made by the legal systems of the past; where it was put forward at all, the degree of logical abstraction was often extremely low. In the main, the "system" has predominantly been an external scheme for the ordering of legal data and has been of only minor significance in the analytical derivation of legal propositions and in the construction of legal relationships. The specifically modern form of systematization, which developed out of Roman law, has its point of departure in the logical analysis of the meaning of the legal propositions as well as of the social actions. The "legal relationships" and casuistry, on the other hand, often resist this kind of manipulation, as they have grown out of concrete factual characteristics.

In addition to the diversities discussed so far, we must also consider the differences existing as to the technical apparatus of legal practice; these differences to some extent associate with, but to some extent also overlap, those discussed so far. The following are the simplest possible type situations:

Both lawmaking and lawfinding may be either rational or irrational. They are *formally* irrational when one applies in lawmaking or lawfinding means which cannot be controlled by the intellect, for instance when recourse is had to oracles or substitutes therefor. Lawmaking and lawfinding are *substantively* irrational on the other hand to the extent that decision is influenced by concrete factors of the particular case as evaluated upon an ethical, emotional, or political basis rather than by general norms. "Rational" lawmaking and lawfinding may be of either a formal or a substantive kind. All formal law is, formally at least, relatively rational. Law, however, is "formal" to the extent that, in both substantive and procedural matters, only unambiguous general characteristics of the facts of the case are taken into account. This formalism can, again, be of two different kinds. It is possible that the legally relevant characteristics are of a tangible nature, i.e., that they are perceptible as sense data. This adherence to external characteristics of the facts, for instance, the utterance of certain words, the execution of a signature, or the performance of a certain symbolic act with a fixed meaning, represents the most rigorous type of legal formalism. The other type of formalistic law is found where the legally relevant characteristics of the facts are disclosed through the logical

analysis of meaning an
nitely fixed legal conc
abstract rules are forr
process of "logical ratic
nificance of extrinsic elements and thus softens the rigidity of concrete formalism. But the contrast to "substantive rationality" is sharpened, because the latter means that the decision of legal problems is influenced by norms different from those obtained through logical generalization of abstract interpretations of meaning. The norms to which substantive rationality accords predominance include ethical imperatives, utilitarian and other expediential rules, and political maxims, all of which diverge from the formalism of the "external characteristics" variety as well as from that which uses logical abstraction. However, the peculiarly professional, legalistic, and abstract approach to law in the modern sense is possible only in the measure that the law is formal in character. In so far as the absolute formalism of classification according to "sense-data characteristics" prevails, it exhausts itself in casuistry. Only that abstract method which employs the logical interpretation of meaning allows the execution of the specifically systematic task, i.e., the collection and rationalization by logical means of all the several rules recognized as legally valid into an internally consistent complex of abstract legal propositions.

Our task is now to find out how the various influences which have participated in the formation of the law have influenced the development of its formal qualities. Present-day legal science, at least in those forms which have achieved the highest measure of methodological and logical rationality, i.e., those which have been produced through the legal science of the Pandectists' Civil Law, proceeds from the following five postulates: viz., first, that every concrete legal decision be the "application" of an abstract legal proposition to a concrete "fact situation"; second, that it must be possible in every concrete case to derive the decision from abstract legal propositions by means of legal logic; third, that the law must actually or virtually constitute a "gapless" system of legal prop-

...s, or must, at least, be treated as if it were ...n a gapless system; fourth, that whatever can-not be "construed" rationally in legal terms is also legally irrelevant; and fifth, that every social action of human beings must always be visualized as either an "application" or "execution" of legal propositions, or as an "infringement" thereof, since the "gaplessness" of the legal system must result in a gapless "legal ordering" of all social conduct. . . .

The Concept of Legitimation in the Sociology of Law

Alan Hyde

I. Introduction

Why do populations obey their leaders? Why is revolution, or lesser disobedience, not more common? From where do people derive the beliefs they hold about the meaning of justice in the abstract, the fairness of their leaders, or the justness of the societies in which they live? Why do legal institutions such as courts and legislatures pronounce particular norms instead of other norms? What is the impact of legal decisions and pronouncements?

It is a considerable understatement to call these big questions. Even if any single question could be answered satisfactorily, the relationship of that answer to the other questions would be obscure. With so little known about the answers to any of these questions, it may seem churlish or foolhardy to criticize any serious attempt to come to grips with them.

Nevertheless, many contemporary attempts to answer these questions start from a particularly weak conceptual base—the concept of "legitimacy" and "legitimation." Although it may be surprising that one concept should figure so prominently in the answers to such different questions, it is used commonly in contemporary theories of obedience and revolt, in popular conceptions of justice, and in the behavior of legal institutions and personnel. In this article I hope to survey contemporary usage of "legitimacy" and "legitimation;" to appraise methods for identify-ing them in order to determine whether either exists in measurable form; to evaluate three unfortunate effects of overuse of the concepts in studies of law; and to suggest alternative formulations potentially more fruitful for answering the above questions. Specifically, most research explaining conduct through legitimacy should rather investigate rational grounds for action. This revised research will be equally clear and much more sensitive to differences among legal doctrines and among individuals.

In the sense in which it is most commonly encountered, the "legitimacy" of a social order is the effective belief in its binding or obligatory quality. The term appears in Max Weber's *Economy and Society* as one of several possible "motives" for social action. By definition, Weber closely associates "legitimacy" with stability:

> Action, especially social action which involves a social relationship, may be guided by the belief in the existence of a legitimate order. The probability that action will actually be so governed will be called the "validity" (*Geltung*) of the order in question.
>
> Thus the validity of an order means more than the mere existence of a uniformity of social action determined by custom or self-interest. . . . Only . . . will an order be called "valid" if the orientation toward [determinable] "maxims" occurs, among other reasons, also because it is in some appreciable way re-

garded by the actor as in some way obligatory or exemplary for him. Naturally, in concrete cases, the orientation of action to an order involves a wide variety of motives. But the circumstance that, along with the other sources of conformity, the order is also held by at least part of the actors to define a model or to be binding, naturally increases the probability that action will in fact conform to it, often to a very considerable degree.

"Legitimacy" in Weber's sense thus involves, at the outset, a definition and two hypothesized causal relationships. "Legitimacy" is a state of widespread belief; namely, the belief that an order is obligatory or exemplary. Moreover, the belief is a reason for action. It is distinct from custom or self-interest and thus may either cause, or be associated with, certain behavior that is not explainable wholly through the factors of custom or self-interest. Finally, it is associated with *more* conformity than custom or self-interest; in general, the greater the legitimacy, i.e., the greater the observed belief in the obligatory qualities of an order, the greater the conformity to the norms believed legitimate.

. . . For decades, commentators on American law have assumed—prematurely, in my view—the correctness of the Weberian model. They have then gone on to argue that law and legal institutions, in America at least, play a key role in the process of legitimation. The general theory is that the procedures, rituals, ideology, and substantive decisions of legal institutions, particularly judicial institutions, measurably shape American popular beliefs in the legitimacy of government and the American sense of obligation and loyalty to the nation. . . .

There is . . . a large body of theory that rests on the supposedly significant contribution of law and legal institutions to popular belief in legitimacy and hence to political action or nonaction of various types. Despite the common resort to this model, the actual process that it describes remains extremely obscure as an empirical or behavioral matter. How do the legal ideas enter, let alone

shape, popular consciousness? What is the impact of popular belief on political action—put simplistically, do beliefs produce action, or is it the other way around? How can one identify "legitimacy" and how does the political stability associated with "legitimacy" differ from order supported exclusively by habit, fear of sanctions, or self-interest?

I am convinced that the Weberian model— law to belief to behavior—at best is problematic and unproven and at worst is probably wrong. In this article I hope to raise some doubt about the Weberian model and its widespread acceptance by American legal scholars. . . .

II. Does the Modern Order Rest on Legitimacy?

A. What Is Legitimacy?

Late at night, at a clear intersection with no drivers to be seen on any side, Joe Driver stopped at a stop sign. Why? His stop, after all, delayed his return home, cost him gasoline and wear on his brakes, and denied him some psychic gratification in driving fast.

There is, social science would hold, no single reason why this Joe, or other Joes, stopped at the stop sign. Partly it was unthinking habit, the reflex on seeing a red octagon. Partly it was fear of a police cruiser lurking unseen. Partly it was fear of other hazards, cars or pedestrians, that might not be visible. Partly it was a desire to avoid the disapproval of passengers, a disapproval that might stem from their fear or sense of the rightness of stopping at stop signs. Partly it was an obscure sense in Joe or his passengers that everyone everywhere is better off if everybody stops at stop signs. The question is whether there are any additional motives for Joe's action. Those who believe that there are call these "legitimacy."

In the passage from Weber quoted above, legitimacy is introduced as one of several possible motives for "adhering" to a social order. One may adhere to a social order; that is, one may conform to its rules and norms, because one accepts the order as a model or believes it binding. There are, however, as in Joe's case, other reasons to adhere to an order. One may act "from motives of pure expediency," to further one's individual ends. This is the case if one obeys out of fear of sanctions. It is also the case if one obeys because one rationally decides it is in one's interest to do so in the particular case. Finally, one may adhere to an order "through the fact that the corresponding behavior has become habitual."

All three Weberian motives for obedience—habit, expediency, and legitimacy—are ideal types; they are not encountered in pure form. Indeed, Weber held that all political order is based ultimately on force. Further, "in concrete cases, the orientation of action to an order involves a wide variety of motives." Moreover, "[t]he transitions between orientation to an order from motives of tradition or of expediency [on the one hand] to the case where on the other a belief in its legitimacy is involved, are naturally empirically gradual.". . .

. . . I agree that [no] sociological study of obedience, *disproves* legitimacy. I ask of the reader only a serious agnosticism toward the concept. For if we can explain energy conservation, resistance to desegregation and political protest entirely as the result of reason and habit, do we need the concept of legitimacy? When states' actions basically are just, compliance can be explained as self-interest. When states' actions are unjust, common experience predicts the heavy application of sanctions. What is the situation then for which legitimacy is a helpful explanation? . . .

III. Does Law Legitimate Anything?

Let us assume, however, that modern populations *are* indeed gripped in the false ideological belief that there is an inherent obligation to adhere to dominant political authority and that this belief has behavioral consequences in the form of obedience. Do legal institutions, legal rituals, or government commands cast in legal form contribute to the formation of this belief? Does law "legitimate" anything?

A. Models of Legitimacy in Legal Literature

I have put the question weakly in speaking of the "contribution" of law to the sense of legitimacy. This is not a modesty found among those who have assumed such a contribution; indeed, the claims made for law's legitimatory power are extraordinary. For Weber, the "belief in legality, the readiness to conform with rules that are formally correct and that have been imposed by accepted procedure" was nothing less than "the most usual basis of legitimacy" in modern societies. For Jerome Frank, law was "a substitute for those attributes of firmness, sureness, certainty and infallibility ascribed in childhood to the father." Law was for the benefit of the public not the lawyers, who recognized the inadequacies of law but preferred to bamboozle the public. For Thurman Arnold, law was an effective dissuader to protest:

> [T]he function of law is not so much to guide society, as to comfort it. . . . Though the notion of a 'rule of law' may be the moral background of revolt, it ordinarily operates to induce acceptance of things as they are. It does this by creating a realm somewhere within the mystical haze beyond the courts, where all our dreams of justice in an unjust world come true. . . . From a practical point of view it is the greatest instrument of social stability because it recognizes every one of those yearnings of the underprivileged, and gives them a forum in which those yearnings can achieve official approval without involving any particular action which might joggle the existing pyramid of power.

Then in terms explicitly Weberian: "Law represents the belief that there must be something behind and above government without which it cannot have permanence or respect."

Postwar legal analysts less critical of the law's purported "comforting" effect on the public did not doubt the existence of this effect, or its efficacy. Robert Dahl's much-cited formulation that "the main task of the [Supreme] Court is to confer legitimacy on the fundamental policies of the successful coalition" struck a responsive chord among his New Haven neighbors. Charles L. Black, Jr. based his defense of judicial review entirely on the Supreme Court's purported role as a legitimator of the inherently problematic actions taken by a national government of limited powers:

> What a government of limited powers needs, at the beginning and forever, is some means of satisfying the people that it has taken all steps humanly possible to stay within its powers. That is the condition of its legitimacy, and its legitimacy, in the long run, is the condition of its life. And the Court, through its history, has acted as the legitimator of the government. In a very real sense, the Government of the United States is based on the opinions of the Supreme Court.

Talcott Parsons' analysis was similar. While Alexander Bickel did not regard this supposed fact as a sufficient justification for judicial review, he had no doubt that it exists. "Not only is the Supreme Court capable of generating consent for hotly controverted legislative or executive pressures; it has the subtler power of adding a certain impetus to measures that the majority enacts rather tentatively."

> To declare that a statute is not intolerable in the sense that it is not inconsistent with the principles whose integrity the Court is charged with maintaining—that is something, and it amounts to a significant intervention in the political process, different in degree only from the sort of intervention marked by a declaration of unconstitutionality. . . . [T]he Court can generate consent and may impart permanence.

The problem for Bickel was that the Court, either carelessly or without principle, might legitimate political action. The remedy, of course, was the decision-avoidance techniques that Bickel called the "passive virtues."

The repeated use of the *term* "legitimate" should not obfuscate the fact that several distinct models are operating here. They share the basic Weberian model, law to belief to action. According to all these models, something about legal decisions engenders a public belief in legitimacy, which translates into obedience and adherence. There are, however, fundamental differences among these scholars on the questions of *how* law legitimates—what exactly about law engenders belief in legitimacy. There are also differences, to be considered in the next section, about what exactly is legitimated—the laws themselves, their makers, or the entire social order.

For Weber, the legitimating quality of legal decisions did not come primarily from the substantive values they projected in particular cases. Rather, their legitimacy inhered in their reasoning. I will term this, following Weber's usage elsewhere, *formal* legitimation. Ideally, under this model the legitimating consequence of a legal norm depends not at all on the substantive content of the norm but entirely on the legal form. Knowing that the provenance of a particular legal proposition was correctly and formally derived from what H. L. A. Hart would call "secondary rules," one could not only conclude that this was "law," but also could infer the likely public reaction; namely, adherence. For Bickel, in particular, legal decisions legitimate social norms because of their reasoned form.

For other theorists, such as Thurman Arnold, not just any norm could be legitimated through legal decision. Under this model of "*substantive* legitimation," legal norms derive their impact from correspondence to substantive values already held by the population.

Legal scholarship also has employed different models concerning *what* a legal decision legitimates. For Weber, Arnold, and Frank, legal decisions legitimated an entire *order*. For Dahl, Bickel, and Black, judicial decisions legitimated only the specific *norm* they pronounced and the political institutions, notably Congress or the President, that had enacted or acted upon the norm in question. . . .

Despite these differences, all these theorists employed the same basic model—law to belief to action. None adduced the slightest empirical evidence for the existence of the supposed effect on public belief called legitimation. No opinion survey supported Frank's claim that the public sought certainty in law. Nor was there empirical support for Arnold's claim that the public anticipated satisfaction of its needs through law, let alone his claim that the propensity to revolt was affected by the accessibility of legal institutions. Black did not explain who needed to be convinced of the legitimacy of the national government's actions (though his book was entitled *The People and the Court*). Nor did he explain why the decisions of yet another national political institution should convince, or had convinced, anyone of the rightness of national power. Bickel's command of example and counterexample unaccountably failed him whenever he propounded the assertion, repeated several times throughout *The Least Dangerous Branch*, that the Supreme Court's upholding of the constitutionality of some government practice exerted considerable political impact. The other works cited are similarly barren of empirical analysis.

[. . .]

As it happens, the questions of public awareness of legal norms, public perception of legal institutions, and public reaction to legal norms are not entirely open questions. They are the raw stuff of political science and sociology of law journals. Such studies, reviewed below, offer little support for the model of legitimation. Weberian formal legitimation in particular appears quite implausible. These studies show that the public has little awareness of courts, thinks poorly of the few judicial decisions of which it has knowledge, and, most importantly, cares much more about the substantive value of a legal decision than its legal form or pedigree. As a result it is difficult to support the idea that legal behavior contributes to public obedience irrespective of the substantive norms advanced. The possibility remains that once popular norms are known to legal actors, their efforts to reflect such norms might be predictable and might contribute slightly to obedience. Yet this removes the interesting feature of legitimation and makes it totally dependent on another independent set of substantive values.

B. Formal Legitimation: Do Norms Gain Popular Adherence Simply by Virtue of Being Pronounced by Legal Institutions?

Anthropologists of law do not assume as a working proposition that, as legitimation theory would have it, there is any tendency for popular behavior or belief to reflect legal norms as such, at least without considerable force of sanctions. Indeed, articles discussing the lack of impact of legal norms on behavior are as common as any other sort of article in the anthropology of law literature. Legitimation theory . . . starts from the converse assumption that legal norms as such do influence popular belief and behavior. What is the support for this proposition, as applied to the contemporary United States?

1. The Public Has Very Low Awareness of Legal Institutions and Decisions

The judicial institution whose public salience has been most studied is the United States Supreme Court. These studies strike to the core of legitimation theory, for the United States Supreme Court differs little from other courts in the force of its sanctions. Furthermore, the Supreme Court receives regular attention in the newspapers and mass media, while coverage of lower courts is limited essentially to the occasional notorious criminal, desegregation, or institutional reform case. The Supreme Court ought to be the legitimator *par excellence*. Indeed, some legitimation theories are limited to the United States Supreme Court and the supposed tendency of its decisions, for good or ill, to legitimate the particular norm advanced and the national political institutions that originally legislated or promulgated it.

Yet one review of the literature on public opinion concluded: "there is supporting evidence for the view that the Supreme Court and its decisions have such low salience as to render improbable popular acceptance of governmental action because of public knowledge that policies have been approved by the justices." Less than half the population can name a single Supreme

Court policy or decision they liked or disliked. Less than half the population can select as many as three correct topics from a list of eight possible *areas* in which the Supreme Court might have made a decision. The Supreme Court appears to be the *least* visible institution in the political socialization of American children. Other studies continually show low public awareness of the Supreme Court and even less awareness of the substance of its decisions. The same story could be told about lower courts.

This low salience of courts is a problem for all legitimation theory, although its implications vary for different theories. Norm legitimation, in particular, becomes implausible. If the population does not know the norms that the courts pronounce, they can hardly regard the norms of their authors as newly legitimate. Order legitimation is on firmer ground. People still might feel more loyal to an order because of its courts, even if they do not know—perhaps particularly if they do not know—just what the courts do. After all, there is considerable diffuse communication about legal norms. Particularly if people have generally favorable views of courts as compared with other institutions of government, courts with low salience still might legitimate an order.

2. The Public Has a Low Opinion of Courts

Unfortunately for legitimation theory, it appears that people do not have a particularly high opinion of courts and do not comply instinctively with judicially announced values when these conflict with values propounded by other governmental or nongovernmental sources. In public opinion polls, the Supreme Court typically gets less support than Congress or the President. Opinions of lower courts are even less warm.

3. Even Members of the Public with High Opinions of Courts Display Little Discernible Behavioral Conformity with Judicial Opinions

Much more important than general attitudes about courts is the problem of whether people actually comply with judicial decisions. As discussed above, obedience to law is correlated with rational factors of self-interest, such as fear of sanction and only poorly correlated with the sense of approval or disapproval of the lawmaking institution. Further, the enormous literature on the "implementation," generally arduous, or "impact," frequently exiguous, of judicial decisions dispels any simple hypothesis of an inherent tendency to obey law because of its formal qualities.

One recent study specifically attempted to identify belief in Supreme Court myths and to relate this belief to the propensity to obey hypothetical, but plausible, Supreme Court decisions on busing and curfews. Unqualified obedience to hypothetical decisions, with which respondents substantively disagreed, was attributed to legitimacy. The college student respondents were high believers in myth. "Only a quarter of the respondents deny any substantive significance to black robes and less than a third admitted that the Court would respond to political demands." Yet there was *no* correlation between propensity to obey the hypothetical Supreme Court decisions and belief in the myth. Nor was there a correlation between this propensity and diffuse, positive orientation to the Court, or specific agreement with the Court in five areas.

When courts are viewed as one of several sources of norms, their comparative weakness becomes more apparent. For example, studies have attempted to find shifts in obedience when people learn that certain behavior is legal or illegal. However, the "subject's moral opinions evidently were more strongly influenced by knowledge of the consensus among their peers as to whether the given acts were good or bad than by knowledge of the existence of laws on these matters."

> There appears to be a comparatively small but nevertheless significant tendency for some people to alter their views of the morality of some actions in accord with laws specifying that these actions are legal or illegal. Knowledge of the existence of these laws, however, does not have as much effect in changing the moral judgments as knowledge of a consensus of opinions among one's peers.

How do these findings affect the validity of the various legitimation theories identified above? Formal legitimation theory appears to be a very weak theory. It is not that there is *no* tendency to obey law against one's own preferences; some school boards comply with Supreme Court decisions on prayer, and some respondents change their moral opinions upon learning something is illegal. Rather, such an influence on behavior is a very weak one. In determining which standards of conduct are obligatory, people seem to care a great deal more about the substance or content of the standard than they do about a legal source or pedigree. Indeed, they may evaluate the legitimacy of the source by their approval of the substantive norm. Obligation is in part a function of the correspondence between legal norms and previously held values or the values of one's peers. Of course, people may comply with legal norms for more fundamental reasons. Legal norms are backed by sanctions, and may in turn trigger the more important informal sanctions of peer groups and other "semiautonomous fields." There are few experimentally identifiable people, however, for whom legal values as such have any sort of privileged legitimating effect. In the words of E. P. Thompson: "[P]eople are not so stupid as some structuralist philosophers suppose. They will not be mystified by the first man who puts on a wig.". . .

C. Substantive Order Legitimation: Does Law, by Projecting Certain Ideas Already Held by the Population, Legitimate Ruling Orders?

Under a considerably weaker version of legitimation theory, there is no necessary propensity on the part of the population to adhere to the norms of the legal system just because they have been promulgated properly. Nor do legal rules have any inherent tendency, by virtue of the procedural correctness of their promulgation or other formal aspects, to promote adherence or loyalty. Instead, certain ideas or principles inherent in particular legal rules, by virtue of their correspondence to views already held by the population, are claimed

to convince the population that their rulers and lawmakers are fair, just, looking out for the nation's interest, and the like. . . . The model is Thurman Arnold's: legal institutions project values, these values are accepted by the population because they converge with their own values, and the acceptance of these values in turn legitimates the entire order. The model frequently is applied to the study of legal doctrine or other products of legal institutions.

Alan Freeman, for example, has dissected brilliantly the twists and turns of Supreme Court doctrine in race discrimination cases, particularly the constant ideological projection of images such as equality of opportunity. He then concludes that Supreme Court doctrine legitimates existing patterns of racist maldistribution. Indeed, its "function" is "*merely* legitimizing." This is accomplished, much as Thurman Arnold long ago suggested, when the doctrine "holds out a promise of liberation," which makes it "convincing," and then "refrain[s] from delivering on the promise."

Similarly, Isaac Balbus has analyzed the behavior of urban criminal courts and has shown empirically their fundamental adherence to constitutional norms of criminal procedure even during so-called race riots. While the constitutional norms are partially abandoned, they are not wholly jettisoned. Balbus suggests that legitimation explains this observed behavior of legal institutions. Such features of American criminal procedure as the constraint of state prosecutorial authority by formal rules, the presumption of innocence, and other rights of the criminal defendant, "the state can abrogate only at the . . . risk of delegitimation. . . ."

Principles of criminal procedure or antidiscrimination law undoubtedly may be described as ideological. There are problems, however, with the move from ideology to legitimation, or the attribution of independent causative force and behavioral impact to particular ideological structures. Such a move is undermined by the studies in the sociology and anthropology of law cited above. If legal decisions and rules are largely unknown to the population, not well-regarded when known, and cannot be shown to influence belief or behavior in the absence of sanction, how could they, by projecting particular values, legitimate an order?

One response is to trivialize the concept of legitimation. For example, if "majesty, justice, and mercy," "promise[s] of liberation," the rights of criminal defendants or other "yearnings of the underprivileged" are indeed popular, and are publicly announced norms of a particular regime (whether announced through the legal system or otherwise), then the regime that announces those norms and appears to be pursuing them is, I suppose, somewhat more likely to become popular among the population. In other words, people like governments that say what the people want them to say. This sort of correlation is unexceptionable. In view of the low levels of popular awareness and approval of the legal system, it is hard to imagine that legal ideas, even at best, would be terribly effective in promoting popular loyalty to a regime. I suppose nevertheless that a regime that professes popular legal ideas is likely to be more popular than one that professes unpopular legal ideas. If this is all that substantive order legitimation theory of the Thurman Arnold variety says, it is probably true but hardly interesting.

In other formulations, however, legitimation theory is put forward either as a theory of disobedience and revolt or as a theory of the behavior of legal institutions. People do not revolt, *because* of the effects of the legitimation process begun by legal institutions. The doctrinal or other behavior of courts may be predicted, *if* one understands that some or all of their behavior is legitimating. Although theories of disobedience and revolt and of legal behavior are worthy theories, I believe that the legitimation concept would not play much part in an adequate version of either theory. . . .

IV. Why Should We Abandon the Concept of Legitimation?

. . . I hope to show, . . . that legitimation tends to enter sociological accounts of law in order to perform one of three functions. First, it may perform

an evaluative function under the guise of sociology. Second, it may explain away anomalies so as to preserve a structural-functional approach under which all law contributes to the maintenance of a social system. Third, legitimation may offer an attractive way of discussing the sociological effects of law without addressing its substantive moral content.

None of these vices is inherent in the concept of legitimation, properly defined; yet they are frequently associated with it. The vices could be avoided by starting from the premise that obedience is largely a function of rational factors, such as perceived self-interest and fear of sanctions. This reconceptualization would open up new realms of inquiry, and direct research toward more realistic explanations of obedience, revolt and the behavior of legal institutions. . . .

A. Freedom from Evaluation Disguised as Social Science

The criticism of social institutions is a most worthy task. It is not a task, however, for which the concept of legitimation is helpful. Social institutions may be just or unjust, rational or irrational; they might or might not be consented to in Habermas's communication community. However, there was a time when it was thought inappropriate to address such questions in law schools and departments of sociology and political science. Instead it became customary to describe unjust or irrational institutions as "illegitimate."

This usage—even when employed by as brilliant a practitioner as Jürgen Habermas—has the unfortunate tendency of collapsing the normative into the descriptive. Criticism of a social institution as illegitimate, where unaccompanied by substantive moral argument, is limited to the implication that people will not obey the order. Yet obedience is normally a descriptive claim that adds nothing to the normative analysis. . . .

Naturally normative questions can be disguised as descriptive questions in the absence of the word "legitimate." I think, however, that there is an unfortunate history of using the term "legitimate" to free someone from arguing on moral grounds for a contested moral claim.

B. Freedom from Functionalism

Why does an able scholar like Douglas Hay assert that the ideology of the criminal law, "more than any other social institution, made it possible to govern eighteenth-century England without a police force and without a large army"? In his theory, Hay adopts an undefended assumption, the assumption of functionalism. He treats legal behavior as a social system, every aspect of which must serve the needs of the ruling class. Having adopted this functionalist premise, Hay then uses the legitimation concept to explain ostensibly dysfunctional elements of the system. For example, the opportunities for the display of mercy that existed in the eighteenth-century English criminal law were dysfunctional, according to Hay, in protecting the property of the rich. The apparently dysfunctional element is made functional, however, if said to legitimate the system.

Hay's work illustrates the role that "legitimation" usually plays in a theory of law. This may be seen most clearly in an overtly normative theory like Charles Black's defense of judicial review. Black takes the democratic critique of the Supreme Court to be that the Court is dysfunctional for democracy since it is an unelected, unresponsive body with power to check political majorities. In defense, Black then must define a function for the Supreme Court consistent with an ideology of political democracy. Thus, he theorizes that the Supreme Court was created, notwithstanding a lack of expressed motivation on the part of the actual founders, to legitimate the actions of national governing coalitions.

This analysis is paradigmatic even in ostensibly descriptive theory. Each theorist who employs legitimation—Weber, Frank, Arnold, Dahl, Bickel, Lipset, Lowenthal, Schwartz, the neo-Marxists—begins by positing a legal system under which every element is functional for some purpose. Then the apparent anomalies—the doctrines and institutions that apparently do not maintain

"democratic theory" or "ruling class authority," or simply are untrue (like "legal certainty")—are said to perform the function of legitimating the whole system. Thus, as always in structural-functional analyses, everything contributes to the maintenance of the equilibrium of the whole, and the system remains closed.

None of this has any place in an adequately political account of law, and it is thus all the more surprising that Marxists should be so drawn to functionalist analysis. If law is a terrain of political struggle, many of its institutions and doctrines will be temporary compromises and lines of truce, subject to renegotiation. These institutions and doctrines should not be regarded as system-maintaining or functional. One of the major benefits of abandoning the concept of legitimation would be a corresponding abandonment of the assumption that every element of a legal system contributes to the maintenance of the whole system, or that legal "systems" exist as coherent and autonomous entities.

C. Freedom from Sociological Formalism

There is a tradition, stemming from Weber, of defining law entirely through formal criteria. A philosophic tradition influenced by Weber has developed sophisticated techniques for the identification of "law" without any reference to its substantive content. Legitimacy, as employed by Weber, is a sociological theory that does the same thing. That is, "law" is distinguished from other forms of social control, communication, and moral life by *formal* criteria—its due enactment through formally correct procedures, or pedigree. Having identified the subject without employing any criteria relating to its substantive values, one then can make sociological predictions about its anticipated effects. In Weber's case, this is the hypothesized relationship between "law," defined formally, and obedience due to belief in legitimacy. It is this relationship that, when tested, appears to lack any empirical support whatever. There simply are no demonstrations of such behavioral consequences linked to formal criteria.

In a very real sense, the concept of legitimation continually directs scholars towards just this
error. Law is assumed to have certain effects on
the population, either because of its formal criteria or its substantive values, which are not analyzed morally but are simply *assumed* to reflect
popular values. The effect either is or is not found.
The concept of legitimation makes it easy to follow Weber and ignore the relationship between
the substantive moral values of the law and behavioral change.

The problem disappears once one abandons
reliance on the concept of legitimation and assumes heuristically that obedience stems from
rational factors. Determining the extent to which
this is true in the individual case necessitates inquiry into whether, for whom, and in what sense
law is "rational." Since Weber proposed his theory, social science has attempted to avoid this
inquiry. Yet all its efforts in the Weberian mode
demonstrate that obedience, compliance, and revolt *cannot* be understood as a unified reaction to
a value-free phenomenon called formal law.

In other words, it makes a difference if, in
asking why Joe Driver stops at the stop sign, one
assumes the answer will implicate Joe's sense of
his rational self-interest. This difference affects
the research program and its conclusions. In any
subjective case, the rational evaluation of self-
interest will be shaped by falsehoods, ideology and
cultural misunderstandings. Nevertheless, these
can be studied. Further, if Joe's obedience is treated
as a question of reason, the impact of sanctions,
formal and informal, centralist and pluralist, will
not be neglected. By contrast, if obedience is
treated as a function of attitude, survey questions
must be refined endlessly to find the right index
for belief in legitimacy. It appears however that
this effort is unlikely to result in criteria that will
ever predict Joe's obedience—or revolt.

Let me illustrate this point by describing an
article—a good, interesting article—that cannot
discover what it sets out to find because it operates in a framework of Weberian legitimacy. Many
studies might have been chosen for this purpose;
I have selected this study because it is imaginative,

valuable, and informative in empirical terms. This
particular study attempted to discover the impact
of the national adoption of the Medicare and
Medicaid programs on the attitudes and behavior
of physicians.

In 1964 and 1965 (Time 1), 1025 physicians
in private practice in New York State were interviewed and asked their views on what were then
the proposals that subsequently became Medicare
and Medicaid. The physicians were subdivided
randomly into two subsamples. One group was reinterviewed subsequent to the bills' passage but
prior to their effective dates (Time 2, May–June
1966). The other group was reinterviewed about
six months after the bills' implementation (Time 3,
January–April 1967). Attitudinal shifts between
Time 1 and Time 2 thus reflect the effect of the law
prior to actual experience with it; shifts between
Time 1 and Time 3 reflect the combined effect of
the law and short term experience with it. The
design thus attempted to separate the effect of the
law itself from the effects of its implementation.

Nationally, the organized medical profession
bitterly opposed Medicare and considered a boycott. At Time 1 only thirty-eight percent of the
practitioners favored a Medicare-type bill. By
Time 2 this level had risen to seventy percent. By
Time 3 the percentage in favor had gone up to
eighty-one percent.

I have suggested that data of this sort could be
interpreted from two starting points: one that attributes compliance to legitimacy, and one that
attributes compliance to rational factors. The two
starting points yield sharply different interpretations of the data.

The author operates in a framework of Weberian legitimation. "What can be asserted . . . is
that the law itself had a large effect on the physicians' attitudes toward Medicare even before it
was implemented." For the author, this is a convincing demonstration "that for the law to influence attitudes it does not necessarily have to
change behavior first." "[L]aw may 'legitimate'
opinion." In true Weberian fashion, these conclusions are reached with no analysis whatever of the
substantive provisions of the Medicare legislation.

By contrast, the hypothesis that the shift in physicians' attitudes implicates a good deal of rational judgment opens up a series of questions not part of this author's research program. It is entirely consistent with the data to assume what popular wisdom has always maintained, that, as the Medicare legislation took shape, physicians realized they would make enormous sums of money from it with negligible government interference. This view is deliberately crude and cynical of course. The point is that a research design based on a "legitimation" framework permits easy conclusions about the effect of law on attitudes without considering the provisions of the law itself. Yet not surprisingly, studies on compliance repeatedly reveal, when so directed, that people care far more about the substance of a law than about its pedigree.

Now of course it is possible within a legitimation framework to keep an eye on the substantive provisions of the law studied. Possible, but hardly easy. The legacy of hypothesized responses to law, just because it is law, has led to an unwillingness to grapple with the substantive moral provisions of legal doctrine. Yet sociology cannot hope to explain a phenomenon like physicians' cooperation with Medicare without analysis of the doctrinal provisions of the law in question. This necessarily involves quasi-evaluative questions, including whose interests the law serves, the law's ideological basis, and the like. It also involves inquiry into the social setting in which the law

operates, including the presence or absence of informal sanctions reinforcing state sanctions. It simply appears that one cannot get close to the phenomena of obedience and revolt without grappling with these substantive features of law. The conceptualization of obedience and revolt as *rational* processes, while no panacea, clearly orients research into substantive law and into actors' beliefs, ideals, and rational interests.

The concept of legitimation, in short, has no clear operational meaning, nor agreed upon empirical referent. It is difficult to disentangle operationally from other motives for obedience. Whatever the index chosen for its measurement, however, legitimacy cannot be shown to be as significant in explaining obedience as rational calculation, including evaluation of self-interest and sanctions. It leads researchers into easy hypotheses about the effect of legal phenomena without the necessity of empirical support. It leads social scientists into subjective evaluative claims without the burden of normative argument. It preserves a sterile functionalism and blinds researchers to the possibility that law is merely a terrain of combat, and is neither system-maintaining nor functional. It leads research away from substantive legal doctrine and toward unlikely hypotheses of attitudinal and behavioral change merely because something is law. Nor does it capture social facts not equally capturable by theories of compliance premised on rationality. In short, we would be better off abandoning the concept of legitimation.

Max Weber on Law and the Rise of Capitalism

David M. Trubek

I. Law in *Economy and Society*

Max Weber dedicated much of his energy to explaining why industrial capitalism arose in the West. While he recognized that this was an historical issue, Weber did not limit himself to historical methods. Rather, he attempted to construct a sociological framework which could guide historical research. This framework identified the main analytic dimensions of society and the concrete structures that correspond to them. Weber focused on polity, social structure, economy, religion, and law, and the political, social, economic, religious, and legal structures of given societies. He felt that these dimensions, with their associated structures, must be separated and investigated so that their interrelationships in history can best be understood. Using these methods, he argued, particular events in history can be explained.

The "event" he sought to explain was the fact that the modern system of industrial (or "bourgeois") capitalism emerged in Europe but not in other parts of the world. Law, he felt, had played a part in this story. European law had unique features which made it more conducive to capitalism than were the legal systems of other civilizations. To demonstrate and explain the significance of these features for economic development, Weber included the sociology of law within his general sociological theory. Thus the monumental treatise *Economy and Society*, which sets forth a comprehensive analysis of his sociological thought,

includes a detailed discussion of the types of law, a theory of the relationship between law and the rise of industrial capitalism, and comparative sociological studies which attempt to verify his theory.

Weber's decision to include law within a general sociological theory can be explained not only by his personal background as lawyer and legal historian, but also by the methods he employed to trace the rise of the distinctive form of economic activity and organization he called bourgeois capitalism. Weber was concerned with explaining the rise of capitalism in the West. This meant he had to discover why capitalism arose in Europe and not in other parts of the world. The way to do this, he thought, was to focus on those aspects of European society which were unique, and which, therefore, might explain why capitalism developed there. This technique is clearly seen in his sociology of law and sociology of religion. The latter examines the relationship between unique features in Western religious life and "the spirit of capitalism," while the former identifies unique features of Western legal systems which were especially conducive to capitalist activity.

While Weber believed that Western law had particular features which helped explain why capitalism first arose in Europe, he did not think the West alone had "law." Weber had a broad concept of law that embraced a wide range of phenomena in very different societies. Nevertheless, he drew sharp distinctions between the legal systems of different societies. Most organized societies have "law," but the European legal system differs significantly from others. He developed typologies that permitted him to distinguish European law from the legal order of other civilizations, and then conducted historical studies designed to show the origins of the unique features of European law.

At the same time, through parallel theoretical analysis, Weber found it possible to show how a certain type of legal system fitted the needs of capitalism. Finally, he returned to history in order to demonstrate that, of all the great civilizations— Europe, India, Islam, China—*only* Europe developed this particular type of law. Since, at the same time, capitalism arose first in Europe, this analysis suggested very strongly that European law played an important role in the emergence of the capitalist economic system.

Weber stressed his belief that the unique legal aspects of European society were not the mere result or reflex of economic phenomena. He explicitly and repeatedly denied that the special features of European legal systems were caused by capitalism itself. Rejecting the Marxian deterministic theory which held that legal phenomena were caused by underlying economic forces, he demonstrated that what was unique in the European legal systems had to be explained by such noneconomic factors as the internal needs of the legal profession, and the necessities of political organization. Economic factors—specifically, the economic needs of the bourgeois classes—were important but not determinative in shaping legal institutions of Europe.

These institutions differed from those of other civilizations in their formal and structural qualities—or as Weber somewhat misleadingly put it, in their degree of "rationality." The uniqueness of European law—and the affinities between this system and capitalism—lay not so much in the content of substantive provisions as in the forms of legal organization and the resulting formal characteristics of the legal process. Weber's contrasts between the legal systems of Europe and such civilizations as China did not focus on the presence or absence of specific rules of law, although these were not ignored. Rather he was concerned with such questions as whether legal organization is differentiated or is fused with political administration and religion, whether law is seen as a body of manmade rules or as a received corpus of unvarying tradition, whether legal decisions are determined by prior general rules or are made on an ad hoc basis, and whether rules are applied universally to all members of a polity or if specialized law exists for different groups.

The European legal system was distinct in all these dimensions. Unlike the legal systems of other great civilizations, European legal organization was highly differentiated. The European state separated law from other aspects of political activity. Specialized professional or "status" groups of lawyers existed. Legal rules were consciously fashioned and rule making was relatively free of direct interference from religious influences and from other sources of traditional values. Concrete decisions were based on the application of universal rules, and decision making was not subject to constant political intervention.

Thus Weber believed that European law was more "rational" than the legal systems of other civilizations, that is, it was more highly differentiated (or autonomous), consciously constructed, general, and universal. But he also attempted to show that no other civilization had been capable of developing this type of legal order. European law was the result of the interaction of many forces. Its ultimate form was shaped not only by very distinct features in Western legal history— especially the Roman law tradition and aspects of medieval legal organization—it was also molded by general and often distinct trends in the religious, economic, and political life of the West. The other civilizations he studied lacked this special legal heritage, and failed to develop the religious ideas, political structures, and economic interests which facilitated the growth of rational law in Europe.

The failure of other civilizations to develop rational law helped explain why only in Europe could modern, industrial capitalism arise. Weber believed that this type of capitalism required a legal order with a relatively high degree of "rationality." Since such a system was unique to the West, the comparative study of legal systems helped answer Weber's basic question about the causes of the rise of capitalism in Europe.

II. Reconstructing Weber's Analysis: The Concept of Law and Its Relationship to Domination

To understand how Weber reached these conclusions, it is necessary to reconstruct the details of his argument. The position I have stated in the preceding paragraphs emerges from a synthetic analysis of the various discussions of law and capitalism in his work. Because Weber did not give us a finished, systematic treatment of these themes, I shall attempt a reconstruction that will permit us to understand why Weber chose to focus on the autonomy, generality, and universality of the European legal system; why he felt that such a system could only have come into existence in Europe; and why such a system should be necessary for, or at least highly conducive to, capitalist economic development.

A. Weber's Concept of Law: Coercion, Legitimacy, and Rationality

There are certain central themes in the Weberian discussion of law. Law is associated with organized coercion, with legitimacy and normativeness, and with rationality. These elements deserve separate consideration.

Weber is frequently cited for the famous definition of law set forth in chapter I of *Economy and Society*, in which law is identified merely with organized coercion, or power. In establishing the fundamental concepts of his sociological system Weber stated that:

> An order will be called . . . *law* if it is externally guaranteed by the probability that physical or psychological coercion will be applied by a *staff* of people in order to bring about compliance or avenge violation.

There is no doubt that Weber stressed the coercive quality of law. As I shall demonstrate, legal coercion is a key feature of Weber's model of a functioning market economy. Nevertheless, further analysis reveals that Weber used a much more complex concept of law than the one quoted. Indeed, seen in context, the very definition itself suggests that coercion was only one pole of Weber's idea. The other was a concept of law as one form of "legitimate order," a term Weber uses to refer to any structured source of guidelines for right conduct.

Thus, in the Weberian scheme, law is a subclass of a category called legitimate or normative orders. All such orders are (1) socially structured systems which contain (2) bodies of normative propositions that (3) to some degree are subjectively accepted by members of a social group as binding for their own sake, without regard for purely utilitarian calculations of the probability of coercion. . . .

[T]he essential elements of Weber's broad concept of "law" are that it be a system of standards, maxims, principles, or rules of conduct, to some degree accepted as obligatory by the persons to whom it is addressed, and backed by a specialized enforcement agency employing coercive sanctions. To the extent that sanctions are applied in accord with a system of rules, law is said to be "rational."

Weber was concerned with possible variations along two dimensions of this definition. Law, as Weber conceived it, can be said to vary in its degree of *rationality* and in the nature of its *legitimacy*. The degree of law's rationality is, furthermore, related to the nature of its legitimacy. Weber discussed historical variations along these dimensions in order to determine their significance for the rise of capitalism.

1. Variations in Legal Rationality: The Types of Legal "Thought"

In order to explore the historical significance of legal systems, Weber constructed ideal types of different legal orders. These types were methodological artifices which permitted him to examine and compare the legal systems of concrete societies. They did not reflect any particular concrete legal system, but rather included complexes of typical features that can be found in real systems and which highlight the problems that Weber wanted to explore.

Weber's typology of legal systems must be seen in the context of his overall analysis of legal "rationality." It attempts to differentiate those dimensions of legal organization and the law-society relationship which he believed influenced rationality. The various types, therefore, chart differences that exist between the way legal systems handle the characteristic problems of formulating authoritative norms ("lawmaking") and of applying such norms to specific instances ("lawfinding"). These are distinguished in ways that are designed to measure degrees of rationality....

Weber himself classified legal systems into distinct categories depending on how law is both made and found. Law may be found and made either *irrationally* or *rationally*. Law can be either (1) formally or (2) substantively irrational, or (3) substantively or (4) formally rational. Finally, formally rational law can be "formal" either in an "extrinsic" or "logical" sense.

There are thus two major dimensions of comparison: the extent to which a system is formal, and the extent to which it is rational. If these terms are analyzed, one finds that "formality" can be considered to mean "employing criteria of decision intrinsic to the legal system" and thus measures the degree of systemic autonomy, while "rationality" means "following some criteria of decision which is applicable to all like cases" and thus measures the generality and universality of the rules employed by the system....

Formally irrational legal decision-making is associated with prophetic decisions or revelation. Decisions are announced without any reference to some general standard or even to the concerns of the parties of the dispute. The criteria of decision making is intrinsic to the legal system but unknowable; there is no way the observer can predict the decision, or understand why it was reached.

Substantively irrational decisions apply observable criteria but these are always based on concrete ethical and practical considerations of the specific cases. It is possible to understand these decisions after the fact, but unless a system of precedent arises, it is difficult to generalize from the concrete cases. Substantively rational decision-making employs a set of general policies or criteria, but these are of some body of thought extrinsic to the legal system—religion and political ideology are examples of such extrinsic systems. To the extent that the overarching principles of the external thought system are understood, it is possible to apprehend rationally how the system will function. But this is only true to a limited degree, for the manner in which the precepts of the external system will be translated into legal decisions may vary. Thus, while this type is more capable of formulating general rules than the previous two, it is less likely to do so than logically formal rationality. In comparison with this fourth type, these three types of legal systems, therefore, display a low degree of differentiation, a low degree of generality of rules, or both. As a result it is difficult to predict the types of decisions they will reach.

This is not true of European law, which Weber identified with logically formal rationality. This type of system combines a high degree of legal differentiation with a substantial reliance on pre-existing general rules in the determination of legal decisions. Indeed, these two features are closely related.

What did Weber mean by "logically formal rationality"? And why does it lead to general, universally applied rules? Legal thought is *rational* to the extent that it relies on some justification that transcends the particular case, and is based on existing, unambiguous rules; *formal* to the extent that the criteria of decision are intrinsic to the legal system; and *logical* to the extent that rules or principles are consciously *constructed* by specialized modes of legal thought which rely on a highly logical systemization, and to the extent that decisions of specific cases are reached by processes of specialized deductive logic proceeding from previously established rules or principles. Since in such a system, court decisions can only be based on previously established *legal* principles, and since the system requires these to be carefully elaborated, normally through codification, legal decisions will be based on *rules*, and these will be general as well as derived from autonomous *legal* sources. . . .

In this system, "abstract" legal propositions are organized systematically in the form of a civil code; judges are to apply the code using specific modes of professional logic; not only is all human action "ordered by law," but what law allows no other social force can deny.

2. The Relationship between Political Structure and the Legal System: The Types of Domination and the Types of Law

With the special features of European law in mind, Weber's theory of the genesis of this structure must be examined. Under what conditions did European law arise? Why did this system only develop in Europe? The answers to these questions require analysis of Weber's political sociology, for, in this part of his work, Weber asserted a mutual relationship between political and legal structures. The European or "modern" legal system could only emerge under distinct political conditions. Its existence was intimately linked to the rise of the modern bureaucratic state. Yet, at the same time, this type of state was itself dependent on a legal system of the modern type.

In his political sociology, Weber constructed ideal types of political systems or forms of "domination" (legitimate authority). These are organized in accordance with the basic claim these systems or regimes make to have their commands obeyed. The classification is made by the typical conditions of legitimacy, the primary justification regimes offer for their power over others. Weber selected this aspect of political systems as the basis for classification because, he felt, it constitutes "the basis of very real differences in the empirical structure of domination."

Weber identified three ideal or pure forms of legitimization. These are called traditional, char-

ismatic, and legal "domination." Members of a social organization will treat commands as legitimate because they are issued in accordance with immutable custom, because they are issued by an individual with extraordinary or exemplary characteristics, or because they rest on conscious legal enactment. . . .

Weber established a close relationship between the types of domination and the types of "legal thought." Legal domination is based on logically formal rationality, which can exist only in the context of legal domination. Moreover, he suggested that as "law" (in the generic sense) evolved to modern, rational law, so the form of domination evolved toward the modern state, a creation and creature of this type of law.

This becomes clear only upon detailed examination of these two ideal types. Legal domination is said to exist when the following conditions prevail: (1) There are established norms of general application; (2) there exists a belief that the body of law is a consistent system of abstract rules, and that administration of law consists in the application of these rules to particular cases and is limited to these rules; (3) the "superior" is himself subjected to an impersonal order; (4) obedience is to the law as such and not to some other form of social ordering; and (5) obedience is owed only within rationally delimited spheres (juridiction).

Thus, the particular concept of "law" contained in the notion of logically formal rationality is included as one of the essential elements of a system of legal domination. And, at the same time, only logically formal rationality can maintain the "consistent system of abstract rules" necessary for legal domination. No other type of legal thought can create systematic general norms and guarantee that they, and only they, will determine the outcome of legal decisions. . . .

Weber underscored the relationship between legal domination and European law by describing the other types of domination. Just as formally rational law is necessary to create a situation under which domination can be rationally legitimized, so other forms of legitimization discourage the rise of rational law. "Traditionalism places serious obstacles in the way of formally rational regulations . . . ." In traditional societies, according to Weber, one cannot have specific, purposefully enacted law (legislation), for such a procedure would be inconsistent with the ruler's claim to legitimacy. Commands will only be obeyed if they can be related to unchanging, eternal principles. Furthermore, the traditional ruler must base any actual regulation of the economy on "utilitarian, welfare, or absolute values." This is true because, while his legitimacy is based on adherence to traditional principles, successful domination requires him also to maintain the economic welfare of his subjects. Such a situation, Weber concluded, "breaks down the type of *formal* rationality which is oriented to a technical legal order." Charismatic authority, too, discourages the rise of modern rational law; Weber observed that bureaucratic (or legal) authority "is specifically rational in the sense of being bound to intellectually analyzable rules; while charismatic authority is specifically irrational in the sense of being foreign to all rules."

From this analysis, it is apparent that European law differs from other types of law in several dimensions. Unlike other types, European law develops bodies of rules, which are applied through formal procedures guaranteeing that the rules will be followed in all cases. For these reasons, it curbs the arbitrary action of the ruling groups, and is, partly as a result, highly predictable. Thus, under European law, the rules governing economic life are easily determined; this type of legal order reduces one element of economic uncertainty. This calculability of European law was its major contribution to capitalist economic activity. . . .

B. The Rise of "Legalism"

What emerges from this complex system is the picture of the growth of a certain kind of society. In this society, the primary source of normative ordering is a logically consistent set of rules constructed in a specialized fashion. These rules are created by the use of highly specialized forms of thought which allow the construction of an intel-

lectual system which can be applied only by trained professionals. While the values reflected in this set of norms have their source outside the specialized profession, they only become reflected in rules to the extent that they are incorporated in the intellectual system constructed by the professionals. And only legal rules so constructed are employed in the resolution of disputes between members of the society. All behavior not so regulated is formally free.

If this system is to function, there must be a clear differentiation of law from other sources of normative ordering. Ultimately, law must supersede other systems that might have a grip on men's loyalties. Law must become both autonomous and supreme.

Law must become separate from power and religion if it is to reach its goal of formulating and maintaining unambiguous, general rules. Weber constantly stressed that "power has its reasons that reason cannot understand," that rulers will constantly be tempted to sacrifice universal principles for particular, expedient goals. In the language of American constitutional theory, power wielders will be "result oriented." Similarly, where law is mixed with religion, pressures will emerge to sacrifice generality for concrete ethical ends.

But it is not enough for law to become separate from other sources of social control. It is not enough that rules exist in some abstract sense. They must come to control all social life, and law must supersede other forms of normative order. If it does not, legal rules will have limited social impact.

Such legal autonomy entails a differentiated legal structure. Unique skills, roles, and modes of thought are necessary if a society is to create and maintain universal rules. A highly specialized profession must exist to nurture and maintain these qualities. Since unique modes of thought are an essential element of the social structure of modern law, highly specialized training must exist.

This model may be called "legalism," to suggest a society dominated by an autonomous rule system. In this model, rules are obeyed because they are believed to be rationally enacted. Given the high degree of differentiation of legal machinery, and the decline of other forms of social control, men in this lawyer's utopia live in a highly calculable universe. They know, or can learn, what their rights and duties are, for they can predict with a high degree of certainty when legal coercion will be employed, and, at the same time, know that no other source of social control will constrain the behavior law allows.

Unique conditions in European history, Weber argued, led to the emergence of legalism. Religious, political, economic, and legal factors contributed to this development. In the West, religious and secular law were separated, thus allowing a divorce of legal and ethical norms. At the same time, the bureaucratization of the Catholic Church, and its Roman law heritage, led canon law to become significantly more rational than most theocratic legal orders. And European kings, in their struggles for power with other groups in the polity, found it necessary to create bureaucratic staffs and to enter into alliances with rising bourgeois interests. To further their own self-interest, both the administrative staff and the merchant groups demanded more rational and calculable legal systems, demands which patrimonial rulers found difficult to refuse, even though the result was in some way a limitation of their powers.

Finally, autonomous developments in legal life provided an element essential to realization of this thrust toward legal rationality. A major development was the separation of lawfinding and lawmaking, a phenomenon Weber found especially accentuated in early German law. This development was a necessary condition for the establishment of conscious lawmaking and thus for the secularization of the law. This differentiation occurred more fully in Western systems. Only in the West, moreover, did there arise the idea of a universal "natural" law that suggested the possibility of transcending particularistic rules and time-honored traditional norms. Additionally, the influence of Roman law, with its special logical techniques, added another unique feature to European law. The universities of continental Europe had developed a systematic study of Roman law, employing

highly abstract, logical techniques. From these universities emerged specialized practitioners trained to think of law as a science. It was the existence of this group of legal notables, trained in methods of legal analysis, that made possible the codification and rationalization of the law which was demanded by the various political and economic groups. A viable, rational legal technique, merged with strong political and economic needs, gave birth to modern legal rationality. These developments, in turn, strengthened the modern bureaucratic state, which lays its claim to obedience on the ground that it can and does create and maintain a system of rational rules. Thus, rational law and legal domination developed in a symbiotic relationship. And as they developed, they superseded other forms of social control.

One of the most important elements of European legal history, and one of the key concepts for an understanding of legalism, is Weber's treatment of the emergence of a distinct legal profession. This event was not only unique; it was absolutely essential for the emergence of logically formal rationality and underlies much of the contemporary dynamics of legalism.

Weber argued that only in the West did lawyers emerge as a distinct "status group." A status group is an organization founded on the basis of formal education, occupational prestige, or a distinct style of life. Status groups may be formed on the basis of shared ideas, such as political beliefs or religious faith. Since men form concrete interests as a result of membership in such groups, they become committed to the ideas that have shaped the organization. In this way these groups become historical factors by which ideal—as opposed to material—interests become the basis of social conflict. Status groups affect history because men will struggle to maintain the ideas that underlie the groups to which they belong.

Ideas about the nature of law may have this group-forming quality, and group needs may foster the development of distinct legal conceptions. The emergence of a distinct legal profession in the West not only fostered the growth of the idea of law as an autonomous technique of social ordering; it also meant that such an idea became the basis of real social conflict. Logically formal rationality is an extreme version of the basic idea that law is a consciously shaped autonomous technique that can be applied to resolve social conflict. Such an idea could only arise where the legal profession becomes differentiated, and once it arises it becomes the basis of the social cohesion of the lawyers as a status group. Thus, once legalism is established, conflicts can arise between the lawyers, with their commitment to the idea of a fixed and formally derived law, and political and economic factions that advocate specific substantive policies or economic results which threaten the legal autonomy formalism tries to maintain.

III. Legalism and Capitalism: A Reconstruction of Weber's Theory of Law in Economic Life

We now have most of the elements needed to understand Weber's theory of the relationship between the rise of modern law and capitalism. We have examined his legal sociology, which identifies distinctive types of legal systems, and his political sociology, which shows that the structure of power determines to some degree the type of legal order that can exist. We have seen why Weber thought legalism developed in Europe. Now we must turn to his economic sociology, in which the dynamics of the market are developed. This analysis will show why capitalism and legalism are intimately related.

In his economic sociology, Weber stressed the importance for capitalist development of two aspects of law: (1) its relative degree of *calculability*, and (2) its capacity to develop *substantive* provisions—principally those relating to freedom of contract—necessary to the functioning of the market system.

The former reason was the more important of the two. Weber asserted that capitalism required a highly calculable normative order. His survey of types of law indicated that only modern, rational law, or logically formal rationality, could provide

the necessary calculability. Legalism supported the development of capitalism by providing a stable and predictable atmosphere; capitalism encouraged legalism because the bourgeoisie were aware of their own need for this type of governmental structure.

Legalism is the only way to provide the degree of certainty necessary for the operation of the capitalist system. Weber stated that capitalism "could not continue if its control of resources were not upheld by the legal compulsion of the state; if its formally 'legal' rights were not upheld by the threat of force." He further specified that: "[T]he rationalization and systematization of the law in general and . . . the increasing calculability of the functioning of the legal process in particular, constituted one of the most important conditions for the existence of . . . capitalistic enterprise, which cannot do without legal security."

Weber never worked out in detail a model of capitalist production which might explain why legal calculability was so important to capitalist development. I have developed such a model, and I believe that underlying Weber's repeated emphasis on legal calculability is a vision similar to this latter-day ideal type.

The essence of the model is the conflict of egoistic wills, which is an inherent part of competitive capitalism. In pure market capitalism of the type idealized in microeconomics texts, each participant is driven to further his own interests at the expense of all other participants in the market. Theoretically, the profit motive is insatiable, and is unconstrained by any ethical or moral force. Thus, each actor is unconcerned with the ramifications of his actions on the economic well-being of others.

At the same time, however, economic actors in this system are necessarily interdependent. No market participant can achieve his goals unless he secures power over the actions of others. It does little good, for example, for the owner of a textile plant to act egocentrically to further his interests if at the same time he cannot be sure that other actors will supply him with the necessary inputs for production and consume his product. If suppliers do not provide promised raw materials, if workers refuse to work, if customers fail to pay for goods delivered, all the ruthless, rational self-interest in the world will be of little value to the textile producer in his striving for profits.

Now if all the other actors were nice, cooperative fellows, our textile manufacturer might not have to worry. Others would play their roles in the scheme and he would come out all right. But this may not always happen because they are, by hypothesis, as selfish as he is. Thus, they, too, will do whatever leads to the highest profit; if this means failing to perform some agreement, so be it. And since one can assume that there will frequently be opportunities for other actors to better themselves at the expense of providing him with some service or product necessary to the success of his enterprise, our hypothetical businessman lives in a world of radical uncertainty.

Yet, as Weber constantly stressed, uncertainty of this type is seriously prejudicial to the smooth functioning of the modern economy. How can the capitalist economic actor in a world of similarly selfish profit seekers reduce the uncertainty that threatens to rob the capitalist system of its otherwise great productive power? What will permit the economic actor to predict with relative certainty how other actors will behave over time? What controls the tendency toward instability?

In order to answer these questions, Weber moved to the level of sociological analysis. The problem of the conflict between the self-interest of individuals and social stability—what Parsons calls "the Hobbesian problem of order"—is one of the fundamental problems of sociology, and, to deal with it, Weber constructed his basic schemes of social action. Weber recognized that predictable uniformities of social action can be "guaranteed" in various ways, and that all of these methods of social control may influence economic activities. Actors may internalize normative standards, thus fulfilling social expectations "voluntarily." Or they may be subjected to some form of "external effect" if they deviate from expectations. These external guarantees may derive from some informal sanctioning system or may involve organized coercion. Law is one form of organized coercion. All types of control may be involved in guaranteeing stable power over economic resources; factual control of this type, Weber observed, may be due to custom, to the play of interests, to convention, or to law.

As I have indicated, however, Weber believed that the organized coercion of *law* was necessary in modern, capitalist economies. While internalization and conventional sanctions may be able to eliminate or resolve most conflict in simpler societies, it is incapable of serving this function in a way that satisfies the needs of the modern exchange economy. For this function, law, in the sense of organized coercion, was necessary. Weber stated:

> [T]hough it is not necessarily true of every economic system, certainly the modern economic order under modern conditions could not continue if its control of resources were not upheld by the legal compulsion of the state; that is, if its formally "legal" rights were not upheld by the threat of force.

Why is coercion necessary in a market system? And why must this coercion take legal form? Finally, when we speak of *legal* coercion, do we mean state power, regardless of how it is exercised, or do we mean power governed by rules, or legalism? Weber gives no clear-cut answer to these questions. The discussion suggests answers but the issues are not fully developed. And the most crucial question, the interrelationship between the need for coercion and the model of legalism, is barely discussed at all. However, I think answers to the questions can be given which fit coherently with other aspects of his analysis.

Coercion is necessary because of the egoistic conflict I have identified above. While Weber never clearly identified this conflict, he himself was aware of it. Some principle of behavior other than short term self-interest is necessary for a market system. Tradition cannot function to constrain egoistic behavior because the market destroys the social and cultural bases of tradition. Similarly, the emerging market economy erodes the social groupings which could serve as the foci for enforcement of conventional standards. Indeed, the fact that the type of conflict I have described comes into existence is evidence of the decline of tradition and custom. Only law is left to fill the normative vacuum; legal coercion is essential because no other form is available.

A second reason why the necessary coercion must be legal is tied to the pace of economic activity and the type of rationalistic calculation characteristic of the market economy. It is not enough for the capitalist to have a general idea that someone else will more likely than not deliver more or less the performance agreed upon on or about the time stipulated. He must know exactly what and when, and he must be highly certain that the precise performance will be forthcoming. He wants to be able to predict with certainty that the other units will perform. But given the potential conflict between their self-interests and their obligations, he also wants to predict with certainty that coercion will be applied to the recalcitrant. The predictability of performance is intimately linked to the certainty that coercive instruments can be invoked in the event of nonperformance.

In this context, it becomes clear why a calculable legal system offers the most reliable way to combine coercion and predictability. Here the model of legalism and the model of capitalist dynamics merge. A system of government through rules seems inherently more predictable than any other method for structuring coercion. Convention is inherently too diffuse, and, like custom, was historically unavailable given the market-driven erosion of the groups and structures necessary for effective constraint of egoism. Like Balzac, Weber saw how the decline of family, guild, and Church unleashed unbridled egoism. Pure *power*, on the other hand, is available in the sense that the state is increasingly armed with coercive instruments. But untrammeled power is unpredictable; wielders of power, unconstrained by rules, will tend not to act in stable and predictable ways. Legalism offers the optimum combination of coercion and predictability.

It is here that the significance of legal autonomy can be seen. Autonomy is intimately linked

to the problem of predictability. The autonomous legal system in a legalistic society is an institutional complex organized to apply coercion only in accordance with general rules through logical or purely cognitive processes. To the extent that it truly functions in the purely logical and, consequently, mechanical manner Weber presented, its results will be highly predictable. If it is constantly subject to interference by forces which seek to apply coercion for purposes inconsistent with the rules, it loses its predictable quality. Thus Weber observed that authoritarian rulers (and democratic despots) may refuse to be bound by formal rules since:

> They are all confronted by the inevitable conflict between an abstract formalism of legal certainty and their desire to realize substantive goals. Juridical formalism enables the legal system to operate like a technically rational machine. Thus it guarantees to individuals and groups within the system a relative maximum of freedom, and greatly increases for them the possibility of predicting the legal consequences of their actions. . . .

IV. A Deviant Case and the Problems of Historical Verification: Legalism and Capitalism in England

Weber's ideal-typical analysis of economy, polity, and law told him that law contributed to capitalism in large measure because of its calculability. Moreover, he stressed that only logically formal rationality, the autonomous legal system with universal and general rules, could guarantee the needed legal certainty. When he tried to verify this historically, the record did not completely support his analysis. This led him to qualify but never really abandon his basic thesis.

In his attempts to struggle with the historical record, Weber pointed repeatedly to aspects of legal life that were important for capitalist development, but inconsistent with a high degree of logical formalism. For example, at one point, he

explicitly recognized that there is a potential conflict between legal rationalism of the logically formal type and a legal system's creative capacity to
generate the new substantive concepts and institutions required by changing economic situations.
He also noted the way in which legal autonomy
can frustrate economic expectations. But these
insights, which might have caused a more fundamental reappraisal of the model, did not affect his
tendency to stress repeatedly the importance of
legal calculability, and the identification of calculability with logical formalism.

Since his methods are as important as his
theory, it is useful to examine the deviant case that
particularly troubled him in this area. This was
the problem of English development. Nowhere in
his sociology of law is the struggle between concept and history, between theory and fact, more
apparent than in his attempts to deal with the
relationship between the English legal system and
capitalist development in England. He returned
to this issue several times. His somewhat ambiguous and contradictory discussion of this issue presents a picture of Weber the historian battling with
Weber the sociological theorist.

As Weber analyzed the relationships between
law and economy in English history, the nation's
growth presented two major problems for his theories. On the one hand, England seemed to lack
the calculable, logically formal, legal system that
he frequently identified as necessary for initial
capitalist development. On the other hand, capitalism, once it became established in England, had
little, if any, appreciable effect on the rationalization of English law.

From Weber's perspective, the English legal
system presented a stark contrast to the continental systems. "[T]he degree of legal rationality is
essentially lower than, and of a type different
from, that of continental Europe." In its "fundamental formal features" the English system differs
from the judicial formalism of the continental
system "as much as is possible within a secular system of justice . . . ." Nevertheless, capitalism had
first emerged in England, and England was undoubtedly a formidable capitalist regime.

These findings presented several logical possibilities. First, they could refute the notion of any
systematic relationship between law and economy.
Second, they might suggest that the ideal type of
logically formal rationality did not focus on the
truly important features of legal life in economic
development. Third, they might indicate that England was in some way an exception to an otherwise historically valid set of generalizations. In
his discussion of the "England problem," Weber
adopted all three of these mutually inconsistent
positions.

In a series of brief and contradictory passages,
Weber suggested all of the following hypotheses:
(1) The English legal system offered a low degree
of calculability but assisted capitalism by denying justice to the lower classes. (2) England was
unique in that it achieved capitalism "not because
but rather in spite of its judicial system." The
conditions allowing this, however, did not prevail
anywhere else. (3) The English legal system, while
far from the model of logically formal rationality,
was sufficiently calculable to support capitalism
since judges were favorable to capitalists *and* adhered to precedent.

If these contrasting positions indicate that
Weber had no clear image of English history in
mind, they also reflect his concern with the issue
of legal calculability and his tendency to equate it
with one mode of legal thought—a mode of
thought which clearly was not well developed in
England. His constant temptation was to maintain
the key importance of calculability, and deal with
England either as an exception to the theory that
legal calculability and capitalism are related, or as
an exception to the idea that logically formal rationality and calculability necessarily go together.
Although clearly aware of other possible economically relevant dimensions of English legal life,
class control or substantive rules for example, he
returned time and again to the feature that his
underlying model told him was crucial. His last
statement on the issue adopted the third position,
thus maintaining the importance of *calculability*
while sacrificing the centrality of logically formal
rationality with its emphasis on logical techniques

as a means to guarantee autonomy. But this position is basically consistent with the overall analysis, since a system controlled by capitalists will presumably be quite predictable, at least from the capitalists' point of view. Since Weber thought such capitalist control was rarely possible, he did not see the English situation as a threat to the basic model. Moreover, the English judiciary was to a significant degree independent of the state, so that autonomy in this sense remains part of the model. Because of this latter aspect of English legal life, some observers have argued that England did develop a truly "rational" legal system before the rise of capitalism, and that the major flaw in Weber's analysis was the false distinction he drew between English and continental law.

V. Legalism and the Legitimization of Class Domination

Up to this point, "capitalism" has been presented as a vague abstraction. While Weber thought that capitalism was in some ways the most rational possible economic system, he was no apologist for it. He could be scathingly critical of the moral effects of this system. These criticisms can be seen in several points; they emerge clearly in another part of the sociology of law where Weber takes up an issue raised by Marx: the role of legalism in legitimizing capitalist domination.

Legalism served more than purely economic functions under capitalism. Weber showed how the idea of an autonomous legal system dispensing formal justice legitimizes the political structure of capitalist society.

Legalism legitimizes the domination of workers by capitalists. The relationships between law, the state, and the market are complex. Legalism, while seeming to constrain the state, really strengthens it, and while the system guaranteed formal equality, it also legitimized class domination. Legalism strengthens the state by apparently constraining it, for the commitment to a system of rules increases the legitimacy of the modern state

and thus its authority or effective power. And as the liberal state grows stronger, it reduces the hold of other forces on the development of the market. This strengthens the position of those who control property, since market organization increases the effective power of those individuals and organizations that control economic resources. "[B]y virtue of the principle of formal legal equality . . . the propertied classes . . . obtain a sort of factual 'autonomy' . . . ," Weber observed.

He believed that these effects of legalism stem from the fundamental antimony between formal and material criteria of justice, and the negative aspects of purely formal administration of justice under modern conditions. Formal justice is advantageous to those with economic power; not only is it calculable but, by stressing formal as opposed to substantive criteria for decision making, it discourages the use of the law as an instrument of social justice. In a passage reminiscent of Anatole France's famous quip that the law forbids both rich and poor to sleep under the bridges of Paris, Weber observed:

> Formal justice guarantees the maximum freedom for the interested parties to represent their formal legal interests. But because of the unequal distribution of economic power, *which the system of formal justice legalizes,* this very freedom must time and again produce consequences which are contrary to . . . religious ethics or . . . political expediency.

Formal justice not only is repugnant to authoritarian powers and arbitrary rulers; it also is opposed to democratic interests. Formal justice, necessarily abstract, cannot consider the ethical issues raised by such interests; such abstention, however, reduces the possibility of realizing substantive policies advocated by popular groups. Thus, certain democratic values and types of social justice could only be achieved at the cost of sacrificing strict legalism. Weber also pointed out that formal legalism could stultify legal creativity, and that legal autonomy could lead to results opposed to both popular and capitalist values.

▪ 6 ▪

The Durkheimian Perspective

This chapter focuses on some of the more significant and controversial ideas that have come to form the Durkheimian perspective of legal sociology. The chapter begins with a discussion of Emile Durkheim's most important sociological concepts. Next, the chapter examines the correspondence that Durkheim sees existing between the types of social solidarity and the types of legal system and penal sanctions. Third, Durkheim's statements about the evolution of contract and his ideas about contract's role and place in society are closely analyzed. The chapter concludes with a discussion of the recent critiques that contemporary scholars have made in regard to Durkheim's thoughts on the relationship between law and morality, his ideas about legal evolution and the division of labor, and his methodological procedures and assumptions.

Emile Durkheim: The Sociologist as Moralist

Of the three major problems that most occupied Emile Durkheim's attention—morality, religion, and law—law was the least important and morality the most important. For Durkheim, legal phenomena "were considered to be something rather like particular manifestations or types of moral and/or religious phenomena" (Vogt, 1983:177). It was his continuing interest in the moral elements of social life that strongly informed his views on law and society. Indeed, for Durkheim society itself is a moral phenomenon whose well-being depends on people's commitment to certain moral beliefs and sentiments. Law is simply a reflection of these moral beliefs and sentiments. For instance, if he were alive today Durkheim would probably attribute the success of civil rights legislation to the moral force that derives from the belief that it is wrong to favor one race over another.

Thus, largely as a result of his overriding interest in religion and morality, Durkheim (like Marx) did not articulate a systematic sociology of law. That notwithstanding, he did leave us with an expansive, albeit controversial, explanation of legal evolution. Indeed, as we shall soon see, Durkheim's "interest in law covered all human societies at all points in history and the evolutionary relations between them" (Clarke, 1976:346). In order to gain a better understanding of his legal sociology, let us now briefly examine Durkheim's life and some of the major influences on his thought.

Life and Influences

Emile Durkheim (1958–1917) was born in Epinal, France, to a Jewish family with a long line of rabbis. Shortly after deciding not to become a rabbi himself, Durkheim, at the age of nineteen was admitted to the prestigious Ecole Normale Supérieure in Paris, where he developed a general interest in philosophical doctrine. However, by the time of his graduation from the Ecole in 1882 Durkheim had shifted his intellectual interest to the scientific study of society. Five years later, a sociology course was created for him at the University of Bordeaux, thus giving Durkheim the distinction of being "the first French academic sociologist" (Coser, 1979:143). In 1893, Durkheim defended his doctoral dissertation, *The Division of Labor in Society*, at the University of Paris. Published as a book, the work had a significant impact. It annoyed the classical economists, and thus Durkheim found it difficult to obtain a professorship (Mauss, 1958:2). Later, he founded, edited, and wrote for the very successful and influential journal *L'Année Sociolgique*. By 1913, Durkheim had attained the professorship of "Science of Education and Sociology" at the Sorbonne.

Durkheim's intellectual thought was heavily influenced by the Enlightenment thinkers Montesquieu and Rousseau and their ideas on the holistic view of society and the general will, respectively. Durkheim was also influenced by the German philosopher Immanuel Kant's conception of morality as a principle of social duty. From the titular "father of sociology," Auguste Comte (1760–1825), Durkheim derived his positivistic approach to the study of society and his notion of the "collective consciousness." From Herbert Spencer, he obtained much of his organismic and evolutionary views. German sociologist Ferdinand Tönnies' *Gemeinschaft und Gesellschaft* (1887) influenced Durkheim's ideas about the different types of social *solidarity* (i.e., cohesiveness or integration). Durkheim's emphasis on solidarity may have given his sociological theory what is now considered to be a conservative—that is, functionalist—bias. And while Durkheim may have "sympathized" with the socialism of the Marxists, "he never gave himself to it" (Mauss, 1958:3). To be sure, he considered Marxism nothing more than a collection of "disputable and out-of-date hypotheses" (Lukes, 1985:323).

As will later become evident, the intellectual influences noted above are at the core of the Durkheimian perspective. Before we can discuss his perspective, however, we must first deal with several of Durkheim's key concepts.

Principal Concepts in Durkheim's Sociology

Two of Durkheim's pivotal works are *The Division of Labor in Society* (1893) and *The Rules of Sociological Method* (1895). It is in these groundbreaking books that Durkheim first introduces several of his most influential sociological concepts, which he subsequently employs in his later studies on suicide, religion, education, morality, and punishment. In *The Division of Labor*, Durkheim focuses on what holds society together. In *The Rules*, his concern is with defining the subject matter of sociology. In what follows we shall discuss in some detail four of Durkheim's key concepts as found in the aforementioned books: *social facts, collective consciousness, mechanical solidarity,* and *organic solidarity.*

   Social facts. Seeking to establish sociology as a distinct academic discipline, Durkheim's objective was to outline sociology's proper study. Trying to break away from the analytic individualism popular at the time, he attempted to distinguish sociology from other knowledge-fields (such as psychology, philosophy, and biology) that also, to one degree or another, attempt to explain human behavior. For Durkheim, sociology was to be a science similar in methodology to the natural sciences and thus rooted in the principles of positivism.
   Durkheim postulates in *The Rules of Sociological Method* that the fundamental subject matter of sociology consists of the study of *social facts*. He defines **social facts** as those "ways of acting, thinking and feeling, external to the individual, and endowed with the power of coercion" (1966:3). In other words, according to Durkheim, social facts exist outside of the individual's physical body (and, at least initially, outside of his or her consciousness as well) and, yet, they exert an influence on the individual's behavior.
   Durkheim acknowledges that social facts are not (usually) tangible, physical entities, as in the example of collective tendencies and passions. He argues, however, that social facts must be considered and treated as "things" because they are real. They are just as real as physical objects because they influence, inhibit, and constrain people's actions. In this sense social facts are part of an "objective," external, and demonstrable social reality. They are not, however, always easily observable.
   Durkheim contends that social facts are phenomena *sui generis* (from Latin meaning "of its own kind"). This means that they have an autonomous and distinct existence of their own. Indeed, social facts cannot be reduced to anything else; they are not primarily molecular, biological, chemical, or even psychological in nature. Social facts are different from and more complex than any of these realms of nature. They are independent of the mere will or needs of individuals. States Durkheim: "the determining cause of a social fact should be sought among the social facts preceding it and not among the states of the individual consciousness" (1966:110). Accordingly, social facts can only be explained by other social facts.
   Another "thing-like" quality that is characteristic of social facts is that they are resistant to change and thus persist from generation to generation. They were here before we were born, and more than likely will be here after we are gone. Examples of social facts include gender roles, norms, values, morality, all the social institutions (the family, the polity, the economy, religion, etc.), the suicide rate, the crime rate, and society itself.
   For Durkheim, law is the preeminent social fact. As an institution it has been around for a long time and, because only a few people would desire a society without some kind of legal system, it will undoubtedly continue indefinitely. The law is *coercive* because it constrains people's actions by prohibiting certain behaviors like murder, theft, and prostitution. The law is *real* since its violation will almost invariably lead to very real consequences such as a fine, incarceration, or death.

The law is also experienced as *external* to the individual. People perceive it as being "out there"—an aspect of objective social reality—as, for example, when they talk about "breaking," "running from," or being "outside" the law. Finally, the law is *observable* because we can see legal rules written down in codes, constitutions, law books, and the like.

In treating social facts as things, Durkheim seeks to study these phenomena through positivism, or the application of the principles of the physical sciences. Consequently, he urges the sociologist to abide by the basic tenets of the scientific method, which include empirical investigation through observation and measurement. As we shall see presently, some social facts are extremely difficult to measure because they are nonmaterial in nature. Durkheim therefore proposes that certain indicators that are closely correlated with nonmaterial social facts be identified so that these social facts can be measured indirectly through them. One example of a nonmaterial social fact is the collective consciousness.

Collective consciousness. Durkheim defines the **collective consciousness** (or "collective conscience") as "the totality of beliefs and sentiments common to the average members of a society [which] forms a determinate system with a life of its own" (1984:38–39). A sort of "group mind," the collective consciousness serves as a general regulating moral force. It is the common morality of the community that tells people the difference between right and wrong and guides their behavior. In *The Division of Labor in Society*, Durkheim remarks that the collective consciousness is stronger and more precise in a society with mechanical solidarity than in a society with organic solidarity.

Mechanical solidarity. As an ideal type, **mechanical solidarity** is that cohesiveness existing when the members of a small, traditional, preindustrial community are attracted to one another because of mutual resemblances. In this case, *homogeneity*—or the fact that people are basically alike—creates a strong bonding force that holds this group together. Moreover, there is a consensus or a "communion of minds" as the members share similar beliefs, ideas, tendencies, and sentiments that are clearly placed within a religious framework. Because these people believe very deeply in the same moral system, theirs is a common way of life. Mechanical solidarity is based on the similarity of the consciousness of the members of this society and constitutes a direct link to their collective consciousness. In this context, it becomes almost impossible for any individual to think of himself as different from his fellows. Individual personalities disappear and the members become collective beings as they mechanically follow the commands of the group. Questioning the common way of life is not tolerated and nonconformity is regarded as a moral outrage that must be quickly and severely quelled. Thus, explains Durkheim, "we should not say that an act offends the common consciousness because it is criminal, but that it is criminal because it offends that consciousness" (1984:40).

There is a lower degree of **division of labor** in a mechanical solidarity. In the main, the members of such a community do not perform a wide variety of highly specialized tasks or roles. To be sure, the division of labor is relatively undifferentiated and simple. The jobs that need to be done to sustain the community may be based on traditional expectations of age and gender. For instance, young people may be responsible for the household chores while the elderly may be expected to keep an eye on the children; the men are charged with hunting game and the women's job is to cook the meals.

Although mechanical solidarity generally typifies "primitive," "ancient," "prefeudal," "feudal," and "postfeudal but preindustrial," societies (Clarke, 1976:249), features of this typology may also be found in certain contemporary religious subcultures. The Old Order Amish of rural Pennsylvania, Ohio, Indiana, and southern Ontario are one such example. The Amish community may be identified as a mechanical solidarity for a number of reasons. First, their uniform dress gives the Amish the appearance of homogeneity. "Many American people have seen Amish families, with the men wearing broad-brimmed black hats and the women in bonnets and long dresses" (Hostetler, 1980:3). Second, their division of labor is organized, very simply, along traditional gender roles. "In planting and harvest time one can see their bearded men working the fields with horses and their women hanging out the laundry in neat rows to dry" (Hostetler, 1980:3). Third, their collective consciousness is strong and well-defined. "Amish life is distinctive in that religion and custom blend into a way of life. The two are inseparable. The core values of the community are religious beliefs" (Hostetler, 1980:10). In short,

> By living in closed communities where custom and a strong sense of togetherness prevail, the Amish have formed an integrated way of life and a folklike culture. Continuity of conformity and custom is assured and the needs of the individual from birth to death are met within an integrated and shared system of meanings. Oral tradition, custom, and conventionality play an important part in maintaining the group as a functioning whole (Hostetler, 1980:11).

In sum, mechanical solidarity is that cohesiveness that results from social homogeneity. In a mechanical solidarity, the division of labor is relatively undifferentiated and the collective consciousness is well defined. Let us now look at its counterpart, organic solidarity.

Organic solidarity. An **organic solidarity,** by contrast, is characterized by an extensive and highly differentiated division of labor or *specialization* of occupational tasks. Relying on biological imagery, Durkheim describes this type of cohesiveness:

> On the one hand each one of us depends more intimately upon society the more labor is divided up, and on the other, the activity of each one of us is correspondingly more specialized, the more personal it is. . . . This solidarity resembles that observed in the higher animals. In fact, each organ has its own special characteristics and autonomy, yet the greater the unity of the organism, the more marked the individualization of the parts. Using this analogy we propose to call "organic" the solidarity that is due to the division of labor (1984:85).

In Durkheim's view, the determining cause of the increase in the division of labor is an increase in the **dynamic density,** or amount of interaction that occurs among members of a society. Naturally, a sizable population will contribute to a greater degree of dynamic density. Hence, this type of solidarity is typically characteristic of large, modern, industrial societies.

The members of an organic solidarity do not share a common moral outlook; individuality, not community, rules supreme. The collective consciousness therefore weakens; that is, it becomes more general and abstract. In this case, it is their *heterogeneity,* or the fact that these people possess different talents and pursue different objectives, that contributes to social cohesiveness. This creates a situation of complementary differentiation. Indeed, the dissimilarities present in industrial society create a contractual exchange between autonomous individuals with distinct specialties. Durkheim tersely describes this contractual exchange as "a system of rights and duties joining [people] in a lasting way to one another" (1984:338).

U.S. society is an example of organic solidarity. The performance of a wide variety of essential roles or functions—such as those of cardiologist, judge, professor, meteorologist, writer, plumber—fosters a reciprocal reliance between people. For instance, even though a cardiologist may not agree with her plumber's political orientation she nevertheless needs the plumber to unclog her sink. Similarly, the plumber may not accept his cardiologist's views on say, abortion, but he needs her as a cardiologist to treat his anginal pain. To this extent, there exists a cooperative functioning between the individual members of society as they engage in different occupational specializations and depend on each others skills. In sum, the "social glue" that holds an organic society together is the members' *interdependence according to the division of labor.* By contrast, in the case of a mechanical society, the social bond is a *shared morality* that exists among the members.

Contrary to an organic society, the collective consciousness in a mechanical community is particularly intense because all its members share the same basic feelings concerning morality, values, traditions, and sentiments. They are of one mind. Behaviors that depart from these feelings are considered deviant and vehemently prohibited. Such aberrant actions are seen as an affront or assault on the collective consciousness of the community. Conversely, the collective consciousness of a large organic society is comparatively weaker in constraining and regulating behavior because the members of this "melting pot" hold diverse viewpoints. Because of this cultural diversity, a greater degree of deviance is tolerated. For instance, in general, urbanites are less likely than people living in small, rural areas to be shocked or scandalized by the prevalence of illicit drug use, the latest risqué fashions, or the high rates of violent crime. Indeed, German sociologist Georg Simmel (1971:324–339) characterizes individuals living in the modern metropolis as having a blasé attitude of indifference to many of the people and events around them.

Since they are ideal types, mechanical and organic solidarity are present in every real society, but in varying proportions. Historically, however, Durkheim tells us that there has been a general evolutionary movement from mechanical to organic solidarity. Thus, we may say that as a form of social organization, mechanical solidarity is most likely to be found in "simple," preindustrial communities with a strong collective consciousness and a negligible division of labor. By contrast, organic solidarity best characterizes differentiated, industrialized societies with a weaker collective consciousness and a highly developed division of labor. In the section that follows, we examine the correspondence that Durkheim makes between the forms of social solidarity and the forms of law.

From Repressive to Restitutive Law

Durkheim's interest in law results from his belief, articulated in *The Division of Labor*, that societies develop from a form of organization based on mechanical solidarity to that based on organic solidarity. Durkheim recognizes that these solidarities are extremely broad and ephemeral typologies that do not easily lend themselves to scientific inquiry; that is, to empirical observation and measurement. Nevertheless, because Durkheim regards social solidarity as "a wholly moral phenomenon," and sees morality as the basis of law (law often reflects moral beliefs and sentiments), he concludes that codified law is the "external" and "visible symbol" by which to gauge society's level of integration. In other words, since social solidarity cannot be observed and thus measured directly, Durkheim uses law as a methodological indicator to measure it indirectly. In Durkheim's view, codified law is readily accessible to scientific observation and can be measured in regard to type and amount. For Durkheim, law is an excellent index of group solidarity. Just as the physicist measures heat through certain objectively observable and easily measurable phenomena such as the rise and fall of mercury in a glass tube (Merton, 1934:326), so Durkheim uses law as the "sociological equivalent of a thermometer" (Parkin, 1992:26) to gauge social cohesion. According to Durkheim, there exists a concomitant variation between the type and amount of law and the type and amount of solidarity.

"Thus our method is clearly traced out for us," Durkheim writes in *The Division of Labor*. "Since law reproduces the main forms of social solidarity, we have only to classify [and count] the different types of law in order to investigate which types of social solidarity correspond to them" (1984:28). Quite simply, Durkheim categorizes all legal rules into repressive and restitutive law. More specifically, *repressive (penal) law* encompasses all criminal law. *Restitutive (cooperative) law*, on the other hand, consists of civil law, commercial law, procedural law, administrative, and constitutional law. Durkheim then correlates repressive law with punitive sanctions but sees restitutive law as invoking reconciliatory measures. Moreover, he maintains that the greater the amount of repressive law in a society, the greater the indication of mechanical solidarity; and the greater the amount of restitutive law, the greater the indication of organic solidarity. We now discuss these two types of law in turn.

Repressive Law

Durkheim argues that the laws of a mechanical solidarity as well as the sanctions associated with the violation of those laws are almost entirely repressive. **Repressive sanctions** are those severe punishments arising from the community's moral outrage toward acts that offend the heightened and pervasive collective consciousness. The high degree of homogeneity (cultural similarity) in a mechani-cal solidarity will engender a harsh, passionate societal reaction since an offense against any one person is seen as an offense against the community as a whole.

Repressive sanctions inflict some suffering, loss, or disadvantage on the in-dividual offender. Punishments imposed by penal law are the best examples of repressive sanctions. It is this highly emotional and vengeful attitude, Durkheim maintains, that makes blood-revenge, public tortures, and the execution of con-demned criminals especially prevalent in premodern mechanical societies.

The law of retaliation, or lex talionis, articulated in the law of Moses in the Old Testament as "an eye for an eye, a tooth for a tooth," finds its expression in repres-sive punishments. Anthropologist A. R. Radcliffe-Brown describes the repressive punishment of retaliation in a premodern Australian tribe:

> [W]hen one man has committed an offense against another, the latter is permitted by public opinion . . . to throw a certain number of spears or boomerangs at the former or in some instances to spear him in the thigh. After he has been given such satisfaction he may no longer harbor ill feel-ings against the offender or some member of his group. In regulated ven-geance the offending group must submit to this as an act of justice and must not attempt further retaliation (1965:209).

In Durkheim's view there is a direct causal relationship between repressive law, with its concomitant sanctions, and religious morality. Such a relationship is especially evident in the societies of the ancient Egyptians, Hebrews, and Indians (1984:50). According to Durkheim:

> every penal law is more or less religious, for what lies at its heart is the feeling of respect for a force superior to that of the individual, for a power in some way transcendental, regardless of the particular symbol whereby it impinges upon the consciousness, and this sentiment is at the basis of all religious feeling. This is why, in a general fashion, repression dominates the entire corpus of law in lower societies: it is because religion permeates all legal activity, just as, moreover, it does all social life (1984:94).

Thus, we may say with Durkheim that the type of law that characterizes a mechanical community is repressive law. The repressive sanctions attached to this type of law are punitive and serve as a retaliatory response to the offenses that assault the community's religious sentiments and strong collective consciousness. We now turn our attention to the type of law that characterizes an organic soli-darity, restitutive law.

Restitutive Law

In contrast to the repressive sanctions endemic to a mechanical solidarity, **restitutive sanctions** are prevalent in an organic solidarity, and are conciliatory, not punitive. Their goal is to restore to their previous, normal state the coop-erative, reciprocal transactions (based on rights, duties, privileges, and immunities) between people. According to Durkheim, there is a preponderance of restitutive law (i.e., civil law, commercial law, procedural law, administrative law, and constitutional law) in a modern organic society with its differentiated institutions, specialized occupations, and autonomous individuals. Restitution is illustrative of the redress that a plaintiff seeks in civil court litigation. Compensatory damages, usually in the form of a sum of money, are awarded as payment in a civil suit involving a tort such as breach of contract. In this case the injury (infringement of rights) is not against the morality of society but against the individual. Consequently, the state, as the representative of society, is only tangentially involved in the administration of civil remedies.

Because restitutive law is not deeply rooted in the collective consciousness of an organic solidarity (absent is a universal religious faith), its violation is not likely to evoke stringent measures. Durkheim contends that while "repressive law corresponds to what is the heart and center of the common consciousness. . . . restitutory law springs from the farthest zones of consciousness" (1984:69). As a matter of fact, in an organic society the collective consciousness "ceases to be a major component of the social bond because it comes to express a predominantly *individual* ethos" (Cotterrell, 1977:242). The division of labor gives rise to what Durkheim calls "the cult of the individual," and the secular moral values consist of human dignity, respect for the individual, and humanitarianism.

The primary tasks of restitutive law are dispute resolution, reconciliation, and restoration. In short, its function is to act as a social binding force by maintaining the harmonious equilibrium of interpersonal relations. Durkheim's image of law is similar to that held by the structural-functionalists who see the law as a mechanism of social integration (see Chapter 7).

To summarize, Durkheim uses law as an external and objective index for measuring the degree of social solidarity. Thus, one of his major theoretical contributions in *The Division of Labor in Society* is the idea that as society evolved from a simple mechanical to a complex organic form, the types of law and punishment corresponding to these solidarities evolved from repressive to restitutive.

To be sure, Durkheim's general thesis has its share of detractors (see Merton, 1934; Barnes, 1966; Clarke, 1976; Rueschemeyer, 1982; Lukes and Scull, 1983; and Garland, 1983) as well as a few defenders (Erikson, 1966; Cotterrell, 1977; and Pearce, 1989). And as we shall see later, several scholars have attempted to empirically test his ideas on legal evolution. In what follows, however, we look at what Durkheim has to say about the relationship between the evolution of punishment, social development, and the centralization of political authority.

Penal Sanctions and the Law

As pointed out in the previous section, Durkheim advanced the idea that as the basic structure and organization of societies progressed from the mechanical to the organic type, repressive law would gradually be replaced by restitutive law. Later in his career he returned to the theme of penal law but came to see that the original thesis that he had presented in *The Division of Labor in Society* was inadequate and needed qualification. With the 1901 publication of his essay "Two Laws of Penal

Evolution," Durkheim restated his position but abandoned the original distinction between mechanical and organic solidarity as well as the sharp contrast he had made between repressive and restitutive laws. In this article, Durkheim proposes two interrelated principles relating the transformations in the kind and degree of punishment to social changes. It must be noted, however, that for Durkheim the evolution of punishment is not an uninterrupted, unilinear sequence.

Durkheim refers to the first principle as the **principle of quantitative change** and he looks primarily at the magnitude, severity, and intensity of penal punishment. In the second principle, the **principle of qualitative change,** he focuses on the historical shift from an emphasis on corporal punishment to incarceration. We now examine these two principles.

The Principle of Quantitative Change

As he had done in *The Division of Labor,* Durkheim, in "Two Laws of Penal Evolution" correlates the severity of punishment with the level of social development. In this article he continues to maintain that punishment becomes less severe as societies become more advanced. This time, however, he introduces the idea of *political centralization* and thus contends that punishments are likely to be severe when a society more closely approximates a less advanced type and/or when a society's governmental power is centralized.

Durkheim makes it clear that these two variables explaining the intensity of punishment—social development and political centralization—are wholly independent of each other; that is, society's level of social development is separate and distinct from its degree of political centralization (governmental absolutism). Because centralized absolute power is found among the simpler societies as well as the advanced, Durkheim argues that it is a historically contingent phenomenon independent of any particular type of social solidarity. Moreover, Durkheim "did not consider the two variables to bear equal explanatory weight. Consistent with his usual dim view of political agency, he held that the level of social development was the more decisive factor and that the form of state power was of secondary importance" (Parkin, 1992:35).

What Durkheim is saying in the principle of quantitative change is that the greater the centralization of political authority, the more repressive will be the punishment inflicted on the criminal offender. Conversely, the less centralized, or more differentiated (i.e., democratic), a society's political power structure, the less draconian its penal measures will be. According to Durkheim, governmental power is most absolute when it is concentrated in the hands of a single ruler—be that a monarch, an emperor, a tyrant, or a dictator—and there is a reliance on the more coercive forms of government.

Through an historical analysis of various premodern societies and the punishments they inflicted on the offender, Durkheim demonstrates the principle of quantitative change. For example, he notes that even though the Hebrews did not possess an advanced type of society, due to the fact that they were essentially a democratic people and never developed a tyrannical monarch, they did not use the cruel and aggravated forms of death employed by the Egyptians, Syrians, and

Assyrians. These latter groups beheaded, stoned, crucified, burned, and hanged the offender.

The more advanced city-state of Athens had punishments that were even less harsh than those of the ancient Hebrews. In Athens, corporal punishments virtually disappeared. And, during the highly developed Roman Republic, there were fewer capital punishments in Rome than there were in Athens. Historians, for example, have pointed out that the Tarpeian Rock, located somewhere within the city limits of Rome, was used to execute only traitors and murderers. The accused were either thrown from it (a distance of about eighty feet) or were forced to jump off it. In addition, there was the Tullianum which was a one-room jail. Its lower chamber was Rome's only execution cell, where the condemned were strangled to death. Notwithstanding these forms of execution, historian James Leigh Strachan-Davidson is quite correct in stating that "so far as citizens were concerned, the criminal law of the Roman Republic, in spite of abundant threats of capital punishment, became in practice the mildest ever known in the history of mankind" (1969:114).

However, by the time of Imperial Rome, when the emperors exercised autocratic rule, penal law carried greater punishments and torture and capital crimes increased. Historian Edward Peters tells about suspected traitors who were tortured under orders from four Roman emperors: Tiberius, Caligula, Claudius, and Domitian:

> Suetonius (*Tib.* 61–2) details with great maliciousness the steps by which Tiberius sought out real and imagined conspiracies, so that "every crime was treated as capital," even to the point at which a friend of the emperor's, invited from Rhodes, was absent-mindedly put to the torture because the emperor assumed that he was simply a new informant. "While Caligula was lunching or reveling, capital examinations by torture were often made in his presence" (*Cali.* 32). Claudius "always exacted examination by torture" (*Claud.* 34), and Domitian, "to discover any conspirators who were hiding, tortured many of the opposite party by a new form of inquisition, inserting fire into their private parts, and he cut off the hands of some of them" (*Dom.* 10) (Peters, 1986:23).

Crimes of lese majesty, which were unknown in feudal times, appeared in fourteenth-century Europe with the development of monarchic absolutism and reached their zenith in the seventeenth century. Because these crimes carried the death penalty, executions grew in number during this period. Moreover, as European society became progressively differentiated, the administration of punishment was itself affected by the specialized occupations of inquisitor and executioner, occupations specifically charged with inflicting punitive sanctions. However, punishment became less cruel in the eighteenth century as the power of the monarchies declined and gave way to less centralized governments.

Thus, as we have already seen in Chapter 2, the eighteenth century witnessed a decrease in the number of offenses subject to the death penalty as well as the abolition of various forms of corporal punishment. We may say, in sum, that "the course of penology is toward progressive amelioration, and where significant exceptions take place in this trend they are to be accounted for by the changes in the allocation of power in the central government" (Tiryakian, 1964:263). Let us now examine Durkheim's second principle: the principle of qualitative change.

The Principle of Qualitative Change

In the principle of qualitative change Durkheim states that the more brutal forms of punishment will give way to a more humane alternative, namely, *incarceration*. According to him, the deprivation of liberty through incarceration tends to become increasingly the preferred form of punishment as society progresses and becomes more secular. It is important to note that Durkheim is not saying that repressive law is going to disappear entirely. Although crimes would be punished more leniently in the future, they would be punished nevertheless. "There is not in reality, therefore, a general weakening of the whole apparatus of repression," declares Durkheim, "rather, one particular system weakens but it is replaced by another which, while being less violent and less harsh, does not cease to have its own severities, and is certainly not destined to an uninterrupted decline" (1983:131).

Durkheim further proposes that the social practice of incarceration passes through several stages of historical development. Originally, the earliest prisons were not used as places of punishment but only as places of temporary detention. This was the case, for example, in Athens, where the offender, like Socrates, was detained in prison only while awaiting trial. Although incarceration began to make an appearance during Socrates' time, it was never fully seen as the sole mode of penal sanction. Similarly, in Republican Rome jails were primarily used as temporary holding places for prisoners. The Lautumiae was a jail located on the outskirts of the Forum. Its cells, which could accommodate about fifty prisoners, were usually empty. Although lictors, or public servants, were recruited to stand guard duty, security was usually lax. Essentially, the idea of the prison was a foreign one to the Romans. Incarceration did not occur in premodern societies because criminal responsibility was seen as collective. In this case it is not just the offender who is considered guilty but the entire clan or family to which he or she belongs. It therefore becomes unnecessary to imprison the offender since in the case of flight others remain who can be punished in the offender's stead.

Gradually, prisons became institutions for the administration of penal sanctions where offenders were systematically subjected to all sorts of torments. The dungeons and torture chambers of the absolutist monarchs of seventeenth-century Europe are prime examples of this type of prison. Following the collapse of these authoritarian regimes, and their replacement by less-centralized governments, incarceration came to signify something different from the administration of direct physical cruelty on the offender. As society advanced, prisons lost their character of preventive custody and acquired their "pure" form as they became places of long-term confinement. Loss of liberty was considered a distinctive penal form and came to replace corporal punishments. As sociologist Frank Parkin correctly points out, "prisons were needed in order that punishment could be made less violent" (1992:37). Once loss of liberty became accepted as a penalty in its own right, the various types of torture and execution were abolished. "If locking offenders away had not been available as an option," asks Parkin rhetorically, "how could penal law have evolved along more humane lines?" (1992:37).

By the eighteenth century, the penal nature of the prison had become accepted and incarceration became the model of punishment. Indeed, the prison became the "necessary and natural substitute for other punishments which were fading away" (Durkheim, 1983:120). At this time in the United States, for example, the death sentence had been abolished for almost all but a handful of offenses and a term in the penitentiary became customary. Opening in 1776, the Walnut Street jail in Philadelphia was the first prison in the United States. Others soon followed. Auburn State Prison and Sing Sing Prison of New York opened in 1819 and 1825, respectively. Eastern Penitentiary of Philadelphia and Charlestown Penitentiary of Massachusetts opened in 1829. In 1831, France dispatched the social observers Alexis de Tocqueville and Gustave Auguste de Beaumont to investigate the penitentiary system of the United States. Tocqueville and Beaumont wrote about American penologists: "they have caught the *monomanie* [craze] of the penitentiary system, which to them seems the remedy for all the evils of society" (1964:80).

Thus far we have seen that Durkheim advanced two principles in explaining the evolution of punishment in regard to type and severity. In the principle of qualitative change Durkheim tells us that as society progresses and becomes more secular, incarceration replaces corporal punishment as the preferred penalty. In the principle of quantitative change, he explains that punishments inflicted upon the offender will be especially severe when a society is relatively undifferentiated and/or when its governmental power is absolute. We now turn our attention to how Durkheim sees the evolution of quantitative punishment as corresponding to the evolution of two fundamental types of criminality.

Types of Criminality

Durkheim identifies two types of criminality: religious crimes and human crimes. **Religious crimes** are acts directed against collective things having a transcendent or mystical character, while **human crimes** are acts injuring only the individual or his or her property. Sir Henry Maine made a similar distinction between types of crime when he wrote that there are "laws punishing sins" and "laws punishing torts."

Religious crimes. Religious crimes, which are offenses against religion, state authorities, traditions, and the like, are predominant in less-developed societies and seriously violate the collective consciousness of those societies. Because government leaders and deeply cherished moral values are seen as having a quasi-religious aura, the religious crimes committed against them are considered sacrilege and blasphemy. In this case the collective consciousness, or that shared framework of sacred moralities, is assaulted severely; the acts are regarded as reprehensible; and, as a consequence of the community's moral outrage, the punishments are particularly intense.

In these simple societies, where political power is monopolized by one individual like a monarch, that individual assumes the attributes of a deity and is elevated to a superhuman level. Consequently, crimes against the society are really crimes against the absolute sovereign who makes the laws. Crimes against the king are seen as acts against divinity and are considered an abomination. Thus, says Durkheim, wherever political power is absolute, violations of the law are always treated as religious criminality and punishment becomes an emotional act of vengeance.

Religious crimes provoke a strong punitive response because they are seen as more odious. Although many, if not most, crimes are committed by the public against their own kind and not against the despot or his functionaries, such crimes are nevertheless treated as if they were offenses against the state. This is because the laws of the land "are supposed to emanate from the sovereign and express his will, so the principle violations of the law appear to be directed against him" (Durkheim, 1983:129). Thus, any breach of the despot's laws—laws endowed with a divine quality—is interpreted as a religious crime and violently repressed. In this context, the function of punishment is to reaffirm group solidarity and restore the sacred collective consciousness violated by the criminal.

Human crimes. According to Durkheim, compared to religious crimes, society views human crimes (murder, theft, rape, fraud, and so forth) as less revolting because they involve only the private interests of the individual victim who is not seen as a religious or sacred entity. These types of crime predominate in more advanced, differentiated societies where the collective consciousness has lost its stern, religious character. Here the trend is away from the ethic of collective responsibility and toward what sociologist Steven Spitzer calls "the 'individuation' of the offended object" (1979:211). In modern legal systems, criminal and victim possess equal standing. Human crimes are not punished too heavily because one person's injury does not threaten the entire society. States Durkheim: "The offense of man against man cannot arouse the same indignation as an offense of man against God" (1983:125). As the coercive force of the collective consciousness grows weaker— that is, as society becomes increasingly secular—crime is no longer considered a desecration and an act of impiety against the collectivity. Consequently, the collective outbursts of anger, outrage, indignation, and irrational vengeance are delimited and tempered.

As noted earlier in this chapter, in an advanced society there emerges a secular morality—that is, a new collective consciousness—based on the values of human dignity, respect for the individual, and humanitarianism. Accordingly, there is an increasing sentiment of mercy and sympathy for the offender who suffers the pains of punishment. Durkheim tell us that the "sentiments protecting human dignity," which lead us to "respect the life and property of our fellows," arose out of "the sympathy which we have for man in general" (1983:124). Similarly, Michel Foucault points out that by the eighteenth century the masses could sympathize with the accused and "the people never felt closer to those who paid the penalty than in those rituals intended to show the horror of the crime and the invincibility of power [to punish] . . . exercised without moderation or restraint" (1979:63). By this time, reformers like Cesare Beccaria were calling for the abolition of excessive punishment and public executions. Because of this increase in public sympathy as well as the fact that crimes were no longer regarded as sacrilegious, punishments became progressively milder.

Later in this chapter we shall discuss some of the criticisms made against Durkheim's principles of quantitative and qualitative change. For now, however, we turn our attention to another idea that makes up part of his legal sociology: the evolution of contract and contract law.

The Evolution of Contract and Contract Law

Durkheim's thoughts on contracts and contract law were first articulated in *The Division of Labor in Society*. His most developed sociological insights into the evolution of the contract, however, are found in a series of lectures that he gave at the University of Bordeaux and, later, at the Sorbonne. These lectures were subsequently translated into English and published as a book under the title *Professional Ethics and Civic Morals*.

In what follows we will look at Durkheim's statements concerning the evolution of contract as found in *Professional Ethics*, and then we will turn once again to *The Division of Labor in Society* and examine his ideas about contract's role and place in society. However, before we engage ourselves in these issues, we must first identify those social arrangements giving rise to the juridical bond of contract.

The Juridical Bond of Contract

Although the contract is a wholly social phenomenon, according to Durkheim, it did not develop as an institution until a very late date. To be sure, Durkheim's explanation of its evolution echoes Sir Henry Maine's idea of the progression of legal history from status to contract. As we saw in Chapter 2, Maine postulated that the idea of contract is buttressed by the fact that individuals enter into volitional agreements with each other. Such autonomous and free arrangements could only occur after a de-emphasis on the individual's ascribed status, which emanated from family and group ties. In a similar vein, Durkheim states that the juridicial bond of contract derives from either (1) "a state or condition in being, of things or of persons" (for example, the slave who by virtue of social status is legally bound to the master), or (2) "a state not yet in being of things or of persons, but simply desired or willed on both sides" (1957:176).

In the first arrangement, the bond of contract, with its rights and duties, is a unilateral relationship. In antiquity, for instance, the master had rights over the slave but the slave had no rights over the master. By contrast, the second type of arrangement emphasizes the *willful* and *bilateral* rights and duties of the contracting parties. Here, the contractual bond is realized only after the traditional status of the thing or person in question is changed. For example, in modern industrial society the status relationship between master and slave is transformed into the contractual relationship between employer and employee. Within the contract of employment, the employee acquires certain rights and duties toward the employer, while the employer, in turn, acquires certain rights and duties toward the employee. Moreover, it is said that both parties enter this relationship of mutual obligations of their own free will. Thus, for Durkheim, the true contract arises only when there is a "declared agreement of the wills" between the two bargaining parties.

According to Durkheim, the true contract has its basis in the second type of arrangement. In this case there is no intermediary between the contracting parties. Durkheim defines contract, very simply, as "relations according to law having as their origin wills that are in agreement" (1957:177). We shall see that only after the individual achieves some degree of independence from the sacred force of the community's collective consciousness can he or she engage in this type of contractual relationship. As we noted in the previous sections, the force of the collective consciousness decreases as the division of labor increases. And, as will be explained later, the development of the contract is closely connected with the development of the division of labor. In addition, the contract evolves as society progresses from mechanical to organic solidarity. However, it is in mechanical solidarity where the sacred origin of contract is to be found.

The Sacred Origin of Contract

Durkheim traces the origin of the juridical bond of contract—its rights and duties—to the sacred status of certain persons or things. As we have already seen, in a simple mechanical solidarity, where the force of the collective consciousness is especially intense, the community itself acquires a sacred aura. Indeed, Durkheim maintains repeatedly that divinity is only the symbolic form of the society. In this context, the individual, in awe of the group's supreme power, will invariably be obligated to the group as well as to the other members who engage in the common way of life. His or her relations with the community as a whole and with the members individually will be reverential and emotionally close. To be sure, this relationship is a unilateral one: the community as a sacred entity has certain rights over the individual but the individual has no rights over the community.

Durkheim explains the contract's evolution from a bond that is based on a unilateral, sacred, coerced, and unequal relationship to a bond based on a bilateral, secular, free, and equitable relationship between contracting parties. He considers five major types of contract in his analysis of its evolution:

1. The blood covenant
2. The *real* contract
3. The contract of solemn ritual
4. The consensual contract (or contract by mutual consent)
5. The contract of equity (or the just contract)

Together, these types comprise a sequence of historical stages delineating the progression from the "pseudo" contract of the past to the true contract of the present and beyond. We now turn our attention to a short discussion of each of these five types of contract.

The blood covenant. In the case of the **blood covenant**, members of a group with a strong collective consciousness have certain rights and duties toward each other because they share a common sacred quality. Literally or figuratively, they see themselves as being of the same blood. When these individuals wish to create relations with others outside their group, they simulate artificial bonds symbolizing the natural ties they have with their kind. As an artificial bond, the blood covenant took several forms. It could consist, for example, of two individuals mingling their blood thus becoming "blood brothers." An illustration of this phenomenon is found in Mafia member Joseph Valachi's account of his induction into the Cosa Nostra. Valachi tells of being asked for his trigger finger at his initiation ceremony before forty members of the Cosa Nostra. His finger was pricked with a pin and squeezed until it bled. At this point the Mafia Don announced, "This blood means that we are now one Family" (Maas, 1968:98).

The Christian rite of communion, where the believers partake of the body and blood of Christ, is another form of blood covenant. This ritual sharing of the sacred blood symbolizes the contract made between God and the community of believers. In the Roman Catholic tradition, for example, Jesus' Last Supper is re-created in the sacrament of communion as the priest lifts the chalice and proclaims to the congregation: "Jesus took the cup and gave it to his disciples and said: 'Take this all of you and drink from it. This is the cup of my blood; the blood of the new and everlasting *covenant* which will be shed for you and for all so that your sins may be forgiven.'"

The **real** *contract.* The second type of contract, the ***real*** **contract,** occurs only with the actual transfer and delivery of a thing, thus giving rise to a duty of debt. For example, in the Roman loan called *mutuum*, the loan was concluded when its object (a sum of money or an amount of **fungibles**—goods that can be replaced in quantity and quality) was handed over to the debtor. In this contractual agreement, a buyer has the right to receive the thing purchased but also has the duty to pay for it. In later times, a symbolic article without value, such as a straw or a glove (in Germanic law), was substituted for the actual object of exchange.

The contract of solemn ritual. The third type of contract, the **contract of solemn ritual,** involved the declaration of an oath. The words of the oath, said in ritual form, were endowed with a sacred force that served to bind the participants. The contracting parties carefully uttered a specific phrase in accordance with a consecrated formula. The formal pronouncement of the oath made the words sui generis; that is, it gave them an identity of their own. This idea still exists today when people say they "give their word."

The oath in the contract of solemn ritual was said to invoke a divine being who served as intermediary or **guarantor** (one who answers for the performance of another's duty) of the promises made and exchanged. The deity was said to be offended if the participants failed to fulfill the terms of the agreement. Consequently, breach of the pact was considered a sacrilege and the retaliatory penalty inflicted on the offender was especially severe. An example of the solemn contact is found in the thirteenth-century practice of compurgation. **Compurgation** consisted of a gathering of twelve reputable people who were brought together by the accused and who would swear to his or her innocence. Supposedly, no one would think of lying for fear of being punished by God.

According to Durkheim, the participants in the solemn contract are bound by two duties. First, the bargaining parties are under an extreme obligation to fulfill

their promises because they have sworn an oath to the highest moral authority—
the deity. Second, the promisor becomes closely bound to the promisee because the
promisor's oath, by detaching his or her words and projecting them outwardly,
enables the promisee to possess them as if they were tangible things. "Our word,
once given," states Durkheim, "is no longer our own" (1957:196). Because of its
strong binding force, the contract of solemn ritual is employed whenever the ties
to be made are of supreme importance. This, for example, is the case with the
marriage contract when it is forged in the context of a religious ceremony.

    The consensual contract. The contract of solemn ritual diminished as soci-
ety's religious traditions began to weaken and fade. A fourth type, the **consensual contract,** emerged when sales and purchases of commodities and property
became more frequent. As these new demands of economic life increased, it became impractical and inexpedient to engage in the ritual formalities of the solemn
contract.

    Unlike the solemn contract, which relied on the backing of sacred forces, the
consensual contract is legitimated by the sanctions of positive law. In this way, the
consensual contract protects not only the rights of the community but also the
rights of the individual. Further, the consensual contract creates a bilateral bond of
reciprocal duties between the two transacting parties; that is, each party plays the
dual role of creditor and debtor, promisor and promisee. "The two parties declare
at one and the same time that they consent to the exchange on the conditions
agreed between them" (Durkheim, 1957:200).

    The consensual contract differs from the solemn contract in that not only is
there an external element, an exchange of goods, but there must also be an internal
element—a psychological agreement to the terms of the bargain. Durkheim
considers the consensual contract the first "true" contract because the bargaining
parties freely agree to the terms of the bargain. Indeed, its principal feature is the
declaration of wills. Durkheim tells us that the transfer involved in the consensual
contract is an *internal state of mind* as it pertains to the will or intention of the
bargaining parties. If intention and will are absent, or if they are not freely given,
the contract is considered invalid. The binding force of the consensual contract is
thus internal or psychological and not based on a formal ritual or the transfer of a
physical object. Neither **duress** (the coercion of a contracting person to act contrary to his or her will) nor an intermediary is involved in the bargaining relationship. It is a *bona fide* (from Latin meaning "in good faith") contract because the
parties enter into it with an attitude of sincerity and through mutual consent.

    The contract of equity. In addition to considering the internal state of mind of
the transacting parties, the **contract of equity** also considers the *external consequences* of the agreement. Durkheim maintains that only by regarding both the
internal and external aspects of the bargain can a truly equitable, objective, and just
contract be realized. He states: "A just contract is not simply any contract that is
freely consented to, that is, without explicit coercion; it is a contract by which
things and services are exchanged at the true and normal value, in short, at the just
value" (1957:211).

Even though an individual voluntarily enters into a contract, this does not necessarily mean that the transaction will turn out to be a fair one for him or her. Contractual consent can be obtained through **fraud** (an intentional act of deception used by one party to gain advantage over the other). Fraud prevents one of the contracting parties from fully knowing what they are agreeing to. Suppose that Smith purchases a racehorse from Jones based on the latter's statements that the horse is a thoroughbred with a pedigree from the Thoroughbred Owners and Breeders Association. Smith later discovers that the horse is actually a crossbred. In this case of fraud, Smith, as the deceived party, may engage in the legal **rescission** or unmaking of the contract and collect rescissory damages.

In the contract of equity the notion of constraint recedes into the background while the idea of exploitation becomes ever more important. Durkheim contends that the exploitation of one person by another rouses our indignation. He attributes the interest in exploitation to the organic solidarity's increased feeling of sympathy, or altruism, which we acquire for our fellow citizens. In "Two Laws of Penal Evolution," he had characterized this moral sentiment as "the sympathy which we feel of every man who suffers" (1983:125–126).

Durkheim argues that in order to ensure against exploitation in contractual transactions, goods and services should only be exchanged at a fair price. In other words, what one party receives must be equivalent to what he or she gives and vice versa. On the related issue of how to prevent contractual inequalities, Durkheim proposes a measure that, coming from him, seems quite radical: the abolition of inheritance. Durkheim considers inheritance to be the great culprit that upsets the balance of social equality because the individual who inherits wealth or property has the unfair advantage of imposing his or her will on the other party by forcing them to sell the goods or services being exchanged at a price below their real value. Thus, in Durkheim's mind, the idea behind the discontinuance of inheritance is that all parties will volitionally enter the contractual relationship on common footing. He believed that this reform would ultimately produce a truly just contract because it will transcend the inequities that derive from the accident of birth or from family status.

It is somewhat ironic that Durkheim, who "never gave himself" to socialism, would support one of socialism's central tenets—the abolition of inheritance—in order to arrive at a completely fair contract. This notion makes sense, however, only when we realize that for Durkheim, "inheritance goes against the whole spirit of individualism that inheres in a society marked by an extensive division of labor" (Milovanovic, 1988:34). Merit based on individualism, and not status based on membership in a collectivity, is what Durkheim sees as being important in a society with a highly developed division of labor. Furthermore, he asserts that this organic society must rest firmly upon contractual foundations. Let us now see what makes up these contractual foundations.

The Division of Labor and Contractual Relationships

Durkheim contends that the main social function of contract is not to encourage the exchange of goods and services between parties, but to ensure their regular cooperation and thus maintain the equilibrium of society. To be sure, because it gives rise to reciprocal obligations, the contract becomes "the supreme legal expression of cooperation" (1984:79). In Durkheim's view, the composite division of labor, or the specialization of tasks in organic society, depends on that form of cooperation that is best expressed by the contract.

Contracts, as symbols of exchange, help to harmonize those social relationships taking place between persons performing specialized and distinct functions. Some of these functions, for example, are manifest in the commercial code regulating such contracts specific to commerce as those made between agent and principle, between carrier and consignor, and between insurer and insured. In other words, each contracting party needs the other. But even in collaborations such as these, we find a certain amount of competition as each self-interested party "seeks to obtain at least cost what he needs, that is, to gain the widest possible rights in exchange for the least possible obligations" (Durkheim, 1984:160). If the solidarity between the competing parties is to be preserved, however, every contractual outcome must be the result of a compromise. Such a compromise must be a position of equilibrium; "one that steers a middle course between the interests that are in competition and their solidarity with one another" (Durkheim, 1984:160).

The purpose of contractual law is to maintain social equilibrium by regulating and determining the contract's legal outcome. It does this by constraining the bargaining parties to respect each others' rights and duties and, in the process, it helps to achieve a fair compromise by ensuring that the goods and services exchanged are of equivalent social value. Durkheim, however, makes it clear that the role of contract is not to abolish competition but only to moderate it. To be sure, he sees the contract as a precarious truce that can assuage disputes only temporarily. Nevertheless, Durkheim is quick to point out that contracts also express the general *consensus* existing in society. This consensus is reflected in the special ties that originate in the agreement of wills between contracting parties.

In sum, Durkheim sees the contract as having a pivotal, albeit limited, role to play in the maintenance of society. As Durkheim sees it, the law of contracts, through its authority to regulate, "constitutes the foundation of our contractual relationships" (1984:161). In light of the aforementioned statements, it is easy to see why Durkheim calls one of the important varieties of organic solidarity "contractual solidarity."

Thus far in this chapter we have seen that Emile Durkheim's sociology of law can be understood only when considered within the context of organic and mechanical solidarity and the division of labor. To be sure, Durkheim's interest in law holds only to the extent that he uses it, as a material social fact, to measure a nonmaterial social fact: the degree of social solidarity. As such, Durkheim correlates repressive law with mechanical solidarity and restitutive law with organic solidarity.

Later, as he analyzes the evolution of punishment, Durkheim abandons his distinction between mechanical and organic solidarity, as well as repressive and restitutive law, but retains the idea that an advanced society is characterized by a highly differentiated division of labor. In the essay "Two Laws of Penal Evolution," Durkheim introduces the notion of political centralization and states that punishments are most severe when a society does not have a highly differentiated division of labor and when its governmental power is absolute. He further contends that the severity of penal measures also depends on whether the offense is an act committed against the private interests of the individual—human crime—or an act committed against collective things possessing a sacred character—religious crime. Religious crimes are more prevalent in less-developed societies, where political power is centralized. These crimes are punished harshly because they are seen as acts against divinity. By contrast, human crimes are predominant in highly advanced societies where the collective consciousness encourages mercy and sympathy for the offender.

Finally, in our analysis of Durkheim's legal sociology we examined his views on the evolution of contract and its role and place in society. We noted that Durkheim identifies five types of contract that make up a historical sequence tracing contract's evolution from the bond based on a unilateral, sacred, coerced, and unequal relationship to the bond based on a bilateral, secular, free, and equitable relationship between parties. Lastly, we discussed Durkheim's contention that the contract's main function is to ensure solidarity by encouraging social relations of cooperation and compromise between parties performing specialized and distinct roles. In sum, we may say that the whole of Durkheim's sociology of law is premised on the notion of contractual solidarity.

In the remainder of this chapter we look at how Durkheim's ideas concerning social solidarity, repressive and restitutive law, the functions and evolution of punishment, the division of labor, and contractual legal relations have been extended and criticized by contemporary legal scholars.

Neo-Durkheimian Contributions to the Durkheimian Perspective

The previous sections of this chapter were devoted primarily to a discussion of the theoretical notions about law, crime, and punishment initially advanced by Emile Durkheim in *The Division of Labor in Society*. In the sections that follow, we return to many of those same themes but this time we will look at how they have been tested empirically by contemporary research. What follows, therefore, is a survey of those studies that have subjected Durkheim's legal sociology to the rigors of quantitative and qualitative research in an effort to evaluate its validity. We will see that the bulk of this research is extremely critical of his theses. In fact, social theorist Lewis Coser is quite correct when he states that criticism of Durkheim's theoretical work is so pervasive today that it has become a "minor cottage industry" (1984:xxiv). Be that as it may, it is hard to imagine that Durkheim, who spent much of his career arguing that sociology should be oriented toward empirical research, would have disapproved of the motivation behind these studies. Before we examine those studies that are particularly critical of the Durkheimian perspective, let us first look at those studies largely supportive of Durkheim's contentions about law and morality.

Law and Morality

Durkheim sees morality as the basis of law because law usually represents the moral beliefs and sentiments of a community. In this section we examine Durkheim's ideas concerning law and morality by looking at three studies, one empirical, the other two more theoretical, supporting much of what he said about these ideas.

The first study, conducted by Lonn Lanza-Kaduce and his colleagues, bolsters Durkheim's contention that the violation of criminal law will invoke strong feelings of moral condemnation. The second study, by Yale sociologist Kai Erikson, builds upon Durkheim's thesis that punishing criminal law violators helps bring together the "upright" citizens of a community by giving them a common sense of morality. The third study, by Albert Bergesen, extends Durkheim's notion that crimes threaten the moral boundaries of a society and shows that crimes may also threaten its political boundaries. Let us begin by looking at the relationship between law and normative attitudes.

The Law and Normative Attitudes

As noted previously, in an attempt to measure the type and amount of social solidarity, Durkheim distinguished between criminal law and civil law and their corresponding repressive and restitutive sanctions. Moreover, he distinguished between these two types of law on the basis of the kinds of *normative attitudes* (i.e., beliefs, feelings, sentiments, or opinions) they reflect.

According to Durkheim, criminal laws, which are abundant in a mechanical solidarity, "are inscribed upon everyone's consciousness, all are aware of them and feel they are founded upon right" (1984:34). Since criminal laws reflect the community's commonly held beliefs, when they are violated they will arouse strong feelings of anger and moral indignation in the community members. As a consequence, the community will demand that the offender suffer repressive measures. Civil laws, by contrast, "do not correspond to any feeling within us, . . . they have no deep roots in most of us" (Durkheim, 1984:69). Like criminal laws, civil laws also derive their authority from public belief, but it is not a belief involving widespread consensus; rather, it is "specific to certain sectors of society" (Durkheim, 1984:82). That is to say that the diverse specialized groups in an organic solidarity will not be acquainted with all of the laws but only those legal rules that directly impact upon them.

In short, we may say that criminal laws are pervasive in a mechanical solidarity and reflect a community's commonly held beliefs. These laws are known throughout the community and their violation will arouse strong feelings of moral condemnation. On the other hand, civil laws, which abound in an organic solidarity, have only selective interest for specialized groups, are not known throughout the society, and do not arouse strong feelings of moral condemnation.

In *The Division of Labor in Society*, Durkheim puts constitutional law in the same category as civil law. He stipulates that both types of law are characteristic of organic society and both involve restitutive sanctions. However, sociologist Lonn Lanza-Kaduce and his colleagues (1979) contend that the manner in which constitutional law is conceptualized in the United States—as a body of law protecting citizens' civil liberties from government encroachment—makes it more akin to criminal law. Thus, they argue that virtually all of the features that are relevant to criminal law should apply equally to constitutional law. However, Lanza-Kaduce et al. maintain that repressive sanctions are inappropriate to violations of constitutional law because this type of law contributes to organic, not mechanical solidarity.

In the context of the aforementioned statements derived from Durkheim's theory of law, Lanza-Kaduce et al. formulate five sets of hypotheses:

1. There is a high degree of knowledge about criminal and constitutional laws and a lower degree of knowledge about civil laws across society.
2. Because there is a high degree of knowledge about criminal and constitutional laws, there is a high degree of legitimacy to be attributed to criminal and constitutional laws. Where there is a high degree of knowledge about certain civil laws, there will be a high degree of legitimacy attributed to those laws. Conversely, where there is a low degree of knowledge about certain civil laws, there will be a low degree of legitimacy attributed to those laws.
3. Violations of criminal and constitutional laws will evoke a high degree of moral condemnation from society. Violations of civil laws will evoke a relatively low degree of moral condemnation.
4. When criminal laws are violated, society will call for repressive sanctions to be inflicted on the offender. When civil or constitutional laws are violated, society will call for restitutive remedies to be imposed on the offending party.
5. When criminal laws prohibit behavior that is morally condemned by the public, the moral beliefs will remain unchanged. However, when those criminal laws are repealed, the moral beliefs will be moderated and legitimacy withdrawn. When civil laws prohibit certain behavior, the public will support their legitimacy and sanctions. When the civil laws are repealed, the public will stop supporting their legitimacy and sanctions.

In order to test these five hypotheses, Lanza-Kaduce et al. collected data from a group of students in junior high school, high school, and college. The students were presented with six vignettes describing behaviors associated with criminal, civil, and constitutional law. They were then asked to morally evaluate these behaviors, assess the law's legitimacy, and indicate the appropriate sanction for the behaviors. The researchers found that:

1. Fifty-six point four percent of the respondents had knowledge about criminal law; 66.4 percent had knowledge about constitutional law; and 39.1 percent had knowledge about civil law.
2. Fifty-eight point three percent of the respondents saw criminal law as legitimate; 76.2 percent saw constitutional law as legitimate; and 41.1 percent saw civil law as legitimate.
3. Fifty-two point two percent of the respondents considered criminal law violations to be very wrong morally; 63.9 percent considered constitutional law violations to be very wrong morally; and 26.9 percent considered civil law violations to be very wrong morally.

4. Twenty-seven point two percent of the respondents advocated repressive sanctions in response to criminal law violations; 5.9 percent advocated repressive sanctions in response to civil law violations; and 5.2 percent advocated repressive sanctions in response to constitutional law violations.

5. Twenty-five point six percent of the respondents moderated their moral beliefs after being told that the conspiracy vignette of two persons making extensive plans to steal, but not acting upon those plans, did not violate the criminal law.

In general, the study's findings supported all five sets of the hypotheses that Lanza-Kaduce and his colleagues had deduced from Durkheim's legal theory. We now turn our attention to another study that not only supports Durkheim's theoretical notions about crime, morality, and punishment, but also builds elegantly on those notions.

Ritual Punishment and Moral Solidarity

In the previous section we reiterated the fact that Durkheim saw a close association between morality and the law. In this section we look more closely at Durkheim's contention that the function of punishment is to strengthen a community's moral solidarity.

Durkheim suggests in *The Division of Labor in Society* that the ritual punishments inflicted on law violators serve to bring together the "honest," "upright," and "respectful" citizens of the community and give them the opportunity to reaffirm their commitment to shared values and a common identity. In other words, rituals of punishment help tighten the bonds of social solidarity. This cohesiveness occurs as the anger generated by the criminal offense produces a dynamic density in the community, creating a situation in which the consciences of the individual members are integrated in a common sense of morality. Durkheim cogently describes this phenomenon:

> Crime . . . draws honest consciousnesses together, concentrating them. We have only to observe what happens, particularly in a small town, when some scandal involving morality has just taken place. People stop each other in the street, call upon one another, meet in their customary places to talk about what has happened. A common indignation is expressed. From all the similar impressions exchanged and all the different expressions of wrath there rises up a single fount of anger, . . . anger which is that of everybody without being that of anybody in particular. It is public anger (Durkheim, 1984:58).

Kai Erikson agrees with Durkheim's idea that punishing criminal law violators contributes to the community's solidarity. Erikson, however, extends this thesis and suggests an interesting addendum: that a disruption of the community's solidarity will compel the community to seek out criminals to punish. Let us see how Erikson explains this notion and how it is premised on the concept of boundary maintenance.

Boundary maintenance. As we have indicated, in Durkheim's view, breaches of the criminal law reveal to people the interests they share in common and call their attention to the central values of their community's collective consciousness. Continuing with this argument, Erikson tells us that, besides occupying a geographical space (physical territory), all societies also occupy a cultural space (moral territory). A community's cultural space, he says, provides a meaningful reference point for its members since contained within its boundaries are the core moral values defining that community's "way of life" and giving it its particular identity. Thus, any challenge to these moral boundaries will be interpreted as a threat to the community's cultural integrity. States Erikson: "A human community can be said to maintain boundaries . . . in the sense that its members tend to confine themselves to a particular radius of activity and to regard any conduct which drifts outside that radius as somehow inappropriate or immoral" (1966:10). Thus, when deviants challenge the normative outlines of a society they are actually helping to highlight and accentuate those contours for the rest of the group. Through their actions, deviants provide a point of contrast that gives the norms some scope and dimension. It is ironic that only by having criminals occasionally test the outer edges of acceptable behavior can the "upright" citizens learn *where* the moral boundaries are figuratively located and, accordingly, they can also learn *who* they are as a community.

Penal rituals (e.g., criminal trials, excommunication hearings, courts-martial), in which the deviant offender is publicly confronted by the community's anger and indignation, act as boundary-maintaining devices because they demonstrate where the line between moral and immoral behavior is drawn. "Each time the community moves to censure some act of deviation, . . . and convenes a formal ceremony to deal with the responsible offender, it sharpens the authority of the violated norm and restates where the boundaries of the group are located" (Erikson, 1966:13).

Two related sociological insights may be derived from the foregoing remarks. First, we may say that when a community is engaged in the task of shaping its cultural identity—that is, of realizing its way of life—that community will need to produce deviants. The reason for this is that in the process of defining the nature of deviance, the community is also defining the moral boundaries of its new way of life. Second, when a community feels that a particular form of deviant behavior is threatening the security of its established cultural identity, it will impose very severe sanctions against that behavior and devote much time and energy to rooting it out. These two notions are aptly illustrated in Erikson's classic study in the sociology of deviance, *Wayward Puritans* (1966).

In a brilliant attempt at testing Durkheim's ideas about punishment and solidarity, Kai Erikson relies on a sociohistorical account of how the Puritans of seventeenth-century Massachusetts Bay Colony dealt with deviant conduct. In what follows we first examine some background characteristics of this community and its inhabitants. Next, we look at the three "crime waves" that took place during the first century of the community's founding and see how Erikson explains these episodes.

The Puritans and their legal system. The Puritans were a sect of English Protestants who sought to completely "purify" the Anglican Church of all Roman

Catholic influences. Unable to accomplish their objective, a group of about 1,000 of these Puritans left England in early 1630, intent on founding a model Christian community—a true Bible Commonwealth—in the uncertain wilderness of New England, or what was at that time known as Massachusetts Bay Colony.

During the first years of the colony's existence, its legal system consisted of a patchwork of rules brought together from two diverse and largely incompatible sources of law: the sacred authority of Scripture and the secular common law of England. Along with this hybrid of a legal system there existed a General Court composed of the ruling elite of the community: the ministers and magistrates. Indeed, it was the ministers who, acting in their capacity as accredited Bible scholars, settled most questions of law during the early years of the Massachusetts Bay Colony.

Erikson contends that three "crime waves" that took place during the first six decades of the settlement's founding helped the Puritans to define and redefine the moral boundaries of their community. These three crises were the Antinomian heresy, the Quaker persecutions, and the witchcraft hysteria in Salem Village.

The Antinomian heresy. The Antinomian heresy began in 1636, a mere six years after the Puritans first arrived on the bay and during a time when they were struggling to found a viable community in an ungodly and hostile land. Although the Puritans were never tolerant of differences of opinion concerning their way of life, their new environment created in them an even stronger conviction to protect their values against subversion by dissident forces. Accordingly, the Puritan magistrates and ministers believed that if they were to successfully establish a cultural identity for their community, it was necessary that a disciplined orthodoxy be tightly imposed on their congregations. This orthodoxy was in essence a new theology proclaiming that God had entered into a covenant with the Puritans as a community and was only ready to deal with them through their government leaders. And even though the ministers could not hold political office, they nevertheless wielded tremendous power since they played a leading role in determining who among the settlers had experienced a true religious conversion and so deserved the privileges of the community.

Presently, a woman from Boston, Anne Hutchinson, began to criticize the character and competence of the local ministers. An accomplished biblical scholar in her own right, Hutchinson felt that almost none of the colony's ministers were qualified to judge whether a person had been saved. She soon attracted a large number of followers who eventually formed a major partisan faction. A serious skirmish erupted between the Hutchinson faction and the community's ruling elite.

The church officials of Puritan Massachusetts saw Hutchinson's attempt to undermine their authority as a heresy that blurred the political outlines along which they were trying to establish their unique identity as a community. Believing that their righteous way of life was being jeopardized, the magistrates and ministers promptly accused her of heresy, tried, convicted, excommunicated, and banished her from the colony.

The Quaker persecutions. By the time that the Quaker persecutions began in 1656, a number of important changes had taken place in the Puritan Bay Colony;

changes that would help to resolutely secure the community's territorial identity. To begin with, a comprehensive legal code, *The Laws and Liberties of Massachusetts*, had been compiled in 1648 after critics accused the Puritan government officials of violating the laws of England (McManus, 1993:10). In addition, the Cambridge Platform had been adopted that same year to give the churches a formal constitution. But the most significant change was the fact that the Puritans of Massachusetts found themselves cut off from their brethren in England. Certain political transformations in that country had made the English Puritans more tolerant of other religious opinions. And because such tolerance was anathema to the Massachusetts Puritans, they became theologically isolated from the country that gave them birth.

In light of these changes, Erikson describes the colony's road to maturation during this period as he states that "the subjective principles of Puritanism slowly hardened into a solid network of institutions." And now that the Puritans had firmly established their community, a new generation of elders and leaders was charged with guarding its distinctive way of life against foreign intrusions and ensuring that its institutions were not disrupted in any way. Such intense vigilance and defensiveness, says Erikson, "is often associated with people who are no longer sure of their own place in the world, people who need to protect their old customs and ways all the more narrowly because they seem to have a difficult time remembering quite who they are" (1966:114). Thus, it is at this point that the community, if it is to continue to survive, needs to renew and reaffirm its moral boundaries, to recreate its cultural identity.

One way in which a community can recreate its cultural identity is by seeking out and severely punishing offenders who threaten the security of its group life. Thus, according to Erikson, it is understandable why just at the time when they were trying to find a new sense of their own identity, the Puritans should discover heretics in their midst. These heretics came as an unwelcomed religious sect known as the Quakers. Because the Quakers did not show any commitment to the Puritan spirit of theocratic discipline (they lived apart from the rest of the community) and refused even to abide by the community's most trivial conventions (they would not remove their hats in the presence of magistrates), the Puritans quickly instituted a campaign of persecution against them.

The first Quakers to "invade" the Massachusetts Bay Colony in 1656 were two housewives who, once discovered, were quickly deported. As other Quakers entered the colony and converted some of the settlers, the Puritan authorities began to administer harsh penalties. That same year, a law against "that cursed sect of heretics lately risen up in the world" was enacted by the colony's General Court. It ordered: "that what person or persons soever shall revile the office or persons of magistrates or ministers, as is usual with the Quakers, such persons shall be severely whipped or pay the sum of five pounds." These punishments seemed only to spur the Quaker missionaries into ever more vigorous activity. The Puritans, therefore, made penalties for infringing the law even more severe by including ear cropping, imprisonment, hard labor, mutilation, beatings, banishment, and execution. Nevertheless, the greater the cruelties inflicted on the Quakers, the more they increased their level of lawbreaking. Indeed, legal historian Edgar J. McManus charges that the Quakers actually provoked persecution and glorified in the reprisals they suffered (1993:184). He further contends that the Quakers were clearly a force of social destabilization intent on undermining the group cohesion of the Massachusetts Bay Colony. In any event, the Puritan violence against the Quaker heresy reached a fevered pitch until 1661, when King Charles II of England intervened and prohibited the use of either corporal or capital punishment in cases involving the Quakers.

The witches of Salem Village. Between the end of the Quaker persecutions in the mid 1660s and the beginning of the witchcraft hysteria in 1692, the colony experienced a series of unprecedented political calamities. These trying times can be characterized as a period of apprehension, alarm, and impending doom—with the settlers growing more and more pessimistic about their future. Their uncertainty concerning the colony's fate stemmed from several factors. First, a series of harsh arguments took place in 1670 between the magistrates and ministers of the colony. This strife threatened to tear the alliance, which, forty years earlier, had been indispensable in creating the community's unique way of life. Second, in 1675, a brutal and costly war broke out with a confederacy of Indian tribes. Third, in 1679, Charles II ordered that an Anglican Church be established in Boston. Fourth, in 1686, the King revoked the charter that had given the colony its only legal protection. Finally, and most significantly, the Puritan community, which depended on a high degree of harmony and group feeling, was being racked by internal dissension in the form of legal disputes, personal feuds, and open political bickering. It was while the people of the colony were preoccupied with their internecine fighting that the witches decided to strike.

The witchcraft frenzy began in early 1692 when a group of teenage girls in Salem Village began to scream uncontrollably, suffer convulsions, grovel on the ground, and fall on their hands and knees and make noises like the barking of a dog. The girls were said to be bewitched, and, encouraged by the Puritan ministers, began to identify the witches who were allegedly tormenting them. They named three women in the village and accused them of practicing witchcraft, the devil's conspiracy against the colony. Further accusations were made and more suspects were arrested, so that by spring the Salem jail was overflowing with people awaiting trial. That summer the first criminal trials were held as panic and fear spread throughout the colony. By autumn, scores of persons had been condemned and twenty-two had been executed: nineteen were sent to the gallows, one was pressed to death under a pile of rocks, and two died in prison. Not one of the suspects brought before the court was ever acquitted.

One year after it began the witchcraft hysteria came to a abrupt halt as the governor and the other leading men of the colony began to doubt the teenage girls' accusations. A new session of the Superior Court of Judicature acquitted many of the suspects. The governor signed reprieves for those had been condemned, released many others who were in prison, and issued a general pardon to all persons still under suspicion.

Erikson convincingly argues that the three "crime waves" that besieged the Massachusetts Bay Colony—the Antinomian heresy, the Quaker persecutions, and the witchcraft hysteria in Salem village—helped the Puritans to define and redefine the moral boundaries of their community. Had these crimes not taken place, and had the Puritans been less vigilant in seeking out criminals to punish, it is doubtful that the colony would have maintained its cultural identity as long as it did.

By building on the work of Durkheim, Erikson has advanced a most persuasive argument in *Wayward Puritans*. He tells us that deviants perform a needed social function by patrolling the outer edges of a community's moral territory. Further, as they violate the law and are subsequently subjected to ritual punishment (in the form of excommunication, banishment, public execution, etc.), these deviants provide a contrast that gives the community members some sense of their own cultural identity. Finally, in having their cultural identity renewed and reaffirmed, the community members experience a greater sense of solidarity. In the next study we see how Albert Bergesen extends Durkheim's and Erikson's theoretical ideas and uses them to formulate his own thoughts about political witch-hunts.

Political Witch-Hunts

Basing his ideas on the Durkheimian tradition of understanding crime and ritual punishments in maintaining social solidarity, sociologist Albert Bergesen (1984) proposes a general explanation of political witch-hunts. His specific focus is on those individuals who are said to have committed political crimes and their persecution by the state. The types of political crimes examined by Bergesen are those subversive activities involving "accusations of *plotting* to overthrow the government, *conspiring* with *foreign agents* and *disloyal elements* to 'deliver the nation into the hands of the enemy,' and engaging in *seditious* and *treasonous* activities of all kinds" (1984:141). "Crimes of this sort," writes Bergesen, "are accompanied by a sense that the society is in some way *contaminated* and *polluted* [from within] . . . and that a *collective cleansing* is required to *purify* the fabric of social life" (1984:141–142). The processes of cleansing and purifying society of subversive elements involve the ritual persecution of political criminals; that is, the witch-hunt. Historical examples of these types of witch-hunts are illustrated in the public persecutions conducted by the Jacobins during the French Revolution, the Soviets during the Stalin purges of the 1930s, the Chinese during the Great Cultural Revolution, and the Americans during the era of McCarthyism.

Bergesen identifies four common characteristics shared by all political witch-hunts:

1. Political witch-hunts have a sporadic nature to them because subversive activities seem to come in certain dramatic outbursts. Accordingly, there does not exist a steady rate of political crime. This suggests that when the society experiences a crisis—some threat to its collective identity—there is a sudden increase in the discovery of political criminals (i.e., "traitors," "counterrevolutionaries," "subversives," and other imaginary enemies of "the Republic," "the Revolution," or "the Nation").

2. Because there exists a general fear that the goals and interests of the society are being undermined by criminals from within, political witch-hunts are characterized by a great sense of severity and pressing urgency—a feeling that some action needs to be taken immediately in order to protect the cultural and physical existence of the society as a whole.

3. Political witch-hunts have a hysterical nature about them. During upsurges in political crime waves, the most diverse and seemingly nonpolitical acts are defined as criminal. Innocent groups and persons are accused, tried, and punished for crimes allegedly committed against the collective purposes of the society. In short, the hunting of subversives gets "out of control" in the witch-hunt.

4. Political witch-hunts make full use of public ritual. They dramatize—through "show trials," printed confessions, investigating committees, and other degradation ceremonies—the danger of conspiratorial plots to national security as well as the apprehension and punishment of subversives. We may say, then, that the defining characteristics of witch-hunts are their ritual, pomp, hysteria, drama, and terror.

In formulating his explanation of when and why political crimes and their subsequent witch-hunts occur, Bergesen relies on the theoretical ideas of Durkheim and Erikson and proposes a theory of political crime.

Bergesen's Theory of Political Crime

As previously noted, Durkheim and Erikson see crime as an attack on the moral boundaries of a community. However, in his analysis of political witch-hunts, Bergesen differs from Durkheim and Erikson in two important respects. First, he maintains that the boundaries in question are not just moral, they are also political. Second, he asserts that the boundaries constitute the identity of the community, not just as a cultural entity, but as a sovereign political entity—that is, as a *nation-state*. Thus, according to Bergesen, political crimes, or any acts seen as a threat to the collective existence, attack the moral and political boundaries of the nation-state. Furthermore, the collective existence of the modern nation-state is represented in its political parties. Bergesen classifies contemporary nation-states as being multiparty states, two-party states, or one-party states. Let us briefly look at each of these in turn.

Multiparty states. Found throughout Europe, *multiparty states* abide by "proportional representation," an electoral procedure ensuring that there exists a correspondence between the proportion of votes a party receives and the number of legislative seats it is awarded. Proportional representation, therefore, gives the constituent interests of the various political parties in that society a formal role in the making of collective decisions. In this case, the national legislature represents a wide variety of political interests.

Two-party states. The electoral arrangement of *two-party states* (which characterizes the party system of the United States, with its Democratic and Republican parties), is based on plurality or simple majority vote. This means that, in order to win an election, a political party is required to obtain more votes than its nearest competitor. In a two-party state, the party that loses the election does not have its constituent interests fully represented in the national decision-making process (in the office of the president and in Congress).

One-party states. In *one-party states* (e.g., Nazi Germany, Russia during the Soviet era, North Korea, China), a single party acts both as the representative of the interests of the nation as a whole and as the agency for carrying out those interests. According to Bergesen, the more the national interests are represented at the expense of specific constituent interests the more a society becomes politicized; that is, *more areas of moral life are infused with ultimate political meaning.* Bergesen hypothesizes that, in terms of party systems and electoral arrangements, "this means that we should expect multiparty states to be, on the average, the least politicized and one-party states the most, with two-party systems somewhere in between" (1984:160).

How the criminal act is defined depends to what degree the moral boundary that has been attacked is infused with transcendent political meaning. The more politicized a society (e.g., the one-party state) the more likely that "ordinary" crime (e.g., theft) is seen as an act against the values and purposes of the state (e.g., "sabotage"). In another society, with a lower degree of politicization, where the boundaries are not infused with political meaning (e.g., multiparty states), the violation of the same moral boundary is seen as an ordinary crime and not as a threat and danger to the collective existence of a nation-state. Bergesen states: "What is experienced as an ordinary nonpolitical crime versus a political crime therefore has less to do with what was actually done than with whether the moral boundary in question was infused with political meaning" (1984:164). On the basis of the aforementioned comments, Bergesen surmises that it is expected that one-party states have the highest volume of political crime (engage in the most political witch-hunting), followed by two-party and then multiparty states.

Elaborating on the Durkheimian notion that an individual violation of the moral order creates crime, Bergesen stipulates that the violation of a *politicized* moral order creates *political* crime. And building on the Eriksonian thesis that in order for a community to renew and reaffirm its cultural identity, it needs to engage in the ritual persecution of imaginary enemies, Bergesen generates three propositions:

1. The more politicized a society, the more political crime is manufactured, and the greater the frequency of political witch-hunts.
2. The more a society's moral order is infused with political meaning, the more "ordinary" crime is defined as political.
3. Given a boundary crisis, the more politicized a society, the more ritually manufactured political crime will be found in more areas of social life, including those areas that have nothing to do with the real interests of the state.

By extending and amplifying Emile Durkheim's theoretical ideas, Bergesen and Erikson have shown us how the cumulative development of sociological knowledge takes place. More generally, in this section we have seen how the evidence provided by Lanza-Kaduce et al., Erikson, and Bergesen has largely supported three of Durkheim's general statements regarding law and morality: (1) criminal law violations arouse intense feelings of moral indignation; (2) the ritual punishing of criminal law violators gives a community a strong sense of morality; and (3) violating the criminal law serves to accentuate the moral boundaries of a community. In the next section we take a different turn as we consider those empirical studies that largely refute Durkheim's theses concerning legal evolution and the division of labor.

Legal Evolution and the Division of Labor

In this section we look closely at several studies conducted by researchers attempting to test some of the central theoretical claims advanced by Durkheim in *The Division of Labor in Society*. The first collection of studies is specifically designed for evaluating his notion about the relationship between legal evolution and societal complexity. And, although these studies do indeed point out some serious shortcomings in Durkheim's work, we must bear in mind that much of this research has theoretical and methodological flaws.

In the last study to be discussed, the concept of the division of labor takes center stage and is assessed for its effectiveness in explaining in what social situations contract law is most likely to be invoked for regulating conflicts between labor and management. This study seems to give only minimal support to Durkheim's hypotheses. His hypotheses, however, cannot be completely disconfirmed on the evidence of these findings alone. To be sure, much more empirical research is needed before a truly informed decision can be made, one way or the other, about Durkheim's sociology of law. Let us now look at the empirical studies of several scholars who have critiqued Durkheim's thesis concerning the evolution of punishment: that, with increasing societal complexity, there is a movement from the preponderance of repressive law to that of restitutive law.

Legal Evolution and Societal Complexity

Legal sociologists Richard D. Schwartz and James C. Miller's (1964) study on the development of legal institutions casts grave doubt on the validity of Durkheim's thesis concerning the evolution of punishment. In their study, which was based on a cross-cultural analysis of fifty-one preindustrial societies, Schwartz and Miller demonstrate that, with very few exceptions, legal institutions do indeed follow a path that parallels the growth of societal development. This path of legal evolution, however, turns out to be the opposite of what Durkheim had postulated in his thesis. Thus, in direct contradiction to Durkheim, the authors' ethnographic data strongly suggest that restitutive, not repressive, legal structures, occur in mechanical solidarities based on a simple division of labor.

Schwartz and Miller typify the legal organization of their sample societies on the basis of three institutional criteria of development: "counsel," "mediation," and "police." By *counsel* is meant the "regular use of specialized non-kin advocates in the settlement of disputes." *Mediation* has to do with the "regular use of non-kin third party intervention in dispute settlement." And the concept of *police* refers to the "specialized armed force used partially or wholly for norm enforcement" (1964: 161). Schwartz and Millers' sample revealed that eleven societies showed none of the three criteria; eighteen had only mediation; eleven had only mediation and police; and seven had mediation, police, and specialized counsel.

Progressing from the simplest to the most complex societies, Schwartz and Miller discovered that mediation, police, and counsel follow a standard sequential order. Specialized mediation arises first. This is followed by the appearance of a distinct police force to enforce laws and, later, by the development of a specialized counsel to represent claimants and defendants. Thus, it is only in relatively complex societies that evidence can be found of repressive legal structures such as police and counsel, while the most simple societies—in which even a basic division of labor is absent—depend on mediation (conciliatory restitution) as the primary mechanism for achieving formal social regulation.

Schwartz and Miller further charge that one problem in testing Durkheim's thesis arises from the fact that he introduced "organization" in distinguishing between the repressive and restitutive systems of law. The difficulty, they say, is that Durkheim very broadly described the organization of repressive law as consisting of the "assembly of the people." On the other hand, in characterizing the organization of the restitutive legal system, Durkheim identifies some very specialized legal organizations such as consular courts and industrial and administrative tribunals, as well as specialized legal officials such as magistrates, lawyers, and the like. Schwartz and Miller contend that by arguing that restitutive law exists only in highly complex organizational forms, Durkheim "virtually ensured that his thesis would be proven—that restitutive law would be found only in complex societies" (1964:166, n.30).

The authors conclude their study by stating that, "restitutive sanctions—damages and mediation—which Durkheim believed to be associated with an increasing division of labor, are found in many societies that lack even rudimentary specialization. Thus Durkheim's hypothesis seems the reverse of the empirical situation in the range of societies studied here" (Schwartz and Miller, 1964:166).

Durkheim is rescued. Professor Upendra Baxi (1974) of the University of Delhi advances three important criticisms against the Schwartz-Miller study that serve to "rescue" from refutation the Durkheimian thesis on legal evolution. First, Baxi argues that by defining police as a *specialized* armed force, Schwartz and Miller ensure that their counterthesis is correct. After all, specialization is, by definition, not to be found in simpler societies based on mechanical solidarity. Baxi further contends that the repressive sanction of police is only one of many ways by which a society can enforce and punish offenses against itself. Consequently, simple societies may indeed engage in the coercive implementation of norm enforcement in ways that do not require a specialized police force. He maintains that Schwartz and Miller failed to look at alternative measures (e.g., authoritative decision-making by the tribal chieftain) that exist in simple societies and that may be just as repressive as the police.

Second, Baxi maintains that nowhere in *The Division of Labor in Society* does Durkheim state or imply that restitutive sanctions are altogether absent from simple societies. Rather, says Baxi, Durkheim uses relative terms—"proportions" and "preponderances"—when speaking about the amount of punishment found in the various types of social solidarity. Thus, finding some restitutive sanctions in simple societies does not disconfirm Durkheim's thesis, since restitutive sanctions and repressive sanctions are not mutually exclusive.

Finally, Baxi claims that the Schwartz-Miller criticism regarding Durkheim's inconsistent application of the criterion of organization to repressive and restitutive law is basically irrelevant. Baxi posits that Durkheim did not introduce any criterion of organization because his concern "is not at all with *how* the sanctions are organized but with *why* they are organized" (1974:651). Baxi concludes by stating that the Schwartz-Miller study does not in any way refute the Durkheimian thesis.

Durkheim's theory of punishment revisited. Utilizing a list of cross-cultural sample societies similar to that used by Schwartz and Miller, Suffolk University sociologist Steven Spitzer (1975) reexamines the relationship that Durkheim claimed to exist between a society's level of complexity and the type of punishment on which it relies. Spitzer distinguishes several types of punishment based on their degree of severity and classifies the sample societies according to which type they used.

Extending his analysis beyond what Schwartz and Miller had done in their study, Spitzer also attempts to test the hypotheses that Durkheim advances in the principles of quantitative and qualitative change. These hypotheses are:

1. The greater a society's degree of political centralization (governmental absolutism), the more severe its punishments will be.
2. The variable of political centralization is separate and distinct from the variable of social development.
3. The more advanced a society, the greater is the preponderance of human crimes to religious crimes.
4. The more advanced a society, the less harshly it will punish human crimes.
5. As society develops, the deprivation of liberty through incarceration tends to become the preferred form of punishment.

Spitzer's findings reveal the opposite of Durkheim's hypotheses *at almost every point!* Spitzer arrives at the following conclusions:

1. Severe punishments are found more frequently in advanced societies, while simple societies are more likely to be characterized by milder punishments.
2. Although political centralization does indeed produce severity of punishment, the level of social development is also associated with the degree of political centralization, which appears to be associated in turn with greater reliance on repressive sanctions.
3. While it is true that religious crimes are punished more severely, religious crimes are more common in advanced societies.
4. More advanced societies are generally characterized by more severe punishments coupled with a greater preponderance of religious crimes.
5. Even though incarceration has emerged as an alternative form of punishment along with the development of society, other deprivations of liberty,

such as banishment and punitive slavery, have also emerged as repressive measures in advanced societies.

Notwithstanding the shortcomings of Durkheim's thesis on punishment, Spitzer rightly credits him for making explicit what too making investigators had previously ignored: the fact that punishment is deeply rooted in the structure of society. To be sure, Durkheim may be credited for inspiring many students of punishment (Rusche and Kirchheimer, 1939; Hay et al., 1975; Ignatieff, 1978; Foucault, 1979; and Linebaugh, 1992) to seriously consider social structural factors like the economy, ideology, and culture in explaining the historical development of penal methods.

Like the studies that we have discussed thus far, the next study we look at also attempts to test Durkheim's notion about the type of social solidarity determining the type of legal system and penal sanctions to be used. This time, however, Durkheim's thesis is tested, not by comparing societies varying in size and complexity, but by comparing two modern Israeli settlements.

Law and punishment in two Israeli settlements. English sociologist Michael Clarke (1976) attempts to test Durkheim's ideas about legal evolution. Clarke does this by using Schwartz's (1954) study of two Israeli agricultural settlements that have a similar population size but have very different systems of social control.

The settlement "that most approximates Durkheim's mechanical solidarity" (Clarke, 1976:252) was a collective, or kvutza, where there was no private property, everything was shared equally, and many activities were subject to public observation. Members shared a common way of life, living in community-owned housing, eating together in a communal dining hall, using communal washing and showering facilities, and placing their children in communal nurseries and schools. In short, virtually all social relations were the subject of general public knowledge. Perhaps what is most significant from a Durkheimian point of view is that the kvutza was characterized by a shared division of labor; that is, the farming and maintenance jobs were rotated so that everyone had the experience of working at all jobs.

In Schwartz's study the other community was a semiprivate property settlement, or moshav. Here the members had a high degree of autonomy in farming their own land. Thus, work was usually conducted alone. In addition living arrangements were private, and many activities—showering, washing, child rearing, reading, listening to the radio, and the like—were carried out in the privacy of the moshav home. Moreover, there was a great degree of social isolation as each family's separate house was often set quite far from other farms.

Aside from these differences, the two settlements were very similar in terms of their superficial characteristics. Both were founded by Eastern European settlers in 1921, and both were engaged in cultivating the same kinds of crops on about the same amount of land (about 2,000 acres) with roughly the same population (about 500 members).

The legal systems of these two communities were not similar, however. To resolve disputes, the moshav developed a formal system of legal control that was centered around its Judicial Committee—a specialized agency charged with enforcing the community's rules. The committee was given the authority to hear complaints by members against each other and to enforce rulings by invoking punitive sanctions such as fines and even banishment from the community. Moreover, the committee operated according to written procedures and enforced a set of codified rules. Hence, we may argue, following Durkheim, that the moshav's member's interdependence—premised on the specialized and autonomous division of labor in which they engaged—is what prompted the emergence of formal legal regulation in that settlement

The kvutza, by contrast, had no counterpart to the moshav's Judicial Committee. On the kvutza, the members' intense and frequent face-to-face interaction provided an effective means of informal, nonlegal control, based on public opinion. In other words, the constant intimate contact that occurred between members during the course of their daily regime is what prevented undesirable behavior. Since kvutza life meant engaging in continuous interaction with others, each member could be subjected to a wide variety of subtle and not-so-subtle forms of negative public opinion. Such social disapproval was communicated by the ways in which members glanced at an individual, spoke to them, passed them a requested tool or dish of food, assigned them work, gave them instructions, and so forth. Because public opinion was the major informal sanction for which members developed a great sensitivity and respect, no special committee or set of written rules or procedures was needed.

Clarke's contention is that Schwartz's study of the two Israeli settlements provides empirical evidence disproving Durkheim's thesis concerning legal development. According to Clarke, the study shows that "penal sanctions, let alone harsh ones, were irrelevant to the case that most approximates Durkheim's mechanical solidarity (the Kvutza), *precisely because of the nature of that solidarity*" (1976:252, emphasis added). We may continue Clarke's reasoning and argue, conversely, that in the moshav—the settlement that Clarke, comparatively speaking, considers as being more approximate to Durkheim's organic solidarity—penal sanctions were regularly employed by its Judicial Committee.

While Clarke's arguments against Durkheim may not be entirely persuasive, it is worth noting that his critique is one more in a long line of attempts to debunk Durkheim's theory of legal evolution. Thus far we have examined those studies that have attempted to test Durkheim's ideas about legal development and societal complexity. We now turn our attention to a study that considers the relationship between legal invocations and the division of labor.

Legal invocations and the division of labor. Premising their study on the Durkheimian view of legal invocations, sociologists B. C. Cartwright and Richard Schwartz (1973) examine those mechanisms that influence the invocation of legal norms. They also look at how widely these norms are invoked, as well as how their invocation is related to social situation and legal experience.

The Durkheimian view of legal invocations implies that laws will be widely called upon because the general public requires normative regulation in its day-to-day conduct. Correspondingly, people actively seek and adopt laws for the purpose of reducing the tensions of stressful situations.

Durkheim tells us that in complex urban areas with a high population density and a well-developed division of labor, conflictual relations will arise from the social exchanges that take place between persons performing specialized and distinct functions. In this case, contract law is called upon to help resolve these conflicts by regulating the transactions. This is especially true, says Durkheim, as regards the disputes that exist between labor and management in large-scale industrial firms.

Social situations in which the division of labor is highly differentiated and specialized—i.e., large-scale industrial firms and cities with a high population density—create relations that can only be described as conflictual because each self-interested party "seeks to obtain at least cost what he needs" (Durkheim, 1984:160). Thus, the law is called upon to harmonize these relations and ensure a pattern of regular cooperation between the transacting parties. Cartwright and Schwartz formulate a proposition that encapsulates Durkheim's general view on the invocation of legal norms in large-scale industrial firms located in cities with a high population density: "since the rates and costs of exchange transactions and the occasions for potential conflict are greatly accelerated in large firms and urban areas, the invocation of legal norms will also be accelerated in large firms and urban areas" (1973: 342). In other words, the Durkheimian view postulates two causal chains: the first chain links firm size to legal invocation, and the second chain links urban areas to legal invocation.

Cartwright and Schwartz attempt to test the Durkheimian view of legal invocation by using empirical data derived from their research on the legal regulation of labor-management relations in two Indian jurisdictions (urban Bombay and rural Mysore). These data deal with the labor-management disputes heard before India's quasi-judicial, regulatory agencies known as the Industrial Tribunals. (The dispute-resolution process has two other stages that precede and follow the tribunal hearings: conciliation before a labor commissioner and an appellate hearing before the supreme court.)

Most of the disputes that arose in industrial firms with an extensive and highly differentiated division of labor revolved around labor-management negotiations for union contracts. The object of the tribunals, then, was to resolve labor-management disputes through arbitration by getting both parties to agree to the terms of the union contract.

Cartwright and Schwartz measured the concept of *legal invocation* by the number of times that firm managers involved in labor-management negotiations made reference to decided cases (court decisions). In looking at the two causal chains that the Durkheimian model postulates, Cartwright and Schwartz discovered the following. In the first chain they found that *firm size* (measured by the total number of firm employees) is related to the *division of labor* in the firm (measured by the total number of unions in the firm); the division of labor is related to *contractual complexities* (measured by the total number of labor-management agreements); and the variable of contractual complexities is related to legal invocations. In the second chain they found that *population density* (measured by the population of the urban area where the firm is located) is positively related to legal invocations, but the intervening variable of *industrial conflict* (measured by the number of strikes and written complaints made by employees) had a relatively weak influence on the relationship. Cartwright and Schwartz also found that the division of labor in a firm does not seem to produce industrial conflict; and when controlled for population density and contractual complexity, no causal link appears to exist between industrial conflict and the frequency of legal invocations.

Simply put, the results of the second causal chain reveal that: (1) if a firm is located in a large urban area, this does not mean that there will be more strikes and complaints in that firm; (2) because a firm has a high level of differentiation and specialization, this does not mean that there will be more strikes and complaints in that firm; and (3) because strikes and complaints occur in a firm; this does not mean that court decisions will be cited with greater frequency during labor-management negotiations. It is significant to note that these results seem to clearly negate Durkheim's contentions that, (a) social situations characterized by a highly developed division of labor and great population density will create conflicting social relationships, and (b) in situations of conflicting social relationships the law will be called upon to help regulate, harmonize, and integrate those relationships.

Cartwright and Schwartz then propose that industrial conflict need not be limited to strikes and complaints. Rather, *litigation activity* (measured by the total number of appearances before the labor commissioner, the Industrial Tribunals, or the appellate courts) is another means by which to consider labor-management disputes. Taking this variable into consideration, Cartwright and Schwartz discover that there is a significant causal link from both population density and the division of labor in a firm, to the presence of litigation activity. And litigation activity is directly related to the invocation of decided cases. This revised model, then, seems to confirm the Durkheimian view of legal invocations.

In this section we examined those empirical studies that evaluate Durkheim's notions about the relationship between legal evolution and societal complexity, and the relationship between legal invocations and the division of labor. We noted that those studies aiming to test Durkheim's first notion reveal several shortcomings in his theoretical claims. Moreover, the study seeking to verify Durkheim's second notion provided only weak support of his hypothesis. While these studies were largely concerned with Durkheim's *theoretical ideas*, in the next section we look critically at the shortcomings of his *methodological procedures and assumptions*.

Methodological Procedures and Assumptions

Sociologist Joseph Sanders (1990) has recently argued that some of the weaknesses of longitudinal studies on trial courts stem from these studies' excessive macrolevel view of litigation. Sanders states that this macro focus, which considers social structural factors, has been emphasized at the expense of the micro focus, which considers individual behavior. He further claims that the procedures and assumptions of Durkheim's methodology have been responsible for skewing this focus in the macro direction.

According to Sanders, Durkheim's methodology has had a greater influence on the longitudinal study of courts than on any other area of sociolegal studies. However, as we have already seen, most of Durkheim's work concentrates on macrolevel social facts. Sanders says that the problem with this concentration on social facts is that Durkheim pays little attention to the microlevel individual behaviors through which the social facts produce their effects.

Durkheim's methodological procedure is to compare *social rates* of various phenomena (i.e., crime, suicide, etc.). One assumption underlying this methodological procedure is that the effects of social change can be observed without looking closely at the microprocesses of individual behavior. Durkheim's procedure has been employed in the longitudinal study of courts because it is there that the litigation rate, as a dependent variable, demands explanation. As a result, researchers have looked at how a number of independent variables (urbanization, economic changes, social development, cultural changes, religious orientations, etc.) have influenced the litigation rate.

Sanders points to several problems that are inherent in employing Durkheim's methodology. First, there is the problem of *vagueness*. Sanders maintains that because most of the longitudinal studies make their arguments at the macrolevel, there is ambiguity about how the independent variables affect the dependent variable (the litigation rate). Related to the vagueness problem is the problem of determining what is an independent variable, what is a dependent variable, and what is "only" an indicator. Adding to the ambiguity of the longitudinal studies is the choice of a rate for the dependent variable of litigation—the dispute rate, the litigation rate, the trial rate, or the appellate rate?

The problem of *validity* is associated with these rates because they are measured by indicators. For example, the dispute rate has been estimated by measuring, among other indicators, population, business activity, and automobile accident rates. Unfortunately, it is not known how well any of these indicators actually measure the rate chosen to constitute the dependent variable.

Sanders calls for an alternative line of analysis that remedies the problems of vagueness and validity that are inherent in Durkheim's macrolaw focus. His suggestion is to pay greater attention to the interplay of macro- *and* microlegal processes that exists in litigation disputes. Sanders sees the dependent variable of litigation not as a rate but as "an aggregation of individual behaviors." Therefore, instead of looking at macrolevel litigation *rates*, Sanders argues that we should really be looking at microlevel litigation *behaviors*.

Sanders proposes a theory for the longitudinal study of courts that begins at the macrolevel of organizational structure, moves down to a microlevel of individual behaviors, and then goes back up again. Such a theory explicitly explains how microprocesses transform macroeffects to individual behaviors and connects microbehaviors to macrochange. This macro-to-micro link becomes evident only when we begin to see litigant behavior as behavior that occurs within the courts *as organizations*, and litigant behavior as altering the courts' organizational structure by bringing about changes in the substantive and procedural legal rules. Thus, instead of following Durkheim's methodology, which focuses only on macrolevel litigation rates, Sanders recommends that researchers doing longitudinal studies of courts consider the relationship between macrolevel organizational structures (the courts) and microlevel litigant behavior (court decisions, bargains, disputes, etc.). Sanders's alternative line of analysis leads us to study the fundamental sociological question of how one set of organizational structures is transformed by individual behavior into another set of organizational structures.

SUMMARY

In this chapter we saw how the Durkheimian perspective—which relies on a penetrating examination of the moral elements of social life—has yielded sociological theories to explain the evolution of law, punishment, and contract. Taken together, these theories constitute Emile Durkheim's sociology of law.

We began with a discussion of some of Durkheim's key concepts, including the collective consciousness, the division of labor, and social solidarity. We noted that a society's collective consciousness is the moral force that regulates people's behavior. This moral force is stronger and more precise in a mechanical solidarity than in an organic solidarity. On the other hand, the division of labor, or specialization of tasks, is more highly developed in an organic solidarity than it is in a mechanical solidarity.

Durkheim reasoned that since social solidarity is a moral phenomenon and morality is the basis of law, the law, therefore, can be used to measure the degree of social solidarity. Thus, he argued that the greater the amount of repressive law in a society, the greater the degree of mechanical solidarity and the greater the amount of restitutive law, the greater the degree of organic solidarity. Durkheim further maintained that there has been a general evolutionary movement from mechanical to organic solidarity. These preliminary remarks set the stage for our discussion of Durkheim's theories about punishment and contract.

First, we looked at Durkheim's ideas concerning the evolution of punishment as encapsulated in his principles of quantitative and qualitative change. The principle of quantitative change states that punishments are likely to be harsh in premodern societies with an undifferentiated division of labor and an undifferentiated political power structure. The principle of qualitative change, on the other hand, states that in modern societies incarceration replaces torture and execution as the preferred mode of punishment.

We next looked at the five types of contract that Durkheim identified in his analysis of its evolution: the blood covenant, the *real* contract, the contract of solemn ritual, the consensual contract, and the contract of equity. This was followed by a brief discussion about the main social function of contract, which, according to Durkheim, is to encourage cooperative relations between persons performing specialized and distinct tasks. Contract law regulates these reciprocal relations and thus gives rise to a type of organic solidarity that is based on contract: contractual solidarity.

Turning our attention to the neo-Durkheimian contributions, we then examined those contemporary research studies that have empirically tested Durkheim's thoughts on the relationship between law and morality, his ideas about legal evolution and the division of labor, and his methodological procedures and assumptions. These studies have supported as well as refuted Durkheim's hypotheses in the sociology of law.

We proceeded by examining three studies that support Durkheim's comments concerning the relationship between law and morality. In the first study, we saw that Lonn Lanza-Kaduce et al. substantiated Durkheim's contentions that criminal laws reflect a society's moral beliefs; that there is a high degree of knowledge of criminal laws across society; that violations of criminal laws evoke a high degree of moral condemnation; and that society will call for repressive sanctions to be inflicted on the offender.

By way of introducing the second study, we briefly discussed Durkheim's idea that punishing criminal law violators contributes to the community's solidarity. We then considered Kai Erikson's *Wayward Puritans*, where he demonstrates that a disruption of the community's solidarity will compel the community to seek out criminals to punish. Accordingly, Erikson argued that ritual punishments, where the offender is publicly confronted by the community's moral indignation, act as boundary-maintaining devices because they reveal where the line between moral and immoral behavior is drawn.

In the third study, we saw how Albert Bergesen extended Durkheim's and Erikson's ideas about crime and ritual punishments and used them to formulate his theory of political crime. In essence, Bergesen's theory states that the more a society's moral order is infused with political meaning, the more "ordinary" crime is defined as political.

Next, we discussed several empirical studies that attempted to test Durkheim's ideas about legal evolution and the division of labor. More specifically, we examined those studies evaluating Durkheim's notions about, the relationship between legal evolution and societal complexity, and the relationship between legal invocations and the division of labor.

The studies seeking to test Durkheim's first notion were conducted by Richard D. Schwartz, James C. Miller, Steven Spitzer, and Michael Clarke. These researchers concluded that Durkheim's ideas concerning the relationship between legal evolution and societal complexity—that, with increasing societal complexity, there is a movement from the preponderance of repressive law to that of restitutive law—has some serious weaknesses. The study by B. C. Cartwright and Richard Schwartz examined Durkheim's ideas on the relationship between legal invocations and the division of labor. In contrast to the previous studies, this one provided some support for Durkheim's contention that contract law is invoked to resolve disputes between labor and management occurring in large-scale industrial firms and cities with a high population density and a high division of labor.

Finally, we concluded our analysis of the neo-Durkheimian contributions to the Durkheimian perspective by critiquing Durkheim's methodological procedure (of comparing social rates) and methodological assumption (that the effects of social change can be observed without examining individual behavior). Joseph Sanders argued that Durkheim's methodological procedures and assumptions have given longitudinal studies on trial courts an excessive macrolevel focus on litigation. Thus, Sanders suggests that researchers conducting these studies consider the relationship between macrolevel organizational structures *and* microlevel litigant behavior.

Having devoted Chapters 4, 5, and 6 to reviewing the Marxian, Weberian, and Durkheimian perspectives of legal sociology, we may conclude that these three perspectives share several commonalities. First, we saw that, *as sociologists*, Karl Marx, Max Weber, and Emile Durkheim made their theoretical contributions to legal sociology from *outside* of the legal profession. Second, we noted that despite the points of disagreement extant between the sociolegal theories of these three classical thinkers, their common objective was to analyze the law in order to better understand society. Third, the three nineteenth-century theorists consistently looked not to legal doctrine but to *social phenomena*—economics, morality, religion, politics, and the like—for their explanations of the law's role in society.

In Chapters 4, 5, and 6 we also examined the substantive contributions made by the neo-Marxian, neo-Weberian, and neo-Durkheimian scholars who have produced their work within the classical perspectives laid down by Marx, Weber, and Durkheim. By amplifying, extending, critiquing, and testing the classical thinkers' ideas, these contemporary scholars have contributed greatly to the theoretical development of legal sociology.

As will become increasingly evident in the next two chapters, it is only through a thorough acquaintance with the classical perspectives of Marx, Weber, and Durkheim that we can truly appreciate the contemporary sociological paradigms of structural-functionalism and conflict theory.

The Evolution of Punishment

Emile Durkheim

... [W]e shall seek to establish and to explain two laws which seem to us to prevail in the evolution of the apparatus of punishment. It is quite clear that we shall direct our attention only to the most general tendencies; but if we succeed in introducing a little order into this confused mass of facts, however imperfect it may be, our labors will not have been in vain.

The variations through which punishment has passed in the course of history are of two sorts, quantitative and qualitative. The laws governing each of these are, of course, different.

The Law of Quantitative Change

This may be formulated as follows:

The intensity of punishment is greater the more closely societies approximate to a less developed type—and the more the central power assumes an absolute character.

Let us first explain the meaning of these propositions. The first of them does not really need much further definition. It is relatively easy to determine whether one social type is more or less advanced than another: one has only to see whether they are more or less complex and, as to the extent of similar composition, whether they are more or less organized. This hierarchy of social types, moreover, does not imply that the succession of societies takes an unilinear form; to the contrary, it is certain that the sequence must rather be thought of as a tree with many branches all diverging in greater or lesser degree. But, on this tree societies are found at differing heights, and are found at differing distances from the common trunk.[1] It is on condition that one looks at in this way that one can talk in terms of a general evolution of societies.

The second factor which we have distinguished must concern us at more length. We say that governmental power is absolute when it encounters among the other social functions nothing which serves to counterbalance it and to limit it effectively. In reality, the complete absence of all such limitations is nowhere to be found: one might even say that it is inconceivable. Traditions and religious beliefs act as brakes on even the strongest governments. Beyond this, there are always certain lesser social institutions which now and then are capable of making themselves felt and resisting governmental power. The subordinate elements which are subjected to a supreme regulatory function are never deprived of all their individual energy. But this factual limitation may be in no sense legally required of the government which submits to it; although it exercises a certain amount of care in the exercise of its prerogatives, it is not held back by written or by customary law. In such a case, it exercises a power which we may term absolute. . . .

Therefore, what makes the central authority more or less absolute in character, is the degree to which all counterweights organized with a view to restraining it are missing. One can therefore foresee that this kind of power structure comes into being when all the directive functions of society are more or less completely brought together into one and the same hand. In fact, because of their vital significance, they cannot be concentrated in one and the same person, without giving him an extraordinary hold over the rest of society, and this dominance is what is meant by the term absolutism. The person who wields such an authority finds himself possessed of a power which frees him from any collective restraint, and which to some extent means that he only takes into account himself and his own whims and can impose all his wishes. This hypercentralization releases a social force *sui generis* which is of such intensity that it dominates all the others and holds them in thrall. And this does not simply amount to a *de facto* dominance, but is seen as being as of right, for the person who has such a privilege is possessed of such an aura of prestige that he seems to be in a sense superhuman; as a consequence we do not even conceive that he could be subject to ordinary restraints, as it the common run of humanity. . . .

. . . Nothing is more simple than the rule of some barbarian chieftains; nothing is more absolute.

This observation leads us to another more closely related to the issue at hand: namely the fact that the degree to which a government possesses an absolutist character is not linked to any particular social type. Indeed, if one may find such a government as often in an extremely complex society as in a very simple one, it is no more tied exclusively to primitive societies than to other types. . . .

. . . This is why these two causes of the evolution of punishment—the nature of the social type and of the governmental organ—must be carefully distinguished. For being independent, they act independently of one another, on occasion even in opposite directions. For example, it happens that, in passing from a primitive type of society to other more advanced types, we do not see punishment decreasing as we might have expected, because the organization of government acts at the same time to neutralize the effects of

social organization. Thus, the process is a very complex one.

Having explained the nature of the law, we must now show that it conforms to the facts. Since there can be no question of examining every society, we shall choose the ones we are going to compare from among those where penal institutions have reached a certain degree of development and are known fairly precisely. For the rest, as we have tried to show elsewhere, the essence of a sociological explanation does not lie in piling up facts, but rather in organizing series of regular variations whose terms are bound together as closely as possible, and which are also sufficiently wide-ranging.

In a very large number of ancient societies death pure and simple is not the supreme punishment; it is augmented, in the case of those offenses deemed most frightful, by further torments which are aimed at making it still more dreadful. Thus, among the Egyptians, above and beyond hanging and beheading, we find burning at the stake, "death by ashes," and crucifixion. In the case of punishment by fire, the executioner used to begin by inflicting numerous wounds in the hands of the criminal using sharpened stakes, and only after this was the latter placed on a fire and burned alive. "Death by ashes" consisted of suffocating the condemned man to death under a pile of ashes. "It is even probable," says Thonissen, "that the judges were accustomed to inflicting on the criminals whatever additional suffering they felt was required by the nature of the crime or the exigencies of public opinion." The Asian peoples would seem to have taken cruelty to even further lengths.

Among the Assyrians, criminals were thrown to ferocious animals or into a fiery furnace; they were cooked to death in a brass pot placed over a slow fire; they had their eyes put out. Strangulation and beheading were spurned as being too mild! Among the various tribes of Syria, criminals were stoned to death, they were shot full of arrows, they were hanged, they were crucified, their ribs and entrails were burned with torches, they were drawn and quartered, they were hurled from cliffs

... or they were crushed beneath the feet of animals, etc.

The code of Manu itself distinguishes between an ordinary death sentence, consisting of beheading, and a severe or aggravated death sentence. The latter was divided into seven categories: impalement on a pointed stake, being burned to death, being crushed to death under an elephant's feet, judicial drowning, having boiling oil poured into one's ears and mouth, being torn apart by dogs in public, being cut into pieces with razors.

Among these same peoples, the ordinary death sentence was widely used. It is impossible to list all the offenses punished in this way. A single fact illustrates how numerous they were: according to Diodore's account, one Egyptian king, by banishing those condemned to death into the desert, managed to establish a new city there, and another, by employing them in a program of public works, succeeded in building numerous dikes and digging canals.

Punishments symbolic of the crime committed were used as less drastic penalties than the death sentence. Thus in Egypt, forgers, those who altered public documents, used to have their hands cut off; rape of a free-born woman was punished by castration; spies had their tongues torn out, etc. Likewise, after the laws of Manu, the tongue of man in the lowest caste who had gravely insulted the twice-born[2] was to be cut out; a Sudra who had the audacity to sit down next to a Brahmin was to be branded on the buttocks, etc. Over and above these characteristic mutilations, all sorts of corporal punishment were customary in one tribe or another. This type of punishment was usually inflicted at the discretion of the judge.

The Hebrews certainly did not possess a higher type of society than these other peoples; indeed, the concentration of the society only occurred at a relatively late period, under the monarchy. Before this, there was no Israeli nation, but merely a more or less autonomous grouping of tribes or clans, which only united briefly if faced by a common threat. And yet Mosaic law is much less harsh than the law of Manu or the sacred books of Egypt. Capital punishment is no longer accompanied by the same refined cruelties. It even seems that, for a considerable period of time, stoning was the only way it was done; it is only in the rabbinical texts that there is mention of burning, beheading and strangulation. Mutilation, so widely practiced by the other Oriental peoples, is only mentioned once in the Pentateuch. True, the principle of retaliation, when the crime involved wounding someone, might involve mutilation; but the guilty party could always escape this by means of a financial settlement; this practice was only forbidden in case of murder. As for other physical punishments, which are reduced to whipping, they were certainly used for a great number of offenses, but the maximum penalty was fixed at 40 lashes, and in practice this number was really 39. Where does this relative mildness come from? From the fact that among the Hebrews absolutist government was never able to establish itself on a lasting basis. We have seen that for much of the time they lacked any sort of political organization. Later on, of course, a monarchy was formed; but the king's power remained very limited: "There always existed a very lively belief in Israel that the king was there for the sake of the people and not the people for the sake of the king; he ought to seek to help Israel, and not to further his own self-interest." Even though certain individuals occasionally succeeded, by dint of their personal prestige in winning an exceptional degree of authority, the temper of the people remained profoundly democratic.

Yet we have been able to see that the penal law still remained a very harsh one there. If we move from the preceding sorts of society to the City-State, which is without doubt a more advanced type of society, we observe a more marked decline in the severity of punishment. Although capital punishment at Athens was, in certain instances, accompanied by other penalties, this was, nevertheless, highly exceptional. Such punishment consisted, in principle, of death by drinking hemlock, by the sword, by strangulation. Symbolic mutilation disappeared. It even seems that the same thing happened with corporal punishment, except for the slaves and, perhaps, the lower classes. Yet Athens, even viewed at its apogee, represents a relatively archaic form of the City. Indeed, organization based on the clan system (gene, phratries) was never as completely obliterated there as it was at Rome, where, from a very early period, curias and gentes became mere historical survivals, of whose meaning even the Romans themselves were uncertain. Consequently the system of punishments was much harsher at Athens than at Rome. First, Athenian law, as we noted above, did not completely avoid adding other punishments to the death sentence. Demosthenes alludes to culprits being nailed to the gallows; Lyseas cites the names of assassins, highwaymen, and spies beaten to death; Antiphon speaks of a poisoner dying on the rack. Sometimes death was preceded by torture. Besides this, the number of offenses for which the death penalty was invoked was considerable: "Treason, harming the Athenian people, assaults on the political institutions debasing the national law, lying to the tribune of the people's assembly, abuse of diplomatic office . . . extortion, impiety, sacrilege, etc., etc., immediately brought forth the intervention of 'The Eleven.'"[3] At Rome, on the other hand, capital crimes were much less numerous and the *Leges Porciae*[4] limited the employment of capital punishment throughout the Republic. Beyond this, except for totally exceptional circumstances, execution was never accompanied by lesser tortures, or by any further mistreatment. Crucifixion was only permitted for slaves. Moreover, the Romans were apt to boast of the relative leniency of their system of punishment . . .

But when, with the advent of the Empire, governmental power tended to become absolute, the penal law became more severe. First, the number of capital crimes grew. Adultery, incest, all sorts of offenses against public morals, and above all the constantly growing number of crimes of lesemajesty were punished by death. At the same time, harsher forms of punishment were instituted. Burning at the stake, formerly reserved for political crimes of an exceptional nature, was used against arsonists, the sacrilegious, sorcerers, par-

ricides, and certain other crimes of lese-majesty; the sentence '*ad opus publicum*' was established, and mutilations visited upon some classes of criminals (for example, castration in the case of certain offenses against public morals, severing the hands of forgers, etc.). Finally, torture made its appearance; it was the Imperial period that the Middle Ages was later to borrow from.

If we move on from the City to the case of Christian societies, we observe punishment evolving according to the same law. . . .

The apogee of the absolute monarchy coincides with the period of the greatest repression. In the seventeenth century the forms of capital punishment in use were still those we have just enumerated. Beyond this, a new punishment was introduced, the galleys, and this form of punishment was so terrible that the wretches condemned to it would sometimes sever their own arm or hand in order to escape it. The practice was even so common that a decree of 1677 made it punishable by death. As for corporal punishments, these were countless: there was the ripping out or the piercing of tongues, cutting off of lips, cutting or tearing off ears, branding with a hot iron, beating with cudgels, the cat-o'nine tails, the pillory, etc. Finally, we must not forget that torture was used not only as a means of getting information, but also as a means of punishment. At the same time, the number of capital crimes increased because the crimes of lese-majesty were growing ever more numerous. . . .

The Law of Qualitative Change

The law which we have just established refers exclusively to the severity or the quantity of punishments. The one which will now concern us is concerned with their qualitative aspects. It may be formulated thus:

> *Deprivations of liberty, and of liberty alone, varying in time according to the seriousness of the crime, tend to become more and more the normal means of social control.*

Primitive societies almost completely lack prisons. Even in the laws of Manu, there is at most one passage which seems to concern itself with prisons: "Let the king place all the prisons on the public highway, so that the criminals, hideous and humiliated, may be exposed in full view of everyone." Yet such a prison has a completely different character than ours; it is more nearly analogous to the pillory. The guilty party was held prisoner so that he could be put on display and also because imprisonment was a necessary condition of the punishments being imposed on him; but not because this itself was the punishment. That consisted rather of the harsh existence imposed on all the detainees. The silence of the Mosaic law on this point is even more complete. There is not even a single mention of prison in the Pentateuch. Later on, in the Chronicles, in the book of Jeremiah, one does come across passages which speak of prisons, of fetters, of damp dungeons; but, in all these cases what is in question is preventive custody, places of detention where people accused of crimes, are held while awaiting trial, and where they had to submit to a régime of greater or lesser severity, depending on their particular circumstances. It is only in the book of Ezra that imprisonment appears, for the first time, as a punishment properly so-called.[5] In the ancient law of the Slavs and the Germans, punishments simply involving deprivation of liberty would seem to have been similarly missing. The same was true of the old Swiss cantons until the nineteenth century.

In the City-States such punishments had begun to make their appearance. Contrary to what Schoemann says, it seems certain that at Athens imprisonment was inflicted as a special punishment in some situations. Demosthenes expressly states that the tribunals were empowered to punish by imprisonment or by any other punishment. Socrates speaks of life imprisonment as a penalty which could be invoked against him. Plato, outlining in *The Laws* the plans of the ideal city, proposes to repress quite a large number of offenses by imprisonment, and we know that his utopia is nearer to historical reality than it was at one time thought to be. However, everyone recognizes that

at Athens this type of punishment remained little developed. In the orators' speeches, prison is most often put forward as a way of preventing the flight of those accused of a crime or as a convenient way of forcing some debtors to pay their debts, or indeed as a supplementary form of punishment, a *prostimema*. When the judges restricted themselves to imposing a fine they had the right to supplement this with a term of five days in the public prison with one's feet shackled. At Rome, the situation was not very different. "Prison," states Rein, "was originally no more than a place for preventative detention. Later it became a means of punishment. However, it was rarely used, except for slaves, soldiers and actors."

It is only in the Christian societies that it has completely developed. The Church, indeed, from very early on was accustomed to prescribe temporary detention or life in a monastery for some criminals. At first this was thought of as no more than a means of surveillance, but later on incarceration, or imprisonment properly so-called, came into existence, being regarded as genuine punishment. The maximum sentence was permanent solitary confinement in a cell which had been bricked up, as a sign of the irrevocability of the sentence.

It is from here that the practice passed over into the secular legal system. However, as imprisonment was simultaneously used as an administrative measure, the sense in which it was a punishment remained for a long time rather ambiguous. It is only in the eighteenth century that criminologists ended up agreeing to recognize imprisonment as a kind of punishment in certain definite situations, when it was for life, when it was substituted by a commutation for the death penalty, etc.; in a word, every time it had been preceded by a legal investigation. With the penal law of 1791, it became the basis of the system of control, which, other than the death penalty and the pillory, consisted of no more than various kinds of imprisonment. Nevertheless, imprisonment by itself was not considered a sufficient punishment; but deprivations of another kind were added to it (belts or chains which the inmates had to wear, and a miserable diet). The Penal Code of 1810 left aside these additional penalties, except for hard labor. The two alternative punishments involving deprivations of liberty scarcely differed from one another except in respect of the amount of time during which the prisoner was shut up. Since that time, hard labor has lost a great part of its distinctive character and is tending to become simply another kind of imprisonment. At the same time, the death penalty has been utilized less and less frequently; it has even disappeared completely from some legal codes, to such an extent that virtually the whole field of punishment is now found to consist in the suppression of liberty for limited period of time or for life.

Explanation of the Second Law

Having shown how punishment has varied through time, we will now seek the causes of the established variations; in other words, we shall try to explain the two laws previously established. We will begin with the second.

As we have just seen, incarceration first appears only as a simple preventive measure; it later takes on a repressive character, and finally becomes equated with the very notion of punishment. To account for this evolution, we must in turn search for what gives birth to imprisonment in its original form—and then see what has determined its subsequent transformations. . . .

. . . No doubt at first sight it would seem just common sense that from the day that the prison would have served a useful function for societies, men would have had the idea of building it. In reality, however, this development presupposes the realization of certain conditions without which it could not come about. In practice, it implies the existence of sufficiently spacious public establishments, run on military lines, managed in such a manner as to prevent communications with the outside, etc. Such arrangements are not improvised on the spur of the moment. Indeed, there exist no traces of them in primitive societies. The very meager, very intermittent public life which then exists requires nothing more for its develop-

ment than a place for popular assemblies. Houses are constructed with exclusively private ends in mind; in places where there are permanent chiefs, their houses are scarcely distinguished from the others; temples themselves are of relatively late origin; finally, ramparts do not exist, for they appeared only with the rise of the City State. In these conditions, the concept of a prison cannot arise.

But as the social horizon extends, as collective life, instead of being dispersed in a multitude of small centers where it can only be weak, is concentrated in a more limited number of places, it becomes at the same time more intense and more continuous. Because this sphere assumes greater importance, so the dwelling places of those who direct it are transformed. They are enlarged, they are organized in terms of the wider and more permanent functions which are laid upon them. The more the authority of those who live there grows, the more their homes are marked off and distinguished from the rest of the dwellings. They take on a lofty air, they are protected behind higher walls, deeper ditches, in such a way as to visibly mark the line of demarcation which henceforth separates the holders of power from the mass of their subordinates. The conditions for the creation of the prison are now present. What makes one suppose that the prison must have arisen in that way is that in the beginning it often appears in the shadow of a royal palace, in the outbuildings of temples and similar buildings. Thus, in Jerusalem we know of three prisons during the period of the invasion of the Chaldeans: one was "at the high gate of Benjamin," and we know that the gates were fortified places; another was in the court of the royal palace; and the third was in the house of a royal functionary. In Rome, it is in the royal fortress that the most ancient prisons are found. In the Middle Ages, it is in the manorial castle, in the towers of the ramparts which surround the towns.

Thus, at the very time when the establishment of a place of detention was becoming useful in consequence of the progressive disappearance of collective responsibility, buildings were arising which could be utilized for this purpose. The prison, it is true, was still only a place of pre-trial detention. But once that it had been set up on this basis, it quickly assumed a repressive character, at least partially. In fact, all those who were thus kept prisoner were suspects; they were also most frequently those suspected of serious crimes. Furthermore, they were subjected to a severe regimen which was already virtually a punishment. Everything that we know about these primitive prisons, which, let it be remembered, are still not penitentiaries in the strict sense, paints them in the blackest of colors. In Dahomey, the prison is a hole, in the form of a pit where the condemned wallow in refuse and vermin. In Judaea, we saw that they used dungeons. In ancient Mexico, it consisted of wooden cages where the prisoners were kept; they were scarcely fed. In Athens, the prisoners were subjected to the dishonorable punishment of shackles. In Switzerland, to make escape more difficult, they put iron collars on the prisoners. In Japan, the prisons are called hells. It is natural that a sojourn in such places should have been very early considered as a form of punishment. Petty crimes, especially those which have been committed by the people of slender means, the *personae humiles*, as the Romans called them, were dealt with in this way. It was a penalty which the judges could impose more or less arbitrarily.

As to the juridical development of this new punishment from the time of its formation onward, it can be accounted for by combining the preceding considerations with the law relating to the progressive weakening of punishment. In practice, this weakening takes place from top to bottom of the penal code. In general, it is the most serious punishments which are the first to be affected by this regression, that is to say, which are the first to grow milder, then to disappear. The process begins with the diminution of the aggravated forms of capital punishment, which continues until the day is reached when they are completely done away with. The crimes to which capital punishment is applied are gradually curtailed; mutilations are subject to the same law. It follows from this that lesser punishments must be developed to fill the gaps which this regression produces. In proportion as the penal law abandons the archaic forms

of repression, new forms of punishment invade the free spaces which they then find before them. Now the various modes of imprisonment are the last punishments to develop. At first, they are lowest in the scale of penalties, since they begin by not being punishments at all, properly so called, but only the condition of true repression; and for a long time, they retain a mixed and indecisive character. For this reason, the future was reserved for them. They were the necessary and natural substitutes for the other punishments which were fading away. But from another perspective, they were themselves influenced by the trend towards moderation. This is why, whereas originally they were mingled with other hardships to which they were occasionally only ancillary, they are gradually disentangled from them. They are reduced to their simplest forms, which is to say, to deprivation of liberty alone, varying only with respect to the length of that deprivation.

Thus, the qualitative changes in punishment are in part dependent on the simultaneous quantitative changes it undergoes. In other words, of the two laws which we have established, the first contributes to an explanation of the second. Thus, the time has now arrived to explain it in its turn.

Explanation of the First Law

In order to facilitate this explanation, we will consider the two factors which we have distinguished separately; as the second is the one which plays the least important role we will leave it on one side for the moment. Let us look, therefore, at how it is that punishments become less severe as one moves from the most primitive to the most advanced societies, without bothering ourselves temporarily with those perturbations which may be due to the more or less absolute character of governmental power. . . .

Since punishment results from crime and expresses the manner in which it affects the public conscience, it is in the evolution of crime that one must seek the cause determining the evolution of punishment.

Without it being necessary to go in detail into the proofs which justify the distinction, we think it will be readily conceded that all acts deemed criminal in every known society may be divided into two basic categories: those which are directed against collective things (whether ideal or material, it matters not) of which the principal kinds are offenses against public authority and its representatives, the mores, traditions and religion; and those which only injure the individual (murders, thefts, violence and fraud of all types). These two forms of criminality are sufficiently distinct that there is every reason to designate them by different words. The first may be called religious criminality because outrages against religion are the most essential part of it, and because crimes against tradition or chiefs of state have always had a more or less religious character; the second, one might term human criminality. Granting this distinction, we know that the penal law of primitive societies consists almost exclusively of crimes of the first type; but, as evolution advances, so they decline, while outrages against the person take up more and more space. For primitive peoples, crime consists almost uniquely in not performing cult practices, in violating ritual prohibitions, in straying from ancestral morality, in disobeying authority where it is quite firmly established. By contrast for the European of today, crime consists essentially in the injury of some human interest.

Now, these two kinds of criminality differ profoundly because the collective sentiments which they offend are not of the same type. As a result, repression cannot be the same for one as for the other.

The collective sentiments which are contradicted and offended by the criminality characteristic of primitive societies are collective, as it were, in a double sense. Not only have they the collectivity as their subject, so that they are found in the majority of individual consciences, but more than that *they have collective things as their object*. By definition, these things are outside the circle of our private interests. The ends to which we are thus attached infinitely surpass the narrow horizon we each have as individuals. It is not us personally with which they are concerned, but with the collective existence. Consequently, the acts which we must perform in order to satisfy them do not correspond to our own individual inclinations; but rather they do violence to them since they consist in all kinds of sacrifices and privations which a man has to impose upon himself whether it be for the purpose of humoring his god, to conform to custom, or to obey authority. We do not have an inclination to fast, to mortify ourselves, to forbid ourselves one or another kind of meat, to sacrifice our favorite animals on the altar, to inconvenience ourselves out of respect for custom, etc. Consequently, just as with the sensations which come to us from the external world, such sentiments are in us but not of us; even exist, in a sense, in spite of us; and they appear to us in this way in consequence of the constraint which they exercise over us. We are thus obliged to alienate them, to assign as their cause some external force, just as we do for our sensations. Moreover, we are obliged to conceive of this force as a power which is not only extraneous, but even superior to us, since it gives the orders and we obey them. This voice which speaks within us in such an imperious tone, which enjoins us to do violence to our nature, can come only from a being other than ourselves, and one, moreover, which dominates us. In whatever special form men have portrayed it (god, ancestors, august personages of all kinds), it always has in its relation to them something transcendent, superhuman about it. That is why this part of morality is wholly imbued with religiosity. The duties which it prescribes for us bind us to a personality which infinitely surpasses our own; the collective personality, which we may think of as a pure abstraction, or with the help of what are properly religious symbols, the guise in which it most frequently appears.

In the case of crimes which violate these sentiments and which consist of the neglect of special obligations, these cannot fail to appear to us as directed against these transcendent beings, since they do indeed strike at them. It is because of this that they appear exceptionally odious; for an offense is the more revolting when the person offended is higher in nature and dignity than the offender. The more one is held in respect, the more abominable is lack of respect. An act which is simply reprehensible when directed at an equal becomes sacrilegious when it concerns someone who is superior to us; the horror which it produces can therefore only be calmed by a violent repression. Normally, when simply trying to please his gods, the faithful man must submit to a thousand privations if he is to maintain regular relations with them. To what privations must he not be subjected when he has outraged them? Even were the pity which the guilty party inspires quite strong, it could not serve to effectively counterbalance the indignation aroused by the act of sacrilege, nor, consequently, to modify appreciably the punishment; for the two sentiments are too unequal. The sympathy which men experience for one of their kind, especially one disgraced by an offense, cannot restrain the effects of the reverential fear which they feel for the divinity. In the face of a power which is so much greater than him, the individual appears so insignificant that his sufferings lose their relative importance and become a negligible quantity. For what is an individual's suffering when it is a question of appeasing a God?

It is otherwise with collective sentiments which have the individual for their object; for each of us is an individual. What concerns humankind concerns us all; for we are all men. Consequently we take sentiments protecting human dignity personally to heart. Of course, I do not mean to say that we respect the life and property of our fellows out of a utilitarian calculation and to obtain from them a just reciprocity. If we reprove acts which lack humanity, it is because they offend the sentiments of sympathy which we have for man in general, and these sentiments are disinterested precisely because they have a general object. . . .

Consequently, the conditions of repression are no longer the same as in the first case. There is no longer the same distance between the offender and the offended; they are more nearly on the same level. This is the more so as, in each particular case, the victim of the crime offers himself in the guise of a particular individuality, in all respects identi-

cal to that of the transgressor. The moral scandal which the criminal act constitutes is, therefore, less severe, and consequently does not call for such violent repression. The offense of man against man cannot arouse the same indignation as an offense of man against God. At the same time, the sentiments of pity which he who suffers punishment evokes in us can no longer be so easily nor so completely extinguished by the sentiments he has offended and which react against him; for both are of the same nature. The first sentiments are only a variety of the second. What tempers the collective anger, which is the essence of punishment, is the sympathy which we feel for every man who suffers, the horror which all destructive violence causes us; it is the same sympathy and the same horror which inflames this anger. And so the same cause which sets in motion the repressive apparatus tends also to halt it. The same mental state drives us to punish and to moderate the punishment. Hence an extenuating influence cannot fail to make itself felt. It might appear quite natural to freely sacrifice the human dignity of the transgressor to the outraged divine majesty. But there is a real and irremediable contradiction in avenging the offended human dignity of the victim by violating that of the criminal. The only way, not of eliminating the difficulty (for strictly speaking it is insoluble), but of alleviating it, is to lessen the punishment as much as possible.

Seeing as, in the course of time, crime is reduced more and more to offenses against persons alone, while religious forms of criminality decline, it is inevitable that punishment on the average should become weaker. . . .

But, you may say, if this is the case, how is it that punishments attached to crimes against persons participate in the general decline? For, if they have declined less than the others, it is still certain that they too are, in general, less harsh than they were two or three centuries ago. If, however, it is in the nature of this type of crime to call forth less severe punishments, the effect should have shown itself from the first, as soon as the criminal character of these acts was formally recognized; punishments directed against them ought to have immediately and at a single stroke attained the degree of mildness which they allow of, rather than becoming progressively milder. But what determines this progressive softening, is that at the time when these crimes, having remained for a long time on the threshold of the criminal law, were brought within it and finally classed as part of it, religious criminality held almost complete sway in this area. As a result of this preponderant situation, it began by pulling into its orbit those new offenses which had just been created and marked them with its imprint. So much so, that just as crime is essentially conceived as an offense directed against the divinity, so crimes committed by man against man are also conceived on this same model. We believe that they also repel us because they are defended by the gods and, by the same token, outrage them. The habits of mind are such that it does not even seem possible that a moral precept can have a sufficiently well-founded authority if it does not derive from what is at the time considered as the unique source of all morality. Such is the origin of these theories, still so widespread today, according to which morality lacks all basis if it does not rest upon religion, or, at the very least, on a rational theology; that is to say, if the categorical imperative does not emanate from some transcendent being. But to the extent that human criminality develops and religious criminality recedes, the former shows more and more clearly its own physiognomy and distinctive traits, such as we have described. It frees itself from the influences to which it used to be subjected and which prevented it from being itself. If, even today, there are a good many people for whom the penal law, and more generally all morality, are inseparable from the idea of God, yet their number is diminishing; and even those who lag behind in this archaic conception are no longer as narrowly tied to these ideas as a Christian of earlier times used to be. Human morality progressively sheds its primitively confessional character. It is in the course of this development that that regressive evolution of punishments which makes the most grave breaches in the prescriptions of this morality occurs.

But a reciprocal influence must be noted, for as human criminality gains ground, it reacts in its turn on religious criminality and, so to speak, assimilates it. If it is offenses against persons which constitute the principle crimes today, offenses against collective things (crimes against the family, against morals, against the State) nevertheless still exist. However, these collective things themselves tend to lose more and more that religiosity which formerly marked them. From the divinities which they were, they are becoming human realities. We no longer hypostatize the family or society in the form of transcendent and mystical entities; we see scarcely more than human groups who coordinate their efforts with a view to achieving human goals. As a result, crimes directed against these collectivities partake of the characteristics of those which directly injure individuals; and punishments which are aimed at the former themselves become milder.

Such is the cause which had determined the progressive weakening of punishments. One can see that this result is produced mechanically. The manner in which collective sentiments reacted against crime changed because these sentiments changed. New forces came into play; the result could not remain the same. This great transformation has not taken place with a view to a preconceived end nor under the direction of utilitarian considerations. But, once accomplished, it finds itself quite naturally adjusted to useful ends. For the very reason that it had necessarily resulted from the new conditions in which societies found themselves placed, it could not be other than in relationship and harmony with those conditions. In fact, the intensity of punishments serves only to make individual consciences aware of the force of collective constraint; so it is useful only if it varies with the same intensity as this constraint. It is fitting that it becomes milder as collective coercion becomes lighter, more flexible, becomes less inaccessible to free examination. Now this is the great change produced in the course of moral evolution. Although social discipline, of which morality properly so-called is only the highest expression, progressively extends its field of action, it loses more and more of its authoritarian rigor. Because it becomes more human, it leaves more room for the spontaneity of individuals; it even solicits it. It has therefore less need to be violently imposed. And for this to occur, the sanctions which assure it respect must also become less constricting on all initiative and thought.

We may now return to the second factor of penal evolution, which we have up until now left out of account; namely the nature of the means of government. The preceding considerations will readily allow us to explain the manner in which they act.

In truth, the constitution of absolute power necessarily has the effect of raising the one who wields it above the rest of humanity, making of him something superhuman; the more so as the power with which he is armed is more unlimited. In fact, wherever the government takes this form, the one who controls it appears to people as a divinity. When they do not make an actual god of him, they at the very least see in the power which is invested in him an emanation of divine power. From that moment, this religiosity cannot fail to have its usual effects on punishment. On the one hand, offenses directed against a being so palpably superior to all its offenders will not be considered as ordinary crimes, but as sacrilegious acts and, by virtue of this, will be violently repressed. From this stems the exceptional position that the penal law assigns to crimes of lese-majesty among all peoples subjected to an absolutist government. From another point of view, as in these same societies almost all the laws are supposed to emanate from the sovereign and express his will, so the principal violations of the law appear to be directed against him. The reprobation which these acts arouse is thus much stronger than if the authority to which they cause injury was more dispersed, and consequently more moderate. The fact that it is concentrated at this point, rendering it more intense, also makes it more sensitive to all who offend it, and more violent in its reactions. Thus the gravity of most crimes is heightened by degrees; consequently, the average intensity of punishment is extraordinarily increased.

Conclusions

. . . Seeing with what regularity repression seems weaker the further one goes in evolution, one might believe that the movement is destined to continue without end; in other words, that punishment is tending toward zero. Now, such a consequence would be in contradiction with the true sense of our law.

In fact, the cause which has determined this regression would not produce its attenuating effects indefinitely. For it does not result from a kind of sluggishness of the moral conscience which, gradually losing its strength and its original sensitivity, would become more and more incapable of all energetic penal reaction. We are not more complacent today than formerly toward all crimes indiscriminately, but only toward some of them; there are some, on the contrary, towards which we are more severe. However, those to which we show increasing indulgence, turn out to be also those which provoke the most violent repression, inversely, those for which we reserve our severity call forth only moderate punishments. Consequently, as the former, ceasing to be treated as crimes, are removed from the penal law and give place to others, it must necessarily produce a weakening of the average punishment. But this weakening can last only as long as this substitution goes on. The moment must come—and it has almost arrived—when this will be accomplished, when offenses against the person will fill the whole of criminal law, or even when what remains of the other offenses will be considered no more than an appendage of the previous sort. Then the movement of retreat will cease. For there is no reason to believe that human criminality must in its turn regress as have the penalties which punish it. Rather, everything points to its gradual development; that the list of acts which are defined as crimes of this type will grow, and that their criminal character will be accentuated. Frauds and injustices, which yesterday left the public conscience almost indifferent, arouse it today, and this sensitivity will only become more acute with time. There is not in reality, therefore, a general weakening of the whole apparatus of repression; rather, one particular system weakens, but it is replaced by another which, while being less violent and less harsh, does not cease to have its own severities, and is certainly not destined to an uninterrupted decline. . . .

NOTES

1. See *Règles de la Methode Sociologique* Ch. 4.
2. The term used by Durkheim is *Dwidjas*, which refers to any members of the three higher castes, i.e., the twice born. [Eds]

3. "The Eleven" refers to a committee of eleven people charged with making sure that punishments prescribed by the Athenian courts were carried out. [Trs.]
4. Three laws of the second century BC which stated that no Roman citizen should be put to death without trial. [Trs.]
5. "For all those who will not obey the law of your God and the king's law, let them be immediately brought to justice and let them be condemned either to death or to exile . . . or to imprisonment." (Ezra 7.26)

Law and Durkheimian Order:
An Empirical Examination of the Convergence
of Legal and Social Definitions of Law

Lonn Lanza-Kaduce, Marvin D. Krohn,
Marcia Radosevich, Ronald L. Akers

Unlike most theorists, Durkheim distinguishes between types of law so that the resulting comparative definitions of criminal and civil law violations coincide with legal realities while having extralegal referents. While the type of law was not one of the major theoretical concepts in the *Division of Labor*, it did appear as an indispensable variable in Durkheim's investigation of the relationship between societal complexity (simple versus differentiated) and social solidarity (mechanical versus organic). Indeed, criminal and civil law (with their attendant sanctions) were used as the indices of the types of solidarity (Durkheim, 1933:64). It was because Durkheim saw solidarity itself as an emergent moral phenomenon, primarily located in society, that he focused on a societal variable like law rather than on individual sentiments. However, to justify his use of criminal and civil law as the proxy variables for mechanical and organic solidarity, it was necessary for Durkheim to offer some detail outlining the association he saw between type of law and the cohering moral order. To do this, he was forced to recognize that the types of solidarity had corresponding levels of feeling states in individuals (Durkheim, 1933:56, 67, 79–80, 105–106, 226–229). Moreover, because the domain of ethics was seen to be an integral part of the domain of law (Durkheim, 1933:426–427), it is not surprising that he defined criminal versus civil law largely in terms of evaluative attitudinal referents. It is because of this that the association between normative attitudes and legal definitions has theoretical significance.

Criminal Law

The nature of the consensus posited by Durkheim varied depending on the type of societal cohesion. Durkheim was most explicit in the case of mechanical solidarity. Because mechanical solidarity was borne of the similarity and likeness of the commonly held collective conscience, it had certain features which were definitionally related to its proxy variable, the criminal law. Criminal definitions were "graven in all consciences, everybody knows them and feels that they are well-founded" (Durkheim, 1933:74). Accordingly, we would hypothesize a high degree of knowledge about criminal law definitions across society and we would expect a high degree of legitimacy to be attributed to them. Moreover, Durkheim (1933:80) states "that an act is criminal when it offends strong and defined states of the collective conscience." Derivatively, criminal violations should not only be considered morally wrong by the large majority of the population, but they should be considered to be very wrong. Durkheim argues that there is consensus about the intensity of moral feeling that accompanies criminal definitions. (See also Chambliss, 1974). However, because crime does exist and is normal in society, Durkheim proposes a consensus that is something less than unanimous (Durkheim, 1933:103; see also Simpson, 1963:61–64). In addition, because the collective conscience has been offended and is in need of explanation, the appropriate sanction is repressive punishment rather than restitution (Durkheim, 1933:69, 85–103).

So, although "the penal reaction is not (always) uniform" in cases of criminal law violations (Durkheim, 1933:101), we would expect repressive sanctions to be advocated.

Finally, it is this expiatory or retributive nature of sanctioning on behalf of the collective conscience that raises the issue of the "declaratory argument"; that is, does the law's declaration of a norm lend symbolic support to that norm and tend to induce agreement with it and conversely does the removal of the law undermine support for the norm (Walker, 1964; Walker and Argyle, 1964).[1] Because Durkheim posited widespread consensus in criminal law matters antecedent to the formal legal enactment, criminalizing an existing norm has less significance for his analysis than does decriminalizing a behavioral standard. Durkheim showed greater appreciation than did Sumner (1906) for the complexity of the relationship between law and custom and recognized that law would act back on and affect folkways (see Durkheim, 1933:83, 84, 476).

Derivative from a Durkheimian analysis and central to the declaratory argument is the issue of what happens when law's symbolic power is removed—when a criminal law is repealed. Bankston and Cramer (1974:258) state that the "Durkheimian perspective would lead us to suspect that, if the reaction of society becomes less severe, the consequence would be a lessening of social solidarity and commitment to the norm" (see also Gusfield, 1968:55). A withdrawal of the authoritative symbol of unity by decriminalization would be a serious assault on the mutuality of common beliefs. It is a reasonable extension to hypothesize, therefore, that a change in normative attitudes might accompany repeal of the criminal proscription. More specifically, conduct that was once morally condemned might be less severely evaluated, less severe sanctions might be advocated, and legitimacy might be withdrawn after people learn that the criminal proscription has been removed or that the behavior is not legally proscribed. On the other hand, when a widespread consensus is reaffirmed by announcing criminal proscriptions already anticipated, little attitude change would be expected.

Civil Law

Durkheim was less clear, and perhaps contradictory, about the definitional relationship between civil law and features of organic solidarity. In order to achieve organic solidarity, Durkheim saw the need for an underlying consensus among parts (1933:360); our specialized relations resulting from the division of labor had to be regulated (1933:353–373). However, unlike criminal law proscriptions, civil law definitions did not need to correspond to any sentiment in a majority of us (1933:112). Nevertheless, they did have some generality due to the functions they fulfilled and it was from opinion that their authority was derived (1933:127). Indeed, the rules of conduct embodied in the civil law were thought to have grown from the habits and customs of the mutual dependence from which organic solidarity arose (1933:366). However, the relationship between law and custom was not a simple one; "very often the law cannot be detached from the customs which are its substratum, nor the customs from the law which realized and determines them" (Durkheim, 1933:426). For example, contract law—the juridicial expression par excellence of the cooperation underlying organic solidarity (1933:123)—determines in a very real way consequences of relations not contracted for and imposes duties and obligations in addition to those negotiated (1933:214). It is the willingness of society to intervene to order diverse relations such as in contracts that allows Durkheim to consider organic solidarity as a societal phenomenon; society has a stake over and above the interested parties in a dispute because it feels the repercussions (1933:155). Civil law is the organization of social life (1933:65) that benefits society's members and accordingly wins their support except where it forces a division of labor that does not reflect their natural differences (1933:373–388). The nature of the consensus in organic solidarity is based more on the recognized functional interdependence among people than on specific value agreement. This renders the task of hypothesizing more difficult.

While, on one hand, civil law definitions are not seen to reside in commonly held sentiments, on the other hand some generality is expected due both to functions civil laws perform and to the customs from which they derive. Consequently, the degree of knowledge about civil law is less predictable than it was in the case of criminal law. It can be hypothesized with confidence that there should be less knowledge about civil law definitions than there is about criminal law ones. Whether the majority is knowledgeable about a particular civil law probably depends more on the specific subject of the law itself (Durkheim, 1933: 127), that is, how it fits in the nexus of functional interdependency. Nor can one expect legitimacy to be attributed to the legal norm unless its legal status is known. Accordingly, legitimacy might be expected to be lower when the legal status of a norm is unknown. However, when the legal status is supplied, the legitimacy attributed to it should be high because the civil law is the means by which the diverse interdependent relations of society are ordered to the benefit of all. Moreover, because civil law breaches do not correspond to very active sentiments (1933:127), the level of moral condemnation would be expected to be less severe and less consensual than it was for criminal law violations. In addition, because civil breaches impair the functioning of well-ordered relations, the purpose of any sanctions are primarily to restore smooth operation of the system; they are restitutive, therefore, and not expiatory (1933: 111).

What effect the declaratory argument would have on attitudes circumscribed by civil law is open to alternative interpretations. It may be argued, consistent with Durkheim, that because civil law addresses issues of less moral importance than does criminal law, governmental action, being symbolic of public authority, would be more influential in altering normative attitudes about these less central matters. Alternatively, because civil law enjoys far less evaluative consensus to begin with and is instrumental in integrating via restitution rather than through the expression of public outrage, altering a civil law prescription may have less impact on relevant attitudes than would criminalization or decriminalization. Actually, both approaches may be accurate depending on the particular attitude under consideration. Zeitlin (1968:268–269) argues that Durkheim restricted morality to those norms which occasion repressive, penal-like sanctions. Accordingly, *moral* condemnation is most closely linked to criminal-like norms in a Durkheimian analysis so that people's moral evaluations might be relatively indifferent to and unaffected by official civil law definitions. However, because civil law definitions and sanctions help to order and restore diverse or disrupted relations, the government as a recognized integrating mechanism may exert more influence in civil law matters on "nonmoral" normative attitudes like legitimacy or sanctioning preferences. Therefore, we expect shifts in legitimacy and advocated sanctions consistent with the civil law when people are informed of its normative stance on the matter in question, but we anticipate stability in the moral evaluations of civil law matters.

Constitutional Law

Even though Durkheim subsumed constitutional law under the civil law rubric, we have isolated it for separate consideration because its role in the American legal system does not correspond to the continental tradition with which Durkheim was familiar. To Durkheim constitutional law determined both what normal governmental functions are and what their relations among each and with other functions in society should be (1933:126). Accordingly, it was logically considered to be part of the civil law which reflected organic solidarity because it ordered diverse relations. While this encompasses one of the primary thrusts of constitutional law, such a conceptualization fails to entail the body of law proscribing limitations on government encroachment of individual liberties such as are enumerated in the Bill of Rights. It is this second major theme of American constitutionalism that warrants separate examination. To the extent that the Bill of Rights (and certain of the other amendments) represents our dedication to the individual and his/her civil liberties, such constitutional provisions may assume a unique role in a Durkheimian analysis.

> (As organic solidarity progresses in advanced societies) common conscience is (not) threatened with total disappearance. . . . There is even a place where it is strengthened and made precise: that is the way in which it regards the individual . . . the individual becomes the object of a sort of religion. We erect a cult in behalf of personal dignity [Durkheim, 1933:172].

It seems that the emphasis of constitutional provisions on individual liberties would be viewed by Durkheim as a modern facet of the collective conscience which was associated historically with mechanical solidarity. Accordingly, this theme of constitutional law may be more akin to criminal law than to civil law and should enjoy a high degree of consensus. People would be expected to have as much knowledge about constitutional matters as criminal ones; they should be more informed of protected civil liberties than they are of civil law relations. We might expect the moral condemnation extended to unconstitutional actions to be more like that of criminal violations than the less severe evaluations accorded to civil law breaches. In addition, given the posited consensus, a high degree of legitimacy should be attributed to constitutional law provisions protecting human rights. However, the expected relationship between civil libertarian safeguards and sanctions is more problematic. While the emphasis on the individual may be an expression of the modern collective conscience, it does not contribute to mechanical solidarity like criminal law does. If repressive sanctions express a mechanical solidarity associated with the law of property and inherigroup (1933:106), they would be inappropriate for a body of law which emphasizes individualism. Indeed, individualism and the commonality of mechanical solidarity are opposing forces (1933:129–130). Inasmuch as constitutional law that safeguards individual rights dictates what government must refrain from doing, it produces negative or abstentive relations resembling those of the negative solidarity associated with the law or property and inheritance and the law of delicts and quasi-delicts (torts) (see 1933:115–119). Because restitutive sanctions are associated with negative solidarity for these other law areas, the same might be expected in the instance of constitutional law.

There is room for extending Durkheim alternatively on the relationship of the declaratory statement to civil rights constitutionalism. On the one hand, it is reasonable to think that beliefs residing in the collective conscience would relate to the sense of justice of those societal members who subscribe to them (see Lukes, 1972). Indeed, regulation to the contrary was seen as "forced" and could give rise to conflict. Accordingly, it would be consistent with Durkheim to expect that governmental interference with libertarian norms would be resisted. Following this line of reasoning the moral evaluations of, the sanctions advocated for, and the legitimacy attributed to norms embodied in constitutional safeguards would not change due to government withdrawal of these protections. However, there are countervailing considerations. To the extent that government comes to symbolize public authority, its actions may exert influence over individual sentiments. According to this emphasis, shifts might be expected in normative attitudes due to learning of government postures taken on various libertarian norms. While no a priori predictions can be made with confidence, the data may shed some light on the relationship between government action and attitudes.

Summary of Hypotheses

Five sets of contrasting hypotheses addressing the issues of legal knowledge, legitimacy of the norm, moral evaluation, advocated sanction, and changed evaluations when the official legal definition is removed or provided, can be derived from Durkheim. First, we would expect a high level of knowledge about criminal law and constitutional law and a lower degree of knowledge about civil law norms. Second, the legitimacy attributed to criminal and constitutional law definitions should be high; that accorded to civil law definitions should be low when the legal status of the norm is unknown but it should increase markedly and approach the legitimacy accorded criminal and constitutional definitions when the legal status of the civil law rule is provided. Third, criminal and constitutional law violations should be more severely condemned morally by a broad range of people; civil law breaches should reflect less consensus. Fourth, the sanction advocated in the case of violations of criminal law definitions should be more repressive while those favored for civil and constitutional law breaches should be more restitutive.

The fifth set of hypotheses investigates the effects on normative attitudes of being informed that a legal norm either does or does not apply to a situation. For criminal matters, when the criminality of behavior is confirmed, normative attitudes will remain unchanged; however, when it is stated that the behavior is not criminal, moral evaluations and sanctioning preferences should be moderated and legitimacy withdrawn. For civil law concerns, only nonmoral attitudes (legitimacy and advocated sanctions) will be altered consistent with the position adopted by the law (i.e., law or no law). No certain hypotheses could be offered for civil libertarian constitutional situations.

Methodology

Sample

Data were collected on an adolescent sample drawn from a population of seventh through twelfth grade boys and girls enrolled in two junior high schools and one senior high school in a midsized Iowa community (approximately 60,000) and from a college sample from a midwestern university. The 414 adolescent respondents represent 77 percent of those in the selected classes. The college sample was composed of 240 students enrolled in four introductory sociology courses that satisfied general social science requirements at the university. Participation for both samples was voluntary and only those present on the day of administration

completed questionnaires. Later, two more college classes were used to form a control group ($N=120$) in order to examine testing effects.

Measurement of Variables

Part I of the questionnaire presented six vignettes describing conduct that had legal relevance although not all of the activities were unlawful. The vignettes included two examples from criminal, civil, and constitutional law areas. The criminal law vignettes described an arson situation revolving around the transferred intent of a person whose careless, indifferent conduct with regard to some gasoline resulted in catching a building afire and a conspiracy story where two persons made extensive plans to steal but did not act on them. The civil law matters included a landlord-tenant problem where the renter moves out without providing notice and a labor example where the employer dismisses and does not rehire striking workers. Both of the civil law relationships are specifically mentioned by Durkheim as being germane to organic solidarity (1933:124–125). The constitutional law area focused on the procedural due process violations committed by a public school principal in expelling a student and on the search and seizure tactics of a police officer in a traffic encounter.

Each vignette was followed by questions on the morality (five-point scale ranging from very right to very wrong), legal legitimation of the rule (whether or not the law should exist), legality (whether the law does exist), and the advocated sanction (ordinal response categories which were later collapsed into repressive and restitutive categories). Part I of the questionnaires was collected on its completion and prior to respondents answering Part II.

The same vignettes were repeated in Part II. The control group was asked to morally evaluate the behaviors, assess the rules' legitimacy, and indicate the appropriate sanctions once again with no additional information provided. The moral evaluation, legitimacy, and advocated sanction questions were repeated for the experimental group as well. However, on half of the vignettes (the arson, rent, and due process situations) the respondents were first told that the behaviors in question violated the criminal, civil, or constitutional law and for the other three situations (the conspiracy, labor, and search vignettes) the respondents were told that the conduct did not violate the relevant area of law. This permitted us to investigate law as an independent variable particularly when responses were controlled for by the knowledge perceptions obtained in Part I. By providing information that a behavior was either lawful or unlawful, we could manipulate people's perceptions of the legal status of the norms and simulate either decriminalization or criminalization to study the respective effects on normative attitudes.

In presenting this manipulation, two questions arose: (1) Would such a short time span between the initial presentation and this manipulation of legal knowledge preclude any chance of a significant treatment effect? (2) If change did occur, could we attribute it to a treatment effect or to a systematic testing effect? We are able to address these issues with preliminary analysis of the data.

First, we did indeed observe a significant change in the expected direction in legitimation, advocated sanction and moral evaluation for some of our vignettes after explicitly stating whether or not behavior was against the law in our high school and college sample. Second, to investigate whether these changes were indeed due to the manipulation (treatment) or simply an artifact of the testing procedure, we utilized the control sample of college students. With this comparison sample the questionnaires were administered the second time without any information given regarding the legal status of the behavior; rather the vignettes were simply repeated in their original form. Overall, we did not observe much variation between the responses to the first and second presentation among the control group. Only one of eighteen possible before and after measures taken among the control respondents was significant at the .001 level; ten or eighteen comparisons were significant for the treatment group.[2] When mean change scores

for the control group are compared with mean change scores for the treatment group (the high school and first college sample) on the eighteen items, we found that for eight of the comparisons the treatment effect is significantly greater than any change in the control group. Four more treatment-control differences reach significance if a more lenient decision-rule about the critical value ($\propto = .01$) is accepted. In those instances where there is not a significant difference, it is generally due to the fact that the manipulation did not have a significant effect rather than there being very much change on the mean change scores for the control group.

Results and Discussion

Tables 1 through 4 present data relevant to the five sets of hypotheses advanced earlier. Our first hypothesis predicted that our sample would have more accurate knowledge of criminal and constitutional law items than it would have of civil items. With one exception our hypothesis is confirmed by the results presented in Table 1. The extent of legal knowledge concerning the conspiracy item is lower than we anticipated. However, in spite of this the mean percentage of those with accurate knowledge of criminal and constitutional law items is still significantly greater than that for the civil law items.

In examining our second hypothesis concerning the legitimacy extended to the legal norm (whether or not the norm should be embodied in the law), we again observe the same pattern (Table 1). That is, while the mean percentages for the combined criminal and constitutional law items are significantly greater than for the civil law items, the conspiracy item elicits less consensus on the legitimacy of the legal norm. Overall, however, the Durkheimian hypotheses about legitimacy were supported.

Because support for the hypotheses derived from Durkheim's theory of law presented in the *Division of Labor* would be stronger except for the conspiracy item, it warrants further investigation. Conspiracy may be an aberrant criminal law

Table 1. Extent of Legal Knowledge and Legitimacy of the Norm before Being Informed of Its Legal Status (in percentage)

Type of Law	Correct	Knowledge Perceptions		Legitimacy	
		Didn't Know	Incorrect	Legitimate	Illegitimate
Criminal Law:					
Arson	70.2	12.0	17.8	77.0	23.0
Conspiracy	42.5	11.5	46.0	39.6	60.4
Average	56.4[a]	11.8	31.9	58.3[b]	41.7
Civil Law:					
Rent	33.6	13.7	53.8	33.3	66.7
Labor	45.6	19.8	34.6	49.0	51.0
Average	39.1	16.7	44.2	41.1	58.9
Constitutional Law:					
Due Process	66.7	8.5	24.8	75.8	24.2
Search	66.0	8.4	25.6	76.7	23.3
Average	66.4[c]	8.4	25.2	76.2[d]	23.8

a. Significantly greater than the average for civil law items ($P < .001$; $T = 12.63$; $df = 653$).
b. Significantly greater than the average for civil law items ($P < .001$; $T = 5.43$; $df = 653$).
c. Significantly greater than the averages for both criminal law ($P < .001$; $T = 6.69$; $df = 653$) and civil law ($P .001$; $T = 17.86$; $df = 653$).
d. Significantly greater than the averages for both criminal law ($P < .001$; $T = 11.16$; $df = 653$) and civil law ($P<.00$; $T = 16.61$; $df = 653$).

item despite its general moral condemnation (see Table 2) because one of the elements of criminal definitions to Durkheim was precision. (see Durkheim, 1933: 79). Because of uncertainty as to when conspiracy constitutes a completed criminal act, conspiracy is considered by legal students to be inchoate and accordingly it is this feature that may have rendered responses somewhat aberrant.

In Table 2 it can be seen that constitutional and criminal law violations were considered to be very wrong morally about twice as often as was the case for civil law breaches (64 percent and 52 percent to 27 percent). Over three-fourths of the respondents thought each of the criminal and constitutional law violations were wrong or very wrong (indicative of wide normative consensus) while less than two-thirds thought the civil law breaches were wrong. Unlike the knowledge and legitimacy questions, moral evaluations to the conspiracy vignette were not so markedly different from those of the other criminal law item.

When significance tests were performed on the differences in means for the respective areas of law, only the difference in moral evaluations between constitutional and criminal law areas failed to reach significance at the .001 level. Again, these findings are exactly what the hypotheses led us to expect: the moral condemnation in both criminal and constitutional matters is strong and more severe than in civil law relations.

While Table 3 does not provide evidence of a widespread advocacy of repressive sanctions for criminal law violations, it does indicate that repressive sanctions are much less likely to be advocated for civil and constitutional breaches than for criminal violations. On reexamination of Durkheim, this relative preference for repressive sanctions in criminal matters is all that should have been expected. To Durkheim, the function of the repressive sanction was to restore and reinforce mechanical solidarity. In a modern industrial society like our own, cohesion would flow from the

Table 2. Moral Evaluations of the Described Conduct before Being Informed of the Legal Status of the Norm Involved (in percentage)

Type of Law	Very Wrong	Somewhat Wrong	Neither Right nor Wrong	Somewhat or Very Right
Criminal Law:				
Arson	55.9	34.6	8.8	0.8
Conspiracy	48.5	28.6	18.7	4.2
Average	52.2[a]	31.6	13.7	2.4
Civil Law:				
Rent	29.0	49.8	14.7	6.4
Labor	24.7	26.1	15.1	34.1
Average	26.9	38.0	14.9	20.3
Constitutional Law:				
Due Process	79.9	17.5	0.8	1.8
Search	47.9	29.2	9.9	13.0
Average	63.9[b]	23.4	5.4	7.4

a. Significantly greater than the average for civil law items ($P < .001$; $T = 16.60$; $df = 653$).
b. Significantly greater than the average for civil law items ($P < .001$; $T = 19.37$; $df = 653$).

Table 3. Sanctioning Preferences by Nature of the Sanction in Response to Described Conduct (in percentage)

Type of Law	Nothing	Restitutive Sanctions	Restitutive (Penal) Sanctions
Criminal Law:			
Arson	7.1	56.5	36.4
Conspiracy	82.0	—	18.0
Average	44.6	—	27.2
Civil Law:			
Rent	58.1	38.1	3.8
Labor	43.9	48.1	8.1
Average	51.0	43.1	5.9
Constitutional Law:			
Due Process	4.9	91.1	4.0
Search	12.5	81.0	6.5
Average	8.7	86.0	5.2

division of labor rather than from the collective conscience; repressive sanctions lose much of their primacy or organic solidarity replaces mechanical solidarity. As a result of this and the continued rationalization of punishment that Durkheim predicted would accompany the rise in organic solidarity, repressive sanctions may be advocated less frequently than formerly. (See Durkheim, 1933: 287–291 and Durkheim, 1973).

Although tangential to a Durkheim analysis, another aspect of the advocacy of sanctions worth noting was the wide agreement among the respondents about the appropriateness of "specific performance" remedies rather than money damages for constitutional violations. Specifically, the oft-attacked "exclusionary rule" (unconstitutionally seized evidence cannot be introduced at trial) was the sanction of choice for the unconstitutional search by the wide majority of young people (60 percent of the sample) indicating, perhaps, that its merits are more appealing when juxtaposed against alternative remedies than when discussed in the abstract. Specific performance in the way of expunging the school record was nearly unanimously advocated (90 percent of the sample) in the due process example.

In addition to examining the frequency data to assess the extent of consensus on given normative attitudes for a particular law area, we also calculated the degree of dispersion of the responses in order to obtain another indicator of consensus. Variances will be small and indicate less dispersion or more consensus about responses unless they are unduly inflated by extreme scores. After combining responses for both vignettes for each of the three law areas into single civil, criminal, and constitutional law measures, significance tests for the differences between variances of correlated samples were computed (see Taylor, 1972). In line with our predictions, the degree of consensus in

moral evaluations as measured by the variances for criminal (T=3.724, df=652) and constitutional law matters (T=4.561, df=652) is significantly greater than that for civil law items (P<.001). Also, as was expected, the variance of the constitutional law area did not vary significantly from that for criminal law (T=.802, df=652). However, using this method of assessing the degree of consensus on the legitimacy measures did not yield significant differences among any of the law areas. Nonstandardized response alternatives for the sanctioning question across the six law items prevented using this approach to assess the consensus on sanction preferences by area of law.

Our final set of hypotheses investigated the declaratory argument. The propositions concerned what effect providing information that a legal norm either did or did not exist to proscribe the conduct in question would have on evaluations of legitimacy of the law, moral evaluation of the conduct, and advocated sanctions. As predicted the only major shift in moral evaluations (significant at the .001 level, T= –11.26, df=557) occurred when respondents were informed that there was no law proscribing criminal conduct (Table 4). Over one-fourth of the sample moved from viewing conspiratorial behavior as very wrong to a more tolerant moral assessment after being told that the conduct

Table 4. Changes Occurring in Moral Condemnation, Legitimacy, and Advocated Sanction after Being Informed of the Legal Status of the Norm (in percentage)

Type of Law	Morally Very Wrong	Norm Is Legitimate	No Sanction	Restitutive Sanction	Repressive Sanction
Criminal Law:					
Arson (Law)	–5.3	+12.2[a]	–3.1	+0.6	+2.4
Conspiracy (No Law)	–25.6[a]	–15.6[a]	+5.4[b]	—	–5.5
Civil Law:					
Rent (Law)	–1.1	+38.6[a]	–25.0	+20.8[a]	+4.3
Labor (No Law)	–1.7	–0.8	+6.8[a]	–5.0	–1.9
Constitutional Law:					
Due Process (Law)	–1.2	+14.3[a]	–1.0	–4.4	+5.4
Search (No Law)	–7.4	–2.5[a]	+8.5[a]	–7.4	–1.1

a. Change scores showed a significant difference from the pretest at the P < .001 level.
b. The change was significant at the P < .01 level.

did not constitute a crime.[3] Only slight changes occurred when respondents were informed that norms applicable to the labor and search situations were not incorporated into civil and constitutional law. As suspected, informing the respondents that legal norms did exist in the arson and rent examples had almost no effect on the subsequent moral evaluations; nor did knowledge alter moral assessments for the due process situation.

When nonmoral normative attitudes were discussed previously (legitimacy and advocated sanctions), our hypotheses were more uncertain. However, recall that Durkheim posited a widespread consensus prior to the formation of criminal law definitions and that we deduced that there would be similar prior agreement for civil libertarian safeguards. This consensus led us to expect no substantial shift in nonmoral normative attitudes when people were informed of the existence of criminal norms although we were more cautious in predicting about constitutional standards. The results presented in Table 4 support our interpretation for the advocated sanction measures. There was no significant change in sanctioning preferences for the arson example even though the shift to repressive sanctions for the due process item was significant ($P<.001$; $T=5.38$; $df=562$). The increase in the percentages of those extending legitimacy was greater than anticipated and statistically significant for both the arson ($P<.001$; $T=5.79$; $df=574$) and due process ($P<.001$; $T=6.52$; $df=572$) situations. However, the shifts for the civil law rent item were even greater. After learning of the civil law norm 40 percent of the respondents thought that no legal standard should exist changed their minds.[4] The shift in sanctioning preferences for the civil law rent item was nearly as dramatic. Of the sample 25 percent ceased to believe that nothing should happen to the renter and advocated some sanction (usually restitutive) on learning that a civil law norm existed. Our hypothesis that due to the lack of consensus in civil law matters the authority embodied in the law should produce marked changes in nonmoral attitudes toward consistency with the civil law position when people are informed of the law's existence was clearly supported by our data.

In the opposite context (that is when the respondents were told that a legal standard did *not* exist to proscribe the conduct described in the vignettes) there were limited but significant changes in the sanctions advocated for all three law areas. The shifts in legitimacy for the labor and search were small but that for the search was statistically significant ($P<.001$; $T=3.80$; $df=558$). However, more than 15 percent of the sample moved from attributing legitimacy to withholding it for the criminal law item after being told that the conspiratorial behavior was not illegal ($P<.001$; $T=8.45$; $df=555$).

From the foregoing, it must be concluded that law qua law operates as an independent variable. Learning of the legal status of a norm affected related normative attitudes in a way that was not uniform across all law areas but varied by whether the norm addressed a criminal, civil, or civil libertarian constitutional law matter. The removal of a criminal law proscription potentially relaxes moral views about the formerly prohibited behavior. This has not been demonstrated for civil and constitutional law provisions. Withdrawing the legal standard was also shown to affect the legitimacy extended to the norms and what sanctions were advocated in the event of breach for all of the law areas. When the opposite context was examined—informing respondents of the existence of legal norms regulating specified conduct—the greatest effect occurred in the civil law area. While moral evaluations remained largely unchanged for all law areas in this context, the most striking shifts in legitimacy and advocated sanction occurred with the civil law item. Notable, but less dramatic, shifts occurred in the legitimacy measures for criminal and constitutional law but little effect was evidenced for these latter law areas in sanctioning preference. It seems that once people learn something is against the law, they are more likely to think it should be (see also Podgorecki, 1973) particularly for civil law matters. It also appears that in civil law areas people may believe some form of sanction is in order where they previously did not just because they learn of the existence of an applicable civil law norm.

This prompts us to conclude that while other students (Evan, 1962; Zimring and Hawkins,

1971) have speculated about the conditions under which law is successful in implementing social change, they have overlooked a basic variable—the distinction between types of law suggested by Durkheim. Our data indicate that the basic divisions of law are not arbitrary but represent real differences in normative orientations that may either catalyze or inhibit attitude change.

NOTES

1. While other students have discussed the "educative" (Andaneas, 1971) or "socializing" (Zimring and Hawkins, 1971) effects of the criminal law's sanctions, the declaratory argument more narrowly focuses only on attitude change due to the mere declaration or removal of the law absent any other circumstances. No threat of punishment or probability of enforcement, no preexisting custom or behavioral compliance, no courtroom drama or public sanctioning are necessarily entailed within the purview of the declaratory argument.
2. Two more differences between the pretest and posttest means are statistically significant if a more lenient decision rule of .01 is employed.
3. Unfortunately, this was the only item which yielded a significant shift for the control sample (suggesting a contesting effect) when moral condemnation was remeasured on Part II of the questionnaire. However, the treatment group evidenced significant change over and above that shown by the control group. For further discussion, see Lanza-Kaduce (1978).
4. This shift occurred among those whose knowledge perceptions were not correct at the pretest. Although we expected the shift in legitimacy for civil law matters that resulted among those whose original legal knowledge perceptions were incorrect, we failed to anticipate that this would occur in criminal and constitutional areas of law as well. Interestingly, changes in legitimacy attributions for five of the six items varied significantly by whether people's knowledge perceptions were confirmed or contradicted. The only other attitude changes that showed significant differences by amount of prior knowledge of the law were sanctioning preferences for both civil law examples. For other normative attitudes and other items, the mere declaration of the legal position evidently can operate either by reinforcing and confirming accurate knowledge perceptions or by correcting mistaken notions about the law, because no

change differences by level of prior knowledge were found in these instances.

REFERENCES

Andeneas, J. 1971. "The Moral or Educative Influence of Criminal Law." *Journal of Social Issues* 24(2):17–31.

Bankston, W. B., and J. B. Cramer. 1974. "Toward a Macro-Sociological Interpretation of General Deterrence." *Criminology* 12(3):251–280.

Chambliss, W. J. 1974. "Functional and Conflict Theories of Crime," pp. 1–23 in *Module* 17. New York: MSS Modular.

Durkheim, E. 1933. *The Division of Labor in Society* (George Simpson, trans.). New York: Free Press.

———. 1973. "Two Laws of Penal Evolution." (T. A. Jones and A. T. Scull, trans.). *Economy and Society* 2:285–307.

Evan, W. M. 1962. "Law as an Instrument of Social Change." *Estudies de Sociologia* 2(August):167–176.

Gusfield, J. P. 1968. "On Legislating Morals: The Symbolic Process of Designating Deviance." *California Law Review* 56:54–73.

Lanza-Kaduce, L. 1978. "Disintegration Or Rebellion: The Law-Morality Debate." M.A. thesis, University of Iowa.

Lukes, S. 1972. *Emile Durkheim: His Life and Work.* New York: Harper & Row.

Podgorecki, A. 1973. "Public Opinion On Law," pp. 65–100 in A. Podgorecki, W. Kaupen, J. Van Houtte, P. Vinke, and B. Kutchinsky (eds.) *Knowledge and Opinion about Law.* South Hackensack, N.J.: Fred B. Rothman.

Simpson, G. 1963. *Emile Durkheim.* New York: Thomas Y. Crowell.

Sumner, W. G. 1906. *Folkways: A Study of the Sociological Importance of Usages, Manners, Customs, Mores, and Morals.* Boston: Ginn.

Taylor, P. A. 1972. *An Introduction to Statistical Methods.* Itasca, IL: F. E. Peacock.

Walker, N. 1964. "Morality and The Criminal Law." *Howard Journal* 11(3):209–219.

——— and M. Argyle. 1964. "Does the Law Affect Moral Judgments?" *British Journal of Criminology* 4(October):570–581.

Zeitlin, I. M. 1968. *Ideology and the Development of Sociological Theory.* Englewood Cliffs, N.J.: Prentice Hall.

Zimring, F., and G. Hawkins. 1971. "The Legal Threat As An Instrument of Social Change." *Journal of Social Issues* 27(2):33–48.

Punishment and Social Organization:
A Study of Durkheim's Theory of Penal Evolution

Steven Spitzer

[. . .]

Hypotheses

The essential relationships in Durkheim's analysis of penal evolution may be summarized as follows.

Hypothesis 1: The greater the complexity and dynamic density of a society, the less severe punishment will be, other things being equal.

Hypothesis 2: The more absolutist political structures become, the greater the deviation from the trend toward leniency.

Hypothesis 2a: Variations in political structure will occur independently of changes in basic social forms.

Hypothesis 3: The greater the complexity and dynamic density of a society, the greater the proportion of individual to collective crimes, other things being equal.

Hypothesis 4: The greater the complexity and dynamic density of a society, the less severely collective crimes will be punished, other things being equal.

Hypothesis 5: As punitive systems evolve, punishment will increasingly assume the form of the deprivation of liberty, other things being equal.

Method

Durkheim was sensitive to the problems involved in formulating and verifying general evolutionary laws. In his own analysis he utilized historical examples as "a preliminary means of coming to grips with reality" and was aware that "this leads one now and then to what are merely gross approximations" (1973:285). Although much of the historical evidence regarding punishment remains fragmentary and obscure, a strategy for systematically examining Durkheim's insights is available to the modern researcher. By comparing culturally distinctive social systems at a given point in time, it is possible to shed light on the long-term process of evolutionary change. Specifically, cross-cultural evidence can be utilized to explore the relationship between differing levels of structural differentiation and forms of social control. The Human Relations Area Files provide a major resource in this regard, and a number of studies—including investigations of legal evolution (Freeman and Winch, 1957; Schwartz and Miller, 1964; Wimberley, 1973)—have successfully explored developmental hypotheses through the use of these data. The present research draws upon a sample of societies from these files to test relationships between social organization and penal response.

The 48 societies utilized by Wimberley (1973) in his study of legal evolution provided a preliminary sample for the present analysis. This sample differed slightly from that employed earlier by Schwartz and Miller (1964), which in turn was derived from an investigation of societal complexity by Freeman and Winch (1957). Six societies analyzed by Wimberley were not included in the Human Relations Area Files at the University of

298

Pennsylvania as of July, 1974. Each of the remaining 42 societies was examined in terms of the adequacy of information on punitive controls by consulting categories 68 (offenses and sanctions), 625 (police), 692 (judicial authority), 696 (execution of justice), and 697 (prisons and jails). Through this procedure an additional 7 societies were found to have incomplete and/or unreliable data on punishment and were excluded from the sample. Thirty-five societies remained. To re-establish a sample size of 48, thirteen societies with appropriate punishment data were added through a process of random selection within each of the geographic areas sampled—North America, Asia, Africa, Middle East, Occania, Russia, South America and Europe. The number of societies in each geographic region was determined according to procedures adopted by Freeman and Winch (1957).

In order to test Durkheim's theory, all forms of punishment were analyzed within each of the 48 societies. Four patterns of punitive control, each reflecting a somewhat different level of "punitive intensity," were distinguished and societies were assigned to one of the four types. In most of the societies investigated, control systems were relatively informal and data on punishment were primarily *behavioral*—based on direct observation or second-hand accounts of punishment-in-action. In relatively complex societies, where controls were more formal, impersonal and regularized, evidence was typically available for both punishment-on-the-books (prescribed legal norms) and punishment in practice. Wherever possible, an effort was made to classify societies in terms of punishment as it was actually applied, although this proved more difficult in the case of the most complex societies studied.

Punishments reported in Type I societies were the most severe and included aggravated capital punishment, mutilation, torture and severe corporal penalties for a wide range of offenses. Type II societies were characterized by less physical violence against offenders, and even though torture and mutilations were occasionally carried out, they did not represent routine features of official control. Societies classified as Type III might also rely on physical punishments for crime, but these sanctions were generally restricted to mild corporal punishment and capital punishment "pure and simple." Material penalties were found more frequently in societies of this type. Societies of the final type (IV) were distinguished by the dominance of material sanctions (e.g. fines, compensation in kind, confiscation or destruction of the offender's property) and/or confinement as modalities of punishment. In these societies the most "primitive" physical penalties are either unknown or extremely rare.

The classification of societies is reported in Table 1. The logic of Durkheim's approach, which suggests that the evolution of punishment is developmental rather than cumulative, is reflected in this classification. In contrast to the process of legal evolution, where advanced forms (e.g. legal counsel) presuppose and build upon prior evolutionary stages (police, courts, mediation), punishments do not *accumulate* in any simple linear sense. Instead, Durkheim argues that the acquisition of more advanced (lenient) controls requires the dropping out of primitive (severe) penal types.

In addition to the analysis of punishment, data were gathered on crime in the societies sampled. Through an analysis of legal norms and perspectives on offensive behavior it was possible to classify punishable crimes in each society as either *individual* (i.e., having individuals and their property as objects) or *collective* (i.e., crimes against religion, moral beliefs, or the state). Crimes where a corporeal victim did not exist (e.g. violations of ceremonial rites), where victimization was diffuse (e.g. "social dangerousness"), and where victimization was restricted to "public authority and its representatives" (e.g. disloyalty) were coded as collective. Crimes involving injury to specific victims (e.g. murder, theft, assault) were designated as individual. For certain categories of sexual and moral offenses, where *both* individual and collective victimization might be assumed (cf. Durkheim, 1973: 300), decisions were made on a case by case basis. For instance, adultery was classified as a collective offense in societies where it was regarded as an attack against long-standing sexual taboos or the

Table 1. Societies by Punishment Type

Society	Type I	Type II	Type III	Type IV
Aranda	X			
Ashanti	X			
Azande	X			
Balinese	X			
Cambodians	X			
Chagga	X			
Cuna	X			
Inca	X			
Iranians	X			
Koreans	X			
Saudi Arabia	X			
Siwans	X			
Turkestan	X			
Vietnamese	X			
Buka		X		
Chuckchee		X		
Creek		X		
Jivaro		X		
Mbundu		X		
Nootka		X		
Zuni		X		
Cayapa			X	
Comanche			X	
Crow			X	
Guana			X	
Hottentot			X	
Indonesians			X	
Iroquois			X	
Kazaks			X	
Lapps			X	
Lepcha			X	
Maori			X	
Serbs			X	
Thonga			X	
Albania				X
Andamanese				X
Czechs				X
Formosan Aborigines				X
Georgia				X
Ifugao				X
Navaho				X
Nuer				X
Riffians				X
Siriono				X
Somali				X
Soviet Union				X
Woleaians				X
Yurok				X

family as a sacred social form, while in societies such as Thonga (Junod, 1927:196–198) and the Andamanese (Radcliffe-Brown, 1922:50) it was coded as individual since these societies viewed it in much the same way as property theft. Generally, sexual offenses were categorized as collective if they were culturally defined in terms of taboo or kinship rules (e.g. incest), and individual if they were defined as an abrogation of individual rights (e.g. rape in certain societies).

A measure of social complexity was available for many of the societies through a previous study by Freeman and Winch (1957). Evidence on population, political organization and other features of these societies was also culled from Murdock's *Ethnographic Atlas* (1967). This information provided a more complete basis for examining the relationship between punishment and social structure in most of the societies explored.

Findings

The *first hypothesis* asserts that punitive intensity is inversely related to societal complexity and dynamic density. Freeman and Winch ratings of complexity were available for 30 of the societies sampled. According to this scale, societies are progressively more complex to the extent that they cumulatively acquire a symbolic medium of exchange, officially organized punishment, full-time specialized priests, full-time specialized teachers, full-time bureaucrats unrelated to a government head and a written language. If a society was char-

acterized by three or less of these characteristics (money, official punishment, and religious specialization) it was defined as simple, while societies reaching the fourth, fifth or sixth level (educational specialization, bureaucracy and written language) were defined as complex. The relationship between punishment type and social complexity is presented in Table 2.

Instead of confirming Durkheim's general law, this table suggests that severe punishments are found more frequently in relatively differentiated societies, while simple societies are more likely to be characterized by lenient forms. The fact that the negative evidence is stronger in the case of simple societies is especially interesting because it cannot be argued that political structure confounds the relationship between social complexity and punitive forms. Since simple societies do not possess a differentiated political system, distortions in the relationship between punishment and social organization cannot be attributed to fluctuations in political power *per se*.

Although "dynamic density" involves more than the concentration of population alone (cf. Schnore, 1958; Lukes, 1972), Durkheim clearly singles out "social condensation" as the basis of fundamental social change. The *Ethnographic Atlas* (1967) describes settlement patterns for 37 of the societies studied. Sixteen of these societies were made up of compact and relatively permanent settlements (i.e., relatively concentrated), while the remaining twenty-one were designated as either migratory bands, separated hamlets, neighborhoods and dispersed homesteads, or seminomadic

Table 2. Societal Complexity by Punishment Type

	Punishment Type				
	I	**II**	**III**	**IV**	**Total**
Simple Societies	11.7%	23.5%	23.5%	41.2%	
	(2)	(4)	(4)	(7)	17
Complex Societies	46.2%	7.7%	15.4%	30.8%	
	(6)	(1)	(2)	(4)	13
Total	8	5	6	11	30*

* Data on societal complexity (Freeman and Winch, 1957) were only available for thirty of the forty-eight societies studied.

Table 3. Societal Concentration by Punishment Type

	Punishment Type				
	I	II	III	IV	Total
Dispersed Societies	14.3%	14.3%	38.1%	33.3%	
	(3)	(3)	(8)	(7)	21
Concentrated Societies	56.2%	18.8%	6.2%	18.8%	
	(9)	(3)	(1)	(3)	16
Total	12	6	9	10	37*

* Data on societal concentration (Murdock, 1967) were only available for thirty-seven of the forty-eight societies studied.

communities (i.e., relatively dispersed). Table 3 describes the distribution of relatively concentrated and relatively dispersed societies across punishment types.

As in the case of societal complexity, the data fail to support the hypothesis relating social organizations to punitiveness. Relatively dense societies are more likely to employ harsh sanctions, while lenient controls are found with greater frequency when societies are relatively dispersed.

The *second hypothesis* concerns the impact of political absolutism on the evolution of punitive controls. Potential support for this hypothesis is found in an examination of the societies which employed the most severe penalties (Type I). All of these societies (see Table 1), with the exception of the Aranda, exhibit a relatively high level of political integration and absolute power is exercised by a single ruler (i.e., prince, emperor, chief, king, sheik) or venerated elite. But if Durkheim's analysis is correct it is not enough to argue that absolutism produces severity in punishment; political "hypercentralization" must be essentially uncorrelated with social development (*Hypothesis 2a*).

One means of examining the nexus between political and social organization is by looking at the extent to which the societies studied varied in terms of political integration. According to the *Ethnographic Atlas*, 60 percent of the simple societies were characterized by a relative absence of political integration, while 85 percent of the complex societies possessed at least "minimal states." The problem with this finding is that Freeman

and Winch (1957) included "government" as one of their measures of complexity, and therefore assume (rather than explore) the relationship between political and social structural change.

To provide a more meaningful test, the data on political integration were analyzed in terms of social concentration. The results of this cross-classification, which are reported in Table 4, indicate that concentrated societies are likely to be politically integrated, while dispersed societies usually lack structures of authority beyond the family. At the very least, this finding casts doubt on Durkheim's assertion that political and social changes are unrelated. More generally, the relationship between social and political concentration supports the conclusion that social condensation may be basic to the emergence of the modern state (cf. Fried, 1967).

Durkheim explained the weakening of repressive controls in terms of the changing nature of

Table 4. Societal Concentration by Political Integration

	Political Integration		
	High	Low	Total
Dispersed Societies	38.1%	61.9%	
	(8)	(13)	21
Concentrated Societies	87.5%	12.5%	
	(14)	(2)	16
Total	22	15	37

what constitutes crime. The *third hypothesis* asserts that increased complexity and social density will be associated with a movement from collective crimes to offenses where the victim is individually defined. The uneven quality of the data made it impossible to estimate reliably the exact proportion of individual to collective crimes defined in each society. However, a comparison could be made between societies in which collective crimes were relatively commonplace and those in which they were not. Twenty-four of the forty-eight societies defined, and applied major penalties to, *three or more* categories of collective crime, including political (e.g. treason, sabotage, sedition) and/ or moral (e.g. violation of sacred ceremonies, incest, witchcraft) offenses. The remaining societies (24) gave greater emphasis to individual (e.g. murder, assault, theft) and less to collective crimes (see Appendix). Table 5 presents a comparison of these two groupings in terms of societal complexity and concentration.

Although the evidence is far from conclusive, it clearly challenges the contention that collective definitions of deviance disappear as societies become more complex. To the extent that these data suggest developmental tendencies they do not

permit us to conclude that "crime is reduced more and more to offenses against persons alone" or that "religious forms of criminality decline." However, if we recall (Table 2 and 3) that more differentiated societies are likely to apply harsher rather than milder penalties, then Durkheim may have been correct in assuming that offenses against collective objects tend to be punished more severely. The question is raised, then, whether Durkheim was incorrect in asserting that conceptions of deviance increasingly assume more individualized forms, but correct in associating punitiveness with collective definitions of crime.

To explore this issue, the distribution of societies identifying three or more and less than three collective crimes was analyzed within each punishment type. Table 6 indicates that societies employing harsh punishment are more likely to define deviance in collective terms. In fact, moving from the most severe (Type I) to the least severe (Type IV) levels of punishment, the proportion of societies with three or more collective definitions declines progressively.

A case by case examination of "lenient" societies (Types III and IV) also reveals that when they do resort to severe punishment, it is often

Table 5. Societal Type by Criminal Definitions

Societal Types	Distribution of Criminal Definitions		Total
	Societies Defining Three or More Collective Crimes	Societies Defining Less Than Three Collective Crimes	
Simple	35.3% (6)	64.7% (11)	17
Complex	69.2% (9)	30.8% (4)	13
Total	15	15	30
Dispersed	42.8% (9)	57.2% (12)	21
Concentrated	56.3% (9)	43.7% (7)	16
Total	18	19	37

Table 6. Punishment Type by Criminal Definitions

Punishment Type	Distribution of Criminal Definitions		
	Societies Defining Three or More Collective Crimes	Societies Defining Less Than Three Collective Crimes	Total
I	71.4% (10)	28.6% (4)	14
II	57.1% (4)	42.9% (3)	7
III	46.2% (6)	53.8% (7)	13
IV	28.6% (4)	71.4% (10)	14
Total	24	24	48

because the offense involved violates collective rather than individual crimes. Thus, for example, although the Navaho (Valkenburgh, 1937) and Thonga (Junod, 1927) rely primarily on systems of compensation, they both define witchcraft as an exceptional crime and punish it by death. To the extent that these instances are representative, the link between collective definitions and punishment appears to exist within, as well as between structures of punitive response.

The *fourth hypothesis* addresses the process of punitive substitution described by Durkheim. To account for the character of penal evolution and establish the limits of leniency, Durkheim argued that individual crimes come to be punished more severely as societies evolve. The evidence considered thus far offers little support for this proposition. More advanced societies are generally characterized by harsher penalties coupled with a larger number of collective crimes. Accordingly, we have little reason to assume either that the number of individual crimes defined and punished expands with the process of social development, or that these crimes come to be punished more severely.

A more precise investigation of this relationship was achieved by rating each society in terms of whether it punished individual or collective

crimes more severely, or whether both categories were handled in approximately the same way (see Appendix). Twenty-one societies (43.8 percent) punished individual crimes more severely, sixteen (33.3 percent) applied harsher punishment to collective offenses, and eleven (22.9 percent) societies punished neither individual nor collective crimes more severely. Table 7 describes the relationship between foci of punitive control and the major features of social organization studied (complexity and concentration). As in the case of Table 5, the direction of the relationship is more explicit for the complexity than the concentration variable. Nevertheless, it seems reasonable to infer that undifferentiated societies are likely to punish individual infractions more severely, while more developed societies generally reserve extreme punishments for collective crimes. To the extent that one type of crime comes to replace another as the most severely punished, the data suggest that the sequence is more likely to involve a shift from an emphasis on individual to collective definitions than vice versa.

Finally, the *fifth hypothesis* focuses on the deprivation of liberty as a form of punitive control. In his investigation of qualitative change, Durkheim equated the deprivation of liberty with incarceration. It is not surprising, therefore, that he was

Table 7. Societal Type by Punitive Emphasis

| Societal Type | Punitive Focus | | | |
	Human Crimes	Neither Type	Collective Crimes	Total
Simple	52.9%	35.3%	11.7%	
	(9)	(6)	(2)	17
Complex	7.7%	23.1%	69.2%	
	(1)	(3)	(9)	13
Total	10	9	11	30
Dispersed	52.4%	33.3%	14.3%	
	(11)	(7)	(3)	21
Concentrated	37.5%	18.7%	43.8%	
	(6)	(3)	(7)	16
Total	17	10	10	37

able to establish a connection between confinement and the emergence of modern societies. The history of modern Europe and America supports the hypothesis that incarceration became a more and more popular mode of punishment (cf. Rusche and Kirchheimer, 1968; Rothman, 1970). Nonetheless, there is an important flaw in this approach. The deprivation of liberty, as one dimension of repressive control, need not take the form of physical confinement within a structure designed for detention. It may also involve methods of segregation, deprivation and exclusion which, although functionally comparable to incarceration, do not require the creation of a specialized physical facility.

An analysis of punitive reactions within the sample societies reveals that the Soviet Union and Czechs rely predominantly on incarceration, while three other societies (Lepcha, Serbs and Albanians) occasionally impose restrictions on physical mobility as a means of punishment. But in addition to these examples, *banishment* and/or *punitive slavery* is utilized by twenty-four societies (see Appendix) as a means of segregating, coercing and systematically excluding deviants. We may extend Durkheim's analytical model by asking whether banishment and slavery are in any way "function-

ally equivalent" to contemporary methods and by exploring the relationships between these "deprivations" and other modalities of punitive response.

The distribution of slavery and banishment according to various levels of punishment is presented in Table 8. Dividing societies into those characterized by punitive slavery (or slavery combined with banishment), and those employing banishment alone, an interesting pattern appears. When banishment is found without punitive slavery societies are likely to be classified as relatively lenient, but when punitive slavery is present levels of punishment tend to be more severe.

Several observations are suggested by these results. First, banishment may operate as a punishment of last resort in societies based primarily on restitutive controls. To the extent that these societies are what Fried (1967) has called "simple egalitarian" and are based on principles of reciprocity (Dalton, 1968), status differences do not have to be protected through repressive controls. Moreover, since these societies are not likely to have a well-developed state, serious or persistent offenders are most easily killed immediately (without "refined cruelties"), or excluded from the group. Exclusion is normally permanent, although in a few societies (e.g. Andamanese, Siriono,

Table 8. Punishment Type by Forms of Control

Punishment Type	Patterns of Control		Total
	Societies with Punitive Slavery or Both Slavery and Banishment	Societies with Banishment Alone	
I	67%	33%	
	(6)	(2)	8
II	67%	33%	
	(2)	(1)	3
III	20%	80%	
	(1)	(4)	5
IV	12.5%	87.5%	
	(1)	(7)	8
Total	10	14	24

Albania) exile may be imposed on a temporary basis.

The concentration of punitive slavery in societies with the most severe penalties may indicate that slavery is simply one more manifestation of a repressive control system. It may also be argued, however, that these societies—distinguished by gross disparities in wealth and social rank—require an extensive and brutal system of sanctions (including punitive slavery) to guarantee their survival. If the latter explanation is correct then it would appear that methods of social confinement, including punitive slavery, must be understood in relationship to structures of authority and privilege in social life.

Discussion

The evidence developed here raises serious questions about Durkheim's perspective on punishment and social change. To summarize: (1) The severity of punishment does not decrease as societies grow more concentrated and complex. On the contrary, greater punitiveness is associated with higher levels of structural differentiation. (2) While variations in political structure are related to punitive intensity, these variations are neither historically contingent, nor idiosyncratic. (3) Although the "religiosity" of deviance is correlated with punitiveness, collective crimes are more common in complex than simple societies. (4) Controls involving social and geographic segregation are not represented by incarceration alone and are not peculiar to advanced societies.

The discrepancies between Durkheim's observations and the data presented are important because they force us to re-examine his approach to the explanation of social order, social change and methods of control. If punishment is related to social organization, but not in the way that Durkheim describes, then we must investigate his assumptions about society, as well as the nexus between social organization and patterns of punitive response. If we can better account for the results by making different assumptions about the nature of society, then these findings are valuable in more than a narrow negative sense.

Two major assumptions of Durkheim's model are challenged by the findings reported here. These are the interrelated assumptions of *normative priority* and *emergent control*. Throughout his work Durkheim tried to identify the mechanism which coordinated and integrated social life. While the basis of interdependence might vary according to social type, it was the *conscience collective* which invariably played an important role. Because he viewed the collective conscience as the substructure of any society, Durkheim was willing to argue that beliefs shaped the character of social practices and institutions, rather than the reverse. Accordingly, he argued that transformation in punishment will reflect changes in the strength and nature of shared beliefs.

Even though the data suggest a connection between beliefs and punishment, we need not assume that beliefs cause punishment. Instead, we may argue that sentiments and sanctions are correlated because they perform a similar function—the maintenance of hegemonic control. From this point of view, beliefs act as legitimations or rationalizations which bolster a specific set of social arrangements. The significance of beliefs, therefore, will not depend on the "maturation" of the society *per se*, but will correspond to its requirements for social control. The more repressive a given system of domination is, the more important both punishments and beliefs will be in securing social order. Punishment, in this sense, is an instrumental mechanism for preserving the structure of social life, and although beliefs may complement formal sanctions, they do not produce these sanctions.

If the structure of punishment springs full blown from underlying beliefs, then it is reasonable to conclude that formal controls reflect a common consciousness, rather than specific interests. However, when we acknowledge the *instrumental* rather than *emergent* quality of punishment a number of relationships are rendered less obscure. If punishment is instrumental in consolidating a particular system of domination, then we can explain why greater concentration and complexity lead to harsher and more extensive punitive controls. This would seem to be particularly true in societies where the development of political integration has just begun. As Dubow (1974) has pointed out, simple societies and established nation-states have less need for excessive punishments than emerging states—who must impose homogeneity on heretofore autonomous groups. These emerging states come to rely on powerful

collective definitions and naked force because they have neither "models to build on or to reject" (Fried, 1967:232), nor do they have other means of exacting obedience and labor power (which Durkheim described as "organic society"). While market economies may use "laws of the market" to regulate labor and institutionalize inequality, redistributive economies (Polanyi, 1944) must resort to political and ideological controls to support the concentration of wealth. Societies based on redistribution are also distinguished from reciprocal economies, which regulate labor through bonds of friendship, kinship or status. Institutions of slavery are common in redistributive economies because these societies cannot depend on social obligation (principles of reciprocity) or a labor market to insure a commitment to labor beyond that necessary for subsistence.

If the relationship between punitive intensity and social development is actually curvilinear—in the sense that sanctions are lenient in simple egalitarian (reciprocal) societies, severe in non-market (redistributive) complex societies, and lenient in established market societies—then the limitations of Durkheim's approach are as much a function of his selection of evidence as his theoretical presuppositions. Durkheim established the plausibility of a linear hypothesis by excluding the most undifferentiated societies from his analysis and identifying complexity with market systems (i.e., economic systems which are controlled, regulated and directed by markets alone). He reinforced that hypothesis by viewing complex non-market societies (e.g. Imperial Rome, ancient Egypt, mercantile France) as atypical, rather than intermediate, developmental forms.

The interpretation outlined above is consistent with the finding that: (1) the intensity of punishment is related to the level of political integration within pre-industrial societies; (2) collective definitions of crime are found more frequently in complex, non-market societies than simple societies; (3) simple egalitarian societies are more likely to use material sanctions than hierarchical or stratified societies; and (4) slavery is likely to be institutionalized as both a means of organizing productive labor and controlling selected deviants in societies utilizing the harshest sanctions, while banishment is more consistent with patterns of social control dominant in "lenient" (simple) societies.

Whatever its shortcomings, Durkheim's approach to the study of punishment provides a valuable model for the study of social control. In linking the nature of control to the organization of society Durkheim makes explicit what too many investigators ignore—the fact that punishment is deeply rooted in the structure of society. Whether we determine that Durkheim's explanation must be specified or completely disregarded, one thing is clear: the investigation of punishment must be sensitive to the political and economic dimensions of social life. Although the present research has only been a preliminary step in this regard, it has at least raised the questions that must be asked if an understanding of the relationship between punishment and social structure is to evolve.

REFERENCES

Dalton, George. 1968. *Primitive, Archaic and Modern Economies: Essays of Karl Polanyi.* Boston: Beacon Press.

Dubow, Fred. 1974. "Nation-Building and the Imposition of Criminal Law." Presented at the Annual Meeting of the American Sociological Association.

Durkheim, Emile. 1973. "Two Laws of Penal Evolution," T. Anthony Jones and Andrew T. Scull (trs.) 2 *Economy and Society* 285.

Freeman, Linton C., and Robert F. Winch. 1957. "Societal Complexity: An Empirical Test of a Typology of Societies," 62 *American Journal of Sociology* 461.

Fried, Morton H. 1967. *The Evolution of Political Society.* New York: Random House.

Junod, Henri A. 1927. *The Life of a South African Tribe.* London: Macmillan and Company.

Lukes, Steven. 1972. *Emile Durkheim: His Life and Work.* New York: Harper and Row.

Murdock, George Peter. 1967. *Ethnographic Atlas.* Pittsburgh: University of Pittsburgh Press.

Radcliffe-Brown, A. 1922. *The Andaman Islanders.* Cambridge: Cambridge University Press.

Rothman, David J. 1970. *The Discovery of the Asylum.* Boston: Little, Brown and Company.

Rusche, Georg, and Otto Kirchheimer. 1968. *Punishment and Social Structure.* New York: Russell and Russell.

Schnore, Leo F. 1958. "Social Morphology and Human Ecology," 63 *American Journal of Sociology* 620.

Schwartz, Richard D. and James C. Miller. 1964. "Legal Evolution and Societal Complexity," 70 *American Journal of Sociology* 159.

Valkenburgh, Richard F. Van. 1937. "Navaho Common Law II: Navaho Law and Justice," 9 *Museum of Northern Arizona, Museum Notes* 51.

Wimberley, Howard. 1973. "Legal Evolution: One Further Step," 79 *American Journal of Sociology* 78.

Appendix

Societies	Punishment Type	Criminal Definitions	Freeman-Winch Rating	Settlement Patterns	Political Integration	Punitive Emphasis	Slavery/ Banishment
Albania	IV	Individual	—	Dispersed	High	Individual	Banishment
Andamanese	IV	Individual	0	Dispersed	Low	Neither	Banishment
Aranda	I	Collective	0	Dispersed	Low	Neither	—
Ashanti	I	Collective	5	Concentrated	High	Collective	Slavery
Azande	I	Collective	0	Dispersed	High	Collective	Slavery
Balinese	I	Collective	4	Concentrated	High	Neither	Banishment
Buka	II	Collective	0	Dispersed	Low	Neither	—
Cambodians	I	Collective	—	Concentrated	High	Individual	Slavery
Cayapa	III	Collective	—	Dispersed	Low	Individual	—
Chagga	I	Collective	4	Dispersed	High	Collective	Slavery
Chuckchee	II	Collective	0	Dispersed	Low	Individual	Slavery
Comanche	III	Individual	—	Dispersed	Low	Individual	—
Creek	II	Individual	5	Concentrated	High	Collective	Banishment
Crow	III	Individual	—	Dispersed	High	Individual	—
Cuna	I	Collective	4	Concentrated	High	Neither	—
Czechs	IV	Collective	6	Concentrated	High	Collective	—
Formosan Aborigines	IV	Individual	0	—	—	Individual	—
Georgia	IV	Individual	—	—	—	Individual	Banishment
Guana	III	Collective	—	—	—	Neither	Banishment
Hottentot	III	Collective	0	Dispersed	High	Neither	—
Ifugao	IV	Individual	0	Dispersed	Low	Neither	—
Inca	I	Collective	—	Concentrated	High	Collective	Banishment
Indonesians	III	Collective	—	—	—	Collective	Slavery
Iranians	I	Individual	—	Concentrated	High	Individual	—
Iroquois	III	Collective	—	—	—	Collective	Banishment
Jivaro	II	Individual	0	Dispersed	Low	Individual	—
Kazaks	III	Individual	0	Dispersed	Low	Individual	Banishment
Koreans	I	Collective	6	Concentrated	High	Collective	Slavery
Lapps	III	Individual	6	Dispersed	Low	Individual	—
Lepcha	III	Individual	3	Dispersed	Low	Individual	—
Maori	III	Collective	4	Concentrated	High	Collective	—
Mbundu	II	Individual	3	Concentrated	High	Individual	Slavery
Navaho	IV	Individual	5	Dispersed	Low	Collective	—
Nootka	II	Collective	—	—	—	Collective	—
Nuer	IV	Collective	—	Dispersed	Low	Individual	—
Riffians	IV	Individual	6	Concentrated	High	Neither	Banishment
Saudi Arabia	I	Individual	—	—	High	Individual	—
Serbs	III	Individual	—	—	Low	Individual	Banishment
Siriono	IV	Individual	0	Dispersed	Low	Individual	Banishment
Siwans	I	Individual	1	Concentrated	High	Individual	—

Appendix (continued)

Societies	Punishment Type	Criminal Definitions	Freeman-Winch Rating	Settlement Patterns	Political Integration	Punitive Emphasis	Slavery/Banishment
Somalia	IV	Individual	—	Dispersed	High	Neither	Banishment
Soviet Union	IV	Collective	6*	—	High	Collective	—
Thonga	III	Collective	2	Dispersed	High	Neither	—
Turkestan	I	Individual	—	—	—	Individual	—
Vietnamese	I	Collective	6	Concentrated	High	Collective	Slavery
Woleaians	IV	Collective	0	—	—	Collective	Banishment
Yurok	IV	Individual	1	Concentrated	Low	Individual	Slavery
Zuni	II	Individual	—	Concentrated	Low	Collective	—

*Not included in original Freeman-Winch study but rated in terms of available evidence.

• 7 •

Structural-Functionalism

We may say with confidence that the origins of sociology's contemporary theories are, by and large, found in the classical works of Marx, Weber, and Durkheim. In other words, the nineteenth-century theoretical perspectives formulated by these three thinkers have inspired twentieth-century sociology to develop its own distinctive paradigms.

In Chapter 1 we defined *paradigm* as a theoretical perspective, school of thought, or intellectual tradition that reflects a particular set of ideas and assumptions regarding the nature of people and society. We also indicated that several competing paradigms currently exist in sociology and that each provides the sociologist with a different view of social reality. Finally, we stated that those sociological paradigms that have most influenced the sociology of law are *structural-functionalism* and *conflict theory*.

In this and the following chapter, we discuss both of these paradigms in turn and see how they have been used toward the development of a modern sociology of law. This chapter introduces structural-functionalism by presenting a few of its key concepts. Relying on these concepts, the chapter then examines the legal system's social functions. We will see that the law's principal function is that of integration through social control. The chapter then looks at the legal system as an autopoietic unit, or as a coherent entity that reproduces itself, regulates itself, and refers to itself. Finally, the chapter concludes with an analysis of the empirical study of the social functions of law.

Structural-Functionalism: Society as an Integrated System

Structural-functionalism was the preeminent sociological paradigm during the 1940s and 1950s. Indeed, it was so popular that Kingsley Davis, in his presidential address to the American Sociological Association in 1959, took the position that functionalism was, in effect, synonymous with sociological analysis. Although Davis acknowledged that there were several variants of functionalism, he describes those traits most frequently cited as characterizing functional analysis in general:

311

Functionalism is most commonly said to *do* two things: to relate the parts of society to the whole, and to relate one part to another. Almost as common is the specification of *how* it does this relating—namely, by seeing one part as "performing a function for" or "meeting a need or requirement of" the whole society or some part of it (1959:758).

Accordingly, structural-functionalism sees society as a *system* made up of differentiated and interrelated structures. In applying a systematic analysis to human societies, this paradigm focuses on (1) the *functional imperatives,* or "needs," that a social system must satisfy in order to ensure its survival; (2) the *interconnecting structures* (institutions or "subsystems") that satisfy these needs; and (3) the way that all the institutions reorganize to bring the social system back to an ideal state of harmony or *equilibrium.* Thus, "to speak of the *function* of an institution *for* a society or *for* another institution in that society is a way of asking what the institution does within the system to which it is relevant" (Davis, 1959:772).

In their examination of how social systems maintain and restore equilibrium, functionalists regard shared norms and values as fundamental to society. They tend to emphasize *consensus,* or the fact that individuals will be morally committed to the existing social structures. For functionalists, voluntary cooperation and general consensus is what holds the social system together. Thus, any conflicts or disruptions that arise must be quickly and efficiently resolved and mitigated so that the social system can preserve *order.*

In sum, structural-functionalists take a holistic view of society. As such, they see society as an integrated system made up of distinct structures performing specialized tasks but working together to help the system maintain an orderly state of equilibrium. The differentiated and interrelated structures achieve social equilibrium in two ways. First, by fulfilling the needs of the social system, and second, by subduing disorder in the social system. For a more detailed understanding of the functionalist paradigm let us now examine its beginnings in sociology and anthropology.

The Beginnings of Functionalism in Sociology and Anthropology

Sociology and functionalism both had their official beginnings in the work of Auguste Comte. Comte's *organic analogy of society* (which he derived from biology) set the stage for the systemic and structural-functionalist sociological approaches. Just as a biological organism is made up of different parts, Comte argues, so too is the social organism composed of various structures, each playing a vital role.

We have thus established a true correspondence between . . . the Social Organism in Sociology, and that of the Individual Organism in Biology. . . . If we take the best ascertained points in Biology, we may decompose structure anatomically into *elements, tissues,* and *organs.* We have the same things in the Social Organism; and may even use the same names.

I shall treat the Social Organism as definitely composed of the Families which are the true elements or cells, next the Classes or Castes which are its proper tissues, and lastly, of the cities and Communes which are the real organs (Comte, 1875:239–40; 242).

Like Comte, Herbert Spencer also made wide use of the organic analogy. Spencer, however, gives particular emphasis to the *differentiation* of society. As we saw in Chapter 2, Spencer believed that as the social organism progressed and increased in size and density there would result greater **differentiation**—that is, an increased complexity concerning the mutual dependence of unlike parts of the system. Social theorist Walter Buckley states that Spencer's views were derived from the principles of biological functionalism, "according to which an organism is an integrated whole made up of certain differentiated organs or structures through which certain functional requirements for the survival or effective operation of the organism are typically met" (1957:239). Comte and Spencer's organic analogy had a pervasive influence on sociological thought throughout the nineteenth century.

Without a doubt, Emile Durkheim had the most significant intellectual influence on sociological functionalism. In taking an organicist approach, Durkheim regards society as a sui generis whole that is not reducible to its constituent parts. Durkheim sees each of these parts, or social facts, as meeting certain "general needs of the social organism." For example, Durkheim explains that the function of ritualized punishment is to bring together the collective sentiments of the offended community. In so doing, punishment satisfies a vital need of society, the need for social solidarity.

> [T]he social reaction that we call "punishment" is due to the intensity of the collective sentiments which the crime offends; but, from another angle, it has the useful function of maintaining these sentiments at the same degree of intensity, for they would soon diminish if offenses against them were not punished (Durkheim, 1966:96).

Furthermore, in viewing social conditions as either *normal* or *pathological*, Durkheim makes it clear that social organisms have equilibrium points. A pathological state is such because it "disturbs the normal functioning of society" (Durkheim, 1966:54). On the other hand, Durkheim calls normal those "social conditions that are the most generally distributed" (1966:55). In other words, what is *average* in a particular society is what is normal because it serves to maintain balance in the system. By contrast, what is *deviant* is pathological because it upsets that balance. While all social facts demonstrate these concepts, Durkheim relies on the social fact of crime to illustrate the normal and the pathological.

Crime is said to be normal (that is, average or usual) because it exits in all societies. "No doubt it is possible that crime itself will have [pathological] forms, as, for example, when the rate is unusually high. . . . What is normal, simply, is the existence of criminality, provided that it attains and does not exceed . . . a certain level" (Durkheim, 1966:66). Not only does an average amount of crime contribute to the equilibrium of a society, Durkheim contends that crime also provides a function; that is, *it plays a useful role*. One useful role that crime plays is that it brings about social change. States Durkheim: "Crime implies not only that the way remains open to necessary changes but that in certain cases it directly prepares these changes. Where crime exists, collective sentiments are sufficiently flexible to take on a new form, and crime sometimes helps to determine what form they will take" (1966:71).

Thus, in Durkheim's view, social facts are functional because they satisfy the general needs of society and because they play a useful role in that society. In a word, social facts are functional because they are *beneficial* to society.

Functionalist analysis emerged as much from anthropology as from sociology. To be sure, theorists from one discipline usually attribute the development of their ideas to the influence of functionalism in the other discipline. Two of the most eminent functionalists in social anthropology were A. R. Radcliffe-Brown and Bronislaw Malinowski.

Arthur R. Radcliffe-Brown (1881–1955), in his book *Structure and Function in Primitive Society* (1952), takes great care in explaining the utility of the concepts of structure and function as employed in social anthropology. Like Durkheim, he believes all social phenomena are the immediate result of the social structure. But unlike Durkheim, who restricted his sociology to the study of social structure (i.e., social facts), Radcliffe-Brown is also interested in the activities of people, and contends that social activities and social structure can only be studied in relation to each other. He contends that the relationship between social activities and the social structure constitutes a functional unity that produces a certain degree of harmony in the social system. Radcliffe-Brown states that function "involves the notion of a *structure* consisting of a *set of relations* amongst *unit entities*, the *continuity* of the structure being maintained by a *life-process* made up of the *activities* of the constituent units" (1965:180). Furthermore, much like Durkheim, Radcliffe-Brown posits that the "*function* of any recurrent activity, such as the punishment of a crime, . . . is the part it plays in the social life as a whole and therefore the contribution it makes to the maintenance of the structural community" (1965: 180).

Bronislaw Malinowski (1884–1942), in his study of premodern island culture off the coast of New Guinea, identified functionalism with system interrelations and *reciprocity*. According to him, the real units of culture are institutions—that is, the general and relatively stable sets of activities organized to meet critical needs. He says that institutions provide a function, a useful activity, as they satisfy certain societal needs and thus help maintain social equilibrium. In addition, society's equilibrium is sustained by **reciprocity**, the mutual give-and-take principal, which reigned supreme among the Trobriand islanders Malinowski was studying (Malinowski, 1982:46–47).

Malinowski notes that, with the Trobrianders, this principle of reciprocity is not based primarily on the exchange of utilitarian goods but on the continuous mutual exchange of symbolic gifts such as necklaces, armlets, fish, and yams. Thus, for the Trobrianders, reciprocity constitutes "the fundamental impulse to display, to share, to bestow [and] the deep tendency to create social ties" (Malinowski, 1984:175). In this view, the Trobrianders' network of mutual exchange has as its function the *integration* of social life.

In his slim volume *Crime and Custom in Savage Society* (1926), Malinowski discusses "primitive law," which he characterizes as "the various forces which make

for order, uniformity and cohesion" (1982:2). The primitive law of the Trobrianders is enforced, not by coercion, Malinowski tells us, but by "a specific mechanism
of reciprocity and publicity inherent in the structure of their society" (1982:58).
Thus, the islanders conform their behavior to the law not because they fear legal
reprisal, but because theirs is a society that demands reciprocal and binding obligations. Moreover, according to Malinowski, one of primitive law's main functions
is that it satisfies a biological need that is necessary for survival: the need to share.
Therefore, following Malinowski, we may conclude that the law has three main
functions: (1) at the cultural level it fulfills the need for having regular and stable
sets of activities (i.e., institutions); (2) at the structural level it meets the need of the
regulation of behavior; and (3) at the biological level it satisfies the need to share.
In concluding, Malinowski reiterates that the end result of the functions of law is
social integration.

In the next section we continue our analysis of structural-functionalism by
examining the theoretical contributions of Robert K. Merton and Talcott Parsons.
In particular, we focus on Merton's concepts of manifest and latent functions and
dysfunctions, and Parsons's elaboration of the concept of the social system.

Manifest and Latent Functions and Dysfunctions

Sociologist Robert K. Merton takes the functionalism developed by Malinowski,
Radcliffe-Brown, and other anthropologists who studied premodern cultures, and
reformulates it for use in the study of modern complex societies. Merton (1968:
81–87) rejects the three postulates accepted by functionalist anthropology: (1) the
postulate of the functional unity of society, (2) the postulate of universal functionalism, and (3) the postulate of indispensability.

The postulate of the functional unity of society states that every cultural activity or
belief is beneficial, not only for society as a whole but for every person living in that
society. *The postulate of universal functionalism* holds that all social structures have
positive consequences for society. *The postulate of indispensability* advances two interrelated assumptions: (1) that there are certain functions that must be performed or
the society will cease to exist, and (2) that certain social structures are indispensable
for fulfilling each of these functions. In his reformulation of functionalist theory,
Merton offers alternatives to these postulates as he introduces the notion of *dysfunctions*, and makes a clear distinction between *manifest and latent functions*.

Functions, Merton stipulates, "are those observed consequences which make
for the adaptation or adjustment of the system." **Dysfunctions,** by contrast, are
"those observed consequences which lessen the adaptation or adjustment of the
system" (1968:105). This last concept had been ignored in the postulate of universal functionalism, which stressed the idea that *all* functional units contributed in
a positive manner to the maintenance of the social whole. However, Merton proposes that any item may have both functional (positive) and dysfunctional (negative) consequences. According to him, these consequences are relative to the
experience of different groups in society and therefore the question to be asked is,
"Functional for whom?" In this view, an item that may be functional for one group

may be quite dysfunctional for another. (This point approximates the theoretical approach taken by conflict theory in Chapter 8.)

Merton refers to **manifest functions** as "those objective consequences contributing to the adjustment or adaptation of the system which are intended and recognized by participants in the system." Conversely, **latent functions** are "those which are neither intended nor recognized" (1968:105). Because of Merton's reformulation, the concept of function is now used in the more general and neutral sense of *consequences*, which may contribute positively or negatively to the social system and which may be intended or unintended. Let us see how the concepts of manifest and latent functions empirically apply to the case of the Norwegian Law on Housemaids.

The Norwegian Law on Housemaids, which belongs tangentially to labor legislation, was issued by the Norwegian Parliament in 1948. Legal sociologist Vilhelm Aubert (1967a) examines the manifest and latent functions of this law.

When enacted by the left and the conservative legislators of parliament, this piece of legislation produced two seemingly conflicting manifest functions that clearly reflected the political views of the opposing parties. From the left standpoint, the law served the interests of housemaids as employees by improving their working conditions. This view is called the "reform" argument. From the conservative standpoint, the law was intended to serve the interests of the housewives as employers by protecting the privacy of the home. This opposing view is referred to as the "status-quo" argument. In its attempt to improve the working conditions of housemaids (the reform argument), the law limited working hours to ten a day; clearly defined overtime (a minimum payment for overtime was stipulated and overtime beyond a certain number of hours per week was prohibited); allowed the housemaid to demand a written contract and payment every other week; and allowed her to demand one free afternoon a week and every other Sunday.

Two years after the law was passed, Aubert and his associates conducted a study to determine the law's influence on housemaids and housewives. This was accomplished by measuring the extent to which the housewives and their housemaids had complied to its rulings on working hours, overtime, payment, and so on. The researchers concluded that the law had been relatively ineffective in improving working conditions for housemaids for two main reasons.

First, the legal language employed was so technical that it made the law incomprehensible to most housemaids and housewives. As a result, many of them had little intimate acquaintance with the new piece of legislation. Simply put, neither of these two parties knew what the law required of them. Second, the law was enforced only weakly and the sanctions for its violation were vague. Consequently, the chances of a housemaid instigating legal procedures against a nonconforming employer were very low. Because of these two factors, the law did not adequately fulfill its manifest function of reforming working conditions. Nevertheless, Aubert tells us that the law did accomplish a latent function completely unrelated to improving the working conditions of housemaids or protecting the privacy of the housewives' homes. This latent function had to do with the left and conservative legislators' need for compromise in parliament. Compromise was one way of resolving or ameliorating the conflicts that continually arose between the two legislative groups.

According to Aubert, the least controversial and most convenient argument in favor of passing the law was that it did, on the whole, correspond to established customary practice that had traditionally guided the relationship between housemaids and housewives (the status-quo argument). Therefore, the law would only affect the exceptional cases that were in real need of change (the reform argument). This compromise satisfied both the left and conservative political groups in parliament. Thus, while the law's manifest functions may not have been accomplished to any appreciable degree, the law nevertheless did serve the latent function "of restoring peace and harmony in a situation where opposing interests might tear politicians and others apart" (1967a:112).

Merton's concepts of manifest and latent, functions and dysfunctions alert us to the fact that the consequences of social structures may be intended or unintended, positive or negative. We now turn our attention to Talcott Parsons's contributions to the functionalist paradigm and his focus on the social system.

The Social System

Talcott Parsons (1902–1979) was arguably the foremost exponent of functionalism in the United States during the 1940s and 1950s. To this day, his theory of social systems continues to stimulate theoretical discussion in many quarters of the sociological community. Although he devoted relatively limited attention to the law, as we shall see throughout the remainder of this chapter, several sociologists have used Parsons's theoretical notions in explaining the social functions of the legal system. We begin this section with a brief discussion of Parsons's major concepts.

Parsons's sociology began with his voluntaristic theory of action, which he first proposed in his book *The Structure of Social Action* (1937). According to Parsons, the starting point of sociological analysis is the "unit act." The unit act involves the social actions taken by individuals. Social actions are voluntaristic and meaningful because motivated individuals, after some consideration of the existing (situational and normative) conditions, voluntarily and rationally decide which means to pursue in achieving a particular goal.

In what is perhaps his most well-known work, *The Social System* (1951), Parsons maintains that several social actions are interrelated into a pattern that can be conceptualized as a *social system*. For Parsons, a social system "consists in a plurality of individual actors *interacting* with each other in a situation which has at least a physical or environmental aspect" (1951:5–6). Thus, a **social system** refers to any unit in which numerous interactions occur, ranging from the interactions that take place between people to those that take place between societies. (In this chapter we will direct most of our comments to the interactions or *interchanges* that take place between institutions). Consequently, we may see society as a social system and the institution of law as one of its component **subsystems.** Or, we may consider law as the social system and the courts and legal profession as its subsystems.

Parsons further contends that in order to develop and survive, all social (sub)systems must meet four **functional imperatives:** (A) Adaptation, (G) Goal attainment, (I) Integration, and (L) Latency (AGIL). These four functional imperatives are the needs that every social system must satisfy in order to operate effectively and remain viable as a system.

Adaptation means that the system must obtain from its environment certain necessary resources and then distribute them throughout the system. *Goal attainment* means that the system must define and prioritize its goals and then mobilize its resources and energies to achieve those goals. *Integration* means that the system must regulate, coordinate, and facilitate the intra- and interrelationships of its constituent subsystems. As such, it must manage the input/output exchanges among the other neighboring systems. The system must also manage the relationship among the other three functional imperatives (A, G, L). *Latency* (pattern maintenance/ tension management) means that the system must maintain conforming behavior by motivating individuals to display that behavior. It also means that the system must resolve the tensions and strains that individuals may experience. In short, the performance of the AGIL functions ensures that conflicts, deviance, and other disruptions are properly controlled and that the social system keeps its equilibrium. By employing Parsons's AGIL scheme we can now examine how the legal system performs its social functions.

The Legal System and Its Social Functions

As indicated above, all social systems must satisfy all four of the functional imperatives if they are to preserve their equilibrium. Nevertheless, when analyzed at the societal level, some subsystems (institutions) are particularly adept at performing one function better than the others. For example, the *economic system* performs the adaptation function by controlling the environment for the purpose of producing and allocating those goods and services that satisfy the wants of society as a whole.

The goal-attainment function, which has to do with a social system obtaining what it needs in order to survive, is fulfilled by the *political system*, or "polity." The polity meets this functional requisite by pursuing system objectives and mobilizing resources to that end. According to Parsons, "the goal of the polity is to maximize the [power] of the society to attain its system goals" (Parsons and Smelser, 1956:48).

The function of latent pattern-maintenance refers to the individual in a social system having a motivational commitment to act in accordance with consensual normative expectations. Because society expects its members to conform to conventional behavior, it must provide institutionalized values (originating in religious beliefs, ideology, etc.) that, through the process of socialization, are internalized by the individual. Parsons defines values as "conceptions of the desirable society . . . held in common by its members" (1960a:122). The *educational, familial, and religious systems* meet the pattern-maintenance function by inculcating individuals with society's shared values. In this way, the social system controls the personality of the individual.

Being very specific about the integrative function, Parsons says that it is principally concerned with two things: (1) "the maintenance of a state of internal 'harmony' or absence of 'conflict' among the units of the system" (1953:625), and (2) "the mutual adjustments of . . . subsystems from the point of view of their 'contributions' to the effective functioning of the system as a whole" (1961:40). The *legal system*—and most notably the appellate courts and the legal profession—performs the integrative function by facilitating, or *adjusting*, the interchanges among the various subsystems thereby creating social harmony.

Parsons (1961:58–59) lists three processes of adjustment that the legal system must employ if it is to effectively perform its integrative function. First, the legal system must articulate its laws at a high level of generality. Generality provides broad interpretations of the law, thus giving the various subsystems (e.g., religion, education, etc.) sufficient time and opportunity to adjust to the changing legal environment. For example, when the U.S. Supreme Court ruled in *Brown v. Board of Education* (1954) that racial desegregation occur "with all deliberate speed," it was being vague and indefinite as to when the change should take place. This vague and indefinite phrase, however, gave the schools and other public institutions the freedom to desegregate at a responsible pace, thereby keeping social disruption to a manageable level.

Second, the legal system must have laws that are neither too rigid nor too flexible; that is, legislative, judicial, and administrative rulings and decisions need to be stated in such a way that social changes do not readily threaten their legitimacy or compromise their integrity. For example, the Eighth Amendment of the U.S. Constitution, which prohibits "cruel and unusual punishments," was enacted in 1791. At that time, the framers did not consider branding and ear cropping to be cruel and unusual punishments and thus they legally permitted these practices. By today's standards, however, branding and ear cropping are seen as barbarities to be constitutionally prohibited. Thus, while the wording of the Eighth Amendment has not changed since it was written by the framers, this law has a measured degree of plasticity that allows it to adapt to society's changing normative standards. Over two hundred years later, the Eighth Amendment remains legally authoritative and textually intact.

Third, in order for the legal system to adjust social interchanges it must engage in **social control,** or the process that regulates individuals' behavior and minimizes deviance. According to Parsons, the legal system needs to control individuals' motivations and sentiments by redefining what they want. To illustrate Parsons's point we may look the American cultural value of aspiring to monetary success. While this type of success may be obtained through theft, prostitution, drug dealing, and any number of deviant ways, the legal system must ensure that only conventional actions are taken to achieve this objective. Thus, while individuals want monetary success, it is the law's responsibility to convince them that they must want it legitimately. By controlling people's motivations and sentiments, the law coordinates the social interchanges between cultural value and social wants and subsequently contributes to the integration of society.

To summarize, Parsons maintains that the legal system performs the integrative function by adjusting or coordinating the interchanges among the various components of society. He then lists three processes of adjustment that the legal system must employ if it is to effectively perform its integrative function. These are: (1) the laws must be stated at a high level of generality; (2) the laws must possess a measured degree of plasticity; and (3) the legal system must operate as a mechanism of social control. In the next section we examine the last process in greater detail.

Law as a Mechanism of Social Control

Law, Parsons tells us, "consists in a body of norms or rules governing human conduct in social situations" (1954:372). Employing his systems-functional approach, Parsons (1962) gives two major reasons why law should be treated as a generalized mechanism of social control. First, law is an institution dealing with patterned rules, concerning behavioral expectations and obligations, to which various **sanctions,** or penalties for nonconformity, are applied. Second, law has a general function of regulating *any* social relationship. Thus, in Parsons' view the law's regulative interventions help to maintain the order and harmony of the social system.

As indicated above, for Parsons, the law's primary function is *system integration.* Accordingly, the law "serves to mitigate potential elements of conflict and to oil the machinery of social intercourse" (Parsons, 1962:58). Moreover, the legal system also provides *normative consistency;* that is, it must systematically regulate interactions by impartially subjecting all people to the same general expectations and obligations. Conversely, normative inconsistency means that legal rules must not subject individuals to incompatible expectations or obligations.

However, before the functions of system integration and normative consistency can be accomplished, the courts must provide institutionalized responses to four major questions that will arise in a large-scale, highly differentiated society. These are the questions of *sanctions, jurisdiction, legitimation,* and *interpretation,* and may be formulated respectively as follows:

1. If I fail to comply with the legal norms, what sanctions will apply and who will apply them?
2. What authority has jurisdiction in defining and imposing the legal norms and to what situations does a given rule apply?
3. What justifies those legal norms that obligate me to fulfill the expectations of others with whom I interact?
4. What is the meaning of these general rules and how should I interpret them in light of the particulars of a given situation?

Parsons contends that the legal system is closely integrated with the political system with respect to the question of *sanctions,* or enforcement. Coercion—the threat of negative punishments, including physical force, for not performing an expected or obligatory behavior—may be used as a sanction in enforcing the legal rules. If the enforcement of law through physical coercion is monopolized by the political system (i.e., the state), then the legal system must have a close association with it. Another integrative link is found between the two systems in regard to **jurisdiction**—the territorial range of legal authority or control—since it is the polity that determines what territory and who within that territory is subject to the sanctions.

However, the legal system is more autonomous from the political system as concerns the questions of interpretation and legitimation. The legal system's own **legitimation,** or validity, creates a justification for compliance to its laws; that is, in the absence of political influence, the legal system's procedural law (e.g., the U.S. Constitution) gives authority to the legal system's substantive law (statutes). Moreover, Parsons maintains that all law, in order to act as a legitimate mechanism of social control, must, at bottom, have the backing not of values that are purely political, but of values that are religious or quasi-religious. For example, in American society the legitimation process is carried on in the name of two fundamental values: freedom and equality (Bourricaud, 1981:279). The founding fathers framed the Constitution on the basis of these values, or "inalienable rights," that take on a quasi-religious quality.

In Parsons's view, **interpretation,** or meaning endowment, is the legal system's central function. Interpretation may be *rule focused* or *client focused.* The rule-focused aspect of interpretation concerns the integrity of the legal system itself. It resides with the judiciary, especially with the appellate courts such as the U.S. Supreme Court. At the appellate level, the legal and political systems are very closely integrated. For instance, the selection of Justices to the U.S. Supreme Court is a preeminently political process. Candidates for the Court are nominated by the executive organ (the president) and confirmed by the legislative organ (the Senate).

On the other hand, there also exists "a relative independence of the judiciary from both executive and legislative organs" (Parsons, 1960b:144). This independence is due, in large measure, to the professionalization of the judicial role. Appellate court judges, who are lawyers and not politicians, usually have lifetime appointments and cannot be removed from office, nor can the executive branch of government influence the judges' judicial decisions.

The client-focused aspect of interpretation is located with the attorney. The lawyer's professional and impersonal relationship with the client focuses on giving private advice to the client, depending on the client for payment, and enjoying a privileged confidential relation with the client. Put another way, the lawyer's relationship to the client is focused "on situations of actual or potential social conflict and the adjudication and smoothing over of these conflicts" (Parsons, 1962:63). The rule-focused and client-focused aspects of the law, as well as their corresponding mechanisms, all serve to facilitate the interpretive function of the legal system.

In short, we can see that, as concerns the questions of sanctions and jurisdiction, there is clearly a system integration between the law and the polity, which ensures normative consistency. On the other hand, Parsons has also shown that there exists a relative autonomy between the legal and political systems in regard to the questions of legitimation and interpretation. However, the degree of system integration notwithstanding, both the law and the polity function to mitigate social conflict.

Elsewhere, Parsons (1954) states that the *legal profession* performs the necessary functional requisites for integrating the legal system itself. He refers to the legal profession as an "intermediate mechanism" that integrates in two ways. First, it integrates the legal system by relating the law through interpretation of the specific practical situation faced by the client. In other words, the attorney explains to the client what the client's rights and duties are relative to the case. In so doing the attorney fosters a closer relationship between the client and the law. Second, the legal profession integrates the legal system by maintaining the internal consistency of the precedent system of legal rules. Put another way, lawyers give the legal system stability and coherency when they follow stare decisis.

Parsons further contends that the legal profession, in its independent mediating role, balances the goals of legislation against those goals set by the polity, against particular client problems, and against the need for internal consistency. All this leads Parsons to state approvingly that "the legal profession has a place in our social structure, and performs functions on its behalf" (1954:381). In sum, the legal profession, like the law, is also an integrative mechanism.

Parsons makes it clear that the law performs its basic function of system integration most effectively in a society with a high degree of value consensus and a low degree of enforcement through physical coercion. Restated, the law operates best in a free and open society. Thus, according to Parsons, the law is different from those forms of social control usually found in authoritarian and closed societies. He describes three characteristics of the law that differentiate it from other forms of coercive social control.

First, Parsons states that, unlike other social control mechanisms, the law lays particular stress on procedural matters like limiting and separating the powers of government. The law maintains social freedom and social order because it demarcates and delimits not only the powers of the executive office and the appellate courts but also its own powers of lawmaking.

Second, Parsons distinguishes the law from those types of social control that operate through the mass media (television, radio, newspapers, etc.) and "those that operate more privately and subtly in relation to the individual." An example of the former type of social control is propaganda; an example of the latter type is psychotherapy. Parsons considers psychotherapy as a form of social control because it exposes the patient "to a situation where forces can be brought to bear which are capable of breaking through the vicious circle of the generation of deviant motivation" (1951:313). It appears, therefore, that Parsons does not see law as having either the mass influence of propaganda nor the individualized influence of psychotherapy.

Third, Parsons posits that the law must be distinguished from those mechanisms of social control, like politics and religion, "that focus on the solution to the fundamental problems of value orientation involving decisions for the system as a whole." Thus, according Parsons, the law as a generalized mechanism of social control cannot be equated with a specific political doctrine like liberalism or a religious doctrine like Christianity, both of which have their own unique conceptions of the desirable society.

In sum, Parsons viewed law as a generalized mechanism of social control that achieves its primary function of systems integration by adjusting the interchanges among the various subsystems. As a mechanism of social control, the law works best in a free and open society. As such, the law imposes limits on itself, does not operate at the mass or individualized level of influence, and does not provide us with a conception of the desirable society. Roger Cotterrell, professor of legal theory at the University of London, states that the importance of the systems-functional approach for the sociology of law "is that Parsons's analysis makes possible a clear specification of law's location within this comprehensive picture of relationships between functional elements in social systems" (1992:81–82). In the next section we see that in reformulating Parson's functionalism, sociologists have recently produced a vision of the legal system as an autopoietic unit.

The Legal System as an Autopoietic Unit

Neofunctionalism, or a reconsideration, reinterpretation, and reformulation of Parsonian theory, emerged in the mid-1980s as a new theoretical development. The neofunctionalists' efforts to reappropriate Parsons have led them to elaborate more fully on certain aspects of his sociology. One of these efforts has been the further extension of Parsons's **theory of differentiation.** A product of social change, *differentiation* refers to the notion that postmodern society and its institutions have become more specialized, autonomous, technical, and abstract. Neofunctionalists Jeffrey Alexander and Paul Colomy depict this social condition as follows:

> Institutions gradually become more specialized. Familial control over social organization decreases. Political processes become less directed by the obligations and rewards of patriarchy, and the division of labor is organized more according to economic criteria than by reference simply to age and sex. Community membership can reach beyond ethnicity to territorial and political criteria. Religion becomes more generalized and abstract, more institutionally separated from and in tension with other spheres (1990:1).

A highly differentiated, postmodern society requires that neofunctionalists develop a new vision of law. With this in mind, let us now turn our attention to the legal sociology of neofunctionalist Niklas Luhmann.

Luhmann's Neofunctionalist Sociology of Law

In order to analyze a variety of social phenomena, including the law, German sociologist Niklas Luhmann has constructed an abstract conceptual scheme in the Parsonian tradition. Luhmann's conceptual scheme is a general theory of postmodern social systems.

In Luhmann's view, a *system* refers to any entity that draws and maintains a boundary that distinguishes its special internal environment from the external environment. Because its environments are highly complex, a system must reduce *environmental complexity*. If environmental complexity is not reduced, the system will be unable to selectively structure interrelated actions and will cease to exist.

Reducing environmental complexity is the basic functional need of all systems. According to Luhmann, environmental complexity may be reduced in time, space, and symbolic terms by delimiting all actions to the past, present, or future; the number of relations possible; and the number of symbols used to communicate. In other words, simplicity is achieved by paring down the number of actions conceivable to a system.

A *social* system, Luhmann tells us, is first of all a meaning system. Meaningful communication is the basic element of all social systems. Thus, a social system is said to exist when the actions of several people become meaningfully interrelated through the mechanism of *communication*. Luhmann (1977) further maintains that a postmodern social system is characterized by *functional differentiation*, or the fact that each of its single subsystems (the legal, economic, political, religious, etc.) performs a distinct and highly specialized function that cannot be fulfilled by any other subsystem. Luhmann is primarily interested in the internal operations of the functionally differentiated social system.

Finally, Luhmann contends that a postmodern social system is **autopoietic,** that is, it reproduces itself (self-producing), regulates itself (self-regulating), and continually refers to itself by distinguishing itself from its environment (self-referential). An autopoietic system cannot communicate with the environment or any other system. Since there are no such exchanges, communication is created, produced, and constituted by other communications within the system itself. In other words, a social system communicates only with itself.

The main characteristic of an autopoietic system is *reflexivity* (that is, the ability of the system to observe itself). On the basis of reflexivity, the system can choose to reproduce or not reproduce itself (that is, it can create its own decay or engage in further sociocultural evolution). The system's continuous regeneration is an inherently restless and dynamic process that (paradoxically) contributes to its self-maintenance and stability. Let us now see how the foregoing concepts produce a theoretical vision of the law as an autonomous system of communication.

The Law as an Autonomous System of Communication

According to Luhmann, environmental complexity, which is created by the infinite number of experiences and behaviors that are possible in the social world, is based on contingency. *Contingency* refers to "the danger of disappointment and the necessity to take risks" (Luhmann, 1985:25) by a person in light of the complexity of the environment. In other words, the more functionally differentiated a society, the greater the number of risks that individuals take in making decisions about how to relate to their complex environment. This is the case because, relative to a mechanical solidarity, in an organic solidarity (to use Durkheim's terms) there are many more people performing many more varied roles. Such a situation also increases the number of disappointments that a person experiences when making an incorrect decision in relating to others. Needless to say, the whole process creates a tremendous amount of uncertainty for everyone concerned.

Expectations reduce uncertainty by decreasing the number of risks and disappointments that a person will experience. The social system also prepares individuals to deal meaningfully with disappointments by helping them to foresee disappointments and by stabilizing their behavior when they are disappointed (otherwise deviance and other dysfunctional side effects are likely). Normative expectations serve to stabilize the disappointed individual's behavior by encouraging him or her to cling "to expectations despite disappointments" (Luhmann, 1988:22).

Luhmann describes *law* as "generalized normative behavioral expectations" (1985:77). He further states that the "law must be seen as a structure that defines the boundaries and selection types of the societal system. . . . [L]aw is essential as structure, because people cannot orient themselves towards others or expect their expectations without the congruent generalization of behavioral expectations" (1985: 105). Let us see how Luhmann's description of law plays itself out at the systems level.

According to Luhmann, a postmodern legal system is characterized by *positivity*, or the process by which the legal system makes, selects, validates, and changes the law. People accept the validity of legal decisions because the latter are made and selected by components of the legal system: the legislature and the courts.

The legal system becomes more positive as it becomes more differentiated and autonomous from the other social systems. While it is certainly true that the legislature (i.e., Congress) is part of the political system, the legislature can only make law in accordance with procedures stipulated by an element of the legal system (i.e., the Constitution). Moreover, as the legal system becomes increasingly independent from the other sectors of society, it performs a unique social function: it brings about general agreement concerning the behavioral expectations of different members of society. Put another way, the law contributes to normative consensus. Luhmann explains that the law accomplishes this task through the "exploitation of conflict perspectives" (1988:27). In other words, the legal system uses the resolutions of misunderstandings arising in social interaction as standards for helping people to determine which behavioral expectations they can expect and to avoid disappointment. The law also helps to resolve the conflicts that will inevitably emerge in the process of communication.

However, because social expectations and the meanings of interactions (i.e., acts of communication) between people are always changing, the legal system must also change. By revising its legal decisions, the law can deal with contingencies as they arise and adapt to its environment. The legal system has a mechanism that structures the making and changing of its legal decisions—procedural law. Procedural law regulates substantive law. In other words, the legal system engages in self-reflexivity because it uses first-order legal rules to make and change second-order legal rules. We may say that the autonomous legal system, in circular fashion, produces and reproduces a network of communications that allows it to communicate with itself. Let us look more closely at how the self-reflexivity of the legal system allows it to observe itself and communicate with itself. Our focus will be on one element of our legal system, the Federal Constitution.

Reflexivity and Self-Amendment

We begin with the eminently reasonable and heady question posed by legal philosopher Peter Suber: "If a constitution has an *amendment clause* (a provision describing or prescribing how to amend that constitution), then can that clause be used to amend itself?" (1990:xi). While the attempt to seriously grapple with this question is best left to others, we may nevertheless use its premise as a launching point for our discussion of the law's reflexivity.

The amendment clause of the U.S. Constitution is found in Article V and specifically explains the procedures by which a constitutional amendment may be proposed and ratified. The amendment clause, however, does not stipulate that it itself cannot be *amended* (changed by adding, deleting, or rephrasing). Therefore, theoretically at least, the amendment clause can be used to *repeal*, or annul, itself. This is an example of a system that creates its own destruction. Self-destruction aside, the Constitution does have the ability of continuous regeneration through self-amendment. To date, the U.S. Constitution has been amended sixteen times since the first ten original amendments—the Bill of Rights—were ratified in 1791.

To take but one example of the Constitution's continuous regeneration through self-amendment, the amendment clause of Article V allowed the proposal and ratification of the Eighteenth Amendment (National Prohibition) in 1919. It also allowed for the repeal of the Eighteenth Amendment by the Twenty-First Amendment in 1933. The salient point here is that the legal process is self-referential and occurs *within the system itself.* Moreover, the circular communication taking place within the system helps the system to constitute itself as a unity. As Luhmann explains: "Only the law can change the law. Only within the legal system can the change of legal norms be perceived as change of the law. . . . [T]he legal system reproduces itself by legal events and only by legal events" (1990:229). But not only does the legal system engage in autopoietic regeneration, it also engages in self-validation. Only the law can validate the law, and the law can only validate the law.

The legal system is self-referential and cannot communicate with its external environment. Because of the circularity of its communication, Luhmann refers to the legal system as a *normatively closed system.* This means that it "is a system of legal operations using normative self-reference to reproduce itself and to select information" (Luhmann, 1990:230). The illustration of constitutional self-amendment has shown this to be the case. However, the legal system is at the same time a *cognitively open system.* This means that the "legal system, basing itself on its normative self-reference, is an information-processing system, and it is able to adapt itself to changing environments" (Luhmann, 1990:230). As the legal system "learns" from its external social environment, it reinterprets itself according to the needs and demands of that environment. In the final analysis, the "law has to fit the society around" (Luhmann, 1990:235).

To be sure, Luhmann's sociology of law is exceedingly theoretical and abstract. Like Parsons, he has pitched his theory at a very high level of generality. This allows Luhmann to explain a great deal about the functioning of the legal system. By the same token, Luhmann's legal sociology appears to have limited practical utility. In the final section of this chapter we take a different track from that of analyzing the abstractions of Parsons's and Luhmann's theoretical frameworks and look instead at the empirical study of the social functioning of law.

The Empirical Study of the Social Functioning of Law

The next major functionalist whose work we examine, the Polish sociologist Adam Podgorecki, differs from Parsons and Luhmann in at least one fundamental respect: Podgorecki regards the sociology of law as an *empirical* science to be used in explaining the social functioning of law. This difference notwithstanding, Podgorecki provides a functionalist conception of law and society similar to that held by Talcott Parsons.

Podgorecki (1974) begins by distinguishing the sociology of law from the traditional study of jurisprudence. In Podgorecki's view, jurisprudence in Cold War Poland, consisting of the philosophy of law and the Marxist theory of law, was primarily engaged in abstract reflection and, therefore, virtually useless for practical application. Jurisprudence, as such, has been largely unsuccessful in explaining how the law really functions in society. By contrast, Podgorecki contends that the "natural" concern of the sociology of law is the study of the *functioning of law*. (By "functioning of law," Podgorecki means nothing more elaborate than the law's efficient and effective operation in the social system. His use of the concept is undoubtedly simpler that than of Parsons and Luhmann). For Podgorecki, the sociology of law differs from jurisprudence in regard to four significant characteristics: (1) the working law characteristic; (2) the social engineering characteristic; (3) the empirical research characteristic; and (4) the characteristic of social reality. In the next sections we examine, in some detail, each of these four characteristics of the sociology of law.

The Working Law Characteristic

Podgorecki describes legal sociology's working law characteristic as follows:

> The sociology of law aims at grasping law in its working, thus to determine the range of efficiency of short- or long-range impacts of law; it tries to find out what kinds of *legal instrument* are most suited for *remodeling* political attitudes, economic relationships, or human interaction; it seeks to discover whatever *negative by-products* ensue from law; it exposes the myths about how law functions and points out whatever elements of truth may reside in them, and inquires into their origin (emphases added, 1974:7).

In proposing the working law characteristic of the sociology of law, Podgorecki relies on the ideas of several thinkers whom we have previously discussed. For example, as will be recalled from Chapter 2, Roscoe Pound suggested that we should study not just the law "in the books" but also the law's concrete operations; that is, the law "in fact." We can also see the influence of Robert Merton in the above quote. Merton's attention to latent dysfunctions (what Podgorecki calls "negative by-products") sheds new light into the law's practical workings. Moreover, the ideas of Oliver Wendell Holmes and of the legal realist Karl Llewellyn—regarding the origins of law, their exposure of the myths of how the law functions, and their explanations of how judges arrive at judicial decisions—are also an inspiration to Podgorecki's sociology of law.

In short, the working law characteristic focuses the sociological study of law on the practical, the instrumental, the utilitarian, and the "remodeling" of society. Let us now see how the last focus is achieved through the social engineering characteristic.

The Social Engineering Characteristic

Podgorecki describes the second characteristic of the sociology of law as follows: "The main objective of sociological investigations into the functioning of law is to provide expert advice for social engineering, allowing for rational and effective remodeling of the human condition" (Podgorecki, 1974:8). At the heart of Podgorecki's legal sociology is this utilitarian idea of using the law as an instrument to plan and realize social change for the purpose of helping the social system achieve its desired goals.

Social engineering, or what Podgorecki has alternatively referred to as *sociotechnique*, is more practical in its application than general sociology:

> Whereas [general] sociology deals with the formulation and verification of statements concerning the relationships between diverse elements of social life, sociotechnique is concerned with how these statements and relationships can be used to bring about desired changes. [General s]ociology aims at discovering the nature of social reality, whereas sociotechnique aims at rational change of that reality (Podgorecki, 1963:48).

Social engineering through the law is the task of legal policy. According to Podgorecki, *legal policy* "would incorporate the more or less general sociological regularities and the values embodied in the system of law, and would offer practical directives aiming at rational social change, to be instrumentally brought about by law" (1974:10). Podgorecki further contends that in order to effectively and efficiently engage in social engineering, legal policy requires a set of theories that are couched at the middle-range level of abstraction.

The notion of the **middle-range theory** was first proposed by Robert K. Merton (1968) in reference to *empirical* generalizations that focus on particular phenomena. From such theories specific hypotheses can be derived, operationally defined, and empirically tested. The idea of the "theories of the middle range" was advanced by Merton in reaction to Parsons's all-encompassing, and highly abstract, grand theoretical scheme. Indeed, Podgorecki himself "mistrusts any closed system or grand theory of law . . . because its synthetic ambitions compel it to neglect empirical findings" (Ziegert, 1977:165). Seeing the sociology of law as largely empirical, Podgorecki formulates the middle-range hypothesis that he calls "the three levels of the functioning of law." Let us briefly look at this hypothesis and its relation to the social engineering characteristic of law.

The Hypothesis of the Three Levels of the Functioning of Law

Podgorecki (1967) maintains that people will have a high or low opinion about a particular law depending on the *prestige* that they attribute to it. It is on this basis that they will decide whether to accept or reject that law. Three variables, which

Podgorecki describes as acting like "prisms," influence people's attitudes about the law.

The first variable has to do with how people interpret the law within a particular type of *socioeconomic system*. The second variable has to do with the interpretation given to the law by those persons who are part of a particular reference group or *subculture*. The third variable has to do with the interpretation given to the law based on the *individual personalities* of the legislators who enacted the law as well as the people to whom the law is directed. Because the variables operate at three different levels of social reality, we may say that the personality variable functions within the framework of the subculture variable and the subculture variable functions within the framework of the socioeconomic variable. Like prisms, each of these variables may "refract," in various directions, the impact that an abstract law has on the attitudes of the people to whom it is addressed.

Podgorecki illustrates how the first variable, the socioeconomic system, influenced the meaning of Article 93 of the Polish Penal Code that made it a crime to forcibly change Poland's constitution. Prior to the Soviet Union gaining control of Poland in 1945, Article 93 protected the Polish constitution, which upheld a capitalist economy. After Soviet control of Poland in 1945, Article 93 was subsequently used to support a socialist economy in that country. This example shows how the same law is interpreted differently based on which socioeconomic system—capitalism or socialism—is in place.

In regard to the second variable, the subculture, Podgorecki lists six types of subcultures and their interpretive positions relative to the law: (1) the positive; (2) the negative; and (3) the neutral; as well as subcultures of, (4) people who are ultimately affected by the law; (5) people shaping the law; and (6) people administering the law. Let us see how the law is refracted in types (2) and (4) above; that is, in a negative subculture of people who are ultimately affected by the law.

As a grouping of criminals, the Mafia is a subculture because it has its own value system, or code of honor, called "omerta" (Cressey, 1969). The Mafia is a *negative subculture* because its members—with their involvement in racketeering, extortion, providing illicit goods and services, and so forth—reject the values of, and have little respect for, the valid legal system. Consequently, Mafiosi will be *ultimately affected by the law* in a manner different from that of a group of college students. Put in different words, relative to law-abiding college students, Mafiosi will have a very different opinion of, and respond differently to, a law like the Racketeer Influenced and Corrupt Organization Act (RICO).

Regarding the third variable, that of individual personality factors, Podgorecki notes that these factors account for the various attitudes toward the law. Personality factors include *sociodemographic traits* (age, education, occupation) and *psychological traits* (insecurity, inhibition, social maladjustment). Podgorecki contends that personality factors play an important role in influencing the meaning of the law and legal behavior. For instance, white-collar workers with relatively high levels of education, who lack feelings of insecurity, and who are between the ages of thirty-five and forty-nine, are more likely to obey the law than individuals who do not possess these demographic and psychological traits.

Taking the three-level hypothesis in its entirety, Podgorecki concludes that a law functions least effectively when it operates in an unpopular socioeconomic system that is subject to the antagonistic influence of a negative subculture and that is received by antilegalistically oriented individuals. The upshot is that Podgorecki considers the three-level hypothesis of the functioning of law a useful mechanism for social engineering. The three-level hypothesis tells the legislator "where to look for the social environments and individuals who are apt to fulfill the directives of law and, also, where resistance may arise" (Podgorecki, 1974:236).

The Empirical Research Characteristic

Legal sociology's third salient characteristic is that it "makes an effort to shape its studies so as to make them useful for practical applications" (Podgorecki, 1974:8). As a way of shaping its studies, Podgorecki insists that legal sociology employ those research methods available to it. These include the historical-descriptive method (involving evaluations of historical accounts about law and society), the ethnographic-comparative method (i.e., field research), the method for the analysis of legal materials, the experimental method, and the questionnaire and interview method. These research techniques permit the sociologist to collect empirical data that can later be applied practically in a rational effort at remodeling the human condition.

The Characteristic of Social Reality

The last characteristic of the sociology of law is that it "struggles with reality, trying to describe it in empirical terms and to give a fuller and clearer image of it than we now possess" (Podgorecki, 1974:8). As such, the sociology of law must be actively involved in pragmatic research.

Before the actual operations of social engineering are begun, the sociologist must have an exact knowledge about the practical conditions he or she is analyzing. Podgorecki argues that this knowledge is obtained through "social diagnosis." **Social diagnosis** involves fully describing, through concrete research, social phenomena in a very simple way and without having to explain them through an abstract theoretical framework (Podgorecki, 1968:67). To be sure, Podgorecki is not against using abstract theory to better understand social reality. The important point for him, however, is to formulate middle-range hypotheses that consider the practical *motives* of individuals. If used properly, says Podgorecki, "the concept of social system could lead towards thinking in categories of a total social engineering" (1971:27).

In short, Podgorecki sees the sociology of law as a practical science concerned with establishing legal policy as well as a theoretical discipline concerned with studying the functioning of law. We now turn to what Podgorecki has to say about the functioning of law.

The Functioning of Law

In Podgorecki's view, the law can only be truly effective if it is based on a sociological theory that anticipates the law's functional and dysfunctional consequences. This theory must consider the psychosocial factors that influence people to obey the law. Understanding what motivates people to engage in legal behavior will help the legislator in drafting effective law.

From the foregoing comments it is clear that Podgorecki does not base the law's principal functioning on the use of coercive sanctions. Indeed, with only passing regard to political coercion, he gives the following theoretical-descriptive definition of law: *"law is a social norm which is based on four reciprocal elements belonging to the parallel parties and containing two corresponding pairs of rights and duties"* (1974:272). This definition forms Podgorecki's tetrad conception of law.

The tetrad conception of law. In his definition of law Podgorecki implicitly distinguishes between social norms and legal norms. Legal norms, he maintains, consist of a **tetrad**, or a set of four rights and duties. Accordingly, each party in a bilateral relationship has a right and a duty in relation to the other party or, as Podgorecki said, "the tetrad conception of the law is based on the principle of accepted reciprocity" (Podgorecki, 1974:273). For example, in a business transaction the seller has a duty to surrender the product to the buyer after the latter has purchased it. Conversely, the buyer has a duty to pay for the product before it is surrendered. The seller, in turn, has a right to payment and the buyer has the right to own the product. Therefore, for Podgorecki, any social relationship involving the mutual reciprocity of rights and duties possesses a legal-normative character. This notion shares several obvious commonalities with Malinowski's idea that law is based on the principle of reciprocity and binding obligations. And much like Parsons and Luhmann, Podgorecki also sees the law as fulfilling certain basic functions: (1) integration, (2) petrification, (3) motivation, (4) education, and (5) reduction.

The five functions of law. The *integrative* function of law occurs when the parties involved in a reciprocal relationship exchange rights and duties. As we have seen, this function has been underscored by every theorist that we have considered in this chapter. Podgorecki reiterates the law's integrative function by explaining that the very act of exchange brings cohesiveness to the relationship.

It appears that Podgorecki's functions of petrification, motivation, and education can be subsumed under Parsons's functional imperative of latency. It will be recalled that latency refers to the fact that social systems maintain the institutionalized patterns of conformist behavior by socializing and motivating individuals to display such behavior. The educational, familial, and religious systems meet the latency function by transmitting values and norms to individuals.

According to Podgorecki, the law's function of *petrification* serves to institutionalize interpersonal relationships thus making them semipermanent fixtures of the social structure. Moreover, the *motivation* function impels individuals to act in accordance with those normative expectations prescribed by the legal system. Simply put, the law motivates people to engage in conformist behavior.

Podgorecki's fourth function of law is that of *education*. Podgorecki contends that through the process of socialization, the law instructs people to habitually engage in conformist behavior.

Finally, integration and petrification, says Podgorecki, lead to the *reduction* function of law. That is, the law reduces the number of possible relationships between people and, in the process, simplifies and gives order and predictability to a complex social world. This last function appears to closely parallel Luhmann's notion of reducing environmental complexity.

In conclusion, we may say that Podgorecki's view of law and society is generally shared by those sociologists and anthropologists whose work has been informed by structural-functionalism. However, relative to the other theorists, Podgorecki's sociology of law tends to be much more practical and empirical. For him, legal sociology's ultimate objective is to formulate middle-range hypotheses that will aid sociologists, legislators, and policymakers in engineering rational changes in the human condition through the law. These changes can be realized, however, only when we have an empirical understanding of how the law functions in social reality.

SUMMARY

Structural-functionalism is one sociological paradigm that has greatly influenced the sociology of law. This chapter introduced structural-functionalism and explained how functionalists view society as an integrated system comprised of differentiated and interrelated subsystems. Functionalists believe that the object of the social system is to preserve order and maintain equilibrium. The system accomplishes this objective by meeting its needs and by regulating the behavior of individuals. In regard to the latter initiative, the system must ensure that individuals engage in cooperative behavior and abide by the consensual norms and values of society.

We began a detailed understanding of structural-functionalism by examining its nineteenth-century beginnings. We first noted that Auguste Comte's organic analogy of society (an analogy subsequently adopted by Herbert Spencer and others) set the stage for the systemic and structural-functionalist approaches of the twentieth century. Next, we discussed Emile Durkheim's major statement concerning functionalist analysis: Social facts are functional or beneficial to society because they satisfy society's general needs and play a useful role.

Following this, we turned our attention to the functionalist work of anthropologists A. R. Radcliffe-Brown and Bronislaw Malinowski. Radcliffe-Brown stressed the interplay between social structure and social activities. By considering both of these phenomena, Radcliffe-Brown was able to see society as a functional unity. In his view, the relationship between structure and activity produces harmony in the social system.

Malinowski also considered the functional interplay between social structure and social activity in his study of "primitive" law. According to him, primitive law has three main functions: (1) it creates institutional patterns of activity by telling people what they should expect from each other, (2) it regulates social behavior by demanding that people engage in reciprocal and binding obligations, and (3) it satisfies the biological need to share. The end result of these functions is that the law contributes to social integration.

We next looked at Robert K. Merton and Talcott Parsons's contributions to the structural-functionalist paradigm. Merton's concepts of manifest and latent functions and dysfunctions shifted the paradigm's theoretical focus from "benefits" to "consequences." Accordingly, sociologists now see the consequences of social structures and social activities as being positive or negative, intended or unintended. Parsons, on the other hand, advanced the notion of social system. As a social system, society is made up of institutional subsystems. According to Parsons, in order to operate at optimum capacity all social (sub)systems must perform the four functional imperatives of adaptation, goal-attainment, integration, and latency. Following a brief discussion of Parsons's concept of social system and the functional imperatives, we began a specific examination of the legal system and its social functions.

Parsons maintained that the legal system is particularly adept at performing the integrative function since it adjusts, coordinates, and facilitates the interchanges among the various subsystems. In so doing, the law mitigates social conflicts. Parsons further argued that the legal system must engage three processes of adjustment in order to effectively perform the integrative function: (1) the law must be articulated at a high level of generality, (2) the law must have a measured degree of plasticity, and (3) the law must function as a generalized mechanism of social control. These processes of adjustment, he stated, ultimately lead to system integration.

Aside from its primary function of system integration, Parsons contended that the law also provides the function of normative consistency. However, before these two functions can be accomplished, the law must deal with the questions of sanctions, jurisdiction, legitimation, and interpretation. In answering these questions Parsons showed that the law is more or less autonomous from the polity. Moreover, he showed that the law acts as a generalized mechanism of social control and operates best in a society with a high degree of value and normative consensus and a low degree of coercive enforcement.

We next considered Niklas Luhmann's view of the legal system as an autopoietic unit, or an autonomous system that reproduces itself. In this regard we noted that, through the process of self-amendment, U.S. constitutional law has reproduced itself sixteen times since 1791. We further noted that since the legal system is self-referential, it cannot communicate with its external environment but it can "learn" from it. As such, the law is able to respond and adapt to political, economic, and other changes.

Finally, in the last section of the chapter, we examined Adam Podgorecki's empirical study of the social functioning of law. He described the sociology of law as a pragmatic science invested with the working law characteristic, the social engineering characteristic, the empirical research characteristic, and the characteristic of social reality. Endowed as such, Podgorecki believed that the sociology of law must engage in the rational and effective engineering of society. However, Podgorecki also stated that unless law- and policymakers understand the law's efficient and effective operation in the social system—that is, its functioning—the law cannot be used as an instrument for bringing about rational social change.

As we have seen in this chapter, the structural-functionalist paradigm underscores the *consensual* norms and values of society, the social system's orderly state of *equilibrium*, and the law's ultimate function of social *integration*. In the next chapter we examine the alternative paradigm to structural-functionalism, conflict theory.

The Law and Social Control

Talcott Parsons

From a variety of points of view I think it can be said that law and sociology have an unusually wide area of overlapping interests. But for various reasons the exploration of these interests and the implications of the relationships have not been very adequately pursued. Perhaps the very extent to which sociology is such a young discipline plays a major part in bringing about this situation.

It may be useful to call attention, at the start, to two salient general considerations about the law as seen from a social scientist's point of view. In the first place, law is not a category descriptive of actual concrete behavior but rather concerns patterns, norms, and rules that are applied to the acts and to the roles of persons and to the collectivities of which they are members. Law is an aspect of social structure but one that lies on a particular level, which should be carefully specified. In a certain set of sociological terms I should call it an institutional phenomenon. It deals with normative patterns to which various kinds of sanctions are applied. This is a level that on general sociological grounds it is important to distinguish from that of the concrete structure of collectivities and roles in them.

The second salient characteristic of law is that it is nonspecific with respect to functional content at lower levels. Functional content, understood in the usual sociological senses, refers to such categories as economic, political, and a variety of others. There is law defining the Constitution and political processes within it. There is a law of

business and of labor and the relations of business to labor. There is a law of the family, of personal relationships, and a variety of other subjects. Indeed *any* social relationship can be regulated by law, and I think every category of social relationship with which sociologists are concerned is found to be regulated by law in some society somewhere.

It seems justified to infer from these considerations that law should be treated as a generalized mechanism of social control that operates diffusely in virtually all sectors of the society.[1]

Law, of course, is not just a set of abstractly defined rules. It is a set of rules backed by certain types of sanctions, legitimized in certain ways, and applied in certain ways. It is a set of rules that stands in certain quite definite relationships to specific collectivities and the roles of individuals in them. Perhaps we can approach a little closer characterization of the place of law in a society by attempting to analyze some of these relationships, and by showing some of the conditions on which the effectiveness of a system of rules can be held to rest.

The Functions of Law and Some Structural Implications

Let us suggest that in the larger social perspective the primary function of a legal system is integrative. It serves to mitigate potential elements of conflict and to oil the machinery of social intercourse. It is, indeed, only by adherence to a system of rules that systems of social interaction can function without breaking down into overt or chronic covert conflict.

Normative consistency may be assumed to be one of the most important criteria of effectiveness of a system of law. By this I mean that the rules formulated in the system must ideally not subject the individuals under their jurisdiction to imcompatible expectations or obligations—or, more realistically, not too often or too drastically. In the nature of the case, since they act in many different contexts and roles, individuals will be subject to many particularized rules. But the rules must somehow all build up to a single, relatively consistent system.

In this respect we may suggest that there are four major problems that must be solved before such a system of rules can operate determinately to regulate interaction. (Even though the questions are not explicitly put by the actors, an observer analyzing how the system operates must find some solution to each of them.)

The first problem concerns the basis of legitimation of the system of rules. The question is why, in the value or meaning sense, should I conform to the rules, should I fulfill the expectations of the others with whom I interact? What in other words is the *basis* of right? Is it simply that some authority says so without further justification? Is it some religious value, or is it that I and the others have some natural rights that it is wrong to violate? What is the basis of this *legitimation?*

The second problem concerns the *meaning* of the rule for me or some other particular actor to a particular situation in a particular role. In the nature of the case, rules must be formulated in general terms. The general statement may not cover all of the circumstances of the particular situation in which I am placed. Or there may be two or more rules, the implications of which for my action are currently contradictory. Which one applies and in what degree and in what way? What specifically are my obligations in this par-

ticular situation or my rights under the law? This is the problem of *interpretation*.

The third basic problem is that of the consequences, favorable or unfavorable, that should follow from conforming to the rules to a greater or lesser degree or from failing to conform. These consequences will vary according to the degrees of nonconformity and according to the circumstances in which, and reasons for which, deviation occurs. Under a system of law, however, the question of whether or not conformity occurs can never be a matter of indifference. This, of course, is the problem of *sanctions*. What sanctions apply and by whom are they applied?

Finally, the fourth problem concerns to whom and under what circumstances a given rule or complex of rules, with its interpretations and sanctions, applies. This is the problem of *jurisdiction*, which has two aspects: (1) What authority has jurisdiction over given persons, acts, and so on in defining and imposing the norms? (2) To which classes of acts, persons, roles, and collectivities does a given set of norms apply?

We may now attempt to say something about the conditions of institutionalizing answers to these questions in a large-scale, highly differentiated society. At the outset I want to suggest that a legal system must not itself be regarded in an analytical sense as a political phenomenon, although it must be closely related to political functions and processes. The two systems are most intimately related with respect to the problems of sanctions and of jurisdiction. Of these, the connection with respect to sanctions is in a sense the more fundamental.

We may speak of the existence of a continuum of sanctions, ranging from pure inducement to sheer and outright coercion. By inducement I mean the offer of advantages as a reward for actions that the inducer wishes his role-partner to perform. By coercion I mean the threat of negative sanctions for nonperformance of the desired course of action. Both inducement and coercion operate in all social relationships. The basis of the relation of law to political organization lies primarily in the fact that at certain points the question must inevitably arise as to the use of physical force or its threat as a means of coercion; that is, a means of assertion of the bindingness of the norm. If physical force is altogether excluded the ultimate coercive sanction is expulsion, as for example in the case of excommunication from a church. In many cases, however, expulsion will not be a sufficiently severe sanction to prevent undesirable action from taking place. And if it is not sufficient, resort must be had to force. Force is, at least in the preventive sense, the ultimate negative sanction.

Thus if rules are taken sufficiently seriously, inevitably the question will sometime be raised of resort to physical sanction in a preventive context. On the other hand, the use of force is perhaps the most serious potential source of disruption of order in social relationships. For this reason in all ordered societies there is at least a qualified monopoly of the more serious uses of physical force. This monopoly is one of the primary characteristics of the political organization, in its more highly developed forms leading up to the state. If, then, it becomes necessary in certain contingencies to use or threaten physical force as a sanction for the enforcement of legal norms, and if the legitimate use of physical force is monopolized in the agency of the state, then the legal system must have an adequate connection with the state in order to use its agencies as the administrators of physical sanctions.

The problem of jurisdiction is obviously closely linked with that of sanctions. One of the main reasons that the jurisdiction of political bodies is territorially defined is precisely the importance of the use of physical force in their functioning. Physical force can be applied only if the individual to whom it is directed can be reached in a physical location at a given time. It is therefore inherently linked to territoriality of jurisdiction. Hence a legal system that relies at certain crucial points on the sanctions of physical force must also be linked to a territorial area of jurisdiction.

A further source of linkage between law and the state requires me to say a word about the imperative of consistency. On the level of the con-

tent of norms as such, this imperative exerts a strong pressure toward universalism (a trait that is inherent in systems of law generally). I spoke above of consistency from the point of view of not subjecting the same individual to contradictory rules. The obverse of this imperative is the recognition that, when a rule has been defined as a rule, it must be impartially applied to all persons or other social units that fall within the criteria that define the application of the rule. There are inherent limitations in systematizing legal systems, that is, in making them consistent, if this criterion of universalistic application cannot be followed.

In its practical implication this criterion of universalism, however, connects closely with territoriality, because it is only within territorial limits that enforcement of universalistically defined rules can effectively be carried out. It follows from these considerations that enforcement agencies in a legal system are generally organs of the state. They carry a special political character.

Enforcement agencies are, however, ordinarily not the central organs of the state. They are not primarily policy-forming organs but rather are organs that are put at the service of the many different interests that are covered by the rules of a legal system. The fact that even the enforcement agencies are not primarily political is vividly brought out by their relations to the courts. In most legal systems what they may do, and to a considerable degree how they may do it, is defined and supervised by the courts. Where enforcement agencies gain too strong a degree of independence of the courts, it may be said that the legal system itself has been subordinated to political considerations, a circumstance that does occur in a variety of cases.

The interpretive and legitimizing functions in law are even less directly political than are the sanctioning and the jurisdictional functions. First let us take the legitimation function, which concerns to an important degree the relation and the distinction between law and ethics.

We may say that, in the deeper sense, the lawyer as such tends to take legitimation for granted.

It is not part of his professional function, whether as attorney or as judge, to decide whether the existence of a given rule is morally or politically justified. His function rather concerns its interpretation and application to particular cases. Even where, as under a federal system, there may be certain problems of the conflict of laws, it is the higher legal authority—for example, that of the Constitution—that is the lawyer's primary concern, not the moral legitimation of the Constitution itself. Nevertheless, the legal system must always rest on proper legitimation. This may take forms rather close to the legal process itself, such as the question of enactment by proper procedures by duly authorized bodies. For example, legislatures are responsible to electorates. But in back of proper procedure and due authorization of lawmaking bodies lies the deeper set of questions of ultimate legitimation.

In the last analysis this always leads in some form or other either to religious questions or to those that are functionally equivalent to religion. Law from this point of view constitutes a focal center of the relations between religion and politics as well as other aspects of a society.

Turning now to "interpretation," it must be noted that here again there are two basic foci of this function. One concerns the integrity of the system of rules itself; it is rule-focused. The other concerns the relation of rules to the individuals and groups and collectivities on whom they impinge. In a legal sense this latter function may be said to be client-focused. Taken together in these two aspects, the interpretive function may be said to be the central function of a legal system.

The first, the rule-focused aspect of the law, is primarily the locus of the judiciary function, particularly at the appellate levels. The second is the focus of the functions of the practicing legal profession. With respect to the judiciary certain sociological facts are saliently conspicuous. Wherever we can speak of a well-institutionalized legal system, the judiciary are expected to enjoy an important measure of independence from the central political authority. Of course, their integration with it must be so close that, for example, practically always judges are appointed by political authority. But usually (unless holding office for specified terms) they enjoy tenure, they are not removable except for cause, and it is considered most improper for political authority to put direct pressure on them in influencing their specific decisions. Furthermore, though not a constitutional requirement in the United States it is certainly general practice that judges, the more so the higher in the system, must be lawyers in a professional sense. This is not a function ordinarily open to the ordinary lay citizen.

Furthermore, the judicial function as part of the attorney's function is centered in a special type of social organization: the court. This is an organization that directly institutionalizes the process of arriving at decisions. This is done, of course, through the bringing of cases to the court for adjudication, in the course of which not only are the rights and obligations of individual petitioners settled but the rules themselves are given authoritative interpretations. We might perhaps say that authoritative interpretation in this sense is perhaps the most important of the judicial functions.

With respect to the legal profession in the sense of the practicing attorney, there is a conspicuous dual character. The attorney is, on the one hand, an officer of the court. As such he bears a certain public responsibility. But at the same time, he is a private adviser to his client, depending on the client for his remuneration and enjoying a privileged confidential relation to the client. This relation between lawyer and client parallels, to an interestingly high degree, that between physician and patient, its confidential character being one of the principal clues to this parallel. It is focused, however, on situations of actual or potential social conflict and the adjudication and smoothing over of these conflicts. It is not primarily person-oriented as the health-care functions are, but rather social relationship-oriented.

Performance of the interpretive function is facilitated, we have said, by such structural devices as "judicial independence" from political pressure, professionalization of the judicial role, and institutionalization of the decision-making process. . . .

Law and Other Mechanisms of Social Control

Despite these general ways in which lawyers, as professionals, contribute to social control, it is important to note certain crucial differences between law and other control mechanisms. A useful point from which to approach the distinction, and from which to make clear its functional importance, is the set of remarks made above in connection with the functions of legitimation and interpretation.

From the combination of the interpretive function and that of legitimation, we may begin to understand some of the reasons for the emphasis in the law on procedural matters. As Max Weber put it, "the rationality of law is formal rather than substantive." Certainly one of the basic conceptions in our Anglo-Saxon legal systems is that of due process. Here, of course, it even goes to the point where the question of substantive justice may not be an issue, and injustice may have no legal remedy so long as correct formal procedure has been observed. It may be noted that if pressure becomes strong with reference to either the question of enforcement or the question of legitimation, it may operate against the integrity of the procedural traditions and rules. People who are sufficiently exercised about questions of substantive justice and injustice are often not strong respecters of complicated legal procedure. Similarly, if disobedience to law is sufficiently blatant and scandalous, there may be a demand for direct action that altogether by-passes the rules of procedure.

From this point of view, it may become evident that the prominence of and the integrity of a legal system as a mechanism of social control is partly a function of a certain type of social equilibrium. Law flourishes particularly in a society in which the most fundamental questions of social values are not currently at issue or under agitation. If there is sufficiently acute value conflict, law is likely to go by the board. Similarly it flourishes in a society in which the enforcement problem is not too seriously acute. This is particularly true where

there are strong informal forces reinforcing conformity with at least the main lines of the legally institutionalized tradition. In many respects, modern England is a type case of this possibility.

Law, then, as a mechanism of control may be said to stand in a position midway between two other types of mechanisms:

(a) On the one hand, there are two classes of mechanisms that focus primarily on the motivation of the individual: those that operate through the media of mass communication—through the distribution and allocation of information and the concomitant emotional attitudes; and those that operate more privately and subtly in relation to the individual. Though there are many of these latter mechanisms, a particularly conspicuous one in our own society, administered by a sister professional group, is that of therapy. The line of distinction between questions that can be handled by legal procedure and those that involve therapy is a particularly important one.

(b) In another direction, the law must be distinguished from those mechanisms of social control that focus on the solution of fundamental problems of value orientation involving basic decisions for the system as a whole, rather than regulation of the relations of the parts to each other. Politics and religion both operate more in this area, and because of this difference it is particularly important to distinguish law from politics and religion.

Finally, it may perhaps be suggested that law has a special importance in a pluralistic liberal type of society. It has its strongest place in a society where there are many different kinds of interests that must be balanced against each other and that must in some way respect each other. As I have already noted, in the totalitarian type of society, which is in a great hurry to settle some fundamental general social conflict or policy, law tends to go by the board.

Both individually and collectively, law imposes restraints on precipitate and violent action. I might recall the words with which the recipients of law degrees are greeted by the President of Harvard University at every commencement. He says, "You are now qualified to help administer those wise restraints which make men free."

NOTE

1. Of course it is better adapted to some problems of social control than to others. It is notorious that the more refined and settled sentiments of individuals cannot be controlled by legal prescription. Nevertheless, it is one of the most highly generalized mechanisms in the whole society. It is located primarily, as I said, on the institutional level. It is not isolated but is one of a family of mechanisms of control. At the end of this discussion I will sketch its relations to one or two others.

Three Levels of the Functioning of Law

Adam Podgorecki

There is a view, tacitly accepted by almost all theorists and practitioners, that a legal enactment, legitimately issued and marked by valid authority, functions automatically. Is it really so?

The paradox is that a lawmaker always devotes very much effort to prepare his normative act, but—as a matter of principle—is not interested in its efficiency; he can be compared with a person who sends a letter by registered mail but fails to put down his own address, assuming naively that the post office will find the addressee even if he has moved out, or has become ill and has been sent to the hospital. Similarly, the science of law is interested mainly in the origin of law, its sources and its interpretation, but not in the actual functions performed by it. The only legal reality for lawyers is the world of legal enactments. Often they fail to see the real world behind it, although that is what the enactments are meant to refer to.

The hypothesis of the three levels of the functioning of law states the following: an abstract legal precept enacted by the legislature influences social behavior through a threefold connection. The first independent variable in the process is the content or meaning of the letter of the law in the given social and economic system where it is an element of the valid legal pattern. The second independent variable is the type of subculture functioning within the larger social and economic system as a link between the directives of the lawmakers and the actual behavior of people to whom the law is addressed. The third independent vari-

able can modify, in various directions, the actual functioning of an abstract legal precept within a given social and economic system and within a given legal subculture. It represents the personality types of those who are the ultimate agents carrying out the legal directives. An abstract legal precept begins to function (and to be expressed in social behavior) when it reaches its interpreter in the form of a complex conjunction. The constituent parts of such a conjunction are: the precept in itself and three meta-norms: the first derives from the character of the social and economic system, the second takes its contents from the definite legal subculture, and the third follows from the personality of the individual who makes the decision to behave lawfully.

This scheme might appear to be another abstract model, built of synthetic definitions. However, we shall present considerations and data from empirical studies, aiming to prove that this model is an attempt at a synthesis of empirical observations.

Article 93, paragraph 2 of the [Polish] penal code of July 15, 1932, valid until January 1, 1970, stated: "Whoever attempts to change by force the constitution of the Polish state is liable to a term of imprisonment of not less than ten years, or until the end of his life." In a somewhat modified version (article 79 of the Polish Army penal code) this regulation has been valid for many years in the People's Poland. Thus, the same precept has been functioning within a social and economic system quite different from the one that existed when it was issued. Its functioning, however, has been quite different. Before the war (1939) it protected the system of private property, the means of production and large land estates, a political system within which the communist party was illegal; the main task of this precept was to prevent the realization of the conditions which prevail now [1974]. After 1945, until 1970, the same precept has had a quite different meaning. It was aimed against the system in which it had been issued, since the repression provided by it threatened those who wanted to restore the capitalist system.

The proposition that a legal precept can be regarded as a vessel with contents poured into it by the actual conditions of its functioning is also confirmed when we analyze the detailed data concerning several institutions of a legal system. . . .

The general statement that the action of an abstract legal precept depends on various extraneous elements which, while the law remains unchanged, modify its contents, adapt and fit it into the changing social and economic situations, could be further justified by other similar examples. However, it is not necessary to multiply examples. The significant point is that in general the same legal norm can act in various ways under different systemic conditions. It can function as it used to; the direction of its impact can shift totally; it can cease to have any effect at all (although it has remained valid and legitimate); or its influence can in part be modified.

Our former distinction between legal principles and legal prescriptions finds a particular application in the present context if we take into account that the social system is a variable factor. Let us remember that a legal principle is a piece of law based on social acceptance and inculcated into the common legal sentiment of a group, or several groups, or of the whole society. Although every legal principle is written down in the form of a legal precept, it is additionally supported by several norms of custom, ethics, social interaction, etc. On the other hand, legal prescriptions deal above all with the formal, procedural aspects of behavior, and they are addressed to professionals who are versatile in handling them. Legal prescriptions form the base of the legal constructions.

Sometimes the constructions are also supported by elements of principles giving them social meaning. Now, if we take this distinction into account, it can easily be seen that a change of a social system would have a different influence upon the legal principles and the legal prescriptions. When the social, economic and political structure undergoes some changes, and when the new administrative machinery has already been established, it is easier to introduce new prescriptions than to modify the principles. Since legal principles are not susceptible to rapid changes—if only because of their deep social rooting—it is much easier to change the conditions of their application, the categories of persons to whom they apply, the procedures of their realization, etc.

Sometimes revolutionary changes (which cause social and economic changes without parallel changes in the major parts of the legal system) offer what can be considered experimental situations clearly revealing the role of the independent variable denoted as the social and economic system. However, if the changes are introduced gradually and inconspicuously, an illusion can arise that the new system contributes nothing to the independently functioning legal norms. Thus, we may conclude that the first prism through which the legal precept is refracted on its way from lawmakers to those whom it concerns, is the set of social and economic conditions in the given type of social system.

In every society there is a set of general social values such as ideas, knowledge, art, institutions, patterns of behavior, material products, etc., which together constitute the culture of the society. On the other hand, various narrower social environments and circles within a society cherish their different, specific subcultures. Their peculiarities are that the values cherished by the particular subcultures are typical for them only and they frequently contribute little to the general cultural store. But in cases when the subcultures are socially negative, their influence upon the encompassing culture of the whole society can be more or less noxious or destructive. Very often, if we observe behavior occurring in some specific environments, e.g., among artists, soldiers, hippies, or students, we cannot understand what is going on without considering the peculiarity of the observed social group.

There are also legal subcultures. Besides the valid legal system, in every society (if we leave aside the primitive societies which usually do not have valid legal systems) there is something else, described as legal sentiment, legal feeling, intuitive law, etc. Without going into semantic niceties here let us say that in every society there is some degree of obedience to law and it has a certain prestige; there are always moral attitudes, customs and social patterns which support or impede the functioning of the whole legal system. The total set of habits and values related to acceptance, evaluation, criticism and realization of the valid legal system can be called the general legal culture of the society. The legal culture can be more or less developed, and its particular parts can disclose various degrees of harmonization with the rest. As we have already mentioned, deviations from the principles of the general legal culture occur, for in various environments law is administered and realized in various ways. The types of the czarist Russian "chinovniki" (officials of minor rank) as sketched by Chekhov or by Dostoyevski represent a quite peculiar legal culture. There are also negative legal subcultures of criminals, e.g. thieves with their complex set of habits and rituals, their rules about distribution of loot, their moral and honor codes, their "dintoira" (Polish slang for a tribunal of thieves; the lynch law of criminals settling their disputes), old age security measures, etc.; all such institutions involve elements of the *sui generis* "law" of the group, although this law is at odds with the general legal order. As we know from the study by Z. Bozyczko,[1] there is a principle forbidding a thief to take away his partner's wife or mistress, in particular when he is in prison. It is forbidden to hamper another pickpocket at work; on the contrary, if one notices that another works without sufficient protection, one should provide a "curtain" ("wall"), without the right to claim part of the profit for such service. The military subculture, highly formalized, is based less on

the respect of attractive legal principles and more on the habit of obedience to the actual directives and orders of superiors. One of the most remarkable observations on the negative hooligan subculture—particularly strongly opposed to existing legal principles—reports that a person who passes from this subculture to one of people seeking a more stable status as a result of marriage, almost overnight begins to accept a legal subculture which is incompatible with that of his former group.[2] ...

... [S]everal types of legal subculture can be discerned. We can speak about negative, positive, or neutral legal subcultures. We can also speak about the legal subculture of people who are ultimately affected by law (to whom legal norms are addressed), about the legal subculture of people shaping the law (deputies, members of councils, administrators), and about the legal subculture of people administering or realizing law (the so-called minions of the law, professionally inducing others to lawful behavior).

The most puzzling problem for traditional formalist lawyers is the existence of negative legal subcultures. They ask, how on earth can a negative legal subculture exist if valid law is in principle positive? In spite of such naive (or based on pretended ignorance) statements, there are data pointing to the existence of broader or narrower negative legal subcultures. Studies of recidivism show that imprisonment is not very effective in discouraging repetitious crime. Recidivists have their own outlook and legal awareness, their own peculiar evaluation of law consisting of negative judgments about legal precepts as well as legal institutions. Here are some typical attitudes: "Only some people are afraid of punishment." "Punishment (in prison) is no obstacle to anyone." "People who are not afraid of stealing are not afraid of punishment either." "If someone is out to steal, he'll do it, punishment or not." "If someone is about to do something, he will do it anyway, even if a dozen cops were on guard." "It can happen to anyone—that he gets caught and nobody minds." "As to myself, no prison would stop me from stealing." Another recidivist, thirty years old, "laughs out of the courts and prisons." "Only a

sucker is afraid of prison, or if he falls under recidivism for the first time" (i.e., if he is put in a cell
with recidivists). "Prison won't help or scare those
who steal; they don't while they're in, and as soon
as they get out, they'd do it again even before they
get home." "No punishment will stop him; he
must make a break and stop by himself."[3] These
declarations clearly illustrate the atmosphere of the
recidivist subculture from which the re-socializing
function of punishment is returned as a table-
tennis ball.

Another study revealed that the percentage
of juvenile delinquents having collaborated with
adults in criminal actions did not exceed 9 percent
of all the juveniles sentenced for offenses;[4] this
proves that it is not adults who push the juveniles
toward delinquency. Other investigations suggest
that there is a specific intervening factor involved.
With reference to his research data Cz. Czapów
has pointed out that the three basic features of the
negative juvenile delinquent subculture mentioned
in the literature have been found empirically in Polish investigations also. The features are: malevo-
lence, negation of all values, and the non-pragmatic
character of damage or injury.[5] Of course, not all
offenses committed by juveniles are direct effects
of the negative influence of the legal subculture,
and not all offenses by juvenile delinquents are
committed in groups. But, what has been committed by team work (and the percentage is as
high as 34–39 percent) bears the imprint of criminal collusion—and thus of the criminal subculture.

From the above data we can conclude that a
negative legal subculture (or, rather, anti-culture)
influences the behavior of those to whom the legal
norms are addressed. In turn, different investigations indicate that legal behavior and, in particular, legal decisions taken by the so-called minions
of the law also depend on specific legal subcultures
typical of their professional circles. For example,
studies show that the practice of prosecutors in
similar cases—prosecuting juvenile delinquents
cooperating with adult criminals—can be quite
different. A thorough statistical analysis of this
problem supports "a suspicion that what determines the percentage of this category of cases sent

to regular courts are not actual differences between situations in various parts of the country,
but rather the *local practices of prosecutors*"[6] (emphasis by the present author). Thus, a definite
judicial *usus*, or a specific clerical subculture, may
cause deeds which are identical from the point of
view of their normative qualification to be handled differently in practice.

Another study of the practical activities of
courts concerned Norwegians who refused to be
drafted into the army (conscientious objectors). It
showed that there were essential differences in the
practice of decision-making by various courts.
Namely, courts in southern and northern Norway
clearly displayed different styles in handling such
cases. The differences could be explained, on one
hand, by the specific features of the accused (e.g.
the accused was an emotional atheist, a Nord-
lander, and an unskilled worker, who refused to be
drafted from the outset) and, on the other hand,
by the peculiar styles of verdict-making prevailing
in the different circles of judges.[7]

> The investigations carries out, point to a reg-
> ularity which concerns all the law-breakers:
> what is usually defined as an offense—its dis-
> covery and hearing in court—is a result of
> two processes. The first of them involves the
> trespassers, the other is related to the court
> authorities. This principle, revealed by our
> investigations, has obviously great and impor-
> tant consequences, as I believe, for various
> important fields of criminology. . . .

Summing up what we have said about legal
subcultures and using the quoted results of various empirical studies as illustrations, we can say
that the second prism, through which a legal message is refracted on its way from the law-makers
to those for whom it is aimed, is the specific
content of a legal subculture influencing the attitudes of those who create the law or who control
its creation. Thus, within the same social and economic system, various types of legal subcultures
cause or determine various types of legal behavior.
However, even within the same socioeconomic system and the same legal subculture, legal

and illegal actions of particular subjects will be different because of the personality differences among people to whom the law is addressed. As has been said, different types of psycho-social determination generally bring out various attitudes toward law. For example, the following categories of people tend to obey the law more strictly than others: people in the age brackets from 35–49 and above 60 years; people with proportionately higher education; white-collar workers; individuals whose parents belong to the intelligentsia; people without feelings of insecurity; people with few personal contacts; and rationalistically minded people engaged in social activities (although the latter also reveal some law-related cunning).

On the other hand, the following categories more often than others admit a wish to by-pass or to disobey (break) the regulations of law: those in the 25–34 age bracket; people uneducated or with elementary education; unskilled workers (breaking the law); persons with symptoms of insecurity; dogmatically minded persons (by-passing law); psychically inhibited persons (breaking the law); frustrated persons; those without a clear hierarchy of values; and those who are not engaged in social activity. . . .

. . . Thus, the third prism though which legal regulations are refracted on their way from the legislator to those to whom they are addressed are various personality types.

In our considerations on the hypothesis of the three levels of functioning of law we have intentionally left out, as factors of minor importance in this context, the extensive category of formal, semantic and procedural framework which can influence the transmission of information about legal norms. Thus, we have ignored the contents intended by the lawmakers as well as the actual contents of the legal enactments; the valid interpretations (authentic—done by the legislator himself) of such contents; the sources of information about laws (official publications, mass media, the experiences of the legal profession, individual and other informal experiences, etc.); the ways the normative acts are brought to life by the minions of the law; the changing directives of those ways;

opinions about them, etc. All this has been set aside, because our main focus was an attempt to grasp the most significant or strategic variables determining the functioning of law.

The multilevel conception of the working of law proposes, as we have said, three basic variables: the type of social and economic system, the type of legal subculture, and the personality type. We can develop this hypothesis further referring to the familiar proposition of social engineering that the degree of acceptance of received information depends on the degree of acceptance of the authorities giving this information; this proposition is relevant if we admit that a legal norm is a special (protected by its sanction) kind of information. We can expect any given normative act to work efficiently in proportion to the degree of acceptance of the discerned three variables. Thus, optimal effectiveness can be expected from a normative act functioning within an accepted social and economic system, supported by a pro-legal subculture and realized by legalistically-minded individuals. In turn, the least efficient would be a regulation functioning within an unaccepted system which is subject to an antagonistic influence of an anti-legal subculture, and which is received by anti-legalistically oriented individuals. An example illustrating this is the attitude of the Polish population toward the enactments of the occupant's authorities during the Second World War. In real life the three factors interact in various ways and ideal types can rarely be found. The intensity of influence in a concrete social system is an important prerequisite of effective action since it shows where to look for the social environments and individuals who are apt to fulfill the directives of law and, also, where resistance may arise. This shows that the three-level hypothesis of the functioning of law is important for social engineering, too. . . .

* * *

. . . It seems rational . . . to distinguish between two incompatible delineations of the law: the practical and the theoretical. The practical (fixed for clearly utilitarian reasons, to give a judge or a lawyer a guide-line between law and non-law) would say that the law is a norm generated by proper authority and supplied with compulsory sanctions. This type of definition, useful as it is, originated different branches of the law and was polished by the analytical work of jurisprudence. The task of the theoretical definition is not a practical one: it aims to say what law is and how it functions in social reality.

The theoretical answer to the question "What is law?" would be this: *law is a social norm which is based on four reciprocal elements belonging to the parallel parties and containing two corresponding pairs of rights and duties.*

Neither state, nor subject, is able to tell which social norms belong to the category of legal ones. Some norms which are not legal from the point of view of the state (they don't have the compulsory sanction) are legal nevertheless because they operate as such. Being recognized as such by subjects they act in the same way in which they would function having the full support of the state control apparatus. Some norms are legal even if subjects are unable to perceive the links between reciprocal elements, even if they have a feeling of duty and right without the recognition of the corresponding dyad of duty and right. When a 35-year-old teacher from a highly industrialized country is deeply convinced that he is the only owner of Mount Everest and that all people have a duty to respect his rights to this mountain, his conviction (contrary to L. Petrazycki's view) is not a legal one: it does not correspond to the reciprocal attitudes of duties and rights of any real party. But if a Mafia leader demands obedience and gives dangerous orders, then he behaves according to the law: his rights to do so are recognized, several of his comrades accept the duty to obey and—this is quite important—he has a corresponding *duty* to protect his subordinates, while they have a legitimate claim to his protection. Only this tetrad of duties and rights constitutes the law. Usually the reciprocal dyads correspond—according to the principle of "*do ut des*"—to each other. But how does one determine the law when they don't? The very fact that the complementary interplay of dyads might be disrupted (or not recognized at all) creates a need for a judge or, better, an agency which (after a search for power-related elements: rights and duties) declares its existence (or lack of it).

The tetrad conception of the law is based on the principle of accepted reciprocity. Should an Indian chief give a mountain to a lawyer as a gift, his action would have several consequences. According to this act he would have a duty to surrender the land which he is giving and also by the act of donation he would be obliged to accept the right on the part of the lawyer to possess the land in question. It is obvious (from the point of view of living, intuitive law) that the chief, according to his act, also acquires some right to certain services from the recipient of his gift. The recipient has, even if this is not recognized by the official law, the duty to discharge these services. If the case were a sale of the mountain the four bonds which tie together duties and rights would be even more visible—and more digestible for legal dogmatists. Then the chief would be bound by duty to turn over the land, and the lawyer bound to pay the price; on the other hand the chief would have the right to demand the payment and the lawyer the right to possess the mountain. Unilateral perception of duty and right and insistence on them might, in special circumstances, change social reality. But is such a case the change of social reality is a condition triggered by deviance: results in no response, reciprocity—social resonance. Bilateral perception of duties and rights constitutes several regularities which match attitudes and behavior. Social life allocates duties and rights in patterns which are designated by accumulated experience collected by many repetitions or careful analysis of exceptional cases. Thus, the grandfather has (under certain conditions) a duty to leave the property to his grandson, having also a right to insist on proper conduct. The grandson on his side has a right to expect the transfer of the property at the proper time and a duty to respect his grandfather. The rights and duties cemented by the rule appear especially clear when the links between them are sharply broken (grandson killed his grandfather).

The court of the USA said in the case of *Riggs v. Palmer*, "no one shall be permitted to profit by his own fraud, or to take advantage of his own wrong, or to found any claim on his ingenuity, or to acquire property by his own crime" (*Riggs v. Palmer*, 115 N.Y. 506, N.E. 188(1889)). It would be a mistake to assume that this case creates an entirely new rule. But it does serve a special function, and is spelled out in order to prevent the improper allocation of obligations and claims (as L. Nader would say: "it makes the balance").

If the law is understood as such a tetrad, then it is easy to explain why it fulfills its five basic functions: (1) integration, (2) petrification, (3) reduction, (4) motivation, and (5) education.

Indeed, the law integrates the mutual expectations of behavior of two parties (through the reciprocally-structured duties and rights) in a way that is consistent with the general values existing in a given social system.

The *integrative* function of the law could be summarized the following way:[8]

> Law may, according to this conception, fulfill an integrative function by stimulating the processes of integration successively on various levels of social organization with the following objectives: system integration (integration of social sub-systems); institutional integration (integration of social roles and institutions); and social (personal) integration (integration of individuals and groups): objectively and subjectively.

Another description of this function of the law is given by Shang:[9]

> Of old, the one who would regulate the empire was he who regarded as his first task the regulating of his own people; the one who could conquer a strong enemy was he who regarded as his first task the conquering of his own people. For the way in which the conquering of the people is based upon the regulating of the people is the effect of smelting in regard to metal or the work of the potter in regard to clay; if the basis is not solid, then

people are like flying birds or like animals. Who can regulate these? The basis of the people is the law.

The law—through trial and error—selects those interpersonal relations which, in the forms of tetrads, satisfy changing social needs. In this way the law *petrifies* those schemes of behavior which are recognized as successful and functional. It may be said that law labels as positive only felicitous manifestations of human relations which are generated in the changing laboratory of society. The unsuccessful forms, after several trials, are rejected and abandoned, very seldom undergoing petrification. They may, however, be perpetuated in obscure institutions, disrupted by cognitive dissonance.

Both the processes of integration and those of petrification lead to a *reduction* in the number of acceptable types of interhuman behavior. The number of possible types of interrelations between people among themselves or between themselves and social institutions is vast and complex. Order and predictability are unattainable within such a complicated social fabric. Because each case in its specificity differs from all others, the rules which are generated in connection with a particular case are not applicable generally. This variety of social situation leads to a need for simplification, a reduction of factual possibilities: the law, through its abstract categorization, gives such a possibility. Experimentally established tetrads reduce the endless possibilities for social interrelations to manageable schemes of behavior, the ramifications of which have already been recognized and tested as socially essential and strategic.

Another function of the law is : behavior's *motivation* (the regulation of individual attitudes and performances). The legal norm contains a normative appeal and is, at the same time, informative: this type of behavior is prohibited and that is supported by the legal system. Knowledge of this sort gives individuals the opportunity to select behavior which will enable them to operate successfully inside the parameters of the legal system. Thus, knowledge of legal norms does condition the actor to behave in the manner prescribed by the basic values of the legal system. But even more: the actor is not only motivated to avoid those actions not included in the pre-demanded pattern but is also educated (through the repeated process of reinforcement) to act in a mode fixed by this pattern. Educational function of the law—from this point of view—could be regarded as an extension of the motivational one.

It is observed that from an enormous number of options, the law enforces that which has already been tested and found useful and just as an acceptable relationship between two parties. The final function is the *educational* one. But rewards and punishments not only motivate behavior, but also, in the long run, socialize and educate. Rewards reinforce desirable performances, thus creating positive habits. Punishments can be used to reduce or eliminate situations which generate undesirable behavior or can be used, as B. Skinner says, to break contingencies under which punished behavior is reinforced through this type of training. According to L. Petrazycki the law alters originally difficult patterns of behavior into patterns molded by habit. . . .

NOTES

1. Z. Bozyczko, *Kradziez kieszonkowa i jej sprawca*, Warsaw, 1962.
2. C. Czapów, *Mlodziez a przestepstwo*, Warsaw, 1962.
3. S. Szelhaus, *Mlodociani recydywisci*, Warsaw, 1960, pp. 181–2.
4. J. Jasinski, "Ksztaltowanie sie przestepczosci nieletnich w Polsce w latach 1951–1960 w swietle statystyki sadowej," *Archiwum kryminologii*, vol. 2, Warsaw, 1964, p. 134.
5. C. Czapów, *op. cit.*
6. J. Jasinski, *op. cit.*, p. 38.
7. V. Aubert, "Conscientious objectors before Norwegian military courts," in G. Schubert (ed.), *Judicial Decision Making*, New York, 1963, p. 219.
8. M. Los, "Law as an integrative system," unpublished paper presented at the Conference of Sociology of Law, Nocdwijk, 1972.
9. *The Book of Lord Shang*, London, 1928, p. 285 (trans. by J. J. L. Duyvendak).

· 8 ·

Conflict Theory

In the previous chapter we saw how the structural-functionalist paradigm has made an enormous contribution to the development of a contemporary sociology of law. In this chapter we look at conflict theory and how this approach has also left its imprint on sociolegal theory and research.

This chapter discusses conflict theory's key concepts by contrasting them with the basic tenets of structural-functionalism. The chapter first presents a general description of the conflict model of society. We then examine the notions of competition and dissensus and their role in the legal sphere. Next, we consider some of the theoretical statements proposed by a few of the more visible conflict theorists. The chapter then focuses on how the elite social classes have historically manipulated certain laws in order to maintain their economic and political positions. This is followed by a discussion regarding the legislative measures taken by powerful cultural groups in imposing their morals and values on other, less powerful groups. Finally, the chapter addresses how law is used as a weapon in social conflict.

Conflict Theory: Society as an Arena for Conflict

The structural-functionalist approach, and in particular Talcott Parsons's singular interest in the social system, is critiqued severely by British sociologist Ralf Dahrendorf in his highly influential article "Out of Utopia" (1958a). In this essay, Dahrendorf argues that structural-functionalism assumes a utopian or unreal image of society because it highlights the benefits but disregards the detriments resulting from the interdependence of social institutions. He further contends that Parsons's systems-functionalist approach is biased because it focuses on stability, harmony, and consensus ignoring society's other face, the one dealing with the problems of *dissensus, conflict,* and *coercion.*

The functionalists' detachment from the negative aspects of the social system engendered an intellectual trend in sociology that Dahrendorf calls "the conservatism of complacency." In other words, because functionalists neglect to undertake a critical analysis of the social system and its subsystems (including the legal one), their sociology implicitly legitimates and justifies the status quo. Dahrendorf proposes the **conflict model of society** as an alternative sociological paradigm. He maintains that if the social conflict model is to provide a more realistic picture of society than that proposed by structural-functionalism, it must presuppose four essential points:

1. Every society is subjected at every moment to change: social change is ubiquitous.
2. Every society experiences at every moment social conflict: social conflict is ubiquitous.
3. Every element in a society contributes to its change.
4. Every society rests on constraint of some of its members by others (1958b: 174).

A model premised on these four factors underscores the process of social change and views conflicts as struggles between social groups.

Despite Dahrendorf's pioneering efforts in constructing an analytical model of social conflict, this theoretical approach did not originate with him. Its legacy, as we saw in Chapter 4, can be traced to the Marxian tradition of the nineteenth century. Indeed, Dahrendorf, having been initially influenced by Marx, proclaims that "the sociological theory of conflict would do well to confine itself for the time being to an explanation of the frictions between the rulers and the ruled" (1958b: 173). However, conflict theory's most contemporary manifestation is grounded, not in Marx's statements on political economy, but rather in German sociologist Georg Simmel's (1858–1918) work on small groups. As such, today's conflict theorists have virtually abandoned the Marxian emphasis on class oppression and instead focus, more broadly, on the clash of group interests. Let us examine some of Simmel's statements concerning social conflict and the law.

Simmel, Conflict, and the Law

Viewing conflict as a normal part of the social order, Simmel regards legal relations within the context of superordination-subordination interactions as being reciprocal, not just oppressive. For him, the seemingly one-sided action of the superior giving the law and the subordinate receiving it is actually a bilateral and contractual relationship. Law is possible, Simmel states, only when the subordinate acquiesces to its demands. In short, Simmel considers conflict as merely an intense form of social interaction.

Simmel also comments on a specific type of conflict, *competition*, and its relation to the law. According to him, competition is an indirect conflict that is neither offensive nor defensive. Destroying or in some way harming the competitor is not competition's objective. Simmel describes competition as those "conflicts which consist in parallel efforts by both parties concerning the same prize" (1969:57). In this sense, competition is seen as pure, honest, legitimate, and useful to society. However, when competition employs such means as violence, damage to property, fraud, and **slander** (i.e., the act of making false charges against an individual in order to damage that individual's reputation), then it is said to be *illegitimate*.

Because illegitimate competition has the potential to harm society, the law must intervene to regulate it.

The antitrust laws aptly illustrate Simmel's notion of illegitimate competition. **Antitrust** legislation, which includes the Sherman Act (1890) and the Federal Trade Commission Act (1914), outlaws such practices as price-fixing and the creation of corporate monopolies. The Sherman Act prohibits unreasonable restraints upon and monopolization of trade, which means, among other things, that business corporations may not form cartels (combinations) for the purposes of limiting economic competition. Competition between businesses is said to benefit the market economy and the consuming public because it produces the highest quality product at the lowest price. However, when several corporations consolidate themselves (monopolization) in order to set artificially high prices on their products (price-fixing) and subsequently drive smaller competitors out of business, this type of direct conflict becomes illegal. Such conflict is economically detrimental to both the business competitor and the consumer. In essence, we may say that Simmel saw competition as being functional as well as dysfunctional for society.

Simmel (1950) contends that it is possible to identify patterns of conflict, cooperation, and competition in the social associations called the *dyad* and the *triad*. According to Simmel, the relationship between two parties forms the simplest sociological formation, the **dyad.** A third party appears in the **triad** and, thus, the form of social interactions is fundamentally altered. Simmel states that the non-partisan third party may function either as a mediator with the intent of bringing together two disputing parties in order to produce harmonious agreement between them, or else function as an arbitrator who balances the disputing parties' contradictory claims against one another and eliminates what is incompatible in those claims.

Relying on these Simmelian ideas, legal sociologist Vilhelm Aubert (1963) classifies the types of interpersonal conflict that arise in a dyadic relationship between two individuals or two groups, the sources of these conflicts, and the ways of resolving these conflicts.

For Aubert, two types of interpersonal conflict can be readily distinguished in regard to whether they involve *interests* or *values*. A **conflict of interests** has its source in *competition*. In this case, conflict arises from a situation of scarce resources as when two parties desire the same thing but the amount available is not sufficient to satisfy each of them completely and for all time. Such a situation may occur, for example, when the proprietors of the only two supermarkets in town compete over the same limited pool of potential customers.

By contrast, a **conflict of values** has its source in *dissensus*. Here, two parties disagree strongly with each other's (religious, moral, ideological, political) beliefs. Pro-choice and pro-life groups, for instance, disagree fundamentally over whether the abortion of a human fetus is, in fact, murder, and therefore immoral and illegal. Because the two parties are also competing over the scarce resources (i.e., positions of power and authority) needed to propagate their beliefs, a conflict of values is almost always intermingled with a conflict of interests. In Aubert's analysis, all social conflicts can be traced back to dissensus and/or competition.

Two ways of resolving conflict based on competition are through compromise and bargaining. In the case of *compromise*, the opposing parties negotiate a give-and-take exchange in such a way that the gain of one party is not entirely the loss of another. For example, when jurors are divided in their opinions concerning a criminal case and cannot reach a verdict, some of them may surrender their strongly held opinions in return for others relinquishing their similarly strong views on another issue concerning the same case. (A *compromise verdict* is prohibited or limited in many jurisdictions.) In the case of *bargaining*, on the other hand, there is essentially no conflict between the parties because they both possess a mutual understanding in that they desire and seek a contractual **quid pro quo** (from Latin meaning "something for something") exchange. Contrary to compromise, nothing is surrendered in the case of bargaining.

However, an interpersonal conflict involving pure dissensus cannot be settled through compromise or bargaining because the adversaries are interested only in keeping their values and beliefs intact. Thus, in Aubert's view, dissensus is best resolved through the informal mechanisms of *mediation* and *arbitration*. **Mediation** involves the interposing of a third nonpartisan element between two conflicting parties for the purpose of persuading them into a mutually agreed settlement. In this case, "the triadic situation may come to settle the conflict at very much the same point where the two parties would have converged if they had been willing to carry on with their bargaining" (Aubert, 1963:39). **Arbitration** involves the resolution of a dispute by an impartial third party (other than a judge) whose decision is binding. In both mediation and arbitration the disputants attempt to minimize their losses. This raises the question of why, if informal and private modes of dispute settlement like mediation and arbitration are available, do many disputants seek **litigation,** or trial lawsuits, before a court of law when this mechanism involves the risk of total loss for one of the parties?

Aubert (1967b) proposes eight reasons why conflicting parties may prefer legal settlement with its all-or-none character over the less coercive out-of-court options such as compromise, bargaining, mediation, and arbitration.

1. Complete knowledge into all aspects of the case may be lacking, and, as a consequence, people may tend to overestimate their chances of winning.
2. Lawsuits have a moral tinge, and the disputing parties may feel they need to retain their aggression against each other as a matter of moral principle.
3. The litigants may be so agitated and aggressive that, for them, compromise and bargaining are full of unpleasantness and out of the question.
4. Some parties may have interests beyond the specific case, such as a desire to have their rights and duties officially identified and clarified.
5. Lawyers may have personal reasons to instigate a lawsuit (for occupational rewards like status and money, for example), even in those cases where it would be more rational from the client's point of view to work toward a compromise settlement out of court.
6. There may be conflicts in which one of the parties assumes that it is going to lose a lawsuit but may choose to let itself be forced to pay in full rather than agree voluntarily to a partial payment.

7. In some conflicts the object of the dispute may be indivisible (for example, a child in a divorce case), making bargains and compromise irrelevant.
8. Conflicting parties may choose litigation because they see it as a game of chance and are attracted to the risks involved.

Based on Aubert's statements it is clear that public lawsuits in our adversarial legal system not only escalate disputes, they also impede the making of agreements that may mutually benefit each of the antagonistic parties. In this sense we may say that formal legal conflict, like illegitimate competition, leads to social dysfunctions. Let us now consider how legal conflict may produce social functions.

The Functions of Legal Conflict

As we have already seen, Simmel tells us that competition as a type of conflict may be functional, as when it benefits the market economy, or it may be dysfunctional, as when it leads to price-fixing and monopolization. In a series of sixteen general propositions derived chiefly from Simmel's theories, Boston College sociologist Lewis Coser (1956) considers conflict within the functionalist paradigm and reveals some its positive consequences.

In regard to legal conflicts, Coser maintains that they benefit society in two related ways. First, legal conflicts lead to the creation and modification of new laws, and second, the new laws in turn create new institutional structures charged with enforcing the new laws (1956:126). The events surrounding the landmark U.S. Supreme Court decision *Brown v. Board of Education* (1954) will serve to illustrate Coser's two proposed functions of legal conflict.

In 1896, the Supreme Court, in *Plessy v. Ferguson*, upheld the Jim Crow practice of segregating the races in public places. This meant that the individual states could continue to provide separate facilities for Caucasians and Negroes. For instance, African American passengers in railway trains had to ride in separate "Colored" cars. Provided the accommodations were equal in every way, the Court did not see this racial segregation as violating the requirement of the Fourteenth Amendment that "no state shall deny the equal protection of the laws" to its citizens.

After *Plessy*, a number of individuals and antisegregation groups, in particular the National Association for the Advancement of Colored People (NAACP), began to forcefully challenge the practice of public racial segregation. For them, the "separate but equal" doctrine was discriminatory and unconstitutional. They maintained that separate facilities were inherently unequal, and by the 1950s the NAACP had begun to wage a litigation campaign against segregated schools.

In 1954, the U.S. Supreme Court, in *Brown v. Board of Education*, set a precedent in establishing new policies in interracial relations with its decisions forbidding official segregation in elementary and secondary public schools. The Court unanimously concluded that "separate but equal" educational facilities deprived African American children of equal educational opportunities. Moreover, the Court intimated that racial segregation in elementary schools was psychologically harmful to African American children because it retarded their educational and mental development. Accordingly, the nation's highest court called for desegregation "with all deliberate speed."

Although the *Brown* decision had specifically addressed only the desegregation of the public schools, numerous laws were enacted during the ensuing post-*Brown* years ending Jim Crow in a variety of social settings. For example, just ten years after the Supreme Court decision the Senate passed the Civil Rights Act of 1964, which forbade racial discrimination in public facilities such as buses, public parks, and lunch counters.

The enforcement mechanisms needed to ensure compliance with these new desegregation rulings were subsequently institutionalized. Under the Civil Rights Act of 1964, for instance, any state or local government practicing racial discrimination was ineligible to receive federal aid. The Elementary and Secondary Education Act of 1965 made sizable federal funds available to school districts that complied with the desegregation orders. The Department of Justice could bring lawsuits against school districts that refused to desegregate, and the Department of Health, Education and Welfare also put pressure on public schools to integrate their faculties.

The events preceding *Brown* support Coser's statement that legal conflicts "lead to the modification and creation of law." The events following the *Brown* decision show us how "the application of new rules leads to the growth of new institutional structures centering on the enforcement of these new rules and laws." Coser's message is that conflict leads to progress and in the long run, legal conflict may be functional for society.

In the next section we peruse the work of four of the more prominent conflict theorists—Ralf Dahrendorf, Thorsten Sellin, George Vold, and Richard Quinney—and consider how their ideas concerning the clash of group interests have relevance to the sociology of law.

The Clash of Group Interests

The development of conflict theory gained new vigor with the publication of Dahrendorf's *Class and Class Conflict in Industrial Society* (1959). Although initially influenced by the thought of Karl Marx, Dahrendorf departed from Marx's focus on the conflict between the social classes and looked instead to the conflict between interest groups. Thus, for Dahrendorf, social inequities have their basis not only in economics but also in bureaucratic and political *power.* Simply put, those with power give orders and those without power take orders. Power relations of superordination and subordination, says Dahrendorf, form the basis of antagonisms between groups. He distinguishes three broad types of groups that contribute to social conflict: "quasi-groups," "interest groups," and "conflict groups." The members of these groups share certain common interests.

Quasi-groups are aggregates of people occupying identical power positions and holding latent interests or unconscious role expectations. The population of retired American workers constitutes a quasi-group. The quasi-group may have conflicts of interest with other groups, but these conflicts are not usually overt. People from a quasi-group may be recruited into an interest group.

Interest groups are organized associations of people mobilized into action by virtue of their membership in the group. They share manifest interests or conscious goals. Dahrendorf states that interest groups are the real agents of group conflict. The American Association of Retired Persons (AARP) is one example of an interest group. The AARP is a national organization with over 32 million members whose goal is to improve health care, worker equity, and other aspects of living for people fifty years of age and older.

Conflict groups emerge out of interest groups. Conflict groups attempt to instigate revolutionary social change, sometimes through violent means. Examples of conflict groups include the Provincial Irish Republican Army (IRA) of Northern Ireland, the Islamic Jihad of the Middle East, and the Zapatistas of Mexico.

Although Dahrendorf does not deal directly with the law, his conflict model of society may easily be adopted in analyzing legal issues. For example, his conflict-coercion perspective portrays law as nothing more than a product of group interests. Accordingly, interest groups attempt to sway lawmakers through their lobbying activities. Those groups with sufficient political power determine the law and use it to safeguard their values. Consider how legislation is influenced by such powerful political interest groups involved on opposite sides of the issue of gun control—those groups opposing a legislative ban on handguns (National Rifle Association) and those desiring a legislative ban on handguns (Handgun Control, Inc.)—and abortion—those groups that are pro-choice (Planned Parenthood and the National Organization of Women) and those that are pro-life (Operation Rescue and Missionaries to the Preborn). Contrary to the integration-consensus perspective derived from structural-functionalism, conflict theorists argue that the law is not a neutral expression and codification of society's values. Instead, the law is the outcome of power politics and interest group conflict.

Two decades before Dahrendorf introduced the conflict-coercion perspective to sociology, criminologist Thorsten Sellin had relied on an early variant of conflict theory to explain the creation of criminal law. In *Culture Conflict and Crime* (1938), he presents a theory of crime in which he relates cultural adaptation to criminal behavior.

Sellin begins with the idea that society is composed of different cultural groups, each of which maintains its own *conduct norms*, or systematized rules that dictate to its members what is "normal" social behavior under certain circumstances. By regulating the members' conduct and life situations, these rules serve to protect the social values of the group. However, in a complex society made up of many divergent cultural groups, there is a greater chance that there will be a clash of conduct norms. The outcome is *culture conflict*.

According to Sellin, culture conflict is manifested in the legal sphere when the conduct norms of the dominant social group (e.g., the white, Anglo-Saxon, Protestant, middle class) are reflected and embodied in the criminal law; that is, when behavior that the dominant group views as abnormal and wrong is criminalized and punished. What is more, the criminal law may be inconsistent with the conduct norms of the less influential groups (e.g., racial and ethnic minorities). The result, Sellin contends, is a higher incidence of criminality among those individuals who have not adapted to the values, ideology, and lifestyle of the more influential group.

To illustrate his point, Sellin cites the case of a Sicilian father in New Jersey who kills the sixteen-year-old seducer of his daughter. The father is surprised that he is arrested for murder because, to his way of thinking, he was only defending his daughter's honor in accordance with traditional Sicilian culture. For Sellin, then, criminal behavior is behavior that is in conflict with the dominant groups' conduct norms. Let us now see how the ideas of conflict criminologist George Vold parallel those of Sellin.

Like Sellin, Vold's intention is to explain how crime emerges from group behavior. However, unlike Sellin, who focuses on the conflict of group *norms*, Vold chooses to emphasize the conflict of group *interests* and begins with the premise that all groups have certain interests that they try to maintain and improve. When one group encroaches on another group's interests, the latter group will protect its position through active resistance. During the struggle, the groups may seek the state's coercive authority to help them defend their rights and safeguard their interests. The conflict then takes on a political bent, and whichever group marshals the greatest number of legislative votes determines if there is to be a law that hampers and curbs the interests of the other group.

> The whole political process of lawmaking, lawbreaking, and law enforcement becomes a direct reflection of deep-seated and fundamental conflicts between interest groups and their more general struggles for the control the police power of the state. Those who produce legislative majorities win control over the police power and dominate the policies that decide who is likely to be involved in violation of the law (Vold, 1958:208–209).

We may take as an example conscientious objectors, who, during wartime, refuse to participate in war activity because of ideological or moral reasons. Conscientious objectors are considered criminals because they are members of a minority group whose beliefs and behaviors (pacifism at all times) are legally opposed by the more politically powerful majority group supporting the war effort. For Vold, criminal behavior is minority group behavior and its development is a political process.

Richard Quinney is another criminologist working within the conflict paradigm. Quinney (1970) credits Dahrendorf, Vold, and other proponents of the conflict model for inspiring him to formulate his theory of **the social reality of crime.** The theory consists of six propositions explaining the development of crime and criminal law through social conflict. Let us examine each of the propositions in turn.

1. Quinney begins with the premise that no behavior is inherently criminal. For him, crime is simply a *definition* of behavior that is conferred on some persons by those in positions of power. It follows then, that the greater the number of criminal definitions (i.e., criminal laws) formulated and applied, the greater the amount of crime.

2. Quinney contends that criminal laws exist because some segments of society are in conflict with others. By formulating criminal laws, the powerful segments are able to control the behavior of the powerless segments. Thus, those groups that have the power to have their interests represented in public policy regulate the formulation of criminal laws.

3. Quinney states that "criminal definitions are applied by the segments of society that have the power to shape the enforcement and administration of criminal law" (1970:18). Consequently, legislators, police, prosecutors, judges, and all those involved in the enforcement and administration of criminal law represent the powerful groups and work to protect their interests.

4. Quinney argues that compared to those powerful segments that formulate and apply criminal laws, the powerless segments of society, whose behaviors are not represented in formulating and applying criminal laws, are more likely to act in ways that will be defined as criminal.

5. Quinney maintains that the most critical criminal conceptions are held by the powerful segments of society. These conceptions, which are disseminated through the mass media (newspapers, magazines, television, etc.), are widely accepted by other people in society as their own view.

6. The five aforementioned propositions are collected into a composite statement: "The social reality of crime is constructed by the formulation and application of criminal definitions, the development of behavior patterns related to criminal definitions, and the construction of criminal conceptions" (Quinney, 1970:23).

What Quinney is saying in these six propositions is that the interests (desires, values, and norms) of the politically powerful segments of the population are incorporated into the criminal law. Thus, by formulating criminal law, these dominant groups perpetuate and maintain their interests over those who are less influential. This political process involves coercion and conflict. In a word, crime is what those with power define it to be.

Conflict theorist Randall Collins (1975) contends that, in contrast to functionalist systems theory, which is influenced by its adherents' commitment to an ideological conservatism, conflict theory, being intrinsically more detached from value judgments, will make sociology into an objective science with causal statements, greater explanatory power, and a comprehensive body of principles. Although Collins's optimism about conflict theory's scientific quality remains to be realized, it is quite clear that, since the 1950s, conflict theory has developed into a pivotal paradigm in sociology. In the sections that follow we see how Jerome Hall, William J. Chambliss, Joseph R. Gusfield, and Troy Duster have employed conflict theory in explaining the historical evolution of the laws on theft, vagrancy, alcohol consumption, and narcotic drug addiction.

Economy, Crime, and Law in Renaissance England

In this section, we apply the conflict paradigm in analyzing the law in historical perspective. In particular, we focus on the development of the English criminal laws of theft and vagrancy during the time when feudalism began to disintegrate in England. We begin with a brief historical overview of the socioeconomic conditions that helped to shape the laws of theft and vagrancy.

The invasion of Britain by the Anglo-Saxon tribes of North Germany, between 400 and 600 C.E., accentuated Britain's transition from tribalism to feudalism (Jeffery, 1957). These invaders were warriors and farmers with their families. Each family unit received a share of land from which it gained economic subsistence. By the fifth century, all land in England was land held under the control of private landlords. Anyone occupying the lord's land owed the lord military or agricultural services. In the tenth century, everyone was required by law to have a lord. By 1200, the transition to feudalism was complete: political authority was in the hands of landlords; the king was the supreme landlord; the economic organization was agricultural and the feudal manor was the economic unit; and each person occupied land belonging to the lord and was attached to this land through a personal-legal relationship known as the tenure system.

With the emergence of feudalism in England, a new legal system came into existence. At first, the law was under the control of the feudal lords. But during the reign of King Henry II (1154–1189), feudal justice was replaced by state justice and the law emerged as the sole prerogative of the Crown. According to criminologist C. Ray Jeffery, "As a *legal* system, feudalism means a body of institutions creating obligations of service and duty—a military service on the part of the vassal and an obligation of protection on the part of the lord with regard to the vassal" (1957:649). By the fifteenth century, feudalism was in decline. Let us see how this transformation in the economic system of England led to changes in the criminal laws of theft.

Property and Theft Laws

In his influential book *Theft, Law, and Society* (1952), legal scholar Jerome Hall shows how a judicial decision rendered in the Carrier's Case in 1473 reflected the social conflicts that emerged from the changing political and economic conditions of Renaissance England. In this important case, which involved the crime of theft, Hall illustrates that legal decisions are often influenced by sociological factors that are seemingly independent of the law. He outlines the basic facts of the Carrier's Case: "the defendant was hired to carry certain bales to Southampton [England]. Instead of fulfilling his obligation, he carried the goods to another place, broke open the bales and took the contents. He was apprehended and charged with felony [i.e., theft]" (1952:4).

In 1473, all the different kinds of theft with which we are now familiar were not legally recognized. At that time most theft was considered **larceny,** or the wrongful taking and carrying away (asporting) of personal property without the owner's consent and with the intent to deprive the owner of it permanently. A necessary element of larceny is *trespass,* or the carrying away of moveable property such as a cow or a piece of furniture. As a result, the crime of **embezzlement,** which consists of obtaining rightful possession of property with the owner's consent and subsequently depriving the owner of that property permanently, did not legally exist at the time of the Carrier's Case. Moreover, not until 1506 did English common law distinguish between possession and custody.

The Carrier's Case was discussed before the highest tribunal in England, the Star Chamber. Only one judge contended that the carrier was not guilty of theft because he had not gotten possession of the bales by stealth. The judge reasoned that the carrier had legally obtained the bales and, since there had been no *vi et armis* (from Latin meaning "by force of arms"), no robbery had been committed. This judge further maintained that because the carrier had not trespassed, he could not larcenously take what he already possessed. The Star Chamber, nevertheless, found the defendant guilty of larceny. How it is that the judges rendered this verdict in contradiction to the legal precepts of the time?

As we noted in Chapter 5, one of the chief characteristics of English common law is that it abide by stare decisis. The judges of the Star Chamber, however, asserted that they had not departed from the legal precedent that mandated that trespass be an essential element in larceny. They reasoned that trespass occurred when the carrier broke open the bales. He had legal possession of the bales, they argued, but not their contents. "Breaking bulk" constituted trespass, thus terminating the carrier's legal possession.

It may be said that the innovative line of legal argumentation that the judges presented in the Carrier's Case complied with, and at the same time departed from, stare decisis. This argumentation is congruent with Sir Henry Maine's concept of **legal fiction,** or "any assumption which conceals, or affects to conceal, the fact that a rule of law has undergone alteration, its letter remaining unchanged, its operation being modified . . . The *fact* is . . . that the law has been wholly changed; the *fiction* is that it remains what it always was" (1970:25).

A simple analysis of the Carrier's Case does not reveal the entire story behind the verdict and its legal fiction. For further understanding we must consider the political and economic conditions influencing the court's decision. Edward IV was King of England at the time that the Carrier's Case was decided. The king was a despot who instituted a reign of terror and often interfered in judicial matters, conceivably manipulating the decisions of the Star Chamber. Furthermore, himself a trader and industrialist who had amassed a great fortune, Edward championed the business interests of the burgeoning mercantile class.

The Carrier's Case was decided at a time of great economic transition. During this period, between the decline of feudalism and the beginning of capitalism, revolutionary changes were taking place in English society. Most notable was the recent advent of commerce and industrialization. As a merchant, Edward found it advantageous to safeguard the mercantile class from the misappropriation of its property. Thus, he guaranteed foreign merchants the successful transportation of their goods throughout England.

In light of these political and economic factors, it becomes apparent why the Star Chamber needed to find the carrier guilty of larceny. The Carrier's Case vividly illustrates how the English legal system protected the economic interests of the new mercantile class, not through the creation of law but through a particular judicial decision.

Changes in Vagrancy Statutes

Similar to Hall, legal sociologist William Chambliss (1964) takes a sociohistorical approach in his analysis of law. However, instead of considering the laws of theft, Chambliss looks at the connection between the English laws of vagrancy and the social setting in which these laws emerged, were interpreted, and took form. More specifically, Chambliss illustrates the relationship between the changing interests of the dominant groups in society and the changes in the vagrancy statutes.

Chambliss begins his analysis in the year 1349, when the first true vagrancy law was passed in England. This law made it a crime to give alms to any who were unemployed while being of sound mind and body. By 1360, the punishment for any able-bodied person under sixty years of age who was idle was fifteen days imprisonment.

Chambliss explains that the Black Death, the bubonic plague epidemic in Europe during the fourteenth century, was the primary factor responsible for propelling the enactment of the vagrancy statutes in England. The pestilence killed at least 50 percent of the English population and subsequently decimated most of the labor force. This drastic reduction of workers was especially problematic for England's economic system of feudalism, which depended on a cheap and ready supply of labor. Even before the plague, however, the availability of cheap labor had started to diminish as the manorial lords began to sell the serfs their freedom. Chambliss contends that the Black Death and the declining serf population made necessary the creation of legislation operating as a form of social control: the vagrancy laws. In essence, then, the laws against vagrancy were enacted for the purpose of forcing the much needed laborers to work for the landowners at low wages.

By the turn of the sixteenth century, and with the rapid decay of feudalism, the services of the serfs were no longer required. Instead, England's economy was beginning to rely increasingly on commerce and industry. These changes in the socioeconomic structure of England brought about corresponding changes in the laws of vagrancy.

Because foreign merchants engaged in commerce were frequently robbed by English citizens, the vagrancy laws evidenced a shift from a concern with the availability of cheap labor to a concern with criminal activities. The vagrancy laws were now used as a means of controlling the behavior of thieves and highwaymen preying on merchants transporting goods. The 1530 statute stated very clearly who was engaging in vagrancy—someone who gives no reckoning of how he or she makes a living and makes use of unlawful games and plays—and applied the most severe sanction to date for its violation: corporal punishment. Five years later, vagrancy became a crime punishable by death.

Chambliss states that his sociological analysis of the law of vagrancy demonstrates the importance of vested interest groups like the feudal landowners, and later the mercantile class, in the emergence and/or alteration of laws. In the next section we analyze how a certain cultural group uses the law to advance, not its economic and political interests, but its way of life.

Conflict, Law, and Morality

University of Illinois sociologist Joseph Gusfield also employs an historical analysis in his study of law and society. But, contrary to Hall and Chambliss, who examine how the elite classes manipulate the law to maintain their economic and political interests, Gusfield demonstrates how a particular cultural group employed Prohibition legislation to symbolically uphold its *status*—deference, prestige, and position in society—at the expense of another cultural group. Along with other proponents of conflict theory, Gusfield points out that in a pluralistic society like the United States, "to assume a common culture or a normative consensus . . . is to ignore the deep and divisive role of class, ethnic, religious, status, and regional culture conflicts which often produce widely opposing definitions of goodness, truth, and moral virtue" (1968:55–56). In contrast to the Marxists, who underscore the exclusive role of economics in their explanations of legal conflict, Gusfield analyzes how *morality* compelled the American middle-classes to impose, via the law, their abstemious lifestyle on others.

Abstinence as a Status Symbol

Gusfield posits that Americans have traditionally possessed great faith in the power of the law to rectify the ills of society. Because it has been our history that behavior considered to be bad, sinful, or immoral is often quickly criminalized, moral reform through the law has been a common American practice. Moral reform is precisely what the Temperance movement of the nineteenth century attempted to achieve as it sought to change the behavior of that subculture of "immoral" people who indulged in the drinking of alcohol. More to the point, Temperance efforts at reform were a way by which a certain cultural group—composed of nativist, rural, middle-class evangelical Protestants—sought to "preserve, defend, or enhance the dominance and prestige of its own style of living within the total society" (Gusfield, 1986:3).

This cultural group, which we may refer to as the Dry forces, consisted of **moral entrepreneurs,** or crusading reformers involved in creating rules in order to correct what they perceived to be a social evil: the drinking patterns of ethnic groups. Although they are often fervent and self-righteous in their holy mission, moral entrepreneurs "typically want those beneath them to achieve a better status" (Becker, 1963:149).

Those drinkers who threatened the moral culture of the Dry forces, and therefore needed to be reformed and controlled, consisted mainly of immigrant, urban, lower-class Catholics and German Lutherans, whose "cultures did not contain a strong tradition of Temperance norms which might have made an effective appeal to a sense of sin" (Gusfield, 1967:184). Further, these ethnic groups were generally ranked at the bottom of the American social and economic scale and thus held limited political power.

According to Gusfield, in order to retain the dominance of their way of life, which they felt was being threatened by the immigrant population, middle-class Protestants defined abstinence as a status symbol that conferred esteem, prestige, and respectability. Abstinence also indicated membership into their group.

Gusfield explains that during the 1840s and 1850s, the Temperance movement attempted to "convert the sinner" through *assimilative reform*. That is to say that the abstinent reformer sought to persuade drinkers to alter their "immoral" consumptive habits by inviting them to membership in the middle class. At this time, the temperance reformer could afford to take this sympathetic approach "because he felt secure that abstinence was still the public morality. It was not yet somebody else's America" (Gusfield, 1986:6). However, by the last quarter of the nineteenth century, when the middle classes no longer saw their conventional way of life as dominant—that is, as the U.S. became more urban, secular, and Catholic—the tactic changed to the more hostile and conflictual one of *coercive reform* through legislation. Gusfield asserts that the middle-class demand for laws limiting alcoholic consumption seemed to increase as the immigrant drinking groups began to gain social and political power and deny the validity of the middle-class abstinence ideology.

Coercive reform culminated in national Prohibition in 1919, when Congress ratified the Eighteenth Amendment to the U.S. Constitution prohibiting the manufacture, sale, and transportation of intoxicating liquors. Gusfield explains that the establishment of Prohibition laws was a battle in the struggle for status between two divergent styles of life: middle-class abstinence and lower-class drinking culture. But even when the Prohibition laws were disobeyed and not enforced, the respectable status of the abstinent middle-classes was nevertheless honored in the breach, since it was *their* law that drinkers had to avoid.

In this analysis of the designation of middle-class morality, Gusfield makes a distinction between the instrumental and symbolic functions of legislation. He states that on the one hand, the law's *instrumental function* lies in its enforcement and the fact that legislation clearly influences people's behavior. For example, in light of the Eighteenth Amendment, brewery owners ceased manufacturing beer because failure to do so would have subjected them to legal sanctions. On the other hand, Gusfield states the *symbolic function* gives meaning to the law as a symbol. As such, the law "symbolizes the public affirmation of social ideals and norms" and therefore "glorifies the values of one group and demeans those of another" (Gusfield, 1968:57).

The instrumental and symbolic prominence of national Prohibition in the form of the Eighteenth Amendment illustrates what sociologist Troy Duster refers to as "the legislation of morality" (1970). To be sure, up until the 1920s, the Dry forces, as a cultural group, clearly possessed the political clout and organization to publicly and legally define as deviant the lower-class immigrant Irish, Italian, and German drinking cultures. Shortly after the passage of Prohibition, however, the drinking issue became a political conflict pitting the cultural values of one group (the middle-class Temperance movement) against the cultural values of another group (the ethnic immigrants). "When those once designated as deviant achieve political power," remarks Gusfield, "they may shift from disobedience to an effort to change the designation itself" (1968:62). In this view, the group that comes to dominate in the struggle over power and status is socially positioned to legally determine which behaviors will be prohibited and defined as deviant and which behaviors will be accepted and regarded as conventional. The repeal of the Eighteenth Amendment, only fourteen years after its ratification, marked two social changes in the cultural landscape of America: (1) the decline of the old, rural, middle-class values and, more specifically, the emphasis given to the moral supremacy of abstinence; and (2) the increased urban political influence and popularity gained by the immigrant drinking cultures.

The upshot of Gusfield's argument is that when different cultural groups are engaged in status conflicts, the law is determined by the group with the most power. Let us now examine, within the context of conflict theory, an issue similar to that of the legal regulation of alcohol consumption, namely, the legal regulation of narcotic drug use.

Law, Drugs, and Moral Judgment

What Gusfield did to the issue of alcohol consumption, Troy Duster, in his book *The Legislation of Morality* (1970), does to the issue of drug addiction: he sees the law's infiltration on the area of drug addiction as stemming from the conflict of group interests. Duster states that at the turn of the century, narcotics such as heroin and morphine could, without a doctor's prescription, be bought inexpensively at any pharmacy or mail-order house in the United States. Most of the purchases were made by the upper and middle classes, and no moral stigma was attached to the use of such drugs. Within two decades, however, there occurred a remarkable transformation in moral judgment concerning narcotics usage. By 1920, the purchase and use of these drugs by the lower-classes was considered not only criminal but also bad and wrong. Let us see how this transformation resulted in legislation that morally condemned the lower-class drug addict.

The drug that most influenced American's attitudes about narcotics was the exceptionally effective painkiller, opium. In the mid-nineteenth century, morphine, a derivative of opium, was legally obtainable and widely regarded as a cure for a variety of ailments including cholera, food poisoning, and even boredom. The first hypodermic injections of morphine were administered in 1856. In addition, cocaine was isolated from the coca leaf at around this time. Eventually, it too had achieved widespread popularity and was commonly used as a general tonic for sinusitis and hay fever. Cocaine was a favorite ingredient in medicines, Coca-Cola, and wines.

The following passages from Sir Arthur Conan Doyle's 1890 novel *The Sign of the Four*—featuring his fictional and highly popular, gentleman-detective Sherlock Holmes—illustrate how narcotics were freely used by "respected" individuals. (The following first-person account is given by Holmes's loyal assistant, Dr. Watson):

> Sherlock Holmes took his bottle from the corner of the mantelpiece and his hypodermic syringe from its neat morocco case. With his long, white, nervous fingers he adjusted the delicate needle, and rolled back his left shirt-cuff. For some little time his eyes rested thoughtfully upon the sinewy forearm and wrist, all dotted and scarred with innumerable puncture-marks. Finally he thrust the sharp point home, pressed down the tiny piston, and sunk back into the velvet-lined armchair with a long sigh of satisfaction. . . . Three times a day for many months I had witnessed this performance, but custom had not reconciled my mind to it. . . .
>
> "Which is it to-day?" I asked. "Morphine or cocaine?"
>
> He raised his eyes languidly . . . "It is cocaine," he said; "a seven per cent solution. Would you care to try it?" . . . "But consider!" I said, earn-

estly. "Count the cost! Your brain may, as you say be roused and excited, but it is a pathological and morbid process, which involves increased tissue-change, and may at least have a permanent weakness. . . . Remember that I speak not only as one comrade to another, but as a medical man to one for whose constitution he is to some extent answerable" (Doyle, 1984:713–714).

It is significant that Dr. Watson's concern for Holmes's addiction is not based on morality but rather on the fact that his friend's condition is a "pathological and morbid process." By the latter part of the nineteenth century, many of Dr. Watson's real-life American counterparts had become increasingly alarmed about the population's pathological addiction to morphine.

In 1898, heroin, a derivative of morphine and three times stronger, was discovered and hailed as a cure for morphine addiction. The new drug was used frequently and no prescription was necessary for its purchase. By the turn of the century, addiction to opium derivatives had become fairly widespread among the higher and middle classes. Moreover, those citizens who had become addicted to these drugs were seen, nonjudgmentally, as unwitting victims of a physiological affliction. In other words, narcotics addiction among higher-income persons was not considered a problem of weak will or low moral character. Nevertheless, by 1920, and "despite the fact that all social classes had their share of addicts, there was a difference in the way lower class addicts were regarded. This difference was exacerbated when legislation drove heroin underground, predominantly to the lower classes" (Duster, 1970:10).

The demographic profile of the average drug addict changed dramatically during the first two decades of the twentieth century. In 1900, most drug addicts were middle-aged women of the higher classes who had been supplied narcotics by their physicians and in their use of patent medicines. In 1914, however, Congress, in an attempt to control narcotics usage, passed the Harrison Narcotic Act, and the average addict became the younger man of the lower classes. Let us see how this transformation came about.

The Harrison Narcotic Act stipulated three major provisions. First, it required everyone who produced and distributed narcotics to register with the federal government. Second, it obliged all who bought or sold narcotics to pay an excise tax. Third, the act mandated that unregistered persons could purchase drugs only with a physician's prescription, and that such a prescription must be for legitimate medical purposes. Because of the act's last provision, most physicians ceased treating the drug addict. That is to say, physicians decided that they were not in a position to determine what constituted a *legitimate* medical use of narcotics. "The decision about what is legitimate medical practice," writes Duster, "rests ultimately outside the medical profession in the moral consensus which members of society achieve about legitimacy" (1970:15). In *Webb v. U.S.* (1919), the U.S. Supreme Court ruled that a physician's prescription for narcotics was illegal if it was "issued for the purpose of providing the user with morphine sufficient to keep him comfortable by maintaining his customary usage."

Thus, with all legal sources cut off, the addict was left with no alternative but to turn to the black market and the drug pusher. Morality had now merged with the law as evidenced by the fact that as the righteous condemnation of the lower-class drug users increased, the drug laws became tougher. For instance, the Boggs Amendment of 1951 set a mandatory minimum prison sentence of ten years for repeat offenders, and the Narcotic Drug Control Act of 1956 allowed the death penalty for the sale of drugs to minors. As Duster pointedly puts it, "America's moral hostility comes faster and easier when directed toward a young, lower-class Negro male, than toward a middle-aged, middle-class white female" (1970:21).

Clearly, moral hostility is "related to the view of the drug addict as representing a world outside conventional society" (Gusfield, 1968:71). Thus, in stark contrast to the functionalist argument that the law reflects the moral consensus of the community, we have seen that with the issues of drinking and drug use, the need for the law appears to be greatest when consensus is least likely to be achieved.

In the concluding section of this chapter we consider what sociologist Austin T. Turk says about how law is used as a weapon in social conflict.

The Power of Law

Austin Turk compares the functionalist-consensus model with the conflict-coercion model and shows that they yield contrasting theoretical views of law. On the one hand, if we assume that social order is achieved through consensus among the members of society, emphasis will be given to the "power-conferring" benefits rather than the coercive aspects of law. On the other hand, if social order is seen as "largely a pattern of conflict among parties seeking to protect and improve their life chances . . . then legality becomes an attribute of whatever words and deeds are defined as legal by those able to use their advantage and machinery for making and enforcing rules" (Turk, 1969:30–32).

Turk posits that in order to develop a neutral and empirically-grounded legal theory, both the law's noble and "seamier" sides must be considered. This idea echoes Dahrendorf's contention that in emphasizing consensus, equilibrium, and integration, functionalism produces a utopian view of society that has no bearing on empirical reality. Consequently, for Turk, a methodologically superior and objective conception of law must take into account social diversity, conflict, and change.

Five Types of Legal Power

In his article "Law as a Weapon in Social Conflict" (1976), Turk asserts that the law is power. As such, it is a weapon that can be controlled and mobilized. He then indentifies five types of power or resource control represented by the law:

1. Police power
2. Economic power
3. Political power
4. Ideological power
5. Diversionary power

Police power, or the control of the means of direct physical violence, is evident when an economically influential country has the support of a United Nations Security Council resolution authorizing it to instigate military action against another country. This situation occurred when the United States sought U.N. support in demanding the complete withdrawal of Saddam Hussein's Iraqi troops from Kuwait after Hussein had occupied that Persian Gulf country in the summer of 1990.

Economic power, or the control of the production, allocation, and/or use of material resources, is determined by legislative enactment. For example, the imposition of a municipal ordinance that substantially raises property taxes may prohibit the lower classes from establishing residence in the city and force low-income property owners already living in the city to move out.

Political power refers to the control of decision-making processes. This type of power may be exercised, for example, when the executive branch of government influences the judicial or legislative branches, much like the Crown influenced the Star Chamber in the Carrier's Case.

Ideological power, or the control of definitions of values, as we have seen, occurred when, through the passing to the Eighteenth Amendment, a certain segment of the American population, the nativist middle-class, had its moral sentiments about sobriety upheld. Abstinence from alcoholic drink was not only a legal requirement, it was also an ideological orientation.

Diversionary power, or the control of human attention and living-time, means that the law attracts people's attention toward it and away from concerns that would be more threatening to authorities in power. For example, in discussing this type of power, Temple University legal sociologist Robert L. Kidder (1983:92) points out that during India's campaign for independence from Britain, 1920 to 1942, the Hindu nationalist leader Mahatma Gandhi called on all Indians to boycott the English courts because he saw his people's energy and time being wasted on lawsuits against each other when they should really be making a concerted effort to rid India of British control.

Taken together, Turk's five types of legal power conceptualize the law as a weapon that is controlled and mobilized by one group for the purpose of extolling its own interests at the expense of the interests of another group. This process produces social discord. Building upon his idea that law may be used as a weapon, Turk then proposes a conflict theory based on twelve empirical propositions that explain how law creates, intensifies, and fails to resolve inter-group antagonisms.

Turk's Conflict Theory of Law

The twelve propositions delineated by Turk constitute a theory of law that explains when and how conflict is managed by controlling and mobilizing the five types of legal power mentioned above. According to Turk, such a theory is "able to deal with conflict management as a problematic outcome instead of a defining characteristic of law as a social and cultural phenomenon" (1976:284).

The first proposition. The idea put forth in Turk's first proposition is that the ready availability of legal resources contributes to social conflict because disputing parties are impelled to make use of these resources for the purposes of protecting or advancing their interests. To illustrate, after the Civil War many Southern whites feared that African Americans would gain independent political power. In order to ensure that this did not occur, the Democratic party of the South set up a variety of legal and extralegal restrictions preventing African Americans from participating in politics. After the U.S. Supreme Court overturned a Texas law banning African Americans from voting in the political primary, that state authorized the Democratic party to set up its own admissions standards for voting. The Court then overturned that restriction on the grounds that the state of Texas was ordering the party to be its agent of discrimination. In their next countermove, the Southern states maintained that the Democratic party was a "private" association and thus not subject to governmental demands. The Supreme Court responded by ruling that the party lost its private character when it performed state functions such as the political primary. When one legal resource did not help Southern whites achieve their objective—to disqualify African Americans from registering to vote—they used other restrictive devices, including the poll tax, literacy tests, residence requirements, and gerrymandering. In this way, the law was used as a weapon by Southern whites in their legal war against African Americans (Wirt, 1970:56–59).

The second proposition. In the second proposition, Turk states that the group maintaining control over nonlegal sources of power also controls legal power. Conversely put, the group that lacks political or economic power also lacks legal power. For example, the Nineteenth Amendment to the U.S. Constitution gave nationwide suffrage to women since prior to the amendment's ratification in 1920 they could not vote in presidential elections. Denying women the political power to vote also meant denying them certain legal powers such as serving on a jury, because in many jurisdictions jurors are chosen from voter registration lists.

The third proposition. According to the third proposition, legal power denies the existence of certain social conflicts by making it difficult to articulate and manage them. Simply put, what the law does not recognize does not legally exist. For example, prior to Congressional passage of the National Labor Relations Act in 1935, workers were prohibited from organizing and engaging in collective bargaining with management. When workers were involved in these activities, they were beaten, imprisoned, or shot. This very real clash between labor and management was not a part of legal reality. Because it did not legally exist, the courts did not attempt to regulate such disputes.

The fourth proposition. The fourth proposition advances the notion that where power differences between groups are not extreme, the law encourages litigiousness (lawsuits). Unlike people in many countries, every American citizen possesses (ideally at least) an equal amount of legal power. This equality of legal power is provided by the Fourteenth Amendment, guaranteeing Americans the equal protection of the laws. Because legal power is relatively equitable and fairly accessible in the United States, it is no surprise that Americans, more than any other people, bring an extensive amount of litigation against each other. This practice only serves to exacerbate social conflict. As legal historian Jerold Auerbach explains: "Litigation is the all-purpose remedy that American society provides to its aggrieved members. But as rights are asserted, combat is encouraged; as the rule of law binds society, legal contentiousness increases social fragmentation" (1984:10). The staggering increase of personal injury lawsuits indicates a litigious society that breeds discord.

The fifth proposition. In the fifth proposition, Turk asserts that the wide availability of law reduces the likelihood that warring parties will settle their disagreements through nonlegal, less costly, and more informal means such as mediation. In contrast to **adjudication,** a public method of conflict resolution practiced by the courts through formal law, mediation is an alternative form of dispute resolution rooted in informal justice.

The sixth proposition. According to the sixth proposition, the law may intensify antagonisms when it creates new social categories, boundaries, and roles—with their corresponding rights and duties. Social interactions previously ignored or discreetly managed are now brought out into the open for legal inspection and, in the process, create new conflicts. A case illustrating this point is that of Minnesota second-grader Cheltzie Hentz, who claimed that some boys had been using obscene and "naughty language" with her while riding the school bus. This matter prompted the U.S. Department of Education office of civil rights to conduct a sexual harassment inquiry that contributed to a defensive posture taken by the school district. Seven-year-old Cheltzie was the youngest person ever to prompt a federal inquiry of this type (*The Milwaukee Journal,* December 1, 1992).

The seventh proposition. The fact that procedural law determines what information is or is not admissible in a court of law may impede or prevent the resolution of conflicts. According to the seventh proposition, even though certain evidence may be of great significance to the disputants, if it is regarded as highly subjective or qualitative, that evidence, according to the formalist Anglo-American legal system, is not seen as pertinent to the case and thus excluded. On the other hand, legal systems that are less formal-rational may consider a wide range of extralegal testimony.

The anthropologist E. L. Epstein, in his study of the African Urban Courts in Northern Rhodesia, describes a case showing how testimony considered irrelevant by an English lawyer, is regarded as significant by the Urban Court. In this case, the complainant tells the court that she was going to visit her home in Kawambwa. Her friend, the defendant, gave the complainant two pieces of cloth to give to her mother who also lived in Kawambwa. The complainant took the cloth but it was subsequently stolen from her. When the complainant told her friend about the theft, the friend did not believe her. The complainant then brought the case to the Urban Court. When the Court inquired what she wanted, the complainant replied "No, there is nothing." After a few further inquires, the Court passed judgment telling the disputants not to do this sort of thing again, but to go and live peacefully together. Epstein explains that this case "is in essence an inquiry into the norms of friendship" (1958:202). Such a case, however, would not be heard in an American courtroom since it does not strictly deal with legal matters. Furthermore, much of the testimony would be considered immaterial. Excluding or distorting important information, says Turk, leads to an inadequate understanding of the conflict. Consequently, the dispute may never be truly settled.

The eighth proposition. The eighth proposition states that the law fails to resolve disputes because it regulates the symptoms and not the sources of the conflict. In seeking to minimize their political or social cost, the law hides the real issues contributing to a conflict when it gives undue emphasis to the artificial ramifications of a dispute. For example, legal debates over affirmative action and "reverse discrimination" have focused on whether racial quotas and ethnic/racial diversity should be permitted or forbidden in education settings. These debates, however, deflect attention away from the more critical issue of the structured social inequality of minority groups. Because of its superficial character, the law may be seen as just "another device for out-positioning an opponent or for gaining time to mobilize or regroup one's non-legal forces" (Turk, 1976:286) and not seen as an instrument for dealing with the larger social issues that produced the conflict in the first place.

The ninth proposition. The ninth proposition maintains that when a conflict is legalized, communication between the disputants becomes stilted, limited, and circumspect. This formalization of verbal exchanges in legal proceedings makes it difficult for the two disputing parties to exchange information that may lead to a genuine settlement. Lawyers control much of what their clients say as they prepare them for litigation:

> Houston lawyer David Berg writes that "most [attorneys] trim the sail of the testifying client a bit too much . . . who among us has not warned the client, "Before you tell me your side of the story, let me tell you what the law is in this area," or "If you say that, you'll lose." Or who, wincing at his client's explanation, has not reminded the client, "Well, that's not how your boss remembers it," or "Aren't you really telling me . . ." (as cited in Olson, 1991:240).

The lawyer's intentional manipulation of the client's discourse prevents the disputing parties from candidly communicating their true thoughts and sentiments.

The tenth proposition. The tenth proposition states that legal decisions may create the illusion that a dispute has been resolved without actually settling it to the satisfaction of all the parties involved. The abortion controversy, for instance, was far from settled in 1973 when the U.S. Supreme Court decided, in *Roe v. Wade,* that women had a constitutional right to choose to have an abortion during the first six months of pregnancy. Because the Court is not really a final arbiter in such controversial matters, "instead of resolving the abortion issue, the decision in *Roe v. Wade* unleashed a flood of new cases upon the Supreme Court, each one requiring the Court to reconsider the abortion issue through examination of statutes passed in reaction to *Roe*" (Smith, 1992:130). Turk tells us that "to the extent that law produces illusory instead of real conflict resolutions, it not only aggravates existing conflicts but also makes future conflicts more likely, and likely to be worse" (Turk, 1976:287).

The eleventh proposition. In the eleventh proposition, Turk maintains that our formalist system of law creates the illusion that legal agents (i.e., judges, lawyers, police) are unbiased and impartial. Because legal authorities will inevitably fall short of this idealized claim, the law contributes to cynicism, evasion, and defiance with respect to normative expectations and decisions. For example, in April 29, 1992, just hours after a California jury acquitted four white police officers charged with using excessive force against African American motorist Rodney King, random acts of lawlessness broke out in South-Central Los Angeles. What had appeared for many people to be a clear case of police brutality was, after the verdict, considered a gross miscarriage of justice. The legal system and the Los Angeles police department were cynically seen as racist and biased. The shock of the verdict triggered the worst rioting in twenty-five years.

The twelfth proposition. The twelfth proposition states that as law contributes to social change it may, at least in the short run, produce and exacerbate conflicts. Social change through legislation means that the ideas, interests, and values previously engendered by the old law are replaced by different ideas, interests, and values when the new law is introduced. Thus, the group whose way of life was reflected in the old law is shunted aside. This phenomenon is illustrated by the repeal of national Prohibition with the ratification of the Twenty-First Amendment in 1933. The values and lifestyle of the Dry forces were replaced by the values and lifestyle of the Wet forces.

In short, what Turk is advancing through his propositions is the idea that, far from performing an integrative function that stabilizes social relations and mollifies disputes, law stirs up conflict. Those groupings in the population that hold the power of law use it as a weapon to safeguard and further their own interests. In other words, the creation of law is more likely to be a result of conflicts among different subcultures with different norms than an expression of general consensus.

SUMMARY

We began this chapter by introducing conflict theory as an alternative to structural-functionalism. We saw that whereas Talcott Parsons's systems-functionalist approach underscores stability, harmony, and consensus, the conflict tradition focuses on disensus, conflict, and coercion. The conflict tradition has its legacy in nineteenth-century classical theory. In particular, it has roots in Karl Marx's statements concerning class struggle and political economy. Yet, most contemporary conflict theorists have been influenced less by Marx and more by Georg Simmel's ideas on group conflict. Nevertheless, applying either Marx's or Simmel's notions of dissensus, conflict, and coercion to an analysis of the law yields a legal sociology of conflict.

We noted that unlike Marx, Simmel viewed conflict as reciprocal, not just oppressive. Moreover, Simmel considered the type of conflict called competition to have functions as well as dysfunctions for society. More recently, Lewis Coser has revealed the functions that social conflict in general and legal conflict in particular have produced. According to Coser, legal conflict is functional because it may lead to beneficial social change. More to the point, legal conflict creates new laws and new institutions to enforce those new laws.

Next, by examining the theoretical work of Ralf Dahrendorf, Thorsten Sellin, George Vold, and Richard Quinney, we saw how the conflict model of society has been applied to the sociology of law. Beginning with Dahrendorf, we learned of his position that power relations produce antagonisms between interest groups—like the American Association of Retired Persons (AARP), the National Rifle Association (NRA), and the National Organization of Women (NOW)—that have their specific interests to advance and defend on the legislative battlefield.

Turning next to Thorsten Sellin, we observed that his theory of crime envisions a society composed of divergent cultural groups with distinct conduct norms. Culture conflict occurs when these groups' opposing conduct norms collide. Culture conflict, Sellin explained, finds its legal expression when the conduct norms of the dominant cultural group are codified in criminal law.

In our discussion of George Vold, we considered his idea that crime is created from the conflict between different groups who desire to protect their interests. The conflict is transformed into a political struggle as one group vies for sufficient legislative influence to outlaw the actions of the members of the competing group. The group with the most political power determines what laws are enacted, what actions violate those laws and thus constitute criminal behavior, and how the state is to enforce those laws.

We next examined Richard Quinney's theory of the social reality of crime. He argued that the criminal law reflects and protects the interests of the politically powerful segments of the population. It follows, then, that for Quinney, no behavior is inherently criminal; rather, criminal behavior is what those in power define it to be.

Following an analysis of work of the aforementioned theorists, we took an historical approach to illustrate how the unfolding development of the laws on theft, vagrancy, alcohol use, and narcotic use has been propelled by the social conflict taking place between rival groups. Focusing on Renaissance England, we surveyed the transformations in the laws of theft and vagrancy as they occurred within the context of the political and economic conditions of the time.

Turning our attention to the Carrier's Case of 1473, we saw how Jerome Hall convincingly revealed why the Star Chamber, under royal mandate to protect the economic interests of the burgeoning mercantile class, had to find the carrier guilty of larceny, even if it meant creating a legal fiction. Similarly, in his study of the vagrancy laws of England during the fourteenth through the sixteenth centuries, Chambliss demonstrated how these laws were manipulated to provide the feudal landowners with cheap labor and protect foreign merchants from robbery. Chambliss showed that the landowners and merchants protected their economic interests by using the vagrancy laws to control the English masses.

Continuing with an historical analysis of law, we next considered the late-nineteenth and early-twentieth-century legislation intended to regulate the use of alcohol and narcotics in the United States. We saw how Joseph Gusfield employed the basic precepts of the conflict-coercion model in explaining how one cultural group—composed chiefly of nativist, rural, middle-class evangelical Protestants—relied on coercive legislative reform to temper the drinking practices of another cultural group—the immigrant, urban, lower-class Catholics and Lutherans. In this case, Prohibition legislation not only played an instrumental role by attempting to control the consumptive habits of the immigrant lower-classes, it also played a symbolic role by exalting and revering the abstinent moral culture of the nativist middle-classes.

Troy Duster also viewed legislative attempts to moralize the use of narcotics as the result of group conflict. He explained that initially most drug addicts were the respectable citizens of the upper and middle classes. However, the Harrison Narcotic Act of 1914 made drug use illegal, compelled physicians to stop treating drug addiction, and forced lower-class addicts to turn to the black market and the drug pusher. By 1920, lower-class drug use was seen as a crime as well as a problem of low moral character. The drug laws became tougher as the moral condemnation of the lower classes increased. The point is that legal coercion is employed when members of conventional society use the law to impose their morality on members of marginal groups.

In concluding this chapter, we considered Austin Turk's thesis that the law does not always promote integration as the functionalists suggest; rather, it sometimes creates greater frictions and antagonisms in society. Turk conceptualized the law as a weapon invested with police power, economic power, political power, ideological power, and diversionary power. As a weapon of power, the law is wielded by one group to advance its interests over another group. Attempting to formulate a conflict theory of law, Turk listed twelve propositions that reveal the law's discordant side.

In the next chapter we consider critical legal studies, a legal tradition that shares some common ground with both conflict theory and the Marxian perspective. Similar to sociological jurisprudence and legal realism, critical legal studies developed within the law schools and not within the discipline of sociology. And, like sociological jurisprudence and legal realism, we shall see that critical legal studies has the potential to contribute much to legal sociology's ongoing development.

A Sociological Analysis of the Law of Vagrancy

William J. Chambliss

With the outstanding exception of Jerome Hall's analysis of theft[1] there has been a severe shortage of sociologically relevant analyses of the relationship between particular laws and the social setting in which these laws emerge, are interpreted, and take form. The paucity of such studies is somewhat surprising in view of widespread agreement that such studies are not only desirable but absolutely essential to the development of a mature sociology of law.[2] A fruitful method of establishing the direction and pattern of this mutual influence is to systematically analyze particular legal categories, to observe the changes which take place in the categories and to explain how these changes are themselves related to and stimulate changes in the society. This paper is an attempt to provide such an analysis of the law of vagrancy in Anglo-American Law.

Legal Innovation: The Emergence of the Law of Vagrancy in England

There is general agreement among legal scholars that the first full fledged vagrancy statute was passed in England in 1349. As is generally the case with legislative innovations, however, this statute was preceded by earlier laws which established a climate favorable to such change. The most significant forerunner to the 1349 vagrancy statute was in 1274 when it was provided:

> Because that abbeys and houses of religion have been overcharged and sore grieved, by

the resort of great men and other, so that their goods have not been sufficient for themselves, whereby they have been greatly hindered and impoverished, that they cannot maintain themselves, nor such charity as they have been accustomed to do; it is provided, that none shall come to eat or lodge in any house of religion, or any other's foundation than of his own, at the costs of the house, unless he be required by the governor of the house before his coming hither.[3]

Unlike the vagrancy statutes this statute does not intend to curtail the movement of persons from one place to another, but is solely designed to provide the religious houses with some financial relief from the burden of providing food and shelter to travelers.

The philosophy that the religious houses were to give alms to the poor and to the sick and feeble was, however, to undergo drastic change in the next fifty years. The result of this changed attitude was the establishment of the first vagrancy statute in 1349 which made it a crime to give alms to any who were unemployed while being of sound mind and body. To wit:

> Because that many valiant beggars, as long as they may live of begging, do refuse to labor, giving themselves to idleness and vice, and sometimes to theft and other abominations; it is ordained, that none, upon pain of imprisonment shall, under the color of pity or alms, give anything to such which may labor, or

presume to favor them towards their desires; so that thereby they may be compelled to labor for their necessary living.[4]

It was further provided by this statute that:

> . . . every man and woman, of what condition he be, free or bond, able in body, and within the age of threescore years, not living in merchandise nor exercising any craft, nor having of his own whereon to live, nor proper land whereon to occupy himself, and not serving any other, if he in convenient service (his estate considered) be required to serve, shall be bounded to serve him which shall him require . . . And if any refuse, he shall on conviction by two true men, . . . be committed to gaol till he find surety to serve. And if any workman or servant, of what estate or condition he be, retained in any man's service, do depart from the said service without reasonable cause or license, before the term agreed on he shall have pain of imprisonment.[5]

There was also in this statute the stipulation that the workers should receive a standard wage. In 1351 this statute was strengthened by the stipulation:

> An none shall go out of the town where he dwelled in winter, to serve the summer, if he may serve in the same town.[6]

By 34 Ed 3 (1360) the punishment for these acts became imprisonment for fifteen days and if they "do not justify themselves by the end of that time, to be sent to gaol till they do."

A change in official policy so drastic as this did not, of course, occur simply as a matter of whim. The vagrancy statutes emerged as a result of changes in other parts of the social structure. The prime-mover for this legislative innovation was the Black Death which struck England about 1348. Among the many disastrous consequences this had upon the social structure was the fact that it decimated the labor force. It is estimated that by the time the pestilence had run its course at least fifty per cent of the population of England had died from the plague. This decimation of the labor force would necessitate rather drastic innovations

in any society but its impact was heightened in England where, at this time, the economy was highly dependent upon a ready supply of cheap labor.

Even before the pestilence, however, the availability of an adequate supply of cheap labor was becoming a problem for the landowners. The crusades and various wars had made money necessary to the lords and, as a result, the lord frequently agreed to sell the serfs their freedom in order to obtain the needed funds. The serfs, for their part, were desirous of obtaining their freedom (by "fair means" or "foul") because the larger towns which were becoming more industrialized during this period could offer the serf greater personal freedom as well as a higher standard of living. . . . And [Bradshaw] says regarding the effect of the Black Death:

> . . . in 1348 the Black Death reached England and the vast mortality that ensued destroyed that reserve of labor which alone had made the manorial system even nominally possible.[7]

The immediate result of these events was of course no surprise: Wages for the "free" man rose considerably and this increased, on the one hand, the landowners problems and, on the other hand, the plight of the unfree tenant. For although wages increased for the personally free laborers, it of course did not necessarily add to the standard of living of the serf, if anything it made his position worse because the landowner would be hard pressed to pay for the personally free labor which he needed and would thus find it more and more difficult to maintain the standard of living for the serf which he had heretofore supplied. Thus the serf had no alternative but flight if he chose to better his position. Furthermore, flight generally meant both freedom and better conditions since the possibility of work in the new weaving industry was great and the chance of being caught small.[8]

It was under these conditions that we find the first vagrancy statutes emerging. There is little question but that these statutes were designed for one express purpose: to force laborers (whether personally free or unfree) to accept employment at a low wage in order to insure the landowner an adequate supply of labor at a price he could afford to pay. Caleb Foote concurs with this interpretation when he notes:

> The antimigratory policy behind vagrancy legislation began as an essential complement of the wage stabilization legislation which accompanied the break-up of feudalism and the depopulation caused by the Black Death. By the Statutes of Laborers in 1349–1351, every able-bodied person without other means of support was required to work for wages fixed at the level preceding the Black Death; it was unlawful to accept more, or to refuse an offer to work, or to flee from one country to another to avoid offers of work or to seek higher wages, or to give alms to able-bodied beggars who refused to work.[9]

In short, as Foote says in another place, this was an "attempt to make the vagrancy statutes a substitute for serfdom."[10] This same conclusion is equally apparent from the wording of the statute where it is stated:

> Because great part of the people, and especially of workmen and servants, late died in pestilence; many seeing the necessity of masters, and great scarcity of servants, will not serve without excessive wages, and some rather willing to beg in idleness than by labor to get their living: it is ordained, that every man and woman, of what condition he be, free or bond, able in body and within the age of threescore years, not living in merchandise, (etc.) be required to serve ...

The innovation in the law, then, was a direct result of the aforementioned changes which had occurred in the social setting. In this case these changes were located for the most part in the economic institution of the society. The vagrancy laws were designed to alleviate a condition defined by the lawmakers as undesirable. The solution was to attempt to force a reversal, as it were, of a social process which was well underway; that is, to curtail mobility of laborers in such a way that

labor would not become a commodity for which the landowners would have to compete.

Statutory Dormancy: A Legal Vestige

In time, of course, the curtailment of the geographical mobility of laborers was no longer requisite. One might well expect that when the function served by the statute was no longer an important one for the society, the statutes would be eliminated from the law. In fact, this has not occurred. The vagrancy statutes have remained in effect since 1349. Furthermore, as we shall see in some detail later, they were taken over by the colonies, and have remained in effect in the United States as well.

The substance of the vagrancy statutes changed very little for some time after the first ones in 1349–1351 although there was a tendency to make punishments more harsh than originally. ...

The tendency to increase the severity of punishment during this period seems to be the result of a general tendency to make finer distinctions in the criminal law. During this period the vagrancy statutes appear to have been fairly inconsequential in either their effect as a control mechanism or as a generally enforced statute.[11] The processes of social change in the culture generally and the trend away from serfdom and into a "free" economy obviated the utility of these statutes. The result was not unexpected. The judiciary did not apply the law and the legislators did not take it upon themselves to change the law. In short, we have here a period of dormancy in which the statute is neither applied nor altered significantly.

A Shift in Focal Concern

Following the squelching of the Peasant's Revolt in 1381, the services of the serfs to the lord "... tended to become less and less exacted, although in certain forms they lingered on till the seventeenth century ... By the sixteenth century few knew that there were any bondmen in England ... and in 1575 Queen Elizabeth listened to the prayers of almost the last serfs in England . . . and granted them manumission."[12]

In view of this change we would expect corresponding changes in the vagrancy laws. Beginning with the lessening of punishment in the statute of 1503 we find these changes. However, instead of remaining dormant (or becoming more so) or being negated altogether, the vagrancy statutes experienced a shift in focal concern. With this shift the statutes served a new and equally important function for the social order of England. The first statute which indicates this change was in 1530. In this statute (22 H.8.c. 12 1530) it was stated:

> If any person, being whole and mighty in body, and able to labor, be taken in begging, or be vagrant and can give no reckoning how he lawfully gets his living; . . . and all other idle persons going about, some of them using divers and subtil crafty and unlawful games and plays, and some of them feigning themselves to have knowledge of . . . crafty sciences . . . shall be punished as provided.

What is most significant about this statute is the shift from an earlier concern with laborers to a concern with *criminal* activities. To be sure, the stipulation of persons "being whole and mighty in body, and able to labor, be taken in begging, or be vagrant" sounds very much like the concerns of the earlier statutes. Some important differences are apparent however when the rest of the statute includes those who ". . . can give no reckoning how he lawfully gets his living"; "some of them using divers subtil and unlawful games and plays." This is the first statute which specifically focuses upon these kinds of criteria for adjudging someone a vagrant.

It is significant that in this statute the severity of punishment is increased so as to be greater not only than provided by the 1503 statute but the punishment is more severe than that which had been provided by *any* of the pre-1503 statutes as well. For someone who is merely idle and gives no reckoning of how he makes his living the offender shall be:

. . . had to the next market town, or other place where they [the constables] shall think most convenient, and there to be tied to the end of a cart naked, and to be beaten with whips throughout the same market town or other place, till his body be bloody by reason of such whipping.[13]

But, for those who use "divers and subtil crafty and unlawful games and plays," etc., the punishment is ". . . whipping at two days together in manner aforesaid."[14] For the second offense, such persons are:

> scourged two days, and the third day to be put upon the pillory from nine of the clock till eleven before noon of the same day and to have one of his ears cut off.[15]

And if he offend the third time ". . . to have like punishment with whipping, standing on the pillory and to have his other ear cut off."

This statute (1) makes a distinction between types of offenders and applies the more severe punishment to those who are clearly engaged in "criminal" activities, (2) mentions a specific concern with categories of "unlawful" behavior, and (3) applies a type of punishment (cutting off the ear) which is generally reserved for offenders who are defined as likely to be a fairly serious criminal.

Only five years later we find for the first time that the punishment of death is applied to the crime of vagrancy. We also note a change in terminology in the statute:

> and if any ruffians . . . after having been one apprehended . . . shall wander, loiter, or idle use themselves and play the vagabonds . . . shall be eftfoons not only whipped again, but shall have the gristle of his right ear clean cut off. And if he shall again offend, he shall be committed to gaol till the next sessions; and being there convicted upon indictment, he shall have judgment to suffer pains and execution of death, as a felon, as an enemy of the commonwealth.[16]

It is significant that the statute now makes persons who repeat the crime of vagrancy a felon. During this period then, the focal concern of the vagrancy statutes becomes a concern for the control of felons and is no longer primarily concerned with the movement of laborers.

These statutory changes were a direct response to changes taking place in England's social structure during this period. We have already pointed out that feudalism was decaying rapidly. Concomitant with the breakup of feudalism was an increased emphasis upon commerce and industry. The commercial emphasis in England at the turn of the sixteenth century is of particular importance in the development of vagrancy laws. With commercialism came considerable traffic bearing valuable items. Where there were 169 important merchants in the middle of the fourteenth century there were 3,000 merchants engaged in foreign trade alone at the beginning of the sixteenth century.[17] England became highly dependent upon commerce for its economic support. Italians conducted a great deal of the commerce of England during this early period and were held in low repute by the populace. As a result, they were subject to attacks by citizens and, more important, were frequently robbed of their goods while transporting them. "The general insecurity of the times made any transportation hazardous. The special risks to which the alien merchant was subjected gave rise to the royal practice of issuing formally executed covenants of safe conduct through the realm."[18]

Such a situation not only called for the enforcement of existing laws but also called for the creation of new laws which would facilitate the control of persons preying upon merchants transporting goods. The vagrancy statutes were revived in order to fulfill just such a purpose. Persons who had committed no serious felony but who were suspected of being capable of doing so could be apprehended and incapacitated through the application of vagrancy laws once these laws were refocused so as to include ". . . any ruffians . . . [who] shall wander, loiter, or idle use themselves and use themselves and play the vagabonds . . ."[19]

The new focal concern is continued in 1 Ed. 6. c. 3 (1547) and in fact is made more general so as to include:

Whoever man or woman, being not lame, impotent, or so aged or diseased that he or she cannot work, not having whereon to live, shall be lurking in any house, or loitering or idle wandering by the highway side, or in streets, cities, towns, or villages, not applying themselves to some honest labor, and so continuing for three days; or running away from their work; every such person shall be taken for a vagabond. And . . . upon conviction of two witnesses . . . the same loiterer (shall) be marked with a hot iron in the breast with the letter V, and adjudged him to the person bringing him, to be his slave for two years . . .

By 1571 in the statute of 14 El. C. 5 the shift in focal concern is fully developed:

All rogues, vagabonds, and sturdy beggars shall . . . be committed to the common gaol . . . he shall be grievously whipped, and burnt thro' the gristle of the right ear with a hot iron of the compass of an inch about; . . . And for the second offense, he shall be adjudged a felon, unless some person will take him for two years in to his service. And for the third offense, he shall be adjudged guilty of felony without benefit of clergy.

And there is included a long list of persons who fall within the statute: "proctors, procurators, idle persons going about using subtil, crafty and unlawful games or plays; and some of them feigning themselves to have knowledge of . . . absurd sciences . . . and all fencers, bearwards, common players in interludes, and minstrels . . . all juglers, pedlars, tinkers, petty chapmen . . . and all counterfeiters of licenses, passports and users of the same." The major significance of this statute is that it includes all the previously defined offenders and adds some more. Significantly, those added are more clearly criminal types, counterfeiters, for example. It is also significant that there is the following qualification of this statute: "Provided also, that this act shall not extend to cookers, or harvest folks, that travel for harvest work, corn or hay." . . .

And a provision is made for giving more money for maintaining the gaols. This seems to add credence to the notion that this statute was seen as being significantly more general than those previously.

It is also of importance to note that this is the first time the term *rogue* has been used to refer to persons included in the vagrancy statutes. It seems, *a priori*, that a "rogue" is a different social type than is a "vagrant" or a "vagabond"; the latter terms implying something more equivalent to the idea of a "tramp" whereas the former (rogue) seems to imply a more disorderly and potentially dangerous person.

The emphasis upon the criminalistic aspect of vagrants continues in Chapter 17 of the same statute:

> Whereas divers *licentious* persons wander up and down in all parts of the realm, to countenance their *wicked behavior*; and do continually assemble themselves armed in the highways, and elsewhere in troops, *to the great terror* of her majesty's true subjects, *the impeachment of her laws*, and the disturbance of the peace and tranquillity of the realm; and whereas many outrages are daily committed by these dissolute persons, and more are likely to ensue if speedy remedy be not provided. (Italics added)

With minor variations (e.g., offering a reward for the capture of a vagrant) the statutes remain essentially of this nature until 1743. In 1743 there was once more an expansion of the types of persons included such that "all persons going about as patent gatherers, or gatherers of alms, under pretense of loss by fire or other casualty; or going about as collectors for prisons, gaols, or hospitals; all persons playing or betting at any unlawful games; and all persons who run away and leave their wives or children . . . all persons wandering abroad, and lodging in alehouses, barns, outhouses, or in the open air, not giving good account of themselves," were types of offenders added to those already included. . . .

Before leaving this section it is perhaps pertinent to make a qualifying remark. We have emphasized throughout this section how the vagrancy statutes underwent a shift in focal concern as the social setting changed. The shift in focal concern is not meant to imply that the later focus of the statutes represents a completely new law. It will be recalled that even in the first vagrancy statute there was reference to those who "do refuse labor, giving themselves to idleness and vice and sometimes to theft and other abominations." Thus the possibility of criminal activities resulting from persons who refuse to labor was recognized even in the earliest statute. The fact remains, however, that the major emphasis in this statute and in the statutes which followed the first one was always upon the "refusal to labor" or "begging." The "criminalistic" aspect of such persons was relatively unimportant. Later, as we have shown, the criminalistic potential becomes of paramount importance. The thread runs back to the earliest statute but the reason for the statutes' existence as well as the focal concern of the statutes is quite different in 1743 than it was in 1349.

Vagrancy Laws in the United States

. . . The control of criminals and undesirables was the *raison de etre* of the vagrancy laws in the U.S. This is as true today as it was in 1750. As Caleb Foote's analysis of the application of vagrancy statutes in the Philadelphia court shows, these laws are presently applied indiscriminately to persons considered a "nuisance." Foote suggests that ". . . the chief significance of this branch of criminal law lies in its quantitative impact and administrative usefulness."[20] Thus it appears that in America the trend begun in England in the sixteenth, seventeenth and eighteenth centuries has been carried to its logical extreme and the laws are now used principally as a mechanism for "clearing the streets" of the derelicts who inhabit the "skid roads" and "Bowerys" of our large urban areas.

Since the 1800's there has been an abundant source of prospects to which the vagrancy laws have been applied. These have been primarily those persons deemed by the police and the courts to be either actively involved in criminal activities or at least peripherally involved. In this context, then, the statutes have changed very little. The functions served by the statutes in England of the late eighteenth century are still being served today in both England and the United States. The locale has changed somewhat and it appears that the present day application of vagrancy statutes is focused upon the arrest and confinement of the "down and outers" who inhabit certain sections of our larger cities but the impact has remained constant. The lack of change in the vagrancy statutes, then, can be seen as a reflection of the society's perception of a continuing need to control some of its "suspicious" or "undesirable" members.[21]

A word of caution is in order lest we leave the impression that this administrative purpose is the sole function of vagrancy laws in the U.S. today. Although it is our contention that this is generally true it is worth remembering that during certain periods of our recent history, and to some extent today, these laws have also been used to control the movement of workers. This was particularly the case during the depression years and California is of course infamous for its use of vagrancy laws to restrict the admission of migrants from other states.[22] The vagrancy statutes, because of their history, still contain germs within them which make such effects possible. Their main purpose, however, is clearly no longer the control of laborers but rather the control of the undesirable, the criminal and the "nuisance."

Discussion

... This analysis of the vagrancy statutes ... has demonstrated the importance of "vested interest" groups in the emergence and/or alteration of laws. The vagrancy laws emerged in order to provide the powerful landowners with a ready supply of cheap labor. When this was no longer seen as

necessary and particularly when the la. were no longer dependent upon cheap labor . were they a powerful interest group in the society the laws became dormant. Finally a new interest group emerged and was seen as being of great importance to the society and the laws were then altered so as to afford some protection to this group. These findings are thus in agreement with Weber's contention that "status groups" determine the content of the law.[23] The findings are inconsistent, on the other hand, with the perception of the law as simply a reflection of "public opinion" as is sometimes found in the literature.[24] We should be cautious in concluding, however, that either of these positions are necessarily correct. The careful analysis of other laws, and especially of laws which do not focus so specifically upon the "criminal," are necessary before this question can be finally answered. ...

NOTES

For a more complete listing of most of the statutes dealt with in this report the reader is referred to Burn, *The History of the Poor Laws*. Citations of English statues should be read as follows: 3 Ed. 1. c. 1. refers to the third act of Edward the first, chapter one, etc.

1. Hall, J., *Theft, Law and Society*, Bobbs-Merrill, 1939. See also, Alfred R. Lindesmith, "Federal Law and Drug Addiction," *Social Problems* Vol. 7, No. 1, 1959, p.48.
2. See, for example, Rose, A., "Some Suggestions for Research in the Sociology of Law," *Social Problems* Vol. 9, No. 3, 1962, pp. 281–283, and Geis, G., "Sociology, Criminology, and Criminal Law," *Social Problems* Vol. 7, No. 1, 1959, pp. 40–47.
3. 3 Ed. 1. c. 1.
4. 35 Ed. 1. c. 1.
5. 23 Ed. 3.
6. 25 Ed. 3 (1351).
7. [Bradshaw, F. *A Social History of England*, p. 54].
8. *Ibid.*, p. 57.
9. Foote, C., "Vagrancy Type Law and Its Administration," *Univ. of Pennsylvania Law Review* (104), 1956, p. 615.

10. *Ibid.*
11. As evidenced for this note the expectation that "... the common gaols of every shire are likely to be greatly pestered with more numbers of prisoners than heretofore ..." when the statutes were changed by the statute of 14 Ed. c. 5 (1571).
12. Bradshaw, *op. cit.*, p. 61.
13. 22 H. 8. c. 12 (1530).
14. *Ibid.*
15. *Ibid.*
16. 27 H. 8. c. 25 (1535).
17. Hall, *op. cit.*, p. 21.
18. *Ibid.*, p. 23.
19. 27 H. 8. c. 25 (1535).

20. Foote, *op. cit.*, p. 613. Also see in this connection, Irwin Deutscher, "The Petty Offender," *Federal Probation*, XIX, June, 1955.
21. It is on this point that the vagrancy statutes have been subject to criticism. See for example, Lacey, Forrest W., "Vagrancy and Other Crimes of Personal Condition," *Harvard Law Review* (66), p. 1203.
22. *Edwards v. California*, 314 S: 160.
23. M. Rheinstein, *Max Weber on Law in Economy and Society*, Harvard University Press, 1954.
24. Friedman, N., *Law in a Changing Society*, Berkeley and Los Angeles: University of California Press, 1959.

Law as a Weapon in Social Conflict

Austin T. Turk

... Not to deny either that law often does contribute to conflict management or that the quest for a just and secure social order is honorable and necessary, the objectives in this paper are (1) to note certain fundamental limitations of what may be termed the moral functionalist conception of law; (2) to marshal arguments for a conception of law free of those limitations—i.e., the conception of law as a form or dimension of social power (as empirically more a partisan weapon in than a transcendent resolver of social conflicts); and (3) to formulate a set of basic empirical propositions about law and social conflict to which the power conception of law directs sociolegal research.

Law as Conflict Management

To *define* law as a means of conflict management is to leave theory and research on law and society without an analytical framework independent of particular ethical and theoretical preferences and aversions. While it may facilitate critiques of totalitarian or bureaupathic decisions and actions taken "in the name of law," such a definition appears at the same time to impede the development of an understanding of law in which evidence of its regulatory functions is integrated with evidence of its disruptive and exploitative uses and effects. Merely condemning the seamier side of law as perversions or departures from "the rule of law," and attributing them to human fallibility or wickedness, encourages neglect of the possibly systemic linkages between the "good" and "bad" features of law as it is empirically observed. Moreover, insofar as the moral functionalist conception of law has directly or by default encouraged such neglect, it has left sociolegal research vulnerable to charges of bias favoring certain culture-specific ideas and institutions, and helped to provoke the radical counter-assertion that exploitation and disruption constitute the defining reality of law while regulation is only illusion and suppression (see Lefcourt, 1971; Zinn, 1971; Quinney, 1974.)

A related difficulty with the moral functionalist conception of law is that *legal* means of conflict management tend to be equated with *peaceful* ones; and there is a strong inclination to assume that consensual, non-coercive methods are the only really effective ways of preventing or managing conflicts. ...

At a more general theoretical level, the moral functionalist conception of law impedes efforts to approach the scientific ideal of unbiased inquiry by encouraging investigators to define their research problems in terms of theoretical models derived from "natural law" and/or "functional-systems" assumptions. First, the bias introduced by natural law philosophy, even though secularized (cf. Selznick, 1961), leaves researchers unable to deal convincingly (i.e., in strictly naturalistic and empirically demonstrable propositions) with the observation or view that any idea of justice is founded ultimately upon faith, not upon empirical criteria (Stone, 1965). Second, many crucial methodological and theoretical issues are not resolved but evaded to the extent that research begins with, instead of testing, the assumptions (a) that legal phenomena constitute a system, (b) that the system-referent is empirically obvious, or at least readily determined, and (c) that the system embodies the meritocratic or egalitarian prerequisites for social welfare. In particular, boundedness and the other assumptions of systems modeling are left unexamined, as are the conventional or traditional understandings of what are "legal things," while—despite the recognition of structured inequities in particular instances (e.g., Nonet, 1969)—there is no conceptual resolution of the issues raised by the fact that the prerequisites, however, defined, for the welfare or survival of *some* are not necessarily consistent with the prerequisites of *all*.

To summarize briefly, the major limitations of the moral functionalist conception of law for the purposes of sociolegal research are that it (1) introduces cultural bias into research by defining away the disruptive and exploitive aspects of law, (2) tends to equate legal with consensual methods or processes of conflict management, which are presumed to be more effective than coercive means, and (3) encourages research in which natural law and/or functional-systems assumptions are taken for granted. If research on law and society is to be even relatively unbiased by culturally, ethically, methodologically, and politically partisan assumptions, a more neutral and empirically-grounded conception of law is needed. The remainder of this paper is devoted to an attempt to develop such a conception.

Law as Power

It must be granted that people may use the language of norms and generally, more or less consciously, accept their constructions as binding in the absence of a centralized enforcement agency, or indeed of any reliable means of forcing conformity. However, as has already been observed, it is equally clear that they may come to believe that their interests are better served by violating the normative expectations of others. In this connec-tion, the increasingly formal articulation of such expectations and the recognition or invention of the right to seek or attempt their enforcement (Hoebel, 1954:28) implies the increasing inability of people to get along with one another solely on the basis of tacit or consensual understandings. Furthermore, the persistence and growth of law as a cultural (symbolic, perceptual) and social (interactional, relational) reality is at least a kind of evidence that people have not yet found that they can do without such formalization, whether by a return to primitivism or by attaining some new consensual plateau. The effort to develop an adequate conception of law must, therefore, begin by recognizing the centrality of diversity and conflict in social life wherever law—provisionally understood as the process of formally articulating normative expectations—is discernible.

Given the law is intimately linked with social diversity and conflict, the most parsimonious explanation of the linkage seems to be that people find they cannot trust strangers. As the scale and complexity of social relatedness increase, so does the diversity of human experiences. The more diverse the experiences people have had, the more diverse their perceptions and evaluations of behavioral and relational alternatives may be. The greater the diversity of perceptions and evaluations, the greater may be the variability in what is perceived as justice in the specific terms of everyday life. (The implied distinction is between "norms in action" versus whatever similarities might be found in terms either of a general belief in justice as an abstract value, or of verbal responses to hypothetical questioning regarding the substantive meanings and relative importance of various normative statements or labels.) Aware that others' ideas of justice may vary from their own, people try—in accord with their own ideas and interests as they understand them—to maintain or gain control of, or to contest or evade, the processes by which normative expectations come to be formally articulated and enforced across, rather than only within, the boundaries of culturally homogeneous groups (whether the salient boundaries be those of families, clans, tribes, nations, or other groupings).

The empirical reality of law—apparently well understood in practice if not in theory—seems then, to be that it is a set of resources for which people contend and with which they are better able to promote their own ideas and interests against others, given the necessity of working out and preserving accommodative relationships with strangers. To say that people seek to gain and use resources to secure their own ideas and interests is, of course, to say that they seek to have and exercise *power*. While the meaning of power is far from settled, a convenient starting point is to view power as the control of resources, and the exercise of power as their mobilization in an effort to increase the probability of acceptable resolutions of actual or potential conflicts.[1] Although it helps to recognize that "law is power," a more specific conceptualization of what *kinds* of resource control are possible is necessary if we are to arrive at a useful understanding of what the general proposition means. I see five kinds of resource control, all represented in the cultural and social structural reality of law. These are (1) control of the means of direct physical violence, i.e., *war* or *police* power; (2) control of the production, allocation, and/or use of material resources, i.e., *economic* power; (3) control of decision-making processes, i.e., *political* power; (4) control of definitions of and access to knowledge, beliefs, values, i.e., *ideological* power; and (5) control of human attention and living-time, i.e., *diversionary* power.[2]

1. Having the law on one's side in a conflict implies that one can rightfully use or call upon others (allies, champions, or the authorities claiming jurisdiction over the area, people, or matters involved) to use violence to support one's claims against others. Modern polities are characterized by the presence and availability of control agencies specializing in the accretion, organization, and use of the means of violence, and asserting the principle that violence is—excepting more and more narrowly defined emergency situations—a resource reserved for official use only. Decisions by authorities, including decisions regarding the respective claims of disputing parties, are accom-

panied by the implied threat of physical coercion should any of the affected parties refuse to act in accord with such decisions.

2. People's life chances are affected just as decisively by how much their economic power is enhanced or eroded by law. The invention and elaboration of property and tax laws, in particular, reflect and help implement decisions on (1) what kinds of activities, products, and people should be rewarded more and what kinds less, and (2) how great should be the range between maximum and minimum rewards. . . .

3. The formulae and procedures of legal decision-making are integral to the workings of politically organized societies. . . . While non-legal factors clearly affect political struggle in general and organizational decision-making in particular, the law—as the most authoritative record of events and as the definitive model, criterion, and arbiter of rightness—is itself a political resource of major importance.

4. Legal concepts and thought-ways develop in the course of pragmatic efforts by men to comprehend problems of social interaction so as to manage them—including the problematics of dominating the lives of other people. Though not in this regard different from other products of such efforts, law as culture has an especially strong impact upon the frames of reference people use to give meaning to their situations. . . . Yet, the greatest importance of law as an ideological resource probably lies not in the facts of deliberate or inadvertent intervention on behalf of some perceptual alternatives versus others, but in the fact that legalism is the cultural bedrock of political order. The very concept of legality is designed to promote adherence to the ground rules of conventional politics (Turk, 1972:15–16)—which amount to agreement among contending parties on the supreme value of their common membership in a polity which must be preserved.

5. Human attention and living-time are finite resources—a trite but profoundly consequential observation. Insofar as the rhetoric and the real workings of law occupy men's attention and time to the exclusion of other phenomena—perhaps of greater import for the probability and quality of life—the law exerts diversionary power. . . . Preoccupation with the law, especially in its more attractive and innocuous aspects, not only diverts attention from potentially more dangerous concerns (from the perspective of authorities, *de facto* including loyal oppositions) but also reinforces the sense of law as an overwhelming, scarcely challengeable reality and criterion of reality. . . .

[I]n the power conception of law students of law and society are offered a methodologically tenable definition of the scope of their inquiry that includes it within the social scientific enterprise without reifying, mystifying, or obscuring the legal-nonlegal distinction. Given then the availability and amorality of legal power, the formulation and testing of propositions about the exercise of such power become central concerns for the scientific study of law as it is, as distinguished from doctrinal or applied research on behalf of law as someone believes it should or must be.[3] Because of the availability of so much work on law as a regulator and the relative paucity of work on law as a source and means of conflict, there is a particular need for propositions about ways in which law may generate or sharpen social conflicts. Accordingly, an effort has been made to develop several propositions indicating what seem to be the major ways law promotes or facilitates conflict. To the extent that these and related propositions are sustained and elaborated with greater precision in further research, they are expected to constitute the basis for a theory of law able to explain the conditions when and how conflict management may be accomplished by the control and mobilization of legal resources—i.e., a theory able to deal with conflict management as a problematic outcome instead of a defining characteristic of law as a social and cultural phenomenon.

Propositions: Law and Social Conflict

1. The availability of legal resources is in itself an impetus to social conflict, because conflict-ing or potentially conflicting parties cannot risk the possible costs of not having the law—or at least some law—on their side. When legal resources are not available or are negligible, parties are forced or able to rely upon nonlegal power to deal with the problematics of social interaction; law is irrelevant except perhaps in the loose sense of a generally recognized right of self-help for aggrieved parties able to assert it (cf. Hoebel, 1954: 25–28). As law becomes available, it becomes relevant as a contingency which must be met. It then becomes necessary to act so as to gain or increase control of legal resources, if only to neutralize them as weaponry an opponent might employ. The point is illustrated in the long effort by American southern whites to use the "white primary" and other ostensibly legal devices (Wirt, 1970:56–71), supplemented by extralegal and illegal ones, to prevent blacks from using resources formally granted them by emancipation and subsequent legal enactments and decisions.

2. Given pressure to contend for control of legal resources, differential nonlegal power can be expected to result at least initially in corresponding differences in legal power. The party with greater legal as well as non-legal power may then be able to increase its edge over weaker parties, even to the extreme of excluding the weaker altogether from access to the legal arena, cutting him off from even the opportunity to advance his claims and defend his interests "legally." For instance, since the formation of the inegalitarian South African nation in 1910, the weaker nonwhites have had their legal position steadily eroded, losing between 1936 and 1955 even voting rights guaranteed by the "entrenched clauses" of the South Africa Act (May, 1955:47–78; see also Sachs, 1973:143–145 and *passim*)—South Africa's constitution until it was superseded by the Republic of South Africa Constitution Act, 1961.

3. Legal power provides both the opportunity and the means to accomplish the effective denial of the reality of conflicts by making it impossible or inordinately difficult for them to be articulated and managed—as amply demonstrated in the long and stubborn effort to deny legal recognition and support for the effective unionization of agricultural laborers (McWilliams, 1942; Tangri, 1967; Galarza, 1970).

However, the persistent recurrence of struggles against economic, racial, and other forms of domination and exploitation make it clear that issues which cannot be couched in the language of law, or will not be accepted as actionable or justiciable, eventually have to be fought out in non-legal arenas—where resolutions may be achieved, but often at greater cost and with less durability. It is, of course, true that the lack of appropriate legal mechanisms for managing some issues may result from unintended as well as intended actions. Nonetheless, even though the denial of access to law may be explicable in objective terms, "objective" denial appears to be just as real in its consequences as "subjective."

4. Where power differences are rather less extreme, the availability of legal resources may encourage litigiousness—a word indicative of the fact that the presence of law encourages its use by parties hoping to improve their positions by methods relatively less dangerous or costly than non-legal power struggles, especially with formidable opponents. Parties confronting more powerful opponents may be encouraged to hope that by threatened or actual recourse to law they will be able to reduce, eliminate, or reverse initial power differences, or merely to extract some concession. For example, Nonet (1969: 81–83, 133–137) concluded that the New Deal turned law into an ally rather than an enemy of American trade unionism, so that the unions were encouraged to pursue a policy of self-help through legal advocacy instead of relying upon administrative procedures for handling workmen's compensation claims. On the other hand, stronger parties moving against weaker ones may find it advantageous to cloak their moves with legitimacy, especially to minimize the chance of third-party intervention on behalf of the underdog—as in the use of antitrust, conspiracy, right-to-work, and other laws to impede the development of effective labor unions (Blumrosen, 1962; Nonet, 1969: 81–83).

5. Apart from encouraging litigiousness, the availability of legal facilities decreases the pressure upon conflicting parties to resolve disputes in terms of the non-legal resources they can mobilize. Informal and private settlements, or at least accommodations to non-legal power differences (e.g., race relations "etiquette") seems less likely where the parties have the option or hope of legal recourse. Similarly, where an older legal system is giving way to a newer one, as in the Northern Rhodesian (Zambian) copperbelt, parties without recourse in the older system (e.g., young men protesting against the power of their wife's kin to intervene in marital and familial affairs) may be encouraged to appeal "to norms irreconcilably opposed to those of the traditional tribal system" (Epstein, 1958: 222).

6. Articulation in law of social categories, boundaries, and roles—with their associated rights and obligations—can sharpen old conflicts and produce new ones. Heightened awareness of the problematics of social interaction and relatedness can decrease the chances of resolving or avoiding conflicts, because "bringing things out into the open" frequently hardens existing boundaries, cleavages, and inequities (whether objectively or perceptually "real") by making it less easy to ignore, tacitly live with, or quietly and informally erase or change them. Rather than a transformation of conflict into a form more amenable to a reasonable resolution, legalization of a conflict can amount to an escalation that makes genuine settlement more difficult. Recognition of such possibilities has often been used for resisting the use of law as an instrument of social change—e.g., the views of some southern moderates, as well as conservatives, in the 1950's regarding the probable impact of the U.S. Supreme Court's desegregation decisions (Tumin and Rotberg, 1957).

7. Legal procedural norms are often used to exclude or distort information essential to an adequate comprehension of empirical problems, and thus can impede or prevent conflict resolution. In particular, legal distinctions between admissible and inadmissible evidence tend to work against consideration of perceptual, or subjective factors—those perhaps not objectively important or recognizable by legal criteria but extremely important in terms of what is significant to some or all of the involved parties. European, especially Anglo-American, legal systems have frequently been critically contrasted with non-European systems (e.g., Epstein, 1958, 198–223; Gibbs, 1963; several of the selections in Nader, 1969) in which there are few if any restrictions upon what may be considered in determining the contextual significance of facts. These non-European systems emphasize the qualitative more than the formal aspects of what is seen as a continuing rather than an episodic relationship between the disputing parties. Similarly, though in a different vein, "bourgeois legalism" has been rejected by Marxists in favor of "socialist legality," where the emphasis is asserted to be (and in non-political cases normally is) upon the education of disputants and offenders to social awareness and responsibility (Berman, 1966: 277–384).

8. Legal formulae and processes tend to emphasize the limitation and cessation of overt conflict behavior, discouraging not only all-out battles of principle but even the recognition that at least some social conflicts are zero-sum, not variable-sum (e.g., czars vs. communists: white racists vs. black revolutionaries).[4] To a considerable extent, law is oriented to regulating the *symptoms* of conflict without getting at the more intractable problems of removing the *sources* of conflict. However tactical concern with symptoms may sometimes be dictated by a strategic concern to minimize political or other costs of dealing with those sources. Consider the frequently noted judicial preference, supported by and expressed in such operating principles as *stare decisis* and *certiorari*, for carefully delimited case-specific issues rather than open confrontations over the political and economic premises of "the given order." Nonetheless, insofar as the legalization of conflicts does no more than limit the means of conflict and/or obfuscate the real issues, as in zero-sum struggles, some or all of the conflicting parties may come to view legalization as simply another device for out-positioning an opponent or for gaining time to mobilize or regroup one's non-legal forces—an attitude characteristic of both revolutionaries and counter-revolutionary police agents.

9. The tactics required to accomplish a legal settlement can conflict with those required to accomplish a genuine settlement. Where communication between disputants may be essential for them to become aware of common interests with priority over those at issue, communication may be precluded by the risk of disclosing injurious facts, violating rules against collusion, or otherwise weakening or contaminating the case at hand. The terminology and style of public legal conflict—as in verbal exchanges in legislative and judicial proceedings—may emphasize instead of correcting the affective and cognitive biases associated with conflict. Obtaining formal, open concessions from opponents in the course of legal struggle can make it more difficult for them to back down or accept defeat, and can reduce the chances of building a fund of mutual trust with them as a way of making further conflicts more amenable to resolution. Such considerations appear to explain the reluctance of businessmen to conduct their transactions in strictly legalistic terms (Macaulay, 1963), as well as the opposition of many academics to more explicit legalization of faculty-student relationships.

10. Legal decisions may prematurely signal the end of conflicts without actually resolving them. The processes of legal hearing, trial, and appeal often amount to rituals of dispute-settlement resulting in only illusory resolutions of conflicts, i.e., formal decisions that seem to settle disputes but do not do so on terms acceptable or even tolerable to the losers (and sometimes also the winners). Not only may dissatisfied parties be forced to seek redress by non-legal means in such present conflicts but the pretense of conflict resolution which they have experienced as the reality of law in action may make them far less willing to enter the legal arena in future conflicts. To the extent that law produces illusory instead of real conflict resolutions, it not only aggravates existing conflicts but also makes future conflicts more likely, and likely to be worse. Racial conflicts, for instance, have clearly not been resolved in South Africa by the legalization of a policy of racial separation—to be gradually accomplished during a "transitional" period of *dejure* white domination

(Sachs, 1973), or in North America by the legalization of a policy of racial integration—to be gradually accomplished during a "transitional" period of overcoming *de facto* white domination "with all deliberate speed" (compare Blaustein and Ferguson, 1962, with Swett, 1969, Moore, 1971, and Balbus, 1973).

11. Insofar as legal culture is incongruent with the social-behavioral realities of legal power as exercised by authorities, the law itself promotes cynicism, evasion, and defiance with respect to normative expectations and decisions—even among its representatives and practitioners (on lawyers, see Blumberg, 1967; on police, see Galliher, 1971). The law provides authorities with the cloak of claimed impartiality, a difficult claim impossible to live up to always and entirely. Apart from predispositions arising from their social origins, legal officials develop at least a partiality on behalf of their own organizational and career interests (Aubert, 1963) and routines for categorizing and handling cases with as little effort and risk as possible (Cicourel, 1968: 170–242).

Moreover, whether or not authorities try to be unbiased, the intent of the law can never be identical with the effect of the law as experienced. Even the most "understandable" differences between interpretation and interpretation, interpretation and action, or action and action, may not be "understandable" to affected parties who believe themselves—probably correctly—to be disadvantaged by the outcome. Credit, tenancy, welfare, and other laws affecting economic opportunities, privileges, and liabilities have often been shown to work systematically against the poor (Caplovitz, 1963; Carlin, Howard, and Messinger, 1966; tenBroek, 1966).

The crucial point is that bias is not just a matter of intention or even objective behavior, much less a matter only of due process under formal rules. Bias is also—and for the tasks of conflict regulation most important—a matter of perception and inference. Law *believed* to be biased may be just as ineffective, or worse, as law that *is* biased.

12. Legal changes that precipitate or facilitate non-legal social and cultural changes inevitably—barring the improbable case of unanimity on the meaning and desirability of the changes—sharpen and produce conflicts. As new law supersedes old, older ideas and interests may be shunted aside or demoted to lower priority ratings—as will be those people whose identifications and commitments are defined in terms of those ideas and interests. Nowhere is the fact of law as a party with its own interests to safeguard and enhance, potentially in conflict with others, more inescapable to people than when legal power serves to override, subvert, or simply reject their values and ways. Regardless of the possible long-run impact of legally promoted changes, the short-run impact will certainly be some contribution to increasing and exacerbating conflicts—most especially conflicts between legal authorities and at least some of those over whom authority is claimed. The degree of conflict resulting from legal changes will, of course, vary with the type of innovation, the social characteristics of those affected, and other factors (Zimring and Hawkins, 1971), from the relatively mild conflicts of conventional politics to the extreme conflicts resulting from legal intrusions into matters of sacred belief and practice—as in the Bolshevik attempt of the 1920's to impose sexual equality upon the largely Moslem peoples of Soviet Central Asia (Massell, 1968).

Conclusion

. . . It had been argued in this paper that the most prevalent conception of law orienting contemporary sociolegal research—the "moral functionalist" conception of law as in essence a means of conflict regulation—is in this and other respects demonstrably inadequate for the purposes of scientific research, however useful it may be for other purposes. A far more adequate alternative, it has been further argued, is the power conception of law, which recognizes in law a set of resources whose control and mobilization can in many ways—as indicated in a series of propositional statements—lead toward instead of away from conflicts. While the specifics undoubtedly need extension, elaboration, and qualification, the formulation offered here will have served its purpose if it stimulates sociolegal theorists and researchers to be more alert to the often subtle realities of power and conflict. In any case, there should be no quarrel over the fact that law may indeed contribute to conflict management—not least by its role in creating, sustaining, denying, and changing the perceptions and understandings by which people live.

NOTES

1. "Control" means the availability or accesibility of resources, varying from the extremely limited access of the helpless, through the shared access of competitors or allies, to the exclusive access of the almighty. "Resource" means anything of biological or cultural significance for human welfare. The distinction here between controlling and mobilizing resources is analogous to that which Etzioni (1968: 314–317) makes between "assets" and "power." However, his concept of "power" is much more restricted, or truncated, in that it refers only to mobilization against resistance and excludes much of what is involved in the control and mobilization of symbolic resources. With rather unnecessary inconsistency, he defines "persuasive power" as "exercised through the manipulation of symbols" (358) after suggesting that "the assets from which power is generated are much more scarce than the symbols which are the main base of communication" (335) and arguing that "communication" can be substituted for "power" (336).

2. My conscious indebtedness for terms and ideas used in this effort to sort out the forms and dimensions of power is mainly to Russell (1938), Schermerhorn (1961), and Gamson (1968).

3. While the distinction is essentially that proposed by Jerome Hall (1963:42) between "normative" or "humanistic legal sociology" (which he approves) and "scientific legal sociology" or "legal science" (which he disapproves), there is no compelling reason to oppose these two kinds of inquiry to each other. The point is merely that for those whose primary aim is to develop scientific knowledge of law as a social and cultural phenomenon an appropriately objective conception of law is essential. For those with other primary objectives, the moral functionalist or some other "committed" conception may well be more useful.

4. Whether or not all human conflicts are in principle transformable into variable-sum terms, and therefore resolvable by consensual means, it appears that

in empirical, historically specific, rather than philosophical terms there are limits to the ability and willingness of people collectively to accomplish such transformations.

REFERENCES

Aubert, Vilhem. 1963. "Competition and Dissensus: Two Types of Conflict Resolution," *Journal of Conflict Resolution* 7:26–42

Balbus, Isaac D. 1973. *The Dialectics of Legal Repression: Black Rebels Before the American Criminal Courts.* New York: Russell Sage Foundation.

Berman, Harold J. 1966. *Justice in the U.S.S.R.: An Interpretation of Soviet Law.* Cambridge: Harvard University.

Black, Donald J. 1972. "The Boundaries of Legal Sociology," *Yale Law Journal* 81 (May) 1086–1100.

———. 1973. "The Mobilization of Law," *Journal of Legal Studies* 2 (January):125–149.

Blaustein, Alpert P. and Clarence C. Ferguson, Jr. 1962. *Desegregation and the Law: The Meaning and Effect of the School Segregation Cases.* New York: Vintage Books.

Blumberg, Abraham S. 1967. "The Practice of Law as a Confidence Game: Organizational Cooptation of a Profession," *Law and Society Review* 1 (June):15–39.

Blumrosen, Alfred W. 1962. "Legal Process and Labor Law: Some Observations on the Relation between Law and Sociology," Pp. 185–225 in William M. Evan (ed.), *Law and Sociology.* New York: Free Press of Glencoe.

Caplovitz, David. 1963. *The Poor Pay More.* New York: The Free Press.

Carlin, Jerome E., Jan Howard, and Sheldon L. Messinger. 1966. "Civil Justice and the Poor: Issues for Sociological Research," *Law and Society Review* 1 (November):9–89.

Chambliss, William J. and Robert B. Seidman. 1971. *Law, Order, and Power.* Reading, Mass: Addison-Wesley.

Cicourel, Aaron V. 1968. *The Social Organization of Juvenile Justice.* New York: Wiley.

Diamond, Stanley. 1971. "The Rule of Law Versus the Order of Custom," Pp.115–144 in Robert P. Wolff (ed.), *The Rule of Law.* New York: Simon and Schuster.

Epstein, A. L. 1958. *Politics in an Urban African Community.* Manchester: Manchester University.

Etzioni, Amitai. 1968. *The Active Society.* New York: The Free Press.

Galarza, Ernesto. 1970. *Spiders in the House and Workers in the Field*. South Bend: University of Notre Dame.

Galliher, John F. 1971. "Explanations of Police Behavior: A Critical Review and Analysis," *Sociological Quarterly* 12 (Summer):308–318.

Gamson, William A. 1968. *Power and Discontent*. Homewood, Ill.: Dorsey.

Gibbs, Jack P. 1968. "Definitions of Law and Empirical Questions," *Law and Society Review* 2 (May):429–446.

Gibbs, James L., Jr. 1963. "The Kpelle Moot: A Therapeutic Model For the Informal Settlement of Disputes," *Africa* 33:1–11.

Hall, Jerome. 1963. *Comparative Law and Social Theory*. Baton Rouge: Louisiana State University.

Hoebel, E. A. 1954. *The Law of Primitive Man*. Cambridge: Harvard University.

Lefcourt, Robert (ed.). 1971. *Law Against the People*. New York: Vintage Books.

Macaulay, Stewart. 1963. "Non-Contractual Relations in Business: A Preliminary Study," *American Sociological Review* 28 (February):55–67.

Massell, Gregory J. 1968. "Law as an Instrument of Revolutionary Change in a Traditional Milieu: The Case of Soviet Central Asia." *Law and Society Review* 2 (February):179–228.

May, Henry J. 1955. *The South African Constitution* (third edition). Cape Town: Juta.

McWilliams, Carey. 1942. *Ill Fares the Land: Migrants and Migratory Labor in the United States*. Boston: Little, Brown.

Moore, Howard, Jr. 1971. "*Brown v Board of Education*: The Court's Relationship to Black Liberation." Pp. 55–64 in Robert Lefcourt (ed.), *Law Against the People*. New York: Vintage Books.

Nonet, Philippe. 1969. *Administrative Justice: Advocacy and Change in a Government Agency*. New York: Russell Sage Foundation.

Quinney, Richard. 1974. *Critique of Legal Order*. Boston: Little, Brown.

Russell, Bertrand. 1938. *Power: A New Social Analysis*. London: Allen and Unwin.

Sachs, Albie. 1973. *Justice in South Africa*. Berkeley: University of California.

Schermerhorn, Richard A. 1961. *Society and Power*. New York: Random House.

Selznick, Philip. 1961. "Sociology and Natural Law." *Natural Law Forum* 6:84–108.

Stone, Julius. 1965. *Human Law and Human Justice*. Stanford: Stanford University.

Swett, Daniel H. 1969. "Cultural Bias in the American Legal System." *Law and Society Review* 4 (August): 79–110.

Tangri, Beverly S. 1967. *Federal Legislation as an Expression of United States Public Policy Toward Agricultural Labor, 1914–1954*. Berkeley: University of California, unpublished Ph.D. dissertation.

tenBroek, Jacobus (ed.). 1966. *The Law of the Poor*. San Francisco: Chandler.

Tumin, Melvin M. and Robert Rotberg. 1957. "Leaders, the Led, and the Law: A Case Study in Social Change." *Public Opinion Quarterly* 21 (Fall):355–370.

Turk, Austin T. 1969. *Criminality and Legal Order*. Chicago: Rand McNally.

———. 1972. *Legal Sanctioning and Social Control*. Washington, D.C.: Supt. of Docs., U.S. Government Printing Office, DHEW Pub No. (HSM) 72–9130.

Wirt, Frederick M. 1970. *Politics of Southern Equality: Law and Social Change in a Mississippi County*. Chicago: Aldine.

Wolff, Robert P. (ed.). 1971. *The Rule of Law*. New York: Simon and Schuster.

Zimring, Franklin, and Gordon Hawkins. 1971. "The Legal Threat as an Instrument of Social Change," *Journal of Social Issues* 27(2):33–48.

Zinn, Howard. 1971. "The Conspiracy of Law," Pp. 15–36 in Robert P. Wolff (ed.), *The Rule of Law*. New York: Simon and Schuster.

• 9 •

Critical Legal Studies

In the preceding chapters we have considered the classical and contemporary perspectives in the sociology of law. As such, we have been concerned with the theoretical statements made by nineteenth-century sociolegal scholars as well as with the twentieth-century sociological paradigms that have informed legal sociology. We now come to the last, and most contemporary, of the theoretical traditions in law to be discussed in this book: *critical legal studies.*

The purpose of this chapter is to examine how critical legal studies has attempted to demystify and delegitimate the legal doctrine of liberal democratic societies. We begin with an explanation of critical legal studies' critique of liberal legal doctrine. Next, we demonstrate how the "methodologies" of sociological theory, critical theory, and deconstructionism are used by critical legal scholars to expose the inconsistencies and contradictions of contract law. This chapter also focuses on the ideological conflicts in private law disputes that result from opposing worldviews concerning society and humanity; the contradictions of contract doctrine arising from the problems of power and knowledge; and why critical legal studies fails to consider the needs and experiences of women and minorities.

Critical Legal Studies: Trashing Liberal Legalism

Critical legal studies (CLS) is an intellectual trend that has had an enormous influence on legal scholarship during the last two decades. The first conference on critical legal studies was held in Madison, Wisconsin, in the spring of 1977. Since then, the CLS scholars, or the Critics, have produced a noteworthy body of literature in which they critique **liberal legal doctrine,** or that set of legal concepts meant to safeguard from political interference an individual's personal freedom to engage in contractual agreements in order to promote his or her self-interest. The Critics charge that the doctrine of liberal legalism is full of contradictions and inconsistencies. As a result, they contend that the principle of the rule of law, which has been at the core of liberal political theory since the seventeenth century, is a myth (Altman, 1990). The CLS critique strikes at the heart of the legal systems of liberal democratic societies such as the United States, Canada, and England.

391

It is to legal realism (see Chapter 3) that CLS owes a major intellectual debt. According to the Critics, CLS is a direct descendant of American legal realism (Tushnet, 1986:505). Indeed, the CLS and the realist traditions share one fundamental notion: the belief that politics and law are virtually inseparable. They see political power as having a marked influence on the process of lawmaking and, more significantly, on the process of judicial decision-making. This observation is fundamentally a critique of the liberal legal premise, which argues that law and politics are wholly separate entities and which asserts that judges, as neutral arbitrators, make court decisions that are immune from political and ideological influences. The CLS extension of the realist critique occurs as the Critics explore more deeply the doctrinal tenets proposed by liberal legalism. In essence, CLS advances a social theory with the objective of emancipating individuals from the dominant liberal legal ideology. The Critics contend that this freedom can be realized only by transforming the existing social, political, and economic institutions.

The Critique of Liberal Legal Doctrine

Critical legal studies focuses its critique on four aspects of liberal legalism: indeterminacy, antiformalism, contradiction, and marginality (see Trubek, 1984). Let us examine each of these four aspects in turn.

Indeterminacy. The Critics reject the idea that the law is constituted as a coherent set of rules, or a logically ordered "system." Precisely because it is not structured as a system, the law cannot provide conclusively fixed—determinant— answers to all legal questions and situations. The law, therefore, is said to be *indeterminate*. The idea that the law always prescribes a single correct and logical answer in judicial decision-making is patently false, say the Critics.

Antiformalism. The Critics discount the notion that there exists an autonomous and neutral—that is, formal—mode of legal reasoning. They contend that judges, when using their legal skills, do not arrive at court decisions that are independent of their ideological and political persuasions. Mark Tushnet of the Georgetown University Law Center makes it clear that judges, "for political, intellectual and personal reasons, choose to announce doctrines that advance the interests of one or another segment of a fragmented society" (1980:1388). The CLS critique against liberal legal doctrine, therefore, is one of *antiformalism*. Moreover, the connection between the CLS critique of formalism and the challenge to liberal political theory is that liberal political theory depends on formalism. Thus, for the Critics, law and politics are closely intertwined and cannot be separated.

Contradiction. The CLS theorists see liberal legalism as a collection of divergent concepts expressing competing views of society and social relations. In short, liberal legal doctrine is characterized by *contradiction*. For instance, the law maintains that a contract is a private agreement between two parties. However, if one of the parties violates the rules of fair bargaining, that contract is declared invalid by the court. The contract loses it "privateness" and becomes a public matter as soon as the court intervenes to void it. We are then left with the questions: Are bargains made by two individuals private or public matters? Neither? Both? Persuasive arguments, pro and con, can be made for either side of the private-public debate, and the logical inconsistencies of legal reasoning become apparent. CLS scholar Alan D. Freeman states that, "within the world of liberal legal scholarship, every position is refutable, and the product taken as a whole is hopelessly contradictory" (1981:1233).

Marginality. Even if legal contradictions did not exist and there was complete agreement on all of the concepts of liberal legal doctrine, the law would still not be the sole decisive factor in settling interpersonal disputes. In other words, relationships between people are so complex that many other (more important) factors outside of the law need to be considered in judicial decision-making. These extra-legal factors that the judge must take into account reveal that the law is not always central—indeed, it is often *marginal*—to the resolution of social conflicts.

Considering that the law is marginal and thus only tangential to a proper assessment of social relationships, and also considering the fact that it is indeterminate, contradictory, and not a formal system, we may say with University of Wisconsin law professor David Trubek that "'law' itself is not something hard but rather an obscure and vague source of normative guidance. The law, in whose shadow we bargain, is itself a shadow" (1984:578–579).

Ideology. Much of the CLS assault on liberal legalism involves a critique of the social consciousness, or ideology, perpetuated by that doctrine.

Ideology gives us our basic, and quite often implicit, assumptions or worldview about how society should be organized and which social relations are necessary, desirable, and possible. *Legal* ideology also informs this taken-for-granted worldview. Therefore, those ideas that we have about the law—what it is, what it does, and why it exists—find their expression in our society. More to the point, liberal legal ideology is an integral part of *capitalist* society; a society with a free-market economy that contributes to social inequality, power differentials, hierarchy, and other social divisions. In addition, the Critics maintain that liberal legal ideology legitimates capitalist society (and all its institutional arrangements) and capitalist society, in turn, legitimates liberal legal ideology.

Aside from being critics of legal ideology, some CLS scholars also seek to *change* that ideology and the oppressive and exploitative social institutions and human associations that it engenders. Their objective is to construct an alternative worldview, or "countervision" of self and society, that will emancipate individuals from the current institutional setup. Trubek (1984) refers to this action as the "transformative politics" of CLS scholarship, and according to him, it is this quality that gives CLS its *critical* dimension.

Changing how people view the social world and each other is, to say the least, a very difficult task. Besides legitimating things as they are, a worldview also gives *meaning* to our social reality. Meaning forms and informs our consciousness. Like the Marxists, the Critics see the current situation as one of false consciousness, or as "mystical delusions embedded in our consciousness by the liberal legal worldview" (Freeman, 1981:1230–1231). Furthermore, as Trubek explains, "the worlds of meaning that we construct in turn shape and channel what we do and do not do" (1984:592). Put another way, liberal legalism tells us that society, as it is currently organized, is natural and just and that human relations, as they currently exist, are the necessary and desirable ones. A different way of thinking about society and human relations lies outside most people's realm of consciousness.

Trashing. If one technique for doing CLS scholarship can be identified, that technique would be *trashing* (Kelman, 1984). **Trashing** is a generic term for two processes: (1) *demystification,* or "the stripping away of the veneer of apolitical decision-making from the legal process" (Schlegel, 1984:401); and (2) *delegitimation,* or disclosing those possibilities that truly express reality and that can fashion a future that realizes not an abstract, but a substantive notion of justice (Freeman, 1981:1230–1231). In short, through trashing, the CLS theorists seek to lay bare and question the basic premises that underlie liberal legal doctrine. It is these presuppositions (which are usually implicit) that determine our consciousness and thus give meaning to our social world and our interactions with other people. These premises, however, are not always borne out in concrete reality. In other words, there is an inconsistency, and quite often a contradiction, between the *ideas* contained in liberal legal doctrine and the *practical conditions* of everyday life. Freeman's (1981) example of shared values, which he regards as the "most powerful presupposition" in liberal legal doctrine, will serve as an apt illustration of what we are talking about.

According to Freeman, liberal legalism begins with the premise that there is enough of an agreement among people concerning their interests that it is possible to identify shared values. These shared values enable jurists to talk about fundamental concepts endemic to the law such as economic efficiency, equal concern, and representative democracy. Such concepts are then used to evaluate the validity of a particular law. For example, if a certain law is found wanting in representative democracy it is said to exist contrary to the interests of the majority of individuals who believe that every citizen should have an equal voice in the political process. However, the fact is that representative democracy is *not* a pervasive characteristic for all segments of society; the poor, for instance, have less of a say in political matters than the rich. This is a situation where the **de jure** (from Latin meaning "sanctioned by law") aspect of the law contradicts the **de facto** (from Latin meaning "in reality") aspect of society. Or, to put it another way, what liberal legalism presupposes "ought to be," does not correspond with "what is" in the real world of conflict, domination, and hierarchy. Freeman contends that liberal legalism attempts to hide contradictions such as this by leading us to believe that the world is relatively fair and just; promising greater equality but opposing its attainment; and prohibiting the transformation of the social, political, and economic institutions.

The CLS objective is to trash the liberal legal presuppositions and expose the "real" society characterized by hierarchy and power relations based on race, sex, and class. Trashing, the Critics contend, delegitimates the presuppositions of liberal legalism and renders a vision of the world as it really is. In the end, trashing will free people from ideological abstractions and help them to transform society's oppressive institutional arrangements.

CLS Methodologies

According to Debra Livingston, former student editor of the *Harvard Law Review*, critical legal studies "does not have a definitive methodological approach" (1982:1669, n.3). Simply stated, there is no one distinctive way of doing critical legal scholarship. Nonetheless, Livingston explains that CLS does have recourse to the "methodologies" of various disciplines. She identifies three methodologies that CLS borrows from several fields and utilizes to critique liberal legal doctrine: *social theory*, *pure critique*, and *textual explication*.

The methodology of **social theory** is directly derived from sociology. The various sociological traditions—in particular the Marxian perspective, conflict theory, the Weberian perspective, and even structural-functionalism—serve as useful guides for transforming and reconstructing society, human associations, and legal doctrine. Although social theory may produce an alternate vision of society that some would describe as utopian and impractical, it nonetheless provides the Critics with a blueprint for changing the oppressive institutions currently in existence in capitalist society.

The methodology of **pure critique** is also an important part of the CLS arsenal. Pure critique has several intellectual sources, but it is best exemplified by such critical theorists of the Frankfurt School as Herbert Marcuse, Erich Fromm, Max Horkheimer, and Jurgen Habermas. Frankfurt School critical theory has its intellectual roots in the negative dialectics of German philosopher Georg Hegel. Relying on Hegel's *negative dialectics*, Marcuse tell us that we arrive at the true meaning of facts when we deny, through contradiction, those facts that are presented as truth (1960:26–27). For example, one of the dominant values upheld by liberal legalism is that of individual self-interest: people should be allowed to pursue their own happiness in their own way. By contrast, there also exists the cultural value that individuals should consider the well-being of others. Pitting these two values against each other results in a contradiction that gives us a better understanding of liberal legalism and the social context in which it thrives.

Finally, **textual explication**—the explication of legal "texts" (written works) or "stories" (rhetoric)—has to do with the process of *interpreting* (i.e. determining the meaning of) legal principles, concepts, and theory. The techniques of interpretation used by the Critics are borrowed from several sources, including *deconstructionism*. A recent trend in literary criticism, **deconstructionism** involves the strategy of closely reading a text/story for the purpose of penetrating the surface and getting at its hidden meaning and unexpressed assumptions. The text/story is taken apart, deconstructed, and its structure and logic are questioned. In the CLS program, the end result of textual explication is that the underlying inconsistencies and contradictions of liberal legal doctrine are revealed.

In the two sections that follow we examine the ideas of Duncan Kennedy and Clare Dalton and how their work reflects the influence of social theory, pure critique, and textual explication. We begin our discussion by examining Kennedy's statements about the role individualism and altruism have played in liberal legal doctrine.

Individualism and Altruism

Harvard University law professor Duncan Kennedy's "Form and Substance in Private Law Adjudication" (1976), is widely regarded as one of the seminal pieces in the CLS literature. In this article, Kennedy discusses the characteristics of the two antithetical "rhetorical modes," or linguistic styles, influencing substantive legal issues: *individualism* and *altruism*. He also identifies two opposed modes that influence the form in which legal solutions to the substantive problems should be cast: *rules* and *standards*. The relationship between these two sets of rhetorical modes, says Kennedy, is made evident in private law disputes where altruism favors standards and individualism jibes with the use of rules. Both sets of rhetorical modes are based on different utopian visions, or worldviews, of what is right and good. We begin with a discussion of Kennedy's notions regarding rules and standards.

Rules and Standards

Rules are those formal legal norms that direct a judge to respond to the facts of a case in a calculative and determinate manner. By contrast, **standards** are those informal legal norms that direct the judge to tailor his or her judicial decision to the particulars of the case. According to Kennedy, the rules-standards continuum operates at the level of legal *form*. The **form** of law—that is, the way in which law is structured—is characterized as having three dimensions that are regarded as continua: (1) formal realizability of rules vs. informality of standards, (2) generality vs. particularity, and (3) formalities vs. rules designed to deter wrongful behavior. Let us briefly look at each of these dimensions in turn.

Formal realizability of rules vs. informality of standards. As regards the first dimension, formal realizability of rules means that a judge is supposed to apply a rigid law in a technical, mechanical, and principled manner. Ideally, formally realizable rules have two major virtues. First, they safeguard against the ad hoc decision-making of presiding judges, who are supposed "to act in well-defined situations and in well-defined ways" (Altman, 1990:107). This is very similar to Max Weber's contention that a formal rational legal system yields a calculable, efficient, predictable, logical, and universal judicial decision (see Chapter 5). Second, Kennedy states that formally realizable rules provide certainty (and more importantly, advance warning and fair notice) of legal consequences. Because both of these virtues focus on the objective aspects of a situation, formally realizable rules give the law a certain degree of predictability. As we saw in Chapter 5, Weber considers predictability in lawmaking and lawfinding as having a necessary affinity with the high degree of predictability that characterizes that most rational of economic systems, capitalism.

In contrast to a formally realizable rule, an informal standard is a principle applied by a judge in a valuative and subjective way while taking into consideration the specifics of a case. The judge must therefore be situationally sensitive. Because they are based on the judge's personal discretion, informal standards in court cases have the drawback of sometimes being too vague and nonadministrable.

Rules and standards uphold two different sets of values. Whereas rules seek to keep the courts from intruding on the private rights of contracting parties, standards are concerned with protecting the weaker party from unfair advantage.

Generality vs. particularity. In the second dimension, "generality" refers to the multiplicity of issues to which a law can be applied. Although wide-encompassing in scope, generality gives a law a measure of imprecision seen in terms of over- and underinclusion. For example, a rule that sets eighteen as the minimum age at which a person can contract with another party may be overinclusive when it permits the very mature seventeen-year-old to legally back out of an agreement. The problem of underinclusion, on the other hand, occurs when "the minimum age rule for contracts allows me to enforce a contract against a nineteen-year-old who is two or three years behind normal development" (Altman, 1990:108).

As a practical matter, rules, more than standards, are likely to have generality. Realistically, this means that rules are more imprecise and thus more likely to be applied arbitrarily.

Formalities vs. rules designed to deter wrongful behavior. Finally, the third dimension in the rules-standards continuum is the polarity existing between the public sphere of legal institutions (e.g., law enforcement, district attorney's office, prisons) whose purpose is to deter wrongful behavior, and the private sphere of legal institutions, called formalities, whose purpose is "to help parties in communicating clearly to the judge which of various alternatives they want him to follow in dealing with disputes that may arise later in their relationship" (Kennedy, 1976: 1691). As we will see, Kennedy's primary focus is on the formalities of contract law. We now turn our attention to what Kennedy says about individualism and altruism.

Individualism and Altruism

The second set of dichotomous rhetorical modes, individualism and altruism, operate primarily at the **substantive** level of private law—that is, their focus is on the content of the law.

Individualism may be broadly defined as "egotism constrained by a respect for the rights of others" (Kelman, 1987:16). According to Kennedy, the notion of individualism has long been conceptually associated with liberal political theory. Individualism is an ideology legitimating and upholding the notion of individual self-interest. The idea behind this ideology is that individuals are to seek their own interests through self-reliance. Whatever people add to their private stock of social goods, they do so through their own efforts and consequently are not indebted to anyone. The essence of individualism is summed up by the maxim, "Live and let live."

As Kennedy points out, individualism has become the predominant ideology in legal discourse. He identifies altruism as individualism's competing counterpart. By **altruism,** Kennedy means "the belief that one ought *not* to indulge a sharp preference for one's own interest over those of others" (1976:1717). Altruism is expressed through sharing and sacrifice. It is denoted by the scripture verse, "Love thy neighbor as thyself."

As stated previously, rules and standards operate at the level of legal form. As such, these rhetorical modes determine *how* legal discourse will be structured. By contrast, individualism and altruism are most influential at the substantive level. In other words, they determine *what* legal discourse will contain—its content. One of Kennedy's primary interests is the interconnection between legal form and legal substance. For him the conflicting values that rules and standards signify—for example, individual rights vs. others' well-being, privacy vs. community, intrusiveness vs. protection, self-reliance vs. concern—can best be understood in relation to substantive questions about what we should want and about the nature of humanity and society. In other words, depending on what utopian vision we have, we will prefer one set of values and, by implication, one set of rhetorical modes, over another.

Attempting to understand the interconnection between form and substance, Kennedy does two things. First, he gives an account of the historical conflict between the two sets of rhetorical modes. Second, he shows how the rhetorical modes of individualism and altruism, operating at the substantive level, are informed by the rhetorical modes of rules and standards, operating at the formal level. These two objectives are explored in detail below.

The Historical Conflict of the Two Sets of Rhetorical Modes

In tracing the ideological conflict between rules and standards and individualism and altruism, Kennedy delineates three overlapping historical phases that roughly correspond to the periods 1800–1870, 1850–1940, and 1900 to the present.

1800–1870. According to Kennedy, individualism and altruism were not yet conflicting ideologies during the period of 1800–1870. At that time, legal discourse was influenced by both *policy* and *morality*. The first half of the nineteenth century was a time of enormous interest in free-market capitalism and, consequently, the pragmatic arguments of policy, predicated on the idea of encouraging economic development and hence individualism, increasingly began to conflict with the morality, based on the natural law of God, that extolled altruism. A tension characterized legal discourse during this time as "the law aimed at and usually achieved the imposition of a high level of altruistic duty, but had an occasion to make concessions to individualism" (Kennedy, 1976:1727). Through this uneasy alliance of morality and policy it was thought that pure egoism could be forestalled while simultaneously promoting economic growth.

1850–1940. The second historical phase in legal thought, 1850–1940, is generally referred to as the period of legal formalism. (See Chapter 3.) Kennedy calls this phase "Classic individualism." This late-nineteenth-century revolution in the law not only represented a rhetorical shift away from the earlier emphasis on altruism, it also denied that altruism had anything at all to do with basic legal doctrines. Thus, individualism as an ideology gained dominance as it influenced the political, economic, and legal thinking of the time.

During the period of Classic individualism, the law was said to be deduced from such liberal premises as the ideas of natural rights and free will (initially expressed by the Enlightenment philosophers) and self-reliance and free competition (popularized by sociologists Herbert Spencer and William Graham Sumner). The outcome was said to be a determinate legal doctrine that emphasized individual autonomy, freedom, and liberty. Furthermore, this doctrine, except in cases of fault and contract, exempted individuals from being responsible for their effects on others. In other words, aside from contractual duty, which was necessary to the goal of economic development, people had no legal duty to assist one another. Private law purportedly reflected those ideals deeply ensconced in the American cultural values of liberty, private property, and bodily security. Because these ideals were said to determine the substantive content of the law, opposition to the law was seen as a repudiation of the ideals.

1900 to the present. Kennedy's third phase of legal doctrine, 1900 to the present, begins with the rejection of Classical individualism because this ideology failed to show either that the character of American institutions is individualist or that it is possible to deduce concrete legal rules from cultural values like liberty, property, and bodily security. According to Kennedy, contemporary legal thought is again concerned with the 1800–1870 distinction between policy and morality. This time, however, morality is no longer seen as exclusively altruist and policy is no longer seen as wholly individualist. Instead, the modern legal doctrine is characterized by a sense of contradiction because a "conflict of morality with morality and of policy with policy pervades every important issue of private law" (Kennedy, 1976:1731). According to Kennedy, the contradiction in modern private law arises over three conflicting claims: (1) community vs. autonomy, (2) regulation vs. facilitation, and (3) paternalism vs. self-determination.

In the first conflicting claim, that of *community vs. autonomy*, the central question is: What duty does a person have toward another person when there exists no contractual duty between them? The individualist policy is to encourage personal autonomy by restricting the duties of sharing and sacrifice. Kennedy tells us that this restriction could be accomplished in two ways. First, by keeping to a minimum an individual's responsibility for contractual duties. Limiting responsibility opens up the door for people to more freely seek their own self-interest. Second, sharing and sacrifice are restricted by reducing the number of legal excuses that can be used in exempting a person from contractual duty once the duty has been established. Legal excuses oblige the beneficiary of a contractual agreement to share the losses of the **obligor** (the promiser) when for some reason the obligor cannot perform them. Conversely, the altruist policy argues not for the restriction but for the expansion of legal responsibility, as well as for increasing the number of legal excuses. The objective is to encourage solidarity and community.

The second conflicting claim, *regulation vs. facilitation*, has to do with the amount of control the legal system has over a party's use of bargaining power when that party is in conflict with another, weaker and more vulnerable, party. One way in which the law curbs the stronger party's advantage in negotiating is through **incapacitation,** or the instrument concerned with persons' inability to act legally. Incapacitation gives certain people who lack adequate capacity to negotiate (e.g., minors, committed persons, and prisoners) the legal right to void their contracts if they so choose.

The individualist position advocates that the law protect the privacy and personal freedom of the superordinate party by not regulating its conduct (especially in regard to the economic sphere). This policy is one of nonintervention and judicial passivity. In other words, the individualist position maintains that the chief function of the legal system should be facilitative, allowing greater freedom of private action. Alternatively, the altruist response urges the court to regulate the bargaining advantage of the stronger party. This is a way to counteract the power imbalance between the parties and to ensure the distribution of justice.

The third conflicting claim, *paternalism vs. self-determination*, comes into play when a party to an agreement wishes to back out because it has acted in error and contrary to its own interests. We may, along with legal philosopher Anthony T. Kronman, regard paternalism as "any rule that prohibits an action on the ground that it would be contrary to the actor's own welfare" (1983b:763).

The altruist position supports paternalism. The doctrine of fraud is an example of paternalism because it shields and "watches over" the disadvantaged or injured party. Fraud protects the obligor from his or her own folly and gullibility. It does this by allowing the obligor to legally void an agreement that has unfairly resulted in his or her injury. On the other hand, the individualist position on this issue is one of self-determination and contends that people should have the freedom and autonomy "to behave foolishly, do themselves harm, and otherwise refuse to accept any other person's view of what is best for them" (Kennedy, 1976:1737).

Thus far we have discussed the historical conflict of the two sets of rhetorical modes as well as the three major contradictions that characterize modern contract doctrine. We now, with Kennedy, consider how the rhetorical modes of rules and standards at the formal level are linked with the rhetorical modes of individualism and altruism at the substantive level.

How Individualism and Altruism Are Informed by Rules and Standards

Kennedy illustrates the correspondence between form and substance by focusing on the moral, economic, and political arguments influencing modern legal discourse. Because of space considerations, our concern will be limited to the economic arguments advanced by the individualist and pro-rules rhetorical modes.

Kennedy begins his discussion of the relationship between the formal and substantive economic arguments by suggesting that the ideology of individualism is analogous to the pro-rules position. Both strategies favor a policy of nonintervention. The individualist believes that laws (which, by definition, compel or prohibit certain actions) infringe on the individual's freedom and natural rights. The pro-rules advocate concedes that some behaviors must be banned but believes that it should be done indirectly. In this regard, rules are preferred over standards because the former are interstitial and relative. In other words, unlike standards, which are directly applied to the specifics of a case, rules have greater generality and thus permit some behaviors because of their inherent underinclusion, while at the same time prohibit other behaviors because of their inherent overinclusion. Rules, therefore, interfere only indirectly in the privacy of the individual.

A second connection between the formal and substantive levels is made evident when another individualist argument is applied to the economic arena. This argument states that a regime that desires economic success, but does not wish to legally intervene to achieve this goal, must use the sanction of *abandonment*. **Abandonment** means that the state disclaims all duties to come to the aid of its citizens. The individualist believes that a political administration that will let people starve or fall to very low levels of welfare before forcing others to help them will create the most powerful of incentives to economic production and exchange.

Just as the individualist uses abandonment in the economic sphere, so does the pro-rules advocate apply abandonment to the area of formalities. In the latter case, abandonment means that the law will not tailor itself to the specific circumstances of the legal situation. Situationally sensitive decision-making on the part of the judge is disallowed. For example, if a **testator,** or a person who makes a will, fails to sign the will, it is considered null and void regardless of the testator's intentions. Subsequently, there will be no beneficiaries in accordance with the testator's wishes. The upshot of this is that the threat of nullity goads people to properly adhere to the rigid prescriptions required in the execution of a will.

According to Kennedy, individualists favor the use of rules because of the objectives that rules achieve in the legal sphere. Some of these objectives include taking advantage of the incompetence of the partner one is contracting with, looking out for one's best interests, and emphasizing the freedom and autonomy of others. These legal objectives compliment the objectives to be achieved in the economic sphere, namely, high rates of production and exchange. The way to motivate individuals to strive for these economic and legal goals is to punish them if they do not achieve them. The slogans "He who does not work, does not eat" and "Let the buyer beware" exemplify this individualistic/pro-rules approach.

Finally, another economic argument connecting the formal and substantive levels is premised on the doctrine of social Darwinism and praises the notions of the survival of the fittest and the competition of life. At the substantive level, the individualist position contends that those persons with economic power (and who have thus proved themselves more fit to survive in the competitive marketplace) should be free from legal intervention. Only they have the knowledge and competence to wisely use resources and make financial investments. Regulating these activities inhibits the economic growth and production that ultimately benefits society.

At the level of form, the argument for using rules is also based on the doctrine of social Darwinism. Unlike standards, which require the judge to discover the social values inherent in a specific legal situation, rules, because of their high degree of generality, are more arbitrary and difficult to apply to the particulars of a case. The arbitrariness of rules makes those persons with economic power less fearful that legal influence will upset their commercial transactions. In other words, rules minimize the degree of judicial interference on the aggressive activities of self-interested parties.

Kennedy's chief objective in his article is to show that there is, in fact, a connection, in the rhetoric of private law, between individualism and a preference for rules, and between altruism and a preference for standards. The relationship exists because the same moral, political, and economic arguments, for each set of rhetorical modes, are made at the levels of form and substance. What all this boils down to is that our personal positions toward either rules or standards are determined by what vision of society and humanity we favor and what we specifically want to realize within that vision.

In the next section we see how Northeastern University law professor Clare Dalton attempts to deconstruct contract doctrine by revealing its indeterminacy; an indeterminacy based on the tenets of liberal legalism. Additionally, in using feminist theory, Dalton examines the issues of power and knowledge in the agreements of cohabitation between unmarried couples.

Power, Knowledge, and Contract Doctrine

Clare Dalton begins her analysis of contract doctrine by suggesting that the legal discourse of contracts is colored by the underlying issues of *power* (i.e., authority, coercion, regulation, intervention) and *knowledge* (i.e., understanding, interpretation, truth). Before we discuss these and other ideas, it should be noted that Dalton refrains from giving tidy definitions of her terms. The reason for this is that in most cases she is concerned with the duality of concepts. Dalton states that "each pole of a duality is best understood and defined in relation to its opposite, and in fact depends upon an (unavailable) prior understanding of its opposite" (1985:1000). For instance, the only way we can define the "private" is by making reference to the "public," and vice versa. Dalton contends that although contract doctrine would have us believe differently, attempting to categorically define concepts such as these is futile since it is impossible to neatly distinguish between them. The fact of the matter is that there is no real consensus as to the meaning of these terms.

Notwithstanding the absence of precise definitions, we may infer what Dalton means by power by examining the set of questions she provides concerning that issue:

> What separates me from others and connects me to them? What is the threat and the promise to me of other individuals? Can I enjoy the promise without succumbing to the threat? Am I able to create protective barriers that will not at the same time prevent me from sharing the pleasures of community? What is the role of the state in regulating my relations with others? (1985:999–1000).

Although she does not explicitly say so, in posing these questions it appears that, at least in part, Dalton has in mind Duncan Kennedy's (1979) concept of the *fundamental contradiction*. The **fundamental contradiction** is a dilemma denoting the relationship between self and others, and it is simply this: The individual needs others to maintain his or her security and to validate him or her as a person. However, at the same time that others protect and give the individual a sense of self-worth, they can also threaten him or her with physical and existential annihilation. The result is that the individual both needs and fears others.

Kennedy explains how individuals deal with the fundamental contradiction. In order to gain something (some freedoms, validation from others, etc.), individuals must conform to society's expectations. Conformity is a high price to pay because the end result is that we impose on others—and have imposed on us—hierarchical structures of power. The major problem that arises from the issue of power, then, is that, to some extent, others (e.g., a private party or the state) dictate to the individual what he or she can and cannot do. For example, on the one hand, individuals ostensibly have the freedom to contract; on the other hand, that freedom is curbed when it exceeds the limits of what is considered acceptable bargaining behavior. Bearing in mind the fundamental contradiction—the tension between self and others—will help us to understand Dalton when she speaks about power and its problems. Let us now turn to the second issue underlying the legal discourse of contracts, that of knowledge.

The questions that Dalton considers pertinent to the issue of knowledge are the following: "How can I know what others see, what they intend? On what basis can I share my understanding of the world with others? Is there a reality separate from my grasp of it? Is communication possible?" (1985:1000). Dalton seems to believe, along with French philosopher Michel Foucault, that power and knowledge are inextricably linked and that

> power produces knowledge . . . that power and knowledge directly imply one another; that there is no power relation without the correlative constitution of a field of knowledge; nor any knowledge that does not presuppose and constitute at the same time power relations (Foucault, 1979:27).

Dalton contends that the power and knowledge relations arise from, and are connected with, the polar dualities of the private and the public, the objective and the subjective, form and substance, self and others. These categories not only influence how we view the world, they also impose a framework on the legal discourse of contract doctrine. The doctrine of contract permits, shapes, and limits the *stories* we can tell about our relationships with ourselves, one another, and those in power positions. These stories, which emerge from legal discourse, restrict our notions of who we are and who we can be. Nevertheless, if we understand the stories we can begin to demystify legal thinking and, perhaps more importantly, we can comprehend why judges decide contractual disputes the way they do.

Dalton endeavors to reveal how the rules of contract law describe, police, and deny the polar dualities. In essence, her goal is to demonstrate how the problems of power and knowledge contribute to the inconsistency and indeterminacy of the doctrine of contract. We begin by analyzing the polar dualities of private and public.

The Private and the Public

Since around the mid-nineteenth century, contract doctrine has favored the private over the public, the objective over the subjective, and form over substance.

Dalton proposes that this preference for one polar category over another has resulted in the problems of power and knowledge being deflected to a different time and place. Dalton calls this procedure the "strategy of displacement." She insists, however, that the problems of power and knowledge are part of the current reality of contract doctrine; they exist in the here and now. It is only when we stop denying and avoiding these problems that we can begin to deal with them. Considerations of space make it necessary that we limit our discussion largely to the private-public dichotomy as it applies to contract doctrine.

Private-public polar duality. According to Dalton, the private-public polar duality has long dominated the legal language of contracts. However, throughout most of the nineteenth century (but in particular during the period of Classic individualism, as Kennedy calls it) liberal political theory had a marked influence on the doctrine of contract. Consequently, in accordance with the tenants of liberalism, legal doctrine gave primacy to the *private* aspect of contractual duties.

At bottom was the idea that a binding agreement arose only as a result of the volitional wills of the bargaining individuals: a situation where there occurred a "meeting of the minds." In view of this, the focus was on the *subjective intent* of the persons involved in the agreement. The **will theory of contract** celebrated the individual autonomy and freedom of the bargaining parties and, with the exception of duress, rejected the need for judicial intervention. In other words, it advanced the notion that contractual relations were private, equal, and autonomous.

By the latter part of the nineteenth century, however, the legal realists had begun to seriously challenge the doctrinal premise of the "privateness" of contract. They exposed the public aspect of contract and the liberal fiction of state neutrality by arguing that the court, when enforcing contracts, did indeed intervene in disputes between parties; the court exerted its power over contracting individuals. Dalton states that as a consequence of the realist effort, the problems concerning the state's power over individuals as well as the problems of individuals' power over one another, came into focus.

Despite their assault on the privateness of contract and their disclosure of the power relations that are invariably present in bargaining disputes, the realists did not succeed in completely trashing the liberal idea that contracts are private, equal, free, and subjective. According to Dalton, the realists neglected the problem of knowledge as it affects the issue of *interpretation*. "In the hands of the Realists," writes Dalton, "a sensitivity to the problem of power was coupled, by and large, with an apparent lack of sensitivity to the problem of knowledge" (1985:1014). Thus, for Dalton, the realists did not go far enough in analyzing and critiquing the external standards on which the court relied in its attempts to understand and interpret the state of mind of the bargaining parties.

Due in large measure to the realists, the *public* aspect of contract, which to the individualist invokes all the evils of state intervention and the infringement on individual autonomy, has not been entirely neglected. Contract doctrine, however, has attempted to hide and deny its public element through two techniques that "combine-yet-separate" (Frug, 1984) the private-public dichotomy: artificial *conflation*, in which the public is represented as private, and artificial *separation*, "which distracts attention from the public element of the protected 'private' arena by focusing attention on the demarcated (and limited) 'public' arena" (Dalton, 1985: 1010–1011). The use of conflation and separation is illustrated by Dalton as she examines the story told by a particular type of contract, the implied contract.

The implied contract story. Two main types of implied contract may be distinguished: those *implied in law* (or quasi-contracts) and those *implied in fact*. An **implied-in-law contract** is a legal duty created by the state (i.e., the court) when there is no explicit agreement, promise, or intent expressed between parties. The state enforces a legal duty under these circumstances in order to prevent one person from unjustly enriching himself or herself at the expense of another. It is said, by the will theorists in particular, that because the implied-in-law contract is *not* based on the subjective intentions of the parties, it is a fictional, not a "real," contract. Be that as it may, this quasi-contract is seen as essentially public because the judiciary intervenes to enforce the duties.

The **implied-in-fact contract,** on the other hand, involves a tacit understanding between entrepreneurial parties that is inferred from their conduct or circumstances. Contrast this with the **express contract** in which the terms of the agreement are explicitly stated, orally or in writing. Regardless of their differences, the implied-in-fact contract and the express contract are said to be expressly private because their enforceability is based on understanding the subjective intentions of the bargaining parties. Thus, whereas the implied-in-law contract is considered to be public, the implied-in-fact contract is considered to be private.

According to Dalton, however, the legal methods used to argue that contracts implied-in-law are public and that contracts implied-in-fact are private are no longer viable because the legal methods have been separated and conflated. In Dalton's view, legal doctrine makes an artificial separation between the private and public spheres. This separation is a strategy of displacement that hides the fact that the methods used by the court to determine what was intended by the parties in the implied-in-fact contract are virtually indistinguishable from the methods used to determine what was intended by the parties in the implied-in-law contract. Both methods rely on private *and* public standards.

As mentioned previously, the contract implied-in-fact is based on the conduct and circumstances of the bargaining parties (and not, as in the case of the express contract, on their oral or written words). Therefore, in order for a judge to ascertain if there is a contractual duty that needs to be enforced, he or she must interpret the subjective *state of mind* of the disputing parties by understanding their actions during the agreement and by understanding the social context in which the agreement was made. What is occurring in this case is the strategy of displacement— namely, the artificial conflation of the public with the private—and it involves the problem of knowledge.

The problem of knowledge emerges when the judge attempts to understand the individual's personal will at the time the contract was made. Ascertaining *subjective* intent requires the use of *objective* measures of interpretation. Hence, it is misleading to call implied-in-fact contracts "private" when the judge's assessment concerning the parties' state of mind is based on public standards of fair dealing.

The private and public realms of contract doctrine dissolve into each other; the two domains are interrelated. In contradiction to liberal legal doctrine, Dalton concludes that all contracts are as public as they are private.

Despite the major difficulties presented by the problems of power and knowledge, the implied contract story has basically been one where legal discourse has, for over a century, attempted to create a private realm where equal bargaining partners reach binding agreements of their own free will. Let us now see how the private-public polar duality, the strategy of displacement, and the question of power can help us to better understand how judges reach their decisions in cases concerning agreements of cohabitation between unmarried couples.

The Cohabitation Contract

According to Dalton, the nonmarital cohabitant relationship is, legally speaking, at once different from, and similar to, the traditional martial relationship. On the one hand, the relationship of couples living together differs from the marriage relationship because, once the former relationship is dissolved, the court does not permit a cohabitant plaintiff to systematically recover equitable relief in the form of alimony, child support, or distribution of property. On the other hand, the cohabitant relationship is similar to the traditional marriage relationship because both are seen as arrangements between intimates.

The problem of knowledge. Judicial decision on what type of relief to award the cohabitant plaintiff is based on whether the agreement between the nonmarried partners is an express contract or a contract implied-in-law. Credible arguments can be made for and against either type of contract because the methods used by the court to interpret the parties' assent are similar in both cases. In both types of contract, the court may rely on standards that are private (based on the parties subjective intent) or public (based on communal notions of fair bargaining).

It is also possible that the court may not find the presence of *any* type of contract in the nonmarital cohabitant relationship. There are several reasons for this. In the first place, it is commonly assumed that agreements made between intimate individuals in the domestic or family realm (e.g., as between parent and child) are not contractual in any sense. In the second place, agreements between couples living together are not considered express contracts because any written or oral words conveyed are seen as the unselfish language of affection and commitment to the relationship and not as instruments to be used in striking a bargain. Further, nonmarital agreements are also not implied-in-fact contracts because conduct is considered part of the intimate relationship, not part of a business deal. Nor are these agreements implied-in-law contracts because the courts do not regard the cohabitant relationship as a situation where one person is unjustly enriched at the expense of the other since there is a gratuitous exchange of services.

Because the private-public categories are so closely interrelated, in some cases the judges may decide that the cohabitants are bound by express and implied-in-law contracts; in others that they are bound by neither; and in yet others that they are bound by one type of contract but not the other. The process of ascertaining if the nonmarital cohabitant relationship falls within the private or the public realm is also *indeterminate*. As a consequence, several arguments and counterarguments can be made to support or reject either or both positions. For instance, as we have just seen, it may be argued that such an intimate relationship is much too private for the court to find a presence of contract. On the one hand, this position contradicts the traditional liberal tenet that all contracts are essentially private but that court intervention, as in the case of duress, is sometimes necessary (albeit an evil necessity). On the other hand, this position runs counter to the claim that the nonmarital relationship—as a deviant, irregular, or illicit relationship—is much too public, and thus it is the duty not of the courts but of the legislature to regulate this type of arrangement through public law.

In sum, what arises are three contradictory, inconsistent, and inconclusive doctrinal arguments. The first says that the cohabitation emotional relationship is too private, and thus not contractual. The second argument maintains that the agreement is private, and that court enforcement is sometimes needed. The third argument proposes that the nonmarital cohabitation relationship is too public, and that court interference is inappropriate. It quickly becomes evident that the inconsistency of contract doctrine undermines all conventional legal arguments since opposing arguments can be made with equal force. Thus, according to Dalton, contract doctrine is hopelessly indeterminate.

Having considered the problem of knowledge, we now turn to the problem of *male* power as it relates to the cohabitation contract.

The problem of male power. In Dalton's view, attempting to determine fairness of exchange by applying the doctrines of duress and **unconscionability** (a situation in which one party lacks meaningful choice because the terms of an agreement are unreasonably favorable to the other party) is especially problematic in the cohabitation agreement. The principle questions to be asked are: Was coercion involved or did both parties voluntarily assent to the agreement? Did both parties have equal bargaining power relative to each other or was one partner unjustly enriched at the other's expense? In asking these questions, duress and unconscionability bring to light the issues of power and fairness as they exist in the cohabitant relationship.

The issues of power and fairness as they pertain to the cohabitation agreement may, however, be displaced if the judge follows traditional contract doctrine locating intimate relationships in the private sphere and away from court consideration. In this case, the power imbalance in the male-female relationship is ignored as the court refuses to recognize and address the male partner's socially and economically advantageous bargaining position. Dalton maintains that the law's absence from the private sphere contributes to male dominance and female subservience.

Dalton invokes *feminist theory* in order to gain a better understanding of judicial decisions in cohabitation agreements. **Feminist theory** considers the *images of woman and of relationships*, and these notions, Dalton contends, "influence how judges frame rule-talk and policy-talk; in a world of indeterminacy they provide one more set of variables that may persuade a judge to decide a case one way or another" (Dalton, 1985:1110).

According to Dalton, there are two basic images of woman: that of angel and that of whore. If the female cohabitant is portrayed as an angel, she is seen by the judge as unselfishly giving her services (read: sex) to her male partner without expecting any compensation. If she is seen as a whore, the female cohabitant is a seductress with the ulterior and immoral motive of seducing the man for financial gain. Although different in some ways, both images nonetheless present the woman first and foremost as a provider of sex. Regardless of what image the judge may hold of the female cohabitant, sex in this case, and in contrast to the traditional marital relationship, is seen as the basic motivator of the cohabitation agreement. In the cohabitant relationship, sex overshadows all the other services (e.g., career sacrifices, homemaking, child rearing) that the woman provides for her male partner. Consequently, when the court fails to enforce the nonmarital agreement—either because it is too public or too private—it unfairly fails to compensate the female cohabitant for her sacrifices.

To be sure, Dalton's feminist approach provides fresh insight into the problem of male power as it relates to the cohabitation contract. In this sense, Dalton's approach is in agreement with feminist legal scholar Catharine MacKinnon's statement that feminism "comprehends that what counts as truth is produced in the interest of those with power to shape reality" (1983:640). But Dalton's critical inquiry is also important to jurisprudence because it questions why the problems of power and knowledge are not addressed by contract doctrine and suggests how they might be so addressed. In the end, such critical inquiry enables us to see "that the world portrayed by traditional doctrinal analysis is already not the world we live in, and is certainly not the only possible world for us to live in. And in coming to that realization, we increase our chances of building our world anew" (Dalton, 1985:1114).

In the next section we turn our attention to some of the criticisms that have been leveled against the CLS program by women and racial and ethnic minorities. As will become evident, in comparison with the Critics (most of whom are white males), women and minorities have a different perspective on the social world. Thus, because "it really is possible to see things—even concrete things—simultaneously yet differently" (Williams, 1991:150), it is necessary that we consider the alternative perspective; that is, the minority point of view.

Women, Minorities, and Critical Legal Studies

We begin this section by examining the statements of feminist legal scholar Robin West concerning how liberal legalism and critical legal studies can be transformed into an ungendered jurisprudence. We conclude with a discussion of Hispanic law professor Richard Delgado's commentary on the failure of CLS to consider the needs and experiences of racial and ethnic minorities.

Toward an Ungendered Jurisprudence

In her article "Jurisprudence and Gender" (1988), Robin West states that underlying almost all modern American jurisprudence is what she calls the *separation thesis;* that is, the idea that a human being, whatever else he is, is a physically separate, distinct, and "boundaried" individual. West maintains that while the separation thesis may be "trivially true" of men's experience, it is patently untrue of the experience of women. She argues that, unlike men, women are physically and existentially *connected* to other human beings through their biologically based activities of heterosexual intercourse, pregnancy, and breast-feeding. Thus, West contends, by virtue of its explicit or implicit acceptance of the separation thesis, all of modern legal theory—from liberal legal doctrine to critical legal studies—is essentially and irretrievably a *masculine jurisprudence.*

West suggests that one fundamental difference in masculine jurisprudence between liberal legalism and CLS is that, even though both schools accept the separation thesis, they provide two widely different accounts of the male experience of the physical and existential separation of the self from others. According to liberal legalism, the individual's inevitable physical separation from the "other" entails an existential state of, and political right to, autonomy (i.e., privacy, freedom, equality). Liberal legalism, however, also recognizes that the "other" may threaten the individual's autonomy. West describes how this threat is experienced:

> I have reason to fear you solely by virtue of the fact that I am me and you are you. You are not me, so by definition *my* ends are not your ends. Our ends might conflict. You might try to frustrate my pursuit of my ends. In an extreme case, you might even try to kill me—you might cause my annihilation (1988:7).

Critical legal studies also views the individual as separate from the other, but for the Critics this state of physical separation entails not a celebration of autonomy but rather an existential longing for connection and attachment with others. According to the Critics, the individual dreads the loneliness and isolation that his physical separation imposes on him.

In short, West states that liberal legal doctrine values the *autonomy* of the self and fears *annihilation* by the other. By contrast, CLS values *community* with the other and fears *alienation* from the other. West then turns to (nonlegal) feminist theory—which includes "cultural feminism" and "radical feminism"—and shows that it, too, is as fundamentally divided as masculine jurisprudence.

West explains that while most modern feminists agree that women are different from men, they disagree over which differences between men and women are most important. For cultural feminists, the important difference revolves around the issue of pregnancy: women bear children and men do not. For the radical feminists, the important difference between men and women revolves around the issue of heterosexual intercourse: "women," definitionally, are "those from whom sex is taken" while men, definitionally, are those who take sex from women.

West maintains that just as masculine jurisprudence shares the separation thesis, so does modern feminist theory implicitly or explicitly adhere to the *connection thesis:* the idea that, unlike men, women are physically and existentially connected to other human life. Women's connection to other human life engenders values and fears that are entirely different from those values and fears that follow, for men, from the necessity of separation. But, even though cultural and radical feminists share some version of the connection thesis, they nevertheless provide contrasting accounts of women's experience with their physical and existential state of connection.

Cultural feminists maintain that since women are more nurturant, caring, loving, and responsible to others than are men, women long for intimacy with the other with whom they are connected. By the same token, women also learn to dread separation from the other. Radical feminists, on the other hand, believe that women long for independence and, therefore, connection with the other is an invasion of their physical bodies (experienced in intercourse and pregnancy), and an intrusion upon women's existential autonomy (experienced as a violation of their privacy, integrity, and life projects). In sum, cultural feminists maintain that women value physical and psychic *intimacy* with the other and fear *separation* from the other; radical feminists state that women value *individuation* of the self and fear *intrusion* by the other.

West states that the stories that liberal legalism and cultural feminism tell are fundamentally opposed to each other in substance: "Whereas according to liberal legalism, men value autonomy from the other and fear annihilation by him, women, according to cultural feminism, value intimacy with the other and fear separation from her" (West, 1988:28). Further, the stories of CLS and radical feminism also contrast rather than compare. According to the Critics,

> men suffer from a perpetual dread of isolation and alienation and a fear of rejection, and harbor a craving for community, connection, and association. Women, by contrast, according to radical feminism, respond to their natural state of material connection to the other with a craving for individuation and a loathing for invasion (West, 1988:38).

Nor do CLS and cultural feminism mirror each other, since critical legal studies' longing for community is not the same as the cultural feminists' value of intimacy. The difference, says West, is that the intimacy that women value comes naturally to them and can be pictorially described as "a sharing of intersubjective territory," whereas the community that the masculine jurisprudence of CLS strives for does not come naturally to men, "and it is not a sharing of space; at best it is an adjacency" (1988:40).

Major differences also exist between the stories told by radical feminism and those told by liberal legalism. For example, the individuation that women value is not the same as the autonomy that men value. West explains the difference: "Autonomy is something which is natural to men's existential state and which the [political] state might protect [as a right]. Individuation, by contrast, is the material precondition of autonomy. Individuation is what you need to be before you can even begin to think about what you need to be free" (1988:42). In sum, the stories masculine jurisprudence tells about men's experiences contradict the stories feminist theory tells about women's experiences. As West puts it, "the human being assumed or constituted by legal theory precludes the woman described by feminism" (1988:42). The fact of the matter is that current legal theory only describes men's experiences.

West proposes an alternative jurisprudence, one that considers all the stories of human experience as truthfully told by liberal legalism, critical legal studies, cultural feminism, and radical feminism. This would be a jurisprudence that considers the fundamental contradictions of separation and connection that characterize the true experiences of both men *and* women. Such an ungendered jurisprudence would show women as people who simultaneously value intimacy, fear separation, dread invasion, and crave individuation. Only an ungendered jurisprudence can consider the existential, physical, and political needs and experiences of all human beings. Let us now see why CLS fails to consider the needs and experiences of racial and ethnic minorities.

Minority Critique of CLS

According to Richard Delgado (1987), racial and ethnic minorities have found certain elements of the critical legal studies program unappealing and worrisome. As a consequence, a schism has resulted from the fundamental difference existing between what CLS proposes and what minorities seek in their quest for social justice.

Delgado states that while CLS does contain much that is useful for minorities (e.g., its critiques of the private-public dichotomy and of the social order), it also contains four general elements that repel and threaten minorities:

1. The disparagement of legal rules and rights
2. The rejection of piecemeal change
3. Idealism
4. The use of the concept of false consciousness

Delgado states that "much of CLS scholarship in these areas is either risky, since its asks minorities to give up something of value, or unreliable, because it is based on presuppositions that do not correspond to our existence" (1987:303). Let us examine each of these four areas and Delgado's critique of them.

The disparagement of legal rules and rights. We have already seen that CLS views legal rules as unstable and indeterminate. Rights, a special kind of legal rule, are severely criticized by the Critics, who see them as legitimating society's unfair power arrangements. According to the Critics, rights force individuals to look at themselves and others as isolated rights-bearers ("I got my rights") rather than as interdependent members of a community. As such, rights alienate people and make it virtually impossible for them to imagine a nonhierarchical society founded on cooperation and love.

Delgado's counterargument is that while rights and rights-rhetoric may produce feelings of alienation in the critical legal scholars (white males experiencing existential angst), for minorities, rights provide concrete security. Rights, for instance, offer minorities a measured degree of protection and security from blatant and violent racism. Rights serve as a rallying point bringing minorities closer together. And rights provide a protective distance between the victims of racism and their oppressors. In her book *The Alchemy of Race and Rights* (1991), African American law professor Patricia Williams concurs with Delgado as she states that rights elevate minorities to the status of social being because rights demand that society show respectful behavior to everyone.

The rejection of piecemeal change. CLS rejects the idea of piecemeal change, arguing that such a tactic merely postpones people's total emancipation from the ideology of liberal legalism and from the exploitative social institutions of capitalism. Delgado contends that the CLS critique of piecemeal reform is "imperialistic" because it tells minorities how they should interpret events affecting them. Minorities do not know if occasional, small-scale court victories will bring about a just, fair, nonhierarchical, and nonrepressive society in the ethereal future. They *do* know, however, that these legal victories will provide for their needs in the concrete now.

Idealism. The CLS program is idealistic because the Critics claim that a new and better world can be created only after they trash liberal-capitalist ideology and construct an alternative way of thinking. Delgado contends that while the forces of oppression for the Critics—as intellectuals and members of privileged groups— may be mental, the force that holds minorities back is, very simply, racism: "the myriad of insults, threats, indifference, and other 'microaggressions' to which we are continuously exposed" (1987:309). What is more, racism will not be abolished, says Delgado, simply because the Critics demonstrate that legal rules are indeterminate, that rights are alienating, and that law is a reflection of the interests of the ruling class.

The use of the concept of false consciousness. CLS intimates that, because they have no awareness of their denigration, minorities loyally embrace and vehemently defend the very legal rules and social structures that degrade and oppress them. CLS insinuates that this false consciousness blinds minorities to the alienation, lack of justice, conflict, and unfairness inherent in political life. Delgado maintains that minorities find this CLS concept of false consciousness patronizing because it diagnoses "an intellectual disease that exclusively afflicts persons of color" (1987:312).

In Delgado's view, the origins of the dissonance between CLS and minorities (as illustrated in the four areas just discussed) lies with the informality of the CLS program. Critical legal studies rejects formal structures such as rights, rules, and bureaucracies, but embraces informal processes that rely on goodwill, intersubjective understanding, and community. For minorities, however, informality exposes them to an increased risk of prejudicial treatment. Formal rights (e.g., the Civil Rights Act of 1964), on the other hand, help to openly check racism. Delgado contends that the Critics fail to understand the increased vulnerability to which unguided informality subjects minorities because CLS lacks a theory of racism. Critical legal studies naively assumes that racism is just another form of class oppression, a product of a hierarchical social structure. Delgado, therefore, urges CLS to incorporate into its program an approach that formally confronts (i.e., detects, punishes, confines, and combats) racism in public settings. Delgado's evaluative conclusion is that, at this point in time, critical legal studies does not provide what minorities seek.

SUMMARY

In this, the penultimate chapter of the book, we discussed that relatively new trend in legal scholarship known as critical legal studies. We began by noting that the main objective of CLS is to critique liberal legalism by demystifying and delegitimating, or "trashing," its doctrine (rules, mode of reasoning, and ideology). The Critics showed that, contrary to popular belief, the legal doctrine of liberal democracies such as the United States, Canada, and England is inherently indeterminate and contradictory; that the law in these countries neither yields a single correct and logical answer in the process of judicial decision-making, nor does it consist of a coherent set of congruent concepts expressing a common view of society and human relations. The Critics asserted that liberal legal doctrine does, however, legitimate the social, economic, and political inequities created by capitalism. Consequently, some CLS scholars advocate transforming the institutional arrangements of capitalist society in order to emancipate individuals from a world of hierarchy and power differentials.

We also noted that by utilizing the "methodological" approaches of social theory (i.e., the Marxian perspective, conflict theory, the Weberian perspective, and structural-functionalism), pure critique (i.e., the negative dialectics of Frankfurt School critical theory), and textual explication (i.e., deconstructionism), the Critics have had a measured degree of success in trashing liberal legalism and the social arrangements that it engenders.

We then considered Duncan Kennedy's comments regarding the influence of individualism/altruism and rules/standards on private law. According to Kennedy, these sets of rhetorical modes express opposing worldviews about what is right, good, and desirable. Because individualism is the cornerstone of liberal legal doctrine, the law in liberal-capitalist societies like the United States tries to keep the courts from intruding on the individual's right to privately enter into contractual relations for the express purpose of advancing his or her economic interests. Moreover, Kennedy argued that individualists prefer the formality of rules because rules, being imprecise and arbitrarily applied, minimize the degree of judicial interference on contractual activities. Thus, the individualist, pro-rules advocate favors a vision of society and human relations that involves the values of rights, privacy, and self-interest. By contrast, the altruist, pro-standards advocate favors a vision involving the values of sharing, sacrifice, and concern for others. Kennedy, however, argued that liberal legalism is hopelessly contradictory because individualism and altruism have become doctrinally inseparable. This contradiction is illustrated by the three conflicting claims that currently characterize private law: community vs. autonomy, regulation vs. facilitation, and paternalism vs. self-determination.

Turning our attention to Clare Dalton, we discussed how she deconstructed contract doctrine and laid bare its contradictory concepts. We noted that, in Dalton's view, the legal discourse of contracts is greatly influenced by the interrelated problems of power and knowledge. Moreover, she maintained that the problems of power and knowledge emerge from contract doctrine's polar dualities of private/public and subjective/objective.

Dalton showed how the problem of power arises from the contradictory nature of the private/public. The doctrinal premise that all contracts are private, equal, and autonomous is a fiction, said Dalton. The fact is that the court exerts its power when it publicly intervenes in disputes involving unequal power relations and unfair advantage between contracting parties. Likewise, Dalton revealed how the problem of knowledge emerges from the subjective/objective dichotomy. Dalton demonstrated that the subjective always depends on the objective as judges attempt to distinguish between contracts implied-in-law and contracts implied-in-fact. Dalton argued that in order for the judge to determine the parties' subjective state of mind in the implied-in-fact contract, he or she must have an understanding of the objective standards—actions and social context—in which the agreement was made. In sum, contract is as public as it is private and as subjective as it is objective.

Finally, Dalton explained how the private/public dichotomy and the problems of knowledge and power help us to understand the judge's decision to award or not award equitable relief in cases concerning the dissolution of the cohabitation relationship. Since the judge may rely on private or public standards in ascertaining the cohabiting parties' subjective intent, he or she may find the agreement between unmarried couples to be an express contract and/or an implied-in-law contract, or neither. What is more, traditional contract doctrine ignores the power imbalance inherent in the male-female relationship. The end result, said Dalton, is that the cohabitation agreement is legally unfair to women.

We concluded the chapter with a discussion of how critical legal studies has neglected the needs and experiences of women and minorities. We considered Robin West's argument that both liberal legal doctrine and CLS constitute themselves as a masculine jurisprudence. This is so, said West, because these legal theories reflect the physical and existential experiences of men but disregard the experiences of women. Thus, West proposed a jurisprudence that characterizes the true experiences of both men and women; an *ungendered* jurisprudence that considers the existential, physical, and political needs and experiences of *all* human beings.

Finally, we looked at Richard Delgado's criticisms against the CLS program. According to Delgado, the Critics—the majority of whom are white males from privileged backgrounds—base the CLS program on four general presuppositions that are in direct opposition to the worldview of racial and ethnic minorities. Delgado concluded that because the CLS program is too informal and lacks an adequate theory of racism, critical legal studies does not currently provide what minorities seek.

In the next and final chapter we attempt a synthesis of the concepts, theorists, and paradigms that have been highlighted in this book. Such a synthesis will provide us with a conceptualization of the classical and contemporary perspectives in the sociology of law.

Form and Substance in Private Law Adjudication

Duncan Kennedy

This article is an inquiry into the nature and interconnection of the different rhetorical modes found in American private law opinions, articles and treatises. I argue that there are two opposed rhetorical modes for dealing with the substantive issues, which I will call individualism and altruism. There are also two opposed modes for dealing with questions of the form in which legal solutions to the substantive problems should be cast. One formal mode favors the use of clearly defined, highly administrable, general rules; the other supports the use of equitable standards producing ad hoc decisions with relatively little precedential value.

My purpose is the rational vindication of two common intuitions about these arguments as they apply to private law disputes in which the validity of legislation is not in question. The first is that altruist views on substantive private law issues lead to willingness to resort to standards in administration, while individualism seems to harmonize with an insistence on rigid rules rigidly applied. The second is that substantive and formal conflict in private law cannot be reduced to disagreement about how to apply some neutral calculus that will "maximize the total satisfactions of valid human wants." The opposed rhetorical modes lawyers use reflect a deeper level of contradiction. At this deeper level, we are divided, among ourselves and also within ourselves, between irreconcilable visions of humanity and society, and between radically different aspirations for our common future. . . .

I. The Jurisprudence of Rules

The jurisprudence of rules is the body of legal thought that deals explicitly with the question of legal form. It is premised on the notion that the choice between standards and rules of different degrees of generality is significant, and can be analyzed in isolation from the substantive issues that the rules or standards respond to.

A. Dimensions of Form

1. Formal Realizability

The first dimension of rules is that of formal realizability. I will use this term, borrowed from Rudolph von Ihering's classic *Spirit of Roman Law*, to describe the degree to which a legal directive has the quality of "ruleness." The extreme of formal realizability is a directive to an official that requires him to respond to the presence together of each of a list of easily distinguishable factual aspects of a situation by intervening in a determinate way. . . .

At the opposite pole from a formally realizable rule is a standard or principle or policy. A standard refers directly to one of the substantive objectives of the legal order. Some examples are good faith, due care, fairness, unconscionability, unjust enrichment, and reasonableness. The application of a standard requires the judge both to discover the facts of a particular situation and to assess them in terms of the purposes or social values embodied in the standard.

It has been common ground, at least since Ihering, that the two great social virtues of formally realizable rules, as opposed to standards or principles, are the restraint of official arbitrariness and certainty. The two are distinct but overlapping. Official arbitrariness means the sub rosa use of criteria of decision that are inappropriate in view of the underlying purposes of the rule. These range from corruption to political bias. Their use is seen as an evil in itself, quite apart from their impact on private activity.

Certainty, on the other hand, is valued for its effect on the citizenry: if private actors can know in advance the incidence of official intervention, they will adjust their activities in advance to take account of them. . . .

2. Generality

The second dimension that we commonly use in describing legal directives is that of generality vs. particularity. . . . Generality means that the framer of the legal directive is attempting to kill many birds with one stone. The wide scope of the rule or standard is an attempt to deal with as many as possible of the different imaginable fact situations in which a substantive issue may arise.

The dimensions of generality and formal realizability are logically independent: we can have general or particular standards, and general or particular rules. But there are relationships between the dimensions that commonly emerge in practice. First, a general rule will be more over- and underinclusive than a particular rule. Every rule involves a measure of imprecision vis-à-vis its purpose (this is definitional), but the wider the scope of the rule, the more serious the imprecision becomes. . . .

3. Formalities vs. Rules Designed to Deter Wrongful Behavior

There is a third dimension for the description of legal directives that is as important as formal realizability and generality. In this dimension, we place at one pole legal institutions whose purpose is to prevent people from engaging in particular activities because those activities are morally wrong or otherwise flatly undesirable. Most of the law of crimes fits this pattern: laws against murder aim to eliminate murder. At the other pole are legal institutions whose stated object is to facilitate private ordering. Legal institutions at this pole, sometimes called formalities, are supposed to help parties in communicating clearly to the judge which of various alternatives they want him to follow in dealing with disputes that may arise in their relationship. The law of conveyancing is the paradigm here. . . .

II. Types of Relationship between Form and Substance

The jurisprudence of form presented in the last section is common to legal thinkers of many times and places. There seems no basis for disputing that the notions of rule and standard, and the idea that the choice between them will have wide-ranging practical consequences, are useful in understanding and designing legal institutions. But there is more to the matter than that.

The discussion presented a pro-rules position and a pro-standards position, but there was nothing to suggest that these were truly incompatible. A hypothetical lawmaker with undefined purposes could approach the problem of form with no bias one way or another. He could use the analysis to identify the likely benefits of using rules by applying the pro-rules position to the particular circumstances that concerned him. He could then review the opposed position to get an idea of the costs of using rules and the advantages of standards. He might make up his mind to adopt one form, or the other, or one of the infinite number of intermediate positions, by assessing the net balance of advantage in terms of his underlying legislative objective.

From this starting point of "value neutral" description of the likely consequences of adopting rules or standards, there are two quite different directions in which one might press the analysis of legal form. One alternative is to attempt to enrich the initial schema by contextualizing it. This approach involves being more specific both about the particular situations in which lawmakers operate and about the different objectives that they try to achieve in those situations. . . .

The second, and I think more important, approach ignores both the question of how rules and standards work in realistic settings and the question of how we can best solve the problem of fitting form to particular objectives. The purpose of the second line of investigation is to relate the pro-rules and pro-standards positions to other ideas about the proper ordering of society, and particularly to ideas about the proper substantive content of legal rules. . . .

B. Form as Substance

. . . The different values that people commonly associate with the formal modes of rule and standard are conveyed by the emotive or judgmental words that the advocates of the two positions use in the course of debate about a particular issue. Here is a suggestive list drawn from the vast data bank of casual conversation. Imagine, for the items in each row, an exchange: "Rules are A." "No, they

are B." "But standards are C." "On the contrary, they are D."

. . . [W]e will have a better understanding of issues of form if we can relate them meaningfully to substantive questions about what we should want and about the nature of humanity and society. There are two steps to the argument. The first is to set up the substantive dichotomy of individualism and altruism, and to show that the issue of form is one of its aspects. The second is to trace historically and analytically the course of the conflict between the two larger positions.

The method I have adopted in place of contextualization might be called, in a loose sense, dialectical or structuralist or historicist or the method of contradictions. One of its premises is that the experience of unresolvable conflict among our *own* values and ways of understanding the world is here to stay. In this sense it is pessimistic, one might even say defeatist. But another of its premises is that there is order and meaning to be discovered even within the sense of contradiction. Further, the process of discovering this order and this meaning is both good in itself and enormously useful. In this sense, the method of contradiction represents an attitude that is optimistic and even utopian. None of which is to say that any particular attempt will be worth the paper it is printed on.

Rules		Standards	
Good	*Bad*	*Bad*	*Good*
Neutrality	Rigidity	Bias	Flexibility
Uniformity	Conformity	Favoritism	Individualization
Precision	Anality	Sloppiness	Creativity
Certainty	Compulsiveness	Uncertainty	Spontaneity
Autonomy	Alienation	Totalitarianism	Participation
Rights	Vested Interests	Tyranny	Community
Privacy	Isolation	Intrusiveness	Concern
Efficiency	Indifference	Sentimentality	Equity
Order	Reaction	Chaos	Evolution
Exactingness	Punitiveness	Permissiveness	Tolerance
Self-reliance	Stinginess	Romanticism	Generosity
Boundaries	Walls	Invasion	Empathy
Stability	Sclerosis	Disintegration	Progress
Security	Threatenedness	Dependence	Trust [. . .]

III. Altruism and Individualism

A. The Content of the Ideal of Individualism

The essence of individualism is the making of a sharp distinction between one's interests and those of others, combined with the belief that a preference in conduct for one's own interests is legitimate, but that one should be willing to respect the rules that make it possible to coexist with others similarly self-interested. The form of conduct associated with individualism is self-reliance. This means an insistence on defining and achieving objectives without help from others (i.e., without being dependent on them or asking sacrifices of them). It means accepting that they will neither share their gains nor one's own losses. And it means a fair conviction that I am entitled to enjoy the benefits of my efforts without an obligation to share or sacrifice them to the interests of others. . . .

B. The Content of the Ideal of Altruism

The rhetoric of individualism so thoroughly dominates legal discourse at present that it is difficult even to identify a counterethic. Nonetheless, I think there is a coherent, pervasive notion that constantly competes with individualism, and I will call it altruism. The essence of altruism is the belief that one ought *not* to indulge a sharp preference for one's own interest over those of others. Altruism enjoins us to make sacrifices, to share, and to be merciful. It has roots in culture, in religion, ethics, and art, that are deep as those of individualism. (Love thy neighbor as thyself.)

The simplest of the practices that represent altruism are sharing and sacrifice. . . .

IV. Three Phases of the Conflict of Individualism and Altruism

Eighteenth century common law thinking does not seem to have been afflicted with a sense of conflict between two legal ideals. Positive law was of a piece with God's moral law as understood through reason and revelation. In Blackstone, for example, there is no suggestion of recurrent conflicts either about the nature of legal morality or about which of two general utilitarian strategies the legislator had best pursue. The sense of a conflict between systems of thought emerged only at the beginning of the nineteenth century. It has had three overlapping phases, corresponding roughly to the periods 1800–1870, 1850–1940, and 1900 to the present.

A. The Ante-bellum Period (1800–1870): Morality vs. Policy

Individualism was at first not an *ethic* in conflict with the ethic of altruism, but a set of pragmatic arguments perceived as in conflict with ethics in general. Ante-bellum judges and commentators referred to these pragmatic arguments by the generic name of "policy," and contrasted it to "morality." . . .

In this early nineteenth century view, the law aimed at and usually achieved the imposition of a high level of altruistic duty, but had an occasion to make concessions to individualism. . . .

Still, there was no question which of the ethics was primary: we would achieve a social order according to the law of God if we could. We can't, because the ideal is too demanding. We therefore validate a certain amount of conduct inconsistent with altruism but consistent with individualism, hoping that by accepting to this extent the imperfections of human nature we will at least forestall pure egotism, while at the same time promoting economic growth.

B. Classical Individualism (1850–1940): Free Will

Modern legal thought is preoccupied with "competing policies," conflicting "value judgments" and the idea of a purposive legal order, and to that extent has much in common with pre-Civil War thinking. One major difference is the total disappearance of religious arguments, and the fading of overtly moralistic discussion. More important for our purposes, the modern situation has been conditioned by the post-Civil War triumph of what I will call Classical individualism, which represented not just a rhetorical shift away from the earlier emphasis on altruism, but the denial that altruism had anything at all to do with basic legal doctrines. . . .

Classical individualism rejected the idea that particular rules represented an ad hoc compromise between policy and altruist morality. Rather, the rules represented a fully principled and consistent solution *both* to the ethical and to the practical dilemmas of legal order. The contraction of liability that occurred over the course of the nineteenth century was thereby rationalized, and shielded from the charge that it represented the sacrifice of equity to expediency. . . .

The important thing about the Classical position, from our point of view, is that it presented the choice between individualism and altruism as one of all-or-nothing commitment to a complete system. One might accept or reject the individualist claim that our institutions are based on liberty, private property and bodily security. But if one subscribed to these ideas, a whole legal order followed inescapably. To reject the particular applications was a sign either of error or of bad faith, since they were no more than the logical implications of the abstract premises.

If one believed in the first principles and in the possibility of deducing rules from them, then it was easy to believe that the Classical regime was both morally and practically far superior to the state of nature. The restrictions on pure egotism imposed by that regime did not represent a concession to the utopian ideal of altruism. They embodied the individualist morality of self-reliance, the individualist economic theory of free competition, and the individualist political philosophy of natural rights, which set well-defined boundaries to the demand that people treat the interests of others as of equal importance with their own. . . .

Recast in terms of will, the rules of contract law still represented a moral as well as a practical vision, but that vision was no longer perceptibly

altruist. The new premise was that people were responsible for themselves unless they could produce evidence that they lacked free will in the particular circumstances. If no such evidence was available, then they were bound to look to their own resources in performing what they had undertaken. In place of a situational calculus of altruistic duty and an equally situational calculus of economic effects, there was a single individualist moral-political-economic premise from which everything else followed. . . .

. . . "Free will" in law followed from, indeed was simply the practical application of, the freedom of individualist political, moral and economic theory.

C. Modern Legal Thought (1900 to the Present): The Sense of Contradiction

In private law, modern legal thought begins with the rejection of Classical individualism. Its premise is that Classical theory failed to show either that the genius of our institutions is individualist or that it is possible to deduce concrete legal rules from concepts like liberty, property or bodily security. For this reason, morality and policy reappear in modern discussions, in place of first principles and logic. The problem is that morality is no longer unequivocally altruist—there is a conflict of moralities. Nor is policy any longer unequivocally individualist—there are arguments for collectivism, regulation, the welfare state, along with the theory of economic development through laissez-faire. This conflict of morality with morality and of policy with policy pervades every important issue of private law. . . .

In private law, this modern phase of conflict occurs over three main issues, which I will call, somewhat arbitrarily, community vs. autonomy, regulation vs. facilitation, and paternalism vs. self-determination. Each particular debate has a stalemated quality that reflects the inability of either individualism or altruism to generate a new set of principles or metaprinciples to replace the late lamented concepts.

1. Community vs. Autonomy

The issue here is the extent to which one person should have to share or make sacrifices in the interest of another in the absence of agreement or other manifestation of intention. . . .

The individualist position is the restriction of obligations of sharing and sacrifice. This means being opposed to the broadening, intensifying and extension of liability *and* opposed to the liberalization of excuses once duty is established. This position is only superficially paradoxical. The contraction of initial liability leaves greater areas for people to behave in a self-interested fashion. Liberal rules of excuse have the opposite effect: they oblige the beneficiary of a duty to share the losses of the obligor when for some reason he is unable to perform. The altruist position is the expansion of the network of liability and also the liberalization of excuses.

2. Regulation vs. Facilitation

The issue here is the use of bargaining power as the determinant of the distribution of desired objects and the allocation of resources to different uses. It arises whenever two parties with conflicting claims or interests reach an accommodation through bargaining, and the stronger party attempts to enforce it through the legal system. The judge must decide whether the stronger party has pressed her advantage further in her own interests than is acceptable to the legal system. If she has not, then the agreement will be enforced; if she has, a sanction will be applied, ranging from the voiding of the agreement to criminal punishment of the abuse of bargaining power. . . .

The individualist position is that judges ought not to conceive of themselves as regulators of the use of economic power. This means conceiving of the legal system as a limited set of existing restraints imposed on the state of nature, and then refusing to extend those constraints to new situations. The altruist position is that existing restraints represent an attempt to achieve distributive justice which the judges should carry forward rather than impede.

2. Paternalism vs. Self-Determination

This issue is distinct from that of regulation vs. facilitation because it arises in situations not of conflict but of error. A party to an agreement or one who has unilaterally incurred a legal obligation seeks to void it on the grounds that they acted against their "real" interests. The beneficiary of the agreement or duty refuses to let the obligor back out. An issue of altruistic duty arises because the obligee ought to take the asserted "real" interests into account, both at the bargaining stage, if he is aware of them, and at the enforcement stage, if he only becomes aware of them then. On the other hand, he may have innocently relied on the obligor's own definition of his objectives, so that he will have to sacrifice something of his own if he behaves mercifully.

No issue of bargaining power is necessarily involved in such situations. . . .

The individualist position is that the parties themselves are the best and only legitimate judges of their own interests, subject to a limited number of exceptions, such as incapacity. People should be allowed to behave foolishly, do themselves harm, and otherwise refuse to accept any other person's view of what is best for them. Other people should respect this freedom; they should also be able to rely on those who exercise it to accept the consequences of their folly. The altruist response is that the paternalist rules are not exceptions, but the representatives of a developed counterpolicy of forcing people to look at the "real" interests of those they deal with. This policy is as legitimate as that of self-determination and should be extended as circumstances permit or require.

* * *

One way of conceiving of the transition from Classical to modern legal thought is through the imagery of core and periphery. Classical individualism dealt with the issues of community vs. autonomy, regulation vs. facilitation and paternalism vs. self-determination by affirming the existence of a core of legal freedom which was equated with firm adherence to autonomy, facilitation and self-determination. The existence of countertendencies was acknowledged, but in a backhanded way. By its "very nature," freedom must have limits; these could be derived as implications *from* that nature; and they would then constitute a periphery of exceptions to the core doctrines.

What distinguishes the modern situation is the breakdown of the conceptual boundary between the core and the periphery, so that all the conflicting positions are at least potentially relevant to all issues. The Classical concepts oriented us to one ethos or the other—to core or periphery—and then permitted consistent argument within that point of view, with a few hard cases occurring at the borderline. Now, each of the conflicting visions claims universal relevance, but is unable to establish hegemony anywhere.

V. The Correspondence between Formal and Substantive Moral Arguments

This and the two following sections develop the connection between the formal dimension of rules and standards and the substantive dimension of individualism and altruism. This section deals with the issue at the level of moral discourse; those that follow deal with the economic and political issues. The three sections have a second purpose: to trace the larger dispute between individualism/rules and altruism/standards through the series of stages that lead to the modern confrontation of contradictory premises. . . .

There is a strong analogy between the arguments that lawyers make when they are defending a "strict" interpretation of a rule and those they put forward when they are asking a judge to make a rule that is substantively individualist. Likewise, there is a rhetorical analogy between the arguments lawyers make for "relaxing the rigor" of a regime of rules and those they offer in support of substantively altruist lawmaking. The simplest of these analogies is at the level of moral argument. Individualist rhetoric in general emphasizes self-reliance as a cardinal virtue. In the substantive debate with altruism, this means claiming that peo-

ple *ought* to be willing to accept the consequences of their own actions. They ought not to rely on their fellows or on government when things turn out badly for them. They should recognize that they must look to their own efforts to attain their objectives. It is implicit in this idea that they are entitled to put others at arms length—to refuse to participate in their losses or make sacrifices for them.

In the formal dispute about rules and standards, this argument has a prominent role in assessing the seriousness of the over- and underinclusiveness of rules. Everyone agrees that this imprecision is a liability, but the proponent of rules is likely to argue that we should not feel too badly about it, because those who suffer have no one to blame but themselves. Formally realizable general rules are, by definition, knowable in advance. A person who finds that he is included in liability to a sanction that was designed for someone else has little basis for complaint. Conversely, a person who gains by the victim's miscalculation is under no obligation to forego those gains.

This argument is strongest with respect to formalities. Here the meaning of underinclusion is that because of a failure to follow the prescribed form, the law refuses to carry out a party's intention to create some special set of legal relationships (e.g. voiding a will for failure to sign it). Overinclusion means that a party is treated as having an intention (e.g. to enter a contract) when he actually intended the opposite. The advocate of rules is likely to present each of these adverse results as in some sense deserved, since there is no good reason why the victim should not have engaged in competent advance planning to avoid what has happened to him. . . .

The argument of the advocate of "relaxation," of converting the rigid rule into a standard, will include an enumeration of all the particular factors in the situation that mitigate the failure to avoid over- or underinclusion. There will be reference to the substantive purpose of the rule in order to show the arbitrariness of the result. But the ultimate point will be that there is a moral duty on the part of the private beneficiary of the over- or underinclusion to forego an advantage that is a result of the other's harmless folly. Those who take an inheritance by course of law because the testator failed to sign his will should hand the property over to those the testator wanted to receive it. A contracting party *ought not* to employ the statute of frauds to void a contract honestly made but become onerous because of a price break.

This argument smacks as unmistakably of altruism as the argument for rules smacks of individualism. The essential idea is that of mercy, here concretized as sharing or sacrifice. The ethic of self-reliance is rejected in both its branches: the altruist will neither punish the incompetent nor respect the "right" of the other party to cleave to her own interests. Again, the difference between the substantive and the formal arguments is the area of their application. It may well be that the structure of rules falls far short of requiring the level of altruistic behavior that the altruist would prefer. But within that structure, whatever it may be, there are still duties of sharing and sacrifice evoked by the very operation of the rules. . . .

VI. The Correspondence between Formal and Substantive Economic Arguments

The correspondence between the formal and substantive economic arguments is more intricate and harder to grasp than the moral debate. I have divided the discussion into two parts: an abstract statement of the structural analogy of the formal and substantive positions, and an historical synopsis of how the positions got to their present state.

An Abstract Statement of the Analogy

1. Nonintervention vs. Result-Orientation

Suppose a situation in which the people who are the objects of the lawmaking process can do any one of three things: X, Y and Z. The law-

maker wants them to do X, and he wants them to refrain from Y and Z. If he does not intervene at all, they will do some X, some Y and some Z. As an individualist, the lawmaker believes that it would be wrong to try to force everyone to do X all the time. He may see freedom to do Y as a natural right, or believe that if he forbids Z, most people will find themselves choosing X over Y as often as if it were legally compelled. Or he may take the view that the bad side effects of state intervention to prohibit Y outweigh the benefits.

There is still the problem of the *form* of the injunction against Z. There may be a number of tactical considerations that push in the direction either of a rule or of a standard. For example, if the law appliers are very strongly in favor of compelling X, then they may use the discretion inherent in a standard to ban both Z *and* Y, thus smuggling in the substantive policy the lawmaker had rejected. On the other hand, it may be that the nature of the Y-Z distinction defies precise formulation except in terms of rules that will lead to the arbitrary inclusion of a very large amount of Y in the Z category, so that a standard seems the only workable formal mechanism.

In spite of these contextual factors, there is a close analogy between the substantive individualist position and the argument for rules. The individualist claims that we must achieve X through a strategy that permits Y. The rule advocate claims that we can best achieve the prohibition of Z through a rule that not only permits some Z (underinclusion) but also arbitrarily punishes some Y (overinclusion).

What ties the two arguments together is that they both reject result orientation in the particular case in favor of an indirect strategy. They both claim that the attempt to achieve a total ordering in accord with the lawmaker's purpose will be counterproductive. More success will be achieved by limited interventions creating a structure that influences the pattern of private activity without pretensions to full realization of the underlying purpose. In short, the arguments for rules over standards is inherently noninterventionist, and it is for that reason inherently individualist.

The main difficulty with seeing rules as non-interventionist is that they presuppose state intervention. In other words, the issue of rules vs. standards only arises after the lawmaker has decided against the state of nature and in favor of the imposition of some level of duty, however minimal. The point is that *within this structure*, whatever it may be, rules are less result oriented than standards. As with the moral argument, the economic individualism of rules is interstitial and relative rather than absolute.

2. Tolerance of Breach of Altruistic Duty: The Sanction of Abandonment

In the economic area, the analogy between the arguments for rules and those for substantive individualism goes beyond their common nonitnerventionism. Both strategies rely on the sanctioning effect of nonintervention to stimulate private activity that will remedy the evils that the state refuses to attack directly.

The fundamental premise of economic individualism is that people will create and share out among themselves more wealth if the state refuses either to direct them to work or to force them to share. Given human nature and the limited effectiveness of legal intervention, the attempt to guarantee everyone a high level of welfare, regardless of their productivity, would require massive state interference in every aspect of human activity, and still could not prevent a precipitous drop in output. On the other hand, a regime which convincingly demonstrates that it will let people starve (or fall to very low levels of welfare) before forcing others to help them will create the most powerful of incentives to production and exchange. . . .

The advocate of rules as the proper form for private law proposes a strategy that is exactly analogous to that of substantive individualism. The sanction of abandonment consists of not adjusting legal intervention to take account of the particularities of the case. The enforcement of the rule in situations where it is plainly over- or underinclusive involves condoning a violation of altruistic duty by the beneficiary. The motive for this passivity in the face of a miscarriage of the lawmaker's goal is to stimulate those subject to the rules to invest in formal proficiency, and thereby indirectly reduce the evil tolerated in the particular case.

In the area of formalities, the sanction of nullity works in the same fashion as the sanction of starvation in the substantive debate. The parties are told that unless they use the proper language in expressing their intentions, they will fail of legal effect. The result will be that a party who thought he had a legally enforceable agreement turns out to be vulnerable to betrayal by his partner. The law will tolerate this betrayal, although the whole purpose of instituting a regime of enforceable promises was to prevent it. In the area of rules designed to deter wrongdoing, the analogue of the sanction of abandonment is reliance on a rule to alert the potential victims to their danger. Caveat emptor and the rule of full legal capacity at 21 years are supposed to reduce wrongdoing, in spite of their radical underinclusiveness, because they induce vigilance where a standard would foster a false sense of security. Again, the theory is that permitting A to injure B may be the best way to save B from injury. . . .

The basic notion behind these arguments for rules is that ability to manipulate formalities, vigilance in one's interests and awareness of the legally protected rights of others are all economic goods, components of the wealth of a society. The same considerations apply to them as apply to wealth in general. The best way to stimulate their production is to sanction those who fail to acquire them, by exposing them to breach of altruistic duty by those who are more provident. The rule advocate may affirm that "this hurts me more than it does you" as she administers the sanction. But the refusal to tolerate present inequity would make everyone worse off in the long run.

3. Transaction in General

There is a third element to the abstract parallel between substantive and formal dimensions. The argument is that both rules and the substantive reduction of altruistic duty will encourage transaction in general. The classic statement of the substantive position is that of [Oliver Wendell] Holmes [. . .]

. . . [His] implicit premise seems to be that the aggressive action of the injurers, looked at as a class, has greater social value than the activity of the injured inhibited by the removal of protection. In Holmes's thought, this premise is linked to Social Darwinism and the belief in the desirability of conflict in general. As he saw it, the outcome of bargaining under individualist background rules would be to place control of productive resources, and therefore of investment, in the hands of those most likely to use them for the long-run good of the community. Regulatory, paternalist and communitarian objectives are all less important than secular economic growth. The management of growth requires exactly those capacities for aggressive self-reliance that are rewarded under an individualist regime of contract and fault. Regulation, paternalism and communitarian obligation shift economic power from those who know how to use it to those who do not.

The parallel argument about rules is that "security" encourages transaction in general. The minimization of "judicial risk" (the risk that the judge will upset a transaction and defeat the intentions of the parties) leads to a higher level of activity than would occur under a regime of standards. Of course, some people will be *deterred* from transacting by fear of the mechanical arbitrariness of a system of formally realizable general rules. But their activity is less important, less socially desirable than that of the self-reliant class of actors who will master and then rely on the rule system.

The formal argument rests on the same implicit Social Darwinism as the substantive. Security of transaction is purchased at the expense of tolerating breach of altruistic duty on the part of the beneficiary of mechanical arbitrariness. The liberation of the actor's energy is achieved through a kind of subsidy based on a long term judgment that society gains through the actions of the aggressive and competent even when those actions are directly at the expense of the weak. . . .

IX. Conclusion

There *is* a connection, in the rhetoric of private law, between individualism and a preference for rules, and between altruism and a preference for standards. The substantive and formal dimensions are related because the same moral, economic and political arguments appear in each. For most of the areas of conflict, the two sides emerge as biases or tendencies whose proponents have much in common and a large basis for adjustment through the analysis of the particularities of fact situations. But there is a deeper level, at which the individualist/formalist and altruist/informalist operate from flatly contradictory visions of the universe. Fortunately or unfortunately, the contradiction is as much internal as external, since there are few participants in modern legal culture who avoid the sense of believing in both sides simultaneously.

Even this conclusion applies only so long as it is possible to abstract from the context of compromises within the mixed economy and the bureaucratic welfare state. In practice, the choice between rules and standards is often instrumental to the pursuit of substantive objectives. We cannot assess the moral or economic or political significance of standards in a real administration of justice independently of our assessment of the substantive structure within which they operate. . . .

An Essay in the Deconstruction of Contract Doctrine

Clare Dalton

Introduction

Law, like every other cultural institution, is a place where we tell one another stories about our relationships with ourselves, one another, and authority. In this, law is no different from the *Boston Globe*, the CBS evening news, *Mother Jones*, or a law school faculty meeting. When we tell one another stories, we use languages and themes that different pieces of the culture make available to us, and that limit the stories we can tell. Since our stories influence how we imagine, as well as how we describe, our relationships, our stories also limit who we can be.

In this Article, by examining the rules of contract law as applied by judges and elaborated by commentators, I ask whether we can begin to understand the particular limits law stories impose on the twin projects of self-definition and self-understanding. Can we, in other words, expose the way law shapes all stories into particular patterns of telling, favors certain stories and disfavors others, or even makes it impossible to tell certain kinds of stories?

The stories told by contract doctrine are preoccupied with what must be central issues in any human endeavor of our time and place. One set of questions concerns power: What separates me from others and connects me to them? What is the threat and the promise to me of other individuals? Can I enjoy the promise without succumbing to the threat? Am I able to create protective barriers that will not at the same time

prevent me from sharing the pleasures of community? What is the role of the state in regulating my relations with others? The other set of questions concerns knowledge: How can I know what others see, what they intend? On what basis can I share my understanding of the world with others? Is there a reality separate from my grasp of it? Is communication possible? These central questions of power and knowledge devolve from the split between self and other, subject and object, which structures our experience of the world. This Article examines precisely how this split structures our contract doctrine; how doctrine devotes its energies to describing, policing, and disguising the divide.

A. The Project Described

In this Article, I give an account of selected portions of contract doctrine and the themes and problems that permeate them. I demonstrate how our preoccupation with questions of power and knowledge is mirrored in doctrinal structures that depend on the dualities of public and private, objective and subjective, form and substance. I suggest that it is these problems of power and knowledge, these doctrinal structures, which contribute to the inconsistency and substantial indeterminacy of contract doctrine.

In elaborating doctrinal dichotomies, I suggest that contract doctrine consistently favors one pole of each duality: Contract law describes itself as more private than public, interpretation as more about objective than subjective understanding, consideration as more about form than about substance. And I suggest further that while the method of hierarchy in duality allows our doctrinal rhetoric to avoid the underlying problems of power and knowledge, it is an avoidance that is also a confession: The problems are only displaced, not overcome. This displacement is both diachronic and synchronic: The problems are frequently presented as having been then and not now, and equally frequently presented as being there and not here. To answer the strategy of displacement, my account necessarily deals with historical moments in the development of doctrine, as well as with doctrine in its current state. My claim is that the problems are now as well as then, here as well as there. . . .

I. Public and Private

The opposing ideas of public and private have traditionally dominated discourse about contract doctrine. The underlying notion has been that to the extent contract doctrine is "private," or controlled by the parties, it guarantees individual autonomy or freedom; to the extent it is "public," or controlled by the state, it infringes individual autonomy.

Since at least the mid-nineteenth century, the discourse of contract doctrine has tried to portray contract as essentially private and free. At all times, nonetheless, traditional doctrine has uneasily recognized a public aspect of contract, viewing certain state interests as legitimate limitations on individual freedom. But this public aspect has traditionally been assigned a strictly supplemental role; indeed, a major concern of contract doctrine has been to suppress "publicness" by a series of doctrinal moves.

The public aspect of contract doctrine is suppressed differently in each area of that doctrine, and in each historical period. The method of suppression is generally either an artificial *conflation* of public and private, in which the public is represented as private, or an artificial *separation* of

public from private, which distracts attention from the public element of the protected "private" arena by focusing attention on the demarcated (and limited) "public" arena.

The current mainstream treatment of quasi-contracts and implied contracts illustrates doctrine's techniques of separation and conflation. The prevailing position, represented by the *Second Restatement*, but also by cases and commentary from the 1850's to the present, is that quasi-contracts are not contracts at all, but constitute instead an exceptional imposition of obligation by the state in order to prevent unjust enrichment. An artificially sharp line of demarcation is therefore presented as separating quasi-contracts from implied-in-fact contracts, and public from private. But this position obscures the fact that the finding of contractual implication is guided in the so-called "private" sphere by the same considerations that dictate the imposition of quasi-contract. Any inquiry into a party's intent must confront the problem of knowledge—our ultimate inability to gain access to the subjective intent underlying any particular agreement. The indicia or manifestations of intent . . . serve as substitutes for subjective intent. But in relying on this objective evidence, we move from the realm of the private to that of the public. Calling implied contracts based on party intention "private," and thereby ignoring the extent to which their content is shaped by external norms, conflates public with private.

This same pattern of separation and conflation characterizes the doctrines of duress and unconscionability. Like quasi-contract, they are presented in current doctrine as public supplements to the otherwise private law of contract, supplements necessary for policing the limits of fair bargain. The separation of duress and unconscionability from the main body of contract doctrine diverts attention from the fact that the entire doctrine of consideration reflects societal attitudes about which bargains are worthy of enforcement. But even as the technique of separation marks out duress and unconscionability as public exceptions to private contract doctrine, within duress and unconscionability doctrine public and private are conflated—the public grounds for disapproving bargains recast as evidence that there is no private bargain to be enforced. In this arena, the techniques of separation and conflation serve to camouflage critical issues of power—the power of the state to police private agreements, and the power of one private party over another. . . .

A. A Brief History

In the earlier part of the nineteenth century, a will theory of contract dominated the commentary and influenced judicial discussion. Contractual obligation was seen to arise from the will of the individual. This conception of contract was compatible with (and early cases appear sympathetic to) an emphasis on subjective intent: Judges were to examine the circumstances of a case to determine whether individuals had voluntarily willed themselves into positions of obligation. In the absence of a "meeting of the minds," there was no contract. This theory paid no particular attention to the potential conflict between a subjective intention and an objective expression of that intention.

The idea that contractual obligation has its *source* in the individual will persisted into the latter part of the nineteenth century, consistent with the pervasive individualism of that time and the general incorporation into law of notions of liberal political theory. Late nineteenth-century theorists like Holmes and Williston, however, began to make clear that the proper *measure* of contractual obligation was the formal expression of the will, the will objectified. Obligation should attach, they reasoned, not according to the subjective intention of the parties, but according to a reasonable interpretation of the parties' language and conduct. Enforcement of obligation could still be viewed as a neutral facilitation of intent, despite this shift, if the parties are imagined as selecting their language and conduct as accurate and appropriate signals of their intent. Thus, even in this objectified form, the will theory of contract was equated with the absence of state regulation: The parties governed themselves; better yet, each party governed himself.

The Realists made it impossible to believe any longer that contract is private in the sense suggested by this caricature. By insisting that the starting point of contract doctrine is the state's decision to intervene in a dispute, the Realists exposed the fiction of state neutrality. As Morris Cohen argued:

> [I]n enforcing contracts, the government does not merely allow two individuals to do what they have found pleasant in their eyes. Enforcement, in fact, puts the machinery of the law in the service of one party against the other. When that is worthwhile and how that should be done are important questions of public policy.

From this vantage point, the objectivist reliance on intent as the source of contractual obligation was a blatant abdication of responsibility, a failure to address and debate the substantive public policy issues involved in decisions about when and how courts should intervene in disputes between contracting parties.

At its most radical, the Realist critique portrays the "publicness" of contract as overshadowing its "privateness." According to Cohen, "[T]he law of contract may be viewed as a subsidiary branch of public law, as a body of rules according to which the sovereign power of the state will be exercised as between the parties to a more or less voluntary transaction." Thinking about contract from this perspective revealed that the state's interest in maintaining a free enterprise system—while policing its excesses—was at work in doctrines such as duress and consideration. Problems of power—the state's power over individuals, and the power of individuals over one another—came into focus.

This basic challenge to the "privateness" of contract, however, was accompanied by a continuing faith in the ability of courts to understand the agreements made by contracting parties. For example, the contract was felt to restrain the terms on which the court, if it chose to intervene, would favor one party over the other. In the hands of the Realists, then, a sensitivity to the problem of power was coupled, by and large, with an apparent lack of sensitivity to the problem of knowledge, and to the way in which power could be subtly exercised through the interpretation and construction of intention.

In the decades since, the Realist challenge to the "privateness" of contract has been assimilated and defused, a process aided by the incomplete nature of the Realist assault. Thus our principle vision of contract law is still one of a neutral facilitator of private volition. We understand that contract law is concerned at the periphery with the imposition of social duties, that quasi-contract governs situations where obligation attaches even in the absence of agreement, that doctrines of duress and fraud deprive the contracting reprobate of benefits unfairly extorted. But we conceive the central arena to be an unproblematic enforcement of obligations voluntarily undertaken. We excise regulated and compulsory contracts from the corpus of contract doctrine altogether, and create special niches for them, as in labor law and utility regulation. Although we concede that the law of contract is the result of public decisions about what agreements to enforce, we insist that the overarching public decision is to respect and enforce private intention.

Thus, for better than a hundred years, contract doctrine and the commentary it has generated have been characterized by a concern with public imposition and private volition. . . .

B. The Implied Contract Story: Wrestling with the Problem of Knowledge

The implied-in-law or quasi-contract plays a crucial role in sustaining the notion that contract law is essentially private. The implied-in-law contract is portrayed as essentially noncontractual and public, in contrast to the implied-in-fact contract in which the private is dominant. In this account, the implied-in-fact contract is presented as kin to the express contract, the only difference being that the former is constituted by conduct and circumstance rather than words. An examination of how and when courts choose to impose quasi-contractual obligations, however, reveals the essential similarity between this decision and the supposedly dissimilar decision that a given situation evidences implied-in-fact contractual obligations. Thus, although the distinction between the two types of implied contracts accords with our experience—we intuitively know that being bound by one's word is different from being bound by an externally imposed obligation—the methods of legal argument used for over one hundred years to distinguish the two situations do not and cannot hold.

1. *Hertzog:* The Constructive Contract

Hertzog v. Hertzog, decided by the Pennsylvania Supreme Court in 1857, is reputedly the first American case to distinguish the quasi-contract from the implied-in-fact contract. . . .

2. Since *Hertzog: Plus Ça Change* . . .

By the first decades of this century, theorists had begun cautiously to explore the extent to which an objectified will theory required public intrusion on private volition. . . .

[T]he Realist approach to contract involves a radical shift of emphasis from the private to the public aspects of enforcement. Predictably, then, when the Realist Cohen addresses the question of interpretation, he sees and describes its public face. He pinpoints the way in which judges, in the guise of interpretation, "decide the 'equities,' the rights and obligations of the parties. . . . [T]hese legal relations are determined by the courts and the jural system and not by the agreed will of the contesting parties." Cohen also identifies how rules of interpretation serve as state regulation:

> When courts follow the same rules of interpretation in diverse cases, they are in effect enforcing uniformities of conduct.
> We may thus view the law of contract not only as a branch of public law but also as having a function somewhat parallel to that of the criminal law. Both serve to standardize conduct by penalizing departures from the legal norm.

Cohen laments that while the fictional nature of the will theory is at one level a commonplace, it is at the same time ignored, forgotten, or otherwise resisted—in part, because of the force of the traditional language. And indeed, the Realists did generally fail to explore the implications of the will theory's fictional basis. They tended to be much more concerned with problems of coercion and of relief from the bad bargain. The Realist focus was the public-private split as it implicates the problem of power, not the public-private split as it implicates the problem of knowledge. Since the line of inquiry initiated by those such as Costigan has been given only scant attention in the following decades, Cohen's criticism could be leveled with equal force today.

The position taken by the *Second Restatement* is essentially that of Justice Lowrie. The *Second Restatement* divides the universe of contracts along the private-public axis into express contracts, contracts implied-in-fact, and contracts implied-in-law or quasi-contracts. It defines the express contract as an agreement made up of words, either oral or written, and the implied-in-fact contract as one that a court infers wholly or partly from conduct or circumstances. Quasi-contracts, in contrast, are "public." And because they are not concerned with the intentions of the parties, they are not really contracts at all. That quasi-contracts even share the appellation "contract" is a matter of historical accident. Like torts, quasi-contracts are "obligations created by law for reasons of justice." Their noncontractual nature is so essential that they are separated out for treatment in the *Restatement of Restitution*. Only that fact even alerts us that the "reasons of justice" that dictate the imposition of quasi-contractual obligations have to do with the idea of unjust enrichment.

At the same time, the *Second Restatement of Contracts* confesses that this analytically clear distinction between contract and quasi-contract does not always work in practice, that "in some cases the line between the two is indistinct." The *Restatement* attributes the potential for confusion to the difficulties of "Conduct as Manifestation of Assent." Except where formal requirements give words special significance as evidence of agreement, "there is no distinction in the effect of the promise whether it is expressed in writing, or orally, or in acts, or partly in one of these ways and partly in others." But conduct "is more uncertain and more dependent on its setting than are words." The uncertainty of conduct as evidence of agreement can make it unclear whether a particular relationship should be considered contractual or quasi-contractual.

This explanation allows the *Restatement* to save the express contract from involvement in potential confusion between public and private. Words that directly express the parties' intentions make state intrusion unnecessary. Only conduct, inherently more ambiguous and open-textured, threatens the public-private distinction by requiring the interpreter of fact to add his sense of the context to the acts of the parties in order to understand them.

As *Hertzog* demonstrates, however, the division between public and private cannot be so neatly made. Divining intention in order to find an implied-in-fact contract depends on understanding the societal background against which a relationship is formed: A knowledge of private thus requires a knowledge of public. Deciding that a social relationship requires the imposition of a quasi-contract depends on knowing which relationship the parties have entered: A knowledge of public thus requires a knowledge of private. . . .

C. The Story of Duress and Unconscionability: Wrestling with the Problem of Power

The efforts of more than a century have been devoted, as we have seen, to trying to create a private domain in which individuals can reach binding agreements and courts can enforce them, despite the difficulties presented by the problem of knowledge. The story of the doctrines of duress and unconscionability reveals similar efforts over time to create a private domain in which individuals can reach binding agreements and courts can enforce them, despite the difficulties presented by the problem of power. In the context of duress and unconscionability, doctrine wrestles with the power of contracting parties over one another, and the power of the state over both.

The doctrines of duress and unconscionability are self-consciously "public" insofar as they are designed to police the limits of "fair" bargain. They legitimate the exercise of state power to prevent one contracting party from exercising an illegitimate power over the other. Thus, the private deal of the parties—or what appears to be the private deal of the parties—may be overridden in the name of a norm that, under appropriate circumstances, trumps the otherwise prevalent norm of nonintervention.

In a discourse so protective of its private or noninterventionist status, this is a dangerous move that raises a number of interesting questions: Why should contract have to harbor such a public aspect? When is intervention justified? How has this public aspect of contract been reconciled over time with the rest of "private" contract doctrine? What does this particular story reveal about the body of doctrine to which it bears such a dangerously supplemental relationship? While this section will explore all these questions, discussion of the first two figures most prominently in the work of traditional theorists.

The "why" question has both a private and a public answer. The private answer is that since privacy in contract is conceived of as a guarantor of freedom, contracts entered into under coercion are not deserving of that privacy—indeed, under those circumstances, state intrusion becomes the guarantor of freedom. The public answer is that we have some values that occasionally trump our desire for a system of contract in which each party bears full responsibility for protecting his own interests. We conceive some limit to self-interest, some requirement that under certain circumstances contracting parties should look out for one another, and we are prepared to use the power of the state to enforce that obligation.

The "when" question reveals the extent of the problem of power. Three different approaches to the question are embedded in contract doctrine as it has evolved since the nineteenth century. One approach is to focus on the disfavored party, and ask whether that party's assent to the transaction was genuine. Another approach is to focus on the behavior of the favored party, and to rule that some kinds of behavior between contracting parties are unacceptable. A third approach is to look at the terms of the transaction itself, and to determine that some deals are just too lopsided to be enforceable.

The first approach—determining whether the disfavored party genuinely assented—is rendered unworkable by the problem of knowledge. We cannot directly know or ascertain the subjective intent of the disfavored party. Our inquiry therefore becomes indirect—we turn to objective evidence of the party's subjective intent. But in our search for objective evidence we find ourselves abandoning our initial focus, and focusing instead, as the second and third approaches suggest, on the other party's behavior and the terms of the resulting deal. Could anyone resist the pressure exerted by *that* threat, *those* circumstances? Would anyone have voluntarily agreed to *that* deal?

The second and third approaches each embody an assumption that we can distinguish the acceptable from the unacceptable; the attempt to make this distinction throws us directly into the problem of power. We live with two convictions—that we should take care of ourselves and that we should take care of others—and we lack any conceptual or instrumental scheme sufficiently persuasive in its neutrality or its appeal to consensual values to regulate when one impulse should predominate. How, then, should we determine that some self-interested behavior is beyond the pale, but some other is not? How should we determine that some transactions are acceptable in their terms but others are not?

These questions go to the heart of the problem of power—the power of the state to control private arrangements and to evaluate private power relations. Doctrine attempts to deny that these questions can be answered only by recourse to non-neutral and nonconsensual choices. Since doctrine's devices for denial suppress the public aspect of duress and unconscionability, they also serve to reconcile those doctrines with the otherwise private face of contract. . . .

1. Duress as the Absence of Will

Including duress within the core of contract doctrine seemed appropriate, even necessary, to nineteenth century will theorists, who believed that enforcement of contracts was all about implementing the free wills of the parties. They believed contract required assent; voluntarism was the heart of contractual obligation. In developing a body of duress doctrine, the crucial issue was therefore the reality of assent.

The idea that the state could exert control in the name of freedom was easy to assert as an abstraction, but it was difficult in practice to make intervention look like nonintervention. Courts had to make concrete decisions about what was freedom and what coercion in specific contractual situations. They had to struggle with the fact that the whole economic structure quite obviously depended on the law accepting as legitimate countless deals imposed by one party upon another. The judicial identification of "unfreedom" became an uncertain task of drawing lines between acceptable and unacceptable "unfreedom." The line-drawing exercise actually took the form of distinguishing between unacceptable and acceptable behavior by the favored party, although this focus was not made explicit.

. . . The [Supreme] Court chose as its paradigm of duress the situation in which the hand was forcibly guided over the paper, or the gun held at the temple, to produce a signature. Physical force, in short, was the model, with other forms of coercion, such as the force of economic circumstances, going unrecognized.

2. Duress as Substantive Unfairness

The arbitrariness of the choices made by formalist duress doctrine, and particularly its exclusion of economic duress, made it exceptionally vulnerable to attack. As early as the 1920's, Hale noted that all contracting involves a measure of coercion, and that the advantaged person enjoys that position because the legal system has created entitlements for him. This was not only an attack on "free will" as the paradigm of private contract, but was simultaneously an attack on the vaunted neutrality of the state as enforcer of the will of the parties. Following Hale's line of reasoning, one would have to suppose instead that the state actually endorses the imposition of one party's will on the other.

Hale's extremely radical critique calls into question the entire structure of a contract law that purports to be "private," but the critique's revolutionary potential has never been fully realized. Hale's themes were echoed by the Realists, but only to support change in areas where formalism's limited definition of coercion had come to seem inhumane and unrealistic. Employing Hale's insights, the Realists argued that the scope of the doctrine of duress could readily be expanded, and that the doctrine should reflect sensible policies plainly articulated rather than some metaphysical notion of "free will." The Realist message was, "If contract law is to be 'public,' let us be clear what public concerns are being met." . . .

3. Modern Times

The preceding examination of classical and Realist thinking on contract law reveals both a private and a public way of articulating the bases of duress. The private way is to say that what makes some bargains shocking is the way one party is manipulated into an assent that is not "real." The public way is to say that some bargains are so shocking to our norms of decency or equality that we will not enforce them. Classical theorists relied primarily on the private articulation; the Realists shifted the basic articulation of these doctrines to a public mode. In classical doctrine, however, private bumps into public: Doctrinal commitment to a market system based on the exploitation of inequality makes it impossible to judge as "unreal" the majority of coerced assents. Under the Realist view, public bumps into private: The conflict between subjective and objective value, between individualistic policies premised on inequality and dedicated to maintaining the basic market structure, and policies designed to minimize advantage and promote fairness in contractual relationship, can be resolved only by reintroducing a private analysis of assent. In both schemes, standards of good behavior are invoked as a mediating device, without an explicit recognition that they, too, are problematic in the absence of any defined way to sort out those situations requiring altruistic rather than individualistic conduct.

The central question guiding an analysis of current doctrine must therefore be whether it has moved forward in identifying either those public norms that must invalidate private contracts, or those instances in which private intention requires the protection provided by public intervention. I conclude that it has not. I plan to look, briefly, at two areas: the current law of duress and the comparatively new doctrine of unconscionability. My claim is that regardless of whether these doctrines present themselves as "more private" or "more public," they continue to wrestle with both the difficulty of ascertaining subjective intent, and the conflict among policy commitments to subjective and objective value, individualism and altruism.

a. The Modern Law of Duress

. . . If duress is indeed a "public" limitation on freedom of contract, then, at one level, breach of societal norms is a perfectly legitimate basis for invoking the doctrine. Linking the presence of an improper threat to the subjective requirement of actual inducement can then be viewed as an appropriate way of limiting public intervention to protection of the private sphere of autonomy. In practice, however, apart from a somewhat arbitrary list provided by other areas of law, we have as much trouble identifying a breach of societal norms as we do identifying autonomy and its absence. Standards of appropriate behavior prove as elusive as standards of their exchange.

b. Unconscionability

. . . [U]nconscionabilty doctrine is directed to the prevention of oppression and unfair surprise.

In its focus on oppression, it has obvious and strong links to duress; in its focus on unfair surprise, it has similarly obvious and strong links to fraud. One way of explaining the place of unconscionability in the body of contract doctrine is to describe it as the public face of a concern for which duress and fraud then appear as the private expressions. An unconscionable contract is one that shocks the *public* conscience. Duress and fraud concentrate, by comparison, on the effect of the coercive or fraudulent conduct on the contractual capacity of the affected party. Another explanation is that unconscionability is the area in which the Realist insight about coercion is finally enshrined in contract doctrine, as the focus shifts from the model of bad behavior largely unconnected with the operation of the market system to the model of exploitation of economic advantage.

Unconscionability doctrine, however, contains the same tension between public and private, the same preoccupation with the problem of power, that we have already seen characterizes duress. As a result, rather than finally clarifying when the acceptable manipulation of economic advantage shades into unacceptable dealing, unconscionability doctrine reverts to the same endless play around reality of assent, standards of behavior, and inequivalence of exchange.

The newest idea in unconscionability doctrine is inequality of bargaining power. The *U.C.C.* version of unconscionability expressly disclaims any concern with this notion, but the *Restatement* suggests that while "mere" inequality does not make for unconscionability, "gross" inequality does have a role to play.

Even gross inequality is not a conclusive indicator of unconscionability. It is to be used only in conjunction with "terms unreasonably favorable to the stronger party," an analysis that presumes the possibility of substantive measurement. As yet another qualification, the combination of gross inequality of bargaining power and unreasonably favorable terms will only lead to a finding of unconscionability if it demonstrates a failure of process rather than substance: "confirm[ing] indications that the transaction involved elements of deception or compulsion," or alternatively demonstrates a lack of real assent, showing "that the weaker party had no meaningful choice, no real alternative, or did not in fact assent or appear to assent to the unfair terms."

This treatment of unequal bargaining power is paradigmatic of the uneasy way unconscionability doctrine brings together individualism and altruism, public and private. Inequality of bargaining power cannot of itself invalidate agreements, because the *Restatement* recognizes the truth of the Realist insight that every contract is the product of an inequality of bargaining power with respect to the subject of the bargain. The promise that we can correct for "gross" inequality is simply the promise that the worst features of the system can be held in check without threatening the regular operation of the system. The commentary suggests that we could agree on the point at which inequality becomes unacceptable, but it fails to offer any guidance for performing such a calculation. Diverting attention from the issue of equality to the presence or absence of other features of the agreement forestalls the overtly political decisions required to establish such a standard.

D. Summary

In the implied contrary story, we saw how public and private were confounded, how our understanding of implied-in-fact and express contracts requires us to draw on a fund of public information and values that influences our judgment of what we see. Similarly, our imposition of a public quasi-contractual obligation requires us to look for private signals from the parties about their conception of their relationship. Rather than banishing quasi-contract as a dangerous public exception to a private law of contract, therefore, we embraced its lesson that all contract is as public as it is private. . . .

The lessons of duress and unconscionability are similar. The efforts to incorporate these doctrines into the world of private contract through a focus on contractual "will," or to situate them as public exceptions to a rule that traditionally re-

jects interference in private exchanges, necessarily end in failure. . . .

IV. Conclusion: Doctrine, the Cohabitation Contract, and Beyond

. . . In this final section, I will illustrate the poverty of traditional doctrinal arguments by examining the use of contract doctrine in recent cases involving the agreements of nonmarital cohabitants. These opinions deploy many of the doctrinal maneuvers exposed in this Article. Distinctions between private and public realms, between contracts implied-in-fact and contracts implied-in-law, play an important part in the decisions. Interpretive questions and questions about the basis for enforcement—about consideration—also loom large, reiterating the concern with private and public, but couching that concern in the competing terms of subjective and objective, form and substance.

Significantly, the opinions largely ignore the aspect of the public-private debate that appears in contract doctrine as the set of rules governing duress and unconscionability. The concerns of those doctrines—preventing oppression of each party by the other, while preventing oppression of both by the state—are nonetheless highly relevant. For at the heart of these cases lies the problem of power. It is only because the exercise of power in this context is not seen as fitting the traditional rubrics of duress and unconscionability that courts are able to ignore and avoid it. . . .

B. Express and Implied Agreement

The opinions in the cohabitation cases indicate that the distinction between the intention-based express contract and the public institution of quasi-contract may be central to the question of whether to grant relief. As I have earlier argued, however, techniques for interpreting the express contract are indistinguishable from techniques used to determine the presence of a quasi-contractual relationship. If the interpretive techniques employed highlight factors external to the parties and their actual intentions, even express contracts seem very public. If, in contrast, the techniques used have as their stated goal the determination of the parties' intentions, then quasi-contracts appear no less private or consensual than express contracts. The cohabitation opinions employ both public-sounding and private-sounding arguments to reach a variety of conclusions. In some cases courts determine that the parties are bound by *both* real and quasi-contractual obligations, in others that they are bound by neither, in yet others that they are bound by one but not the other. The arguments do not determine these outcomes—they only legitimate them.

In these cases, as in the earlier-discussed *Hertzog*, there is a common presumption that agreements between intimates are not contractual. While this model of association was developed in husband-wife and parent-child cases, nonmarital cohabitants are assumed, for these purposes, to have the same kind of relationship. As in *Hertzog*, express words are taken to be words of commitment but not of contract; conduct that in other circumstances would give rise to an implied-in-fact contract is instead attributed to the relationship. These cases also reach a conclusion only intimated in *Hertzog*: They find no unjust enrichment where one party benefits the other.

One possible explanation for this presumption against finding contracts is that it accords with the parties' intentions. It can be argued that cohabitants generally neither want their agreements to have legal consequences, nor desire to be obligated to one another when they have stopped cohabiting. It can further be presented as a matter of fact that their services are freely given and taken within the context of an intimate relationship. If this is so, then a subsequent claim of unjust enrichment is simply unfounded.

This intention-based explanation, however, coexists in the opinions—indeed sometimes coexists within a single opinion—with two other, more overtly public, explanations that rest on diametrically opposed public policies. The first suggests that the arena of intimate relationships is too

private for court intervention through contract enforcement to be appropriate. In *Hewitt*, for example, the Illinois Supreme Court suggests that "the situation alleged here was not the kind of arm's length bargain envisioned by traditional contract principles, but an intimate arrangement of a fundamentally different kind."

While it has some intuitive appeal, the argument that intimate relationships are too private for court enforcement is at odds with the more general argument that all contractual relationships are private and that contract enforcement merely facilitates the private relationships described by contract. To overcome this apparent inconsistency, we must imagine a scale of privateness on which business arrangements, while mostly private, are still not as private as intimate arrangements. But then the rescue attempt runs headlong into the other prevailing policy argument, which separates out intimate arrangements because of their peculiarly public and regulated status. Under this view, it is the business relationship that by and large remains more quintessentially private.

According to this second argument, the area of nonmarital agreements is too public for judicial intervention. The legislature is the appropriate body to regulate such arrangements; courts may not help create private alternatives to the public scheme. In *Hewitt*, the supreme court directly follows its appeal to the intimate nature of the relationship with an acknowledgment of the regulated, and hence public, character of marriage-like relations. With respect to intimate relations conceived as public, the judiciary can then present itself as either passive or active. The argument for passivity is that judges should "stay out" of an arena already covered by public law. The argument for activity is that judges should reinforce public policy by deterring the formation of deviant relationships, either because they fall outside the legislative schemes organizing familial entitlement and property distribution, or because they offend public morality.

Neither the private nor the public arguments for the absence of contract in this setting are conclusive. Both private and public counterarguments are readily available. If the absence of contract is presented as flowing from party intention, competing interpretations of intention can be used to argue the presence of contract. If, within a more public framework, the court categorizes the concerns implicated by the relationship as private, then an argument can be made that within the boundaries expressly established by legislation, the parties should be free to vary the terms of their relationship without interference by the state. If the focus is the place of cohabitation agreements within the publicly regulated sphere of intimate relationships, then an argument can be made that certain kinds of enforcement in fact extend and implement public policy rather than derogate from it.

The availability of this range of intention-based and policy-based arguments makes possible virtually any decision. A court can find or not find a "real" contract. It can decide that enforcement of a real contract is or is not appropriate. It can decide that while real contracts should be enforced, there is no basis for awarding quasi-contractual relief in the absence of an expressed intention to be bound. It can decide that even in the absence of real contract, the restitutionary claim of the plaintiff represents a compelling basis for quasi-contractual relief. Further, the competing public and private strands of argument—each of which connects to both enforceability and non-enforceability arguments—can be used within the same opinion or other legal text, without the inconsistencies being so apparent as to undermine the credibility of the final result.

C. Manifestation and Intent

Some identifiable, particular patterns do emerge from this overall confusion of public and private arguments. As with all agreements, for example, every aspect of a cohabitation agreement raises interpretive questions that will drive a court to search for the elusive correspondence between subjective intent and manifested form. Even this most private exercise of contractual interpretation thereby opens the doors to the imposition of public values, norms, and understandings. Two interpretive issues in particular recur in the cases. The courts repeatedly consider how to evaluate the relationships out of which the agreements arise. They also repeatedly consider how to evaluate the role of sex in these relationships and in these agreements. This section explores the very different ways in which the opinions treat these issues, within the range of options made available by current doctrine.

Courts frequently invoke the context of cohabitation relationships to avoid enforcing agreements arising out of them. The argument here is essentially that even if such agreements use language of promise, or commitment, or reciprocal obligation, that language must be understood, *in the intimate context in which it is employed*, as not involving any understanding that one party might use a court to enforce a duty forsaken, or a promise broken.

In theory, if the parties make perfectly clear their intention to be legally bound by their agreement, then their intention governs. But this leaves open the question of when a court will find objective manifestations of such an intention to be bound. Will a written agreement be more susceptible to legal enforcement than an oral one? Will an agreement in which the reciprocal obligations relate to a particular piece of property or to a transaction that can be separated out, however artificially, from the affective context of the relationship convince a court that it has crossed the boundary between intimate unenforceability and business-like enforceability? These approaches all find some support in the cases, although their manipulability and their imperfect correspondence to questions of motivation and intention are obvious.

A second common theme employing notions of manifestation and intent is the specific role of sex in the parties' arrangement. The boundaries of this debate are set both by the tradition that precludes enforcement of prostitution contracts for reasons of public policy, and by the acknowledgment that even cohabiting parties may form valid contracts about independent matters. In the case of cohabitation agreements, the question there-

fore becomes whether the sex contemplated by
the parties contaminates the entire agreement to
the point where it is seen to fall within the model
of the prostitution contract, or whether other features of the agreement can be seen as independent
and enforceable.

Judges' differing interpretations of virtually
identical agreements seem to depend quite openly
on either their views of what policy should prevail
or their own moral sense. Rarely does a judge
even appear to make a thorough attempt to understand and enforce what the parties had in mind. . . .

As the courts wrestle with these interpretive
questions, we see them apparently infusing a public element, external to the parties' own view of
their situation, into their assessment of cohabitation agreements. We also can see how this is a necessary result of the tension between manifestation
and intent, of the way in which intent requires
embodiment in manifested forms, even while the
forms require an infusion of substance before they
can yield meaning. Indeed, to accuse judges of
moving from the private to the public sphere is
only to accuse them of the inevitable. If there is
force behind the accusation, it is not *that* they have
made the transition from private to public, but
that they have made the transition *unselfconsciously*,
and that the particular values, norms, and understandings they incorporate are different from the
ones we would have favored, or different from the
ones we think would correspond with those of one
or both of the parties to the agreement.

D. Consideration: Its Substance

Consideration doctrine offers yet other opportunities for the conflation of public and private, and
the introduction of competing values, norms, and
understandings into the resolution of these cohabitation cases. Just as in the area of interpretation, the crucial additions are judicial conceptions
of sexuality, and of woman's role in her relationship with man. Two aspects of consideration doctrine recur in the cases. Each illustrates the proposition that formal consideration doctrine cannot
be implemented without recourse to substance.

Substance, here as elsewhere, can be provided by
assessments of objective value or by investigations
into subjective intent. It is with respect to these
substantive inquiries that ideas about sexuality and
relationship come to play so potentially important
a part.

The first use of consideration doctrine in this
context shows up in the disinclination of courts to
enforce contracts based on "meretricious" consideration. Courts frequently search beyond the express language of the agreement in order to "find"
that sex is at the heart of the deal—specifically
that the woman is providing sexual services in return for the economic security promised by the
man. Insofar as this investigation depends on
divining what the parties had in mind, consideration turns on subjective intent. For these purposes, it matters not at all that "intent" has been
derived from the judge's own feelings about such
relationships, even when the express language of
the parties would appear to point in an opposite
direction.

The treatment of meretricious consideration
also illustrates how consideration may depend on
a finding of objective value. When courts refuse to
enforce contracts based on the exchange of sexual
services for money, they are, for long-standing
policy reasons, declining to recognize sexual services as having the *kind* of value that they will
honor. This decision, based on an objective measure of value, is no different from the decision that
"nominal" consideration will not support a contract. There, too, courts disregard intention in the
name of a policy that depends upon societal recognition of certain sorts of values and delegitimation of others.

The second aspect of consideration doctrine
of interest in this context is the traditional conclusion that the woman's domestic services cannot
provide consideration for the promises made to
her by the man. This is usually linked to the idea
that the relationship itself is not one the parties
see as having a legal aspect. The standard explanation is that the woman did not act in expectation of gain, but rather out of affection, or that she
intended her action as a gift. . . .

E. The Question of Power

Under duress and unconscionability doctrines, policing the "fair" exchange is tied irretrievably to asking whether each party entered into the contract freely, whether each was able to bargain in equally unconstrained ways, and whether the deal was a fair one. I suppose that any of us would find these questions even harder to answer in the context of intimate relationships than in other contexts—harder in that we would require a much more detailed account of the particulars before we could hazard an opinion, and harder in that even this wealth of detail would be likely to yield contradictory interpretations. Yet we acknowledge the importance of these questions in the area of intimate relations; we do not imagine either that most couples wind up with a fair exchange, or that most couples have equal bargaining power vis-à-vis one another.

The doctrinal treatment of cohabitation agreements, however, like the treatment of contracts in general, usually pays little attention to questions of power and fairness. Duress and unconscionability are the exceptions that prove the rule. Those doctrines identify the only recognized deviations from the supposedly standard case of equal contracting partners. Intimate partners are conceived of as fitting the standard model. One consequence of this conception is that courts can justify the failure to enforce cohabitation arrangements as mere nonintervention, overlooking the fact that the superior position in which nonaction tends to leave the male partner is at least in part a product of the legal system. Another is that courts can idealize the private world in which their "nonintervention" leaves the parties, disregarding the ways in which that world is characterized by inequality and the exercise of private power. Yet another is that courts can talk blithely about the intentions of "the parties" in a fashion that ignores the possibility that one party's intentions are being respected at the expense of the other's.

Not all of the cohabitation contract opinions ignore the issues of fairness and power. They are more likely to receive explicit attention when a judge frankly invokes "public policy" instead of relying exclusively on contract doctrine. . . .

Study of the play between public and private, objective and subjective, shows us that these same dichotomies organize not only the strictly doctrinal territory of contract interpretation or consideration, but also the broader "policy" issues that are folded into the cases. Questions of judicial competence, for example, turn out to involve precisely the question of whether a private sphere can be marked off from the public sphere. Similarly, whether enforcement of cohabitation agreements is a pro-marriage or an anti-marriage position turns out to depend on questions of intention and power. Even as this analysis illuminates the policy dimension of the cases, it refutes the claim that the addition of policy considerations can cure doctrinal indeterminacy.

If neither doctrine nor the addition of policy can determine how decision makers choose outcomes in particular cases, the next question is whether the opinions contain other material that illuminates the decision-making process. The dimension of these cohabitation cases that cries out for investigation is the images they contain of women, and of relationship. And since images of women and of relationship are the central concern of feminist theory, I have used that theory as the basis for my inquiry. This does not, of course, foreclose the possibility that other inquiries, in this or other settings, might prove equally possible and promising once doctrine is opened up to make room for them.

I am not claiming that judges decide cohabitation cases on the basis of deeply held notions about women and relationship in the sense that these notions provide a determinate basis for decision. For this to be true, attitudes toward women and relationship would have to be free from contradiction in a way that doctrine and policy are not. I believe instead that these notions involve the same perceived divide between self and other that characterizes doctrine, and are as internally contradictory as any doctrine studied in this Article. My claim, therefore, is only that notions of women and relationship are another source of influence, and are therefore as deserving of attention as any other dimension of the opinions. These notions influence how judges frame rule-talk and policy-talk; in a world of indeterminacy they provide one more set of variables that may persuade a judge to decide a case one way or another, albeit in ways we cannot predict with any certainty. . . .

One powerful pair of contradictory images of woman paints the female cohabitant as either an angel or a whore. As angel, she ministers to her male partner out of noble emotions of love and self-sacrifice, with no thought of personal gain. It would demean both her services and the spirit in which they were offered to imagine that she expected a return—it would make her a servant. As whore, she lures the man into extravagant promises with the bait of her sexuality—and is appropriately punished for *her* immorality when the court declines to hold her partner to his agreement.

Although the image of the whore is of a women who at one level is seeking to satiate her own lust, sex—in these cases—is traditionally presented as something women give to men. This is consistent both with the view of woman as angel, and with the different image of the whore as someone who trades sex for money. In either event, woman is a provider, not a partner in enjoyment. When a judge invokes this image, he supports the view that sex contaminates the entire agreement, and that the desire for sex is the only reason for the male partner's promises of economic support. If sex were viewed as a mutually satisfying element of the arrangement, it could be readily separated out from the rest of the agreement. In most cases, the woman's career sacrifices and child rearing and homemaking responsibilities would then provide the consideration for the economic support proffered by the man. . . .

Epilogue

The stories told by contract doctrine are human stories of power and knowledge. The telling of those stories—like the telling of any story—is, in one sense, an impoverishing exercise: The infinitely rich potential that we call reality is stripped of detail, of all but a few of its aspects. But it is only through this restriction of content that any story has a meaning. In uncovering the way doctrine orders, and thereby creates, represents, and misrepresents reality, I have suggested and criticized the particular meaning created by doctrinal stories, the particular limitations entailed in the telling of those stories. . . .

My story reveals the world of contract doctrine to be one in which a comparatively few mediating devices are constantly deployed to displace and defer the otherwise inevitable revelation that public cannot be separated from private, or form from substance, or objective manifestation from subjective intent. The pain of that revelation, and its values, lies in its message that we can neither know nor control the boundary between self and other. Thus, although my story has reduced contract law to these few basic elements, they are elements that merit close scrutiny: They represent our most fundamental concerns. And the type of analysis I suggest can help us to understand and address those concerns.

By telling my story, I also hope to open the way for other stories—new accounts of how the problems of power and knowledge concretely hamper our ability to live with one another in society. My story both asks why those problems are not currently addressed by doctrine and traditional doctrinal analysis, and suggests how they might be. By presenting doctrine as a human effort at world-making, my story focuses fresh attention on those to whom we give the power to shape our world. My story requires that we develop new understandings of our world-makers as we create them, and are in turn created by them. This kind of inquiry, exemplified for me by feminist theory, can help us see that the world portrayed by traditional doctrinal analysis is already not the world we live in, and is certainly not the only possible world for us to live in. And in coming to that realization, we increase our chances of building our world anew.

• 10 •

Sociology of Law
at Century's End

In this tenth and final chapter we appraise the theoretical terrain we have traversed in the previous nine. Taking measure of the classical and contemporary works that have informed sociology of law over the last one hundred years is no easy task. Nor can we expect that any such effort will do justice to a description and explanation of legal sociology's theoretical development over such a long period of time. Be that as it may, it seems appropriate that, as we approach a new century, we take stock of where we are and where we have been intellectually. This chapter, therefore, attempts to give coherence to sociology of law's past and present by identifying the theoretical themes and orientations found in the works discussed in this book. The chapter closes as I briefly indulge in forecasting where sociology of law may be headed in the twenty-first century.

Theoretical Themes

Five major themes run through the sociolegal works discussed in this book. The first theme concerns the relationship between law and society. All of the theorists—be they classical or contemporary, functionalists or conflict theorists, jurists or sociologists—highlighted the connection between legal phenomena and social structure. To be sure, we noted that despite the points of contention between the theorists, their common objective was always to analyze the law in order to gain greater insight into societal development.

The second theoretical theme, the developmental transformation of law and society, is comprised of three subthemes. First, the theorists mentioned in this book were all engaged in explaining social and legal change. Although some acknowledged that legal change could instigate social change, most theorists like Maine, Sumner, and Pound, recognized that legal modifications usually follow social transformations. Second, whereas some theorists viewed sociolegal change as largely positive, others did not. Beccaria, Spencer, Maine, Marx, and Durkheim generally believed that sociolegal modifications led to greater equality, fairness, and humanitarianism and frequently employed the terms "evolution" and "progress." Weber, on the other hand, saw sociolegal change as having consequences that were both positive (efficiency) and negative (dehumanization). Finally, the theorists perceived the developmental transformation of the law and society as occurring smoothly or fitfully. Spencer, Durkheim, and Parsons considered sociolegal transformations as part of the natural functioning of the social world and maintained that these changes usually transpired in a slow and orderly manner. By contrast, Sumner, Holmes, Marx, and some of the conflict theorists viewed law and society as being resistant to change and believed that social and legal alterations are often realized by coercive reform or revolution. In either case, all of the theorists agreed that there is a certain inevitability to the developmental transformation of law and society.

The third theme concerns the importance that the theorists placed on extralegal factors in their examination of the law. Spencer, Holmes, Pound, the legal realists, Marx, the conflict theorists, and the Critics underscored the interplay between law, politics, and economics. Weber examined politics, economics, and religion in his analysis of the law's formulation and application. Durkheim, Gusfield, and Duster investigated how politics, religion, and morality have a determining influence on legislation. In sum, the theorists treated the law not as an abstract, metaphysical entity but as an empirical, societal phenomenon dependent on social factors.

The fourth theoretical theme pertains to the fact that the majority of the theorists conceptualized the law as a pragmatic instrument used to guide, manage, and order social interactions, the social structure, or both. For example, Sumner and Pound saw law as an institution of social control that regulates human behavior. Being more specific, Durkheim and Malinowski noted that law regulates relations between persons by demanding that they engage in reciprocal and binding obligations. Renner believed that, under socialism, legal norms would rationally regulate labor, power, and goods and therefore coordinate production, distribution, and consumption. Parsons maintained that the legal system is a generalized mechanism of social control that adjusts, coordinates, and facilitates the interchanges among the various subsystems. Podgorecki considered as one of the law's main functions its ability to engage in the rational and effective engineering of society. Finally, the conflict theorists viewed the law as a political weapon that one group adroitly uses to advance and protect its economic interests and moral culture against rival groups. In essence, the theorists considered the law as a regulating social force.

The fifth theme relates to the fact that since most of the theorists attempted to explain the law's role in liberal-capitalist society, a large number of them focused on the private law of contracts and property ownership. For example, Maine argued that as society progresses it accords rights and duties on the basis of private contract. Marx, Balbus, and Stone posited that bourgeoisie law protected two of capitalism's most essential features: contract and private property. Renner contended that property ownership and the employment contract maintained the same structures under feudalism and capitalism. Marx and Weber recognized the exploitative effects of contractual freedom. Durkheim examined the historical evolution of contract and stated that the contract's main function is to foster cooperative relations between people. Kennedy argued that, in liberal-capitalist society, individualism and rules help the law minimize the degree of judicial interference on the individual's right to privately enter into business contracts. Finally, Dalton deconstructed contract doctrine by revealing the contradictory nature of the private/public polar dualities.

To summarize, the five theoretical themes extending throughout the sociolegal works featured in this book are:

1. The correlative relationship between law and society
2. The certainty of social and legal change
3. The influence of extralegal factors
4. The conceptualization of law as a regulatory device
5. The focus on the private law of contracts and property ownership.

Taken together, these five theoretical themes aid us in examining the law in four unique ways:

1. The themes allow us to see the law in broad theoretical perspective; that is, we locate the law within the context of the larger society and, as such, consider its influences at the microlevel of social interaction and the macrolevel of social structure.
2. The theoretical themes assist us in treating the law as a dynamic social phenomenon. Accordingly, the law takes on a character that is evolutionary, transformative, and influential.
3. The five themes help us to regard the law as an independent variable, a dependent variable, and a reciprocal factor. Either way, it becomes apparent that the law is influential to, and influenced by, a variety of social forces.
4. The theoretical themes present us with the opportunity to consider the law from a critical as well as a favorable point of view. Put another way, we become aware of the law's positive and negative consequences on society.

In short, the five theoretical themes common to the works discussed in this text permit not just a jurisprudential but a *sociological* analysis of the law.

Theoretical Orientations

Aside from identifying the themes shared by the sociolegal works, we may also compare and contrast the theories and paradigms examined in this book by placing them along four sets of continua comprised of eight theoretical orientations represented as four polar dichotomies:

1. Positivism-Normativism
2. Formalism-Antiformalism
3. Individualism-Communalism
4. Consensus-Coercion

These four dichotomies are ideal types. Because the theories possess varying degrees of the polar features, they fall at different points on the continua.

1. The first polar dichotomy consists of *positivism-normativism.* "Positivism" is the theoretical orientation that regards sociolegal theory and inquiry as scientific, empirical, and objective. Weber's approach was undoubtedly positivistic as he stressed the need for sociologists to be free from ideological and political biases. Likewise, the sociological movement in law was generally (but not completely) intended to be positivistic. Llewellyn, for example, urged the realists to temporarily put aside the normative question of what "ought to be" so that they can develop a positivist jurisprudence dealing with what "is."

Alternatively, "normativism" is the theoretical orientation that considers and/ or is guided by moral and valuative issues. Following this tradition, Pound argued that law should protect the social interests, or normative claims, that people want satisfied. Neo-Weberians who adopted the normative approach included Martin Spencer, who identified value-rational authority as being legitimized by absolute value norms, and Hyde and Tyler, who demonstrated that substantive moral values and normative issues compel people to obey the law.

2. The second polar dichotomy consists of *formalism-antiformalism.* "Formalism" is the theoretical orientation that treats the law as an internally coherent and gapless system of general rules. Its competing theoretical orientation, "antiformalism," focuses on the law's fluid, dynamic, and inconsistent character. Cesare Beccaria defended legal formalism as he argued that the law should be stated generally and applied systematically. Parsons and Luhmann regarded the law as a coherent system with boundaries. Weber saw legal formalism as a double-edged sword. On the one hand, he acknowledged that formal rational law fostered greater predictability of legal outcome. On the other hand, Weber recognized that its highly technical nature contributed to social alienation. Holmes, Pound, and Llewellyn launched the organized revolt against legal formalism, arguing that the law must meet the ever-changing practical necessities of social life. This legacy has been continued by the Critics who trash liberal legal doctrine by revealing how formalism makes the law indeterminate and contradictory.

3. The third polar dichotomy is *individualism-communalism.* "Individualism" is the theoretical orientation that underscores the private, personal, autonomous, and egoistic features of social and legal life. "Communalism," by contrast, is the theoretical orientation involving that which is public, collective, communal, and altruistic. Maine considered individualism when he argued that as society progressed, property law underwent a transformation from joint-ownership by the family to private ownership by the individual. Spencer and Sumner inveighed against state law meddling in the individual's private affairs. Durkheim also emphasized individualism when he stated that legal punishment is less likely to be harsh in an organic society that celebrates the individual. Nearer to the "communalism" end of the continuum, Renner maintained that, in a socialist economy, the employment contract and property would be "socialized," or given a communal character.

4. The fourth dichotomy involves the polar concepts of *consensus-coercion.* "Consensus" is the theoretical orientation that emphasizes the stability, harmony, and voluntary cooperation of society. Along these lines, Herbert Spencer stated that the law in modern industrial societies originates from the consensus of individual interests. Structural-functionalism, systems theory, and autopoietic theory focused on society's consensual norms and values and asserted that the law mitigated social conflict by performing the functions of integration and normative consistency.

"Coercion," by contrast, is the theoretical orientation that looks at dissensus, culture conflict, class struggle, and social frictions. Holmes, Marx, the neo-Marxists, and some of the Critics maintained that the law reflects, promotes, and protects the interests of the groups possessing the most political and economic power. For example, Hall, Chambliss, Gusfield, Duster, and Turk showed that powerful groups employ legal coercion in changing the social practices of less powerful groups.

To summarize, the theories and paradigms discussed in this text exhibited varying degrees of eight theoretical orientations:

1. Positivism
2. Normativism
3. Formalism
4. Antiformalism
5. Individualism
6. Communalism
7. Consensus
8. Coercion

When utilized individually, each of the theoretical orientations offers the legal sociologist a penetrating and precise (albeit a limited and unidimensional) analysis of sociolegal reality. When employed collectively and in combination with their polar opposites, the eight theoretical orientations provide the legal sociologist with a multidimensional (although often paradoxical and contradictory) picture of sociolegal reality. Let us look at how we may be able to combine, or synthesize, the orientations and other theoretical factors.

An Effort at Synthesis

We have already seen that the theoretical state of present-day legal sociology consists largely of neo-Marxism, neo-Weberianism, neo-Durkheimianism, functionalism, conflict theory, and critical legal studies. These contemporary perspectives are, in large measure, extensions, amplifications, and corrections of the nineteenth-century classical perspectives seeking to explain modern society. However, the end of the twentieth century is, temporally and analytically, a transitional period for legal sociology.

At the present time, sociology of law appears to be on the threshold of a paradigmatic breakthrough as it searches for a mode of theorizing suitable to understanding the different dimensions of postmodern society. But, in contrast to all of the classical and most of the contemporary perspectives, postmodern theorizing relies less on the "science" of causal analysis and more on the "poetry" of rhetoric. Thus, to analyze the law (as does Niklas Luhmann) as a reflexive and self-referential system or to regard legal doctrine (as do some Critics) as discourse and stories, requires a sociolegal theory that has language, or the universal symbolic medium of interpretation and interchange, as its starting point or "basic unit of analysis." To be sure, Luhmann's autopoiesis and the Critics' deconstructionism examine the communication taking place within the normatively closed legal system and the discourse of liberal legal doctrine, respectively. In addition, sociolegal theorizing that focuses on language must address the postmodern questions of legal reflexivity, the multiplicity of legal meanings, and the law's inherent paradoxes and contradictions.

Autopoiesis and deconstructionism are two forms of theorizing that currently stand on the brink of a paradigmatic shift in legal sociology because they consciously and deliberately consider the questions of postmodern social life. As we have seen, these theoretical approaches have as their subjects of analysis the legal system and legal doctrine. Accordingly, they examine, (1) the practice of self observation as it occurs with the legal system and the legal actor; (2) the various meaningful actions of several people constituting a social system and contract doctrine's diverse interpretations of the subjective intentions of bargaining parties; and (3) the paradox of constitutional self-amendment and the doctrinal contradictions existing between the rhetorical modes of individualism/altruism and private/public.

In its cultural sense, postmodernism is an integration of incompatible ideologies and lifestyles. Consequently, postmodern theorizing must likewise involve an integration, or synthesis, of seemingly disparate and diverging theoretical orientations and subjects of analysis.

In my view, sociology of law today must consist of an effort at synthesizing the polar opposites comprising the eight theoretical orientations—positivism (P) and normativism (N); formalism (F) and antiformalism (A); individualism (I) and communalism (COM); consensus (CON) and coercion (COR)—and the two subjects of social analysis: the *legal system* and *legal doctrine*. These syntheses will prove to be a reasonable endeavor because a postmodern approach invariably blurs and subsequently eliminates all traditional theoretical parameters. Finally, these syntheses must take place within the context of *language*. For it is language—in the form of communication, discourse, narrative, and rhetoric—that lies at the center of all modes of postmodern theorizing. Figure 10–1 depicts the effort at theoretical synthesis in sociology of law at the close of the twentieth century.

To illustrate the type of synthesis that I am suggesting, I will take the formalism-antiformalism polar dichotomy as an example. A synthesis of formalism and antiformalism yields a theoretical orientation that concomitantly considers the law's *logical coherence* along with its *inconsistency and indeterminacy*. Moreover, it is a theoretical orientation that analyzes the law as a coherent and indeterminate *bounded unit* (system) that is self-producing, self-regulating, and self-referential, as well as a coherent and indeterminate *set of concepts* (doctrine) that are polar dualities. Finally, it is a theoretical orientation that considers the law as a system where *meaningful communication* is created, produced, and constituted by other communications as well as a doctrine of *legal discourse based on interpretation*. Such a

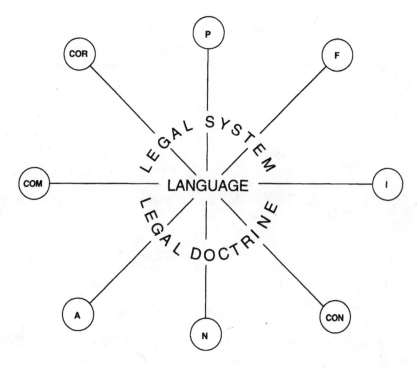

Figure 10–1. A Postmodern Synthesis for Sociology of Law at Century's End

synthesis produces a postmodern theoretical perspective that has, heretofore, been unknown in legal sociology.

I contend that sociology of law will, in the near future, need to engage in many and simultaneous efforts of theoretical synthesis. For only by combining and re-combining, formulating and reformulating, defining and redefining our concepts, theories, and paradigms can we hope to further advance sociolegal thought.

Sociology of law has come of age. It is now a recognized and important aca-demic field destined to continue to impact the discipline of sociology and the pro-fession of law. There is every reason to believe that sociology of law will make significant and exciting theoretical and empirical contributions to future scholar-ship. It is hoped that this book will inspire the students of the twentieth century to become the legal sociologists of the twenty-first.

Figure 10.1. A Postmodern Synthesis for Sociology of Law at Century's End

Bibliography

Adams, H. P. 1972. *Karl Marx: In His Earlier Writings.* New York: Atheneum.

Aichele, Gary J. 1989. *Oliver Wendell Holmes, Jr.: Soldier, Scholar, Judge.* Boston: Twayne Publishers.

Albrow, Martin. 1975. "Legal Positivism and Bourgeois Materialism: Max Weber's View of the Sociology of Law." *British Journal of Law and Society* 2:14–31.

Alexander, Jeffery C., and Paul Colomy. editors. 1990. *Differentiation Theory and Social Change: Comparative and Historical Perspectives.* New York: Columbia University Press.

Altman, Andrew. 1990. *Critical Legal Studies: A Liberal Critique.* Princeton, NJ: Princeton University Press.

Arthur, Chris. 1989. "Editor's Introduction." Pp.9–31. In *Law and Marxism: A General Theory* by E. B. Pashukanis. Translated by Barbara Einhorn. Edited and Introduced by Chris Arthur. Worcester, Great Britain: Pluto Press.

Aubert, Vilhelm. 1963. "Competition and Dissensus: Two Types of Conflict and of Conflict Resolution." *The Journal of Conflict Resolution* 7(1):26–42.

———. 1967a. "Some Social Functions of Legislation." *Acta Sociologica* 10(1–2):98–120.

———. 1967b. "Courts and Conflict Resolution." *The Journal of Conflict Resolution* 11(1):40–51.

Auerbach, Jerold S. 1984. *Justice Without Law? Resolving Disputes Without Lawyers.* New York: Oxford University Press.

Balbus, Isaac. 1973. *The Dialectics of Legal Repression: Black Rebels before the American Criminal Courts.* New York: Russell Sage Foundation.

———. 1977. "Commodity Form and Legal Form: An Essay on the 'Relative Autonomy' of the Law." *Law and Society Review* 11:571–588.

Ball, Harry V., George Eaton Simpson, and Kiyoshi Ikeda. 1961–1962. "A Re-Examination of William Graham Sumner on Law and Social Change." *Journal of Legal Education* 14(3):299–316.

———. 1962. "Law and Social Change: Sumner Reconsidered." *American Journal of Sociology* 17:532–540.

Barnes, Harry Elmer. 1919. "Two Representative Contributions of Sociology to Political Theory: The Doctrines of William Graham Sumner and Lester Frank Ward." *American Journal of Sociology* 25:3–23.

Barnes, J. A. 1966. "Durkheim's *Division of Labour in Society.*" *Man* 1/2:158–175.

Baxi, Upendra. 1974. "Comment—Durkheim and Legal Evolution: Some Problems of Disproof." *Law and Society Review* 8(4):645–668.

Beccaria, Cesare. 1988. *On Crimes and Punishments.* Translated by Henry Paolucci. New York: Macmillan Publishing Company.

Becker, Howard S. 1963. "Moral Entrepeneurs." Pp. 147–163. In *Outsiders: Studies in the Sociology of Deviance.* New York: Free Press.

Beirne, Piers. 1979a. "Empiricism and the Critique of Marxism on Law and Crime." *Social Problems* 26(4):373–385.

———. 1979b. "Ideology and Rationality in Max Weber's Sociology of Law." Pp.103–131. In *Research in Law and Sociology.* Volume 2. Edited by Steven Spitzer. Greenwich, CT: JAI Press.

———, and Robert Sharlet. editors 1980. *Pashukanis: Selected Writings on Marxism and Law.* Translated by Peter B. Maggs. Foreword by John N. Hazard. London: Academic Press.

Bendix, Reinhard. 1962. *Max Weber: An Intellectual Portrait.* Garden City, NY: Doubleday and Company.

Bergesen, Albert. 1984. "Social Control and Corporate Organization: A Durkheimian Perspective." Pp. 141–170. In *Toward a General Theory of Social Control,* Vol.2. Edited by Donald Black. New York: Academic Press.

Berlin, Isaiah. 1973. *Karl Marx: His Life and Environment.* Third Edition. New York: Oxford University Press.

Binns, Peter. 1980. "Law and Marxism." *Capital and Class* 10:100–113.

Black, Donald. 1972. "The Boundaries of Legal Sociology." *Yale Law Journal* 81(6):1086–1100.

———. 1976. *The Behavior of Law.* New York: Academic Press.

Blackstone, Sir William. 1849. *Commentaries on the Law of England.* Four Volumes. New York: W. E. Dean, Printer and Publisher.

Blum, Mark E. 1985. *The Austro-Marxists, 1890–1918: A Psychobiographical Study.* Lexington, KY: The University of Kentucky Press.

Bottomore, Tom, and Patrick Goode, editors. 1978. *Austro-Marxism.* Texts translated and edited by T. Bottomore and P. Goode. With an Introduction by T. Bottomore. Oxford: Clarendon Press.

Bourricaud, Francois. 1981. *The Sociology of Talcott Parsons.* Translated by Arthur Goldhammer. Chicago: The University of Chicago Press.

Buckley, Walter. 1957. "Structural-Functional Analysis in Modern Sociology." Pp.236–258. In *Modern Sociological Theory.* Edited by Howard Becker and Alvin Boskoff. New York: The Dryden Press.

Cain, Maureen. 1980. "The Limits of Idealism: Max Weber and the Sociology of Law." Pp.53–83. In *Research in Law and Sociology.* Volume 3. Edited by Steven Spitzer. Greenwich, CT: JAI Press.

———, and Alan Hunt. 1979. *Marx and Engels on Law.* New York: Academic Press.

Campbell, David. 1986. "Truth Claims and Value-Freedom in the Treatment of Legitimacy: The Case of Weber." *Journal of Law and Society* 13(2): 207–224.

Cardozo, Benjamin N. 1924. *The Growth of the Law.* New Haven: Yale University Press.

Cartwright, B. C., and R. D. Schwartz. 1973. "The Invocation of Legal Norms: An Empirical Investigation of Durkheim and Weber." *American Sociological Review* 38(3):340–354.

Caso, Adolph. 1975. *America's Italian Founding Fathers.* Boston: Branden Press Publishers.

Chambliss, William J. 1964. "A Sociological Analysis of the Law of Vagrancy." *Social Problems* 12(1):67–77.

Clarke, Michael. 1976. "Durkheim's Sociology of Law." *British Journal of Law and Society* 3:246–255.

Cocks, R. C. J. 1988. *Sir Henry Maine: A Study in Victorian Jurisprudence.* Cambridge: Cambridge University Press.

Collins, Randall. 1975. *Conflict Sociology: Toward an Explanatory Science.* New York: Academic Press.

Comte, Auguste. 1875. *System of Positive Philosophy,* Vol. II. London: Longmans, Green, and Co.

Coser, Lewis A. 1956. *The Functions of Social Conflict.* New York: Free Press.

———. 1979. *Masters of Sociological Thought: Ideas in Historical and Social Context.* Second Edition. New York: Harcourt Brace Jovanovich.

———. 1984. "Introduction." Pp.ix–xxiv. In *The Division of Labor in Society* by Emile Durkheim. Translated by W. D. Halls. New York: Free Press.

Cotterrell, Roger. 1977. "Durkheim on Legal Development and Social Solidarity." *British Journal of Law and Society* 4(2):241–252.

———. 1992. *The Sociology of Law: An Introduction.* Second Edition. London: Butterworths.

Cressey, Donald R. 1969. *Theft of the Nation: The Structure and Operations of Organized Crime in America.* New York: Harper and Row.

Currie, Elliot. 1968. "Crimes Without Criminals: Witchcraft and Its Control in Renaissance Europe." *Law and Society Review* 3(1):7–32.

Dahrendorf, Ralf. 1958a. "Out of Utopia: Toward a Reorientation of Sociological Analysis." *American Journal of Sociology* 64(2):115–127.

———. 1958b. "Toward a Theory of Social Conflict." *The Journal of Conflict Resolution* 2(2):170–183.

———. 1959. *Class and Class Conflict in Industrial Society.* Standford, CA: Stanford University Press.

Dalton, Clare. 1985. "An Essay in the Deconstruction of Contract Doctrine." *Yale Law Journal* 94(5): 997–1114.

Davis, F. James. 1957. "The Treatment of Law in American Sociology." *Sociology and Social Research* 42(2):99–105.

———, et al. 1962. *Society and the Law: New Meanings for an Old Profession.* New York: Free Press.

Davis, Kingsley. 1959. "The Myth of Functional Analysis as a Special Method in Sociology and Anthropology." *American Sociological Review* 24(6):757–774.

de Beaumont, Gustave, and Alexis de Tocqueville. 1964. *On the Penitentiary System in the United States and Its Application in France.* Introduction by Thorstein Sellin. Foreword by Herman R. Lantz. Carbondale and Edwardsville, IL: Southern Illinois Press.

Delgado, Richard. 1987. "The Ethereal Scholar: Does Critical Legal Studies Have What Minorities Want?" *Harvard Civil Rights/Civil Liberties Law Review* 22(2):301–322.

Dewey, John. 1924. "Logical Method and Law." *The Cornell Law Quarterly* 10(1):17–27.

Dickens, Charles. 1966. *Oliver Twist.* Edited by Kathleen Tillotson. Oxford, England: Clarendon Press.

Doyle, Arthur Conan. 1984. *Great Works of Sir Arthur Conan Doyle*. New York: Crown Publishers.

Durkheim, Emile. 1957. *Professional Ethics and Civic Morals*. Translated by Cornelia Brookfield. London: Routledge & Kegan Paul.

———. [1895] 1966. *The Rules of Sociological Method*. Eighth Edition. Translated by Sarah A. Solovay and John H. Mueller and edited by George E. G. Catlin. New York: Free Press.

———. 1983. "The Evolution of Punishment." Pp. 102–132. In *Durkheim and the Law*. Edited by Steven Lukes and Andrew Scull. New York: St. Martin's Press.

———. [1893] 1984. *The Division of Labor in Society*. Translated by W. D. Halls. New York: Free Press.

Duster, Troy. 1970. *The Legislation of Morality: Law, Drugs, and Moral Judgment*. New York: The Free Press.

Edleman, Bernard. 1979. *Ownership of the Image: Elements for a Marxist Theory of Law*. Translated by Elizabeth Kingdom. Introduced by Paul Q. Hirst. London: Routledge & Kegan Paul.

Ehrlich, Eugen. [1936] 1962. *Fundamental Principles of the Sociology of Law*. Translated by Walter L. Moll. New York: Russel and Russel.

Eisen, Arnold. 1978. "The Meanings and Confusions of Weberian 'Rationality'." *British Journal of Sociology* 29(1):57–70.

Engels, Friedrich. 1955. "The Housing Question." Pp. 546–634. In *Karl Marx and Friedrich Engels: Selected Works*. Vol. 1. Moscow: Foreign Languages Publishing House.

———. 1959. "Ludwig Fuerbach and the End of Classical German Philosophy." Pp.195–242. In *Marx and Engels: Basic Writings on Politics and Philosophy*. Edited by Lewis S. Feuer. Garden City, NY: Doubleday & Co.

———. 1975a. "Principles of Communism." Pp.341–357. In *Karl Marx–Friedrich Engels: Collected Works*, Vol. 6. New York: International Publishers.

———. 1975b. "On the Critique of the Prussian Press Laws." Pp.304–311. In *Karl Marx–Friedrich Engels: Collected Works*, Vol. 2. New York: International Publishers.

Epstein, E. L. 1958. *Politics in an Urban African Community*. Oxford, England: The University Press of Manchester.

Erikson, Kai T. 1966. *Wayward Puritans: A Study in the Sociology of Deviance*. New York: John Wiley.

Evan, William M., editor. 1962. *Law and Sociology: Exploratory Essays*. Glencoe, IL: The Free Press.

Evans-Pritchard, E. E. 1969. *The Nuer: A Description of the Modes of Livelihood and Political Institutions of a Nilotic People*. New York: Oxford University Press.

Ewing, Sally. 1987. "Formal Justice and the Spirit of Capitalism: Max Weber's Sociology of Law." *Law and Society Review* 21:487–512.

Feaver, George. 1969. *From Status to Contract: A Biography of Sir Henry Maine, 1822–1888*. London: Longmans.

Foucault, Michel. 1979. *Discipline and Punish: The Birth of the Prison*. Translated by Alan Sheridan. New York: Vintage Books.

Freeman, Alan D. 1981. "Truth and Mystification in Legal Scholarship." *Yale Law Review* 90:1229–1237.

Friedman, Lawrence M. 1975. *The Legal System: A Social Science Perspective*. New York: Russell Sage Foundation.

———. 1985. *A History of American Law*. New York: Simon and Schuster.

Frug, Gerald E. 1984. "The Ideology of Bureaucracy in American Law." *Harvard Law Review* 97(6):1276–1388.

Fuller, Lon L. 1934. "American Legal Realism." *University of Pennsylvania Law Review* 82(5):429–462.

———. 1949. "Pashukanis and Vyshinsky: A Study in the Development of Marxian Legal Theory." *Michigan Law Review* 47(7):1157–1166.

Garland, David. 1983. "Durkheim's Theory of Punishment: A Critique." Pp.37–61. In *The Power to Punish: Contemporary Penality and Social Analysis*. Edited by David Garland and Peter Young. London: Heinemann Educational Books.

Geis, Gilbert. 1964. "Sociology and Sociological Jurisprudence: Admixture of Lore and Law." *Kentucky Law Journal* 52(2):267–293.

Gerth, Hans, and C. Wright Mills, editors. 1978. *From Max Weber: Essays in Sociology*. New York: Oxford University Press.

Gilmore, Grant 1977. *The Ages of American Law*. New Haven, CT: Yale University Press.

Grace, Clive, and Philip Wilkinson. 1978. *Sociological Inquiry and Legal Phenomena*. New York: St. Martin's Press.

Grafstein, Robert. 1981. "The Failure of Weber's Conception of Legitimacy: Its Causes and Implications." *Journal of Politics* 43:456–472.

Greenberg, Jack. 1959. *Race Relations and American Law*. New York: Columbia University Press.

Gurvitch, Georges. 1942. *Sociology of Law*. New York: Philosophical Library.

Gusfield, Joseph R. 1967. "Moral Passage: The Symbolic Process in Public Designations of Deviance." *Social Problems* 15(2):175–188.

———. 1968. "On Legislating Morals: The Symbolic Process of Designating Deviance." *California Law Review* 56(1):54–73.

———. 1986. *Symbolic Crusade: Status Politics and the American Temperence Movement.* Second Edition. Urbana: University of Illinois Press.

Hall, Jerome. 1952. *Theft, Law, and Society.* Second Edition. Indianapolis, IN: Bobbs-Merrill.

Hay, Douglas, Peter Linebaugh, John G. Rule, E. P. Thompson, and Cal Winslow. 1975. *Albion's Fatal Tree: Crime and Society in Eighteenth-Century England.* New York: Pantheon Books.

Hilferding, Rudolf. [1910] 1981. *Finance Capital: A Study of the Latest Phase of Capitalist Development.* Edited with an Introduction by Tom Bottomore. From Translations by Morris Watnick and Sam Gordon. London: Routledge & Kegan Paul.

Hirst, Paul Q. 1979. *On Law and Ideology.* Atlantic Highlands, NJ: Humanities Press.

———. 1980. "Law, Socialism, and Rights." Pp.58–105. In *Radical Issues in Criminology.* Edited by Pat Carlen and Mike Collison. Totowa, NJ: Barnes & Noble Books.

Hoebel, E. Adamson. 1978. *The Law of Primitive Man: A Study in Comparative Legal Dynamics.* Cambridge, MA: Harvard University Press.

Holmes, Oliver Wendell. 1873. "Summary of Events— The Gas-Stokers' Strike." *American Law Review* 7(3):582–584.

———. 1897. "The Path of the Law." *Harvard Law Review* 10(8):457–478.

———. 1899. "Law in Science and Science in Law." *Harvard Law Review* 12(7): 443–463.

———. 1953. *Collected Legal Papers.* New York: Peter Smith.

———. [1881] 1963. *The Common Law.* Cambridge, MA: Harvard University Press.

Horwitz, Morton J. 1975. "The Rise of Legal Formalism." *The American Journal of Legal History* 19:251–264.

———. 1977. *The Transformation of American Law: 1780–1860.* Cambridge, MA: Harvard University Press.

———. 1992. *The Transformation of American Law, 1870–1960: The Crisis of Legal Orthodoxy.* New York: Oxford University Press.

Hostetler, John A. 1980. *Amish Society.* Third Edition. Baltimore: The Johns Hopkins University.

Hunt, Alan. 1978. *The Sociological Movement in Law.* London: The Macmillan Press Ltd.

———. 1981. "Marxism and the Analysis of Law." Pp. 91–109. In *Sociological Approaches to Law.* Edited by Adam Podgorecki and Christopher J. Whelan. London: Croom Helm.

———. 1991. "Marxism, Law, Legal Theory, and Jurisprudence." Pp.102–132. In *Dangerous Supplements: Resistence and Renewal in Jurisprudence.* Edited by Peter Fitzpatrick. Durham, NC: Duke University Press.

Hyde, Alan. 1983. "The Concept of Legitimation in the Sociology of Law." *Wisconsin Law Review* 1983 (2):379–426.

Ignatieff, Michael. 1978. *A Just Measure of Pain: The Penitentiary in the Industrial Revolution, 1750–1850.* New York: Columbia University Press.

James, William. 1938. *Selected Papers on Philosophy.* New York: E. P. Dutton and Co.

———. 1975. *Pragmatism.* Cambridge, MA: Harvard University Press.

Jeffery, C. Ray. 1957. "The Development of Crime in Early English Society." *The Journal of Criminal Law, Criminology, and Police Science* 47(6):647–666.

Johnson, Alan V. 1977. "A Definition of the Concept of Law." *Mid-American Review of Sociology* 2(1):47–71.

Kafka, Franz. 1956. *The Trial.* Translated by Willa and Edwin Muir. New York: Modern Library.

Kahn-Freund, Otto. 1949. "Introduction." Pp.1–43. In *The Institutions of Private Law and their Social Functions* by Karl Renner. London: Routledge & Kegan Paul.

Kalman, Laura. 1986. *Legal Realism at Yale, 1927–1960.* Chapel Hill: The University of North Carolina Press.

Kant, Immanuel. 1933. *Immanuel Kant's Critique of Pure Reason.* Translated by Norman Kenny Smith. London: Macmillan and Co.

Kantorowicz, Hermann. 1980. *The Definition of Law.* New York: Octagon Books.

Kelman, Mark G. 1984. "Trashing." *Stanford Law Review* 36:293–348.

———. 1987. *A Guide to Critical Legal Studies.* Cambridge, MA: Harvard University Press.

Kelsen, Hans. 1955. *The Communist Theory of Law.* New York: Frederick A. Prager.

Kennedy, Duncan. 1976. "Form and Substance in Private Law Adjudication." *Harvard Law Review* 89 (8):1685–1778.

———. 1979. "The Structure of Blackstone's Commentaries." *Buffalo Law Review* 28(2):205–382.

———. 1980. "Toward an Historical Understanding of Legal Consciousness: The Case of Classical Legal Thought in America, 1850–1940." *Research in Law and Sociology* 3:3–24. Greenwich, CT: JAI Press.

Kidder, Robert L. 1983. *Connecting Law and Society: An Introduction to Research and Theory*. Englewood Cliffs, NJ: Prentice-Hall.

Kinsey, Richard. 1978. "Marxism and the Law: Preliminary Analyses." *British Journal of Law and Society* 5:202–227.

———. 1983. "Karl Renner on Socialist Legality." Pp.11–42. In *Legality, Ideology, and the State*. Edited by David Sugarman. London: Academic Press.

Kronman, Anthony T. 1983a. *Max Weber*. Stanford, CA: Stanford University Press.

———. 1983b. "Paternalism and the Law of Contracts." *Yale Law Journal* 92(50):763–798.

Lanza-Kaduce, Lonn, Marvin D. Krohn, Marcia Radosevich, and Ronald L. Akers. 1979. "Law and Durkheimian Order: An Empirical Examination of the Convergence of Legal and Social Definitions of Law." Pp.41–61. In *Structure, Law, and Power: Essays in the Sociology of Law*. Edited by Paul J. Brantingham and Jack M. Kress. Beverly Hills, CA: Sage Publications.

Levine, Felice J. 1990. "Goose Bumps and 'The Search for Signs of Intelligent Life' in Sociolegal Studies: After Twenty-Five Years." *Law and Society Review* 24(1):7–33.

Linebaugh, Peter. 1976. "Karl Marx, The Theft of Wood, and Working Class Composition: A Contribution to the Current Debate." *Crime and Social Justice* 6:5–16.

———. 1992. *The London Hanged: Crime and Civil Society in the Eighteenth Century*. New York: Cambridge University Press.

Livingston, Debra. 1982. "'Round and 'Round the Bramble Bush: From Legal Realism to Critical Legal Scholarship." *Harvard Law Review* 95:1669–1690.

Llewellyn, Karl N. 1930a. "A Realistic Jurisprudence—The Next Step." *Columbia Law Review* 30(4):431–465.

———. 1930b. *The Bramble Bush: Our Law and Its Study*. Dobbs Ferry, NY: Oceana Publications.

———. 1931. "Some Realism About Realism—Responding to Dean Pound." *Harvard Law Review* 44(8):1222–1264.

———. 1949. "Law and the Social Sciences—Especially Sociology." *American Sociological Review* 14 (4):451–462.

———. 1960. *The Common Law Tradition: Deciding Appeals*. Boston: Little, Brown.

———, and E. Adamson Hoebel. 1978. *The Cheyenne Way: Conflict and Case Law in Primitive Jurisprudence*. Norman, OK: University of Oklahoma.

Luhmann, Niklas. 1977. "Differentiation of Society." *Canadian Journal of Sociology* 2:29–53.

———. 1985. *A Sociological Theory of Law*. Translated by Elizabeth King and Martin Albrow. Edited by Martin Albrow. London: Routledge & Kegan Paul.

———. 1988. "The Unity of the Legal System." Pp. 12–35. In *Autopoietic Law: A New Approach to Law and Society*. Edited by Gunther Teubner. New York: Walter de Gruyter.

———. 1990. *Essays on Self-Reference*. New York: Columbia University Press.

Lukes, Steven. 1985. *Emile Durkheim: His Life and Work*. Stanford, CA: Stanford University Press.

———, and Andrew Scull, editors. 1983. *Durkheim and the Law*. New York: St. Martin's Press.

Maas, Peter. 1968. *The Valachi Papers*. New York: G. P. Putnam's Sons.

MacKinnon, Catharine A. 1983. "Feminism, Marxism, Method, and the State: Toward Feminist Jurisprudence." *Signs* 8(4):635–658.

Maestro, Marcello T. 1973. *Cesare Beccaria and the Origins of Penal Reform*. Philadelphia: Temple University Press.

Maine, Sir Henry. [1861] 1970. *Ancient Law: Its Connection with the Early History of Society and Its Relation to Modern Ideas*. Gloucester, MA: Peter Smith.

Malinowski, Bronslaw. 1982. *Crime and Custom in Savage Society*. Totowa, NJ: Littlefield, Adams.

———. 1984. *Argonauts of the Western Pacific*. Prospect Heights, IL: Waveland Press.

Marcuse, Herbert. 1960. *Reason and Revolution: Hegel and the Rise of Social Theory*. Boston: Beacon Press.

———. 1968. *Negations: Essays in Critical Theory*. Boston: Beacon Press.

Marx, Karl. 1900. *The Poverty of Philosophy*. Moscow: Foreign Languages Publishing House.

———. 1962. *Capital*. Volumes I–III. Translated by Samuel Moore and Edward Aveling. Edited by

Friedrich Engels. Moscow: Foreign Languages Publishing House.

———. 1972. *A Contribution to the Critique of Political Economy.* Edited with an Introduction by Maurice Dobb. New York: International Publishers.

———. 1973. "The Prussian Press Bill." Pp.134–137. In *The Revolutions of 1848.* Vol. 1. Edited and with an Introduction by David Fernbach. New York: Random House.

———. 1975a. "Debates on the Law on Thefts of Wood." Pp.224–263. In *Karl Marx–Friedrich Engels: Collected Works,* Vol. 1. New York: International Publishers.

———. 1975b. "Debates on Freedom of the Press and Publication of the Proceedings of the Assembly of the Estates." Pp.132–181. In *Karl Marx–Friedrich Engels: Collected Works,* Vol. 1. New York: International Publishers.

———. 1975c. "Comments on the Latest Prussian Censorship Instruction." Pp.109–131. In *Karl Marx–Friedrich Engels: Collected Works,* Vol. 1. New York: International Publishers.

———, and Friedrich Engels. 1964. *The German Ideology.* Moscow: Progress Publishers.

Mauss, Marcel. 1958. "Introduction to the First Edition." Pp.1–4. In *Socialism and Saint-Simon* by Emile Durkheim. Translated by Charlotte Sattler. Edited and with an Introduction by Alvin Gouldner. Yellow Springs, OH: The Antioch Press.

McManus, Edgar J. 1993. *Law and Liberty in Early New England: Criminal Justice and Due Process, 1620–1692.* Amherst: The University of Massachusetts Press.

McManus, J. J. 1978. "The Emergence and Non-Emergence of Legislation." *British Journal of Law and Society* 5(2):185–201.

Mehring, Franz. 1966. *Karl Marx: The Story of a Life.* Atlantic Highlands, NJ: Humanities Press.

Mensch, Elizabeth. 1982. "The History of Mainstream Legal Thought." Pp.18–39. In *The Politics of Law: A Progressive Critique.* Edited by David Kairys. New York: Pantheon Books.

Merton, Robert K. 1934. "Durkheim's Division of Labor in Society." *American Journal of Sociology* 40(3):319–328.

———. 1968. *Social Theory and Social Structure.* New York: The Free Press.

Miller, Perry. 1965. *The Life of the Mind in America: From the Revolution to the Civil War.* New York: Harcourt, Brace and World.

Mills, C. Wright. 1959. *The Sociological Imagination.* New York: Oxford University Press.

Milovanovic, Dragan. 1981. "Ideology and Law: Structuralist and Instrumentalist Accounts of Law." *The Insurgent Sociologist* 10(4), 11(1):93–98.

———. 1988. *A Primer in the Sociology of Law.* New York: Harrow and Heston.

———. 1989. *Weberian and Marxian Analysis of Law: Development and Functions of Law in a Capitalist Mode of Production.* Brookfield, VT: Gower Publishing Company.

Miyahara, Kojiro. 1983. "Charisma: From Weber to Contemporary Sociology." *Sociological Inquiry* 53(4):368–388.

Monachesi, Elio. 1972. "Cesare Beccaria." Pp. 36–49. In *Pioneers in Criminology.* Edited and introduced by Hermann Mannheim. Montclair, NJ: Patterson Smith.

Morris, Herbert. 1960. "Dean Pound's Jurisprudence." *Stanford Law Review* 13:185–210.

Moskowitz, David H. 1966. "The American Legal Realists and an Empirical Science of Law." *Villanova Law Review* 11(3):480–524.

Mullin, Neil. 1980. "Pashukanis and the Demise of Law: An Essay Review." *Contemporary Crises* 4: 433–438.

Nonet, Philippe. 1976. "For Jurisprudential Sociology." *Law and Society Review* 10(4):525–545.

Olson, Walter K. 1991. *The Litigation Explosion: What Happened When America Unleashed the Lawsuit.* New York: Truman Talley Books.

Parkin, Frank. 1992. *Durkheim.* Oxford: Oxford University Press.

Parsons, Talcott. 1937. *The Structure of Social Action.* New York: McGraw-Hill.

———. 1951. *The Social System.* New York: The Free Press.

———. 1953. "Some Comments on the State of the General Theory of Action." *American Sociological Review* 18(6):618–631.

———. 1954. "A Sociologist Looks at the Legal Profession." Pp.370–385. In *Essays in Sociological Theory.* Glencoe, IL: The Free Press.

———. 1960a. "Durkheim's Contribution to the Theory of Integration of Social Systems." Pp. 118–153. In *Emile Durkheim, 1858–1917: A Collection of Essays.* Edited and translated by Kurt H. Wolff. Columbus: Ohio State University Press.

———. 1960b. *Structure and Process in Modern Societies.* Glencoe, IL: The Free Press.

———. 1961. "An Outline of the Social System." Pp.30–79. In *Theories of Society: Foundations of Modern Sociological Theory*. Volume I. Edited by Talcott Parsons, Edward Shils, Kaspar D. Naegele, and Jesse R. Pitts. Glencoe, IL: The Free Press.

———. 1962. "The Law and Social Control." Pp.56–72. In *Law and Society*. Edited by William M. Evan. New York: Macmillan Publishing Company.

———, and Neil Smelser. 1956. *Economy and Society*. New York: The Free Press.

Pashukanis, Evgeny B. 1989. *Law and Marxism: A General Theory*. Translated by Barbara Einhorn. Edited and Introduced by Chris Arthur. Worcester, Great Britain: Pluto Press.

Paul, Julius. 1957. "Foundations of American Realism." *West Virginia Law Review* 60(1):37–54.

Pearce, Frank. 1989. *The Radical Durkheim*. London: Unwin Hyman.

Peters, Edward. 1986. *Torture*. Oxford: Basil Blackwell.

Petrazycki, Leon. 1955. *Law and Morality: Leon Petrazycki*. Translated by Hugh W. Babb with an Introduction by Nicholas S. Timasheff. Cambridge, MA: Harvard University Press.

Phillips, Paul. 1980. *Marx and Engels on Law and Laws*. Totowa, NJ: Barnes & Noble Books.

Phillipson, Coleman. 1923. *Three Criminal Law Reformers: Beccaria, Bentham, Romilly*. London: J. M. Dent and Sons.

Picciotto, Sol. 1979. "The Theory of the State, Class Struggle, and the Rule of Law." Pp.164–177. In *Capitalism and the Rule of Law: From Deviancy Theory to Marxism*. Edited by Bob Fine, Richard Kinsey, John Lea, Sol Picciotto, and Jock Young. London: Hutchinson of London.

Podgorecki, Adam. 1963. "Sociotechnique." *The Polish Sociological Bulletin* 2(8):47–57.

———. 1967. "The Prestige of the Law (Preliminary Research Results)." *Acta Sociologica* 10(1–2):81–96.

———. 1968. "Five Functions of Sociology." *The Polish Sociological Bulletin* 1(17):65–78.

———. 1971. "Practical Usefulness of Sociological Research." *The Polish Sociological Bulletin* 1(23):17–28.

———. 1974. *Law and Society*. London: Routledge & Kegan Paul.

Pollock, Sir Frederick. 1970. "Introduction." Pp. xi–xxiii. In *Ancient Law: Its Connection with the Early History of Society and Its Relation to Modern Ideas* by Sir Henry Maine. Gloucester, MA: Peter Smith.

Pound, Roscoe. [1906] 1937. "The Causes of Popular Dissatisfaction with the Administration of Justice." *Journal of the American Judicature Society* 20(5):178–187.

———. 1907. "The Need of a Sociological Jurisprudence." *The Green Bag* 19(10):607–615.

———. 1908. "Mechanical Jurisprudence." *Columbia Law Review* 8(8):605–623.

———. 1910. "Law in Books and Law in Action." *American Law Review* 44:12–36.

———. 1927. "Sociology and Law." Pp. 319–328. In *The Social Sciences and Their Interrelations*. Edited by William Fielding Ogburn and Alexander Goldenweider. New York: Houghton Mifflin.

———. 1938. *The Formative Era of American Law*. Boston: Little, Brown.

———. [1942] 1968. *Social Control through Law*. Bloomington, IN: Archon Books.

———. 1943. "A Survey of Social Interests." *Harvard Law Review* 57(1):1–39.

———. 1959. *Jurisprudence*. Volumes I–V. St. Paul, MN: West Publishing Company.

———. 1971. "Sociology of Law." Pp.297–341. In *Twentieth Century Sociology*. Edited by Georges Gurvitch and Wilbert Moore. Freeport, NY: Books for Libraries Press.

Quinney, Richard. 1970. *The Social Reality of Crime*. Boston: Little, Brown.

———. 1974. *Critique of Legal Order: Crime Control in Capitalist Society*. Boston: Little, Brown.

Radcliffe-Brown, A. R. [1952] 1965. *Structure and Function in Primitive Society*. With a Foreword by E. E. Evans-Prichard and Fred Eggan. New York: The Free Press.

Radin, Max. 1931. "Legal Realism." *Columbia Law Review* 31(5):824–828.

Redhead, Steve. 1982. "Marxist Theory, the Rule of Law and Socialism." Pp.328–342. In *Marxism and Law*. Edited by Piers Beirne and Richard Quinney. New York: John Wiley & Sons.

Renner, Karl. 1949. *The Institutions of Private Law and their Social Functions*. Edited with an Introduction and Notes by O. Kahn-Freund. London: Routledge & Kegan Paul.

Rheinstein, Max, editor. [1954] 1966. *Max Weber on Law in Economy and Society*. Cambridge, MA: Harvard University Press.

Ritzer, George. 1975. *Sociology: A Multiple Paradigm Science*. Boston: Allyn & Bacon.

———. 1994. *Sociological Beginnings: On the Origins of Key Ideas in Sociology.* New York: McGraw-Hill.

Rueschemeyer, Dietrich. 1982. "On Durkheim's Explanation of Division of Labor." *American Journal of Sociology* 88(3):579–589.

Rumble, Wilfrid E., Jr. 1968. *American Legal Realism: Skepticism, Reform, and the Judicial Process.* Ithaca, NY: Cornell University Press.

Runciman, W. G., editor. 1980. *Weber: Selections in Translation.* Translated by Eric Matthews. Cambridge, Great Britian: Cambridge University Press.

Rusche, Georg, and Otto Kirchheimer. 1939. *Punishment and Social Structure.* With a Foreword by Thorsten Sellin. New York: Columbia University Press.

Salomon, Albert. 1971. "German Sociology." Pp.586–614. In *Twentieth Century Sociology.* Edited by Georges Gurvitch and Wilbert E. Moore. Freeport, NY: Books for Libraries Press.

Sanders, Joseph. 1990. "The Interplay of Micro and Macro Processes in the Longitudinal Study of Courts: Beyond the Durkheimian Tradition." *Law and Society Review* 24(2):241–256.

Savarese, Ralph J. 1965. "American Legal Realism." *Houston Law Review* 3(2):180–200.

Sayre, Paul. 1948. *The Life of Roscoe Pound.* Iowa City: State University of Iowa.

Schlegel, John Henry. 1984. "Notes Toward an Intimate, Opinionated, and Affectionate History of the Conference on Critical Legal Studies." *Stanford Law Review* 36:391–411.

Schur, Edwin M. 1968. *Law and Society: A Sociological View.* New York: Random House.

Schwartz, Richard D. 1954. "Social Factors in the Development of Legal Control: A Case Study of Two Israeli Settlements." *Yale Law Journal* 63(4):471–491.

———. 1966. "From the Editor." *Law and Society Review* 1(1):6.

———, and James C. Miller. 1964. "Legal Evolution and Societal Complexity." *American Journal of Sociology* 70(2):159–169.

Sellin, Thorsten. 1938. *Culture Conflict and Crime.* New York: Social Science Research Council.

Selznick, Philip. 1959. "The Sociology of Law." Pp. 115–127. In *Sociology Today: Problems and Prospects.* Edited by Robert K. Merton, Leonard Broom, and Leonard S. Cottrell, Jr. New York: Basic Books.

———. 1962. "The Sociology of Law." Pp. 50–59. In *International Encyclopedia of the Social Sciences.* Vol.

9. Edited by David L. Sills. New York: The Macmillan Company and The Free Press.

Simmel, Georg. 1950. *The Sociology of Georg Simmel.* Translated, edited, and with an introduction by Kurt H. Wolff. New York: Free Press.

———. 1969. *Conflict and the Web of Group-Affiliations.* Translated by Kurt H. Wolff and Reinhard Bendix. New York: Free Press.

———. 1971. "The Metropolis and Mental Life." Pp.324–339. In *Georg Simmel.* Edited by Donald Levin. Chicago: The University of Chicago Press.

Simmonds, Nigel. 1985. "Pashukanis and Liberal Jurisprudence." *Journal of Law and Society* 12(2):135–151.

Simon, Rita J., and James P. Lynch. 1989. "The Sociology of Law: Where We Have Been and Where We Might be Going." *Law and Society Review* 23(5):825–847.

Skolnick, Jerome H. 1965. "The Sociology of Law in America: Overview and Trends." *Social Problems* (Summer):4–39.

Smith, Christopher E. 1992. *Politics in Constitutional Law.* Chicago: Nelson-Hall Publishers.

Spencer, Herbert. 1880. *First Principles.* New York: Clarke, Given and Hooper.

———. 1898. *The Principles of Sociology.* Vols. I–III. New York: D. Appleton and Company.

———. 1899. *Essays: Scientific, Political, and Speculative.* Vol. I. New York: D. Appleton and Company.

Spencer, Martin. 1970. "Weber on Legitimate Norms and Authority." *British Journal of Sociology* 21(2):123–134.

Spitzer, Steven. 1975. "Punishment and Social Organization: A Study of Durkheim's Theory of Penal Evolution." *Law and Society Review* 9(4):613–635.

———. 1979. "Notes Toward a Theory of Punishment and Social Change." Pp. 207–229. In *Research in Law and Sociology.* Vol. 2. Series editor Rita J. Simon. Guest editor Steven Spitzer. Greenwich, CT: JAI Press.

Starr, Harris E. 1925. "William Graham Sumner: Sociologist." *The Journal of Social Forces* 3(4):622–626.

Stockton, Frank R. 1902. *The Lady, or the Tiger? And Other Stories.* New York: Charles Scribner's Sons.

Stone, Alan. 1985. "The Place of Law in the Marxian Structure-Superstructure Archetype." *Law and Society Review* 19(1):39–67.

Stone, Marjorie. 1985. "Dickens, Bentham, and the Fictions of the Law: A Victorian Controversy and Its Consequences." *Victorian Studies* 29(1):125–154.

Strachan-Davidson, James Leigh. 1969. *Problems of the Roman Criminal Law.* Two Volumes. Oxford: Clarendon Press.

Suber, Peter. 1990. *The Paradox of Self-Amendment: A Study of Logic, Law, Omnipotence, and Change.* New York: Peter Lang.

Sugarman, David. 1987. *In the Spirit of Weber: Law, Modernity and "The Peculiarities of the English."* Working Papers, Series 2. Madison, WI: Institute for Legal Studies, University of Wisconsin-Madison Law School.

Sumner, Colin. 1979. *Reading Ideologies: An Investigation Into the Marxist Theory of Ideology and Law.* New York: Academic Press.

———. 1981. "Pashukanis and the 'Jurisprudence of Terror.'" *The Insurgent Sociologist* 10(4),11(1):99–106.

Sumner, William Graham. 1934. *Essays of William Graham Sumner.* Vols. I–II. Edited with Prefaces by Albert Galloway Keller and Maurice R. Davie. New Haven: Yale University Press.

———. [1906] 1940. *Folkways: A Study of the Sociological Importance of Usages, Manners, Customs, Mores, and Morals.* Boston: Ginn and Company.

Tappan, Paul W. 1961. "Pre-Classical Penology." Pp. 33–49. In *Essays in Criminal Science.* Edited by Gerhard O. W. Mueller. South Hackensack, NJ: Fred B. Rothman and Company.

Thompson, E. P. 1975. *Whigs and Hunters: The Origin of the Black Act.* New York: Pantheon Books.

———. 1991. *Customs in Common.* London: The Merlin Press.

Timasheff, Nicholas S. 1939. *An Introduction to the Sociology of Law.* Cambridge, MA: Harvard University Committee on Research in the Social Sciences.

Tiryakian, Edward A. 1964. "Durkheim's 'Two Laws of Penal Evolution.'" *Journal for the Scientific Study of Religion* 3(2):261–266.

Treiber, Herbert. 1985. "'Elective Affinities' Between Weber's Sociology of Religion and Sociology of Law." *Theory and Society* 14:809–861.

Treves, Renato, and J. F. Glastra Van Loon, editors. 1968. *Norms and Actions: National Reports on Sociology of Law.* The Hague: Martinus Nijhoff.

Trubek, David M. 1972. "Max Weber on Law and the Rise of Capitalism." *Wisconsin Law Review* 3:720–753.

———. 1984. "Where the Action Is: Critical Legal Studies and Empiricism." *Stanford Law Review* 36(1):575–622.

———. 1986. "Review Essay: Max Weber's Tragic Modernism and the Study of Law in Society." *Law and Society Review* 20(4):573–598.

Turkel, Gerald. 1980. "Legitimation, Authority, and Consensus Formation." *International Journal of the Sociology of Law* 8(1):19–32.

Turk, Austin T. 1969. *Criminality and Legal Order.* Chicago: Rand McNally.

———. 1976. "Law as a Weapon in Social Conflict." *Social Problems* 23(3):276–291.

Turner, Bryan S. 1981. *For Weber: Essays on the Sociology of Fate.* London: Routledge & Kegan Paul.

Tushnet, Mark V. 1980. "Post-Realism Legal Scholarship." *Wisconsin Law Review* 1980(6):1383–1401.

———. 1986. "Critical Legal Studies: An Introduction to its Origins and Underpinnings." *Journal of Legal Education* 36:505–517.

Twining, William. 1973. *Karl Llewellyn and the Realist Movement.* Birkenhead, Great Britain: Willmer Brothers Ltd.

Tyler, Tom R. 1990. *Why People Obey the Law.* New Haven: Yale University Press.

Unger, Roberto Mangabeira. 1983. "The Critical Legal Studies Movement." *Harvard Law Review* 96(3):563–675.

Vago, Steven. 1994. *Law and Society.* Fourth Edition. Englewood Cliffs, NJ: Prentice-Hall.

Vogt, W. Paul. 1983. "Obligation and Right: The Durkheimians and the Sociology of Law." Pp.177–198. In *The Sociological Domain: The Durkheimians and the Founding of French Sociology.* Edited by Philippe Besnard. Cambridge: Cambridge University Press.

Vold, George B. 1958. *Theoretical Criminology.* New York: Oxford University Press.

von Savigny, Frederick Charles. 1986. *Of the Vocation of Our Age for Legislation and Jurisprudence.* Birmingham, AL: The Legal Classics Library.

Warrington, Ronnie. 1981. "Pashukanis and the Commodity Form Theory." *International Journal of the Sociology of Law* 9:1–22.

Weber, Max. 1949. *The Methodology of the Social Sciences.* Translated and Edited by Edward A. Shils and Henry A. Finch. New York: The Free Press.

———. 1950. *General Economic History.* Translated by Frank H. Knight. Glencoe, IL: The Free Press.

———. 1958. *The Protestant Ethic and the Spirit of Capitalism.* Translated by Talcott Parsons. New York: Charles Scribner's Sons.

———. 1969. *The Theory of Social and Economic Organization.* Edited with an Introduction by Talcott Parsons. New York: The Free Press.

———. 1978. *Economy and Society.* Vols. I–II. Edited by Gunther Roth and Claus Wittich. Berkeley: University of California Press.

West, Robin. 1988. "Jurisprudence and Gender." *The University of Chicago Law Review* 55(1):1–72.

Westby, David L. 1991. *The Growth of Sociological Theory: Human Nature, Knowledge, and Social Change.* Englewood Cliffs, NJ: Prentice-Hall.

White, G. Edward 1972. "From Sociological Jurisprudence to Realism: Jurisprudence and Social Change in Early Twentieth-Century America." *Virginia Law Review* 58(6):999–1028.

Wigmore, John H. 1937. "Roscoe Pound's St. Paul Address of 1906: The Spark that Kindled the White Flame of Progress." *Journal of the American Judicature Society* 20(5):176–178.

Williams, Patricia. 1991. *The Alchemy of Race and Rights: Diary of a Law Professor.* Cambridge, MA: Harvard University Press.

Wirt, Frederick M. 1970. *Politics of Southern Equality: Law and Social Change in a Mississippi County.* Chicago: Aldine Publishing Company.

Yntema, Hessel E. 1960. "American Legal Realism in Retrospect." *Vanderbilt Law Review* 14(1):317–330.

Ziegert, Klaus A. 1977. "Adam Podgorecki's Sociology of Law: The Invisible Factors of the Functioning of Law Made Visible." *Law and Society Review* 12(1):151–180.

Acknowledgments (continued from copyright page)

Alan Stone, "The Place of the Law in the Marxian Structure-Superstructure Archetype." *Law and Society Review* 19:1, 1985, pp. 39–67. Reprinted by permission of the Law and Society Association and the author.

Max Weber, "Categories of Legal Thought." Reprinted by permission of the publishers from *Max Weber on Law in Economy and Society* edited by Max Rheinstein, Cambridge, Mass.: Harvard University Press. Copyright © 1954 by the President and Fellows of Harvard College. For permission to photocopy this selection, please contact Harvard University Press.

Alan Hyde, "The Concept of Legitimation in the Sociology of Law." 1983 *Wisconsin Law Review* 379. Reprinted with the permission of the *Wisconsin Law Review*. © The University of Wisconsin.

David M. Trubek, "Max Weber on Law and the Rise of Capitalism." 1972 *Wisconsin Law Review* 720. Reprinted with the permission of the *Wisconsin Law Review*. © The University of Wisconsin.

Emile Durkheim, "The Evolution of Punishment." From *Durkheim and the Law* by Steven Lukes and Andrew Scull. Reprinted by permission of St. Martin's Press, Inc. © Introduction, Steven Lukes and Andrew Scull 1983.

Lonn Lanza-Kaduce, et al. "Law and Durkheimian Order: An Empirical Examination of the Convergence of Legal and Social Definitions of Law." Pp. 41–61. In *Structure, Law, and Power: Essays in the Sociology of Law*. Sage Research Progress Series in Criminology, Volume 13. Edited by Paul J. Brantingham and Jack M. Kress. © Notice and reprinted by permission of Sage Publications Inc., and Lonn Lanza-Kaduce and Ronald Akers.

Steven Spitzer, "Punishment and Social Organization: A Study of Durkheim's Theory of Penal Evolution." *Law and Society Review* 9:4, 1975, pp. 618–637. Reprinted by permission of the Law and Society Association and the author.

Talcott Parsons, "The Law and Social Control." Reprinted with the permission of The Free Press, a Division of Macmillan, Inc. From *Law and Sociology* by William Evan, editor. Copyright © 1962 by The Free Press; copyright renewed 1990.

Adam Podgorecki, "Three Levels of the Functioning of Law." Reprinted with the permission of Routledge from *Law and Society* by Adam Podgorecki, 1974.

William J. Chambliss, "A Sociological Analysis of the Law of Vagrancy." © 1964 by the Society for the Study of Social Problems. Reprinted from *Social Problems* Vol. 12, No. 1, (Summer 1964), pp. 67–77, by permission. Reprinted with the permission of the author.

Austin T. Turk, "Law as a Weapon in Social Conflict." © 1976 by the Society for the Study of Social Problems. Reprinted from *Social Problems* Vol. 23, No. 3 (Feb. 1976), pp. 276–291, by permission. Reprinted with the permission of the author.

Duncan Kennedy, "Form and Substance in Private Law Adjudication." *Harvard Law Review* 89(8):1685–1778, (1976). Footnotes omitted. Reprinted with the permission of the Harvard Law Review Association and the author.

Clare Dalton, "An Essay in the Deconstruction of Contract Doctrine." Footnotes omitted. Reprinted by permission of the author, The Yale Law Journal Company, and Fred B. Rothman and Company from *The Yale Law Journal* Vol. 94, pp. 997–1114, (1985).

Name Index

Subject Index